*Interpreting
Educational
Research*

Third Edition

Interpreting Educational Research

An Introduction for Consumers of Research

Daniel R. Hittleman
The City University of New York/Queens College

Alan J. Simon
Metis Associates, Inc., New York

Merrill
Prentice Hall

Upper Saddle River, New Jersey
Columbus, Ohio

Library of Congress Cataloging-in-Publication Data

Hittleman, Daniel R.

    Interpreting educational research: an introduction for consumers of research / Daniel R. Hittleman, Alan J. Simon.—3rd ed.

       p. cm.

    Includes bibliographical references and indexes.

    ISBN 0-13-012859-7

    1. Education—Research. 2. Research—Methodology. 3. Education—Research—Evaluation. I. Simon, Alan J. II. Title.

LB1028 .H537 2002

370'.7'2—dc21   00-053694

Vice President and Publisher: Jeffery W. Johnston
Executive Editor: Kevin M. Davis
Editorial Assistant: Amy Hamer
Production Editor: Mary Harlan
Production Coordination: Linda Zuk, WordCrafters Editorial Services, Inc.
Design Coordinator: Diane C. Lorenzo
Cover Design: Jason Moore
Cover Art: SuperStock
Production Manager: Laura Messerly
Director of Marketing: Kevin Flanagan
Marketing Manager: Amy June
Marketing Coordinator: Barbara Koontz

This book was set in Meridien by Carlisle Communications, Ltd. It was printed and bound by R. R. Donnelley & Sons Company. The cover was printed by Phoenix Color Corp.

Prentice-Hall International (UK) Limited, *London*
Prentice-Hall of Australia Pty. Limited, *Sydney*
Prentice-Hall Canada, Inc., *Toronto*
Prentice-Hall Hispanoamericana, S.A., *Mexico*
Prentice-Hall of India, Private Limited, *New Delhi*
Prentice-Hall of Japan, Inc., *Tokyo*
Prentice-Hall Singapore Pte. Ltd.
Editora Prentice-Hall do Brasil, Ltda., *Rio de Janeiro*

Earlier edition © 1992 by Macmillan Publishing Company.

10 9 8 7 6 5 4 3 2 1
ISBN 0-13-012859-7

To Carol and Carole,
with our love for their continued support of our work

Preface

We intend the third edition of *Interpreting Educational Research: An Introduction for Consumers of Research* to be used in introductory research courses in which elementary and early childhood education teachers, reading/literacy specialists, special education teachers, and content area teachers at the middle and secondary school levels are prepared as consumers rather than as producers of educational research. We provide preservice and in-service teachers with basic knowledge and skills for reading, interpreting, and evaluating both quantitative and qualitative educational research, so that they can make program, curriculum, and instructional decisions based upon those research results. This knowledge base is useful for teachers who collaborate in research projects with college and university faculty and other teachers. In addition, we provide a guide for composing teacher-as-researcher action research projects and syntheses of research.

Through directed learning activities based on current integrated language arts principles and practices for reading and writing content area discourse, we guide readers to independence in the use of techniques for reading, interpreting, evaluating, and writing about education research. The evaluation of education research is approached by us so teachers will become research consumers by understanding the underlying methodological and procedural assumptions used by educators who are research producers. In essence, teachers are guided in research literacy learning to think as research producers.

NATURE OF THE REVISION

Our revisions consist of updating information about how research is produced, providing more recent examples of research methodology, replacing the complete research reports in Appendix B and adding an additional study, and providing current standards for producing action or program evaluation research. The discussions throughout the text are supported with examples of what we feel are good, curriculum-based, quantitative and qualitative research reports representing the fields of elementary-, middle-, and secondary-school general and content-area education, reading/literacy education, and gifted and special education. A very important revision we have made is to update and expand the explanation and interpretation of qualitative research. We have added information about the use of effect size in analyzing quantitative results. The discussion about interpreting and evaluating reviews of research has been revised to reflect current thought about syntheses of research. Information and strategies for locating research reports through the use of electronic databases and the Internet have been updated and expanded. Because we feel that all educators, whether consumers or producers of research, should know and appreciate the criteria for conducting instructional program evaluations, we have added the program evaluation standards that have been established by professional associations.

ORGANIZATION

In this revision, we have maintained the organization and chapter topics of the previous editions. The text is organized into eleven chapters and three appendices. In Chapters 1, 2, and 3, we lead the reader to an understanding of research designs, the general procedures of research producers, and a plan for reading research reports. In Chapters 4 through 9, we present extended discussions of the aspects of research design and methodology and illustrations of the manner in which research producers present them in research reports. In Chapters 10 and 11, we provide information about reading and writing reviews of research and about sources for locating research reports. In the appendices are a glossary of key terms, six complete research reports for additional study and analysis, and ethical standards for conducting educational and program evaluation research.

We begin each chapter with a graphic overview of the content (as shown on page ix) and focus questions so readers can attend to the key ideas of the chapter and the interrelationships portrayed in the structured overview. In the main body of the chapters, we provide techniques for reading, interpreting, and writing about specific sections of research reports. In the activities section at the end of each chapter, we present ways for the reader to gain greater understanding of the key concepts and proficiency in applying the evaluative techniques. For each of these activities, we provide the reader with feedback in which we give samples of how we might respond to our own students' work.

SPECIAL FEATURES

Special features of the text are as follows:

- The text is intended for teachers with a range of backgrounds: generalists, content-area teachers, reading/literacy specialists, special educators, and middle- and secondary-school teachers.
- The examples used throughout the text are drawn from current curriculum-based research literature that these teachers will find relevant to their specific instructional situations. All research designs are illustrated with published research.
- The material is conceptualized for consumers of educational research.
- The text is intended to teach preservice and in-service teachers, in a nonthreatening supportive manner, to read and write about educational research. A step-by-step process leads teachers to understand and use research reports.
- Information is included about strategies for reading both quantitative and qualitative (ethnographic or naturalistic) research.
- The chapters begin with a structured overview of the content showing each chapter's focus in relation to the overall content of the text.

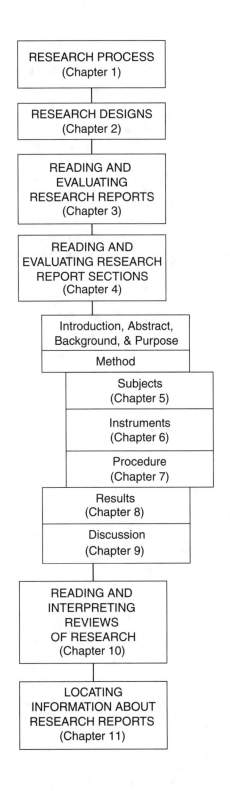

- Specific strategies that have been shown to be effective for the reading of typical content-area texts and the writing of content-area-related expository prose are applied to the reading of research reports and the writing of research evaluations.
- Ample practice is provided for developing readers' skills in evaluating educational research.
- The text provides readers with an understanding of syntheses of research and research meta-analyses and gives guidance in the preparation of action syntheses of research.
- A glossary contains the definitions of all key terms presented in the text. Within the text, key terms are highlighted the first time they are introduced.
- The appendices contain complete research reports for additional practice in evaluating research or for use in class assignments.
- The text is intended to provide teachers with the knowledge and skills to act as teacher-researchers and to create classroom-based action research projects and syntheses of research.

Acknowledgments

No book is published without the support, input, and assistance of others, and we continue to be indebted for the help and assistance of many people. We are grateful for the encouragement and support of our colleagues at CUNY/Queens College, who have used the first and second editions and have provided us with invaluable insights for this revision. We appreciate the comments and critiques of our students and have incorporated many of their ideas in the revision. We also thank our colleagues at Metis Associates, Inc., New York, for their support.

We are fortunate to have had Suzanne Li's assistance in the preparation of Chapter 11. She provided extensive knowledge and insight about both traditional and electronic searches of library resources as well as numerous recommendations for revising and modifying the chapter's content.

We appreciate the constructive comments and reviews by Joe L. Green, Texas Tech University; Anthony Manzo, University of Missouri, Kansas City; and Thomas J. Sheerman, Niagara University. We have given extensive consideration to their concerns and questions and have incorporated many of them in the revision. We also have kept in mind comments and reviews of the second edition by Maurice R. Berube, Old Dominion University; J. Kent Davis, Purdue University; Thomas D. Dertinger, University of Richmond; and Karen Ford, Ball State University. However, we ultimately take responsibility for the interpretations and perspectives about research presented in the text. We also are extremely grateful for the help and assistance by Kevin Davis and Mary Harlan at Merrill, and Linda Zuk at WordCrafters.

Brief Contents

Contents

Chapter 7 **READING AND EVALUATING PROCEDURE SECTIONS**   **123**

Chapter 8 **READING AND INTERPRETING RESULTS SECTIONS**   **172**

Figures and Tables

FIGURES

TABLES

Chapter 1

The Research Process

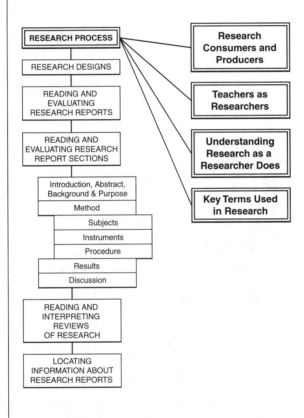

FOCUS QUESTIONS

1. Why do educators conduct research?
2. What is the distinction between research consumers and research producers?
3. What does it mean to understand research as a research producer does?
4. What are some key terms used in research?

[handwritten note: Research is! a) collect info b) analyze info c) apply]

Teachers and schools continually make decisions about instructional activities, such as instructional techniques, classroom management, and student learning. They base decisions on their experiences, other teachers' experiences, and the accumulation of accumulated knowledge about education. Much of the knowledge about teaching and learning comes from educational researchers who seek answers to educational questions or try to clarify some existing educational issue. One sign of a productive profession, such as education, is the systematic attempts by its researchers and practitioners to examine the knowledge base upon which the profession functions. For the purposes of this book, the systematic attempt to examine a knowledge base is called research.

Research is the systematic attempt to (a) collect information about an identified problem or question, (b) analyze that information, and (c) apply the evidence thus derived to confirm or refute some prior prediction or statement about that problem. Educational research is not unique within the total research community; it is the application of some generally accepted systematic procedures to examine the knowledge base of education. Akin to educational research is educational evaluation, the use of research techniques to judge the effectiveness of existing, in-place programs of instruction. For the general purposes of this book, educational evaluation is considered a subarea of educational research.

[handwritten note: 5 Characteristics]

Five characteristics seem indicative of a profession whose members research its knowledge base (Berliner, 1987). First, professionals work at verifying ideas and practices believed to be effective. Often, teachers read about a "new" teaching technique in a professional journal and say, "We've known that all along!" As professionals, however, teachers cannot rely entirely on a common sense approach; intuition needs to be supported and substantiated through research.

Second, professionals work at discovering new ideas and practices. The need for new ideas and practices is almost self-evident and is exemplified by an idea that has been extensively researched, was once new, and is now common in schools: the application of reciprocal teaching, which features guided practice in applying learning strategies (Rosenshine & Meister, 1994).

Third, professionals clarify ideas that are designed to simplify teaching. This is illustrated by research results about cooperative learning procedures when they are applied to problem solving in various subject areas (Qin, Johnson, & Johnson, 1995).

Fourth, although professional educators try to simplify teaching, they often express ideas that may complicate everyone's teaching. An example of this effect is the body of research findings indicating how the learning of many students with disabling conditions is improved in mainstream classes as opposed to self-contained classes (Leinhardt & Pallay, 1982; Madden & Slavin, 1983).

Fifth, professionals discover ideas and practices that are counterintuitive. For example, many educators assume that grouping in self-contained classes according to students' ability permits students to work more effectively with peers and to have instruction adapted to their performance level. Regarding mastery learning, however, research evidence does not seem to support this contention. Instead, it shows that students may achieve more when they are in classes of mixed ability for most of the day. Cross-grade assignments also may increase students' achievement. Limited grouping of students at the same level seems effective only when it is done for specific skill instruction (Slavin, 1987a, 1987b).

RESEARCH CONSUMERS AND PRODUCERS

This book is intended for research consumers—the people who read, interpret, and apply the information systematically collected and examined (researched) by others. Like research producers, research consumers are interested in answering educationally related questions; however, they do so by reading and applying research producers' results, rather than by conducting research.

Research consumers need to read research with a mindset similar to that of research producers—similar, but not the same. Research producers need certain skills to put different phases of educational research into operation. They need technical competence in applying research strategies. Research consumers, on the other hand, need to understand decisions facing research producers, possible alternatives they may consider at those decision points, and implications of researchers' results and conclusions. Also, they need a means of judging the adequacy of research producers' work.

We believe a research consumer can more fully understand educational research by reading research as a research producer does. The research consumer reads research by reconstructing the researcher's message and constructing a meaning from the information on the page—much as students reconstruct a message during an instructional session and then construct its meaning for themselves. The reader may create meanings different from those intended by the writer (as may a listener in response to a speaker). Research consumers reach understanding by reconstructing the ideas of research producers as well as by constructing meanings of their own. A consumer's understanding is constructed from that person's prior knowledge and prior experiences, combined with that person's maturity and his or her proficiency in manipulating research ideas.

Research consumers need to understand the ethical standards by which research producers should be guided in their activities. The American Educational Research Association (AERA) has adopted a set of ethical standards for conducting educational research. Although research producers' compliance with these standards is voluntary, researcher consumers should be aware of their existence and contents. The standards are found in Appendix C.

TEACHERS AS RESEARCHERS

Although the concept of teachers as researchers is not new, our understanding of how important it is for classroom teachers to collaborate with research producers and to produce research themselves about their lives in classrooms has been increasing (Bissex, 1994; Burton, 1991; Donoahue, Van Tassell, & Patterson, 1996; Erickson, 1986; Goodson, 1993; Johnson, 1993; McFarland & Stansell, 1993; Olson, 1990; Santa, 1988; VanDeWeghe, 1992). This text is not intended to create research producers. Even so, the mindset of "understanding research as a researcher does" presented here and the ideas about research methods and research evaluation presented in subsequent chapters will provide teachers with the background knowledge and understanding they need to participate in such research projects.

Teachers need to assume the responsibility of examining their own practices (Erickson, 1986; Patterson & Shannon, 1993). Since teachers are increasingly being held responsible for what and how they teach, they need to take leadership in determining what insights about learning and teaching should be systematically applied in classrooms. It is especially important that classroom teachers collaborate with researchers when changes in curriculum and instructional procedures are being evaluated. Curriculum and instructional leadership should not be expected to come solely from university research centers and state and federal agencies; instead, teachers are being called upon to participate in research that will significantly affect what happens in the classroom. Collaborating in this research

> (1) reduces the gap between research findings and classroom practice, (2) creates a problem solving mindset that helps teachers when they consider other classroom dilemmas, (3) improves teachers' instructional decision making processes, (4) increases the professional status of teachers, (5) helps empower teachers to influence their own profession at classroom, district, state, and national levels, and (6) offers the overriding and ultimate advantage of providing the potential for improving the educational process for children. (Olson, 1990, pp. 17–18)

The research procedures that are often associated with the idea of teachers as researchers are those of qualitative and action research (see the subsection "Action Research" in Chapters 7 and 8 and the section "Preparing Action Reviews of Research" in Chapter 10). Teacher-researcher studies are attempts to explain the experience of teachers and students as they are enacted in actual classrooms. For example, in a study describing the evolution of research questions among elementary- and secondary-school teachers (Baumann, Allen, & Shockley, 1994), teachers posed initial questions about the following classroom-related concerns: motivation, interests, and attitudes; home-school-community links; content reading and learning from text, or functional literacy; assessment; technology; linguistic, racial, and cultural; diversity; and instructional strategies and interventions. Inquiry, reflection, and action characterize what is done by teacher-researchers (Burton, 1991; Patterson & Shannon, 1993). Inquiry is the purposeful observation of all aspects of classroom life. Reflection is the systematic attempt to understand the multiple layers of meaning of what happens in classrooms. Action is the altering of classroom practice as a result of the new understanding. These activities might even be considered a "researching" experience (Burton, 1991, p. 230) in that they are not used to create educational laws, but to reexamine the often hidden dynamics of teaching and learning, look at them in a new light, and take an instructional stance based on what is seen.

UNDERSTANDING RESEARCH FROM THE PERSPECTIVE OF A RESEARCHER

Research producers present the results of their research in reports. (The specific form of those reports is discussed in Chapter 3.) To comprehend a research report fully, the research consumer must understand research producers' processes in conceptualizing, developing, implementing, and reporting research. To illustrate the process, the way in which one research team might develop a project is described below. Although the process is presented linearly for illustrative purposes, research consumers should realize that the process actually may not unfold in such a clear sequence. The researchers may start and stop several times, reject questions and possible solutions, and encounter many pitfalls.

The researchers select a problem area and specify research questions.

From personal experience, professional readings, or discussions with colleagues, our hypothetical research team selects a problem area for study. For example, thoughts arise about the writing performance of middle-school students who are learning disabled. (The differing and often confusing definitions of learning disability will be disregarded here.) These thoughts flow from an array of concerns, a few of which follow.

First, many students with learning disabilities are mainstreamed for particular academic classes. Second, writing skill has increasingly become an issue in the teaching and learning of content areas other than language or communication arts. Third, different writing skills may be needed in different content areas (e.g., science, social studies, mathematics, or technology).

The researchers are concerned about the use to which the resolutions of these issues might be put. These concerns lead to other questions. Are the answers to be applicable only to the students in one specific school, grade level, or class? Are the answers to be used for the students in an entire district, state, region, or nation? Should the writing of students with learning disabilities be compared with that of students who do not have such disabilities?

The next set of concerns deals with the teaching and learning of writing. The researchers wish to know the following: What is the writing performance of students with learning disabilities and how does it compare with that of students without disabilities? What can be done to help the students with disabilities write effectively in the content areas? Of equal importance to the researchers is whether these questions are interrelated or can any one of them be answered without answering the others.

(The question "Why do students with learning disabilities write the way they do?" is also of concern. However, seeking answers to it moves the researcher away from a primary concern with instruction.)

The researchers examine and search journals, books, and databases to review existing research results and define terms.

At this point, the researchers try to find out what other researchers have done to answer these or similar questions. By consulting books, educational encyclopedias, professional journals, and electronic databases, the researchers gain insights about what others have done and what conclusions were drawn from their research. The researchers know their work is based on certain assumptions, one of which is that it will add to the body of educational knowledge. Their aim is to help other researchers and practitioners reach some agreement about the controversy surrounding the teaching of writing to students with learning disabilities.

After reviewing the material from these sources, the researchers conclude that the meaning of certain terms requires clarification. For example, they realize that several terms are defined differently by different researchers: *learning disability, language arts, communication arts, content-area classes, writing, composing, mainstreaming,* and *regular education*. The researchers select an accepted definition or create a new one to enhance communication with other researchers and users of the research.

The researchers formulate researchable questions.

Now they return to the questions about the teaching and learning of writing. A decision must be made about answering one or more of them. They decide to answer three questions and must now determine whether those questions need to be answered in a specific order. The answer is yes, because the answer to the question "What can be done to help students with learning disabilities write effectively in the content areas?" presupposes answers to the others. So, the researchers decide to first answer the questions "What is the writing performance of students with learning disabilities?" and "How does that performance compare with the performance of students without learning disabilities?" (a question of major concern since the researchers wish to examine the writing of students with learning disabilities in mainstream classes).

The researchers select research designs.

The researchers now have three possible studies. (It is possible for the researchers to conduct these three studies as one, but this is not done here so that the three different research plans can be highlighted.) For each, they need a different research plan, or design. **Research designs** are methods for answering questions. Just as skilled craftspeople and artisans have several methods for manipulating their raw material, so do researchers. Some research designs are more appropriate or effective for answering certain questions. Also, more than one plan may be appropriate or effective for answering a particular question.

In the first possible study, the researchers want to describe the writing performance of students with learning disabilities. The description is to be in statistical and in nonstatistical form (see **quantitative research, qualitative research,** and **statistics** in the Glossary). They decide on several activities. They decide to describe the students' processes for beginning a writing task, their topics and organization of ideas, the maturity of their vocabulary and sentence structure, the grammatical form of their works, and the physical aspects of their writing.

To compare the writing of students with learning disabilities with that of students who do not have such disabilities in a second possible study, the researchers will collect the same data from both groups. They plan a statistical and nonstatistical comparison of the two types of students.

For the third possible study, "What can be done to help students with learning disabilities write effectively in the content areas?", the researchers will set up one or more instructional programs and look at them singly and in combination to see which has the greatest effect (or any effect) on the writing performance of these students.

The researchers determine the research method.

The three plans have both common and unique aspects. The common aspects include efforts the researchers must make to determine (a) where and when the research is to occur, (b) with whom specifically the research will be done, (c) with what device students' characteristics and their writing will be assessed, and (d) how they will analyze the information (see **data** in the Glossary) they collected.

In selecting a location, the researchers think about conducting the studies in a special site, such as a college educational clinic or a middle-school classroom. Both have advantages and disadvantages. An educational clinic allows the researchers better control of the data collection environment and the opportunity to make unobtrusive observations and recordings. However, the setting is not educationally natural, since the students need to be brought to it under special circumstances. A classroom lets the researchers observe and collect data in the setting where the students usually learn and work. However, a classroom has distractions that might influence the data collection and the students' performances in ways the researchers may not recognize. After weighing the pros and cons, the researchers decide to conduct all three studies in middle-school classrooms, fully aware that they must make some effort to reduce or eliminate the possible influence of certain distractions.

The researchers describe and select the students to be used in the study.

The researchers are interested in doing the study with middle-school students. The specific group of students for the study is selected with consideration for the ability of the researchers to pass on the results to others in similar urban centers. They select a middle school affiliated with their college because its total student population reflects the range of ability and performance test scores and demographic characteristics of the county as a whole. All students classified as learning disabled in grades five through eight, in both mainstreamed and self-contained classes, are included.

The researchers must describe the students for others, so they collect relevant data normally found in students' permanent records—information such as age, sex, grade level, educational history, and attendance.

The researchers select tests to score the students' writing.

The researchers also begin to document the students' writing performance. To do this, samples of the students' writing in content-area classes are obtained and scored or analyzed by some accepted system (e.g., a rubric). The researchers have the option of using one or more achievement tests or a scoring system known as holistic scoring. Or, they may analyze the students' compositions by nonnumerical analysis.

The researchers conduct the study.

The researchers now have enough information to answer the first question, "What is the writing performance of students with learning disabilities?" To answer the second question, "How does that performance compare with the performance of students without learning disabilities?" the researchers collect the same data about students who do not have learning disabilities. Because it is impractical to collect data about all such students in the middle school, the researchers decide to randomly select a portion of the students without learning disabilities at each grade level.

As the researchers proceed, another question arises. The researchers want to know "Are teachers using any instructional strategies and techniques that seem to enhance the learning of students who are learning disabled?" To answer this question, they set up a series of classroom observations and teacher interviews. They wish to determine possible answers to this question by collecting information about what occurs in classrooms while teaching and learning are happening. As they collect this information, they sort it and seek out patterns of teacher-learner interactions.

To answer their last question, "What can be done to help students with learning disabilities write effectively in the content areas?" the researchers select and prepare instructional activities and collect additional data. Using the information gleaned from other research, from professional sources, and from their classroom observations and teacher interviews, the researchers create or select three instructional programs that have shown promise for teaching students who are learning disabled. The researchers' question now becomes "Which of these instructional programs help the students who are learning disabled write effectively in content area classes?" or "Which of the programs cause the students to write effectively?" The researchers decide how long (for how many days, weeks, or months) the instructional program will last and who will do the actual teaching. They plan to have all content-area teachers in the middle school participate in a special 8-week after-school workshop about implementing one of the instructional programs. The teachers are to use the techniques for the 12 weeks following the workshop.

Additional data about students' writing performance are collected during and after the instructional programs. The researchers now conduct the studies.

✓ *The researchers analyze the data and determine implications of the research.*

After conducting the study and collecting the data, the researchers analyze the data using appropriate statistical (quantitative) and nonstatistical (qualitative) methods. Then, they determine what implications the results have for other researchers and teachers.

✓ *The researchers publish their results.*

After conducting its research, the team produces a written report. For example, after beginning activities to answer their third question, the researchers describe (a) their reason for conducting the study; (b) the conclusions they and others have made about previous research; (c) the steps they took to select the students, the writing scoring procedure, and the instructional activities; (d) the in-service workshop, the instructional programs, and the way they were used in the content area classes; and (e) the statistical and nonstatistical results.

KEY TERMS USED IN RESEARCH

Most key research terms are defined as they occur in this book. A few, however, are introduced now because they underpin most of the discussions. Additional information about these and other key terms is given elsewhere. The Glossary contains all key terms discussed in this book.

variable   In the broadest sense, a variable is anything in a research situation that varies and can be measured. It can be a human characteristic (of students or teachers) or it can be a characteristic of classrooms, groups, schools and school districts, instructional materials, and so on. These characteristics are called variables, and they can be measured. Educationally relevant traits of humans, among many, include age, intelligence, reading scores, learning style, level of motivation, sensitivity to noise, and ethnicity. Educationally relevant other characteristics include, among many, the size of print in textbooks, the number of times an event occurs, the location of schools, the economic status of families, and students' attendance records.

research design   The research design is the plan used to study an educational problem or question. Two basic research designs based on the way information, or data, are collected and analyzed are **quantitative research** (statistical data analysis) and **qualitative research** (nonstatistical, rational data analysis). In the example of the research team used in this chapter, a combination of these two types was used. The team also used three subcategories of quantitative research: descriptive, comparative, and causative. **Descriptive research** provides information about one or more variables. **Comparative research** provides an explanation about the extent of a relationship between two or more variables. **Experimental,** or causative, **research** provides information about how one or more variables influence another variable.

hypothesis   A hypothesis is a tentative statement about how two or more variables are related.

In current practice, many researchers convey the relationship as a prediction, a statement of purpose, or a question. For the causative design used by the research team in our example, the researchers' question "Which of the instructional programs help students with learning disabilities write effectively in content area classes?" could be approached in these forms:

Prediction: Instructional program A will produce a greater improvement in the way middle-school students with learning disabilities write in content-area classes than will instructional program B.

Statement of purpose: The purpose of the study is to determine whether either of two instructional programs helps middle-school students with learning disabilities to improve their writing.

Question: Which of the two instructional programs causes middle-school students with learning disabilities to write more effectively?

subjects   The subjects are the particular individuals used in the research. One group of subjects in the example in this chapter consisted of all students classified as learning disabled in grades five through eight in mainstreamed and self-contained classes in an urban middle school. In the comparative and causative designs, the researchers also used as subjects a small group of students who were not learning disabled. They randomly selected a portion of the students without learning disabilities at each grade level. This selected group is a sample of all the students without learning disabilities in the school. The population is the larger group with which the researchers think their results can be used. They are interested in being able to pass on the results about students with and without learning disabilities in middle school to other educators in other urban centers.

generalizability   When research producers' results can be extended to other groups (e.g., to other students with and without learning disabilities in urban centers), these results are said to have generalizability. That means a research consumer in a different urban center can have confidence in applying the producers' research results because they are applicable to middle-school students with and without learning disabilities in urban centers.

OVERVIEW

The ideas in this book are organized to reflect the phases of research as research producers would go through them. In Table 1.1, the phases of research undertaken by the research team in the example are linked to the information in later chapters.

ACTIVITIES

Each chapter has an activities section in which the book's readers are asked to apply the chapter's content. Two sources of feedback are available to the reader. The first consists of the authors' ideas immediately following the activities. The second consists of the course instructor's feedback.

Table 1.1
Overview of the Research Process

The Research Team's Activity	Phase of Research and Location of Information Within This Text
Selecting a problem area; specifying research questions and defining terms	Reading and Evaluating Introductory Sections, Chapter 4
Searching databases	Locating Information About Research Reports, Chapter 11
Selecting research designs	Research Designs, Chapter 2
Describing and selecting subjects	Reading and Evaluating Subject Sections, Chapter 5
Selecting data collection devices	Reading and Evaluating Instrument Sections, Chapter 6
Conducting the study	Reading and Evaluating Procedure Sections, Chapter 7
Analyzing the data	Reading and Interpreting Results Sections, Chapter 8
Determining implications of the research	Reading and Evaluating Discussion Sections, Chapter 9
Reporting the results	Reading and Evaluating Research Reports, Chapter 3; Reading and Interpreting Reviews of Research, Chapter 10

Activity 1.   Write a summary of the key ideas found in the chapter. The focus questions at the chapter's beginning should be used as a guide to structure your summary.

Activity 2.   Using Table 1.1 as a guide, scan—as opposed to an intensive reading—the research report "Results of an Early Intervention Program for First Grade Children at Risk for Reading Disability" in the chapter's Appendix. (Do not read the Feedback section until you have completed the activity.) As you read the report, locate the particular sections in which information is given. Do not be concerned with fully understanding the report.

FEEDBACK

Activity 1

Why do educators conduct research?

Educators produce research to verify the effectiveness of teaching and learning ideas and practices already in use, to discover new ideas and practices, to develop practices that simplify people's lives, to introduce practices that complicate people's lives, and to discover counterintuitive practices.

What is the distinction between research consumers and research producers?

Research producers need technical competence in applying research strategies—the procedures for conceptualizing, developing, implementing, and reporting research. Research consumers need skills in understanding how researchers undertake research and in reading, interpreting, and applying others' research results.

What does it mean to understand research as a research producer does?

To understand research as a research producer does means understanding research with the mindset of a research producer. To do that, research consumers need to understand (a) the research process and the decisions facing research producers, (b) the possible alternatives research producers consider at those decision points, and (c) the implications of the research producers' results and conclusions.

What are some key terms used in research?

Key research terms are (a) *variable*—anything in a research situation that can vary; (b) *design*—the plan or type of research (research can be quantitative, or statistical, qualitative, or nonstatistical, or a combination); (c) *hypothesis*—a tentative statement about the relationship between two or more variables; (d) *subjects*—the people used in the study; and (e) *generalizability*—the ability of the results from one study to be applied to subjects not used in the study.

Activity 2

Paragraph 1: The abstract, a summary of the entire research report.

Paragraphs 2–9: Background information and what others have found in answering related questions about the topic, and why the authors are doing the research.

Paragraphs 10–11: Statements (predictions) about the researchers' purpose and the results they expect to get in the two studies (first grade and third grade).

Paragraph 12: A description of the children used in the first-grade study.

Paragraph 13: The research design of the first-grade study.

Paragraphs 14–17: A description of the research procedure (intervention) used in the first-grade study.

Paragraphs 18–19 (items 1–10): The tests used to measure the first-grade children's reading performance (see also, paragraph 45).

Paragraphs 20–25: An explanation of the results of the first-grade study. The statistical data are found in Tables 1 and 2 of the study.

Paragraphs 26–27: A description of the children used in the third-grade study.

Paragraph 28: A description of the research procedures used in the third-grade study.

Paragraph 29 (items 1–6): The tests used to measure the third-grade children's reading performance.

Paragraphs 30–34: An explanation of the results of the third-grade study. The statistical data are found in Table 3 of the study.

Paragraphs 35–39: A summary of the purpose and results of the study with ideas about what might have caused the results.

Paragraphs 40–43: The researchers' ideas about how the results can be used for instructional purposes and other research.

Paragraph 46: The reference section, containing all the other research the authors referred to in their report.

McCarthy, P., Newby, R. F., & Recht, D. R. (1995). Results of an early intervention program for first grade children at risk for reading disability. *Reading Research and Instruction, 34*(4), 273–294.

Results of an Early Intervention Program for First Grade Children at Risk for Reading Disability

Patricia McCarthy

Wauwatosa School District
Cardinal Stritch College

Robert F. Newby

Medical College of Wisconsin

Donna R. Recht

University School of Milwaukee

ABSTRACT

Thirty-eight first grade children with low emergent literacy skills who were at risk for difficulty in learning to read were tutored for a median of 58 half-hour sessions in addition to their regular classroom instruction. The tutoring (Early Intervention Program, EIP) focused on word recognition, phonetic application and comprehension in context. The EIP children's word recognition in isolation and in context, reading speed, and comprehension were superior to well-matched controls at completion of tutoring, at the end of first grade, and at third grade. At grade three, the EIP group was equivalent to a group of average-reading classmates on word recognition in context, acceptable accuracy and answering comprehension questions, but not on word recognition in isolation or on reading speed.

The past decade has seen a blossoming of interest in intensive intervention programs for kindergarten and first grade children who are at risk for reading failure. Since transition rooms and retention in grade have not been effective in resolving early achievement delays (Holmes & Matthews, 1984), educators have sought alternative approaches to help children with weak early literacy skills. Several major research studies have shown significant benefits from individual tutorial programs with first grade children. These programs emphasize one-to-one child-specific tutoring in addition to routine classroom instruction. The goal is for children to develop reading and writing strategies so they can learn successfully within a regular classroom. While the present context does not allow a comprehensive review of this previous work, several highlights deserve mention.

The basic theory behind this type of intervention emphasizes the need to interrupt a "causal chain of escalating negative side effects" (Stanovich, 1986, p. 364) that slow-to-develop readers often experience. In an interactive model of reading, the reader constructs meaning from the print. In learning to read, the reader uses background knowledge, recognizes words holistically, and can utilize phonetic strategies within a contextual setting. Children who experience early difficulty learning to read typically come to school with less exposure to print and developmental readiness to devote attention to print (Stanovich, 1986). Alternatively, they are personally impulsive, have difficulty with sustained attention, or are reluctant to take risks in learning activities, which leads to behaviors that are not conducive to learning to read (Clay,

1993a). Their initial reading problems can compound as they receive less text exposure than good readers during the acquisition phase, instruction with reading materials that are too difficult for them, and fewer opportunities to practice their emerging reading skills (Stanovich, 1986). This in turn delays their development of reading automaticity, syntactic mastery, vocabulary knowledge, and conceptual skills (Ball & Blachman, 1991). As Slavin (1993, p. 11) argues, "success in the early grades does not guarantee success throughout the school years and beyond, but failure in the early grades does virtually guarantee failure in later schooling."

(4) The results of previously studied intervention programs have been impressive. Bradley and Bryant's (1985) landmark study demonstrated significant gains in reading and spelling skills with a tutorial program that emphasized manipulation and categorization of sounds with children aged five and one half years to seven years. This study compared two different intervention variations with both non-treated children and children who received the same amount of one-to-one training in semantic rather than phonological categorization. The treatment effects for the two phonologically trained groups remained robust at a third-grade follow-up. Specifically, children receiving forty treatment sessions involving a combination of sound categorization and practice in manipulating word families with plastic letters were almost one year better than the nonspecific effects control group in reading word recognition, and almost one and one half years better in spelling. Ball and Blachman (1991) reported similar initial treatment gains by small groups of kindergarten students who received a combination of phoneme awareness instruction with letters on plastic tiles, sound categorization tasks like Bryant and Bradley's intervention (1985), and training in letter names and letter-sound associations. Training in letter names and letter-sound associations alone did not yield comparable gains. Generalization of Ball and Blachman's (1991) results was limited by their use of a general kindergarten sample rather than an at-risk sample, and they have only reported immediate posttreatment testing rather than long-term follow-up results.

(5) Several research monographs on the Reading Recovery program have been published by the program's directors at the Ohio State University (e.g. Pinnell, DeFord & Lyons, 1988; Pinnell, Lyons, DeFord, Bryk & Seltzer, 1991). Originally developed by Marie Clay (1985) in New Zealand, Reading Recovery tutoring focuses on the individual child as he/she reads and writes connected text. Each one-to-one lesson includes reading familiar easy books which the child has read before, the child writing his/her own stories cooperatively with the teacher, and reading new books. The teacher takes a "Running Record," a form of miscue analysis, on a book each day to provide immediate information regarding the child's reading development. Instruction is thus individualized to each child's needs and focuses on developing good reading strategies, including directional movement, one-to-one matching, self-monitoring, using multiple cue sources, and self-correction. Phonological analysis and decoding skills are emphasized in context and are addressed in writing and included in reading new materials. Children reading in the lowest 20% of their classes who received up to 60 sessions of Reading Recovery instruction have risen to average reading levels by the end of their first grade year, in contrast with children receiving small-group Chapter 1 instruction. Children receiving individual tutoring with the Reading Recovery methods have maintained treatment gains in follow-up testing during the school year after intervention occurred, but a small-group adaptation of the Reading Recovery methods and two alternative individual tutoring models did not yield such gains. Treatment results have been stronger for the approximately three quarters of treatment sample who have been judged to be strong enough readers to be "successfully discontinued" from the program than for the remaining one quarter of the sample who completed the full 60 sessions of intervention without meeting criteria for discontinuation; the latter group has remained below average in long-term follow-up studies.

(6) Wasik and Slavin (1993) reviewed outcome studies on several prominent programs, particularly Reading Recovery and Success for All (Slavin, Madden, Karweit, Dolan & Wasik, 1992). In general, the programs showed substantial treatment gains over the course of the first grade year in contrast with relevant control groups. Programs that included comprehensive models of reading, provided multifaceted instructional interventions, and used certified teachers rather than paraprofessionals tended to achieve stronger results. Follow-up studies have shown that treatment gains persist at least through 3rd grade, and some programs have shown a reduction in retentions or special education referrals over time. Wasik and Slavin (1993) compared different studies by computing treatment effect sizes (differences between treatment group versus control

group on mean posttest or follow-up scores, divided by the posttest or follow-up standard deviation of the control group). In this method, effect sizes that approach or exceed 1.0 are felt to represent substantial treatment gain or maintenance. Some of these studies show decreasing effect sizes from posttest immediately following treatment to follow-up testing several years later, but this modulation in effect size is generally attributable to increasing variability in the outcome measures over time rather than an erosion of the initial mean treatment differences. Wasik and Slavin (1993) interpreted the paradoxically reducing effect sizes in the Reading Recovery studies as a diminishment in the importance of the treatment gains even though the absolute magnitude of the treatment gains were maintained, and they pointed out that the relatively more stable sizes over time in Success for All represented an absolute widening of the differences between treatment groups and control groups over time, probably in response to the continued intervention available to the treatment groups beyond first grade.

(7) While the general value of these programs has been illustrated well in previous research, various important details of the instructional approaches have not been adequately investigated. For example, Iverson and Tumner (1993) added a phonological training element to the standard Reading Recovery program, which shortened the number of sessions that were felt to be necessary before discontinuing students from the program but did not yield incremental gains on most outcome measures in comparison to a standard Reading Recovery comparison group. Outcome measures included a battery of early reading and writing skills (Clay, 1985, 1993b; see also Method for Initial Treatment Study below), the Dolch word list (Dolch, 1939), and a number of phonological processing tests. Because discontinuation criteria were not objectively operationalized or judged by raters blind to treatment condition, and because long-term follow-up data are not yet available, the advantages of the phonological addition in this study remain unclear, beyond the immediate cost-savings of the reduced number of sessions used. None of the previous studies has thoroughly examined the complex interplay among different aspects of the reading process in long-term follow-up, including different types of reading accuracy (i.e. decoding of word lists in isolation, reading accuracy in context, acceptable accuracy without changing test meaning), reading fluency or automaticity (i.e. reading rate), or different types of reading comprehension (i.e., free recall or answering of questions). Early interventions may improve some but not all of these aspects of reading, and the implications of such differential improvement may be important.

(8) The present research program differs from the previous studies in several ways. First, we emphasize integrated reading skills in tutoring. This refers to the child's ability to appropriately combine semantic, syntactic and grapho-phonic cues automatically while reading. This is similar to the Reading Recovery research but contrasts with the Bradley and Bryant (1985) and Ball and Blachman (1991) studies, which focused more narrowly on teaching children to manipulate sounds. Sound manipulation is an important precursor to phonics, hence to success with fluent word identification, but neither study taught reading per se. Second, we examine the reading process in detail at follow-up. The long-term follow-up measures in Reading Recovery (Pinnell et al., 1988) and Success for All (Slavin et al., 1992) focused on unidimensional measures of text reading level and/or standardized achievement tests, with success measured by student reading achievement within the average range. Third, we use carefully matched cohorts of children from equivalent schools for comparison controls. The Reading Recovery research has generally used comparison groups with initial random placement into the Reading Recovery tutoring versus an alternative type of compensatory help, or a random sample of children from the discontinued Reading Recovery treatment group versus a random sample of children from the same grade level. Fourth, teacher training in the present program uses the instructional structure of the Clay (1985, 1993b) model, combined with systematic videotaping and feedback by a support team composed of multiple professionals working in the context of their normal school calendar and school assignments. Reading Recovery trains teachers over a year at a central site. The present program trains teachers to provide feedback to each other as they work with children in their own schools. Training is viewed as staff development that involves increased knowledge about the reading process, increased awareness of child behaviors, and interactive reflection with peers on effective teaching. The Reading Recovery training is beyond the economic and pragmatic constraints of many school systems.

(9) The study presented here demonstrates the effects of the Early Intervention Program (EIP) in the School District of Wauwatosa. This district is located in a middle-class to upper-middle-class suburb of Milwaukee, Wisconsin, and cultural diversity is enhanced by a metropolitan desegregation program. The district has collaborated with a reading/language arts department at a local college and a neuropsychology department at

a medical school for research design and consultation. Prior to implementation of the EIP, first grade children in this school district had little exposure to additional reading help. Concern about children's initial reading difficulty combined with information in the professional literature about the success of Marie Clay's early intervention led to the formulation of the EIP. The EIP was elaborated from the work of Marie Clay (1985, 1991, 1993b) and from available outcome information on Reading Recovery. Pilot research on the EIP started during the 1989-90 school year. Since that time, there have been four yearly cohorts. The present report focuses only on the 1990-91 and 1991-92 cohorts, which have had the longest and most comprehensive follow-up evaluation thus far. For clarity, the present report separates the data into two studies, the initial first grade treatment results and the third grade follow-up results.

(10) In the initial treatment study, we predicted that children receiving EIP in addition to their regular classroom instruction would show greater gain than control children with the same level of reading problems who received only regular classroom placement, in six key areas of early reading development: concepts about print, emerging sight vocabulary (indicated by child-generated written vocabulary), understanding of sound/symbol relationships (indicated by writing to dictation), oral reading accuracy, acceptable reading accuracy that maintained essential meaning in context, and reading comprehension. These predictions were constructed to test the basic notion that specialized intensive intervention should yield positive results at the time of treatment. We did not predict a treatment effect in the reading readiness skill of alphabet recognition, because the regular first grade curriculum was felt to be as likely as the EIP to develop this area.

(11) We also predicted that the initial treatment gains in the six key areas would continue through third grade, and that the EIP children would perform at similar levels as average readers at their schools. These predictions were constructed to reflect the main goal and hope of all specialized intensive early intervention programs since Bryant and Bradley's (1985) classic study, i.e. that children at risk can be helped to "catch up" and stay caught up within the broad range of abilities within their classrooms. Measures of reading rate were added at this point in the program because informal observations as the program developed over time suggested that the previously at-risk children might be lagging in reading automaticity in spite of their gains in other important reading skills. It was expected that treatment effect sizes would modulate over time, as in previous similar studies of intensive intervention programs for children at risk (Wasik & Slavin, 1993).

METHOD FOR INITIAL FIRST GRADE TREATMENT STUDY

Subjects

(12) The subjects were 38 first grade children with low emergent reading skills, 19 from each of two elementary schools in the same suburban school district. Children were drawn from a total of 5 classrooms. These children were identified by their former kindergarten teachers and current first grade teachers as being in the lowest third of their classes in reading skills during the first semester of first grade. The groups from the two different schools were matched as pairs on age, receptive vocabulary skill, Marie Clay's (1985, 1993a) measures of early reading abilities (see Outcome Measures, below), and a global five-point Likert rating of emergent reading skills by their teachers. Two students from each school spoke English as a second language. No students were enrolled in special education or Chapter 1 services at the time of the study.

Experimental Design

(13) Children from one school participated in the EIP program in addition to their regular first grade classroom instruction, and children from the other school received no extra intervention outside their regular first grade classroom placements. Pragmatic concerns regarding teacher assignment to schools, resources for teacher training, and scheduling prevented random assignment of children to treatment groups, so the groups were carefully matched on all outcome measures at pretest. The two schools were located in adjacent neighborhoods in the same school district, and were equivalent in socioeconomic makeup, size, physical facilities, and general curriculum. The communication arts curriculum in this district supports the use of literature for reading instruction. Basals are used as a source of additional stories. Phonics is taught through whole group instruction, conferencing, and developmental writing. The EIP children received a median of 58 (mean 49, range 18 to 82) 30-minute daily one-to-one tutoring sessions during either the fall or spring semesters of first grade.

Intervention

(14) The EIP program was based on the assumption that all children can learn to their own ability within a supportive school environment, and that reading is a learned behavior for which some children require an

active, intensive instructional program for success. Its purpose was to help these targeted readers who needed extra time, individualization and attention to achieve parity with their classmates in reading. Tutoring sessions for the program were scheduled at different times from the children's routine language-arts curriculum involvement within their first grade classrooms, so the intervention represented an "add on" rather than a "pull out" from standard instruction time.

(15) Each EIP lesson involved three ten-minute segments. In the first segment, children reread books that they had covered in previous lessons. Four books of increasing difficulty were utilized on a rotating basis. The goal of this segment was to promote reading fluency and use of the good reader strategies that form the focus of the Reading Recovery Program (Clay, 1993b). In the second segment, children wrote a message of their own composition in standard spelling, with explicit instruction from the tutor in sound segmentation and relations with the alphabetic code. The phonological training involved two strategies: In the Elkonin boxes strategy (Clay, 1985), the child slowly articulated the sounds in a word sequentially while at the same time manipulating corresponding counters. In the "stretch it out" strategy (Clay, 1993; Griffith & Olson, 1992), the child slowly articulated sounds in a word while choosing the appropriate alphabetic symbols to represent sounds. In the third segment, tutors presented new reading material using the guided reading format (Clay, 1991; Ministry of Education, 1985). The basic philosophy of guided reading requires the child to apply good reader strategies to the text independently, with support from the tutor.

(16) The senior author served as program coordinator and provided tutoring to six of the EIP subjects. She trained three additional tutors for the project. Three of the tutors were certified reading specialists, and the fourth had a masters degree in reading with over 20 years experience as a first grade classroom teacher. Throughout the two years of the present study the four tutors met weekly for a two hour training session, which was structured using the cognitive coaching method (Costa & Garmston, 1985). Initially, the team watched videotaped lessons of the coordinator, who modeled instruction with the children. As time went on, each tutor was responsible for presenting a videotaped lesson on a rotating weekly schedule. The videotaped segment addressed theoretical elements of emergent reading and writing, as well as serving as a vehicle for interaction and coaching within the team (Joyce & Showers, 1982). Adherence to the EIP program was monitored by monthly direct observation by the program coordinator, and by examination of the daily running records and lesson plans (Clay, 1985, 1993a) detailing students' performance in the ongoing training sessions.

(17) Students received a maximum of 82 treatment sessions. All but two children were discontinued before the targeted maximum number of 75 sessions was completed, at the point when they were judged by the team of tutors to exhibit strategies of good readers independently in lessons and in the classroom, and when they were judged by their classroom teachers to be reading at or above the average level in their classes. All children were incorporated in the analyses presented below, including the two who simply ended tutoring after 75 or 82 sessions; the latter received a few extra sessions in an attempt to solidify her gains and increase independence.

Outcome Measures

(18) These measures included Marie Clay's (1985, 1993a) Observation Survey, a list of 25 primer level words constructed specifically for the present study, and three story selections from the Wright Company series (Cowley, 1983, 1987a, 1987b). Each child received one story at the preprimer level ("Night-time" for the first year cohort, or "The Seed" for the second year cohort) and one story at the first grade level ("Just This Once" for both cohorts). None of the children had previous exposure to these stories at home or at school. All measures were given at pretest and at posttest (when the EIP member of each pair ended the instruction program), except the first grade level story was given at posttest only because it was too difficult for all children at pretest. Both pretesting and posttesting were completed by one of the EIP teachers or by the reading resource teacher at the control school. The specific variables measured were as follows:

(19) 1. Letter Identification (Clay, 1985, 1993a). The child reads randomly placed upper and lower case letters of the alphabet, with two letters written in different script forms. Credit is given if the letter name, sound or a word beginning with that letter is given. Score is the number correct out of a maximum of 54.

2. Concepts About Print (Clay, 1985, 1993a). The child demonstrates his/her understanding of the conventions of our printed language by responding to questions asked by the teacher as the teacher reads text which includes special features such as upside down print and misspelled words. Examples of concepts evaluated by this text include distinguishing elements in reading, such

as letter, word, top, bottom, front, back, punctuation and one-to-one matching. Score is the number correct out of a maximum of 24.

3. Writing Vocabulary (Clay, 1985, 1993a). The child is asked to write all the words he/she knows within a ten-minute time limit. The teacher can prompt words that the teacher feels the child might know. This measure is an indicator of emerging sight vocabulary. Score is the number of real words spelled correctly, including proper nouns.

4. Hearing and Recording Sounds in Words-Dictation Task (Clay, 1985, 1993a). The child is asked to write a standard sentence that is dictated by the examiner. Correct sounds (phonemes) and letters (graphemes) are credited. This measure is an indicator of phonological analysis skills. Score is the number correct out of a maximum of 37.

5. Primer Level Word List (see Appendix A). The child reads aloud a list of 25 basic words commonly appearing in emergent literature and on high-frequency word lists. The child is provided with a marker to aid visual focus. Two scores are computed: percent of words read correctly within one second, and percent of words read correctly without time limit.

6. Oral Reading Speed in Context. The child orally reads two stories, and the examiner records time to completion. Score is words per minute.

7. Oral Reading Accuracy in Context. The child orally reads two stories, and the examiner notes all miscues (omissions, substitutions, insertions; self-corrections are counted as miscues). Score is the percent of words read correctly.

8. Acceptable Reading Accuracy in Context. On the same stories as in (6), the examiner subtracts from the record of total miscues those miscues that do not change the meaning of the passage and that are syntactically correct. Therefore, self-corrections are not counted as miscues for this computation. Score is the percent of words read acceptably under these criteria.

9. Free Recall Reading Comprehension. On the same stories as in (6), the examiner asks the child to retell the story in his/her own words. Teachers record the child's recollections. One point is given per proposition recalled or inference made. Score is the percent of propositions and inferences from the story that are included in the retelling, in any sequence.

10. Reading Comprehension Questions. On the same stories as in (6), the examiner asks the child six open-ended questions, three of which are explicit and three implicit. A list of correct answers was compiled by the EIP teachers prior to administration. Any answers that varied from this list were judged by the team as a group. Score is the percent of questions answered correctly.

RESULTS OF INITIAL FIRST GRADE TREATMENT STUDY

(20) The two groups were not significantly different on age or baseline test scores at pretest (see Table 1). This result was expected, due to the careful pairwise matching of subjects on the measures. Both groups showed average receptive vocabulary Peabody Picture Vocabulary Test—Revised standard score 98). The present suburban clinical sample was average to low-average in comparison to available urban nonclinical reference groups of first graders in Ohio and six year olds in New Zealand who have been given Clay's measures (third to fifth stanines; Clay, 1993a).

(21) Treatment effects were determined with analysis of covariance on the EIP versus control posttest scores, with pretest scores on the same measures as covariates (see Table 2). To assist in comparing the present results

Table 1   Mean (Standard Deviation) Age and Baseline Test Scores on EIP Versus Control Groups

Variable	EIP (n = 19)	Control (n = 19)	t
Age (years)	6.6 (0.3)	6.6 (0.3)	0.00
Peabody Picture Vocabulary Test-Revised (standard score)	99.7 (12.0)	98.7 (11.7)	0.27
Letter Identification (maximum 54)	49.6 (4.9)	49.0 (5.9)	0.33
Concepts About Print (maximum 24)	15.6 (2.9)	16.0 (3.1)	−0.43
Writing Vocabulary (number of words)	18.7 (14.3)	20.4 (16.1)	−0.35
Dictation Task (maximum 37)	20.0 (12.7)	20.3 (13.2)	−0.06
Word List Reading (maximum 25)	13.3 (10.0)	12.0 (9.1)	0.42
Teacher Rating (maximum 5)	2.2 (0.8)	1.8 (1.2)	0.95

Table 2   Mean Pretest and Posttest Scores for EIP and Control Groups

Variable (form, maximum value)		EIP (n = 19)		Control (n = 19)		F^a	Effect Size[b]
		Pre	Post	Pre	Post		
Reading Readiness							
Letter Identification	M	49.6	53.6	49.0	53.1	0.03	−0.01
(raw, maximum 54)	SD	4.9	1.0	5.9	1.1		
Concepts About Print	M	15.6	20.8	16.0	18.9	15.79***	0.95
(raw, maximum 24)	SD	2.9	1.4	3.1	2.0		
Writing Measures							
Writing Vocabulary	M	18.7	48.9	20.4	38.3	16.98***	0.65
(raw, no maximum)	SD	14.3	11.4	16.1	16.2		
Dictation Task	M	20.0	34.5	20.2	31.2	5.97*	0.50
(raw, maximum 37)	SD	12.7	2.5	13.0	6.6		
Word List							
Flash Presentation	M	50.6	87.7	43.2	74.1	13.54***	0.79
(percent correct)	SD	39.9	11.4	33.5	17.3		
Untimed Presentation	M	53.2	93.1	48.0	80.9	11.41**	0.73
(percent correct)	SD	39.9	9.5	36.3	16.8		
PrePrimer Story							
Oral Reading Speed	M	16.3	52.1	15.6	21.8	11.20**	2.55
(words per minute)	SD	14.0	23.8	5.6	11.9		
Oral Reading Accuracy	M	56.4	94.8	49.3	76.0	10.05**	0.69
(percent correct)	SD	35.5	4.3	39.9	27.2		
Acceptable Accuracy	M	57.9	96.9	51.9	78.3	9.87**	0.67
(percent correct)	SD	36.4	3.0	41.8	27.8		
Free Recall	M	17.4	41.6	22.7	31.7	3.16	0.35
(percent of idea units)	SD	19.0	25.2	25.8	27.9		
Comprehension Questions	M	65.6	93.8	68.5	80.6	9.14**	0.71
(percent correct)	SD	21.1	10.0	25.3	18.6		
First Grade Story							
Oral Reading Speed	M	—	40.6	—	44.1	0.114	−20.17
(words per minute)	SD	—	16.3	—	21.0		
Oral Reading Accuracy	M	—	91.3	—	63.5	17.76***	0.87
(percent correct)	SD	—	8.3	—	31.9		
Acceptable Accuracy	M	—	94.1	—	66.4	17.10***	0.83
(percent correct)	SD	—	7.7	—	33.2		
Free Recall	M	—	13.0	—	8.1	4.87*	0.96
(percent of idea units)	SD	—	5.3	—	5.2		
Comprehension Questions	M	—	88.9	—	50.4	29.43***	1.16
(percent correct)	SD	—	12.1	—	33.1		

[a] F values compare EIP to Control groups on posttest scores, with pretest score on the same variable as the covariate. No variable was significantly different between groups at pretest.
[b]   Effect size = (EIP Posttest Mean − Control Posttest Mean)/Control Standard Deviation.
* $p < .05$,
** $p < .01$,
*** $p < .001$

with other recent research, Wasik and Slavin's (1993) method was used to compute treatment effect sizes. In this method, the difference between the mean posttest scores is divided by the posttest standard deviation of the control group.

(22) Virtually all hypotheses on treatment outcome were confirmed. The EIP group improved significantly more than the control group on concepts about print ($p < .001$), with an effect size approaching one standard deviation (.95). The EIP group also showed sig-

nificantly greater gains than the control group on both writing vocabulary and writing to dictation (p < .05 to .001). The effect sizes for these writing measures were moderate (.50 to .65), approximately one half standard deviation.

(23) The EIP group improved significantly more than the control group on all measures of word reading skill, including both flash and untimed presentation of the word list, oral reading accuracy in context, and acceptable reading accuracy in context, with both the preprimer and first grade level stories (p < .01 to .001). The effect sizes for the reading accuracy measures were substantial (.67 to .87), approaching one standard deviation.

(24) The EIP group made significantly more gains than the control group in answering comprehension questions for both the preprimer and first grade level stories (p < .01 to .001), and in free recall comprehension for the first grade story (p < .05). The effect sizes for these comprehension measures were substantial (.71 to 1.16), approaching or exceeding one standard deviation.

(25) The EIP group was significantly better than the control group for reading speed on the preprimer story (p < .01), but not on the first grade level story (p > .50). The effect sizes for the reading speed measures varied widely (− .17 to 2.55). Both groups showed modest progress on letter identification, but this progress was not different between groups (p > .50), probably because of a ceiling effect on this measure.

METHOD FOR THIRD GRADE
FOLLOW-UP STUDY

Subjects

(26) The subjects consisted of 34 of the 38 children who completed the initial study. Two subjects had moved out of the area and were unavailable for follow-up testing; their matched pairs were also removed from the analyses. Two other subjects had moved to different schools within the area, so follow-up data were obtained by visiting the new schools. Of the 34 children in the follow-up sample, two had been placed in learning disabilities programs, one in a program for emotionally disturbed students, and one in home-schooling.

(27) An average comparison sample of 17 subjects was constructed retrospectively from students at the EIP school. The group of average third graders was selected using two criteria. First, their third grade teachers nominated them as average in reading skills, compared to their classmates. Second, their Total Reading Scores from the Iowa Tests of Basic Skills administered in fall of second grade ranged between normal curve equivalents of 46 and 76.

Procedure

(28) Children were tested individually in middle of their third grade year, 19 to 24 months after the EIP member of each matched pair ended treatment. One follow-up measure, the 4th grade level story, was administered at the end of the third grade year, 24 to 29 months after treatment ended; children enrolled in the second cohort have not yet received the fourth grade level story at the time this report is being prepared for publication. All follow-up testing was done by the senior author.

Follow-up Measures

(29) Follow-up measures were drawn from the Qualitative Reading Inventory (Leslie & Caldwell, 1990).

1. Graded Word Lists. The child reads a series of graded 20-word lists progressing from the primer level up to the point where fewer than 50% of the words are read correctly. Two scores are computed at each grade level: percent of words [read] correctly within one second, and percent of words read correctly without time limit. Only the third grade and fourth grade lists are presented in the present analyses, because of floor or ceiling effects for many subjects on the other lists.

2. Oral Reading Speed in Context. The child orally reads two several-paragraph narrative stories on topics that are familiar to most mid-elementary children. One story is at the third grade level (A Trip to the Zoo) and one at the fourth grade level (Johnny Appleseed). Scoring is the same as in the initial treatment outcome study.

3. Oral Reading Accuracy in Context, using the same stories as in (2). Scoring is the same as in the initial treatment outcome study.

4. Acceptable Reading Accuracy in Context, using the same stories as in (2). Scoring is the same as in the initial treatment outcome study.

5. Free Recall Reading Comprehension, using the same stories as in (2). Scoring is the same as in the initial treatment outcome study.

6. Reading Comprehension Questions, using the same stories as in (2). Scoring is the same as in the initial treatment outcome study, except that eight questions are provided and the scoring criteria from the QRI manual are used.

RESULTS OF THIRD GRADE
FOLLOW-UP STUDY

(30) Follow-up differences were determined with one-way analysis of variance on the scores obtained from the

Table 3 **Mean Third Grade Follow-up Scores for EIP Group, Control Group, and Average Comparison Group**

Variable		EIP	Effect Control	Average	F	Effect of Size[a]
Third Grade Word List	n	16	14	17		
Flash Presentation	M	76.0	65.0	89.1	8.59##	0.58
(percent correct)	SD	19.4	19.0	8.5		
Untimed Presentation	M	80.6	70.0	94.1	11.53++	0.56
(percent correct)	SD	15.4	18.8	5.6		
Fourth Grade Word List	n	14	10	17		
Flash Presentation	M	60.0	42.0	75.9	14.40##	0.91
(percent correct)	SD	14.6	19.8	14.6		
Untimed Presentation	M	70.4	53.4	83.6	11.03##	0.82
(percent correct)	SD	16.5	20.6	11.7		
Third Grade Story	n	17	17	17		
Oral Reading Speed	M	84.8	69.8	119.5	15.62++	0.79
(words per minute)	SD	23.4	18.9	27.0		
Oral Reading Accuracy	M	94.1	89.7	96.9	15.93##	0.80
(percent correct)	SD	3.0	5.5	1.6		
Acceptable Accuracy	M	97.2	93.9	98.4	11.13**	0.75
(percent correct)	SD	2.1	4.4	1.1		
Free Recall	M	36.1	32.3	43.2	2.18	0.32
(percent of idea units)	SD	14.6	11.7	19.2		
Comprehension Questions	M	84.6	71.5	84.7	3.25*	0.65
(percent correct)	SD	16.9	20.1	15.0		
Fourth Grade Story	n	9	9	9		
Oral Reading Speed	M	69.4	65.8	101.2	6.23++	0.15
(words per minute)	SD	19.1	24.3	22.3		
Oral Reading Accuracy	M	94.1	87.4	95.9	5.50*	0.74
(percent correct)	SD	2.8	9.1	2.3		
Acceptable Accuracy	M	96.4	90.2	97.7	4.56*	0.67
(percent correct)	SD	2.7	9.2	1.6		
Free Recall	M	26.7	27.9	28.3	0.04	-0.07
(percent of idea units)	SD	7.9	16.6	12.0		
Comprehension Questions	M	71.1	48.2	53.1	3.10	1.07
(percent correct)	SD	12.5	21.4	25.4		

[a]   Effect size = (EIP Mean − Control Mean)/Control Standard Deviation.
* $p < .05$, with Average = EIP > Control at $p < .05$ in paired comparisons
** $p < .01$, with Average = EIP > Control at $p < .05$ in paired comparisons
$p < .01$, with Average = EIP > Control at $p < .05$ in paired comparisons
++ $p < .01$, with Average > EIP = Control at $p < .05$ in paired comparisons

EIP, control, and average groups during third grade (see Table 3). More sophisticated data treatment with analysis of covariance or repeated measures analysis of variance was not deemed appropriate in this situation, because the two year developmental and learning period since the initial study necessitated completely different, more advanced content on both the word lists and stories.

(31) The follow-up results were more complex than the results of the initial study. Some measures confirmed the follow-up hypotheses completely, i.e. the EIP groups both remained superior to the control group and was equivalent to the average comparison group (noted by asterisks in Table 3). Some hypotheses were confirmed partially (noted by pound signs in Table 3), and some not at all (noted by plus signs or nonsignificant results in Table 3).

(32) The hypotheses were confirmed completely for several measures of contextual reading skill, including oral reading accuracy at the fourth grade level, acceptable reading accuracy at both levels, and answering reading comprehension questions at the third grade level ($p < .05$ to .01). The EIP group showed a trend ($p < .08$) toward better answering of reading comprehension questions than both of the other groups at the fourth grade level. The effect

sizes for these contextual reading differences between the EIP and control groups were substantial, approaching or exceeding one standard deviation (.67 to 1.07).

(33) The hypotheses were partially confirmed for all measures of word-reading skill that had not been confirmed completely, including flash presentation of both the third grade and fourth grade word lists, untimed presentation of the fourth grade word list, and oral reading accuracy of the third grade story (p < .01). On these measures, the EIP group remained superior to the control group but was not equivalent to the average group. The effect sizes for these measures were moderate to substantial, from one half standard deviation to almost one standard deviation (.56 to .91).

(34) The hypotheses for reading speed and for free recall comprehension were not confirmed. The average comparison group was better than both the EIP and control groups on all measures of reading fluency (p < .01), and the EIP and control groups were not significantly better than each other on these measures (p > .10). The three groups were not different on free recall comprehension (p > .10).

DISCUSSION

(35) The present study demonstrated positive benefits from an Early Intervention Program (EIP) for students at risk for reading disability. Children who received a median of 58 one-to-one tutoring sessions during first grade showed better concepts about print, emerging sight vocabulary, understanding of sound-symbol relationships, word recognition skill in isolation and in context, reading speed, and reading comprehension following the tutoring period at the end of first grade than matched children who received only routine classroom placement. As predicted, both the treatment and regular classroom groups achieved reasonable proficiency in alphabet recognition by the end of first grade. Two years later, the treated children still showed better word recognition skill in context and better reading comprehension than untreated children. At the two-year follow-up, the treated children were equivalent to a comparison group of average-achieving classmates in word recognition in context and in reading comprehension, but not in word recognition in isolation or in reading rate. Treatment gains and maintenance by the EIP group were clinically substantial as well as statistically significant, approaching or exceeding effect sizes of one standard deviation of the control group. The present findings are very similar to treatment gains that have been reported by other intensive interventions for children at risk for reading disability (reviewed by Wasik and Slavin, 1993), and are based

on all children who were enrolled in the program, not just those who were successfully discontinued because they reached acceptable, average reading skills before the maximum number of treatment sessions provided.

(36) Several factors probably contributed to the success of the EIP. First, experienced teachers provided instruction, which has tended to produce more positive results than paraprofessionals or briefly trained volunteers (Wasik & Slavin, 1993). Second, instruction was individually shaped by the teacher in the role of the expert evaluator (Johnston & Allington, 1989). Third, informal observation of treated children through running records and daily journals suggested that they became more reflective, increased their self-monitoring and self-correcting, and built strategies to actively construct meaning and patterns in their reading, all of which have been found to characterize successful learners in contrast with less successful learners (Brown, 1980; Johnson & Winograd, 1985; Torgesen, 1982; Vellutino, 1987). Finally, the EIP lessons were provided in non-competitive task-involving contexts that encouraged children to solve problems themselves but to seek help when necessary, reduced feelings of failure, increased cooperation, and engaged children in reading and writing rather than leading to avoidance.

(37) Given the individualized tutoring inherent in the EIP treatment, it was not surprising that the reading word recognition and comprehension performance skills of the children in the EIP group were superior to the classroom-only children in first grade. The critical question was whether the achievement attributed to the 58 individual tutoring sessions would continue past first grade. The two-year follow-up study examined two EIP cohorts (in consecutive years) as third graders compared with their matched controls and compared with average readers, as rated by their teachers and on standardized testing. The EIP readers continued to significantly outperform their matched controls. However, would these EIP readers have the same type of performance as average readers two years after tutoring? The results suggested that the EIP readers achieved like the average readers in their word identification skill in context, in their acceptable word recognition accuracy in context, and in their ability to answer comprehension questions. They were less accurate than average readers in their ability to read isolated words on word lists, and they read more slowly than average readers.

(38) The EIP children have made substantive gains. Although their word recognition in mid-elementary school was not as accurate or rapid as the average group, the EIP children's ability to monitor words for meaning in a story setting was average. Transfer of

these behaviors to classroom settings was encouraged by an emphasis on meaning, interaction with stories, writing opportunities, and assessment measures in classroom instruction. One probable cause of student success at follow-up is this continuity between the individual and classroom approaches in this district. The goal of reading instruction is to help children recognize words in meaningful contexts and to understand what they read. The EIP children appeared to be aware of making reading errors in context, and they knew how to use their reading strategies to self-correct. This extra reading work may have contributed to the EIP children's slower reading speed. In addition, they may continue to be slower in processing words until the words are overlearned through repeated readings in text. The goal of reading is not rapid reading of isolated word lists. The results suggest that the tutoring aids comprehension through the monitoring of words read in context rather than speed or automaticity of word recognition. It is likely that children with low early literacy skills need increased classroom time for processing and/or differentiated instruction as compared to average children. It is important that teachers look beyond word recognition speed as they set expectations for these children.

(39) In the absence of well established quantitative methods for analyzing changes in children's strategic reading behaviors, qualitative observations of EIP children's progress over the course of intervention can be made. Before intervention, children tended to either overuse meaning (usually the pictures) without regard to visual match, or to overuse grapho-phonic cues and not make sense. In either condition, the children often were not concerned with one-to-one correspondence as their production contained either more or less words than the printed text. As tutoring progressed, the children became more aware of the importance of making sense. They became more aware of the use of grapho-phonics to cross check the words they were reading. They also self-monitored, stopping when their word either did not make sense or did not match visually. They began rereading to pick up more cues as well as to maintain one-to-one correspondence between the spoken and written word. The understanding and use of sound segmentation was also observed in their writing. At this point, they began to transfer this ability to decode unfamiliar words when necessary in their reading at the grapho-phonic level. Towards the end of tutoring, children have integrated the semantic, syntactic and grapho-phonic cue systems so that they can use them in coordination to decode unfamiliar words and to self-correct immediately and more efficiently. They appear to use word analysis strategies much as

average readers do but seem to need to apply these strategies more frequently.

(40) One outcome measure did not demonstrate treatment change at posttest or at follow-up, i.e. reading comprehension as measured by free recall. Free recall was included in the study in addition to comprehension questions for the following reasons. Free recall is often demanded in the classroom setting. It is also a more qualitatively comprehensive response to what has been read, as questions can limit child generation. In addition, the process of retelling can enhance children's processing of text information, and this benefit can transfer to the reading of subsequent text (Gambrell, Pfeiffer & Wilson, 1985). However, children in early elementary school need prompts based on the story structure in order to successfully retell stories (Morrow, 1985), and even later elementary school children appear to require practice in order to become proficient in retelling (Gambrell et al., 1985). The EIP in the present study did not specifically train retelling, and the outcome measure in this area did not provide structured prompts, so it is not surprising that no treatment effects were observed in this area. The examiner judgement that is inherent in the free recall measure may render it psychometrically less reliable than other more objective outcome measures, thus less likely to be adequately sensitive to treatment effects.

(41) The results suggest that at risk first grade children profit from individualized one-to-one instruction that emphasizes word recognition and phonetic training in a context-rich environment. The delivery of this instruction can be done by experienced teachers who spend ongoing, cooperative time on site in peer review of their interactions and lessons with children. Results of this study indicate that the intensive weekly teacher interaction and critique provides a less expensive alternative to the year-long intensive Reading Recovery training.

(42) The calculation of effect sizes in the present study, using the method recommended by Wasik and Slavin (1993), both highlights the clinical significance of the EIP findings and allows quantitative comparisons with previous similar research. A recent major review of meta-analysis research on the efficacy of psychological, educational and behavioral treatment (Lipsey & Wilson, 1993) proposed that effect sizes of as little as .20 (i.e. one fifth of a standard deviation difference between a treatment group and a control group) can not be dismissed as practically insignificant. Both the initial and follow-up effect sizes in the present study were substantially higher than .20, ranging from one half standard deviation to over one standard deviation on all measures that showed statistically reliable findings using traditional

parametric tests. The effect sizes immediately after treatment in the present study were comparable to the modal initial effect sizes in the most impactful interventions reviewed by Wasik and Slavin (1993), i.e. Reading Recovery and Success for All. Furthermore, the follow-up effect sizes in both the present study and a number of cohorts in the Success for All program have been comparable to the initial effect sizes, whereas the Reading Recovery follow-ups reviewed by Wasik and Slavin (1993) showed a significant decrement in effect sizes by third grade. The robust maintenance of treatment effects over time in the present study may have been attributable to the integration of the EIP approaches into the ongoing school curriculum, despite the discontinuation of the direct supplemental intervention by the end of first grade. For instance, second and third grade teachers used running records on all children in their classes, and the senior author informally assessed EIP children throughout second and third grades to monitor progress and report on these assessments to classroom teachers.

(43) Several limitations of the present study must be acknowledged. First, the control group did not receive any intervention besides routine classroom placement, so the role of nonspecific effects such as time spent in one-to-one tutoring can not be separated from the role of treatment-specific effects such as the particular curriculum that was used in the EIP. Second, subjects were not randomly assigned to treatment conditions, so a number of extraneous variables may have influenced both initial treatment outcome and long-term maintenance of treatment gains. While each participating school's teaching staff and/or demographic characteristics of the student bodies could have particular potential for such extraneous influence, this district's well-coordinated, unified elementary reading program makes it unlikely that there were extraneous curricular differences between the two schools. Third, standardized individually administered normative outcome measures were not employed, so it is difficult to quantify treatment effects in reference to students outside the school district in which the study took place. On the other hand, the present results are similar enough to the results of the other intervention programs to accept the present findings as robust.

(44) In conclusion, the EIP exemplifies an educational initiative funded by and centered in a public school system. Affiliation with collaborating research centers helped establish an experimental design so that the program's successes could be documented, a necessity in the present climate of pressure on public school budgets. The strong results discussed in this paper have ensured the continued support of this program in the school system. At the same time, it has become ethically inadvisable to continue forming control groups of students with emergent literacy problems who receive no extra intervention in the school district, so current EIP cohorts are being compared to randomly, prospectively selected samples of average classmates based on assessments at the end of kindergarten. The cohorts reported here will also be followed on a longer term basis to substantiate their continued reading success.

APPENDIX A

(45) Word List for Initial Treatment Pretest and Posttest.

and	a	I	to	said
you	he	it	in	was
on	is	go	can	one
look	no	see	down	love
boy	school	mother	like	want

AUTHOR NOTES

(46) This project was supported by a grant from the Wauwatosa School District. We gratefully acknowledge the encouragement of the Wauwatosa School Board and the former Superintendent George Goens; the consultation and collegial support of Robin Gleason, chairperson of the District's Reading Department; the collaboration of Tom Engel, principal of Wilson School, and Mary Weinfurter, reading specialist at Washington School; the tireless teaching by Carolyn Rauen and Kristin Fewel, who were the original tutors for the project, along with the senior author and Robin Gleason; the painstaking organization of materials and data by Kathy Eilbes; and the enthusiastic participation of the children and parents of the District. Correspondence should be sent to Patricia McCarthy, Wilson School, 1060 Glenview Avenue, Wauwatosa, Wisconsin, 53213.

(47) REFERENCES

Ball, E., & Blachman, B. A. (1991). Does phoneme segmentation training in kindergarten make a difference in early word recognition and developmental spelling? *Reading Research Quarterly*, 24, 49–66.

Bradley, L., & Bryant, P. (1985). *Rhyme and reason in reading and spelling*. Ann Arbor: University of Michigan Press.

Brown, A. L. (1980). Metacognitive development and reading. In R. Spiro, B. Bruce, & W. F. Brewer (Eds.), *Theoretical issues in reading comprehension* (pp. 453–481). Hillsdale, NJ: Erlbaum.

Clay, M. M. (1985). *The early detection of reading difficulties*. Exeter, NH: Heinemann.

Clay, M. M. (1991). Introducing a new storybook to young readers. *The Reading Teacher, 45,* 264–272.

Clay, M. M. (1993a). *An observation survey of early literacy achievement*. Portsmouth, NH: Heinemann.

Clay, M. M. (1993b). *Reading recovery: A guidebook for teachers in training*. Portsmouth, NH: Heinemann.

Costa, A., & Garmston, R. (1985). Supervision for intelligent teaching. *Educational Leadership, 42,* 70–80.

Cowley, J. (1983). *Night-Time*. San Diego: Wright Group.

Cowley, J. (1987a). *Just this once*. San Diego: Wright Group.

Cowley, J. (1987b). *The seed*. San Diego: Wright Group.

Dolch, E. W. (1939). *A manual for remedial reading*. Urbana, IL: Geranol.

Gambrell, L. B., Pfeiffer, W. R., & Wilson, R. M. (1985). The effects of retelling upon reading comprehension and recall of text information. *Journal of Educational Research, 78,* 216–220.

Griffith, P. L., & Olson, M. W. (1992). Phonemic awareness helps beginning readers break the code. *The Reading Teacher, 45,* 516–523.

Holmes, C. T., & Matthews, K. M. (1984). The effects of non-promotion on elementary and junior high school pupils: A meta-analysis. *Review of Educational Research, 54,* 225–236.

Iverson, S., & Tunmer, W. E. (1993). Phonological processing skills and the Reading Recovery Program. *Journal of Educational Psychology, 85,* 112–126.

Johnston, P. H., & Allington, R. L. (1989). Coordination, collaboration, and consistency: The redesign of compensatory and special education interventions. In R. Slavin, N. Madden, & N. Karweit (Eds.), *Preventing school failure: Effective programs for students at risk* (pp. 320–354). Boston: Allyn-Bacon.

Johnston, P. H., & Winograd, P. N. (1985). Passive failure in reading. *Journal of Reading Behavior, 17,* 279–301.

Joyce, B., & Showers, B. (1988). *Student achievement through staff development*. White Plains, NY: Longman.

Leslie, L., & Caldwell, J. (1990). *Qualitative Reading Inventory*. Glenview, IL: Scott, Foresman.

Lipsey, M. W., & Wilson, D. B. (1993). The efficacy of psychological, educational, and behavioral treatment: Confirmation from meta-analysis. *American Psychologist, 48,* 181–1209.

Ministry of Education. (1985). *Reading in the junior classes*. Wellington, New Zealand: Department of Education.

Morrow, L. M. (1985). Retelling stories: A strategy for improving young children's comprehension, concept of story structure, and oral language complexity. *The Elementary School Journal, 85,* 647–661.

Pinnell, G. S., DeFord, D. E., & Lyons, C. A. (1988). *Reading Recovery: Early intervention for at-risk first graders*. Arlington, VA: Educational Research Service.

Pinnell, G. S., Lyons, C. A., DeFord, D. E., Bryk, A. S., & Seltzer, M. (1991). *Studying the effectiveness of early intervention approached for first grade children having difficulty in reading*. Columbus: Ohio State University, Martha L. King Language and Literacy Center.

Slavin, R. E. (1993). School and classroom organization in beginning reading: Class size, aides and instructional grouping. In R. E. Slavin, N. L. Kaarweit, B. A. Wasik (Eds.), *Preventing early school failure; Research, policy, and practice*. Boston: Allyn & Bacon.

Slavin, R. E., Madden, N. A., Karweit, N. L., Dolan, L., & Wasik, B. A. (1992). *Success for All: A relentless approach to prevention and early intervention in elementary schools*. Arlington, VA: Educational Research Service.

Stanovich, K. E. (1986). Matthew effects in reading: Some consequences of individual differences in the acquisition of literacy. *Reading Research Quarterly, 21,* 360–407.

Torgesen, J. K. (1982). The learning disabled child as an inactive learner. *Topics in Learning and Learning Disabilities, 2,* 45–52.

Vellutino, F. R. (1987). Dyslexia. *Scientific American, 256,* 34–41.

Wasik, B. A., & Slavin, R. E. (1993). Preventing early reading failure with one-to-one tutoring: A review of five programs. *Reading Research Quarterly, 28,* 179–200.

Chapter 2

Research Designs

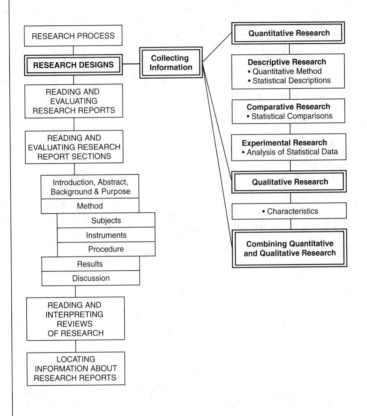

FOCUS QUESTIONS

1. What are the major designs used to conduct educational research?
2. What are quantitative descriptive, comparative, and experimental research?
3. What distinguishes the three types of quantitative research designs from each other?
4. What are the instruments used to collect quantitative data?
5. How are data analyzed in each of the three types of quantitative research designs?
6. What are central tendency and variability, and how are they measured?
7. What are the major purposes for conducting qualitative research?
8. What are the major features of qualitative research?
9. Why might quantitative and qualitative research be combined?

When researchers pose questions about educational problems, there are simultaneous concerns with one or more plans for obtaining answers. The plans, or **research designs,** structure researchers' methods for answering their questions and conducting studies. In current thought about research designs, research is categorized according to the way researchers collect and analyze information and their research purposes. Two basic research designs based on the way information, or data, are collected and analyzed are **quantitative research** and **qualitative research.** Although there are overlapping characteristics in quantitative and qualitative research, they result from different theoretical perspectives about the overall purpose of research. Despite those differences, the two types can be considered as complementary, and they may be combined in a single research project (Lancy, 1993; Slavin, 1992). The two research perspectives share at least four procedural aspects (Hillocks, 1992). Quantitative and qualitative researchers share concerns "in problem finding, in explaining the relationships of data to claims, in theory building, and in explaining particular cases in light of established knowledge and theory" (p. 59). However,

> they can and do focus on different kinds of problems. For example, quantitative methods cannot deal directly with historical problems of cause and effect or the interpretation of unique social phenomena. On the other hand, qualitative researchers find it difficult, if not impossible, to represent the responses of large numbers of individuals to different kinds of stimuli, e.g., different methods of teaching or attitudes toward social conditions or political events. In the sense that the two sets of methods allow researchers to deal with problems of different dimensions in different context, they are complementary (Hillocks, 1992, p. 59).

COLLECTING INFORMATION

Information, or data, for quantitative and qualitative research are collected from direct observation, tests, and survey questionnaires and interviews. Researchers refer to these data collection devices and procedures as **instruments.** (The criteria for determining whether particular instruments accurately collect information are discussed in Chapter 6, Reading and Evaluating Instrument Sections. The use of instruments in qualitative research is also discussed in Chapter 7.)

Researchers usually record direct observation with an observation form, which may consist of questions about the subject's actions or categories of actions. For example, the observer may collect information in response to set questions: "With which children did the target subject play during free-play?" or "Which child started the play?" Or, the observer might tally the subject's actions during a time period according to some predetermined categories: "Subject started play with others," "Others play with subject," "Self-initiated lone play," or "Fringe observer to others' play." In qualitative research, observations are recorded in field notes, which are explained in Chapter 7.

Test information includes scores from **standardized norm-referenced tests,** such as the *Language Assessment Scales,* the *TerrNova* assessment series, the *California Achievement Tests,* the *Iowa Tests of Basic Skills,* and the *Metropolitan Achievement Tests.* The scores also may be from standardized **criterion-referenced tests,** such as the *Stanford Achievement Open-Ended Assessments* or the *Life Skills Tests of Functional Competencies in Reading and Mathematics.* Competency tests also might be created by a researcher or teacher for determining learning style, reading interest, or outcomes of instruction. Some tests are given individually, others are administered to groups. An increasingly popular form of competency test is based on **curriculum performance standards** of federal, state, professional, or other service agencies. An example of this form of test includes the *New Standards Reference Examinations: English Language Arts, Mathematics, Science and Social Studies.*

Questionnaires require the respondent either to write answers to questions about a topic or to answer orally. The answer form may be structured, in that there are fixed choices, or the form may be open, in that the respondent can use his or her own words. When the respondent answers orally and the researcher records the answers, researchers consider the instrument an **interview**. In interviews, the researcher may obtain responses to structured or open-ended questions. Interviews differ from questionnaires in that the researcher can modify the data collection situation to fit the respondent's replies. For example, additional information can be solicited or a question can be rephrased. In addition, researchers use surveys to collect information directly from subjects or from files such as subjects' permanent school records.

QUANTITATIVE RESEARCH

Quantitative research is characterized by the use of statistical analysis. Three basic quantitative research purposes are to describe, compare, and attribute causality. Each of these purposes is fulfilled through the assignment of numerical values to variables and the mathematical analysis of those values. Quantitative research is predicated on the belief that variables should be mathematically measured, and adherents to this approach stress that data should be repeatedly verified. Generally, the quantitative research approach is considered to be objective, that is, "the scientific method."

In **quantitative descriptive research**, the researchers' purpose is to answer questions about a variable's status by creating numerical descriptions of the frequency with which one or more variables occurs. In **comparative research**, the researchers' purpose is to examine numerical descriptions of two or more variables and make decisions about their differences or relationships. In research to attribute causality, or **experimental research**, the researchers' purpose is to draw conclusions about the influence of one or more variables on another variable. They seek to answer "if . . . then" questions: If they do something, then what change will occur in a particular variable?

From the results of experimental research, researchers establish the influence, or **effect**, of one variable on another. Quantitative descriptive and comparative research may show status, patterns, and associations among variables, but studies of those types cannot be used to say that one variable or combination of variables probably does cause a change in, or influence, another variable. Only when researchers follow the plan for attributing causality can they establish that a particular variable may be the reason for a change in another. Causation research, or experimental research, is different from descriptive and comparative research, and that distinction cannot be overstressed (Gall, Gall, & Borg, 1999).

Descriptive Research

Descriptive research is used when researchers want to answer the question "What exists?"

Proportion of Teachers Reporting Percentage of Time They Use
Practices and Activities in Content-Area Instruction

	Practices and Activities				
	Never	1–25%	26–50%	51–75%	76–100%
Instructional context					
Ability groups	34.9	39.4	6.1	10.6	9.1
Cooperative groups	2.9	33.8	30.9	26.5	5.9
Whole class	4.4	10.3	22.1	29.4	33.8
Textbooks	4.6	15.1	21.2	45.5	33.8
Prereading					
Activate prior knowledge	—	28.4	13.4	14.9	43.3
Set purpose	—	28.4	13.4	13.4	44.8
Predict/preview	1.5	37.9	15.2	21.2	24.2
During reading					
Students read silently	9.2	35.4	30.8	18.5	6.2
Students read orally	4.5	23.9	31.3	23.9	16.4
Postreading					
Computer support	34.9	36.4	18.2	7.6	3.0
Workbook/skills center	7.6	45.5	33.3	9.1	4.6

Figure 2.1

Partial Results From a Questionnaire (Adapted From Gillis, et al., 1993, p. 118)

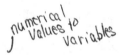
numerical values to variables

Quantitative Descriptive Method.   The quantitative descriptive research method is a procedure involving the assignment of numerical values to variables. For example, Figure 2.1 contains partial results from a questionnaire used in a descriptive study to determine the extent to which teachers use content-area instructional practices and activities that are consistent with current views of reading and learning from text. (Gillis, Olson, & Logan, 1993). These researchers collected data by asking teachers to circle one of five choices to indicate the percentage of instructional time they used various types of student groupings and instructional materials.

Another research team might wish to know "What is the average intelligence of students in gifted programs in a particular county or state?" They collect and tabulate data and find that the average intelligence score of gifted program students is 129. Still another team affiliated with a county library system might wish to know "What is the average reading achievement test score of a sample of beginning sixth-grade students using the public libraries in three local communities?" They collect and tabulate the data and find that the average achievement test grade equivalent score is 6.2.

However, having these two bits of information (average intelligence and average reading achievement score) does not allow the separate teams of researchers to create accurate pictures of the subjects. Average scores may give a limited picture because we know that not all gifted students had an intelligence score of 129 and not all sixth-grade students in each community had scores of 6.2. Also, anyone who observes gifted students and sixth-grade students sees that they differ in many ways other than intelligence or reading performance: personality, preferences and interests, and learning style, to name a few.

Two premises, then, underlie quantitative researchers' collection of descriptive information. First, they should collect and average information for several relevant variables. For the sixth-grade students, other variables relevant to library usage might be age, sex, intelligence, ethnicity, reading interest and preference, proximity of home to the library, and frequency of library usage. Second, after determining the average score for each variable, researchers should determine the extent to which the subjects' scores for each variable cluster near to or spread away from the average score. Two patterns of clustering are common: (a) a clustering of scores around the mean (average) and (b) a clustering of scores either above or below the mean (average). The reporting of this clustering or spreading gives a picture of the subjects' similarity or dissimilarity.

mean

All researchers use descriptive data. Quantitative researchers apply statistical procedures to answer questions about similarities and differences among variables, whereas qualitative researchers apply verbal analyses to answer similar questions.

Statistical Descriptions of Data.   After researchers collect data, they tally them. Figure 2.1 shows the response categories for each answer and the percentage of the total group they represent. From these data, it is possible to get a sense of how most teachers responded and whether there was uniform agreement among them.

However, most researchers following quantitative procedures use other descriptive measures of data, which are **central tendency** and **variability**. Although two common measures of central tendency that researchers use in research reports are the mean and the median, the mean is the measure of central tendency they most often use. The measure of variability of a set of data most often used and the one associated with the mean is the **standard deviation**. The following discussion is only an introduction to these measures. Chapter 8, Reading and Interpreting Results Sections, contains additional information about statistics and criteria for determining whether researchers' use of the mean, median, standard deviation, and other statistics is appropriate. Understanding the concepts of central tendency and variability is essential to understanding quantitative research designs.

gives
a
sense
of average

Both the mean and median give researchers—producers and consumers—a sense of the middle or average score for a variable. The **mean** is an arithmetical average—one adds up individual scores and divides by the number of scores. The **median** is the middle score of a group of scores arranged in ascending or descending order. The mean and median may not be the same for a particular group of scores. For example, the median (middle) score of the following groups is the same (25), but the means (averages) of the two groups are different—the first is 33.57 and the second is 40.86:

10, 15, 20, 25, 40, 50, 75

4, 17, 24, 25, 26, 91, 99

The **standard deviation (SD)** is used with the mean to show how the other scores are distributed around the mean. The use of the SD lets research producers and consumers see how homogeneous (alike) or heterogeneous (varied) a group is. For example, the children entering the kindergarten classes in one school might have a mean age of 64 months (5 years, 4 months) and an SD of 4 months. In this group of kindergartners, most children (approximately two-thirds) would be between 60 and 68 months in age. For another group of children entering kindergarten in another school with the same mean age (64 months) but an SD of 7 months, two-thirds of the children would be between 57 and 71 months in age. The first group of kindergarten children would be more homogeneous in their ages than would be the second group.

Table 2.1

Example of Mean and Standard Deviation Reporting: Means and Standard Deviations of CTBS Test Scores by Group

| | | Testing | | | |
| | | Pre | | Post | |
	Group *n*	M	SD	M	SD
		Vocabulary Test			
Disabled reader					
Instructional level	84	636.56	25.40	660.77	25.61
Frustration 1	88	633.60	27.98	660.02	25.95
Frustration 2	25	630.80	26.80	644.48	35.05
Slow learner					
Instructional level	42	622.76	33.95	641.12	45.55
Frustration 1	51	615.78	39.76	642.27	32.43
Frustration 2	14	604.79	35.31	617.21	48.32
		Comprehension Test			
Disabled reader					
Instructional level	84	637.90	50.77	692.33	41.40
Frustration 1	88	645.75	48.92	692.99	41.76
Frustration 2	25	622.90	61.08	662.40	60.47
Slow learner					
Instructional level	42	603.02	50.06	651.40	49.81
Frustration 1	51	609.65	41.39	652.58	66.38
Frustration 2	14	593.79	45.61	643.64	55.56

Source: Homan, Hines, and Kromrey (1993).

Table 2.1 shows an example of mean and standard deviation reporting. The table reports information from an investigation of the effect of reading placement on reading achievement of at-risk sixth-grade students with reading problems (Homan, Hines, & Kromrey, 1993). The two groups of readers were "disabled reader" and "slow learner." They were tested with two instruments: a vocabulary test and a comprehension test. The table gives the number of subjects (*n*), the mean scores (M), and the standard deviations (SD) for both pre- and posttesting and for groups at three levels of reading performance: Instructional Level, Frustration 1, and Frustration 2. The table shows that on the vocabulary test, a group of 84 disabled readers had an average instructional level pretesting score of 636.56. The standard deviation was 25.40, resulting in the scores of about two-thirds of the students being clustered between 661.96 and 611.16. The same group of students had a posttesting average of 660.77, and about two-thirds of them had scores between 686.38 and 635.16.

Comparative Research

Comparative research lets researchers examine relationships, including similarities or differences among several variables. These variables might represent characteristics of the same group of subjects or those of separate groups. That is, researchers might compare the writing performance and self-concept of members of a single group of subjects, or they might compare the writing performance and self-concept of two groups. Comparative research is more common than is pure descriptive research, but comparative research depends on knowledge generated from descriptive research. All researchers use descriptive data. Quantitative researchers apply statistical procedures to answer questions about similarities, differences, and relationships among variables, whereas qualitative researchers apply verbal analyses to answer similar questions.

Also, researchers can use the statistical comparative data to make predictions. When researchers find two variables that are strongly statistically related, they can use one variable to predict the occurrence of the other. They cannot, however, use relationship information to show that one variable is the cause of a change in another.

For example, a group of researchers conducted a comparative study of Israeli preschool, remedial, and elementary-school teachers' teaching performance. They found consistent differences among the three groups of teachers in affective variables but not in direct, actual teaching behavior. The preschool teachers were seen to be the most flexible, democratic, and expressive in warmth (Babad, Bernieri, & Rosenthal, 1987). The essential aspect to this comparative research is that researchers made no attempt to determine causality. In fact, the researchers state "the results provide no hint as to what might have caused the observed pattern" (p. 414).

Statistical Comparisons of Data.   After researchers following a quantitative procedure collect data, they calculate measures of central tendency (the mean) and variability (the standard deviation) as they do in descriptive research. These measures by themselves, however, do not provide evidence of difference or relationship. One or more statistical procedures can be used to determine whether differences exist between or among groups. Any of the statistical procedures used in comparative research are similar to those used in experimental research. Research consumers must realize that statistical procedures are tools for answering research questions; they are not the research. They help researchers determine whether an apparent difference or relationship is large enough to be considered real. They also help researchers determine the extent to which they can be confident about their research conclusions. (Chapter 8, Reading and Interpreting Results Sections, contains an extended discussion about the research reality, or significance, of differences and relationships.)

One statistical procedure used in descriptive research is the **chi-square.** Table 2.2 contains an example of a chi-square analysis. The information is from a study that examined how teachers responded when students made miscues (deviant oral-reading responses; Lass, 1984). Two types of miscues ([a] attempted pronunciation of word even when wrong and [b] refused or hesitated response) were compared with two types of teacher responses ([a] supplied word and [b] all other kinds of responses). The analysis showed that teachers who dealt with unattempted miscues supplied words more often than they used all other responses combined.

A statistical procedure used extensively in comparative research is **correlation.** Correlations show whether two or more variables have a systematic relationship of occurrence. That is, they help researchers answer questions about the scores: Do high scores for one variable occur with high scores for another (a positive relationship)? or Do high scores for one variable occur with low scores for the other variable (a negative relationship)? The occurrence of low scores for one variable with low scores for another is also an example of a positive relationship.

Table 2.2

Example of Chi-Square Reporting: Attempted Miscues vs.
Refusals/Hesitations and Teacher Response

	Miscues				
	Attempts		Refusals/ Hesitations		
	EO[a]	AO[a]	EO	AO	Raw Total
Teacher response					
Supplied word	105.5	93	13.5	26	119
All other	237.5	250	30.5	18	268
Total		343		44	387

[a]   EO = expected occurrences; AO = actual occurrences.
     $x^2 = 19.83$ with 1 degree of freedom ($p < .001$).
Source: adapted from Lass (1984).

Table 2.3 shows an example of correlation reporting. The table contains information from a study about the relationships between topic-specific background knowledge and measures of total writing quality (Langer, 1984). It shows the obtained relationships among four ways of evaluating students' writing: (a) teachers' marks, (b) a measure of coherence, (c) counting the words and clauses, and (d) a holistic scoring method. The relationship between the holistic scoring method and the teachers' marks is positive and significant—high coherence scores were given to the work of the same students who received high teacher marks. On the other hand, the relationship between coherence and the number of words and clauses, which is negative, was not **significant**. Therefore, the relationship between these two scoring methods can be said to be unrelated (or nonsignificant). (A detailed explanation of significance is in Chapter 8, Reading and Interpreting Results Sections.)

Researchers also use correlations in comparative studies to make predictions. Researchers can predict the existence or occurrence of one variable when a strong relationship has been established between that variable and another. For example, the high positive correlation shown in Table 2.3 between the holistic scoring method and teachers' marks of students' papers might be used to make this prediction: Students' writing that receives high scores through holistic scoring procedures most likely will receive high marks from teachers. Holistic scoring is not the cause of students receiving high marks from teachers. Whatever characteristics make students' writing receive high scores in one scoring method probably are responsible for high scores in the other, but the research data reported in Table 2.3 give no inkling what that third, causative variable is. Thus, researchers' use of one variable as a predictor of another variable or event is not justification for considering the first variable as a causative factor.

Frequently, the same statistic (e.g., *t* test, analysis of variance [ANOVA], chi-square) can be used to analyze the data in descriptive and comparative as well as in experimental research. It is not the statistic that is the distinguishing feature of a research design. Rather, it is the research question, or hypothesis, and the characteristics of the design that distinguish among the three types of quantitative research.

Table 2.3

Example of Correlation Reporting: Relationships Among Writing Measures

	Correlations (*n* papers)		
	Teacher's Mark	Coherence	Words/Clause
Holistic score	.44[a] (57)	.06 (99)	.25 (96)
Teacher's mark	.27 (22)	−.15 (20)	
Coherence	−.10 (96)		

[a] $p < .01$.

Source: adapted from Langer (1984).

Researchers select a statistical procedure that they think will help them answer their research question. Research consumers, then, should not use the type of statistical procedure for determining a researcher's design.

Experimental Research

In experimental research, researchers set out to answer questions about causation. They wish to attribute the change in one variable to the effect of one or more other variables. For example, one group of researchers (Team A) may be concerned with finding answers to questions such as "Will students who receive one type of reading aid (text with focusing questions interspersed every three paragraphs) have better comprehension than students who have a second reading aid (text with key ideas underlined)?" Another research team (Team B) may want to know "Will students who are taught to use calculators for solving mathematical problems do better on final tests than students who do not receive that instruction?"

The influencing variable—the one to which researchers wish to attribute causation—is called the **independent variable**. Independent variables are measurable human and nonhuman characteristics. For example, age (years or months), intelligence (average, above average, or superior), sensitivity to noise (high or low), intensity of light (high or low), frequency of an occurrence (never, sometimes, or often), and teaching style (democratic or autonomous), to name a few, can be independent variables. Sometimes the independent variable is called the experimental variable. When this kind of independent variable is an activity of the researcher, it is called a treatment variable. Researchers manipulate or subcategorize all independent variables; they can study the effects of two or more aspects of the variable by subcategorizing it. In the questions of Team A and Team B above, the treatment, or activity, in Team A's research is type of reading aid (focus questions or underlining). Team B's treatment is type of mathematics instruction (with calculator or without calculator). When nontreatment characteristics, such as age or intelligence, are used as independent variables, researchers can also subcategorize them (e.g., 6-year-olds or 8-year-olds; average or above-average intelligence).

The acted-upon variable—the one being studied for possible change—is called the **dependent variable**. Not all human characteristics can be used as dependent variables. Reading ability is something that researchers might wish to change, as is degree of self-concept or teachers' comprehension-questioning behavior. Something such as age, obviously, cannot be a dependent variable, because individuals' ages are not subject to modification—people will age according to their biological clocks. The dependent variable for Team A is comprehension performance and for Team B is problem-solving performance on tests.

An example of the attribution of causality is found in the research of a team that studied special-education students. They wanted to find out the effect of implementing a process for readying students to transition successfully from special-education resource rooms to regular classrooms for mathematics instruction (Fuchs, Fuchs, & Fernstrom, 1993). They found that special students who received instruction that involved the use of curriculum-based measurement and transitional programming had substantially reduced time spent in special-education math classes and significantly greater math achievement on posttests. In this study, the transitional programming (identifying needs through curriculum-based measurement and teaching needed skills) was the independent variable; math progress was the dependent variable.

The following is an example of the attribution of causality in a study without a treatment. A team of researchers studied how parent configuration (two-parent, mother-extended, or solo-mother) and number of siblings affect, or is the *cause* of, first graders' conformity to a model of student role as measured by their absences, latenesses, and conduct marks (Thompson, Entwisle, Alexander, & Sundius, 1992). Here, differences in first graders' roles as students (dependent variable) were examined to see if they changed as a result of the children's family structure (independent variable, or *causal* factor). However, the researchers did not engage in an activity, or treatment.

Researchers can study the individual or combined effect of several independent variables on a dependent variable, or of one independent variable on two or more dependent variables. An example of experimental research in which two independent variables were examined had the purpose of testing the effects on students' comprehension by providing them with relevant background knowledge and two versions of content-area text (McKeown, Beck, Sinatra, & Loxterman, 1992). In the study, the two independent variables were (a) provision of background knowledge and (b) coherence of the text. The dependent variable was comprehension of the text.

A study in which one independent variable was examined for its effect on several dependent variables set out to determine whether

> text explicitness would enhance children's *silent reading rates, their ratings of story interest, their abilities to recall stories and answer questions about them,* and *ratings of their overall understanding of stories* [italics added to identify the dependent variables]. (Sundbye, 1987, p. 86)

The researcher can conclude that something (text explicitness) caused a change in something else (students' reaction to stories). Researchers can make causative conclusions because they make decisions about the control of variables that are not of concern in descriptive or comparative research. **Control** is the use of procedures by the researchers to limit or account for the possible influence of variables not being studied. They use these controls before the research is done (a priori). The control of these **extraneous variables** can be done in one or more ways. Two ways to develop control in experimental studies are presented below. (Extended discussions of these and other ways to control extraneous variables are found in Chapter 5, Reading and Evaluating Subject Sections, and Chapter 7, Reading and Evaluating Procedure Sections.)

In the study about the use of relevant background knowledge and two versions of content-area text (McKeown et al., 1992), a variable that might possibly affect students' reading comprehension is reading ability. The researchers controlled for the possible effect of students' reading ability by dividing them equally into two groups based on the results of a standardized reading test. This way, the researchers had two groups of comparable readers, and the results could be determined to be the result of factors other than reading ability.

However, other variables might account for researchers' results. To control for the possible effect of such things as students' interest, learning style, general learning ability, and possible researcher bias in selecting the subjects, researchers can use randomization to group the subjects in the treatment groups (those to whom the independent variables were applied). **Randomization** is an unbiased systematic selection or assignment of subjects. When they use randomization, researchers assume that most human characteristics are evenly distributed among the groups.

In the above examples, researchers had the opportunity to manipulate the independent variable before doing the research. Sometimes, however, researchers want answers to questions but cannot manipulate the independent variable for practical or ethical reasons. They realize a condition exists and are unsure about what might have been its cause. For example, researchers might be interested in why some children develop autistic tendencies after birth. They question whether prenatal conditions might account for the development of the autistic tendencies. In such a case, it would be unethical to create an experimental study in which researchers manipulate the prenatal environment. But, by starting with the effect (children with autistic tendencies) and identifying possible causes (nutrition, mother's age, ingestion of abusive substances, or illness), researchers can try to establish a cause-effect relationship. This ex post facto (after-the-fact) research is called causal-comparative research.

The name **causal-comparative research** can be confusing when discussing experimental research. This type of research is comparative because researchers compare possible independent variables to see which variable, if any, has a strong relationship with the already known outcome. It is more than comparative research because the data analysis procedures do more than compare or correlate; the researchers analyze data with the purpose of establishing causality. Since researchers cannot establish a cause-effect relationship experimentally, they do so rationally. They take already intact groups—mothers whose children show autistic tendencies and mothers whose children do not—and compare them statistically under controlled conditions. The groups already differ on the independent and dependent variables. The researchers do not induce differences; they seek to identify one or more preexisting conditions (independent variables) in one group that exist to a lesser degree in the other. When researchers identify one or more conditions, they can attribute causality; however, this attribution may be less strong than in an experimental design where the researchers can control all of the variables.

An illustration of causal-comparative research in education is given in a study about reading comprehension and creativity in the use of English by Blacks (DeLain, Pearson, & Anderson, 1985). The research team

explored the hypothesis that the rich and varied experience of black youth with figurative language outside school would enhance their understanding of figurative language in school texts. Results confirmed that for black students, "sounding" skill, as well as general verbal ability, has a direct influence on figurative language comprehension. Black language ability influences figurative language comprehension indirectly through its effect on sounding skill. For white students, only general verbal ability affects figurative language comprehension. (p. 155)

In this exploratory study, the independent variables, "sounding" or "playing the dozens" and general verbal ability, already existed within and varied between Black and White students. The researchers could not manipulate the variables, nor could they teach the ritual-insult verbal play in a school setting. Also, differences in the dependent variable, understanding figurative language, existed. The researchers, in an ex post facto study, examined the possible causative linkage. They used causal-comparative research to draw conclusions about the positive influence of black youths' ability to "sound" and their ability to understand school-based figurative language.

A limitation of causal-comparative research is that researchers cannot have the same assurance that they do in experimental research about the cause-effect linkage. Often, and whenever possible, causal-comparative results need to be confirmed by experimental research. Causal-comparative research also lacks other controls used by researchers in experimental research. Randomization of subjects among treatments or the creation of closely comparable groups is usually not possible. Also, researchers cannot control the quality of students' previous experiences that relate to the independent variable. And, the people selected for the study may differ on some other variable that the researchers did not consider. These limitations show up in causal-comparative research as an estimate of unaccounted-for influence. When there is a large unaccounted-for influence, researchers must seek and test other independent variables for the possible cause of a recognized result.

Analysis of Experimental Statistical Data.   After data are collected in experimental studies, measures of central tendency (means) and variability (standard deviations) are created. This descriptive information forms the basis of other statistical procedures. When researchers conduct simple one-variable studies, they often use a common statistical procedure known as the *t* test. The *t* **test** is used to determine whether the difference between the means of two groups on a dependent variable is significant; that is, whether the examined results could have happened by chance or whether the researchers can reliably attribute the difference to the influence of the independent variable.

But, as discussed previously, single-variable studies provide limited insight about educational questions. Multiple-variable research requires the calculation of many *t* tests, which is awkward, possibly misleading, and limiting since the interaction among multiple variables cannot be shown by *t* tests. To overcome this limitation, researchers use the **analysis of variance (ANOVA)**. Results of an ANOVA are reported in *F* **ratios**. ANOVAs are used to determine whether differences can be attributed to one or a combination of independent variables.

Table 2.4 contains a common form for reporting ANOVA results. The information is taken from a study about the effect of reading placement (instructional level vs. above-instructional level) and reading potential (disabled reader vs. slow learner) on reading achievement of at-risk sixth-grade students with reading problems (Homan et al., 1993). The results show that there were significant differences for vocabulary achievement based on Potential and Placement. There was no difference shown in vocabulary achievement when Potential and Placement were considered together (Potential × Placement). On comprehension tests, only Potential showed significant

Table 2.4

Reporting of ANOVA Results: Summary Tables for a Two-Way Analysis of Variance

Analysis of Variance of Vocabulary Achievement Scores
by Potential and Placement Level

Source	df	MS	F
Potential (A)	1	9236.14	10.45**
Placement (P)	2	4107.70	4.65*
Potential × Placement (AP)	2	167.09	0.19
Error (S/AP)	298	884.12	
Total	303		

Analysis of Variance of Comprehension Test Scores
by Potential and Placement Level

Source	df	MS	F
Potential (A)	1	38070.15	17.11**
Placement (P)	2	4083.84	1.84
Potential × Placement (AP)	2	1434.62	0.67
Error (S/AP)	298	2224.74	
Total	303		

* $p < .05$; ** $p < .01$.
Source: Homan et al (1993).

differences. (Chapter 8 contains a more detailed discussion of the concepts of significance and ANOVA.)

QUALITATIVE RESEARCH

Qualitative research is a term used for a broad range of research strategies that has roots in the research of the social sciences, especially the field research of anthropology and sociology (Bogdan & Biklen, 1998; Eisner, 1991; Firestone, 1987, 1993; Guthrie & Hall, 1984; Jacob, 1987, 1988; LeCompte, Millory, & Preissle, 1992; Lincoln & Guba, 1985; Marshall & Rossman, 1995; Smith, 1987; Smith & Heshusius, 1986; Van Maanen, Dabbs, & Faulkner, 1982; Wilson, 1977). Terms closely associated with qualitative research are **ethnographic** and ethnologic **research** and interpretive research. Some researchers distinguish between ethnography and ethnology as types of qualitative research methods. For the purposes of this text, the terms ethnography and ethnology are used solely for the type of research undertaken by anthropologists studying whole cultures. They are not used for the work of researchers from education, psychology, and social science who borrow the terms but not the underlying theoretical framework of anthropological ethnography (Jacob, 1989). Some researchers prefer the term "interpretive research" to avoid the connotation of defining research as "nonquantitative" since some sort of quantification can be used (Erickson, 1986).

Characteristics

Qualitative research is characterized not by the use of numerical values but by the use of text—written words—to document variables and the inductive analysis of the collected information. Qualitative researchers are not concerned with numerical (statistical) analysis of the frequency of when or how things happen. They look to inductively answer research questions by examining students and others who influence them in natural contexts, in interaction with other people and objects in their surroundings (Hatch, 1995). Although that approach is often considered subjective, it is based on broad and comprehensive theoretical positions.

Qualitative research can be subcategorized by the expected outcomes of a study (Eisner, 1991; Marshall & Rossman, 1995; Peshkin, 1993). The basic qualitative research purposes are to describe, interpret, verify, and evaluate. In descriptive analysis, the researcher gives an account of a place or process. The purpose is to visualize a situation as a means for understanding what is happening. In interpretive analysis, the researcher explains or creates generalizations. The purpose is to develop new concepts or elaborate on existing ones. The researcher provides insights that might lead to teachers changing their behavior, refining their knowledge, or identifying problems. Interpretive analysis also can be used to develop new theories. In verification analysis, the researcher verifies assumptions, theories, and generalizations. In evaluative analysis, the researcher provides judgments about policies, practices, and innovative instructional practices. The researcher tries to answer questions such as "Has an instructional procedure been implemented? With what impact? What has the process of implementation been like? How has it worked? For whom has it worked? Are there any exceptions?"

Qualitative research has several distinct features (Bogdan & Biklen, 1998; Creswell, 1998; Eisner, 1991; Firestone, 1987; Gay & Airasian, 2000; Guthrie & Hall, 1984; Jacob, 1987, 1988; Lancy, 1993; Lincoln & Guba, 1985; Maxwell, 1998; Putney, Green, Dixon, & Kelly, 1999; Smith, 1987; Smith & Heshusius, 1986; Van Maanen et al., 1982; Wilson, 1977). First, the issue of context is central to qualitative research. One type of context is the conceptual, or theoretical, context. That relates to the theories, assumptions, biases, and beliefs that support a researcher's work. Also, researchers collect data within the natural setting of the information they seek, and the key data collection instruments are the researchers themselves. This means that researchers wishing to study educational questions must collect relevant information at the data source through direct observation and personal interviews. Contexts (i.e., schoolwide situations as well as individual classrooms) do not mean just people and their actions. Contexts can also be considered as the total life situations of students and teachers. Contexts are not static; they shape and are shaped by the people involved (teachers and students) as well as the intentions of instruction, the resources available, and the particular time the events are happening (Graue & Walsch, 1995).

The methods for data collection are participant observing, interviewing, reading diaries, scanning records and files, using checklists, and conducting case studies. The basic premise for these methods is that people do not act in isolation. Their behavior and actions occur in specific social contexts or situations, and, therefore, these behaviors and actions must be studied in their natural settings. Researchers must become part of the natural setting and function as participant observers: in educational environments, students and teachers must accept qualitative researchers as regular members of the classroom and not just as observers.

It is on the point of **participant observer** that some researchers distinguish between qualitative and ethnographic research. If researchers do not collect data in natural settings as total group members, the research may be considered by some researchers as qualitative but not ethnographic. Ethnographic research to them requires researchers to be fully integrated members of the educational environment. This distinction has been called the *insider and outsider perspective* (Lancy, 1993; Van Maanen et al., 1982). The insider becomes part of the group and tries to detail what the members of the group know and how this knowledge guides their behavior. The outsider remains separate and tries to describe aspects of the social situation about which the groups' members may be unaware. Rarely, however, do participant observers function as pure outsiders or insiders.

The second major feature of qualitative research is that the data are verbal, not numerical. Although qualitative researchers may use checklists to count the frequency of occurrences of educational events, behaviors, and activities, these quantifications are for noting trends and not for presenting averages.

Third, qualitative researchers are concerned with the process of an activity rather than only the outcomes of that activity. In educational settings, qualitative researchers look at instructional activities within the total context of classrooms and schools. They want to describe the ongoing interactions occurring during instruction rather than to note only whether the students have increased their test scores.

Fourth, qualitative researchers analyze the data rationally rather than statistically. The outcomes of much qualitative research are the generation of research questions and conjectures, not the verification of predicted mathematical relationships or outcomes. This is an additional key feature of qualitative research. Because some qualitative research is descriptive, many of its data collection procedures are similar to those found in quantitative descriptive research. A distinguishing feature between the two is the use in qualitative research of the search for logical patterns within and among aspects of the research setting. To some researchers, especially those who hold to a strong belief in quantitative analysis, qualitative analysis may seem to lack objectivity. Nevertheless, the contributions of qualitative researchers are their ability to identify and interpret patterns of human responses as a result of their knowledge, experiences, and theoretical orientations to education. (Chapters 7 and 8 contain additional discussions about the role of subjectivity in qualitative research.)

An illustrative qualitative research study involved a field investigation of classroom management from the perspective of high-school students (Allen, 1986). The study was based on the assumption "that classroom contexts interact with students' agenda and result in variations in students' perspectives of the management of the classroom" (p. 438). Data were gathered (a) from the students' perspective, (b) from different classroom management situations, (c) by uncovering the students' agendas, and (d) by analyzing the underlying theoretical constructs. To become part of the groups, the researcher enrolled in a ninth-grade schedule so that he could learn about the students' perspective by taking the role of a student. He wished to gain the students' confidence, so he asked the teachers to treat him as any other student. After the classes began, he avoided contact with the teachers. The researcher attended four morning classes each day and did not volunteer information about himself to the students until they questioned him. Then, he emphasized his student role, deemphasized that of being a researcher, and participated in classwork, activities, tests, and homework assignments. During class he took observational notes under the guise of taking class notes.

Qualitative research views "classroom behavior in the larger context of cultural standards and patterns of behavior, goals of participants, behavior settings, and social influences beyond the classroom. The implications are significant for our understanding of education" (Jacob, 1987, p. 38). From qualitative research, educators can obtain extensive knowledge about educational processes within classrooms, schools, and communities. For example, qualitative research helps educators to gain insights about (a) classroom life and how students function within the particular situation of that classroom, (b) the knowledge and cultural understandings members of a classroom need to participate in social and academic tasks with that environment, (c) the individual and group perspectives and points of view that should be considered for understanding learning within a classroom, and (d) the actions and interactions of students and teachers as they create teaching and learning situations (Putney et al., 1999).

COMBINING QUANTITATIVE AND QUALITATIVE RESEARCH DESIGNS

Currently, many researchers combine the use of quantitative and qualitative research methods. Although there may be purists at either extreme, the use of both methods within a research project can incorporate the strengths of both these types of research. For example, the results from two studies on essay writing were contrasted using qualitative and quantitative data analysis methods (Hartley & Chesworth, 1998). The two studies provided different information about essay writing and indicated that both methods can have their limitations, whether they come first or second. The researchers felt that each method might feed into the other in a sort of sequential reflective chain, or spiral, of assessment.

A mixed methods approach (Jones, 1997) may be of benefit to a researcher for the following reasons:

- Qualitative methods, especially observation or unstructured interviews, allow the researcher to develop an overall "picture" of the subject under investigation. This may guide the initial phases of the research.
- Quantitative analysis may be more appropriate to assess behavioral or descriptive components of a topic.
- The descriptive analysis, such as the sociodemographic profile of the subjects, may allow a representative sample to be drawn for the qualitative analysis. Quantitative research may confirm or deny the representativeness of a sample group for such qualitative research. Thus, the mixed methodology could guide the researcher who is carrying out qualitative research so that his or her sample has some representativeness of the overall population.
- Any topic involves cognitive and affective characteristics, as well as overt behavioral aspects. Thus, a qualitative "core" is appropriate to investigate these aspects by examining the informant's point of view.
- Much research on many topics is still largely exploratory. The use of qualitative methods allows for unexpected developments that may arise as part of such research (i.e., serendipity).
- Quantitative analysis may complement the findings of qualitative methods by indicating the extent of their existence within the subject population.
- Quantitative analysis may confirm or disconfirm any apparently significant data that emerge from the study. Thus, for example, if the level of subject performance, as measured by existing standardized tests, appears to be related to or result from subject behavior, quantitative methods might be used to enable statistical testing of the strength of such a relationship or causative factor.

	Quantitative Research	Qualitative Research
Words used to describe	experimental hard data empirical positivist statistical objective	ethnographic fieldwork naturalistic descriptive participant observation soft data subjective
Key concepts	variables operationalize reliability validity statistical significance replication prediction	contextualization process field notes triangulation insider/outsider perspective meaning is of chief concern making judgments
Design	structured predetermined	evolves over time flexible
Data	statistical operationalized variables measure overt behavior	descriptive field notes documents interviews
Sample	randomized control for extraneous variables size is important	nonrepresentative can be small
Techniques	experiments standardized instruments structured interview structured observation	observation open-ended interview review of documents participant observation researcher as instrument
Data analysis	deductive statistical	ongoing inductive
Problems with approach	control of extraneous variables validity	time consuming data reduction is difficult reliability generalizability nonstandardized procedures

Figure 2.2
Comparison of Quantitative and Qualitative Research

- If such a relationship is determined, then quantitative methods are weaker in providing explanations. Qualitative methods may assist the researcher in understanding the underlying explanations of significant outcome and the underlying process involved in producing that relationship.

Figure 2.2 contains a summary comparison of quantitative and qualitative research.

SUMMARY

Note that the summary is constructed in a question-and-answer format using questions from this chapter's Focus Questions section.

What are the major designs used to conduct educational research?

Two basic research designs based on the way information, or data, are collected and analyzed are quantitative research and qualitative research.

What are quantitative descriptive, comparative, and experimental research?

Descriptive research is done to answer questions about a variable's status. Comparative research is done to make decisions about two or more variables' differences or relationships. Experimental research is done to draw conclusions about the cause-effect relationship between two or more variables.

What distinguishes the three types of quantitative research designs from each other?

Descriptive and comparative research may reveal status, patterns, and associations among variables, but only experimental research can be used to attribute causality.

What are the instruments used to collect quantitative data?

Data are collected with instruments, which are direct-observation forms, tests, and surveys (questionnaires and interviews).

How are data analyzed in each of the three types of quantitative research designs?

In descriptive research, information most often is described with means and standard deviations. In comparative research, in addition to the descriptive measures of data, two common statistical procedures are correlation and the chi-square. In experimental research, common statistical procedures are the *t* test and analysis of variance or ANOVA.

Frequently, the same statistic (e.g., *t* test, ANOVA, chi-square) can be used to analyze the data in descriptive and comparative as well as in experimental research. It is not the statistic that is the distinguishing feature of a research design. Rather, it is the research question or hypothesis and the characteristics of the design that distinguish among the three types of quantitative research.

What are central tendency and variability, and how are they measured?

Central tendency is the average or middle score in a group of scores. The middle score is called the median; the arithmetic average score is called the mean. Variability is the extent to which other scores in the group cluster about or spread from the mean. The variability of a set of data is usually reported as the standard deviation.

What are the major purposes for conducting qualitative research?

The basic qualitative research purposes are to describe, interpret, evaluate, and verify.

What are the major features of qualitative research?

The major features of qualitative research are (a) data are collected within natural educational settings and the major data collection instrument is the researcher observer; (b) data are verbal, not numerical; (c) researchers are concerned with process rather than outcomes alone; and (d) data are analyzed rationally, not statistically.

Why might quantitative and qualitative research be combined?

The use of both quantitative and qualitative research methods within a research project can incorporate the strengths of both types of research and enhance the researcher's results.

ACTIVITIES

Effective learning can be gained from the following activities when they are done with another class student. This peer interacting can follow a simple format:

1. Each student reads and does an activity.
2. Each student explains to the other what the response is and why that response is chosen.
3. The students' responses are compared with the authors' feedback.
4. If there are differences between peer responses or between peer responses and the authors' feedback, students should refer to the text or the course instructor for verification.

Activity 1

For each of the research purposes, questions, and hypotheses listed below indicate (a) the type of research design (descriptive, comparative, experimental, causal-comparative, or qualitative) and (b) the research variables. For experimental or causal-comparative designs, differentiate between the independent and dependent variables. Note that some of the studies have more than one research purpose.

1. This research focused on the ways an adolescent mother for whom English is a second language and who is from a low-income family uses literacy at home, in school, and in the community (McNemar, 1998).
2. The purpose of this study was to describe the procedures that elementary-school principals and teachers use to create classrooms and to examine the effect of these procedures on class composition (Burns & Mason, 1998).
3. Relations between parent attitudes, intrinsic value of science, peer support, available activities, and preference for future science careers were examined for science-talented, rural, adolescent females (Jacobs, Finken, Griffin, & Wright, 1998).
4. Two primary research questions framed the investigation. First, what working knowledge of narrative and informational genres do kindergarten, first-grade, and second-grade children demonstrate in text production tasks? Second, how does their demonstration of this knowledge vary as a function of differential levels or modes of cultural scaffolding?
5. The hypotheses of this study on one wage earner from each household in a small town were that (a) higher levels of education will be associated with higher volumes of certain (but not all) content of reading than lower levels of education and (b) occupational category will be associated with different volumes of certain (but not all) content for reading (Guthrie, Seifert, & Kirsch, 1986).

Activity 2

Using a research report of your own choosing or one from Appendix B, (a) locate the research hypothesis, purpose, or question; (b) indicate the research design; and (c) identify the research variables. For experimental or causal-comparative research, indicate the independent and dependent variables.

FEEDBACK

Activity 1

1. This study was qualitative descriptive. Because it is not entirely possible to identify it as qualitative research from the statement, consider your answer correct if you indicated "descriptive." The researcher wanted to identify the ways in which literacy was used at home, in school, and the community. No comparison among those variables was indicated.

2. The study had two parts, a descriptive and an experimental part. The signal to experimental research was "effect. . . on." In the descriptive part, the researchers were concerned with identifying procedures for arranging classes. In the experimental part, they examined how class creation procedures (independent variable) affected class composition (dependent variable).

3. The study was comparative. The signal was "relationships." The five aspects were compared to see how they related (compared) to each other.

4. The study had two components, descriptive and experimental. The signal to experimental research was "vary as a function of." In the descriptive component, the researchers were looking for what knowledge the students had. In the experimental component, they examined what change (vary) of that knowledge (dependent variable) resulted from differential levels or modes of cultural scaffolding (independent variable).

5. The study was causal-comparative because both the independent variables, "higher levels of education" (Hypothesis a) and "occupational category" (Hypothesis b), were in existence prior to the study. The dependent variable in both parts of the study was "content of reading." Causality *was* presumed—level of education and occupational category would cause differences in reading content.

Activity 2

Discuss your responses with other students and your course instructor.

Chapter 3

Reading and Evaluating Research Reports

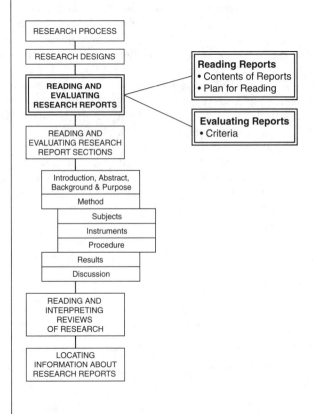

FOCUS QUESTIONS

1. What are the major sections of research reports?
2. What is an effective strategy for reading research reports?
3. What are the criteria for evaluating the quality and appropriateness of research reports?

Research consumers read research reports to increase their general knowledge about educational practice, to acquire knowledge that they can apply in professional practices, and to gain insights about effective instructional procedures that they can use in classrooms.

A **research report** is not research. Research is conducted by systematically collecting information about an identified problem or question, analyzing the data, and, on the basis of the evidence, confirming or disconfirming a prior prediction or statement. A research report is a summary of researchers' activities and results. Research consumers can judge the effectiveness of research producers and the appropriateness of their results and conclusions only by reading and evaluating research reports.

Research reports are pictures of research. They are representations of what researchers have done and how they wish to present their research procedures to the public. Four pictures of research are possible: (a) good research methodology, well reported; (b) good research methodology, poorly reported; (c) poor research methodology, well reported; and (d) poor research methodology, poorly reported. Research consumers' ability will be tested in identifying the second and third pictures. In situation (b), researchers might have conducted appropriate research and reported it inappropriately; in situation (c), they might have conducted inappropriate research and dressed it in the garb of an appropriate research report.

This chapter explains the contents of research reports, presents models of well-written research reports, demonstrates effective report-reading procedures for research consumers, and lists questions for evaluating the quality of research reports. These evaluative questions form the bases for discussions in succeeding chapters about reading and analyzing research methods.

READING RESEARCH REPORTS

Contents of Research Reports

Research reports contain information related to research producers' questions and their research activities. This information is organized to show researchers' efforts in

- Selecting a problem area
- Specifying research questions
- Describing subjects
- Describing instruments
- Explaining procedures and treatments (if appropriate)
- Presenting results based on data analyses
- Discussing implications

The information is generally organized into sections with headings such as Background or Literature Review; Purpose, Questions, or Hypotheses; Method, including Subjects, Instruments, and Procedure; Results; Conclusions; and References.

The **background section** contains (a) an explanation of the researchers' problem area, (b) its educational importance, (c) summaries of other researchers' results that are related to the problem (called a literature review), and (d) strengths from the related research that were used and weaknesses or limitations that were changed.

The background section is often preceded by an **abstract,** a summary of the report. Researchers usually omit the literature review from the abstract.

The **purpose section** contains the specific goal or goals of the research project. These can be expressed as a statement of purpose, as questions, or as a hypothesis. The following is an example from a research report in which both a purpose and specific questions are expressed.

[Purpose]　　The overall focus of this study, then, was to examine the role that varying levels of context and dictionary definitions play in college students' acquisition of new words, assessed under four different testing formats. The following two questions were posed:

[Questions]　　1. Are there significant differences in subjects' abilities to learn and remember new vocabulary words depending on strength of context and adequacy of dictionary definitions?
　　2. Can significant differences in subjects' abilities to learn and remember new vocabulary words as a function of context and dictionary definitions be replicated across four levels of word knowledge? (Nist & Olejnik, 1995, p. 179)

From reading the purpose section, research consumers can identify and classify the type of research and the research variables (independent and dependent when appropriate). In the above example, the words *role, play,* and *acquisition* indicate that something is making something else change. They are clues to the type of research method—in this case, experimental research. In questions Q1 and Q2, the independent variables were "strength of context" and "adequacy of dictionary definitions." In Q2, a third independent variable, "levels of word knowledge," was included. In Q1 and Q2, the dependent variables were "ability to learn" and "ability to remember new vocabulary words."

Sometimes, researchers (e.g., Nist & Olejnik, 1995) do not place their purpose, questions, or hypotheses in a section with a separate heading. In such cases, they include this information in the background section, most often in the section's last paragraph. The following is an example in which hypotheses are stated in a subheaded section. Notice how the researcher predicted the expected results.

Research Hypotheses

The following hypotheses were made:

(a) The onset/rime analogy explanation is a more viable explanation than the phoneme blending explanation for how young children learn to recode unfamiliar graphophonological print phonologically;
(b) the more print words children recognize, the better they are able to make analogies between letter strings representing onsets and rimes in known and unknown words to recode unknown ones phonologically; and
(c) young children's ability to recode unfamiliar print phonologically is constrained when they have difficulty reversing their perceptions of parts and wholes in print. (Moustafa, 1995, p. 468)

The **method section** of research reports usually contains several subsections. These are subjects, instruments, and procedure.

The **subjects section** contains a description of the individuals included in the study, giving general information about such factors as age, sex, grade level, intellectual and academic abilities, and socioeconomic level. It also contains the number of subjects and an account of how the subjects were selected and assigned to groups.

The subjects section is sometimes labeled "Sample" or "Participants." Subjects of research can be parents, teachers, administrators, instructional materials, or even learning environments. The following is a typical subjects section:

> The sample included 118 students from Grades 3 and 6 in three middle-class elementary schools in an urban area of inland southern California. All three schools were ethnically diverse, with approximately 60% White, 30% Hispanic (predominately Mexican-American), 5% Black, and 5% Asian-American students each. Three hundred fifteen students who were asked to participate in the study had, according to school records and teachers' reports, at least average proficiency in English. None was classified as being gifted, having learning or emotional problems, or being involved in special education. One hundred twenty-nine students returned parental consent forms and were included in the original sample. Data from 11 of the students—that is, 6 third graders and 5 sixth graders—were not usable because of problems with tape recording, student absence, and faulty procedure. The numbers and ages of the students who remained in the sample were: 18 boys, 41 girls (mean age = 9.0 years, SD = 0.3) at Grade 3 and 29 boys, 30 girls (mean age = 12.1 years, SD = 0.4) at Grade 6. This sample represented 11 third-grade classrooms (3 to 9 students, median = 5, from each classroom) and 10 sixth-grade classrooms (2 to 9 students, median = 7, from each). (Newman & Schwager, 1995, p. 357)

The **instruments section** contains a description of the data collection instruments: observation forms, standardized and researcher-made tests, and surveys. When instruments are published standardized tests, researchers usually assume the readers' familiarity with them and do little more than name them. (In Chapter 6, Reading and Evaluating Instrument Sections, is an explanation of how readers can obtain information about unfamiliar standardized tests.) When instruments are less well known, researchers describe or give examples of them and give evidence of their effectiveness. If tests other than standardized tests were administered, researchers explain the testing circumstances and the qualifications or training of the test givers and provide information about the test and how it was constructed. If observations or surveys were used, researchers relate how they were done and how the observers or interviewers were trained.

The following is a typical instruments section, which explains in detail how the researchers developed one instrument, an attitude inventory, and which refers to another unexplained test, a cloze test. They are assuming the reader knows what a cloze test is.

INSTRUMENTS

The Student Attitude Inventory (SAI) was used as a pre- and post-test measure. Constructed by the researchers, the SAI contains 33 questions related to five areas: listening (7 items), speaking (7 items), reading (8 items), writing (6 items), and self-perceptions as learners (5 items). The items contained in the SAI were generated from a compilation of statements made by elementary students over a period of four years, who were responding to learning activities presented by preservice teachers during language arts practicum assignments. The practicum assignments included integrated language arts activities and elementary students would spontaneously comment about how much they enjoyed or disliked specific kinds (i.e., listening, reading, speaking, or writing) of activities. Preservice teachers reported students' comments to the university instructors, who sorted the comments according to the area represented. The researchers (i.e., course instructors) pulled from the item groupings the most frequently occurring statements and edited them for content and clarity.

The SAI may be administered individually or in a group setting, with respondents marking the face illustration that best represents their feelings. Five face illustrations are shown at the end of each question, ranging from a big smile to a big frown. Respondents are told that the face illustrations represent the following feelings: very happy, happy, neither happy nor sad, sad, and very sad. The SAI includes questions, such as *Listening:* How do you feel when someone reads a story to you? How do you feel when your teacher tells you the steps to follow in an activity rather than having you read the steps? *Speaking:* How do you feel when someone asks you to tell about something that has happened to you or something that you have done? How do you feel when you are given the chance to tell someone about a story that you have read? *Reading:* How do you feel when you are asked to read written directions and the teacher does not explain them? How do you feel when you have the opportunity to read magazines? *Writing:* How do you feel when you are writing a note to a friend or parent and you do not know how to spell a word? How do you feel when your teacher asks you to write a story? *Self-perceptions as Learners:* How do you feel when you are asked to complete an assignment alone? How do you feel when you are asked to be the leader of a group activity?

A Likert scale, ranging from 5 to 1, is used to score the SAI with 5 representing "very happy" and 1 representing "very sad." Area scores on the SAI are obtained by summing the item responses in each of the five areas. The possible scores for Listening, Speaking, Reading, Writing, and Self-Perceptions as Learners are 35, 35, 40, 30, and 25, respectively. Summing the area scores produces a possible total score of 165. The researchers examined the internal consistency of the SAI and found that alpha coefficients for the area scores were as follows: .74 (Listening), .74 (Speaking), .82 (Reading), .77 (Writing), and .74 (Self-Perceptions as Learners), with .93 being the alpha coefficient for the overall (total) score. The validity of the SAI was examined by correlating the total scores obtained by a sample of 47 elementary students on the SAI with their total scores on the Elementary Reading Attitude Survey (ERAS); the obtained Pearson Product Moment correlation coefficient was .44 ($p < .002$), which the authors considered to be adequate for research purposes.

An oral cloze test was administered at the beginning of the study to determine whether differences existed initially between the treatment and comparison groups in their abilities to meaningfully process oral language. The cloze test contained 9 sentences with deletions representing 3 categories: final, initial, and medial positions (i.e., 3 sentences per deletion category). (Thames & Reeves, 1994, pp. 296–298).

The **procedure section,** a subsection of the method section, contains a detailed explanation of how researchers conducted their study. In descriptive and comparative studies, researchers explain how data were collected and analyzed. In experimental studies, researchers also describe the treatments and how they were administered. If special instructional materials were prepared for the study, they are described and often sample portions are included.

The following example is a typical procedure section. It is taken from an experimental study about the effects of literacy-enriched play settings and adult mediation of the children's play on the children's literacy-related play.

PROCEDURES

Baseline period. Prior to the intervention phase of the study, children's play behaviors during their 1-hour indoor free play time were observed in each classroom over a 2-day period. Following an observational procedure developed by Smith and Connolly (1980), a research assistant first identified a particular child, then recorded (using a small portable tape recorder) the general activity and the specific behavior exhibited by the child for a period of 40 seconds. Ten seconds were used to rest and then to identify the next child for observation. In this manner, children's play behavior in each classroom was observed by two trained research assistants over a 17-minute period, followed by two additional rounds. Because activity spans for this age group generally occur every 10 minutes, this procedure allowed us to observe each child engaged in a variety of play behaviors. Three rounds were recorded each day, for a total of six samples per child over the 2 days. Research assistants were asked not to interpret behavior, but to record only the children's actual behaviors in play. These behaviors were then categorized into demonstrations of handling (focusing on the physical exploration of a literacy object), reading (attributing meaning to environmental and functional print), and writing (attempting to use printed marks as a form of communication) to provide a detailed analysis of children's literacy-based play activities.

Intervention.   Guided by principles established in our previous research (Neuman & Roskos, 1990b; 1992), we redesigned a play area into a literacy-enriched office setting in the six intervention classrooms. Specifically, these changes were defined by: (a) the principle of definition (clearly demarcating play settings from one another); (b) the principle of adaptation (reworking typical play settings to resemble real-life literacy contexts); and (c) the principle of familiarity (inserting a network of prototypical literacy objects into known settings). Thus, through the strategic placement of semifixed structures, like shelves and classroom furniture, we adapted an existing play area (an art table) into an office play setting and included such signs, labels, and common objects as a telephone, calendar, in/out trays, and paper and pencils to encourage literacy interactions through play. In this respect, we interpreted the concept of "office" broadly as any location where daily human affairs may be handled using literacy.

In each setting, we inserted seven alphabetic labels or signs (e.g., OFFICE EXIT). As shown in Figure 1 [not reprinted here], a large "office" sign designated the play setting in each room. Signs in their typical logos were displayed prominently throughout the play space. For example, the word "EXIT" was located above the doorway in each "office"; the "COME IN, we're OPEN" sign was placed in front of the play setting when it was available for play and replaced by "Sorry, We're CLOSED," at the end of each play session. A "time in/time out" sign was displayed on the bulletin board at all times. Each setting also included "Hello, my name is . . ." labels for children as they entered the play area and play money for all "cash" transactions. Our goal, in strategically locating these signs and labels in functional settings, was to simulate a context that might encourage children to read print as if it were in their real-life environment.

In addition, each setting included 10 common functional print items (e.g., telephone book, calendar) that one might see in any typical office, like a gas station or a clinic. Designed to be used by the children, these items were easily available and clustered together in the office setting to enhance sustained literacy interactions. For example, a telephone, telephone book, and message pad were organized together in one area, whereas materials for mailing letters—stationery, envelopes, stamps, and mail box—were placed in an adjacent area. Clustering these items allowed for at least four to six children to play in the office setting at one time.

Following these design changes, parent-teachers and teachers met with researchers and two research assistants to discuss the general procedures of the project. Although we asked that the structural features of the setting and signs and labels remain consistent throughout the study, parent-teachers were encouraged to take responsibility for the office play setting in their respective classrooms, to keep it well-stocked with materials from our storeroom, and to "invent" new projects or scenarios over the course of the project to encourage children to make use of the play setting. Further, because it was important to monitor children's play, parent-teachers were asked to remain around the office area during free play time and not to be drawn into other classroom tasks or activities. Classroom teachers and aides were encouraged to observe and interact with children in areas other than the office play setting.

Parent-teachers from the two intervention groups met separately with the research team. Those assigned to intervene in the office play setting (Group 1) were asked to actively assist young children in their literacy-related play. Didactic teaching of letters or numbers was discouraged; rather, we suggested that what young children seemed to need most were conversations with adults in ways that might serve to integrate their knowledge of the world. For example, adults might contribute to extending a play scene by "taking an order" or helping the child to "write a prescription" or modeling a relevant literacy behavior, like "making a list"—behaviors that were contingent on children's efforts and interests. These examples were designed to give parent-teachers general guidelines for interactions, rather than specific strategies, with the understanding that they themselves might be our most knowledgeable informers.

Those assigned to monitor the office play setting (Group 2) were encouraged to observe children's play, to take notes on the quality of the play behavior, to describe children's favorite activities, to step in when necessary to end a dispute, but not to directly "play" with the children. Basically, they were asked to establish "rapport" behaviors (Wood, McMahon, & Cranstoun, 1980), giving gentle reminders to children that an adult was available if necessary, but with subtle encouragement to interact among themselves.

The office play setting was "open" to children for 3 days a week over a 5-month period. This schedule allowed teachers flexibility in arranging field trips and other special projects on the other 2 days. During the 3 days, the parent-teacher would announce that the office was "open" by displaying the sign, "COME IN, We're OPEN," and encouraging the children to play there during their free time. However, no children were ever assigned to the office play setting; instead, they were allowed to move freely about all areas in the classroom.

During the free play time, the "interactive" parent-teachers, Wanda, Michelle, and Lolita (Group 1), were active participants in children's spontaneous free play in the office. In this group, they were likely to sit at one of the desks with the children by their side and assist in their play activities by using the literacy objects for functional purposes, like "ordering a pizza" or "taking a telephone message." On the other hand, the "monitoring" parent-teacher (Group 2) would first focus on setting the stage in play and then would observe children's ongoing activities. James, for example, would situate himself in a rocking chair outside of the play space and record interesting vignettes to share with us, while the other parent-teachers, Tracy and Nancy, would monitor from inside the office, often cleaning and straightening children's papers. Although children might ask them occasional questions, they would rarely become involved in the play other than to find some materials or to settle a dispute. In neither case, however, were parent-teachers aware of our interest in children's learning of environmental or functional print. Rather, the goal of the project was to encourage children to simply enjoy playing with print.

A research assistant was assigned to each intervention group and visited classrooms twice weekly. The purpose of these visits was to ensure fidelity to the specific intervention treatment, to informally chat with parent-teachers regarding the children's play activities, and to give them positive feedback for their efforts.

Children in the nonintervention classroom continued to engage in their typical free play activities over the 5-month period. In these classrooms, parent volunteers generally provided support for teacher activities, like chaperoning on field-trips or custodial duties, but provided no direct intervention in children's classroom activities.

During the Intervention. To examine the nature of children's literacy interactions, with and without adult assistance, videotaped samples of children's spontaneous free play in classrooms were collected weekly, after the play setting was in place for 1 month. Using a camcorder and a microphone system, a graduate student in language acquisition recorded 15 minutes of play activity in the office play setting in four classrooms per week, for a total of 10 observations per class. These samples yielded a total of 450 minutes, or 7.5 hours of videotaped observation for each intervention group. Rather than focus on individual children, the goal of the videotaping was to obtain samples of children's play themes and literacy interactions with others in the setting throughout the study period.

To examine the influence of the play setting on individual children's play activity, research assistants observed each child's spontaneous play after 8 weeks had elapsed, using the same procedures as in the baseline period.

Following the Intervention. During the final 2 weeks of the study, each child's spontaneous play activity was systematically observed once again by research assistants. After observations were completed, two environmental print measures were administered individually to children in the intervention and nonintervention groups: (a) an environmental word reading task and (b) a functional print task.

The environmental word reading task assessed children's ability to read words from the seven labels and signs placed in the office play setting. Each sign was taken from its context in the setting, and was shown to the child in its customary logo form. In cases where there were several words on the sign, we drew the child's attention to a target word by underlining it from left to right and saying, "What does this say?" Target words were: *office, exit, out, closed, open, hello,* and *dollars.*

The functional print tasks, adapted from Lomax and McGee (1987), measured children's knowledge of the functions and uses of written language associated with the specific types of functional print in the office setting. The child was shown, one at a time, 10 functional items: a page of a telephone book, a calendar, a typed business letter, a message pad, a stamp, a catalogue, a brochure, a calculator, and a "speed-letter" (interoffice memo). He or she was asked to identify the item (e.g., What is this?) first and then asked to identify its function (e.g., What do you use it for?). Answers to the environmental word reading and the functional print tasks were recorded verbatim.

One hundred thirty-eight children comprised the final sample size of the study, representing a loss of 22% of the sample due to long-term absences and family relocations. (Neuman & Roskos, 1993, pp. 100–105, Copyright 1993 by the American Educational Research Association.)

The **results section** contains the outcomes of the researchers' data analyses. This section contains not only the numerical or statistical results (often presented in tables and charts) but an explanation of the importance or educational implications of those results. To many research consumers, results sections are confusing because of the statistical information. (The next subsection of this chapter, A Plan for Reading Reports, explains how these sections can be read. In Chapter 8, Reading and Interpreting Results Sections, are discussions about how to judge researchers' presentations of both qualitative and quantitative data analyses.)

The following example is a typical results section. It is from an experimental study about the effects of focused federal Chapter 1 instruction on first-grade students' literacy. Notice that the results of the statistical analysis were reported as part of the commentary and in tables. The results are presented in relation to three perspectives (see the first paragraph of the extract). The results indicated that (a) students who began the year with few literacy proficiencies made substantial progress, (b) the students in the restructured program made greater progress than students in the regular program, and (c) the Chapter 1 students were performing at the same level as the average students in their classes on reading and writing tasks.

RESULTS

The performances of students in the restructured Chapter 1 program are discussed in relation to three perspectives: (1) absolute performances, (2) comparison to Chapter 1 students in the regular program, and (3) comparison to classmates.

Table 1   Percentage of Students in Restructured and Regular Chapter 1 Programs Attaining Fluency at Various Levels on Text-Level Reading Task[a]

Level of Text	Restructured Chapter 1	Regular Chapter 1
Third grade	13%	—
Second grade	18%	—
First grade	24%	6%
Primer	22%	12%
Preprimer	7%	18%
Predictable book	9%	18%
Below predictable book	7%	47%

[a]   Totals may be slightly less or more than 100 due to rounding of percentages for individual categories.

Table 2   Percentage of Students in Restructured and Regular Chapter 1 Programs at Particular NCE Levels on CTBS-Reading[a]

Level	Restructured Chapter 1	Regular Chapter 1
75–	—	—
50–74	18%	—
33–49[b]	38%	—
25–32	24%	22%
1–24	20%	79%

[a]   Totals may be slightly less or more than 100 due to rounding of percentages for individual categories.

[b]   The second quartile is divided in this manner because 33 NCE had been set as the cut-off for Chapter 1 placement in this district.

Absolute Performances

For parents, teachers, administrators, and, eventually, children themselves, the critical question is, "Can children read grade-level text?" Chapter 1 teachers and administrators also asked the question, "Based on standardized test performances, which children will be eligible for Chapter 1 services next year?" These questions are answered by examining children's absolute levels of performance on reading text and, for Chapter 1 requirements, the standardized test. Table 1 presents the distribution of performances on reading text, and Table 2 presents CTBS—Reading.

In the fall, none of the children in the restructured Chapter 1 program had been able to read even a handful of words independently. In the spring, 77% of the children were able to read at a primer level (which comprises the third quarter of first grade in basal reading programs) or higher, and 55% were reading the first-grade text or higher fluently. Twenty-three percent of the group (10 children) were reading below the primer level, with 3 at the preprimer level, 4 at the predictable book level, and 3 unable to read the predictable book fluently. This group of 10 children had been asked to read the primer text, and their performances were examined on this task. Their average level of fluency was 70%.

Absolute levels were also computed to determine how many children would be designated for Chapter 1 in Grade 2, if the district used a level of 33 NCE as the cut-off. Using that criterion, 56% of the students would no longer be eligible for Chapter 1. If the level for exiting Chapter 1 was lowered to 25 NCE, as had been the case during the year of the project, only 20% of the sample would have remained in Chapter 1.

Table 3   Means and Standard Deviations for Students in Restructured and Regular Chapter 1 Programs at End of Year

Measure	Total Possible		Restructured Ch. 1[a]	Regular Ch. 1[b]	Univariate F for Within-Cell Regression[c]	Univariate F for Program[c]
Reading		X	1.15[d]	.35	12.19**	25.19**
text	3	SD	.84[e]	.32		
Reading		X	27.29	11.38	22.49**	34.28**
words	60	SD	13.44	8.19		
Writing		X	4.36	3.55	11.54**	10.95**
text	6	SD	1.03	1.04		
Writing		X	16.41	6.95	10.59*	29.81**
words	60	SD	8.62	5.11		
CTBS—		X	33.78	19.08	33.73**	43.81**
Reading	99	SD	11.36	5.77		
CTBS—		X	38.25	22.78	9.55*	29.11**
Lang. Arts	99	SD	13.58	9.84		

[a] $n = 45$.   [b] $n = 34$.   [c] $df = 1,76$.

[d] Means adjusted for covariate.

[e] Standard deviations based on residuals.

* $p < .01$.   ** $p < .001$.

Against a standard of conventional reading as measured by ability to read words, none of the children had been able to read at the beginning of the year. At the end of the year, the majority were reading the texts that are designated for the second half of grade one. However, questions remain about the comparability of this growth to students who were in the regular Chapter 1 and classroom programs.

Comparison With Regular Chapter 1 Students

Students in both the restructured and regular Chapter 1 programs scored well below the 33 NCE level on the readiness measure at the beginning of the year, as is evident in the means for the two groups (restructured: $X = 16.42$, $SD = 7.10$; regular: $X = 12.85$, $SD = 6.35$). Since the t of 2.35 for the test of differences between these two groups was significant at $p < .02$, the multivariate analysis of the six dependent variables (reading text, reading words, writing text, writing words, CTBS—Reading, and CTBS—Language Arts) included the readiness scores as a covariate.

The multivariate within-cell effect was significant (Wilks's lambda = .654, $F = 6.27$, $df = 6,71$, $p < .001$), indicating that the readiness performances accounted for a significant proportion of the variance in students' end-of-year performances. The univariate F ratios, which appear in Table 3, indicate a significant difference on all six measures. For most of the measures, the amount of variance accounted for by the readiness measure was in the range of 11 to 14% (CTBS—Language Arts, 11%; writing words, 12%; writing text, 13%; reading text, 14%). The readiness measure accounted for somewhat more of the variance on reading words (23%) and the most on CTBS—Reading (31%). The test for the interaction between readiness and program was not significant (Wilks's lambda = .90, $F = 1.34$, $df = 6,70$, $p < .252$), indicating that the pooled covariance across groups adequately summarized the effect of the readiness measure and a separate analysis of the effect of the covariate within each group was not needed.

Even when the effect of readiness is controlled, the program effect persists, as is evident in the significant multivariate effect for program (Wilks's lambda = .567, $F = 9.02$, $df = 6,71$, $p < .001$). The presentation of univariate F ratios for program in Table 3 shows that differences between students' performances in the restructured and regular programs were significant at the $p < .001$ level for all six measures.

**Table 4   Means and Standard Deviations for Students in Restructured Chapter 1
Programs and Classmates**

		Total Possible	Quintile 1[a]	Quintile 2[b]	Quintile 3[c]	Quintile 4[d]	Quintile 5 (Chapter 1)[c]
Gates-MacGinitie	X		60.38	46.88	41.14	31.13	16.42
(fall)	SD	99	15.54	10.38	18.06	6.49	7.10
Reading text	X		2.61	1.75	1.14	.60	1.22[f]
(spring)	SD	3	.83	.84	.96	.54	.92
Reading words	X		50.79	38.86	28.21	21.28	28.93
(spring)	SD	60	11.22	11.02	14.99	13.53	15.24
Writing text	X		5.29	4.92	4.00	3.53	4.47
(spring)	SD	6	.73	.92	1.10	1.33	1.08
Writing words	X		26.93	19.64	18.43	14.61	17.13
(spring)	SD	60	8.92	9.86	8.65	8.54	8.99

[a] $n = 14$.   [b] $n = 14$.   [c] $n = 14$.
[d] $n = 13$.   [c] $n = 45$.   [f] Observed means.

Absolute levels of performance for the students in the regular Chapter 1 program were also considered and are included in Tables 1 and 2. Approximately 18% of the children in the regular Chapter 1 program had reached a fluency level of primer text or higher, as compared to 77% of the group in the restructured Chapter 1 program. Eighty-three percent of the regular Chapter 1 group read below a primer level (averaging 37% fluency on the primer text). Using the criterion of 33 NCE as a cut-off, all of the Chapter 1 comparison students would return to Chapter 1 in Grade 2. If the cut-off is moved down to 25 NCE, 22% would no longer be eligible for Chapter 1.

Comparison With Classmates

This comparison considered the performances of the students in the restructured Chapter 1 program with those of classmates. Performances of Quintile 5/Chapter 1 students at the end of the year on text-level reading and writing and word-level reading and writing were compared to those of classmates ranging from high (Quintile 1) to medium-low (Quintile 4).

Prior to conducting these comparisons, an analysis was needed to establish that the quintile groups began the year with significantly different levels of readiness. First, spring performances on reading text, reading words, writing text, and writing words were compared for students who had taken the GM in the fall and those who had not. This analysis indicated no significant differences between these two groups ($F = 1.94$, $df = 4,44$, $p < .12$). The group by quintile interaction was nonsignificant ($F = .56$, $df = 12,117$, $p < .86$), indicating that the pattern of no differences between the tested and nontested groups was consistent across the quintiles. These analyses mean that available GM scores can be considered as indicators of a quintile's entry level.

Next, the entry level of Quintile 5/Chapter 1 was compared to those of the other 4 quintiles to determine whether differences existed between groups in fall readiness. The analysis of variance using the reading readiness scores presented in Table 4 showed a significant effect, $F = 47.92$, $df = 4, 71$, $p < .001$. Planned comparisons between Quintile 5/Chapter 1 and each of the other quintiles indicated a significant difference at $p < .01$: Quintile 1, $t = 11.92$; Quintile 2, $t = 7.72$; Quintile 3, $t = 6.06$; and Quintile 4, $t = 2.75$. Quintile 5/Chapter 1 students had a significantly lower entry readiness level than all of the other four groups in the fall.

The next analysis considered whether the performances of the Quintile 5/Chapter 1 students differed from those of any of the other groups at the end of the year. Of particular interest was the question, "Did Quintile 5/Chapter 1 students who began the year with significantly lower reading readiness scores than peers in Quintiles 3 and 4 have comparable performances to these two groups by the end of the year?" It was expected that differences between Quintile 5/Chapter 1 and Quintiles 1 and 2 would still exist since these latter two groups had had substantially higher readiness scores at the beginning of the year.

Analysis of variance indicated that differences across the quintiles existed at the end of the year for reading text ($F = 10.75$, $df = 4,95$, $p < .001$), writing text ($F = 5.28$, $df = 4,95$, $p < .001$), reading words ($F = 9.76$, $df = 4,95$, $p < .001$), and writing words ($F = 3.98$, $df = 4,95$, $p < .01$). The pattern of these differences had changed from the beginning to the end of the year. Except for one planned comparison where Quintile 2 performed significantly better than Quintile 5/Chapter 1, the scores of Quintile 5/Chapter 1 could not be distinguished statistically from those of students in either Quintiles 2 or 3. Quintile 5/Chapter 1 differed significantly from Quintile 4 on reading text ($t = 2.90$, $p < .01$), and the comparison for writing text was marginally significant ($t = 2.06$, $p < .058$). Unlike the beginning of the year, however, Quintile 5/Chapter 1 students had higher scores than students in Quintile 4. Only Quintile 1 had significantly higher scores than Quintile 5/Chapter 1 on all measures (reading text, $t = 5.34$, $p < .001$; reading words, $t = .81$, $p < .001$; writing words, $t = 3.58$, $p < .01$; writing text, $t = 3.25$, $p < .01$).

At the end of the year, Quintile 5/Chapter 1 students had performances that were indistinguishable from those of students who had begun the year substantially ahead of them in Quintiles 2 and 3, and they were ahead of peers in Quintile 4. The only group that had maintained its significant lead over Quintile 5/Chapter 1 consisted of the students who had begun the year as the highest group. (Hiebert, Colt, Catto, & Gury, 1992, pp. 559–564. Copyright 1992 by the American Educational Research Association. Reprinted by permission of the publisher.)

The **discussion** or **conclusion section** contains researchers' ideas about education implications of research results: how results can be used in school settings or what additional research may be called for. Often this explanation is prefaced with a brief summary of research results. When researchers obtain unusual or unexpected results, they discuss possible reasons for these results.

The following example is a typical conclusion section. It is taken from a study that sought information on four dimensions of school-based management [SBM] implementation: school leadership, school climate, student achievement, and community involvement. Notice that it also contains the researchers' recommendations for using their findings.

CONCLUSIONS/RECOMMENDATIONS

The findings of the survey data suggested several conclusions for discussion. Each of the four dimensions of the survey was examined by a combination of four variables, providing for 16 measures of perceptions of SBM effectiveness. One quarter of these measures reported significant interactions between dimension and variable. Each of these significant interactions occurred between the variable of role school category and a particular dimension of the survey.

The assessment of multiple variables to assess effectiveness was suggested by the work of Ogawa and White (1994) and Wohlstetter and Odden (1992). Perhaps not surprisingly, these data suggested that the longer a school is involved in SBM, the greater the perception of effectiveness of the initiative. This perception held true for each of the dimensions—school leadership, school climate, student achievement, and community involvement—used within the study. These data support the findings of Wohlstetter and Mohrman (1996) that "actively restructuring" schools gain in perceptions of effectiveness as they engage in significant SBM programs.

These data are an important endorsement for SBM—a variety of stakeholders perceive that the effectiveness of the reform increases over time in several different areas. The data were in contrast, however, to the work of Robertson, Wohlstetter, and Mohrman (1995), who found that some professionals involved in SBM initiatives for longer than four years were tired and wondered if they could maintain their level of involvement. Too many districts have assumed that SBM occurs with average levels of commitment and energy. This research indicates that active SBM schools place extraordinary demands on personnel involved. The difference in these findings may lie in the level of SBM involvement undertaken by the schools involved in the study to date. The work of Summers and Johnson (1994) supported the importance of the contributions of multiple populations of stakeholders to the success of SBM initiatives.

The following recommendations are made in relation to the conclusions reached through the analysis of the data obtained through the written questionnaire, focus group sessions, and personal interviews in relation to the perceptions of SBM effectiveness.

There are several suggestions that apply to the field of educational administration in general. First among these is the implication that training and professional development are key to the success of an SBM initiative.

Unfortunately, as stated by Bradley (1993), "professional development is the first to be cut" (p. 12) in times of fiscal constraint. The profession needs to stress training and professional development activities in SBM for both administrators and faculty/staff members. Specifically, the training programs should allow the administrator and other stakeholders to become current with the body of SBM literature, and should allow time for reflection on how the SBM concept can be successfully implemented. The data in this study highlight that administrators may be among the most enthusiastic stakeholders regarding an SBM initiative. This asset should not be ignored when planning for SBM implementation. An increase in professional development activities may foster this same positive attitude in faculty/staff members.

A related point in the training arena is that the professional development of administrators and faculty/staff members in finance has been woefully neglected. Significant SBM initiatives, such as those initiated in Chicago, point to the need for expertise in the budgeting and expenditure of funds at the local level. The correct use of resources is essential to a successful SBM initiative. For example, in Chicago, business managers and individual training packages have been allocated to local schools to provide for the accurate usage of local financial resources. Specific strategies such as these are needed to address the legitimate concerns that exist regarding this important aspect of SBM implementation.

A second recommendation for the field generated by the study is to allow for the perceptions of effectiveness of SBM to grow over time. Significantly higher scores regarding perceptions of effectiveness were noted for the groups of schools exposed to SBM over a longer period of time. The researcher believes that a substantial amount of time is needed for the roles and responsibilities of an SBM initiative to be understood and inculcated into the culture of a school district.

However, a balance must be drawn between this period of reflection and the pressing public concerns and perceptions regarding the public schools. It may well behoove our schools to accelerate the rate of SBM implementation.

This aggressive approach would allow for a quicker assessment of the impacts of SBM and allow for the field to make any necessary adjustments in the process in a timely fashion. The forces of competition within education may not permit a more leisurely, extended exploration of the SBM concept.

A third point of consideration for the field is the array of dimensions on which an SBM program can have a positive impact. This study has highlighted that school leadership, school climate, student achievement, and community involvement can all be the beneficiaries of an SBM initiative. As the competition between public and private education escalates in the next century, the school that serves the local community well is a school that is essential to the growth and development of that community. It is incumbent on our public schools to make themselves essential, becoming an integral part of the fabric of improvement within the community. SBM is one method that allows for the increased inputs of all stakeholders. SBM will provide schools with opportunities for increased community integration. Too many schools do not acknowledge the debt they owe to their communities for the support and the responsibility with which they are entrusted.

A final, general recommendation for the field concerns the format of this study. The information related to the perceptions of effectiveness of SBM generated by the written survey was further enriched by both focus group sessions and personal interviews. This approach produced more information than would a single or dual approach. Any study that uses a written survey would be greatly enhanced by augmenting the written data with a series of focus group and personal interview sessions.

AREAS FOR FURTHER STUDY

The findings of this study also suggested several areas for further study. The strong research base promoting community involvement in SBM and the relatively weak concern for the area shown in this study are important. The future researcher might want to target SBM initiatives in which community involvement has been an emphasis to ascertain how this dimension is successfully integrated into an SBM program.

The personal interview data from the study indicated that the role of labor in SBM may be a topic for research. The natural inclination of SBM to promote diversity at local sites may come into conflict with the union/labor mandate to standardize the workplace for its members. This might be a subject of considerable interest.

Several of the authors reviewed (Clune and White 1988; Malen, Ogawa and Kranz 1990; Wohlstetter and Mohrman 1996) found little or no correlation between SBM implementation and student achievement. Given the strong pedigree that SBM brings from the Lawler's (1992) high involvement model, the considerable body of research indicates that better decisions should impact positively on instruction and the strong positive feelings demonstrated in this study, the time is right for a vigorous assessment of the connection between SBM programs and student achievement. (Brown & Cooper, 2000, pp. 82–84).

The **reference section** contains an alphabetical listing of the books, journal articles, other research reports, instructional materials, and instruments cited in the report. Sometimes, researchers follow the reference section with appendices that contain examples of instruments or special materials.

A Plan for Reading Reports

In most research reports, researchers use common terms and organize their ideas similarly. Research consumers, therefore, can read most reports using a basic plan, which has three phases: prereading, reading, and postreading. In the first phase, research consumers determine what they know about the topic before reading and set purposes for reading the report. In the second phase, consumers systematically read parts of the report according to their own purposes. In the last phase, they confirm whether their purposes have been met and learning has occurred.

The reading plan is illustrated with a model research report (see Chapter 3 Appendix). For the first report, a descriptive study using quantitative data collection and analysis (Morrison, Jacobs, & Swinyard, 1999), the reading plan is fully explained with reference to the report's labeled sections. For the second report of experimental research (King, 1994), the sections are labeled, but the reading plan is only outlined.

Guided Reading

First Phase: Previewing and Predicting the Research Report.   The aim of this phase is to determine why you will read the report and what kinds of knowledge or information it presents. It is like a reconnaissance mission to find out what you know about the topic and to predict whether the report meets your intended purpose. It also is a time to determine whether the report is written as a standard research report.

1. Using the research report "Do Teachers Who Read Personally Use Recommended Literacy Practices in Their Classrooms?" (Chapter 3 Appendix), answer the question "Why am I reading this report—to gain knowledge, to apply the knowledge, or to implement an instructional practice?" For this demonstration, we will assume that you desire additional information about the personal reading habits of teachers.

2. Read the report title #1 and the first sentence of the abstract #3.

3. Answer the question "Will reading this report meet my purpose?
   "The answer is yes, because the study looks at teachers as readers, and especially at teachers who are readers and also encourage their students to be readers.

4. Answer the question "What do I know about the topic?"
   On a sheet of paper or in the margin next to the report, list what you already know about factors related to teachers' reading habits. Start with those ideas listed in the title and the abstract's first sentence: teachers who read, recommended literacy practices, and models of reading.

5. Read each of the major headings. Answer the question "Is the report organized using typical section headings?"
   The answer is yes: Background #5 and #6, Purpose #7, Methodology #8 through #10, Results #11 through #18, Discussion #19 through #23, Recommendations #24 through #27, References #28, and Appendix #29 . The researchers have used additional headings and subheadings. They are also important, especially in the Results section, because they help you identify the answers to the researchers' purpose questions.

Second Phase: Reading the Research Report. The aim of this phase is to find information suggested by your purpose for reading and to confirm or modify your list of known information. Your purpose determines whether you read the entire report or only select sections.

6. As you read the report, keep alert to two things: (a) your purpose is to obtain information about teachers who read and what reading practices they recommend for their students and (b) some factors will be added to your list and some will modify or contradict items on your list of factors related to teachers' reading habits and the reading procedures they use in their classrooms. As you read, note that key information regarding the purpose has been printed in boldface type.

7. Read the research report sections in the following order (note that several sections have been intentionally omitted from the list):
   Abstract (3)
   Introduction (4), first paragraph
   Purpose (7)
   Discussion (19–23)
   Recommendations (24–27)

8. You will not read the remaining sections now because the information to meet your reading purpose can be obtained in the previously listed sections.

Third Phase: Confirming Predictions and Knowledge.   The goals of this phase are to verify that your purpose has been met and to immediately recall key information. You should now decide which information supports the proposed research consumer purpose and adds to your knowledge base.

9. Refer to the list you made during the first phase, step 4, and revise it by adding new information and deleting inappropriate information. Answer the question "Were the teachers who read and the reading practices they used similar to those in my own teaching and those of other teachers I know in my school situation so that the insights drawn from the results can be applied there?"

10. Write a short (two- to three-sentence) statement that applies to the proposed purpose for reading the report and contains the report's key points. (The statement should contain information from the boldface text in the report.)

Independent Reading

Using one of the reports in the appendix to this chapter (Morrison et al, 1999), apply the reading plan procedures.

First Phase: Previewing and Predicting the Research Report.   Set your purpose and identify known information about the topic. Determine which sections are to be read.

What possible purpose would you have for reading the research report?

What main headings should be read? (Suggestions: title, abstract, purpose, subjects, procedures, or discussion and conclusion)

Second Phase: Reading the Research Report.   Read the report sections and identify key information. Note whether the researchers' use italics, boldface or other typographical clues as organizational signals.

Third Phase: Confirming Predictions and Knowledge.   Verify that your purpose has been met and recall key information. If the purpose has not been met or if additional information needs to be identified, select sections to be read or reread.

Suggested sections as sources of additional key information: nine (all subsections and Figure 1), ten (all subsections), section 29 (Appendix A).

Suggested sections to be read additionally (if needed): twelve (all subsections).

EVALUATING RESEARCH REPORTS

Informed consumers effectively compare and shop in a store for products by using a set of criteria. Research consumers can "shop" among research reports to identify well-written reports of appropriate methodology. You have already taken the first step in being a research consumer: learning to read research reports like a research producer. The second step is using the questions in Figure 3.1 to evaluate research reports.

The questions are about each of the major aspects of research reports. At this point in your learning, you should not be expected to answer all the questions appropriately. Because the content and length of research reports are often determined by the editors of the journals or books in which the reports appear, our determinations as research consumers about the appropriateness and adequacy of the information in a report will necessarily be subjective. Remember that these subjective decisions change as you gain increased understanding of research methods and research reporting and as you gain more experience in reading and evaluating research

ABSTRACT

Organization. Is information about the major aspects of the research—purpose, subjects, instruments, procedures/treatment, results—included?
Style. Is the abstract brief and clearly written?

INTRODUCTORY SECTION

Problem Area. Are the problem area and its educational importance explained? Are the researchers' assumptions and theoretical perspectives about the topic explained?
Related Literature. Are research studies related to the problem area presented? Has the related research been evaluated and critiqued? Does the intended research logically extend the understandings from the related research?
Hypothesis(es), Purpose(s), Question(s) in Quantitative Research. Is there a purpose that can be studied in an unbiased manner? Are the research variables (independent and dependent, when appropriate) easily identified from the hypothesis, question, or purpose statement? Are key terms or variables operationally defined?
Purpose(s), Question(s) in Qualitative Research. Is the relationship between the study and previous studies explicit? Is there a clear rationale for the use of qualitative procedures? Are researchers' assumptions and biases expressed?

METHOD SECTION

Subjects. Are target populations and subjects, sampling and selection procedures, and group sizes clearly described? Are these appropriate for the research design?
Standardized and Other Instruments. What instruments are used in the study? Are they appropriate for the design of the study? Are the instruments valid for collecting data on the variables in the study and are reliability estimates given for each instrument? Are researcher-made instruments included (or at least samples of the instrument items)? Are the instruments appropriate for use with the target population and the research subjects? In the case of authentic, or performance-based, assessments, what evidence is presented that the devices reflect realistic samples of students' learning?
Design and Procedure in Quantitative Research. Are the research design and data collection procedures clearly described? Is the research design appropriate to the researchers' purpose? Can the study be replicated from the information provided? In experimental designs, are treatments fully explained? Are examples of special materials included?
Design and Procedure in Qualitative Research. Are research questions stated and additional questions generated? Is the method explained in detail? Has researchers' presence influenced the behavior of the subjects? Is there abundant evidence from multiple sources?

RESULTS SECTION

Data Analysis in Quantitative Research. Are the statistical procedures for data analysis clearly described, and are they appropriate for the type of quantitative research design?
Research Validity in Quantitative Research. Are the procedures free from the influence of extraneous variables? Does the study have any threats to its internal and external validity?
Significance in Quantitative Research. Are statistical significance levels indicated? Does the research have practical significance?
Data Analysis in Qualitative Research. Are the processes for organizing data, identifying patterns, and synthesizing key ideas as hypotheses and research questions clearly described?
Research Validity in Qualitative Research. Are there multiple procedures for corroborating research evidence and researchers' judgments?

DISCUSSION SECTION

Discussion (Conclusions, Recommendations). Are conclusions related to answering the research question(s), and are they appropriate to the results? Is the report free from inappropriate generalizations and implications? If inappropriate, are suggestions for additional research provided?

Figure 3.1
Questions for Evaluating Research Reports

reports and writing about them. Your work with this text is a beginning step in acquiring understanding and experience.

The questions presented in Figure 3.1 provide an overview of the discussions in later chapters. The major headings within Figure 3.1 represent common, major headings found in research reports published in professional journals. As you can see by reviewing the previously cited reports, researchers modify these major headings to fit their purposes and to highlight particular information. Research reports in other sources—books, encyclopedias, newspapers, and popular magazines—may have different organizations and formats. Some of these variations are discussed in later chapters.

ACTIVITY

Select a research report from Appendix B at the back of the book or from a professional journal. With one or more partners, other students in the class, read the research report. Use the *peer-interacting procedure* discussed in the Activities section of Chapter 2 and the research report reading plan discussed in this chapter. You and your partner(s) should take turns explaining the reason for selecting sections to be read and the location of key information. Discuss differences you may have about these choices.

FEEDBACK

Discuss your response with your partners, other partner teams, and the course instructor.

Morrison, T. G., Jacobs, J. S., & Swinyard, W. R. (1999). Do teachers who read personally use recommended literary practices in their classrooms? *Reading Research and Instruction, 38*(2), 81–100.

(1)

Do Teachers Who Read Personally Use Recommended Literacy Practices in Their Classrooms?

(2)

Timothy G. Morrison

James S. Jacobs

William R. Swinyard

Brigham Young University

(3)

ABSTRACT

Elementary teachers have been encouraged to serve as models of reading for their students. They have also been advised to implement specific literacy instructional practices in their classrooms. Although such suggestions are common and are considered to be sound advice, the research literature offers limited support for them. In this study, 1874 elementary teachers nationwide were surveyed to determine their level of commitment as readers, as well as to establish their use of recommended literacy instructional practices. Among the results was a significant linear relationship between teachers who read personally and their use of recommended literacy practices in their classrooms. Significant results were also found regarding differences among teachers by grade level, teacher age, and years of teaching experience. Specific recommendations are provided based on results of the survey.

(4) One overriding goal shared by most elementary school teachers is to help students develop the ability and passion for reading that will extend into a lifelong reading habit. Teachers want their students not only to be able to read but also to love to read and choose to read in their leisure time. While the ways to achieve this goal may be debatable, teachers can model reading and provide quality instructional practices to encourage the reading habit.

(5)

TEACHERS AS READERS

Perhaps the most influential teacher behavior to influence their students' literacy development is personal reading, both in and out of school. Modeling of reading (i.e., teachers reading in the presence of children during, for example, a sustained silent reading time) is recommended because children can see that an adult values reading enough that s/he regularly spends time engaging in reading and appears to enjoy it. Mour (1977) argues that "the teacher who reads much would present a more positive and enthusiastic model than would the teacher who reads little" (p. 397).

But teachers involved in personal, recreational reading (i.e., reading out of the presence of children, for example, at home or in the doctor's office waiting room) can also influence the ways they interact with students in literacy settings.

> Just as teachers who write are best able to act as guides for less experienced writers, teachers who see themselves as readers—who are aware of the requirements and strategies of the reader's role—are best able to guide young readers (Andrews-Beck & Rycik, 1992, p. 121).

Although teachers are advised to serve as reading models, there is, unfortunately, little research to support the practice of teachers as readers. Searls (1985) surveyed 64 teachers identified by graduate students enrolled in a university literacy course. She found that these teachers read a great deal. For example, 94% of the teachers reported that they engaged in pleasure reading, 61% said that their students often saw them read, and 68% indicated that they read novels regularly. These figures contrast with results from other studies that reported more pessimistic results (Gray &

Troy, 1986; Mour, 1977; Mueller, 1973). However, critical problems with sampling bias in each of these studies call all of the results into question.

RECOMMENDED LITERACY PRACTICES

(6) Teachers also try to help their students become able readers by providing appropriate literacy instruction. Among the many changes in American literacy instruction occurring in the past 30 years has been the increased use of literature in the classroom for both instructional and recreational purposes. Although the use of literature has increased, basal reading instruction and other forms of more traditional reading instruction continue. Several reports indicate that between 80% and 90% of classrooms in the United States still rely heavily on basal reading programs for the bulk of their reading instruction (Aaron, 1987; Farr, Tulley, & Powell, 1987; Weaver & Watson, 1989). However, teachers are using literature more and more as a major supplement to basal reading instruction. Dillingofski (1993) reports that over 50% of American elementary classrooms use trade books along with basal readers, while 20% use literature only. Lehman, Freeman, and Allen (1994) report that 94% of surveyed teachers agreed or strongly agreed with the recommendation that children's literature should be the primary component of the language arts program in the elementary school. They also indicated that 85% of the teachers read to their students daily and 78% used sustained silent reading (SSR) as a daily practice.

Pressley, Rankin, and Yokoi's (1996) survey of 113 primary grade teachers who were nominated by their supervisors as effective in literacy instruction produced interesting results regarding practices they considered to be critical to their students' literacy development. These teachers reported using literature widely in their work in the classroom. For example, virtually all of the teachers indicated that they read to their students nearly every day and told stories to their students weekly. They reported that they spend 71% of their instructional time with meaning-making activities and only 27% of their time with decoding activities. Nearly three-fourths of the teachers indicated that they read outstanding children's literature to their students, although only 6% of the books they read were informational books. Phonics was taught explicitly by 95% of the primary grade teachers surveyed.

Regie Routman (1996) has worked for over 20 years in public schools helping teachers develop effective literacy programs. She identifies a number of literacy instructional practices she considers appropriate in elementary classrooms, including using children's literature, reading aloud to students regularly, daily sustained silent reading (SSR), discussing literature in small groups, guided silent reading, small group explicit skill instruction, regular miscue analyses, and daily shared reading.

Although many suggestions regarding appropriate literacy instructional practices exist, the research literature has not identified what teachers **use** those activities in their classrooms. Individuals who read extensively may be among those teachers who employ recommended literacy instructional practices. However, the research literature does not address this issue.

PURPOSE OF THE STUDY

(7) The purpose of this study was to examine relationships between two related issues: the personal, recreational reading of teachers with their use of recommended literacy instructional practices in their elementary classrooms. We would expect that teachers who love and value reading in their personal lives will also be better reading teachers—they will use recommended literacy instructional practices and use them more often. Thus, the questions guiding this research are the following:

To what extent are teachers "readers" in their personal lives?

What characterizes teachers who are readers?

Which teachers use recommended literacy instructional practices in elementary classrooms (e.g., do primary grade teachers use these practices more often than intermediate grade teachers; what about teachers with more years of teaching experience; what about older or younger teachers)?

What are relationships between 1 and 2 above-between the personal reading of teachers and their uses of recommended literacy instructional practices?

METHODOLOGY

(8) These research questions were addressed by means of a descriptive study of nearly 2000 elementary school teachers, collected in a national sample. Kindergarten through sixth grade teachers throughout the United States were chosen on a national probability basis.

Measures

(9) Twenty-one items from a larger questionnaire were used to gather information related to elementary teachers' reading practices and their classroom instructional practices. Fifteen of the items focused on teachers' use of recommended literacy instructional practices and six referred to teachers' personal reading habits.

The larger questionnaire was used to collect information about many aspects of elementary teachers' literacy programs, experiences, and practices. The items for the survey were created by or collated from a variety of sources, including one-on-one interviews and group discussions with elementary teachers, visits with publishers' representatives, the personal teaching experience of the authors (both at the elementary and the university level), and a pilot test conducted among preservice teachers. The pilot test examined a larger number of items using a convenience sample of 256 elementary education students enrolled in a senior-level children's literature course. Single-variable and multivariate analyses suggested that some of the items could be dropped and others edited or more fully represented. See Appendix A for a complete list of the 21 items used in this study.

Instructional Practices. The 15 items related to teachers' uses of literacy instructional practices used an 11-point frequency-of-behavior scale, which asked respondents to circle the one number that best reflected "about how many out of the last 10 school days" they had used each activity (scaled from "0" to "10"). For example, a teacher responding "3" to the statement, "Read aloud a picture book to your class," was interpreted as indicating that this activity was used three out of the last ten school days—or in about 30% of that teacher's school days.

Teachers as Readers. The remaining six items examined teachers' perceptions of themselves as readers. These items were measured on a 5-point descriptiveness scale (1 = *not at all; 5 = extremely) based on responses to the item, "How descriptive is this statement of you?"*

The questionnaire also included a number of demographics, including gender, age, years of teaching experience, current grade(s) taught, and other similar information which was used to classify the data.

⑩ *Sampling Procedures*

Names and home mailing addresses for the elementary teachers were obtained from a professional mailing list company. In the second semester of the school year, 3600 questionnaires were mailed to the home addresses of a probability sample of elementary teachers of kindergarten through grade six. Their home rather than school addresses were used because it was believed that the questionnaire would receive a more thorough review during the teachers' quiet moments at home.

Each initial mailout included a cover letter (with all 3600 letters signed in ballpoint by hand), a four-page questionnaire, and a prepaid, self-addressed business-return envelope. Ten days later, all members of the initial sample were sent a reminder postcard. Two weeks afterwards, a third mailing wave was sent to everyone in the sample, including a second copy of the questionnaire, a reminder letter, and a new business-return envelope. The only incentive given was a promise of a copy of summarized results for respondents to those who specifically requested it by writing their name and mailing address on the return envelope.

By the cutoff date, 1874 usable responses had been received, for a usable rate-of-return of 52.3%. Of that number, 70% were respondents to the first mailing wave. Cloud-Silva and Sadoski (1987) indicate that return rates on mailed educational surveys are frequently in the range of 40–60%. A 52% return rate, remarkable in today's junk-mail-intensive environment, provides a sample to accurately reflect the target population's reading aloud practices.

⑪ **RESULTS**

⑫ *Overall*

Table A1 reports the frequencies and percentages of teachers who returned surveys by grade level. Although the majority of the surveyed teachers taught a single grade level, approximately 7% taught a combination of grades. For example, teachers who taught a combination of first, second, and third graders were placed in the Various Primary Grades category on the table. The practice of grouping several grade levels together also occurred in the intermediate grades, so that teachers who taught a combination of grades 4 through 6, for example, were placed in the Various Intermediate Grades category.

A greater number of primary grade teachers responded to the survey than intermediate grade teachers. This may have occurred because primary grades generally have lower class sizes than the upper grades, so there are more primary than intermediate grade teachers. The much lower number of sixth grade teachers compared to the other grades may be due to the placement by school districts of many sixth grade

Table A1   Frequency and Percentage of Teachers Returning Surveys by Grade Level

Grade	Frequency	Percentage
K	216	11.5
1	347	18.5
2	323	17.2
3	275	14.7
Various primary grades	72	3.8
4	245	13.1
5	207	11.0
6	147	7.8
Various intermediate grades	42	2.2
Cumulative	1874	100.0

Table A2 Frequency and Percentage of Teachers Returning Surveys by Gender and Age Range

	Frequency	Percentage
Gender		
Male	145	8.9
Female	1489	91.1
Total	1634	100.0
Age Range		
21–30 years	233	14.2
31–40 years	423	25.8
41–50 years	702	42.8
51–60 years	245	4.9
61–70 years	37	2.3
Total	1640	100.0

Table A3 Teachers as Readers by Grade Level

Grade Level	N	Mean	sd
Kindergarten	216	24.84	5.26
First	347	26.16	4.17
Second	323	25.67	4.54
Third	275	26.09	4.23
Fourth	245	25.76	4.33
Fifth	206	25.88	4.45
Sixth	147	25.73	4.76
Total	1759	25.81	4.49

classes in middle schools rather than in elementary schools. Since the questionnaires were mailed only to elementary school teachers, we may not have included some sixth grade teachers who teach at middle schools.

Table A2 indicates that the vast majority of teachers were female (91.1%), while only 8.9% were male. This proportion represents what we know about the gender distribution of typical elementary school faculties. Of the female teachers, 70% taught in kindergarten through grade three, while 30% taught in grades four through six. Grade levels taught by the males were also disproportionate: approximately one-fourth of the male teachers taught in the primary grades, while three-fourths taught in the intermediate grades.

Table A2 also reports the ages of surveyed teachers. The average age of all teachers was 43.9 years, with more than two-thirds of the teachers falling between 31 and 50 years of age. Also included among our surveyed teachers were some from private schools. However, nearly all of the surveys were returned by public school teachers; only 13 questionnaires were returned by teachers in private schools. Thus, the sample is clearly representative of public school teachers.

⑬ *Teachers as Readers*

Teachers were asked to respond to six items that dealt with their personal reading habits and attitudes (see Appendix A). These items seemed to describe a teacher who valued reading. The items were tested for inter-item reliability and found to surpass the acceptable level of 0.7 (Nunnally, 1978) with an Alpha reliability coefficient of .8274. This suggests that it was appropriate for the six items to be summed to create a single "teacher as reader" construct. This construct was used for several of the analyses of the data.

Teachers were asked to report how descriptive the six statements were of them on a five-point scale (5 = "extremely descriptive," 1 = "not at all"). Three of the

items (2, 3, and 4) were reversed for scoring so that the positive statements about reading were consistently at the high end of the scale. Teachers who felt the statements were "extremely descriptive" of them could score a total of 30 points on the summed construct (five points of each of the six items) and teachers who felt the statements were "very" descriptive of them would score 24.

⑭ *Readers by Grade Level*

The data were examined to determine if teachers as readers differed by grade level taught. That is, we wanted to find out, for example, if primary grade teachers thought of themselves as readers more or less than their intermediate grade teacher counterparts. Table A3 reports the results of the survey on these six items by grade level and indicates that teachers at all grade levels think of themselves as readers. The teachers at all grade levels felt that the items were very or extremely descriptive of them and the results were quite uniform across the grade levels ($F = 2.994$, $df = 1, 1853$, n.s.).

⑮ *Readers by Age*

The teachers were next examined by age by means of a quartile split on the age of the teacher (with ages 22 through 26; 26.1 through 42; 42.1 through 48; and 48.1 through 70). As shown in Table A4, we found a trend of younger teachers having lower reader scores than the older teachers. This result is significant, as is the linear relationship ($F = 8.955$, $df = 1, 1838$, $p < .005$). Results indicated that as the teachers increased in age, they were more likely to be readers; the older teachers were more committed readers than the younger teachers.

⑯ *Readers by Years Teaching*

To examine the extent to which readers differed by number of years of teaching experience, the sample was split into quartiles based on years teaching (1–8 years teaching experience; 9–15 years; 16–21 years;

Table A4   Teachers as Readers by Age

Teacher Age	N	Mean	sd
22–36 years	472	25.32	4.65
36.1–42 years	484	25.79	4.46
42.1–48 years	426	25.95	4.57
48.1–70 years	460	26.19	4.23
Total	1842	25.81	4.49

Table A5   Teachers As Readers by Years of Teaching Experience

Years of Experience	N	Mean	sd
1–8 years	521	5.46	4.49
9–15 years	441	5.95	4.57
16–21 years	462	26.02	4.29
22–47 years	445	95.82	4.60
Total	1869	25.80	4.49

Table A6   Teachers' Use of Recommended Literacy Practices by Grade Level

Grade Level	N	Mean	sd
Kindergarten	147	2.72	1.11
First	298	2.90	1.03
Second	280		1.03
Third	243	2.47	1111
Fourth	208	2.30	1.04
Fifth	180	1.99	1.02
Sixth	127	1.91	1.05
Total	1605	2.51	1.11

Table A7   Teachers' Use of Recommended Literacy Practices by Age

Teacher Age	N	Mean	sd
22–36 years	425	2.64	1.11
36.1–42 years	429	2.55	11.10
42.1–48 years	369	2.38	1.12
48.1–70 years	367	2.48	1.10
Total	1590	2.52	1.10

and 22–47 years). As shown in Table A5, few differences existed in teacher scores according to years of teaching experience, and any differences were not significant ($F = 1.821$, $df = 1$, 1865, n.s.). Thus, length of service as a teacher is not a predictor of teachers who are readers.

(17) *Use of Recommended Reading Practices*

Fifteen of the items on the questionnaire represented literacy instructional practices recommended from the research literature (see Appendix A). Teachers were asked to respond to these fifteen items using an 11-point frequency-of-behavior scale, which asked respondents to circle the one number that best reflected "about how many out of the last 10 school days" they had used each activity (scaled from 0 to 10). For example, a teacher responding "3" to the statement, "Read aloud a picture book to your class," was interpreted as indicating that this activity was used three out of the last ten school days—or in about 30% of that teacher's school days.

The items were examined to see if they represented the same construct (Alpha reliability coefficient = .8040). The fifteen items were found to constitute a single construct dealing with teachers' use of recommended literacy instructional practices, and the fifteen items were subsequently summed to provide a single measure.

The set of analyses discussed here is fundamental to the objectives of this research, for we expected to find that, compared to non-readers, teachers who are readers are more likely to use recommended literacy classroom strategies. First examined was the readers' con-

struct by grade level taught. As shown in Table A6 and Figure A1, the reader scores for teachers using the recommended practices decreased steadily as grade level increased with a range from 2.9 days out of ten for first grade teachers to 1.91 days for sixth grade teachers. This relationship has a significant linear trend (tested by means of an ANOVA relationship, $F = 142.52$, $df = 1$, 1593, $p < .001$). The primary grade teachers in the sample used the recommended literacy practices more than the intermediate grade teachers.

Next studied were reader differences among the teachers by their ages. The age quartiles discussed earlier were again used here, and Table A7 and Figure A2 report the inverse relationship between reader scores and age. Reader scores decreased as teacher age increased (tested by means of ANOVA for a linear relationship, $F = 6.733$, $df = 1$, 1586, $p < .01$). These results indicate that the younger teachers used these instructional practices more than the older teachers.

Finally, teachers as readers were examined by the number of years they had taught. Using the quartiles presented earlier of number of years teaching, we found an inverse relationship between reader and years of teaching experience ($F = 10.558$, $df = 1$, 1603, $p < .001$) as seen in Table A8 and Figure A3. Thus, teachers with fewer years teaching experience employed these literacy instructional strategies more than the teachers with more years of teaching experience.

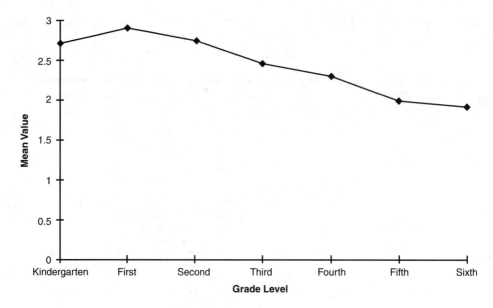

Figure A1 Mean Literacy Practices by Grade Level

(18) *Teachers As Readers and Teachers' Uses of Recommended Practices*

The question that most interested us dealt with possible relationships between our two constructs: teachers as readers and teachers' uses of recommended literacy instructional practices. The relationship between these two constructs was found to be positive ($F = 32.264$, $df = 1$, 1612, $p < .001$), and is shown in Figure A4. This result confirms at the outset of this study: that teachers who see themselves as readers are likely to use recommended literacy instructional practices in their classrooms.

(19)   **DISCUSSION**

Results of this study suggest several areas of discussion that deal with important aspects of literacy instruction. Among these are the prevalence of teachers as readers, older teachers reading more than younger teachers,

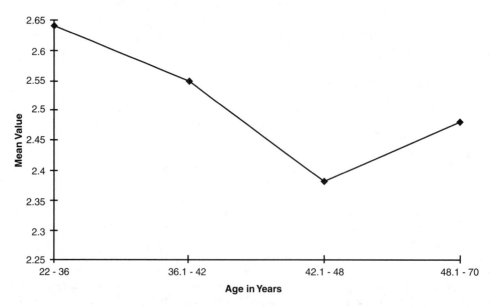

Figure A2 Mean Literacy Practices by Teacher Age

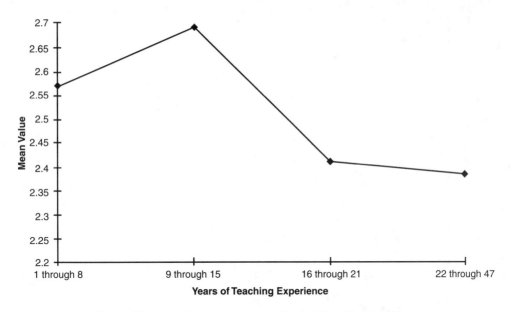

Figure A3 Mean Literacy Practices by Years of Teaching Experience

Table A8 Teachers' Use of Recommended Literacy Practices by Years of Teaching Experience

Years of Experience	N	Mean	sd
1–8 years	461	2.57	1.09
9–15 years	384	2.69	1.09
16–21 years	395	2.41	1.10
22–47 years	367	2.38	1.13
Total	1607	2.52	1.11

teachers' uses of recommended literacy instructional practices, and teachers who enjoy books and use recommended literacy practices in their classrooms.

(20) *Teachers As Readers*

One important finding from this study was that the surveyed elementary teachers reported reading often and enjoying books. The overall mean scores indicated that the statements regarding enjoyment of reading were very or extremely descriptive of them. Although we do not have data to directly compare these results with other adults who are not teachers, the literature shows that the teachers in this survey are probably more committed readers than adults in the general population.

Kaestle, Damon-Moore, Stedman, Tinsley, and Trollinger (1991) report that a consistent trend over the past 50 years has been that adults in the United States do not read a great deal. Specifically, they indicate that only 20 to 25% of adults report having read

a book in the past year. Even though we did not ask teachers in this sample that specific question, results indicate that our sample of teachers probably read more than that. Kaestle et al. (1991) also show that adults with more formal education read more often than those with less education. Because teachers are college educated and deal with literacy instruction of children, they are likely to be more avid readers than adults in the general population. Our results appear to bear out those findings.

(21) *Older and Younger Teachers*

One finding in this study seemed to contradict other results found in the professional literature. We found in this study that older teachers read more than younger teachers. Survey research consistently reports that younger adults (those under 30 years of age) read books and magazines more frequently than adults in all other older categories (Kaestle et al., 1991). Our results indicated the reverse.

In speculating about why that may be, we refer to the type of adults included in this survey. Since all of the adults included in this survey were college-educated, comparisons with the adult population as a whole may be inappropriate. Rather, comparisons should be made with other samples of adults who are all college-educated. When college-educated adult groups are compared with one another, then we may be able to note trends in reading habits among them. For example, it may be that older teachers have more time for recreational

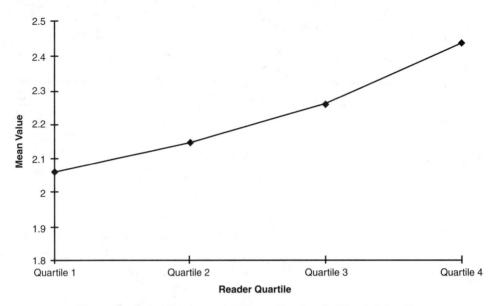

Figure A4 Use of Recommended Literacy Practices by "Reader" Quartile

reading. They may be more established in their lives compared with younger teachers trying to begin a new profession. Because they are older, they have been able to establish the reading habit over a longer period of time compared with their younger peers. However, because no research exists to establish any of these speculations, further study is recommended.

(22) Teachers' Uses of Recommended Literacy Instructional Practices

Two results of this study were that younger teachers and those who are new to the teaching profession use recommended practices more frequently than older teachers. A possible reason for this result may be that these teachers are influenced by their recent teacher preparation courses and experiences. Some of the older, more experienced teachers completed their teacher preparation programs before these more recent instructional practices were validated and encouraged. Another possible reason for the finding may be tied to Lunenburg and Schmidt's notion (1989) that teachers tend to conform to what is expected of them in the culture of schooling. That is, they become more traditional in their teaching behaviors and attitudes over time. Teacher burn-out may also be a possible explanation for these results.

Another result of this study was that primary grade teachers use recommended literacy instructional practices more often than intermediate grade teachers. Primary grade teachers focus a great deal of their attention on helping students acquire literacy skills.

Because of the expectation that children learn to read in the primary grades, primary grade teachers may spend more effort teaching literacy skills than intermediate grade teachers. As children advance in grade levels, the focus of instruction changes from acquisition of literacy skills to application of them in the content areas. Although these may be possible explanations for these results, it is also possible that the types of people who choose to teach in the primary grades may naturally have more interest in reading and books than those who teach in the intermediate grades. Definitive explanations for our results need to come from future research that probes more deeply into teachers' attitudes, opinions, and teaching behaviors.

(23) Teachers Who Enjoy Books and Use Recommended Literacy Practices

Another significant finding from this research was that teachers who more frequently use recommended literacy instructional practices also have more favorable opinions about books and reading.

Many teachers see the influence they can have on their students' literacy development and engage in activities in their classrooms that will hopefully bring about desired results. Teachers are advised repeatedly in the literature to share books with their students. Teachers who place their students in environments where literacy is valued and who provide stimuli for children to engage in literacy activities find that such children increase the amount and type of literacy activity (Morrow, 1990; Morrow, O'Connor, & Smith, 1990).

Work by other researchers reinforces this point. When students have consistent experiences with high-quality literature, their understanding increases in several literacy areas, including story structure (Feitelson, Kita, & Goldstein 1986), comprehension, writing ability and vocabulary (Elley, 1989; Morrow, 1992; Robbins & Ehri, 1994). Teachers who see their role as literacy models for their students may purposely involve themselves in literacy behaviors for the benefit of their students.

(24) **RECOMMENDATIONS**

The results of this study are intriguing and suggest several possible recommendations for teachers. Among these recommendations are that teachers should read personally in their lives, that teachers should make time for reading, and that teachers should share books with children in a variety of ways.

(25) *Teachers Should Read*

Teachers are continually encouraged by literacy professionals to read. By reading children's books, teachers become familiar with many of the books their students are reading. However, by reading any type of text, teachers become more complete individuals. "Our lives outside the classroom makes us better teachers because we are more interesting, vital, and 'real' to be with" (Routman, 1996, p. 170). Teachers should read wherever they are—at home, at the doctor's office, on vacation, and so on.

Teachers can also show their students that they are readers by reading in school so that their students can observe their teachers reading. Many teachers and schools implement a regular sustained silent reading time. Teachers can use this time to read books, showing their students that books and reading are valuable to them. "Achieving this goal [life-long literacy] requires that students be taught by teachers who themselves value reading, as demonstrated by their reading habits and attitudes" (Searls, 1985, p. 233).

(26) *Teachers Need Time for Reading*

Teachers are very busy people with many commitments and obligations. They spend a great deal of time planning instructional activities for their students, arranging optimal learning conditions, and grading student work. However, they need to make time to read. Unfortunately, many teachers may feel guilty when they read children's books. If teachers look upon the time they spend reading books as a professional development activity that will enrich them as teachers, then perhaps they will find more time to keep up with the literature. "The issue is not whether or not I have the time to read (after all, no one will ever give me that time), but whether I will allow myself the joy of being a reader" (Pennac, 1994, pp. 146–147).

Teachers should take the time they have during school hours to read, too. The sustained silent reading time, again, can provide a regular time for teachers to immerse themselves in books. "Teachers who already love reading so much that they always have time to read may engender enthusiasm in their students more easily than teachers who don't" (Hansen, 1987, p. 24).

(27) *Teachers Should Share Books With Children in a Variety of Ways*

When teachers take time to read often and regularly, they will be more effective in their work with children. "[Teachers] who are familiar with children's books are more likely to introduce these books to children. Being familiar with these books helps teachers to appreciate children's literature more and to request a greater selection of books for the school library" (Dillingofski, 1993, p. 32). Effective teachers take advantage of situations that arise in their classrooms to recommend books to children when the need arises.

Sharing books with children in a variety of ways and in a variety of settings is important. Mooney recommends that teachers read to and with their students and also suggests that children be allowed time to read by themselves. Literature is not just for "reading time." Literature can be appropriately used throughout the school day and across the entire curriculum. "The teacher at all levels should devote his/her efforts to leading students into the other worlds that can be found in the pages of books" (Gray & Troy, 1986, p. 179).

(28) **REFERENCES**

Aaron, I. E. (1987). Enriching basal reading programs with literature. In B. E. Cullinan (Ed.), *Children's literature in the reading program* (pp. 126–138). Newark, DE: International Reading Association.

Andrews-Beck, C. S., & Rycik, J. (1992). Teachers reflect on their experience as readers: The literacy club luncheon. *Reading Horizons, 33*, 121–130.

Cloud-Silva, C., & Sadoski, M. (1987). Reading teachers' attitudes toward basal reader use and state adoption policies. *Journal of Educational Research, 8*(1), 5–16.

Dillingofski, M. S. (1993). Turning teachers into readers: The teachers as readers project. *School Library Journal, 39*, 31–33.

Elley, W. B. (1989). Vocabulary acquisition from listening to stories. *Reading Research Quarterly, 24*, 174–187.

Farr, R., Tulley, M. A., & Powell, D. (1987). The evaluation and selection of basal readers. *Elementary School Journal, 87,* 268.

Feitelson, D., Kita, B., & Goldstein, Z. (1986). Effects of listening to series stories on first graders' comprehension and use of language. *Research in the Teaching of English, 20,* 339–356.

Gray, M. J., & Troy, A. (1986). Elementary teachers of reading as models. *Reading Horizons, 26,* 179–184.

Hansen, J. (1987). *When writers read.* Portsmouth, NH: Heinemann.

Kaestle, C. F., Damon-Moore, H., Stedman, L. C., Tinsley, K., & Trollinaer, W. V., Jr. (1991). *Literacy in the U.S.: Readers and reading since 1880.* New Haven: Yale University Press.

Lehman, B. A., Freeman, E. B., & Allen, V. G. (1994). Children's literature and literacy instruction: "Literature-based" elementary teachers' beliefs and practices. *Reading Horizons, 35,* 329.

Lunenburg, F. C., & Schmidt, L. J. (1989). Pupil control ideology, pupil control behavior and the quality of school life. *Journal of Research and Development in Education, 22,* 36–44.

Mooney, M. E. (1990). *Reading to, with and by children.* Katonah, NY: Richard C. Owen Publishers.

Morrow, L. M. (1990). Preparing the classroom environment to promote literacy play. *Early Childhood Research Quarterly, 5,* 537–554.

Morrow, L. M., O'Connor, E. M., & Smith, J. K. (1990). Effects of a strong reading program on the literacy development of at-risk kindergarten children. *Journal of Reading Behavior, 22,* 255–275.

Morrow, L. M. (1992). The impact of a literature-based program on literacy achievement, use of literature, and attitudes of children from minority backgrounds. *Reading Research Quarterly, 27,* 251–275.

Mour, S. I. (1977). Do teachers read? *The Reading Teacher, 30,* 397–401.

Mueller, D. L. (1973). Teacher attitudes toward reading. *Journal of Reading, 17,* 202–205.

Nunnally, J. C. (1978). *Psychometric theory* (2nd ed.). New York: McGraw Hill.

Pennac, D. (1994). *Better than life.* Toronto: Coach House Press.

Pressley, M., Rankin, J., & Yokoi, L. (1996). A survey of instructional practices of primary grade teachers nominated as effective in promoting literacy. *Elementary School Journal, 96,* 363–384.

Robbins, C., & Ehri, L. C. (1994). Reading storybooks to kindergartners helps them learn new vocabulary words. *Journal of Educational Psychology, 86,* 54–4.

Routman, R. (1996). *Literacy at the crossroads: Crucial talk about reading, writing, and other teaching dilemmas.* Portsmouth, NH: Heinemann.

Searls, E. F. (1985). Do you, like these teachers, value reading? *Reading Horizons, 25,* 233–238.

Weaver, C., & Watson, D. (1989). *Report card on basal readers.* Urbana, IL: National Council of Teachers of English Commission on Reading.

Teachers Using Recommended Literacy Practices in Their Classrooms

Few teachers are able to use every activity or approach in the classroom that they *want* to. Think about *the last ten days you have taught.* Of these ten days, in how many days, if any, did you use the following activities? If you did not use the activity circle "0," or circle the number of days out of 10 in which you did use it.

Activity	How many out of the last 10 school days?										
1. Read aloud a picture book to your class	0	1	2	3	4	5	6	7	8	9	10
2. Took your students to the library	0	1	2	3	4	5	6	7	8	9	10
3. Stayed in the library with your students	0	1	2	3	4	5	6	7	8	9	10
4. Children read from a class set of paperbacks	0	1	2	3	4	5	6	7	8	9	10
5. Read a short story in class	0	1	2	3	4	5	6	7	8	9	10
6. Introduced new books to students in your class	0	1	2	3	4	5	6	7	8	9	10
7. Gave students class time for their own reading	0	1	2	3	4	5	6	7	8	9	10
8. Recommended specific book titles to the class	0	1	2	3	4	5	6	7	8	9	10
9. Read from a children's novel to the class	0	1	2	3	4	5	6	7	8	9	10
10. Had children talk to me about books they read	0	1	2	3	4	5	6	7	8	9	10
11. Had children talk in class on books they read	0	1	2	3	4	5	6	7	8	9	10
12. Read aloud from a children's informational book	0	1	2	3	4	5	6	7	8	9	10
13. Read trade books in class for instruction	0	1	2	3	4	5	6	7	8	9	10
14. Read trade books in class for recreation	0	1	2	3	4	5	6	7	8	9	10
15. In class, read aloud books of students' choosing	0	1	2	3	4	5	6	7	8	9	10

Teachers as Readers

Below are some statements teachers could use to *describe themselves* in general terms. For each statement, please circle the one number that best indicates how descriptive the statement is of *you*.

	How descriptive is the statement of you?				
Activity	*Extremely*	*Very*	*Somewhat*	*Slightly*	*Not at All*
I've never really thought of myself as "a reader."	1	2	3	4	5
I think I am a devoted reader.	1	2	3	4	5
I'd like to spend a day reading when I've got the time.	1	2	3	4	5
I get lots of satisfaction from my personal reading.	1	2	3	4	5
I'd rather watch a story on TV or movies than read.	1	2	3	4	5
Frankly, I don't find reading to be very relaxing.	1	2	3	4	5

Chapter 4

Reading and Evaluating
Introductory Sections
Abstract, Background, and Purpose

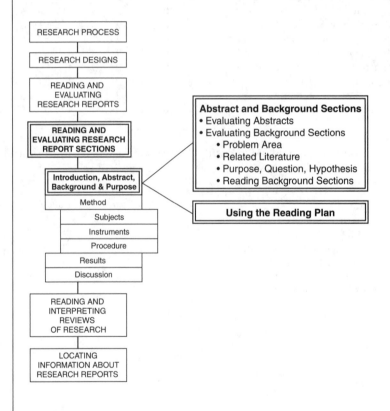

FOCUS QUESTIONS

1. What information should research consumers get from the abstract and background sections of a research report?
2. What criteria are used to evaluate abstracts?
3. What criteria are used to evaluate background sections?
4. What is the plan for reading abstracts and background sections?

In the background section, a researcher introduces readers to the problem area and its educational importance. Researchers also provide brief summaries of other researchers' results that are related to the problem area. The part with these summaries is called the **literature review,** and in it researchers indicate strengths from the related research that were used in their study and weaknesses or limitations that were changed. In many professional journals, the background section is preceded by an abstract, a summary of the report. Most often, researchers omit the literature review from an abstract.

THE ABSTRACT AND BACKGROUND SECTIONS

In the plan for reading research reports discussed in Chapter 3, the abstract and background sections are read first. From these sections, research consumers should be able to answer:

What are the researchers' issues and concerns?

What have other researchers found out about these issues?

What question(s) did the researchers try to answer?

What kind of research was conducted by the researchers, and what variables were being studied?

Were there any independent and dependent variables?

Are the researchers' issues and concerns relevant to me as a professional or to my teaching situation?

The questions for evaluating abstract and background sections (taken from Figure 3.1, p. 61) are the following:

Evaluating Abstracts and Introductory Sections

ABSTRACT

Organization. Is information about the major aspects of the research—purpose, subjects, instruments, procedures/treatment, results—included?

Style. Is the abstract brief and clearly written?

INTRODUCTORY SECTION

Problem Area. Are the problem area and its educational importance explained? Are the researchers' assumptions and theoretical perspectives about the topic explained?

Related Literature. Are research studies related to the problem area presented? Has the related research been evaluated and critiqued? Does the intended research logically extend the understandings from the related research?

Hypothesis(es), Purpose(s), Question(s) in Quantitative Research. Is there a purpose that can be studied in an unbiased manner? Are the research variables (independent and dependent, when appropriate) easily identified from the hypothesis, question, or purpose statement? Are key terms or variables operationally defined?

Purpose(s), Question(s) in Qualitative Research. Is the relationship between the study and previous studies explicit? Is there a clear rationale for the use of qualitative procedures? Are researchers' assumptions and biases expressed?

Evaluating Abstracts

Most abstracts are written in a particular style and manner that facilitates readers' attempts to ascertain whether the research is appropriate for their purposes as consumers. Abstracts contain information about purpose, subjects, instruments, procedure (and treatment when applicable), findings, and conclusions.

Abstracts are usually short, containing 100 to 200 words, and are set in special type or indented to distinguish them from the main body of the research report. Some journals do not require abstracts; the decision is set by the journal editors and advisory boards. Some publications, such as *Psychological Abstracts* and *Current Index to Journals in Education* (CIJE), contain short abstracts that do not have the style and content of journal abstracts. Other publications, such as *Dissertation Abstracts International,* have abstracts 600 to 800 words long that contain more information than journal abstracts. A discussion of these publications and samples of their abstract forms are found in Chapter 11, Locating Information about Research Reports.

The following abstract from a report entitled "Differences in Teaching between Six Primary and Five Intermediate Teachers in One School" illustrates the normal style. The types of information are annotated in the margin. For this demonstration, you should read the abstract for the purpose of finding out whether there is a difference between the two groups of teachers in their communications with their students.

[Purpose]
[Subjects]
[Procedures]

[Data Analysis]

[Results]

This study examined differences between primary and intermediate teachers concerning teacher behaviors, teacher communications, grouping control, and materials. 6 primary classrooms (grades 1 and 2) and 5 intermediate classrooms (grades 4 and 5) were each observed for 4 45-minute periods. In addition, observers, teachers, and 5 students from each classroom responded to 2 vignettes depicting classroom situations and 1 vignette asking respondents to describe a lesson on nutrition. Responses were coded for teacher behaviors, goals, and instructional methods. Analyses of observational data showed that in comparison with teachers in intermediate grades, primary teachers used significantly more sanctions, procedural communications, and total teacher communications. Primary teachers also used a greater proportion of small-group instruction and manipulative materials than did intermediate teachers. Analysis of subjects' responses to vignettes clarified these findings and added further detail. (Van Scoy, 1994, p. 347)

Evaluative question: Is information about the major aspects of the research—purpose, subjects, instruments, procedures/treatment, results—included?

As shown by the margin annotations, the abstract contains information about the major aspects of research. What is not included is the statistical procedure used to code the subjects' responses.

Evaluative question: Is the abstract brief and clearly written?

In the example, the researcher has used only terms that any knowledgeable research consumer would be expected to know. The only technical term used in the abstract (which is explained in this text) is *significantly,* which is a clue that the researcher used quantitative data analysis procedures. The abstract presents the information about the research aspects without unnecessary information.

Researchers sometimes omit specific information and merely refer to the type of information included in the full research report. Such a tactic does not provide report readers with a complete summary and might hinder their understanding of the research because the specific details of the research report are omitted. In the above abstract, the last statement illustrates this weakness. Other statements in abstracts that indicate incomplete information are "The study examined various instructional techniques," "The results are presented," and "The implications of the results are given."

Evaluating Background Sections

Background sections contain three major kinds of information. The first is the problem area and its educational importance. The second is related literature. The third is the research purpose, questions, or hypotheses.

The Problem Area.   In Chapter 1, five characteristics of a profession and its members were enumerated. Briefly, professionals (a) verify existing ideas and practices, (b) discover new ideas and practices, (c) clarify and expand information about ideas and practices, (d) express ideas that complicate educational practice, and (e) discover ideas and practices that are counterintuitive. Researchers try to justify the importance of their research in light of these aspects of professional activity. For example, in a causal-comparative study to determine if gifted and average-ability junior high students differed in learning and study strategies, the researcher indicated that

> In general, we know that gifted students are able to achieve more in school than average-ability students (Scruggs & Cohn, 1983; Scruggs & Mastropieri, 1988). However, we also know that not all gifted children do well in school, and not all are able to achieve to their predicted level. Further research is needed to examine learning and study strategies of gifted children as they compare to less able learners. More information is also needed to determine whether the study strategies of gifted learners are adequate. Therefore, two studies were undertaken to explore these issues. These studies were designed to determine if high-ability junior high students differed from their average-ability peers on learning and study strategies. (Tallent-Runnels et al., 1994, p. 145)

Related Literature.   Researchers also need to examine what others have found to be important. By reviewing relevant research, researchers gain insights about the problem area that should then influence their research questions and methods. During this phase of research, research producers act as consumers. They critically analyze research using questions similar to those in Table 1.1, page 10. As a result of their evaluation, they can

1. Extend knowledge about a problem area. This can be done because the researchers see a next step in answering questions about the problem. For example, after reviewing research about parents who read aloud to their children, one group of researchers realized that no one had described the views of those parents, so their research was concerned with identifying what parents thought about reading to their children (Manning, Manning, & Cody, 1988).
2. Change or revise knowledge about a problem area. This can be done because the researchers see weaknesses or limitations in other researchers' attempts to answer questions about the problem area. For example, after reviewing research about oral reading cue strategies of better and poor readers, a researcher identified several limitations with those studies and made modifications in materials that were used, the reading task assigned to the students, and the number and type of errors evaluated (Fleisher, 1988).

3. Replicate the study. Sometimes researchers wish to redo the research of others. **Replication** means repeating an investigation of a previous study's purpose, question, or hypothesis.

Researchers can replicate research in several ways. First, they can use the same method with different subjects. In this case, the researchers keep the original purpose, method, and data analysis procedure. The subjects have the same characteristics as the original subjects, but they are different people. For example, one team of researchers replicated a study looking at the effect on learning-disabled and slowly developing readers of two instructional programs designed to teach the students how to detect their own errors (Pascarella, Pflaum, Bryan, & Pearl, 1983). In the original study, conducted by two members of the same research team, the subjects were individual students. In the replication, data were analyzed for both individual students and groups because the researchers felt that working with individuals overlooked the "potential interdependencies among individual [student] observations within the same reading group" (p. 270).

Second, in a procedure known as **cross-validation,** the researchers use the same purpose, method, and data analysis procedure to investigate subjects from a different target population. For example, if the subjects in an original study were second and third graders, a different target population might be high-school students.

Third, in a procedure known as **validity generalization,** the researchers use the same purpose, method, and data analysis procedure, but they use subjects from a unique population. For example, if the subjects in an original study were suburban students with hearing impairment, a different population might be rural students with vision impairment.

Fourth, researchers can reanalyze other researchers' data. In this case, no new study is undertaken. For example, after reviewing research about students' silent reading, a team of researchers indicated that the results of one study in particular did not warrant certain conclusions, so they reanalyzed the data presented by the original researchers (Wilkinson, Wardrop, & Anderson, 1988).

Purpose, Question, Hypothesis.   Most examples so far in this text have shown researchers stating their research aims as purposes or questions. This has been done because current practice in research journals is to use this form. Journal editors as well as authorities on effective reading practice often feel that readers of research get a better mindset from purposes and questions than they do from hypotheses. Nevertheless, research reports are often written with traditional hypotheses.

A **hypothesis** is a conjectural statement of the relationship between the research variables in a quantitative study. It is created after researchers have examined the related literature but before they undertake the study. It is considered a tentative explanation for particular behaviors, phenomena, or events that have happened or will happen. A hypothesis is a statement of researchers' expectations concerning the relationship between the variables in the research problem (Gay & Airasian, 2000).

One way to state a hypothesis is as a **nondirectional** (or two-tailed) **hypothesis,** which is a statement of the specific relationship or influence among variables. Researchers use this form when they have strong evidence from examining previous research that a relationship or influence exists but the evidence does not provide them with indications about the nature or direction (positive or negative) of the relationship or influence. The following, taken from a study about the connection between computer technology and reading comprehension, are examples of nondirectional research hypotheses stated to show that differences will exist between variables. Note that the researchers do not state how—positively or negatively—using a computer to mediate manipulations of the text (the independent variable) will influence reading comprehension (the dependent variable).

1. The comprehension of intermediate-grade readers reading expository texts will be affected by using a computer to mediate manipulations of the text.
2. Comprehension of expository text will be affected by varying control of textual manipulations from the reader to the computer program. (Reinking & Schreiner, 1985, p. 540)

If the researchers' evidence supports a statement of the specific way one variable will affect another, then the research hypothesis is stated as a **directional** (or one-tailed) **hypothesis.** The following example contains two directional research hypotheses from a study about the effects of teacher expectations and student behavior.

> The first hypothesis under investigation was that adults who are deliberate and more reserved would be more likely to adopt a task-oriented approach than would adults who are impulsive and highly sociable. Thus the reserved, deliberate adults would make more attempts to structure the task for the child, would more often redirect the child's attention to the task, and would make fewer task irrelevant comments to the child than would the sociable, impulsive adult. In addition [the second hypothesis], compared with inexperienced teachers, experienced teachers are more likely to be task oriented. (Osborne, 1985, p. 80)

In this example, the researcher predicted that teachers' temperament factors (the independent variable) would have a direct effect on how they structure children's tasks (the dependent variable). Not only was an effect predicted, but the particular effect was predicted. The research predicted that teachers with reserved, deliberate temperaments would be more directive and offer fewer irrelevant comments. The second prediction was that teachers' experience (the independent variable) would affect task orientation (the dependent variable) and that experienced teachers would more likely be task oriented.

Another form of hypothesis is the null hypothesis. In contrast to the research hypothesis (directional and nondirectional), the null hypothesis is used exclusively as a basis for statistical analysis and is rarely included in research reports.

Reading Background Sections.   The following, a typical background section, is taken from a report entitled "The Effect of Instruction in Question-Answer Relationships and Metacognition on Social Studies Comprehension." Key information in this background section is annotated.

[Background]   Teachers expect students to be critical readers, comprehending most of the material read in the classroom; but Durkin's (1978–1979) classroom observation studies suggest that while comprehension is expected, it is never taught. Teachers do not 'teach' comprehension during social studies instruction; they merely assess it.

Questions are an integral part of school life. They are used routinely by teachers as a means of gauging student understanding of text. Teachers ask questions, but rarely do they do anything with the student responses—except acknowledge their correctness (Durkin, 1978–1979).

Early comprehension taxonomies first classified questions by type. Pearson and Johnson's (1978) more recent comprehension taxonomy, however, labels questions based upon the demands they make on the reader. In other words, the Pearson-Johnson taxonomy categorizes questions according to the relationship between the question and the answer generated. The Pearson-Johnson comprehension taxonomy recognizes three categories of questions: textually explicit, textually implicit and scriptally implicit.

[Related literature]

Recent research in metacognition has recognized that some children appear to be more capable of processing information efficiently when taught to monitor their own comprehension and to use reading strategies that take into account the variety of reading tasks assigned in school (Brown, 1981, p. 504). Raphael (1982) used the Pearson-Johnson comprehension taxonomy to develop a Question-Answer Relationship (QAR) model which could be used to teach students to successfully respond to four types of questions typically found in content area textbooks. The QAR model categorizes questions based upon the location of the answer generated by a query. The Question-Answer Relationship model considers the demands that questions make upon readers as they strive to arrive at correct responses.

This research study was designed to teach students the QAR model and to provide additional metacognitive instruction in conjunction with the adopted social studies textbook. The social studies instruction provided was used in place of the basal reading instructional program typically employed for reading instruction. Three research questions were posed: Would students, as a result of the QAR and metacognitive instruction, complete the social studies textbook questioning tasks more successfully? How would students perform on the different types of QARs in the social studies text following the treatment? Would student scores on a global reading comprehension measure increase as a result of the social studies QAR-metacognitive instruction? (Benito, Foley, Lewis, & Prescott, 1993)

Evaluative question: Are the problem area and its educational importance explained?

In the example, the researchers succinctly presented the importance of the problem area. Although the first paragraph is short, the researchers indicate the importance of questioning in the teaching of comprehension and substantiate this with references.

Evaluative questions: Are research studies related to the problem area presented? Has the related research been evaluated and critiqued? Does the intended research logically extend the understandings from the related research?

In the third and fourth paragraphs, the researchers provide a summary of relevant research results. In the fifth paragraph, the researchers indicate their two major purposes. What research consumers need to determine is: Do the purposes provide the means for extending the results of the previous research? This question can be answered in relation to the next evaluative question.

Evaluative questions: Is there a purpose that can be studied in an unbiased manner? Are the research variables (independent and dependent) easily identified from the hypothesis, question, or purpose statement? Are key terms or variables operationally defined?

The first research purpose in the example was to determine if students, as a result of the QAR and metacognitive instruction, complete the social studies textbook questioning tasks more successfully. For this purpose, the researchers collected data to examine their claim that these strategies are more effective. The second purpose was to determine how students would perform on different types of QARs in the social studies text following the treatment. It was possible to conduct this comparative and experimental study without bias; the only way research consumers can be confident that no bias was introduced would be to evaluate the method section (this is discussed in the next four chapters). No terms needed special definition.

USING THE RESEARCH READING PLAN WITH ABSTRACT AND BACKGROUND SECTIONS

By using the research reading plan presented in Chapter 3 (see p. 58) for the initial reading of abstracts and background sections, research consumers can efficiently seek out information in a particular order. The abstract and background sections of the report "Learning Science in a Cooperative Setting: Academic Achievement and Affective Outcomes" by Lazarowitz, Hertz-Lazarowitz, and Baird (1994) on the following pages contain annotations to illustrate the suggested order of reading. For this demonstration, you should read the report for the purpose of gaining knowledge about how children can use cooperative group strategies in learning science.

Read the abstract and background sections using the following steps:

1. The title is read to gain a broad overview of the research topic.
2. In this report, the first paragraph of the background section is the abstract. The first sentence of that paragraph is read to gain a general understanding of the researchers' concern.
3. The paragraph containing the researchers' research purposes, questions, or hypotheses is read to gain a specific understanding of the research. This information is usually found at the end of the background section.
4. From reading 1, 2, and 3, research consumers can determine that the purpose (gaining knowledge) will be met by reading the report. In the margin of this text or on a piece of paper, note what you already know about the topic.
5. The remainder of the abstract (the first paragraph) is read to gain a sense of the subjects, research methodology, and findings.
6. The remainder of the background section is read to gain an understanding of cooperative learning and science educators' thoughts about science education, and the related literature subsection is read to understand what other researchers know about cooperative learning in science classrooms.

SUMMARY

The background section contains an introduction to the researchers' problem area and the educational importance they place on their study. Researchers also provide a brief literature review of other researchers' results that are related to their problem area. Researchers usually indicate strengths from the related research that were used in their study and weaknesses or limitations that were changed. Based upon an examination of the related literature, a researcher determines whether to develop a new study or replicate or repeat a study. It is common to find the researchers' purposes at the end of this section. Some research reports contain traditional hypotheses, which often are stated as directional or nondirectional research hypotheses. Nondirectional hypotheses are statements that a possible influence exists but the researcher does not indicate whether it is a positive or negative influence. Directional hypotheses contain statements of the specific way one variable will affect another. In many professional journals, the background section is preceded by an abstract, a summary of the report.

Learning Science in a Cooperative Setting:
Academic Achievement and Affective Outcomes

Reuven Lazarowitz

*Department of Education in Technology and Science, IIT Technion,
Haifa 32000 Israel*

Rachel Hertz-Lazarowitz

*School of Education, Haifa University,
Haifa 31999 Israel*

J. Hugh Baird

*Department of Secondary Education, Brigham Young University,
Provo, Utah 84602*

ABSTRACT

A learning unit in earth science was taught to high school students, using a jigsaw-group mastery learning approach. The sample consisted of 73 students in the experimental group and 47 students who learned the topic in an individualized mastery learning approach. The study lasted 5 weeks. Pretests and posttests on academic achievement and affective outcomes were administered. Data were treated with an analysis of covariance. The results show that students of the experimental group achieved significantly higher on academic outcomes, both normative and objective scores. On the creative essay test, the differences in number of ideas and total essay score were not significant between the groups, although the mean scores for number of words were higher for the individualized mastery learning group. On the affective domain, jigsaw-group mastery learning students scored significantly higher on self-esteem, number of friends, and involvement in the classroom. No differences were found in cohesiveness, cooperation, competition, and attitudes toward the subject learned. The results are discussed through the evaluation and comparison of the two methods of instruction used in this study.

The cooperative learning movement began in junior high schools as part of the desegregation process, aiming at facilitating positive ethnic relations and increasing academic achievement and social skills among diverse students (Aronson, Stephan, Sikes, Blaney, & Snapp, 1978; Sharan & Hertz-Lazarowitz, 1980; Slavin, 1980). However, elementary teachers quickly recognized the potential of cooperative methods, and such methods were adopted freely in elementary schools before becoming widespread on the junior and senior high level. It has only been during the past few years that application of cooperative learning has been studied extensively with these older students.

Cooperative learning methods generally involve heterogenous groups working together on tasks that are deliberately structured to provide specific assignments and individual contributions from each group member. Cognitive as well as social benefits are expected, as students clarify their own understanding and share their insights and ideas with each other as they interact within the group (Deutsch, 1949).

Experiments in the science laboratory have always required students to work in groups of two to four, due to the constraints of experimental processes and limited equipment and supplies. Thus, science courses are a natural curriculum area for examining cooperative learning practices. Now that cooperative methods are being refined to develop particular capabilities in the students, science teachers need to examine ways of structuring specific tasks to achieve the academic, affective, and socialization goals for their students. Although most of the studies of cooperative learning in the high school science classroom have centered around the cognitive outcomes of achievement testing and process skills, affective and social outcomes are also significant with students of this age. But few studies in science classes have attempted to assess such aspects of students' progress.

As part of a previous revision, the science faculty at the high school where this study was conducted developed an exemplary individualized mastery learning (IML) program for teaching science. This program seemed to alleviate the severe motivational problems and the extreme individual differences among the students in this rural/blue-collar community. Students learned to work independently on their science studies. They had almost no lectures and few large group activities. As they worked through their assignments, however, they were free to interact with other students. Looking in on a typical class, one would see several clusters of two or three students working together, sometimes tutoring each other, sometimes just talking through an assignment. Yet at least half of the class members would be working all alone. The importance of the overall social setting in the classroom as it relates to learning (Bruner, 1986, p. 86) and the central function of social interaction as learning occurs (Vygotsky, 1978, p. 106) seemed to have been ignored. Therefore, group mastery learning (GML), a cooperative learning technique, was suggested as an antithesis to IML for teaching science over short periods. The cooperative mode of instruction considers learning as a cognitive as well as a social process, where students interact with each other as well as the teacher.

To bring the social dimension back to science classrooms, the researchers chose to implement GML in Grades 11 and 12. The goal of the study was to investigate the GML's impact of the method on the individual student's academic achievement, creativity, self-esteem, and number of friends and on the overall learning environment of the classrooms. The researchers were also concerned with the students' attitudes toward earth science, the course being taught at the time of the experiment. Both cognitive and affective outcomes for students who participated in the cooperative GML approach were compared with outcomes for students who studied the same topic in an IML approach.

(5) The study addressed a number of questions related to academic and nonacademic outcomes of the two methods of study. First, it sought to determine whether academic achievement of the students taught in the cooperative GML mode would be different from the achievement of students who learned in an individualized method. Second, it sought to determine whether gains or losses would be seen in nonacademic outcomes, such as classroom learning environment, social relations, and students' self-esteem experienced by the students. The results of this study may support more use of cooperative learning in high school science.

LITERATURE SURVEY

(6) The literature concerning cooperative learning methods in science classrooms has shown positive outcomes on many but not all academic subject areas and cognitive skills. Academic achievement has been revealed as significantly higher in studies on earth science (Humphreys, Johnson, & Johnson, 1982); chemistry, biology, and physics (Okebukola, 1985; Okebukola & Ogunniyi, 1984); biology (Lazarowitz, Baird, Hertz-Lazarowitz, & Jenkins, 1985; Lazarowitz & Karsenty, 1990; Lazarowitz, 1991; Watson, 1991); and physics (Scott & Heller, 1991). Group work in junior high school biology classrooms and laboratories enhanced students' learning and research skills. Under cooperative methods of learning, these students developed stronger reporting skills, and at the same time showed greater understanding and enjoyment of the subject matter (Walters, 1988).

In contrast, other studies comparing cooperative and individualized learning have not revealed significant differences in students' academic progress or cognitive development. For example, Sherman (1988) found that teaching ecology in a cooperative mode did not make a difference in students' learning. Tingle and Good (1990) attempted to apply cooperative methods specifically to problem-solving skills in chemistry; they found comparable skills were developed whether students worked individually or in groups.

Although results have not consistently shown the advantage of cooperative learning over more traditional teaching methods for promoting strictly academic achievement in science, studies have consistently shown greater effectiveness on nonacademic aspects of science study. Tingle and Good (1990) also found that cooperative methods resulted in a more supportive climate for learning and in increased student ability to organize projects, divide and assign the work, and take responsibility for completing it. Although these abilities are not necessarily manifest in achievement scoring, all of them are significant in the study of science. The capacity of students to remain on-task while working on science projects is one of those significant related capabilities. Studies have consistently reported that on-task behavior is higher when students learn through cooperative methods as opposed to individualized learning modes (Lazarowitz, Hertz-Lazarowitz, Baird, & Bowlden, 1988; Rogg & Kahle, 1992). Additional learning factors that have been demonstrated to be strengthened by group processes include inquiry skills and self-esteem (Lazarowitz & Karsenty, 1990). The factor of individual differences in preferred learning style was included in cooperative learning research by Okebukola (1988), who reported that students who preferred to learn in the cooperative mode made more progress than they did when they were instructed in a competitive mode.

From this review of existing studies, one may conclude that when science students are given tasks that demand high levels of cognitive skills and/or personal characteristics such as perseverance and positive attitudes toward science, cooperative learning has the potential to contribute significantly to cognitive and affective development.

ACTIVITY

Use the research reading plan and the evaluation criteria on page 58 to read and evaluate the abstract and background sections of the two reports by Jovanovic and King (1998) and Clery (1998) in the chapter's Appendix. Do not refer to the information in the Feedback section until you have fully read and analyzed a passage.

FEEDBACK

Jovanovic and King (1998)

Abstract.   The abstract contains information about the major aspects of the research. It contains information about the researchers' purposes, the subjects, and the results. What is not included is information about the instruments for collecting data and the way the data were analyzed. From the use of the phrases "changes in . . . science attitudes," the researcher consumer can surmise the reported research is experimental. From the use of other phrases, such as "predicted . . . attitudes," "did not participate equally," and "decrease . . . perceptions," the research consumer can surmise that there is a comparative research aspect to this study.

Background.   The background section identifies the problem area and indicates the support from other researchers for the study of gender differences in science teaching. The purpose of the study is specified in the last two paragraphs of this section. From that information, the research consumer can identify the variables being researched: "student behavior" and "hands-on activities." The various comparative research aspects are identified by the following excerpts from the next to last paragraph of the report.

1. "Whether the behaviors performed by students were equally shared by boys and girls"
2. "Whether students' behaviors over the school year related to students' attitudes toward science at the end of the year"

The experimental research aspect of the study is identified by this excerpt from the last paragraph of the report.

1. "Measured changes in students' task value beliefs about science and their perceptions of science ability"

Clery (1998)

Abstract. The abstract contains limited information about the major aspects of the research. It contains the general purpose of the study (see last sentence of the report), a general explanation of the problem area, and some background of the study. It does not, however, contain specific subject characteristics, information about what instruments were used for collecting data or how the data were analyzed, or the specific results.

Background. The problem area and the importance of the topic to educators, not only in Australia, but in other English-speaking cultures allowing home schooling, are explained. The discussion covers the general history of home schooling as related research. The section ends with a general statement of the purpose of the study ("how homeschooled children view their homeschooling experience") and a description of the means for collecting and analyzing the data. From that information, research consumers can surmise that it is a qualitative descriptive study.

Chapter 4 Appendix

Jovanovic, J., & King, S. S. (1998). Boys and girls in the performance-based science classroom: Who's doing the performing? *American Educational Research Journal, 35* (3), 477–496.

Boys and Girls in the Performance-Based Science Classroom:

Who's Doing the Performing?

Jasna Jovanovic and Sally Steinbach King

University of Illinois, Urbana-Champaign

The aim of this study was to examine whether over the school year boys and girls equally share in performing the behaviors required of hands-on activities (e.g., manipulating the equipment, directing the activity, observing) in the performance-based science classroom. In addition, we examined whether these performance behaviors accounted for changes in boys' and girls' science attitudes (i.e., ability perceptions and task value beliefs) at the end of the school year. The sample included 165 students (535 female, mean age = 12.21) in six Grade 5–Grade 8 performance-based science classrooms where the teachers associated with these classrooms were identified not only as exemplary hands-on science instructors but also instructors sensitive to increasing girls' participation in science. Our results indicated that being actively involved in the performance-based science classroom predicted students' end-of-the-year science attitudes. However, boys and girls did not participate equally in these classrooms. Moreover, we found that for girls, but not boys, there was a decrease in science ability perceptions over the school year, suggesting that boys and girls experienced these classrooms differently.

Developing positive student attitudes toward science is a critical part of science learning (Claxton, 1989; Head, 1989). Students' attitudes are linked to their achievement in science and their motivation to persist in science courses in high school and beyond (Kahle & Meece, 1994; Steinkamp & Maehr, 1983; Stoner, 1981). However, national trends indicate that when students reach middle school their interest in science begins to decrease (Jones, Mullis, Raizen, Weiss, & Weston, 1992). Advocates of science education reform believe that to better engage students in science, learning must move from a traditional textbook-focused approach, where students learn by listening and reading, to a performance-based (i.e., hands-on) approach, where learning is an active process involving inquiry and exploration (American Association for the Advancement of Science [AAASI], 1990; National Research Council [NRCI], 1996). The belief is that if students are given opportunities to do science, positive attitudes toward science will be fostered (Hofstein & Lunetta, 1982; Kahle, Parker, Rennie, & Riley, 1993; Okebukola, 1986).

For girls, the goal of fostering positive attitudes toward science is particularly relevant. In a meta-analysis of studies conducted from 1970 to 1991 involving students' science attitudes, Weinburgh (1995) found a persistent gender effect in favor of males, particularly among average and low achieving students. Compared to boys, girls seem less interested in science, attach less importance to science (Schibeci & Riley, 1986; Simpson & Oliver, 1985), and feel less confident of their science abilities (Kahle & Rennie, 1993; Licht, Stader, & Swenson, 1989). Furthermore, there is evidence that attitudes are a stronger predictor of science achievement among girls than boys (Steinkamp & Maehr, 1983; Stoner, 1981).

The gender difference in science attitudes has been attributed, in part, to girls' lack of exposure to science-related activities outside of the classroom (e.g., tinkering with mechanical objects, participating in science clubs); science activities that are familiar to boys (Erickson & Erickson, 1984; Jones et al., 1992; Kahle & Lakes, 1983). Lack of prior experience is thought to undermine girls' confidence to learn (Dweck, 1986; Parsons, Meece, Adler, & Kaczala, 1982), which can lead girls to experience the classroom differently than boys (Good & Stipek, 1983; Johnson & Murphy, 1984). For example, if a girl lacks prior experience with a science content area (e.g., simple machines), she may be less willing to respond to the teacher's questions about this content area. At the same time, teachers' preconceptions about gender differences in science (i.e., that boys are better at science than girls) may lead teachers to call on or to respond to males and females differently (Morse & Handley, 1985; Shepardson & Pizzini, 1992). This prior experience-by-instruction interaction may lead girls to feel less confident than boys about learning science (Qovanovic, Solano-Flores, & Shavelson, 1994).

The promise of moving to performance-based teaching is that the science classroom will become an equalizer by compensating for the disparities between boys' and girls' experiences outside of school (Jenkins & MacDonald, 1989). This assumption, however, rests on boys and girls having equal access to doing science in the classroom. In other words, both boys and girls should be actively performing in the performance-based science classroom. However, research conducted in traditional laboratory science classes has found that boys are more active participants in conducting experiments than girls (Kahle et al., 1993). Tobin and Garnett (1987) found that boys tended to be more involved in manipulating science equipment and directing the activities while girls performed the passive tasks of gathering and organizing the equipment.

If performance-based science classrooms are to succeed in promoting positive attitudes toward science among both girls and boys, these classrooms will have to provide opportunities for all students to perform science. The National Science Education Standards (NRC, 1996) called for students to have access to learning both process and inquiry science skills. This means students should be actively engaged in the behaviors of planning and designing investigations (i.e., directing activities), manipulating variables, making observations, asking questions, recording data, constructing explanations, and communicating ideas to others (NRC, 1996; Willis, 1995). These skills are not necessarily new to science classrooms (Eglen & Kempa, 1974; Tamir, 1974), but they have been emphasized recently as critical to students' conceptual understanding of science. Moreover, it is believed that these skills are best learned in cooperative small groups. The idea is that students will better construct meaning of scientific concepts if they are given the opportunity to share ideas and understanding with their classmates (Roth, 1989; Wheatley, 1991). For example, Webb (1985, 1992) has found that students exhibit learning gains on mathematical tasks when they actively provide content explanations to other students or receive explanations from other group members. Similarly, Swing and Peterson (1982) noted that students' attitudes toward mathematics related to a number of task-related small group behaviors—particularly, providing content explanations.

The aim of this study was to examine students' behaviors while they were engaged in hands-on activities with other students in the performance-based science classroom. More important, we were interested in whether the behaviors performed by students were equally shared by boys and girls. On the assumption that access to doing science will improve student attitudes, we also examined whether students' behaviors over the school year related to students' attitudes toward science at the end of the year after controlling for previous science attitudes and students' science ability. The attitudes we measured were those that have been traditionally related to gender. Specifically, we measured students' task value beliefs about science and their perceived science ability. Eccles and Wigfield (1995) described task value as the degree to which an individual believes that a particular task is able to fulfill personal needs or goals. They identified three positive valence components of task value: interest, or the enjoyment a student derives from engaging in a task; importance, or the degree to which a student believes it is important to do well on a task; and utility, or the degree to which the individual thinks a task is useful for reaching some future goal. *Self-ability* perception is defined as students' performance perceptions, including their expectations for future success. Eccles and her colleagues (1983, 1987) have argued that task value beliefs and ability perceptions are important predictors of students' academic performance and persistence and that male-female differences in these attitudes underlie many of the gender differences in achievement behaviors found in subjects like mathematics and science.

In this study, we measured changes in students' task value beliefs about science and their perceptions of science ability at the beginning and end of the school year. We were therefore able to assess whether changes in students' attitudes related to their behaviors during the school year. Given the reform rhetoric suggesting that girls will benefit from performance-based learning (AAAS, 1990; Council for Educational Development and Research, 1993), we tested the hypothesis that boys and girls have equal access to performing the behaviors required of hands-on activities and that equal access leads to diminished gender differences in science attitudes.

Clery, E. (1998). Homeschooling: The meaning that the homeschooled child assigns to this experience. *Issues in Educational Research, 8*(1), 1–13.

Homeschooling: The Meaning That the Homeschooled Child Assigns to This Experience

Erica Clery

Edith Cowan University

While there are documented cases throughout history of individuals who have received very limited or no formal education and yet have made a significant contribution to society, the long held assumption has generally been that formal education is more likely to lead to success and that a comprehensive education can best be provided to children within an institutionalised setting. However, over the last couple of decades in Australia this assumption has been challenged. There has been an increasing number of families choosing to homeschool who live in areas where mainstream schools are easily accessible. Homeschooling practice varies from family to family. It ranges from families who use a highly structured school curriculum based on material from non-government sources through to those whose children's learning occurs and flows from the contexts and interchanges of daily life. This freedom of choice which homeschooling allows needs to be recognised, not only as challenging a firmly entrenched educational structure, but as offering a viable alternative to families when making educational decisions. This report explores the meaning which homeschooling has to homeschooled children and offers suggestions for future research which focuses on homeschooling from the homeschooled child's point of view.

Consideration of where and in what manner schooling should be provided is significantly influenced by the philosophical base from which such decisions are being made. Various values, beliefs and ideas therefore colour any perception of education and its expected outcomes.

The purpose of education has often been a focus of writers on educational matters and various viewpoints have been espoused within those writings. In the mid nineteenth century Arnold argued that the value of education lay not in its making of men into good citizens or in its vocational uses, but rather in its pursuit of shaping the mind towards perfection (cited in Gribble, 1967, p. 12). According to Whitehead's writings at the turn of the century, the basic aim of education is "to provide for the development of a man of culture who has expert knowledge and who is capable of creative responses" (cited in Bowyer, 1970, p. 314). More recently Holt (1976) asserted that a widely held view of education is that it is about shaping people and making them learn what others think they ought to know. Education is commonly provided in institutions—that is, schools. Apart from those living in remote areas, it is considered usual for children to attend school. However, some families choose to educate their children at home despite other options being available to them.

Hunter asserted that the homeschooling population in Australia is not susceptible to a straightforward census. A reason previously given by Hunter (1990) for the level of support and growth of homeschooling was that some individual parents considered they could offer a superior educational program to that provided by schools in the areas which they considered to be most significant. In revisiting the issue of a resurgence in homeschool education, Hunter stated that the expansion appears to be based on the combination of three factors—parental rights as a priority over government regulation, desire to maintain an exclusive family unit for as long as possible, and the fear of mental, physical or spiritual harm being inflicted on the child within a government-sponsored or supervised school environment (Hunter, 1994, p. 31).

In a small study, Maeder (1995) investigated parental choice of non mainstream schooling for the early education of their children. The results showed an interest in a strongly child centered and holistic approach was indicated by most participants.

Knowles (1987) focused his study on the life histories of parents who teach their children at home. The study found that homeschooling motives were complex and congruent with the life histories of the majority of homeschooling parents who participated in the study. A central factor was identified as parental dissatisfaction with their own experiences in school. Holt (1967) suggested that the advantage of being schooled at home lay in the provision of an environment conducive to the child's natural way of learning. He asserted that parents better understand the ways, conditions, and spirit in which their children learn and are therefore in a better position to encourage them to use and improve the style of thinking and learning natural to them.

Wade (cited in Hunter 1990 & 1994) suggested that there are five main opportunities which homeschools offer over a regular school placement: parents can educate their children according to their own convictions, a non-competitive environment, enhanced social development, enhancement of autonomous and well-timed learning, and the development of parental satisfaction with their own lives and a stronger relationship with their children.

Mooney and Kissane (1985) explored the experiences of four families who were homeschooling. Their study suggests that parents who homeschool expect their children's natural inquisitiveness and eagerness-to-learn to be fostered within a homeschooling environment.

Krivaneck (1988) based his thesis on a study of families whose primary school-aged children were being educated at home. The focus of the research was on the subjective social experience of the children, their understanding of friendship and opportunities for the development of autonomy. The study found a direct correlation between the satisfactoriness of the home-educated children's social experience and parents' attitudes and practices in the area of socialisation. The subjects' understanding of friendship showed the features and limitations normal for age. Contrary to the home educators' expectations, relationships within the family were not unusually close or harmonious. Opportunities available to homeschooled children for self-determination were found to be generally restricted to those aspects of daily life which were somewhat trivial in their consequences.

Brosnan (1991) focused on the psychological growth and development of homeschooled children by examining children's competence, family processes and family environments. He found that homeschooled children in his study had average to above average competency levels. In relation to families acting as a resource for the child, the study indicated that in comparison to families with conventionally schooled children, homeschooled children view their mothers as being much more supportive. They also see their families as being more cohesive and consider that they are much more a part of the decision-making processes within the family. However, no clear link was found between children with above average competency levels and family process resources as a whole.

It is clear there is a lack of studies which have as a major focus examined the interpretation and understanding children have of their home learning experience. Thus the intention of this project was to focus on how homeschooled children view their homeschooling experience, researched from a position of impartiality and using qualitative methods for both collection and analysis of data.

Chapter 5

Reading and Evaluating Subject Sections

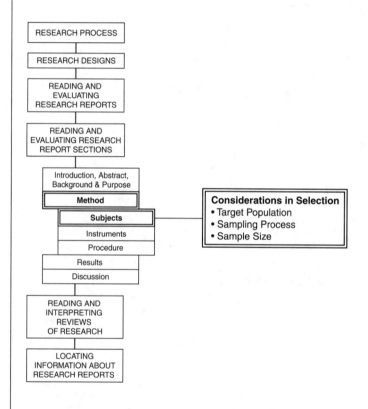

FOCUS QUESTIONS

1. What are populations and target populations?
2. What are subjects and samples?
3. What criteria should be used to evaluate subject sections?
4. What considerations do researchers give to subject selection?
5. What considerations do researchers give to sample size?

In the subject section, which is a subsection within the larger section called the method section, researchers describe the individuals, objects, or events used in their studies. In most cases, researchers wish to apply the answers to research questions to others in addition to their subjects. The hypothetical research team discussed in Chapter 1 were concerned about the extent to which their results could be applied. They were concerned about questions such as the following: Are the answers applicable only to the students in one specific school, grade level, or class? Can the answers be used for the students in an entire district, state, region, or nation?

Of course, subjects can be others besides students: subjects can be teachers, principals, parents, non-school-age individuals (preschoolers or adults), entire groups (e.g., classes, schools, or teams), and so on. They can even be classrooms or school instructional materials.

Subjects can also be nonhuman. For example, subjects can be groups of textbooks or groups of classrooms (the physical aspects of the rooms without consideration for the people in them). In such cases, researchers may be interested in studying the physical characteristics of the books or rooms. In this text, the discussion focuses on human subjects; nevertheless, the same principles of subject selection apply equally to human and nonhuman subjects. Research consumers can use the same criteria for judging the appropriateness of nonhuman subjects as they use for judging the appropriateness of human subjects.

Researchers usually want to use their results to make decisions about a larger group of subjects. That group constitutes the **population**, which is a group of individuals or objects having at least one characteristic that distinguishes them from other groups. Populations can be any size and can include subjects from any place in the world. For example, a population of human subjects could be "students with learning disabilities," or "fourth-grade students," or "beginning teachers." In these cases, the populations are large and include people with many additional characteristics, or variables. The existence of these other variables makes it unlikely that the population will be fully homogeneous and that the research answers are equally applicable to all. "Seventh-grade social studies textbooks" is an example of a nonhuman subject population. Researchers, therefore, narrow the range of the population by including several distinguishing variables. This results in the defining of a **target population**, which is the specific group with which the researchers would like to use their findings for educational purposes. It is from the target population that researchers select the **sample**, which becomes the subjects of their study. Figure 5.1 shows the relationship of the sample to the target population and to the population.

Subject sections contain relevant information about the sample and how it was selected. Subject information might include age, gender, ethnicity (e.g., black, Hispanic, or Native American), ability level (e.g., mental maturity or intelligence), academic performance (e.g., test scores), learning characteristics, affect (e.g., emotional stability, attitudes, interests, or self-concept), and geographic location (e.g., New York State, Chicago, rural/suburban, or Australia). Subject selection information should include the number of subjects, procedures for identifying subjects, methods of actual subject selection, and, in the case of experimental research, steps for assigning subjects to groups or treatments. From a subject section, research consumers should be able to answer the following:

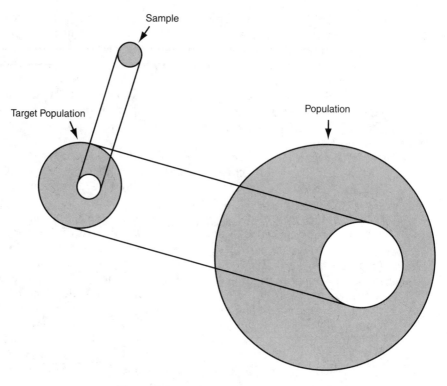

Figure 5.1
Relationship of Sample to Target Population

What was the intended target population?

Who were the subjects?

How were the subjects selected, and did the researchers show bias in their sampling procedures?

Were the subjects truly representative of the target population?

How were the subjects assigned to groups or treatments in experimental research?

Will the research results be applicable to my teaching situation and the students I teach? (Am I part of the target population? Are my students part of the target population?)

Subject sections should be evaluated using the following questions, which are from Figure 3.1, page 61:

Evaluating Subject Sections

METHOD SECTION

Subjects. Are target populations and subjects, sampling and selection procedures, and group sizes clearly described? Are these appropriate for the research design?

CONSIDERATIONS IN SUBJECT SELECTION

In subject sections, researchers should provide information about (a) the target population, (b) the sampling process, and (c) the sample size.

Target Population

Answers to researchers' questions should be applicable to individuals other than those included in the study. The group to which they wish to apply their results is the target population. When researchers can apply their results to the target population, the results are considered to be **generalizable.** An example of how a researcher identified the target population within the larger population is found in a comparative study entitled "Concepts of Reading and Writing Among Low-Literate Adults" (Fagan, 1988). The researcher's purpose was to provide information about the perceptions of reading and writing held by low-functioning adults (the population). The subjects were selected from the target populations. In the following portion of the subject section, the number of subjects is indicated along with descriptions of the target populations. (Specific information about sampling procedures has been omitted from this example.)

A possible purpose for reading the study would be to gain information to help in planning an adult literacy program.

[Subjects]   Two groups of each of 26 adults who were functioning below a grade 9 reading achievement level were selected—one designated as prison inmates and the other as living in mainstream society. Prison inmates were defined as sentenced prisoners in a medium-[Target populations]   minimum correctional institution housing approximately 300 prisoners. Adults living in mainstream society were defined as noninstitutionalized adults, that is not living in prisons, mental, or old age institutions. They were considered "ordinary" people who had freedom of movement, and who could use such city facilities as transportation, recreation, and social interaction. (Fagan, 1988, p. 48)

Because of practical considerations, researchers may not always have equal access to all members of the target population. For example, researchers might wish their target population to be urban, primary-grade students in cities of at least 500,000 people having 20 percent or more Spanish-speaking students. An examination of the U.S. Department of Education census shows that there are at least ten such cities, including Los Angeles, Houston, Miami, and New York. The researchers might be able to use the entire target population as their subjects, or they might choose to select some subjects to represent the target population. More realistically, researchers work with **accessible populations**, which are groups that are convenient but are representative of the target population. Practical considerations that lead to the use of an accessible population include time, money, and physical accessibility.

Researchers should fully describe their accessible populations and their specific subjects so that research consumers can determine the generalizability of the findings. It is the research producers' responsibility to provide the necessary descriptive information about target populations and subjects. It is the research consumers' responsibility to make the judgments about the appropriateness of the subjects to their local situation. In evaluating subject sections, research consumers can be critical of the researchers only if they have not provided complete subject information.

The Sampling Process

If researchers' results are to be generalizable to target populations, the subjects must be **representative** of the population. A representative group of subjects, called the **sample**, is a miniature target population. Ideally, the sample would have the same distribution of relevant variables as found in the target population. It is those relevant variables that researchers describe in subject sections. For example, one researcher (Swanson, 1985) felt it important to keep the same ratio of gender and ethnicity in the sample as found in the target population. She investigated whether socioeconomic status, reading ability, and student self-report reading attitude scores were differentiated by teacher judgments or reading enthusiasm.

> The sample consisted of 117 first-grade students from seven classrooms in a school system located in northeastern Georgia. The rural county has a population of approximately 8,000, of which 37.3 percent is nonwhite. The racial and gender composition of the sample maintained a representative balance. Students repeating first grade, absent during initial testing, and/or not present during reading achievement assessment were deleted from the study. (Swanson, 1985, p. 42)

The most common procedure researchers use to ensure that samples are miniature target populations is **random sampling.** Random sampling works on the principle of **randomization,** whereby all members of the target population should have an equal chance of being selected for the sample (Gall, Borg, & Gall, 1996; Gay & Airasian, 2000; Kerlinger, 1973). And, the subjects finally selected should reflect the distribution of relevant variables found in the target population. Any discrepancy between the sample and the target population is referred to as **sampling error.**

The following does *not* illustrate a random sample because it is not known whether all classes had an equal chance of being selected and whether the students in selected classes represented all the students in the grade level. The classes may have been heterogeneous, but it was not indicated whether they were equal. Although the school principals may have tried to be objective, there may have been an unconscious bias.

> One self-contained, heterogeneous classroom of third-grade students ($N = 22$) and one self-contained, heterogeneous classroom of fifth-grade students ($N = 23$) from a rural school district in the midwestern U.S. participated in the study. The third-grade classroom was one of three in a K–4 building, while the fifth-grade classroom was one of two in a 5–8 building. The participating classrooms were selected by the building principals. (Duffelmeyer & Adamson, 1986, p. 194)

The following is an example of random sampling because each subject had an equal chance of selection from among the students at each grade level.

> Thirty-two children were tested at each grade level; second, third, fourth, and sixth. An equal number was randomly chosen from each of three different elementary schools in a Midwestern city of 50,000. The city is a predominantly white, middle class community. Subjects were replaced by other randomly selected students if they failed a vocabulary reading test. (Richgels, 1986, p. 205)

Random sampling is conceptually, or theoretically, accomplished by assigning a number to each member of the target population and then picking the subjects by chance. One way researchers used to do this was by placing everyone's name in a hat and drawing out as many as needed (Popham & Sirotnik, 1973). A simpler way and one that is more commonly used in current research studies is to assign numbers to each possible subject and then use a list of subjects' numbers randomly created by a computer program. The specific way researchers randomize is not important. The important consideration for research consumers is that a randomized sample has a better chance of being representative of the target population than does a nonrandomized one, and therefore, the researchers' results are more likely to be generalizable to the target population.

In addition to randomly selecting subjects, it is common in experimental studies for researchers to randomly assign the subjects to treatments. The following subject section, from a study about the occurrence of behaviors that reflect social competence components and informational-processing components of problem solving, illustrates this double randomization procedure.

[Random selection]   Subjects for the study were 48 children from a middle-class, midwestern school system who were participants in a larger Logo project. From a pool of all children who returned a parental permission form (more than 80% return rate), 24 first graders (10 girls, 14 boys; mean age 6 years, 6 months), and 24 third graders (13 girls, 11 boys; mean age, 8 years, 8 months) were randomly selected. Children were randomly assigned to either
[Random   Logo or drill and practice treatment groups, so that 12 in each treatment group were from
assignment]   first grade and 12 were from third grade. (Clements & Nastasi, 1988, p. 93)

An extension of random sampling involves stratification. In a **stratified random sample**, the subjects are randomly selected by relevant variables in the same proportion as those variables appear in the target population. One example of nonrandomized stratified sampling is shown in the earlier extract with subjects from Georgia (Swanson, 1985). Although the sample was stratified, the researchers did not indicate whether the subjects were randomly selected. The National Assessment of Educational Progress (NAEP), which is financially supported by the U.S. Department of Education and conducted by the Education Commission of the States, uses a complex form of stratified random sampling.

As with all NAEP national assessments, the results for the national samples were based on a stratified, three-stage sampling plan. The first stage included defining geographic primary sampling units (PSUs), which are typically groups of contiguous counties, but sometimes a single county; classifying the PSUs into strata defined by region and community type; and randomly selecting schools, both public and private, within each PSU selected at the first stage. The third stage involved randomly selecting students within a school for participation. Some students who were selected (about 7 to 8 percent) were excluded because of limited English proficiency or severe disability. (Langer et al., 1995, p. 172)

As indicated previously, subjects may be intact groups, for example, classes to which students have been preassigned. When intact groups are selected, the procedure is called **cluster sampling**. Intact groups are selected because of convenience or accessibility. This procedure is especially common in causal-comparative research.

If a number of intact groups from a target population exist, researchers should randomly select entire groups as they would individuals.

The following subject description, which illustrates cluster sampling, is from a study that examined the instructional organization of classrooms and tried to explain why students achieved in some classes but not in others. Note that the researchers do not indicate whether their "preselected" classes were chosen through random procedures.

> This study was conducted during the math instruction of eight sixth-grade classes in four elementary schools in a school district in southwest Germany. These classrooms had been preselected out of total population of 113 sixth-grade classes in this school district. . . . Altogether, 194 students and their 8 math teachers participated. (Schneider & Treiber, 1984, p. 200)

Regardless of the nature of researchers' sampling procedures, an important concern in all designs is the use of **volunteer subjects.** Volunteers by nature are different from nonvolunteers because of some inherent motivational factor or connection to the researcher.

The following subject section, from a study which examined mothers' deviations from printed text as they read to their children, is an example of using volunteer subjects. Notice, though, that from all volunteers, the researchers randomly selected those involved in the study.

> From a pool of volunteers attending a large university in the Rocky Mountain region, 25 mother-child pairs were randomly selected. All of the mothers either were students or had spouses who were students at the university. Care was taken not to select students enrolled in the teacher education programs of the university, since teacher education students might have been taught specific early book reading methods, i.e., shared book experience. Mothers' ages ranged between 21 and 29 years, with the exception of three in their early 30's. Five comparison groups were formed according to the chronological ages of the children (6, 12, 18, and 24 months, plus or minus two months, and 4 years, plus or minus 4 months). (Martin & Reutzel, 1999).

Results from the use of volunteer subjects might not be directly generalizable to target populations containing seemingly similar, but nonvolunteer, individuals or groups. For example, in the above study, the volunteers may have a distinctive point of view about parenting. The results, then, can be generalized only to a target population with a similar orientation. Or, researchers using volunteers to study the effect of a particular study-skill instruction on social studies achievement might be able to generalize their results only to students who are motivated to learn and use such a procedure in school. Nonvolunteers might need a different kind of instruction to be successful in that subject. Researchers, then, are faced with a seemingly unanswerable question: Can results from research with volunteer subjects be generalized to nonvolunteer subjects?

The issue has wide implications, especially when human subjects are used in experimental research. It has become uniform practice within the educational research community to require the prior permission of subjects. In cases where the subjects are minors (under the age of 18 years), permissions from parents or guardians are necessary. Granting of permission is a form of volunteering. Permission for including human subjects is not a problem in descriptive or correlational research because (a) confidentiality is maintained through the use of grouped rather than individual data collection procedures and (b) such research does not involve intrusive activities. For example, an ethical and legal concern might be raised by subjects when they are assigned to what becomes a less effective treatment. They may say their educational progress was hindered rather than enhanced by the instructional activity.

Sample Size

The size of samples is important to researchers for statistical and practical reasons. There are several practical issues researchers need to consider. In collecting data, researchers must consider factors such as the availability of research personnel, the cost involved in paying personnel and securing instruments and materials, the time available for collecting and analyzing data, and the accessibility of subjects.

More important, researchers who want to generalize from the sample (the smaller group) to the target population (the larger group) should do this with as little statistical error as possible. Statistically, the size of the sample influences the likelihood that the sample's characteristics are truly representative of those of the target population (Gall et al., 1996; Gay & Airasian, 2000; Kerlinger, 1973). That is, the distribution of relevant variables found in the sample should not be significantly different from that of the target population. Any mismatch between the sample and the target population caused by an inadequate sample size will also contribute to sampling error. Clearly, errors associated with sampling are reduced with larger sample sizes. Statisticians frequently examine the *power* associated with sample size as an indication of this error.

ACTIVITIES

Activity 1

Using the focus questions at the beginning of this chapter as a guide, summarize the chapter's key ideas.

Activity 2

Read each of the following subject sections extracted from research reports. The researchers' research purposes have been included for your information. Using the questions and criteria on page 92, evaluate the studies. For each, list questions and concerns you may have about

a. Characteristics of the subjects

b. The sampling procedures

c. The representativeness of the subjects in relation to the target populations

d. The appropriateness of the subjects for the researchers' purposes

EXTRACT A

Purpose: The study examined children's views of the world after they personally experienced a natural disaster—specifically, Hurricane Andrew in South Florida during the summer of 1992.

PARTICIPANTS

Participants were 127 fourth- and fifth-grade students at the two school sites. From a pool of students who personally experienced Hurricane Andrew and whose parents gave written permission for their children to participate, 10 or 11 students were randomly selected from each of 12 groups in terms of ethnicity, SES, and gender. The three ethnic groups included African American, Hispanic of diverse national origins, and White nonHispanic students. Student ethnicity was taken from official school records, as reported by parents. The status of lunch programs is a variable frequently used by education researchers to identify students by socioeconomic status (SES). The two socioeconomic levels were distinguished by including students on free or reduced-price lunch programs in the lower SES group and those who paid for lunch or brought lunch to school in the higher SES group. (Lee, 1999, p. 192).

EXTRACT B

Purpose: The study examined the impact of an intervention targeting economically disadvantaged children in child care centers.

PARTICIPANTS AND SETTINGS

Systematic random sampling procedures were used to select a sample from the larger number of centers receiving the intervention. On the basis of economic need, the majority of centers (255) were from Philadelphia. To take into account the disproportionate number of child care centers in the city, a strategy was devised to oversample five counties (Bucks, Chester, Delaware, and Montgomery in Pennsylvania, and Camden in New Jersey, with a total of 82 centers), and slightly undersample Philadelphia. Philadelphia was partitioned in five separate regions considered to represent differing neighborhoods and economic areas and treated as if they were separate regions. Five centers in each of these 10 regional areas were then randomly selected: five counties and five areas within the metropolitan Philadelphia area for a total of 50 centers. Within each of these centers, four children (two girls and two boys) from two classrooms, one for 3- and one for 4-year-olds, were randomly selected to participate in the study. The initial sample, therefore, represented 50 centers (5 per region) and 100 classrooms (10 per region), for a total of 400 children (40 per region).

At the same time, regional directors were asked for names of comparable child-care centers that would not be involved (e.g., they might have already received a grant from the Foundation for another project or did not have nonprofit status), but shared similar demographic characteristics as those in the Books Aloud program. Ten of these child-care centers agreed to participate; 5 children were then randomly selected from two classrooms in each center, totaling 20 classrooms of 100 children in the designated control classrooms. Tables 2a (the pre and posttest sample) and 2b (the posttest only sample) give the distribution of the sample by age, gender, and ethnicity, as well as by the percentage of children whose parents received subsidies from the government toward the cost of child care as a general measure of income level. (Neuman, 1999, p. 291).

From: Neuman, S. B. (1999). Books make a difference. A study of access to literacy. *Reading Research Quarterly* 34(3), 286–311. Copyright © 1999 by the International Reading Association. All rights reserved.

FEEDBACK

Activity 1

What are populations and target populations?

The larger group of people or objects to whom researchers wish to apply their results constitutes the population, which is a group having at least one characteristic that distinguishes it from other groups. A target population is the specific group to which the researchers would like to apply their findings.

What are subjects and samples?

Subjects are the individuals or groups included in the study. A representative group of potential subjects, called the sample, is a miniature target population. Ideally, the sample would have the same distribution of relevant variables as found in the target population.

What criteria should be used to evaluate subject sections?

From reading the subject sections, research consumers should be able to answer

> What was the intended target population?
>
> Who were the subjects?
>
> How were the subjects selected, and did the researchers show bias in their sampling procedures?
>
> Were the subjects truly representative of the target population?
>
> How were the subjects assigned to groups or treatments in experimental research?
>
> Will the research results be applicable to my teaching situation and the students I teach? (Am I part of the target population? Are my students part of the target population?)

What considerations do researchers give to subject selection?

Subjects should be representative of the large population so results can be generalized from the subjects to the target population. Random sampling, or randomization, works on the principle that all members of the target population have an equal chance of being selected for the sample. The subjects finally selected should reflect the distribution of relevant variables found in the target population.

What considerations do researchers give to sample size?

Research producers and consumers should be sensitive to any mismatch between the sample and the target population caused by an inadequate sample size. The mismatch is a source of error, called sampling error. The probability of making an error relative to sample size is unique to each data analysis procedure.

Activity 2

Extract A. From a very special target population—children who had experienced a natural disaster—the researcher randomly selected a stratified sample using three variables for the stratification. The categories of demographic information about the subjects was provided but no information was provided as to the number of individuals within each group. It can be inferred that approximately 120 to 132 individuals took part in the study. A federal government edict requires parental permission to study children. But, because of the circumstances of the selection criteria (i.e., experience of a disaster), parental approval may be considered a form of volunteering. Although the target population is clear and the sample is a stratified random sample, the results of the study should only be generalized to other children who experienced a similar disaster.

Extract B.   The researcher started with an accessible target population. Then, to offset obtaining a disproportionate sample (i.e., one with a high proportion of representation from Philadelphia), other regions contiguous to Philadelphia were included. To avoid bias in that portion of the sample procedure, the researcher used double-random selection to select the child care centers. First, the centers were randomly selected from those available in the region. Then, within each center, the subjects were randomly selected.

However, the alternate (comparison) sample was identified in a manner that might have introduced bias. That pool was identified by opinion with only the criterion of having "similar demographic characteristics." Since the identified centers "agreed" to participate, there was an element of volunteering in the sample. Also, the criteria for selecting the two classrooms in the centers were not provided. But, within those classrooms, no bias was shown in the selection of subjects since they were randomly selected.

What was not included in Extract B is the table summarizing the demographic information that accompanied the discussion of participants. That table shows that the two groups were proportionately similar in characteristics.

Chapter 6

Reading and Evaluating Instrument Sections

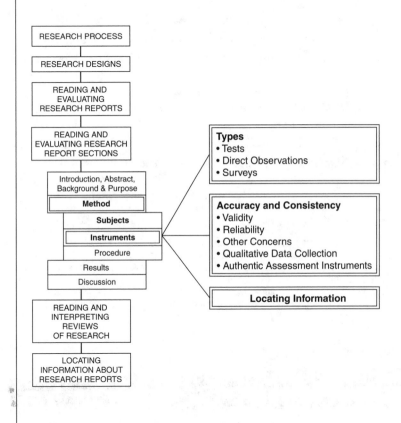

FOCUS QUESTIONS

1. What are the different types of instruments used in research projects?
2. How is information from different instruments reported?
3. What are instrument validity and reliability, and how are they determined?
4. What criteria should be used to determine whether instruments are appropriate for the research?
5. Where can information about instruments be found?
6. How should research report instrument sections be read and evaluated?

Researchers use instruments to collect data within all types of research designs. The term **instruments** is used to denote a broad range of specific devices and procedures for collecting, sorting, and categorizing information about subjects and research questions. Research consumers need to understand (a) what instruments are available to educational researchers, how instruments categorize information, and how data from different instruments are reported; (b) what criteria should be used to determine whether instruments accurately present information; and (c) how instrument sections in research reports should be read and interpreted.

From an instrument section, research consumers should be able to answer the following:

What types of instruments were used?

Were the standardized instruments valid and reliable for the research project?

Were the instruments appropriate for use with the target population and the research subjects?

Will the research results be applicable to my teaching situation and the students I teach because the instruments are appropriate for use with the students I teach?

Instrument sections describing standardized and other instruments should be evaluated using the following questions, which are from Figure 3.1, page 61.

Evaluating Instrument Sections

METHOD SECTION

Standardized and Other Instruments. What instruments are used in the study? Are they appropriate for the design of the study? Are the instruments valid for collecting data on the variables in the study and are reliability estimates given for each instrument? Are researcher-made instruments included (or at least samples of the instrument items)? Are the instruments appropriate for use with the target population and the research subjects? In the case of authentic, or performance-based, assessments, what evidence is presented that the devices reflect realistic samples of students' learning?

TYPES OF INSTRUMENTS

Researchers collect data with tests, direct observation (including observation of student work products, known as authentic assessments), and surveys. These instruments provide data about subjects' characteristics (as reported in subject sections) and about subjects' responses in various situations (as reported in procedure sections) in reports of all three kinds of research. Information about instruments discussed in any section of a research report is usually given in the instrument section.

Tests

Test information includes scores from individual or group standardized norm-referenced tests, standardized criterion-referenced tests, competency tests, and researcher-made tests.

A **standardized test** is one for which the tasks and procedures of administering, recording, scoring, and interpreting are specified so other testers can make comparable measurements in different locations (Harris & Hodges, 1995). The test constructors use accepted procedures and research the test's (a) content, (b) procedures for administering, (c) system for recording and scoring answers, and (d) method of turning the results into a usable form. Everything about the test has been made uniform (standardized) so that if all its directions are correctly followed, the results can be interpreted in the same manner, regardless of where the test was administered.

Standardized tests are of two main types: norm-referenced and criterion-referenced. Norm-referenced tests compare individuals' scores to a standardization, or norming, group. A **norming group** consists of individuals used in researching the standardization of the test's administration and scoring. The section in this chapter called Accuracy and Consistency of Instruments contains a discussion about how to determine the appropriateness of a relationship between a norm group and a target population.

The scores from norm-referenced tests are reported as standard scores (e.g., SS = 53), grade equivalents (e.g., GE = 4.6), percentiles (e.g., 67th percentile, or percentile rank = 67), stanines (e.g., fifth stanine, or stanine 5), scale scores (e.g., scale score = 450), or normal curve equivalents (e.g., NCE = 72). Each of these scores can be used to describe subjects' characteristics or subjects' relative performance. Additional information about the different types of scores is in Chapter 8, Reading and Interpreting Results Sections.

In the following example from a subject section, percentile scores are used to describe the subjects.

Purpose of the study: To determine if subject matter text could be rewritten such that students' comprehension of unfamiliar topic words could be enhanced.

[Sample]   Subjects were 55 eighth grade students enrolled in two state history classes at a university laboratory school. They first were stratified by reading ability according to their reading percentile scores on a standardized achievement test (Stanford Achievement Test, 1981), and then grouped by high and average ability levels. The high ability group, with 28 subjects, had scores ranging from 75–99, with a mean score of 89.28 (SD = 7.14). The average ability group, with 27 subjects, had scores ranging from 12–68, with a mean score of 47.80 (SD = 12.59). (Konopak, 1988, p. 4)

[Percentiles]

On **criterion-referenced tests**, or measurements, students' performance is tested in terms of the expected learner behaviors or to specified expected levels of performance (Harris & Hodges, 1995). Scores on these tests show students' abilities and performances in relation to sets of goals or to what a student is able to do. They do not show subjects' rankings compared with others, as norm-referenced tests do. A standardized criterion-referenced test is one for which the administration and scoring procedures are uniform but the scoring is in relation to the established goals, not to a norm group. In many states, there are proficiency tests for students, which are forms of criterion-referenced tests.

The assessment of students' work and the products of their learning, commonly referred to as *authentic assessment*, has increasingly replaced or supplemented other test data in research. This form of data, similar to criterion-referenced tests, is used to compare students' performance and products (e.g., oral reading, writing samples, art or other creative output, and curriculum-related projects) to specified levels of performance. In authentic assessment, researchers use materials and instruction that are true representations of "the actual learning and activities of the classroom and out-of-school worlds" of the children (Hiebert, Valencia, & Afflerback, 1994, p. 11).

Through using authentic assessment, teachers are expected to provide students with meaningful educational experiences that facilitate learning and skill development as well as greater understanding of what is needed for good performance (Messick, 1994). Specifically,

> authentic assessments aim to capture a richer array of student knowledge and skill than is possible with multiple-choice tests; to depict the processes and strategies by which students produce their work; to align the assessment more directly with the ultimate goals of schooling; and to provide realistic contexts for the production of student work by having the tasks and processes, as well as the time and resources, parallel those in the real world. (pp. 17–18)

Direct Observation

When collecting data from **direct observation,** researchers take extensive field notes or use observation forms to record the information. They may categorize information on forms in response to questions about subjects' actions or categories of actions. These are considered *open-ended* responses. Or, researchers may tally subjects' actions within some predetermined categories during a specified time period (e.g., on a check list), which are considered *closed-ended* responses.

Field notes consist of written narrative describing subjects' behavior or performance during an instructional activity. These notes are then analyzed, and the information is categorized for reporting. The analysis can start with predetermined categories, and information from the notes is recorded accordingly. Or, the analysis can be open-ended in that the researchers cluster similar information and then create a label for each cluster.

The following description of an observational assessment and the information in Figure 6.1 are from a naturalistic investigation (Clements & Nastasi, 1988). Notice how the researchers explain their instrument and provide examples of the behaviors to be categorized.

> *Purpose of the study: To study the occurrence of first- and third-grade students' behaviors that reflect social competence components and information-processing components of problem solving while using computers in school.*

INSTRUMENTS

Observational Assessment of Social Behaviors

The observation scheme was adapted from a more comprehensive instrument (covering six components of social competence) developed by the second author to assess social behaviors (Nastasi & Clements, 1985). Behavioral indicators of social problem solving included cooperative work, conflict, and resolution of conflict. Indicators of effective motivation included self-directed work, persistence, rule determination, and showing pleasure at discovery. [Figure 6.1 top] lists the behaviors observed and provides an operational definition of each. Reliability of the instrument was assessed in previous research; interrator agreement, established through simultaneous coding of behaviors by two observers, was 98% (Nastasi & Clements).

> *Observational assessment of information-processing components.* As stated, initial analysis of the data on social behaviors revealed that (a) one of the most striking differences between the experimental (Logo) and control (drill and practice) groups was in determining rules

Observation Scheme for Social Behaviors

Behavior	Definition
Social problem Solving	
Cooperative work	Child works with another child on an academic task (i.e., jointly engages in computer activity) without conflict (as opposed to cooperative play—engagement in nonacademic activities or conversation not related to the task at hand).
Conflict	Child engages in verbal or physical conflict with another child.
Resolution of conflict	Child reaches successful resolution of conflict, without adult intervention.
Effectance motivation	
Self-directed work	Child initiates or engages in an independent work activity without teacher's coaxing or direction: including constructive solitary or parallel work.
Persistence	Child persists on a task after encountering difficulty or failure without teacher's coaxing or encouragement.
Rule determination	Child engages in self-determination of rules, for example, making plans or establishing parameters of a problem situation. Includes use of verbal heuristic for solving problems.
Showing pleasure	Child shows signs of pleasure at solving a problem or at discovery of new information (e.g., child cheers after reaching a solution).

Observation Scheme for Information-Processing Components

Component	Definition	Examples
Metacomponents		
Deciding on nature of the problem	Determining what the task is and what it requires	"What do we make here?" "We gotto go over here, then put lines around it like our drawing."
Selecting performance components	Determining how to solve the problem: choosing lower order components	"Read the list [of directions] again, but change all the LEFTs to RIGHTs for this side." "How are we gonna make this thing go over this way? We did RIGHT 20. What's 90 − 70 . . . 20, right? We need not RIGHT 90, but 70!" "We got to add these three numbers."
Combining performance components	Sequencing the components selected	"First, you have to get it over that way a little . . . LEFT 45, then FORWARD 30." "We'll make the turtle go up this way about 10, then RIGHT 90 and 10 down, then FORWARD halfway—5—and we're done."
Selecting a mental representation	Choosing an effective form or organization for representing relevant information	No verbalizations recorded
Allocating resources	Deciding how much time to spend on various components	"That's enough time talking. We should draw it." "We go it." Let's think and make sure."
Monitoring solution processes	Keeping track of progress and recognizing need to change strategy	"Put 70." "70? We already did 50 . . . type FORWARD 20." "You're gonna go off the screen, I'm telling you."
Being sensitive to external feedback	Understanding and acting upon feedback	"I know—if it's wrong it goes 'blub, blub, blub' and sinks down."
Performance components	Executing the task; includes encoding and responding	"5 times 7 is 35." "Type R-I-G-H-T-4-5." "It says, 'What is 305 − 78?' "
Other	Miscellaneous; includes off-task and uninterpretable verbalizations	"They're recording us, you know." "I'm tired of this; can we do another game?"

Figure 6.1

Sample Information From an Observational Assessment. (Clements & Nastasi, 1988. Adapted by permission of the publisher.)

and (b) as defined, the construct of rule determination was too general. The rule-determination category involved planning, establishing parameters for problem solving, and use of verbal heuristics. A more detailed framework was needed to differentiate among such metacognitive behaviors. Therefore, a scheme for categorizing information-processing components of problem solving was constructed based on the componential theory of Sternberg (1985). The following metacomponents were delineated in the present study: deciding on the nature of the problems; selecting performance components relevant for the solution of the problem; selecting a strategy for combining performance components; selecting a mental representation; allocating resources for problem solution; monitoring solution processes; and being sensitive to external feedback. Frequencies of behaviors indicative of each metacomponent were recorded. Performance components, used in the actual execution of a task, included such behaviors as encoding, applying, and reporting. These behaviors were relevant to problem solution, but not reflective of metacognitive processing. Because the investigation focused on metacomponential processes, behaviors were not defined more specifically than the "performance" category level. A final category of "other" included off-task behaviors. [Figure 6.1, bottom] presents the definitions and examples of behaviors for each category. Interrater agreement was 87%. (Clements & Nastasi, 1988, p. 95. Copyright 1988 by the American Educational Research Association. Reprinted by permission of the publisher.)

In the above extract, the researchers indicate that the material shown in Figure 6.1 provides an operational definition of each behavior. For example, for the behavior *social problem solving, cooperative work,* they specify the particular subjects' activities that would be counted as an instance of the behavior. An **operational definition** is a definition of a variable that gives the precise way an occurrence of that variable can be seen. In the Clements and Nastasi study, the operational definitions were verbal. Operational definitions can also be test scores. In the Konopak (1988) study discussed earlier, high- and average-ability students were operationally defined by percentile ranges on the Stanford Achievement Test. (To aid research consumers in understanding technical vocabulary and determining the appropriateness of operational definitions, there are specialized professional dictionaries. Chapter 11, Locating Information About Research Reports, contains information about locating and using these dictionaries.)

Surveys

Surveys include questionnaires, interviews including focus groups, scales, inventories, and check lists.

Questionnaires require the respondent to either write or orally provide answers to questions about a topic. The answer form may be *structured* in that there are fixed choices, or the form may be *open-ended* in that respondents can use their own words. Fixed-choice questionnaires may be called **inventories**. They may require subjects to simply respond to statements, questions, or category labels with a "yes" or "no," or they may ask subjects to check off appropriate information within a category.

Questionnaires also are used to collect information from files such as subjects' permanent school records. When the respondent answers orally and the researcher records the answers, the instrument is considered an **interview**. Interviews are used to obtain structured or open-ended responses. They differ from questionnaires in that the researcher can modify the data collection situation to fit the respondent's

1. Approximate number of students in your department:
   undergraduate _____ graduate _____
2. What is your department's emphasis?
   ( ) categorical ( ) cross-categorical

3. Does your department offer a course on *working with parents of exceptional students?*
   ( ) yes ( ) no

   a. Is *working with parents of exceptional students* included as a component of another course?
      ( ) yes ( ) no

   b. Is working with parents of exceptional students offered by another department?
      ( ) yes ( ) no

   c. Is the course required by your department?
      ( ) yes ( ) no

      At what level? (mark each that applies)
      ( ) graduate ( ) undergraduate

   d. Is the course required for certification by your state's Department of Education?
      ( ) yes ( ) no

Figure 6.2
Sample Information From a Questionnaire. (From Hughes, Ruhl, & Gorman 1987)

responses. For example, additional information can be solicited, or a question can be rephrased.

The following explanation of a fixed-response questionnaire is from a descriptive study, and sample questions from that questionnaire are presented in Figure 6.2.

Purpose of the study: To determine the nature, extent, and impact of preservice training for special educators working with parents.

INSTRUMENT

Survey I questionnaire is displayed as [Figure 6.2]. Questions on the survey form included demographic information and series of questions designed to ascertain whether content on working with parents was offered [in college courses preparing special-education teachers] and, if so, to what extent. Respondents whose departments [of special education] offered a course on this topic were asked to provide a course syllabus, which became permanent product data. (Hughes, Ruhl, & Gorman, 1987, p. 82. Copyright 1987 by Teacher Education and Special Education)

The following explanation of an inventory is from a study to develop a way to measure student achievement in terms of a school's local curriculum. Sample items from the inventory are presented in Figure 6.3. Notice that although the instrument was labeled an inventory, its items could easily be restructured as questions.

Purpose of the study: To describe a model for a schoolwide curriculum-based system of identifying and programming for students with learning disabilities.

The final measure used in the [Curriculum-Based Assessment and Instructional Design] (C-BAID) process is the environmental inventory. Its purpose is to assist teachers in identifying factors that may facilitate or impede instruction in the classroom. It is used to provide information once a particular student is determined to be significantly discrepant

Consequences Teacher, target learner, and peer responses to learner behavior (c)

C1   Teacher response to correct answer:
meaningful immediate reinforcement _____
meaningful delayed reinforcement _____
no reinforcement _____

C2   Target learner response to success:
positive _____ negative _____ no response _____

C3   Peer response to target learner's correct answer:
positive _____ negative _____ no response _____

C4   Teacher response to incorrect answer:
immediate feedback _____ delayed feedback _____
modeled correct responses _____
required learner to imitate correct response _____
no corrective feedback _____
punishment or sarcasm _____

C5   Target learner response to incorrect response or failure:
guessed _____
corrected self _____
gave up and said "I don't know" _____
made another response _____ (please describe) _____
sat and said nothing _____
became negative and refused to work _____
became hostile (i.e., engaged in verbally and/or physically aggressive behavior) _____

C6   Peer responses to target learner's incorrect answer:
positive _____ negative _____ no response _____

Figure 6.3
Sample Information From an Inventory. (Bursuck & Lesson, 1987, 17–29)

from peers either academically, in work habits, or both. The checklist used in C-BAID is an adaptation of ones previously developed [by other researchers]. The inventory is based on the ABC model of instruction and thus focuses on the Antecedents, or events taking place prior to or during instruction; the Behavior, or how learners perform; and the Consequences, or events taking place after learners have performed. Many of the variables selected for inclusion in the environmental inventory have been shown to be positively correlated with academic achievement [by other researchers]. The environmental inventory can be conducted by the school psychologist or principal. Classroom teachers may also complete the inventory after a lesson has ended. A portion of the inventory is shown in [Figure 6.3]. (Bursuck & Lesson, 1987, pp. 23, 26)

Scales commonly measure variables related to attitudes, interests, and personality and social adjustment. Usually, data are quantified in predetermined categories representing subdivisions of the variable. Subjects respond to a series of statements or questions showing the degree or intensity of their responses. Unlike data from tests, which are measured in continuous measurements (e.g., stanines 1 through 9, or percentiles 1 through 99), data from scales are discrete measurements, forcing respondents to indicate their level of reaction; common forced choices are "Always," "Sometimes," or "Never." This type of data quantification is called a **Likert-type scale**. Each response is assigned a value; a value of 1 usually represents the least positive response.

The following explanation of a scale is from a study to assess parent attitudes toward employment and services for their mentally retarded adult offspring. Although the report does not include sample items from the survey, the presentation of the results, as shown in Figure 6.4, clearly states that a Likert-type scale was used in the original form.

> *Purpose of the study: To assess parent/guardian attitudes toward employment opportunities and adult services for their own mentally retarded, adult sons or daughters who are currently receiving services from adult community mental retardation systems.*

> The format of the survey for the attitude section was a Likert-type scale. In this section [of the survey], parents were asked to indicate the degree to which they perceived that their sons or daughters were currently exposed to the six qualitative conditions already listed and their opinions regarding the optimal amount of exposure to each practice. Therefore, attitude questions were presented in pairs. The first of the pairs asked for the parents' attitude toward the current situation as they perceived it and the second of the pair asked the parents for the preferred situation on each issue. The first item of the pairs permitted responding on a four-point Likert scale ranging from "never" (1) to "frequently" (4); a "don't know" response was (5). The responses on the second of the paired items regarding preferences employed a five-point continuum, which ranged from "much less than now" (1) to "much more than now" (5) [see Figure 6.4]. (Hill, Seyfarth, Banks, Wehman, & Orelove, 1987, p 12). Copyright © 1987 by The Council for Exceptional Children. Reprinted with permission.

ACCURACY AND CONSISTENCY OF INSTRUMENTS

Researchers are concerned that data they collect with various instruments are accurate and consistent. They wish to be sure they have positive answers to questions such as "Do the data represent real aspects of the variable being measured?" and "Will the data be similar if the instrument is administered a second or third time?" These questions refer to an instrument's validity and reliability. **Validity** refers to the extent to which an instrument measures what it is intended to measure. **Reliability** refers to the extent to which an instrument measures a variable consistently.

Additional information about the validity and reliability of instruments, including that concerning observations, is found in Chapter 7, Reading and Evaluating Procedure Sections.

Validity of Instruments

Instruments have validity when they are appropriate for a specific purpose and a particular population. To use an instrument with confidence, researchers must be able to answer yes to "Does the instrument measure what it is intended to measure at the time it is being used?" and "Are the results generalizable to the intended target population?" These questions imply that instruments are not universally valid. Instruments are considered valid only for clearly identified situations and populations. The creators of instruments (tests, observation procedures, and surveys) are responsible for establishing the validity of their instruments. When researchers use others' instruments, they must present evidence that the instrument is valid for the research project. When researchers create new instruments for their projects, they

Parental Attitudes Toward Working Conditions

Perceptions of Current Working Conditions		Preferred Working Conditions	
Condition	Percent	Condition	Percent
Average current wages		*Preferred wages*	
No pay	41%	No pay	5%
Less than $1/hour	23%	Less than now	.4%
$1.01 to $2.50/hour	10%	Same as now	49%
$2.52 to $3.34/hour	.3%	More than now	25%
Above $3.35/hour	3%	Much more	12%
Don't know	21%	Not sure	9%
Current interaction with nonhandicapped		*Preferred interactions*	
Never	7%	Less than now	2%
Rarely	13%	Somewhat less	4%
Sometimes	22%	Same as now	54%
Frequently	46%	Somewhat more	30%
Don't know	11%	Much more	10%
Currently responsibility and advancement opportunities		*Preferred responsibility and advancement opportunities*	
Never	36%	Less than now	0%
Rarely	13%	Somewhat less	.4%
Sometimes	28%	Same as now	59%
Frequently	25%	Somewhat more	28%
Don't know	17%	Much more	12%
Current level of work without supervision		*Preferred level of work without supervision*	
Never	17%	Less than now	0%
Rarely	13%	Somewhat less	2%
Sometimes	28%	Same as now	52%
Frequently	25%	Somewhat more	29%
Don't know	17%	Much more	17%
Requirements to exhibit "normal" behavior during work		*Preferred level of requirement to exhibit "normal" behavior during work*	
Never	14%	Less than now	3%
Rarely	7%	Somewhat less	5%
Sometimes	16%	Same as now	66%
Frequently	25%	Somewhat more	20%
Don't know	38%	Much more	7%
Current performance of same tasks as nonhandicapped workers		*Preferred level of performance of same tasks as nonhandicapped workers*	
Never	19%	Less than now	9%
Rarely	14%	Somewhat less	3%
Sometimes	19%	Same as now	61%
Frequently	21%	Somewhat more	28%
Don't know	26%	Much more	7%

Vocational Placement

Current placement		*Preferred placement*	
Institution	10.4%	Institution	5.6%
Home (no program)	17.2%	Home (no program)	4,0%
Activities center	23.3%	Activities center	25.6%
Sheltered workshop	43.7%	Sheltered workshop	52.0%
Competitive employment	5%	Competitive employment	12.8%

Attitudes Toward Work
Work should be a normal part of life for my son or daughter.

Strongly Disagree	Mildly Disagree	Not Sure	Mildly Agree	Strongly Agree
4%	2%	18%	18%	60%

Figure 6.4

Sample Information From a Likert-Type Scale. (Hill et al., 1987, 9–23. Reprinted with permission.)

must detail how they established the instrument's validity. Research consumers want to know "Does the instrument provide a real picture?"

An instrument's validity is investigated using one or more of several generally accepted procedures. Even though each procedure can be used to determine an instrument's validity, research consumers need assurance that the particular way an instrument was validated makes it appropriate for a particular research project.

One validation procedure establishes that an instrument has been developed according to a supportable educational, sociological, or psychological theory. The theory can relate to any human characteristic or to any aspect of society. A theory is based on supportable research and tries to explain the nature of human behavior (such as intelligence or learning) and action (such as teaching). A theory's usefulness depends on how clearly it explains those behaviors and actions. A theory should not be considered as complete; it should be considered adequate only for describing a particular set of conditions, but not all conditions. Any theory must be modified or even discarded as new evidence is encountered, and every theory should (a) explain a complex phenomenon (such as reading ability, the nature of learning disabilities, mathematics aptitude, or the social interaction within a classroom), (b) describe how the phenomenon operates, and (c) provide a basis for predicting changes that will occur in one aspect of the phenomenon when changes are made in other aspects. When an instrument's creator demonstrates the instrument as representing a supportable theory, it is said to have **construct validity**. Research consumers should expect every instrument to have construct validity. It is the researcher producers' responsibility to select an instrument with a construct validity appropriate for the research question, purpose, or hypothesis.

In the example that follows, the developers of a reading test, the "Information Reading-Thinking Inventory" (IR–TI), explain their theoretical frame of reference.

> Three principal facts encourage us to believe that a new kind of Informal Reading Inventory [IRI] can address a number of [the technical measurement problems of existing IRIs] and other emerging assessment issues and, more importantly, can result in better decisions in planning instruction. First, the IR–TI was constructed from the start to address some of the technical psychometric issues that have plagued IRIs for five decades. For example, you will see later how we were able to solve the problem of intermixing passage dependent and independent questions rather easily with a design modification that essentially separates the two question types. A second related point is that the IR–TI attempts to be responsive to the new issues that have arisen from recent theories of comprehension and from philosophies of instruction. Chief among these new concerns is the distinction between reconstructing an author's intended meaning (the usual view of comprehension) and the "constructivist" concept of constructing a reasonable interpretation of what one reads. The IR–TI is designed to assess both of these dimensions of comprehension in a manner that grounds it in current theory by acknowledging the "constructivist" ideal of promoting higher-order literacy or literate responses. Third, the movement toward alternative forms of assessment entails reduced emphasis on product measures, such as standardized tests, and greater focus on "process" measures, or performance-based and diagnostic evaluation of the student's thinking, reflection, and strategy choices. Instead of teachers continuing the practice of not assessing at all what cannot be assessed easily and definitively, we urge teachers to use the IR–TI to become more expert in continuing to informally assess critical/creative reading and thinking in a variety of settings and classroom situations. This, again, is the basis of "performance-based" assessment. (Excerpt from *Informal Reading-Thinking Inventory* by Manzo, Manzo & McKenna, 1995. Copyright © 1995 by Harcourt Brace & Company. Reprinted by permission of the publisher.)

A second validation procedure establishes that the instrument is measuring a specific body of information. This is an important consideration, especially when the instrument is an achievement or performance test. An instrument that is intended to measure science achievement should contain test items about the specific information the users (subjects or students) had the opportunity to learn in science classes. For example, achievement tests appropriate for use at the elementary level should contain items that test facts, concepts, and generalizations normally found in typical elementary-school science curricula. When an instrument's creators demonstrate that the specific items or questions represent an accurate sampling of specific bodies of knowledge (i.e., curricula or courses of study), it is said to have **content validity**. Instruments' creators establish content validity by submitting the instruments' items to groups of authorities in the content areas. It is their expert opinions that determine whether the instruments have content validity. Before research consumers can generalize research results, it must be determined that any instruments' content is appropriate (valid) for their educational situation and student population.

In the following example, from a study to assess the perceptions and opinions of students who completed teacher education programs, the researchers explain the source of their questionnaire's content. (The "Dean's Grant" to which they refer was a federally funded grant competition for the development and implementation of preservice teacher preparation models that would prepare regular and special-education teachers for the mainstreaming of special-education students.)

Purpose of the study: To assess the perceptions and opinions of students who completed the teacher education program at a large midwestern university.

A questionnaire comprising four parts was used to survey students. In part 1, respondents rated 34 competency statements related to mainstreaming of handicapped students on two scales. On the first scale, the Coverage Scale, respondents rated the extent to which they thought mainstream content had been covered in their teacher education program. On the second scale, the Knowledge Scale, they rated their knowledge of the mainstream curriculum content. The 34 statements were adapted from competency statements developed during the early years of the Dean's Grant that were still being used as guidelines for infusing mainstream curriculum throughout the undergraduate program. (Aksamit & Alcorn, 1988, p. 54)

A first-level aspect of content validity is face validity. **Face validity** refers only to the extent to which an instrument appears to measure a specific body of information. In other words, "Does the instrument look as if it would measure what it intends to measure?" "Does a mathematics test look like actual mathematical tasks?" Instruments' users, or other subject-area experts, usually establish face validity by examining the test without comparing it to a course of study (curriculum).

A third validation procedure establishes the extent to which an instrument measures something to the same degree as does another instrument. The second instrument must previously have had its validity established by one or more accepted procedures. To establish validity for a new instrument, the instrument's creator administers both instruments to the same group of individuals. The extent to which the results show that the individuals correlated, or scored similarly on both instruments, is an indication of **concurrent validity**. This is a common procedure for establishing a new instrument's validity, but research producers and consumers must interpret the new instrument's results with some caution. They must be sure of the older instrument's construct and content validity. If the older instrument has questionable construct or content validity, the new instrument may not be appropriate even though there is high concurrent validity with that older instrument. Research consumers should expect evidence about the comparison instrument's validity. Research producers should indicate the instrument used to establish concurrent validity and data about the level of correlation.

Information about an instrument's concurrent validity is usually found in studies whose purpose is to develop or assess an instrument. The following example is taken from such a study. It should be noted that the reported negative correlations were a desired result since the two instruments are meant to measure students' behavior in inverse ways.

> *Purpose of the study: To revise and standardize a checklist of adaptive functioning designed for school use at the kindergarten level.*

> ### CONCURRENT VALIDITY WITH WALKER PROBLEM BEHAVIOR IDENTIFICATION CHECKLIST

> [Twenty] students from grade levels kindergarten 2, 4, and 6 . . . were also used to examine the concurrent validity of the revised [Classroom Adaptive Behavior Checklist].

> The teachers of these selected students were asked to complete both the revised checklist and the Walker Problem Behavior Identification Checklist (Walker, 1976), with a return rate of 70%.

> The overall Pearson correlation between the total scores on the revised checklist (where higher scores indicate more adaptive behavior) and on the Walker (where higher scores indicate more problem behavior) was $-.78$ ($df = 54$, $p < .001$). The correlation for kindergarten, grades 2, 4, and 6 were, respectively, $-.77$, $-.84$, $-.86$, and $-.95$. (Hunsucker, Nelson, & Clark, 1986, p. 70)

A fourth validation procedure establishes the extent to which an instrument can predict a target population's performance after some future situation. This **predictive validity** is determined by comparing a sample's results on the instrument to their results after some other activity. An example of predictive validity is the ability of college admissions officers to predict college students' first-year grade point average from their scores on the Scholastic Aptitude Test (SAT).

Reliability of Instruments

Instruments are said to have **reliability** when they are consistent in producing their results. To use an instrument with confidence, researchers must be able to answer yes to "Does the instrument measure what it is intended to measure in a consistent manner?" and "Are the results going to be similar each time the instrument is used?" The implication of these questions for research producers and consumers has to do with dependability and the degree to which the results can be trusted. Reliability is not an either-or phenomenon; reliability is a statistical estimate of the extent to which the results can be considered dependable.*

The creators of instruments (tests, observation procedures, and surveys) are responsible for establishing the reliability of their instruments. When researchers use others' instruments, they must present evidence of the instruments' reliability. When researchers create new instruments for their projects, they must detail how they established the instruments' reliability. Research consumers want to know "Does the instrument give a dependable picture of data?"

---

*There are some test experts (psychometricians) who believe that a test does not have reliability per se. Rather, they believe that reliability is an indication of the consistency of the test results for a particular instance of a test's use.

Evidence of an instrument's reliability is demonstrated with one or more of several generally accepted procedures. Even though each procedure gives only an estimate of an instrument's reliability, research consumers need assurance that the particular way an instrument's reliability was determined deems it appropriate for a particular research project. Whatever procedure is used, the reliability of an instrument is given in a numerical form called the **reliability coefficient**. The coefficient is expressed in decimal form, ranging from .00 to 1.00. The higher the coefficient, the higher the instrument's reliability; that is, the higher the chance that the subject's observed score and true score can be considered similar.

The common procedures for establishing an instrument's reliability are (a) test-retest reliability, (b) equivalent forms reliability, (c) internal consistency reliability, and (d) scorer or rater reliability.

Test-retest reliability, also referred to as *test stability*, is determined by administering the same instrument again to the same subjects after a time period has elapsed. When subjects' results are statistically compared, researchers gain evidence of the instrument's reliability over time, or its stability. It is considered the lowest level of reliability.

Equivalent forms reliability (sometimes called *parallel forms reliability*) is determined by creating two forms of an instrument, differing only in the specific nature of the items; the same subjects are given both forms, and their results are statistically compared. This method results in a much more consequential estimate of reliability than test-retest reliability.

Internal consistency reliability, which is sometimes called *rationale equivalence reliability*, is determined by statistically comparing the subjects' scores on individual items to their scores on each of the other items and to their scores on the instrument as a whole. **Split-half reliability**, a commonly used form of internal consistency, is determined by dividing the instrument in half and statistically comparing the subjects' results on both parts. The most common way to split a test is into odd- and even-numbered items. Most often, this method is used when the test designers want to avoid the additional costs associated with developing a parallel (i.e., equivalent or alternate) form of a test.

Scorer or rater reliability, which is sometimes called *interrater or interjudge reliability*, is determined by comparing the results of two or more scorers, raters, or judges. Sometimes scorer reliability is presented as a percentage of agreement and not as a coefficient.

In the following example, which is taken from a previously cited study about the standardization of a behavior checklist (Hunsucker et al., 1986), two methods of establishing the instrument's reliability are used. Both methods, test-retest and interteacher (or interrater), involve the use of the Pearson correlation formula, which is explained on p. 180.

Purpose of the study: To revise and standardize a checklist of adaptive functioning designed for school use at the kindergarten level.

TEST-RETEST RELIABILITY

Subgroups of 20 subjects from grades kindergarten, 2, 4, and 6 were randomly selected from the normative group to examine the test-retest reliability of the revised checklist. The teachers of these students were asked to complete the checklist twice over a 4-week period (x elapsed days = 31.3), with a return rate of 66.2%.

Using the Pearson correlation coefficient on total checklist scores, test-retest reliability was .72 for kindergarten ($n = 11$), .95 for grade 2 ($n = 11$), .89 for grade 4 ($n = 15$), and .67 for grade 6 ($n = 26$). Using the exact agreement method for specific checklist items (agreements on both occurrence and nonoccurrence divided by total number of items), test-retest reliability was .90 for kindergarten, .92 for grade 2, .90 for grade 4, and .89 for grade 6.

INTERTEACHER AGREEMENT

Subgroups of 15 subjects from grade levels 1, 3, and 5 who were in team-taught classrooms were selected from the normative group to examine interteacher agreement for the revised checklist. Both teachers in the teaching team completed checklists for 68.8% of these selected students.

Using the Pearson correlation coefficient on total checklist scores, interteacher agreement was .92 for grade 1 ($n = 11$), .86 for grade 3 ($n = 10$), and .89 for grade 5 ($n = 10$). Using the exact agreement method for specific checklist items, interteacher agreement was .92 for grade 1, .93 for grade 3, and .86 for grade 5.

(From: Hill, J. W., Seyfarth, J., Banks, P. D., Wehman, P., & Orelove, F. (1987). Parent attitudes about working conditions of their adult mentally retarded sons and daughters. *Exceptional Children 54*: 9-23. Copyright © 1987 by the Council for Exceptional Children. Reprinted with permission.

In the following example, from a study involving the use of various phonemic awareness tests, the researcher uses an internal consistency reliability procedure. Note that although the type of reliability procedure is not indicated, the researcher reports a commonly used statistical formula used—the Cronbach alpha. Another commonly used formula for establishing internal consistency reliability is the Kuder-Richardson formula 20.

Purpose of the study: To determine the reliability and validity of tests that have been used to operationalize the concept of phonemic awareness.

The reliability of each test was determined using Cronbach's alpha. Seven of the tests had high internal consistency, with alpha = .83. The Roswell-Chall (1959) phoneme blending test showed the greatest reliability (alpha = .96) followed closely by the Yopp-Singer phoneme segmentation test (alpha = .95). Two tests showed moderate to high reliability: Rosner's (1975) phoneme deletion test (alpha = .78) and the Yopp rhyme test (alpha = .76). The Yopp modification of Wallach's (1976) word-to-word matching test had the lowest reliability (alpha = .58) for this sample. (Yopp, 1988, p. 168)

Other Concerns About Instruments

The standardization, or norm, group constitutes a key attribute of a standardized test. It is the research consumer's responsibility to ensure that this group, on which the norms of the test have been developed, is comparable to the group to which the consumer wishes to generalize the findings of the research being evaluated. Most often, major test publishers ensure generalization by creating a stratified-sample standardization group. That process usually results in norm groups that are representative of all regions of the country and various ethnic groups in proportion to their population statistics.

A common concern about instruments deals with how and by whom instruments are administered. An instrument may have validity and reliability, but the person using it must be competent and must use it in appropriate settings. For example, certain standardized tests must be administered by fully trained and qualified examiners. Standardized tests requiring special training and certified personnel include the Wechsler Intelligence Scale for Children–Revised and the Stanford-Binet Intelligence Scale, 4th edition. All instruments, whether they are tests, observations, or surveys, should be administered by appropriately trained personnel.

The following three passages illustrate how researchers indicate instrument users' proficiencies.

> *Purpose of the study: To investigate differences in parent-provided written language experiences of intellectually superior nonreaders and accelerated readers.*
>
> *Test Administration.* All 125 potentially gifted children were administered the *Stanford-Binet Intelligence Test* and Letter-Word Identification subtest from the *Woodcock-Johnson Psycho-Educational Battery* by certified examiners. (Burns & Collins, 1987, p. 243)
>
> *Purpose of the study: To compare students' instructional placements as predicted by a standardized test and an informal reading inventory.*
>
> All of the tests were administered over a period of about six weeks (three per grade) by a research assistant trained in the use of both the [Degrees of Reading Power] and the [informal reading inventory]. (Duffelmeyer & Adamson, 1986, p. 195)
>
> *Purpose of the study: To determine the effects of education, occupation, and setting on reading practices.*
>
> *Procedures.* A guided interview was constructed based on a review of previous research in measuring reading practice (Guthrie & Seifert, 1984). Two enumerators were recruited who were paid for their services. They had considerable experience in conducting surveys but were not experienced with reading activity inventories. In a 4-hour training session, they were informed about the purpose of the survey, taken step by step through the inventory, and given a demonstration of its administration. The enumerators individually interviewed an adult wage earner in each designated household. (Guthrie et al., 1986, p. 152)

A factor that may be important in test administration is the familiarity of the examiner to the subjects. Research evidence seems to show that some subjects' scores increase when they are tested by familiar examiners (Fuchs & Fuchs, 1986, 1989). Since researchers cannot always establish examiner-subject familiarity (because of time constraints or expense), research consumers need to be aware of the possible effect on results of subjects' unfamiliarity with examiners.

A second concern is when, in descriptive research, surveys or questionnaires are mailed to potential respondents. A major concern to researchers is the representativeness of the returned surveys or questionnaires. Usually, a return rate of about 70% is considered adequate to ensure that the obtained responses represent those of the entire target population (Gay & Airasian, 2000). When the percentage of returns is lower, researchers should conduct follow-up activities to get additional questionnaires. Also, when the return rate is the minimum acceptable, research consumers should be concerned whether there is a difference in traits between individuals who respond to the questionnaires and those who do not.

Validity and Reliability of Qualitative Data Collection

In many qualitative research studies, the data-gathering instrument is often a participant observer. The question can be raised about the validity and reliability of the data collected by these individuals. In Chapters 7 and 8, there are extensive discussions about understanding the procedures and results of qualitative research. In those discussions, the issues of data collection validity and reliability are addressed.

Validity and Reliability of Authentic Assessment Instruments

Authentic, or performance-based, assessment systems are often criticized for not having rigorous measures of validity and reliability. The major criticisms of authentic assessment deal with issues of the nature of the standards against which student performance is judged (validity) and the ability of educators at different times to apply those standards uniformly (reliability). For example, some educators advocate the use of portfolio assessment, one form of authentic assessment. However, there is no consensus, at this time, as to what constitutes an appropriate portfolio: What should a portfolio contain as samples of a student's work? Who should determine what student work is placed in the portfolio? At what point in the instructional process and how frequently should materials be placed in a portfolio? and, What criteria should be used to determine the quality of a student's work?

Extensive research is being undertaken to answer these and related questions about authentic, or performance-based, assessment (Linn, 1994; Messick, 1994; Swanson, Norman, & Linn, 1995). For there to be validity and reliability in the authentic measurements, these researchers postulate that authentic assessment must be used with the following considerations:

1. Student performances or products used in an assessment should be based on the purposes of the testing, the nature of the subject area being tested, and the instructional theories about the skills and knowledge being tested.
2. Educators should indicate whether the focus of the assessment is the students' products or performances or the knowledge and skills needed to create the products or performances.
3. The selection of tasks to be assessed and the ways they are tested should reflect as much as possible actual school and life situations of the students. That is, the knowledge and performance tasks should be selected from the context of students' learning and should be given in situations that simulate real-life situations.
4. There should be clarity about the outcomes of the assessments in regard to generalizability: Is the assessment being used to generalize to the performance of individuals or large groups? Care should be taken that generalizations are related to, and do not exceed, the intended purpose of the assessment (see item no. 1 above).
5. The method of scoring students' knowledge, products, and performances should be clear, and there should be criteria for determining appropriate outcomes and consistency in the application of those criteria.

LOCATING VALIDITY AND RELIABILITY INFORMATION

Researchers do not always report the available information about instruments' validity and reliability. One reason for omitting validity and reliability information is the extensive reporting of it elsewhere. In such a case, researchers refer readers to the appropriate research report.

In the two examples that follow, the researchers use instruments whose validity information is reported elsewhere. Note that in both examples, the researchers report reliability data established in their research.

Purpose of the study: To improve understanding of the relationships between types of in-service training activities and changes in teaching behavior.

The Stallings Secondary Observation Instrument (SSOI) was used to measure teaching behavior. The validity measures obtained with this instrument in relation to student achievement and attitude has been established in previous studies (e.g., Stallings, Needels, & Stayrook, 1979). High interrater reliability (85% agreement or better) was established for the observers in this study. (Sparks, 1986, p. 218)

Purpose of the study: To investigate the planning and debugging strategies and group processes that predicted learning of computer programming in small groups with students aged 11 to 14.

Six aptitude and cognitive style measures were administered at the beginning of the workshop. These were a test of mathematical computation and reasoning; a test of verbal inference; a short form of the Raven's Progressive matrices (Raven, 1958) to measure nonverbal reasoning ability; and three tests from the Educational Testing Service (ETS) kit of cognitive factor reference tests (French, Ekstrom, & Price, 1963): Surface Development (spatial ability), Gestalt Completion (holistic vs. analytic processing), and Hidden Figures (field independence). Internal consistency alpha for these tests ranged from .64 to .92 in this sample. (Webb, Ender, & Lewis, 1986, p. 246)

Another reason for not including validity and reliability information is the instrument's extensive use in educational and psychological projects. It is assumed that its validity and reliability information is known by most of the research report's readers. This is especially true when researchers use standardized tests such as the Wechsler Intelligence Scale for Children–Revised, the Metropolitan Achievement Tests, or the Woodcock Reading Mastery Tests.

Research consumers can refer to several readily available sources to locate information about instruments' validity and reliability. When the instrument is a standardized test, research consumers can refer to the administration and technical information manuals provided by an instrument's publisher.

Research consumers may find it helpful to rely on reviews of standardized instruments. These reviews can be found in special yearbooks and handbooks, professional journals, and professional textbooks. Chapter 11, Locating Information About Research Reports, contains information about how to locate and obtain authoritative reviews about instruments' validity, reliability, and appropriateness for target populations.

SUMMARY

What are the different types of instruments used in research projects? How is information from different instruments reported?

Instruments are used to denote a broad range of specific devices and procedures for collecting, sorting, and categorizing information about subjects and research questions. Three types of instruments are used in research: tests, observations, and surveys. A standardized test is one for which the tasks and procedures of administering, recording, scoring, and interpreting are specified so that other testers can make comparable measurements in different locations. Standardized tests are of two main types: norm-referenced and criterion-referenced. Norm-referenced tests compare individuals' scores with a standardization, or norming, group. Criterion-referenced tests and various forms of authentic assessment compare students' responses to specified expected learner behaviors or to specified expected levels of performance. Test information includes scores from individual or group standardized norm-referenced tests, standardized criterion-referenced tests, competency tests, and researcher- or teacher-made tests. When collecting data from direct observation, researchers take extensive field notes or use an observation form to categorize the information. They record information on forms in response to questions about subjects' actions or categories of actions. Surveys include a broad range of devices for data collecting, such as questionnaires, individual interviews and focus groups, scales, inventories, and checklists.

What are instrument validity and reliability and how are they determined?

Validity refers to the extent that an instrument measures what it is intended to measure. Reliability refers to the extent that an instrument measures a variable consistently. When an instrument's creator demonstrates the instrument as representing a supportable educational theory, it is said to have construct validity. When an instrument's creator demonstrates the instrument as representing an accurate sampling of a specific body of knowledge, it is said to have content validity. An instrument's creator establishes content validity by submitting the instrument's items to a group of authorities in the content area. It is their expert opinions that determine whether the instrument has content validity. When the subjects' results on one instrument correlate, or result in a similar rank order of scores, with those on another instrument, the new instrument is said to have concurrent validity. A fourth validation procedure establishes the extent to which an instrument can predict a target population's performance after some future situation. This is predictive validity.

The common procedures for establishing an instrument's reliability are (a) test-retest reliability, a measure of the test's stability; (b) equivalent forms reliability; (c) internal consistency reliability; and (d) scorer or rater reliability. Test-retest reliability is determined by administering the same instrument again to the same subjects after a time period has elapsed. When the subjects' results are compared, researchers gain evidence of the instrument's reliability over time, or its stability. Equivalent forms reliability is determined by creating two forms of an instrument. The instrument should be the same in every aspect except for the specific items. The same subjects are given both forms, and their results are compared. Internal consistency reliability, which is sometimes called rationale equivalence reliability, is determined by comparing the subjects' scores on individual items to their scores on each of the other items and to their scores on the instrument as a whole. Split-half reliability, a common type of internal consistency reliability, is determined by dividing the instrument in half and comparing the subjects' results on both parts. The most common way to split a test is into odd- and even-numbered items. Scorer or rater reliability, which is sometimes called interrater or interjudge reliability, is determined by comparing the results from two or more scorers, raters, or judges. Sometimes scorer reliability is presented as a percentage of agreement and not as a coefficient.

What criteria should be used to determine whether instruments are appropriate for the research?

Research consumers should answer the following: What instruments are used in the study? Are they appropriate for the design of the study? Are the instruments valid for collecting data on the variables in the study? Are reliability estimates given for each instrument? Are researcher-made instruments included (or at least samples of the instrument items)? Are the instruments appropriate for use with the target population and the research subjects?

ACTIVITY

Read each of the following instrument sections of research reports. The researchers' purposes have been included for your information. Using the questions and criteria on page 102, evaluate the researchers' instrumentation. For each, list questions and concerns you may have about

 a. The validity of the instruments
 b. The reliability of the instruments
 c. The appropriateness of the instruments for the target population and research subjects
 d. The appropriateness of the instruments for the researcher's purposes

EXTRACT A: PARENTING AND SCHOOL ACHIEVEMENT

Purpose: An examination of the relations between parenting and the school performance of fourth- and fifth-grade children in Asian American, Latino, and European American families.

PARENT QUESTIONNAIRE

A questionnaire was adapted from previous research (Okagaki et al., 1995; Okagaki & Sternberg, 1993; Schaefer & Edgerton, 1985; Small & Luster, 1990) to assess parents' beliefs about education, school achievement, and self-reported parental behaviors. Questionnaires were translated into Spanish and then backtranslated into English by a second translator. Discrepancies were resolved through discussion. The questionnaire consisted of seven sections: (a) educational attainment, (b) grade expectations, (c) childrearing beliefs, (d) self-reported parental behaviors, (e) parental efficacy, (f) perception of child's ability, and (g) demographic information.

Educational attainment. Parents were asked to indicate (a) what the ideal amount of education they would like their child to attain would be (a single item, from 1 = complete some high school education to 6 = get a graduate or professional degree), (b) how much education they expect their child to obtain (a single item), and (c) what the very least amount of schooling they would allow their child to attain would be (a single item).

Grade expectations. Parents indicated on a 4-point scale (1 = very happy: my child did a great job; 4 = upset: I want my child to do better) how they would feel if their child hypothetically brought home certain grades (a separate item for each letter grade from A to F).

Childrearing beliefs. Three subscales were developed to assess the importance parents place on developing autonomous behaviors and attitudes in their children (8 items were adapted from Schaefer and Edgerton, 1985—e.g., How important do I think it is for my child to work through problems on his/her own? and How important do I think it is for my child to think and make decisions on his/her own?), the importance parents place on developing conformity to external standards (8 items adapted from Schaefer and Edgerton, 1985— e.g., How important do I think it is for my child to do what the teacher tells him/her to do?

and How important do I think it is for my child to respect adults and people in authority?), and the importance parents place on parental monitoring of children's activities (16 items adapted from Small and Luster, 1990—e.g., How important do I think it is for me, as a parent, to know what my child does in school? and How important do I think it is for me, as a parent, to know how my child is treated by others at school?). The interitem reliabilities for these subscales were strong (αs = ranging from .78 to .89).

Parental behaviors. The parental behaviors section was divided into two subscales. For each scale, parents indicated on a 6-point scale (0 = rarely; 6 = daily) how frequently they did a specific activity. The first scale consisted of 10 items about activities the parent does to help the child with schoolwork (e.g., How often do you remind your child to study for a test? and How often do you help your child study for a test?). The second scale was composed of eight items related to general activities parents might do with children that would encourage them to read or think about issues or would provide opportunities to observe their parents reading (e.g., How often do you read a magazine at home? and How often do you have your child read a nonschool book at home?). Interitem reliabilities for these scales were strong (both αs = .77).

Parental efficacy beliefs. Six items asked parents to rate the extent to which they agreed or disagreed with statements related to the confidence they felt about their ability to help their child succeed in school (e.g., There are times when I do not understand my child's math homework and There are times when I do not understand my child's reading homework). Items were rated on a 6-point Likert scale (0 = strongly disagree; 6 strongly agree). The interitem reliability for this scale was satisfactory (α = .72).

Perception of child's ability. Parents were presented six items related to their perception of their child's ability to do well in school (e.g., My child usually gets good grades in school and My child usually does not need help with homework). Items were rated on a 6-point Likert scale (1 = strongly disagree; 6 = strongly agree). The interitem reliability for this scale was strong (α = .81). (Okagaki & Frensch, 1998, pp. 129–130.)

EXTRACT B: UNIVERSITY AND URBAN SCHOOL COLLABORATION

Purpose: The study focused on the collaboration component, which involved preservice teachers' interaction in the preschool. The researchers specifically wanted to determine if the field placement enhanced their understanding of the emerging literacy process. In addition, they wanted to investigate the varying roles of the preservice teacher and the effect the roles had on these teachers' knowledge of preschoolers.

INSTRUMENTS

A questionnaire was given to the preservice teachers at the end of the semester to determine their perceptions of the experience. Twenty-three items were rated on the following scale:

1 not at all
2 somewhat
3 pretty much
4 a lot
5 very much

One item assessed the participants' overall enjoyment in the project (I enjoyed participating in the Long Branch preschool project during this semester.). Other more specific aspects of this collaborative venture were explored. Three questions were posed about their participation in the shared book experience (I felt that my participation in the preschool project gave me experience with the shared book reading. I enjoyed reading the children's literature that was utilized in the preschool.). Six questions focused on attitudes involving the Literacy Play Centers (Participating in the Literacy Play Centers gave me insight into the natural and pretend play of three-, four- and five-year-olds. It was a valuable experience to participate in a Literacy Play Center rather than to read about one.). Additional questions were designed to ascertain if the preservice teachers observed developing language patterns, motor skill acquisition, and early attempts at reading and writing (I felt that participating in the Long Branch project gave me a first hand glimpse at early literacy development. I felt that my participation in the preschool project gave me exposure to the developing motor skill patterns of preschoolers; cutting, pasting, coloring.).

Two open-ended questions were also posed regarding the aspects of the project that were viewed as most advantageous for their professional growth as preservice teachers. Their perceptions on the strengths and weaknesses of the preschool program were assessed as well as their comments regarding future program improvement. Open coding was utilized to analyze this data (Strauss & Corbin, 1990). The complete questionnaire appears in Appendix A. (Young & Romeo, 1999, pp. 104–105.)

FEEDBACK

EXTRACT A: PARENTING AND SCHOOL ACHIEVEMENT

The questionnaire is not a standardized instrument. However, it was used in several previously published studies so its content and construct validity have undergone scrutiny and review. The form of the questionnaire used in the present study was adapted from these earlier versions and the authors indicated how conformity in language was determined. The specific questionnaire was not included, but the content of each subsection was detailed, including examples of the specific questions. Also, for each subsection, the manner in which the parents' responses were coded was explained. The data in the subsections were quantified using a Likert-type scale.

For two sections, educational attainment, and grade expectations, the parents' responses dealt with basic demographic information and beliefs. Statistical determination of reliability was not a consideration for those sections.

In four sections, childrearing beliefs, parental behaviors, parental efficacy beliefs, and perception of child's ability, there was a need to ensure that the parents responded in a consistent manner. For those sections, then, coefficients of reliability were determined. The symbol α (the Greek letter alpha) is commonly used to show estimates of a test's reliability (see Chapter 7, Reading and Evaluating Procedure Sections, and the section of Chapter 8 entitled Statistical Significance). The researchers provided information to show the level of reliability for these sections of the questionnaire. In each case, they indicated the results for inter-item or **internal consistency reliability**.

EXTRACT B: UNIVERSITY AND URBAN SCHOOL COLLABORATION

The questionnaire is not a standardized instrument. The content of the device was explained and a copy of the full instrument was included in an appendix. Except for two open-ended questions, the responses were coded using a Likert-type scale. "Open coding," used for the last two questions, is a coding procedure used with analyzing qualitative data.

The researchers did not indicate how the construct and content validity of the instrument were established. It is up to the research consumer, then, to refer to the actual instrument and make such decisions. Also, the researchers did not indicate how reliability was established for the responses to the questions requiring a scaled response. The researcher consumer does not have assurance that the questionnaire had internal consistency and, therefore, may not be able to trust the results.

Chapter 7

Reading and Evaluating Procedure Sections

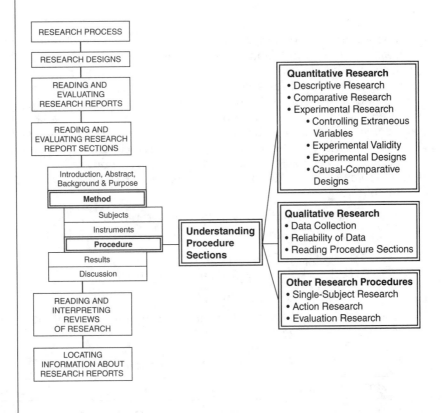

FOCUS QUESTIONS

1. What concerns should research consumers have about research procedures that are common to all research designs?
2. What concerns should research consumers have about research procedures that are specific to quantitative descriptive research designs?
3. What concerns should research consumers have about research procedures that are specific to quantitative comparative research designs?
4. What concerns should research consumers have about research procedures that are specific to experimental research designs?

5. How are extraneous variables controlled in experimental research?
6. What distinguishes simple and complex experimental research designs?
7. What concerns should research consumers have about research procedures that are specific to causal-comparative research designs?
8. What concerns should research consumers have about research procedures that are specific to qualitative research designs?
9. What concerns should research consumers have about research procedures that are specific to single-subject, action, and evaluation research designs?
10. What questions should be used to evaluate procedure sections?

Researchers explain the specific way they conducted their research in procedure sections, which are subsections of method sections in research reports. If the researchers detail their procedures completely, other researchers can replicate the study. From a clear explanation of research procedures, research consumers can evaluate whether the study is free from bias and the influence of extraneous variables. Research consumers need to understand (a) how different types of research designs are implemented as studies (see Chapter 2), (b) what information should be included in procedure sections for the different types of research, and (c) what questions are used for determining whether procedure sections are complete.

From reading a procedure section, research consumers should be able to answer the following:

What research design was used in the study?

What special procedures were used to collect data or conduct treatments?

What special materials were used?

Was the research free from researcher bias?

Can the study be replicated from the given information?

Procedure sections should be evaluated using the following questions, which are from Figure 3.1, page 61:

Evaluating Procedure Sections

METHOD SECTION

Design and Procedure in Quantitative Research. Are the research design and data collection procedures clearly described? Is the research design appropriate to the researchers' purpose? Can the study be replicated from the information provided? In experimental designs, are treatments fully explained? Are examples of special materials included?
Design and Procedure in Qualitative Research. Are research questions stated and additional questions generated? Is the method explained in detail? Has researchers' presence influenced the behavior of the subjects? Is there abundant evidence from multiple sources?

UNDERSTANDING PROCEDURE SECTIONS

Besides understanding principles of subject selection (Chapter 5) and instrumentation (Chapter 6), research consumers need to understand steps taken by research producers to collect data, devise special materials, and implement treatments.

Although there are unique procedures for some types of research, several procedures are common to all types of educational research.

First, research reports should have clear and complete explanations about every step of the research so that other researchers can replicate the study. In all types of studies, there should be clear explanations about the settings from which information is collected or in which treatments were given. Research producers should indicate not only what was done but where and when data collection or treatment procedures were carried out. Research consumers can identify vague procedure sections when there is inadequate information for answering the questions given above.

Another procedure deals with the use of instructional materials. Researchers often study how subjects react to specific materials such as textbooks, stories, maps, graphs, and charts. These may be commercially produced or specially devised by researchers for the study. Research consumers need to be able to judge the appropriateness of the materials for the research situation and for use with the target population. Therefore, researchers should provide citations of published materials and samples of unpublished, specially devised materials.

A third common procedure deals with trying out the research procedures in a pilot study. A **pilot study** is a limited research project with a few subjects that follows the original research plan in every respect. By analyzing the results, research producers can identify potential problems. In descriptive, comparative, and experimental studies, researchers can see whether the data collection instruments (questionnaires, interviews, or observations) pose any problems to the researchers or subjects. Researchers also have the opportunity to examine the need for modifying specially devised materials. Researchers should indicate that pilot studies were conducted and include information about modifications to instruments, materials, procedures, and treatments that resulted from analyses of the pilot study results.

PROCEDURES IN QUANTITATIVE RESEARCH

Descriptive Research

Quantitative **descriptive research** designs deal with statistically explaining the status or condition of one or more variables or events. Research consumers should be concerned that information is valid, objective, and reliable and that variables or events are portrayed accurately.

In observational research, researchers need to be concerned about factors that might affect the replicability of their studies (LeCompte & Goetz, 1982). They need to be sure that the data represent a true picture of what occurred and can be generalized to other situations. This refers to the **validity** of the research. Researchers also need to be sure that they are consistent in identifying aspects of a behavior or event so that others working in the same or similar situations could get similar results. This aspect pertains to the **reliability** of the research.

Several questions can help research consumers determine whether the results from quantitative observational studies are valid.

Could the researchers actually have seen what they reported observing?

Do the researchers' instruments limit or bias the type and extent of data that are collected?

Were the data collection instruments used unobtrusively?

Are their conclusions applicable to other situations and groups?

Could the observers' presence possibly have influenced the collected data (i.e., influenced the way subjects responded or events occurred)?

Could the observers have collected only unique or exotic information (data not representative of usual responses or events)?

Was there a major change in the make-up of the group being observed during the research period?

What status did the researchers seem to have in the group being studied?

Did the researchers seem to select informed subjects from whom to obtain information?

Were multiple observers used and was interrater reliability established?

The following method section is from a quantitative descriptive study.

Purpose of the study: To conduct individualized interviews with middle- and high-school students to better understand their perceptions of teachers' adaptations to meet the special learning needs of students in general education classrooms.

METHOD

Subjects

Subjects were 47 middle-school students (14 seventh graders and 33 eighth graders; 89% Hispanic, 8% Black, and 3% White non-Hispanic) and 48 high-school students (28 eleventh graders and 20 twelfth graders; 82% Hispanic, 1% Black, 16% White non-Hispanic, and 1% Asian-American or East Indian). The two schools attended by these students are located in a large city in the Southeastern United States and include a predominantly Hispanic Population. The median percentile score on the most recent administration of the *Stanford Achievement Test* reading comprehension subtest (Garner, Rudman, Karlsen, & Merwin, 1982) was 34 for the middle school and 45 for the high school.

Subject Selection

An initial subject pool of 164 included all students in target science classes who had returned parent permission slips to participate in the study. We selected a stratified sample that represented low-achieving (LA), average-achieving (AA), high-achieving (HA), students with LD, and students who spoke English as a second language (ESOL). Our goal was to obtain 10 students from each group; however, we were successful in obtaining only 7 LA from the middle school and 8 LA from the high school. In cases with more than 10 students in a stratified group, students were randomly selected from that group to participate in the interviews.

All participating students with LD met school district criteria for classification as LD: significant discrepancy between IQ and achievement test scores, evidence of a processing deficit, and exclusionary criteria to ensure the learning disability was not due to other conditions (e.g., second language learning, physical disability). ESOL students were all classified as "Independent," no longer requiring self-contained ESOL services.

For the purpose of this study, LA students were identified as those students who achieved at stanine levels of 1, 2, or 3 in reading comprehension on the most recent school district administration of the *Stanford Achievement Test*. Students in the AA group were those scoring at stanine levels of 4, 5, or 6, while students in the HA group scored at stanine levels of 7, 8, or 9.

Table 1 Sex, Ethnicity, Mean Reading and Math Stanine Scores for LD, ESOL, LA, AA, and HA Students by Grade Grouping

	Sex		Ethnicity				Reading	Math	
	Female	Male	White	Hispanic	Black	Asian	Comprehension	Comp.	Appl.
	n	n	n	n	n	n	M	M	M
LD									
Middle	5	5	0	9	1	0	1.7	1.7	3.0
High	4	6	1	9	0	0	3.1	3.5	2.9
ESOL									
Middle	5	5	0	10	0	0	4.3	5.1	4.3
High	5	5	0	9	0	1	5.8	6.6	6.7
LA									
Middle	6	1	1	4	2	0	3.0	3.7	3.6
High	4	4	1	7	0	0	2.6	3.6	3.8
AA									
Middle	6	4	0	7	3	0	4.9	5.3	5.0
High	5	5	1	9	0	0	5.4	6.2	6.7
HA									
Middle	5	5	2	8	0	0	7.6	6.7	6.4
High	8	2	2	7	0	0	7.8	7.2	6.9

Note. LD = Learning Disabled; ESOL = English as a Second Language; LA = Low Achieving; AA = Average Achieving; HA = High Achieving.

To ensure that students did not represent more than one subgroup, students who had at some point in their school careers been in self-contained ESOL classes or in programs for LD were omitted from the LA, AA, and HA subgroups. Table 1 provides information on sex, ethnicity, and achievement for all of the subgroups.

Instrument

The instrument used in this study, *The Students' Perceptions of Textbook Adaptations Interview (SPTAI)*, is an adaptation of two previously developed and evaluated instruments, *The Students' Perceptions of Teachers* (Vaughn, Schumm, Niarhos, & Daugherty, 1993) and *The Student Textbook Adaptation Evaluation Instrument* (Schumm et al., 1992).

The SPTAI consists of 11 structured questions, designed to elicit specific information, and follow-up open-ended probes, intended to encourage students to talk freely and to provide a rationale when appropriate (Bogdan & Biklen, 1998). The questions solicit students' opinions about activities, such as experiments or projects that supplement or replace textbooks; prereading activities, such as setting a purpose for reading; activities to be completed during reading, such as study guides or outlines; postreading activities, such as answering questions or writing summaries; activities that promote independent reading skills, such as teaching strategies to aid comprehension; and instructional grouping practices.

Three additional questions were included (a) to elicit information from students regarding their perceptions of the extent to which they think adaptations made for LA students who learn more slowly affected the learning of students who learn quickly; and (b) to determine if there are any other adaptations made by teachers to help students understand difficult material that they like or dislike.

Questions one through eight on the SPTAI are worded to offer students a choice between two hypothetical types of teachers, one who makes a specific adaptation and one who does not. For example, "Some teachers group students by ability levels (for example, putting kids who learn quickly together in one group, and kids who learn more slowly in another group). Some teachers group students so that ability levels are mixed. Which teacher would you prefer? Why?"

Procedures

After the SPTAI was field tested with 10 middle- and high-school students and reviewed by secondary teachers and an outside expert, the instrument was individually administered by trained interviewers. Interviews were tape-recorded, and tapes were audiochecked to ensure that responses had been accurately transcribed.

Coding Procedures

To establish codes for the interview data, two researchers independently read 20 randomly selected interviews (10 high school, 10 middle school). For each question, they searched the responses for common ideas and themes (Strauss & Corbin, 1990), which they used to develop an initial list of categories. The researchers then met to negotiate a mutual set of categories, with examples, for each question.

The two researchers used the categories to independently code the 20 previously selected interviews and then met to compare responses and revise and finalize the categories. The final coding scheme was reviewed by two independent researchers who were experienced in developing coding systems. It allowed the researchers to code each student's preference for the adaptations and his or her rationale.

Using the coding scheme, the two original researchers independently coded the transcribed responses to all the questions. Intercoder agreement was defined as the number of hits (i.e., both researchers coded the student's response in the same category) over the total number of responses. Intercoder agreement was .90. The two researchers conferred to resolve differences in coding. (Vaughn, Schumm, Klingner, & Saumell, 1995)

Comparative Research

In quantitative comparative research, researchers examine the descriptions of two or more variables so they can make decisions about their differences or relationships. Research consumers should use the questions listed for procedures in descriptive research to determine whether the results from comparative research are valid and reliable.

The following method section, which includes the subject and procedure subsections, is from a quantitative comparative study of the different perspectives parents, teachers, and children have about the children's reading difficulties.

Purpose of the study: To examine children's reading difficulties from the perspectives of the children, their parents, and their teachers.

METHOD

Participants

Forty children, their parents, and the children's teachers participated in the study. The children attended a university reading clinic at one of two sites: a midwestern university clinic, operated collaboratively with a regional children's health care facility, (Clinic #1), N = 24; and a southeastern university clinic (Clinic #2), N = 16. The children, grades 1–6 (grade 1: N = 5; grade 2: N = 13; grade 3: N = 8; grade 4: N = 9; grade 5: N = 3: grade 6: N = 2), lived in communities near the clinics. Children were referred to the clinic because of parental and teacher concerns regarding their reading progress. Only those children whose parents and teachers both returned the clinic questionnaire were included in the study. At clinic #1, the children attended either the Fall, 1987, Winter, 1988 or the Fall, 1988 clinic session. There were 16 males and 8 females. Five of the children were African-Americans, seven had repeated at least one grade, and one was receiving special education services. Their average age score on the reading subtest of the *Woodcock Johnson Psychoeducational Reading Test* (Woodcock & Johnson, 1977) was at the 21st percentile. At clinic #2, the children attended the clinic during the Fall, 1988 session. There were 7 males and 9 females. Four of the children were African-Americans, five had repeated a grade, and three received special education services. Discrepancy scores were formed by subtracting the subject's grade placement score on standardized testing (obtained from school folders) from his/her grade level. The average discrepancy was 1.7 years/months.

University students at both clinics conducted the sessions with the children as part of a course in literacy assessment and remediation. Graduate students enrolled in the Master's of Elementary Education program provided the services at clinic #2, while clinic #1 used undergraduate students in their senior year. The university students worked one-on-one with an assigned child.

Materials

Student Interview. We developed an individually administered interview adapted from one by Wixson, Bosky, Yochum, and Alvermann (1984). The interview focused on the child's perceptions of difficulties encountered while reading. After several warm-up questions about reading habits and interests (What hobbies or interests do you have that you like to read about? How often do you read in school? How often do you read at home?), the child was asked to describe any difficulties/problems that he/she had when reading (Why do you think you're here? What difficulties do you have while reading?). If a child gave general answers such as "I need to learn how to read better", or "Reading is hard," the child was asked to elaborate ("I have trouble sounding out words" or "I could read better if I could understand my science book"). The clinicians were instructed that the interview was not to be an interrogation, but rather to follow a discussion format and that probes, such as "Show me what you mean", "Tell me more about that," "Can you give me an example" were to be used to clarify responses.

Parent and Teacher Questionnaires. The first part of the parent and teacher questionnaires included open-ended questions that paralleled those which were listed on the student's. The parent and teacher were asked to list the difficulties or problems the child had when reading (What are your child's/the student's reading difficulties? Why do you feel your child needs special help with reading? What concerns, if any, do you have about this student's classroom reading performance?).

The second part of the questionnaire was designed to assess perceptions of specific reading competencies by examining perceptions of the child's performance across two task conditions—listening to a story and reading independently. These tasks were chosen because they were reading activities that might occur both within the home as well as in a school setting. Twenty-one Likert-scaled items were used. Each item had a six point rating scale, ranging from 1 (hardly ever) to 6 (almost always) as well as an "I don't know" response.

The Likert items focused on comprehension, attitude toward reading and word identification. The comprehension items rated children's text-based and inferential comprehension when listening and when reading independently. Text-based comprehension included 3 items for each task condition (When listening/reading independently, the child can: Remember the story events, identify the central problem in a story, and answer questions when the answer is stated in the story). Inferential comprehension also included 3 items for each task condition (When listening/reading independently, the child can: Identify the main idea of a story, relate story events to real life experiences, and answer questions when the answer is not directly stated in the story). Attitude was evaluated with 1 item for each task condition (the child enjoys listening to a story, and the child enjoys reading).

Word identification included: (a) 2 items that evaluated letter knowledge (knows letter sounds, and can blend letter sounds together), (b) 3 items that evaluated word based strategies (uses letter sounds to identify an unknown word, tries to sound out words, and uses familiar chunks of an unknown word to figure it out), and (c) 2 items that evaluated meaning based strategies (will self-correct errors made when reading aloud, and uses the meaning of the story to figure out unknown words).

Data Collection and Analysis.   The university students, who were trained in appropriate procedures as part of their course work, interviewed each child individually during the first clinic session. The interview took approximately 10-20 minutes. Statements were transcribed verbatim from the interview. Parents completed the questionnaire prior to their child receiving remedial services. Parents were also given a similar questionnaire for their child's teacher to complete and return.

Open-Ended Responses.   The open-ended questions focused on the types of difficulties students experienced while reading. They were coded according to broad categories that emerged after several readings of the student, parent, and teacher responses. The following categories were identified: (a) Word identification—difficulties related to phonics, word identification, fluency and reading aloud, (b) comprehension—difficulties related to word meaning, understanding and remembering information, (c) attitude/behavior towards reading—difficulties related to a dislike or avoidance of reading and/or behavioral problems related to school reading tasks, (d) other (e.g., mention of visual or speech problems), and (e) don't know. Agreement between the two authors was greater than 90% with disagreements resolved through discussion. Children stated fewer problems than did their parents and teachers, and their responses had less elaboration. Responses to the open-ended questions were analyzed using descriptive statistics due to the small number of responses in some cells and because the categories were not discrete as some respondents mentioned more than one problem. The names of the children used in this article are fictitious.

Closed-Ended Responses.   Parents' and teachers' responses to the Likert-scaled items were used to examine the children's comprehension and attitude when listening and when reading independently, as well as word identification strategies. Within the comprehension and word recognition categories, a single value was obtained by averaging across each item's scores. Thus we compared individual scores based on the average rating for all items within the category. (Yochum & Miller, 1993)

Experimental Research

In experimental research, researchers set out to answer questions about causation (Gall, Gall, & Borg, 1999; Gay & Airasian, 2000; Kerlinger, 1973). They wish to attribute any change in one variable to the effect or influence of one or more other variables. The influencing variable—the one that researchers expect to cause change in subjects' responses—is called the **independent variable.** The variable researchers try to change is called the **dependent variable.** Research consumers should be concerned about whether variables other than the independent variables influenced the observed changes in the dependent variable. To have confidence in a study's results, research consumers need to understand (a) how researchers control possible influences of variables other than those under systematic study and (b) how research producers design studies to ensure the validity of their results.

Controlling Extraneous Variables. Variables that might have an unwanted influence on, or might change, dependent variables are called **extraneous variables.** Researchers can restrict the influence of extraneous variables by controlling subject variables and situational variables. **Subject variables** are variables on which humans are naturally different and that might influence their responses in regard to the dependent variable. **Situational variables** are variables related to the experimental condition (i.e., variables outside the subjects) that might cause changes in their responses relating to the dependent variable.

For example, in a study investigating how the learning of syntactic context clues affects students' vocabulary acquisition in science, variables that might influence the results are students' general learning ability (IQ), their reading abilities, and their prior knowledge of the science topic. In this example, researchers can control the possible influence of subject and situational variables by selecting subjects of the same general learning ability and reading ability and by selecting a science topic and materials unfamiliar to all subjects. Another way researchers can account for the influence of these variables is by including them as independent variables. They can do this (a) by selecting students of different general learning and reading abilities and measuring the difference between and among the ability levels or (b) by testing subjects' knowledge of the topic before the treatment and adjusting the after-treatment results to account for their prior knowledge. Obviously, researchers can only use as independent variables those variables that (a) they are aware of and (b) they think might influence the dependent variable.

Probably, randomization is the best way to control subject variables because it accounts for all subject variables, even those not known or suspected by the researchers to influence the dependent variable. Chapter 5 contains a detailed explanation and specific examples of randomization.

Other attempts at controlling extraneous subject variables include creating groups that are homogeneous on one or more variables and the matching of subjects on several variables. These procedures, however, do not ensure that other (and possibly influencing) variables have an equally distributed effect on all groups. When subjects cannot be randomly selected or assigned to groups, researchers can equate them statistically. The procedure known as analysis of covariance (ANCOVA) is used to equate subjects on selected variables when known differences exist. The differences, as measured by pretests, must be related to the dependent variables. (ANCOVA is explained further in Chapter 8, Reading and Interpreting Results Sections.) In the example above, differences in subjects' prior knowledge of a science topic could be used to adjust posttest outcomes statistically.

Experimental Validity. Extraneous variables can invalidate the results of experimental studies in two ways (Campbell & Stanley, 1971; Gay & Airasian, 2000). The first occurs when researchers and consumers cannot attribute their results exclusively to the independent variable(s). The second source of invalidity occurs when the results cannot be used with other subjects and in other educational settings.

When researchers lack assurance that changes to dependent variables can be attributed to independent variables, we say the research lacks **internal validity.** Several factors can affect the internal validity of research. These include the following:

Current Events. Current events include any historical occurrence during the experimental period. For example, a joint U.S. and Russian spacelab project during a study about changing students' attitudes toward science careers might influence the study's outcome. Research consumers may not be aware of the coincidence of such an event during the study, but research producers should strive to be, and they should report it.

Subject Growth and Development.   Subject growth and development includes the physical, emotional, and cognitive maturational changes occurring in subjects and the periodic fluctuations that occur in human responses because of fatigue, boredom, hunger, illness, or excitement. For example, in a study about the influence of daily periods of silent reading on subjects' overall reading performance, changes in reading performance might occur because the subjects matured even without the special reading periods.

Subject Selection.   Subject selection refers to the influence that improper or biased subject selection has on results. This phenomenon is discussed above and in Chapter 5.

Attrition.   Attrition refers to the loss of subjects during experimental research. The reason for subject loss may be important and may unduly influence the results. For example, in a study about the effects on subjects with differing ethnic backgrounds of using calculators for learning of arithmetic number concepts, a major loss of subjects from any group might influence the results. A loss, say, from an ethnic group with a school dropout rate known to be high may result in a small sample with low achievement scores and an erroneous conclusion that individuals from that group do not benefit from using calculators. When attrition occurs, researchers need to determine why the loss occurred.

Testing.   In this context, testing refers to the possible positive and negative influences of pretests on results. For example, subjects' final test scores might be improved because they learned something from taking a pretest. Or, an initial interview might give subjects an inkling about what researchers are studying, thereby influencing their performance on subsequent tasks.

Instrumentation.   In this context, instrumentation refers to the influence of unreliable instruments on results. This phenomenon is discussed extensively in Chapter 6.

Statistical Regression.   **Statistical regression** refers to the tendency of extreme high and low standardized test scores to regress, or move, toward the group mean. That is, very high and very low subjects' scores on pretests seem to come closer to middle scores on posttests—higher scores become lower and lower scores become higher. Research consumers need to understand that this phenomenon may occur "when, in fact, no real change has taken place in the dependent variable" (Kerlinger, 1973, p. 320).

Interaction.   Interaction refers to the effect of several factors on each other. For example, attrition might result because of testing (subjects become threatened by the information they are asked on a pretest), or current events may influence certain subjects because of selection bias (subjects have an advantage because they experienced some event).

   When researchers lack assurance that results can be generalized to other persons and other educational settings, we say the research lacks **external validity.** Several factors can affect the external validity of research. These include the following:

Subject-Treatment Interaction.   Subject-treatment interaction occurs when subjects do not represent a target population and selection procedures produce a sample that is either positively or negatively biased toward a treatment. For example, when researchers use paid subjects, these individuals may undertake the activities solely for the money involved. Volunteer subjects, on the other hand, may have certain personal characteristics (which influence them to be volunteers) that are not present in the target population.

Reactive Effects. Reactive effects refer to special situations that make subjects in a treatment group feel special. One reactive effect occurs when they know they are part of an experiment, or they sense that something special is happening to them. This phenomenon is called the Hawthorne Effect. Another reactive effect occurs when subjects in a comparison or control group know or sense they are in competition with the treatment group, and they produce results above their normal behavior. This phenomenon is called the John Henry Effect, after the legendary railroad builder.

Multiple-Treatment Interaction. This phenomenon might occur when researchers include more than one treatment in a study. For example, in a study to determine which study skills program might be more effective, subjects are given three content-area study strategies: the SQRRR, ReQuest, and Overview methods. If each subject receives instruction about all three, the learning of one might help or hinder the learning of the others. In this case, the order in which subjects learned the strategies might influence the results.

Researcher Effects. Research or experimenter effects refer to the influences imposed on treatments by researchers themselves. For example, when researchers use an experimental instructional program that they developed, they may exert undue (although not conscious) influence on the subjects to use the program successfully. Also, instructional techniques may be complex, and only those with the researchers' knowledge and dedication could effectively implement them.

Research producers cannot control for the effect of all possible extraneous variables. If they were to do this, much research would be difficult, if not impossible, to undertake. So, researchers do two things. They limit or manipulate pertinent factors affecting their studies' validity, and they identify as possible influences other factors that were not controllable or could not be manipulated. Research consumers need to judge whether researchers have missed or underestimated factors that might affect research validity. To do this, research consumers need to understand the experimental designs researchers use to reduce possible effects of extraneous variables.

Experimental Designs. Experimental designs are the blueprints that researchers use in making decisions about the causative effect of one or more variables on other variables. The plans provide researchers with structures for studying one or more independent variables with one or more groups of subjects. Researchers select designs that best fit their purposes, answer questions about causation, and efficiently control extraneous variables.

In studying educational and psychological research, some authorities divide experimental designs into several groups, such as "true experimental," "quasi-experimental," "preexperimental," and "action" research (Gall, Gall, & Borg, 1999; Campbell & Stanley, 1971; Gay & Airasian, 2000; Wiersma, 1995). The criterion for inclusion, or exclusion, from a group is the strictness with which a design controls

| Randomized group 1 (experimental group) | | |
| Pretest | Treatment | Posttest |

| Randomized group 2 (control or comparison groups) | | |
| Pretest | Alternate treatment(s) | Posttest |

| Randomized group *n* (other control or comparison groups) | | |
| Pretest | Alternate treatment(s) | Posttest |

Figure 7.1
Pretest-Posttest Control Group Design

for the effect of extraneous variables. The continuum goes from "true experimental," representing the strictest control, to "action," representing the least strict control. Other authorities consider all designs used to answer questions of causation as experimental (Kamil, Langer, & Shanahan, 1985). These researchers do not identify designs by the above criteria but by other factors. The factors are (a) the number of independent or treatment variables and (b) the extent to which results can be generalized from the immediate subjects to a larger target population.

In the discussion here, experimental designs will be presented as a continuum from simple to complex plans. Simple experimental plans deal with a single independent variable, and complex experimental plans deal with multiple independent variables. In reading and evaluating both sets of plans, research consumers are concerned with the question "How generalizable are the results from the research subjects to other individuals and groups?"

Simple experimental designs deal with one independent variable or have subject selection procedures that limit the generalizability of their results. In Chapter 2, single-variable studies were shown to provide limited insight about educational questions. In Chapter 5, subject selection techniques that produced samples unrepresentative of target populations were discussed. Simple designs are presented here so research consumers can recognize them and understand their limitations.

In some simple experimental designs, two or more groups of subjects are studied with a single independent variable. Subjects are randomly selected and randomly assigned to a group, but each group differs in the experimental condition. An experimental condition refers to how the independent variable is manipulated, varied, or subcategorized. When treatments are involved, one or more groups are randomly designated as treatments or **experimental groups** and the other(s) as **control** (or comparison) **group(s).** In educational and psychological research, a control group is one that has received alternative activities, not the one(s) under study. All groups are given the same pretest and posttest (survey, observation, or test). This simple experimental design is called the **pretest-posttest control group design.**

This simple experimental design is shown diagrammatically in Figure 7.1.

The following method section from a research report includes the subject (sample) and procedure subsections. It is taken from a pretest-posttest control group design that has a single independent variable. The independent variable is an instructional method (IML), so it is called the treatment. Note that there are three dependent variables, but the researchers are trying to determine whether the change in each is attributable to the single independent variable.

Purpose of the study: To assess the effects of learning strategies instruction on the completion of job applications by students identified as learning disabled.

Table 1 Subject Description

	Learning Strategy Instruction (*n* = 16)	Traditional Instruction (*n* = 17)
Gender		
Male	10	10
Female	6	7
Age		
Mean	15.9	16.3
Range	14.5–17.3	14.3–17.5
Race		
White	15	17
African American	1	0
Grade level		
12th	2	3
11th	6	7
10th	6	5
9th	2	2
Years in special education		
Mean	5.9	5.3
Range	4–8	4–9
Percentage of day in special education		
Mode	.50	.50
Range	33–83	33–83
Intelligence[a]		
Mean	98.5	96.2
Range	88–106	84–105
Reading comprehension[b]		
Mean *T*	35.1	33.4
Range	22–43	25–41

[a] Stanford-Binet Intelligence Scale. [b] Iowa Test of Basic Skills.

METHOD

Subjects

Thirty-three students (20 boys and 13 girls) with LD served as participants in the study. All were receiving special education services in a public high school in a city in the Northwest (population 180,000) and were classified as learning disabled by a school district multidisciplinary evaluation team. Criteria for special education classification include deficits in oral expression (as measured by the Northwestern Syntax Screening Test), listening comprehension (as measured by the Carrow Test for Auditory Comprehension of Language), and/or written expression (as measured by the Comprehensive Tests of Basic Skills). Criteria also included a significant discrepancy (at least 2 years below grade placement) between the student's estimated ability and academic performance.

Students were generally from low-SES families (qualified for free and reduced lunch). Table 1 provides additional descriptions of the participants' sex, age, race, grade level, years in special education, percentage of each school day spent in special education, IQ, and achievement.

Setting

All participants were enrolled in a pre-vocational education class for students with learning disabilities. The class was taught by a certificated special education teacher with 6 years of teaching experience at the high school level. The classroom aide was a high school graduate with 8 years of classroom assistance experience. The teacher conducted the experimental sessions during two 60-minute instructional periods. The classroom was approximately 10 m by 15 m and had 25 individual desks at which the participating students sat during the experimental sessions.

Dependent Measures

Student Performance Measures. Three mutually exclusive measures were employed to assess the effects of the learning strategy instruction on the completion of job applications by students: information omissions, information location errors, and a holistic rating of overall neatness of the job application. An omission was scored when a required item was not completed. A location error was scored when the correct information was entered in the wrong location (e.g., writing the information on the line directly below where the information was to be placed). A 5-point Likert-type scale (1 = *very messy* to 5 = *very neat*) was used to obtain a holistic rating of the overall neatness of the job application.

Interscorer agreement for omissions and location errors was determined by having two scorers independently score all of the job applications. The scorers' records were compared item by item. For omissions, agreement was noted when both scorers had marked a response as not present. Similarly, an agreement was noted when both the scorers marked the location of the information as correct or if both scorers had marked the location of the information as incorrect. Percentage of agreement for each measure was computed by dividing the number of agreements by the number of agreements plus disagreements. The percentage of agreement was 100% in both cases.

Interscorer agreement was computed for the holistic rating by having two raters independently rate all of the job applications. A Pearson product moment correlation was then calculated to estimate the reliability of the ratings. The correlation was .78, $p < .05$.

Social Validity Measure. To assess the social validity of the effects of the training, the supervisor of classified personnel at a local university employing approximately 1,200 classified staff was asked the following: "Based on this job application, if you had a position open, would you invite this person in for an interview?" The rating was completed on a 5-point Likert-type scale (1 = *very unlikely*, 3 = *undecided*, 5 = *very likely*). The supervisor rated each application and was unaware of whether it was completed under the learning strategy or traditional instruction condition.

Design

A pretest-posttest control group design was employed. Students were randomly assigned by age and gender to one of two experimental conditions: learning strategy instruction or traditional instruction. This resulted in 16 students (10 boys and 6 girls) being assigned under the learning strategy instruction condition and 17 students (10 boys and 7 girls) under the traditional instruction condition. The results of a preliminary analysis revealed that there were statistically nonsignificant differences in characteristics (i.e., intelligence, achievement, age, years in special education, and percentage of each school day spent in special education) between the two groups.

Procedure

Job Applications. Job applications for entry-level jobs were obtained from eight local businesses. Two of these job applications were selected for the pretest and posttest; two additional applications were used to conduct the training sessions (demonstration and independent practice). Although these job applications were designed to elicit the same general information, the format (e.g., sequence of information and location cues) differed. The same pretest, posttest, and training job applications were used under the learning strategy instruction and traditional instruction conditions.

Preskill Instructional Module.   Students under both conditions (described below) received a prepared instructional module designed to provide the relevant prerequisite vocabulary knowledge necessary to complete a job application. This instruction was conducted, and job application information collected (discussed below), prior to pretesting. The teacher presented the prerequisite vocabulary knowledge module, using a written script, to students under both conditions. The prerequisite information included definitions for the following job application vocabulary words: (a) *birth place*, (b) *nationality*, (c) *previous work experience*, (d) *references*, (e) *maiden name*, (f) *marital status*, (g) *citizenship*, (h) *salary*, and (i) *wage*. Instruction continued until all of the students earned 100% correct on a paper-and-pencil test in which the words were matched with their respective definitions.

Students under both experimental conditions also compiled the information necessary for them to complete a job application, including (a) birth date, (b) social security number, (c) complete address, (d) telephone number, (e) educational experience, (f) previous work experience, (g) references, and (h) felony convictions (if applicable). Students then constructed a job application information card containing this information.

Students under both experimental conditions then completed the pretest job application. The teacher asked them to complete the job application as if they were applying for an actual job. She also explained that typically no one is available to help people complete job applications, and they were to use their job information card for the task. Students were provided as much time as they needed to complete the application. The teacher did not provide the students any assistance during this time. The pretest session was conducted 1 day prior to the training and posttest sessions.

Learning Strategy Instruction Condition.   The job application learning strategy taught in this investigation was designed after analyzing the nature of items included on standard job applications for entry-level jobs obtained from a number of local businesses, and after completing a task analysis of the steps involved in completing a job application. The strategy was also designed in accordance with the needs and skill levels of the students. The principle steps were then sequenced and a first-letter mnemonic device was developed to facilitate students' recall of the strategy steps. This resulted in a six-step strategy called "SELECT."

Students first *S*urvey the entire job application and look for the *E*mphasized words that indicate the type of information requested (e.g., previous experience) and think to themselves, "What information do I have to have to complete the job application?" and "Do I have all of the necessary information to complete the application (check job application information card)?" If not, "What additional information do I need to get?" The students then look closely at the items on the job application for *L*ocation cues that indicate where the requested information is to be entered (e.g., line immediately below the request for information) and think to themselves, "Where does the information go?" Next, they think to themselves, "How much space do I need for the information—How big should I print the information?" and then carefully *E*nter the information requested in the appropriate location. After completing the application, the students then *C*heck to see if the information is accurate (compare with job information card) and that the job application is completed, and think to themselves, "Did I put the right information in the right locations?" If not, "I need to complete another job application." Then, "Did I complete the job application?" If not, "Complete the job application." Finally, the students *T*urn the completed job application into the appropriate individual.

The special education teacher used a five-step procedure to teach the students the job application strategy during an approximately 1-hour instructional session. First, the teacher discussed the goal of the job application strategy instruction procedure (i.e., to help students accurately complete a job application) and why it is important to know how to accurately complete a job application. She also explained how they would be able to use the strategy whenever they applied for a job.

Second, an overhead transparency was used to introduce and discuss the six-step job application strategy. The teacher and students discussed the use of the strategy until it was clear that the students fully understood the steps. This was accomplished through choral responding by the students and informal checks by the teacher.

Third, using an overhead transparency, the teacher modeled the job application strategy by completing a standard job application while "thinking out loud." To actively engage the students, the teacher used prompts to encourage an interactive dialogue with the students throughout the demonstration, for example, "What is it I have to do? I need to . . . " and "How am I doing?" The students were encouraged to help the teacher. After modeling, the teacher and students discussed the importance of using self-questioning statements while completing a job application.

Fourth, students were required to verbally practice the job application strategy steps, including the self-questioning statements, until they were memorized. All of the students were able to do this correctly within a 15- to 20-minute rehearsal period. They were then required to write down the steps and associated self-questioning statements as they worked through a job application. Students were provided only one practice attempt. They were allowed to ask any questions at this time and the teacher provided corrective feedback only upon demand by the students throughout the training session.

Finally, students independently completed the posttest job application. As under the pretest condition, the teacher asked the students to complete the job application as if they were applying for an actual job. She also explained to the students that because there typically is no one there to help them complete job applications, they were to use only their job information card to complete the job application, and that they had as much time as they needed to complete the application. The teacher did not provide the students any assistance during this time. After they completed the posttest job application, the students were asked to independently describe the steps they had used, in an attempt to check whether they had employed the learning strategy. All of the students verbally stated, in sequence, the steps and associated self-questioning statements included in the learning strategy.

Traditional Instruction Condition.   The same job application forms used under the learning strategy condition were used for the traditional instruction condition. During an approximately 1-hour instructional session, the special education teacher (same teacher) first discussed the goal of the job application instruction (i.e., to help students accurately complete a job application) and why it is important to know how to accurately complete a job application. She also explained how they would be able to use the things they learned whenever they applied for a job.

Next, the teacher used an overhead transparency to model how to complete a standard job application. Throughout the demonstration, the teacher explained why it was important to accurately complete job applications and instructed the students to be careful to complete all of the information and to be sure that they put the information in the correct place. To actively engage the students, the teacher used prompts throughout the demonstration, such as "What is it I have to do? I need to . . . " and "How am I doing?" The students were encouraged to help the teacher complete the job application. Students were then required to practice completing a job application. They were allowed only one practice attempt, and they were allowed to ask any questions during this time. The teacher provided corrective feedback only upon request throughout the session.

Finally, the students independently completed the posttest job application. The teacher did not provide the students any assistance during this time. Once again, these conditions (job application, instructions, and amount of time) were the same as those employed under the pretest and learning strategy instruction conditions.

Fidelity of Implementation. Fidelity of implementation was assessed under both experimental conditions by observing the teacher on the day of instruction to ensure that she followed the teaching steps associated with each of the experimental conditions. The primary researcher used a checklist to track whether the teacher fully completed the teaching functions described above under each condition.

From: Nelson, J.R., Smith, D.J., & Dodd, J.M. (1994). The effects of learning strategy instruction on the completion of job applications by students with learning disabilities. *Journal of Learning Disabilities* 27:104–110. Copyright © 1994 by PRO-ED, Inc. Reprinted with permission.

There are some other less-used simple experimental designs. One is the **posttest-only control group design,** in which the experimental and control groups are not pretested. An example of this design is an instance in which researchers have two or more randomized groups engaged in alternative activities, but they do not give a pretest. The groups are assumed to be similar because of randomization, but the differences in group results are determined only by the posttest. This procedure's weakness is that there is no assurance that the groups were equal at the start on the dependent measure (such as a reading test). Also, researchers cannot account for the effect of any subject attrition in each group.

A second simple design is the **nonequivalent control group design.** In it, the groups are not randomly selected or assigned, and no effort is made to equate them statistically. Obviously, when comparison groups are known to be unequal, the research results can occur from many possible causes. A third simple design is the **matched groups design.** In it, the experimental and control subjects are selected or assigned to groups on the basis of a single-subject variable, such as reading ability, grade level, ethnicity, or special disabling condition. A major limitation of this design is the possibility that one or more variables, unknown to and unaccounted for by the researchers, might influence the dependent variable.

For all simple experimental designs, extraneous variables affect the internal and external validity of the research. Research consumers should be wary of generalizing the results of simple design research to other educational settings and populations.

More complex experimental designs deal with multiple experimental and subject variables. Some complex designs are built on the pretest-posttest control group design and are expansions of it. In these complex designs, researchers not only study the effect of one variable on one or more other variables, they study the interaction of these variables on the dependent variable. Above, *subject-treatment interaction* and *multiple-treatment interaction* were noted as threats to research validity. Nevertheless, researchers can use complex designs to account for the effect of these interactions.

Not all complex designs use random selection or assignment of subjects. When randomization is not used, statistical procedures are used to account for the possible influence of the differences between and among subjects. Chapter 8 contains a discussion of these statistical procedures.

Two important threats to research validity are *subject growth and development* and *testing*. They can be accounted for in a design called the **Solomon four-group design.** Using random selection and random assignment, four groups are formed. All four groups are posttested. However, only two groups are pretested. One pretested group and one nonpretested group are then given the experimental condition.

Randomized group 1		
Pretest	Experimental condition	Posttest
Randomized group 2		
Pretest	Alternate condition	Posttest
Randomized group 3		
	Experimental condition	Posttest
Randomized group 4		
	Alternate condition	Posttest

Figure 7.2
Solomon Four-Group Experimental Design

The Solomon four-group experimental design is shown diagrammatically in Figure 7.2.

In addition to the effect of the experimental variable, the possible effects of pretesting can be measured by comparing the posttest results of groups 1 and 3 to groups 2 and 4. If the pretest had an effect, the results of groups 1 and 2 would be higher respectively than those of groups 3 and 4. The possible effect of subjects' growth and development and current events has been controlled because both would have an equal effect on all groups.

The Solomon four-group experimental design is not often used in educational and psychological research, however, because of several limitations. The first limitation is that a large number of subjects is required. In a study employing one independent variable with no factors, approximately 100 subjects (four groups of 25 subjects) would be needed. Each additional independent variable requires another 100 subjects. Therefore, researchers use other experimental designs to control for the effect of pretesting and subjects' growth and development.

Another complex design built on the pretest-posttest control group design is called the **counterbalanced design.** In counterbalanced designs, two or more groups get the same treatments; however, the order of the treatments for each group is different and is usually randomly determined. For this type of design to work, the number of treatments and groups must match. Although the groups may be randomly selected and assigned, researchers often use this design with already existing groups of subjects—for example, when they use all classes in a grade level. A major problem with this design is the possibility of multiple-treatment interaction. Research consumers need to determine that the individual treatments are unique and that one treatment could not directly increase or decrease the effectiveness of another. Figure 7.3 shows the counterbalanced design for a three-treatment, three-group design.

Educational and psychological researchers are often concerned about questions involving multiple variables. Although the Solomon four-group design accounts for the possible influence of some extraneous variables, its use does not allow researchers to easily study two or more independent variables. In the example diagram in Figure 7.2, one independent variable is used with two subcategories: exper-

Group 1	Group 2 (randomized or unrandomized) Pretest (all groups)	Group 3
Treatment C	Treatment B Interim Test 1 (all groups)	Treatment A
Treatment B	Treatment A Interim Test 2 (all groups)	Treatment C
Treatment A	Treatment C Posttest (all groups)	Treatment B

Figure 7.3
Counterbalanced Experimental Design

imental condition and alternate condition. This could represent an experimental science program versus the previously used science program. Many questions are left unanswered in this design. For example, "Does the experimental science program or the existing program produce greater learning with girls?" "With students with learning disabilities?" or "Does the experimental science program lead to greater learning after shorter periods of instruction?" These are questions of interaction. Questions about the interaction of human variables and instructional and environmental situations are important to educators. Teaching and learning involve the interplay of many variables, and they do not occur in isolation.

Questions of interaction are examined in complex experimental designs called **factorial designs,** in which there are multiple variables and each is subcategorized into two or more levels, or factors. The simplest factorial design involves two independent variables, each of which has two factors. This is called a 2 × 2 factorial design. Factorial designs can have any combination of variables and factors. The practical consideration for research producers is having an adequate number of subjects in each subdivision. Generally, 15 subjects per group is considered the minimum, although group size in factorial designs can be as small as 5 subjects.

Figure 7.4 contains examples of three common factorial designs. Notice how the number of groups increases as independent variables and factors increase. Although multivariable designs can provide educators with valuable insights about teaching and learning, research consumers should be wary of research studies containing what seem to be unnecessary factors. When there are too many possible interactions (because there are many groups), the meaning of the interactions could become confusing. Research consumers need to consider whether the number of variables and factors is appropriate. As a general rule, factorial designs in experimental research larger than 2 × 2 × 2 become unwieldy.

The following method section includes subsections of subjects, materials, and procedure. The study is an example of a 2 × 4 × 2 factorial design. The independent variables and their factors are gender (male or female), grade level (3–6), and treatment (experimental or control).

Purpose of the study: To determine the effects of a flexibly paced math program on student achievement.

**2 × 2 Factorial Design
(four groups)**

		VARIABLE 1	
		F1a	F1b
Variable A	FAa		
	FAb		

Example variables:
Variable 1: Student learning ability   Variable A: Science program
  F1a = Has learning disability   FAa = Experimental program
  F1b = Has no learning disability   FAb = Previous program
One example condition: F1a, FAa = Students with learning disabilities using the experimental science program.

**2 × 3 Factorial Design
(six groups)**

		VARIABLE 1		
		F1a	F1b	F1c
Variable A	FAa			
	FAb			

Example variables:
Variable 1: Content-area study technique   Variable A: Gender
  F1a = Summary writing   FAa = Male
  F1b = Questions placed in text   FAb = Female
  F1c = Advance organizer
One example condition: F1a, FAa = Males using the summary writing content-area study technique.

**2 × 2 × 2 Factorial Design
(eight groups)**

		VARIABLE 1			
		F1a		F1b	
		VARIABLE 2			
		F2a	F2b	F2a	F2b
Variable A	FAa				
	FAb				

Example variables:
Variable 1: School grade   Variable 2: Textbook style   Variable A: Reading ability
  F1a = Third grade   F2a = Original textbook   FAa = Above average
  F1b = Sixth grade   F2b = Revised readability textbook FAb = Below average
One example condition: F1a, F2a, FAa = Above-average reading-ability third-grade subjects using the original textbook.

Figure 7.4
Common Factorial Designs

METHOD

Subjects

The participants were 306 students who completed at least one year of a flexibly paced mathematics course at the Johns Hopkins Center for Talented Youth (CTY) between 1985 and 1990. Slightly more than two-thirds of the students were male ($n = 203$). Their grade levels ranged from third to sixth, with the majority from fourth (30%) and fifth (33%) grades. Students qualified for programs through a two-tiered screening process.

The Flexibility Paced Mathematics Course

The major goal of the course was to teach specific mathematics content (arithmetic, pre-algebra, and beginning algebra topics) at a level matched to students' academic abilities and prior knowledge. Students attended 3-hour classes on the weekend for 7 months while concurrently enrolled in their schools. Not only were in-class requirements demanding, an additional 2 to 3 hours a week were required for homework assignments. Class time included a variety of formats: individual work, small-group work, and small-group and whole-class lectures and explanations.

Instructors coordinated the introduction of new material to individual students or small groups and encouraged them to explore a variety of problem-solving strategies (Cauley, 1991; Kamii & Joseph, 1988; Ross, 1989). Small-group collaborations provided an opportunity for students to conceptualize and communicate their ideas. Instructors and their assistants were available for guidance, modeling new skills when appropriate. With artful questioning about facts and strategies, instructors facilitated students' acquisition of new concepts and skills. The instructional approaches and settings used in the course were completely consistent with the Professional Standards advocated by the National Council of Teachers of Mathematics (see CTY, 1992a; NCTM, 1989).

Although the course was unique in many ways, content was not a distinguishing characteristic. The arithmetic curriculum included whole numbers, basic operations, fractions, decimals, percents, ratios, proportion, and measurement. The prealgebra curriculum included geometrical topics, statistics, probability, exponents, integers, variables, and simple linear equations and graphs. The algebra curriculum included beginning algebra topics, such as linear equations, inequalities, polynomials, factoring, and quadratic equations. The commercially available texts used for the course were supplemented by an in-house volume of math exercises, problem-solving activities, and other resources (for a full discussion of the course content, instructional methods, and typical classroom activities, see CTY, 1992a). Again, the character of this course is not a function of any unique content, but rather of the underlying philosophy of flexibility and individualization.

Four characteristics do distinguish the course. First, the curriculum is presented in a linear progression. Students study a topic thoroughly, demonstrate mastery, and then move on. This is in direct contrast with most elementary school mathematics programs that require students to revisit topics year after year. Second, the curriculum is flexibly paced. Instructional pacing is dependent on a student's performance in class and on a variety of standardized and teacher-made assessments. Third, no age or grade-level restrictions are imposed on a student's placement. Instructional placement is determined by the student's entering achievement level. Finally, no arbitrary restrictions are placed on the rate or the range of student progress (e.g., a fourth grader might complete all of the arithmetic sequence and move into the prealgebra curriculum within the 7-month period of the course).

Procedure

At the beginning of the math course, students were given an above-level form of the mathematics subtest from the Sequential Tests of Educational Progress (STEP), a nationally normed and standardized achievement test battery developed by the Educational Testing Service (1971). The intermediate level of the STEP, normed on sixth- through ninth-grade students, was given to students in the third through fifth grades. The advanced level, designed for ninth- through twelfth-grade students, was given to students in the sixth grade. An alternative form of the STEP was administered as a posttest either at the end of the academic year or when a student completed the arithmetic and prealgebra curriculum. (With flexible pacing, completion of a particular math sequence could take from 1 to 7 or more months, depending on a student's initial placement and subsequent pace of learning.) Results from the above-level form of the STEP, using corresponding above-level norms, were used for all pre- and postcomparisons reported in this paper.

In addition to their use for documenting the achievement growth reported in this paper, results from the STEP pretest were also used to help determine a student's initial placement in the class and to establish individualized instructional goals. Through the use of STEP scores and an analysis of a student's errors on the test, instructors were able to identify concepts and skills that a student had already learned and determine topics to be taught. This diagnostic-testing-prescriptive-instruction (DT-PI) approach has been found to be useful in matching students' needs to instruction and thus avoiding unnecessary repetition of already learned material (Durden, Mills, & Barnett, 1990; Lupkowski, Assouline, & Stanley, 1990; Stanley, 1978).

After initial placement, subsequent instruction was based on each student's performance in class and on homework, quizzes, and chapter and cumulative tests. Although students were allowed to move at a flexible, individually appropriate pace with no arbitrary restrictions on how much material they could cover, they were not permitted to move on to beginning algebra until they could demonstrate mastery of the arithmetic/prealgebra topics. "Content mastery" was operationally defined as 90% correct on all teacher-made instruments and chapter tests, as well as a score at or above the 90th percentile on the above-level STEP achievement test, using norms three grade levels above the student's current grade.

Once mastery of the arithmetic and prealgebra content was documented, a student progressed on to beginning algebra topics. Certification of mastery of beginning algebra was defined as a score at the 90th percentile using eight-grade norms on the Cooperative Mathematics Test (COOP), a nationally normed test developed and standardized by the Educational Testing Service (1964). In addition, students had to achieve a standard of 90% correct on all teacher-made assessments. (Mills, Ablard, & Gustin, 1994)

Causal-Comparative Designs.   Causal-comparative experimental research is ex post facto, or after-the-fact, research. Researchers use it in trying to establish one or more causal effects between or among existing conditions. The researchers want answers to questions but they cannot manipulate the independent variable(s) for practical or ethical reasons. They realize a condition exists and are unsure about what might have been its cause. Causal-comparative designs are built on the posttest-only control group design.

A major concern for researchers doing causal-comparative research is that the causal effect should be one-way. The distinguishing variables must precede and be the cause of the differences. For example, Chapter 2 presents a representative causal-comparative study about the effect of black students' figurative language on their school language. The existence of out-of-school language experiences preceded their school language experiences; thus, the causal effect can be only one-way.

In using the causal-comparative design, researchers can randomly select subjects from target populations that differ in respect to one or more variables. Since there are no manipulated, or treated, independent variables, the subjects cannot be randomly *assigned* to groups. The subjects should be similar except for the variables being studied. For example, selection procedures can ensure that subjects are similar in such characteristics as age, socioeconomic status, or intellectual ability, so long as these are not variables that might cause the difference between groups. If it is not possible to select comparable groups, the differences between them can be equated statistically.

For research consumers to generalize the results from causal-comparative studies to other populations and educational situations, they need to be sure that any differences between groups cannot be attributed to one or more important variables that were not accounted for by the researchers. There is always the possibility that these outside variables may be the true causes of the observed differences. Also, they should be sure that researchers' description of the subjects is clear and that operational definitions are used to identify and distinguish the comparison groups. Therefore, research consumers should cautiously interpret the results of causal-comparative research, and they should expect researchers to follow up their tentative results with additional experimental research.

The following method section of a research report contains an example of a causal-comparative design. The researchers sought to determine the effect of a preexisting condition (amount of previous mathematics instruction) on mathematics achievement. It should be remembered that researchers using the causal-comparative design are trying to find causal relationships or predictions.

> *Purpose of the study: To examine the teaching strategies used by mothers of sons with learning disabilities and normally achieving sons.*

METHOD

Subjects

The subjects were 30 boys with learning disabilities (LD), 30 boys without any reported learning problems (NLD), and their mothers. The boys were 8 to 11 years of age, and they were matched for age (LD group: $M = 9.7$ years, $SD = 11.74$ months; NLD group: $M = 9.4$ years, $SD = 7.23$ months). The mean age of the mothers was 37 years. The boys attended second through fourth grade and were drawn from schools in the province of Central Finland; all spoke Finnish as their native language. The control group consisted of boys who, according to their teacher's report, did not manifest learning problems and had not received remedial teaching. Children in both groups were individually administered the Raven Coloured Progressive Matrices (Raven, 1956) (LD group: $M = 25.83$, $SD = 4.09$; NLD group: $M = 31.60$, $SD = 3.08$) and a shortened, 30-item version of the Peabody Picture Vocabulary Test (PPVT) (Dunn & Dunn, 1981) (LD group: $M = 21.93$, $SD = 3.87$; NLD group: $M = 24.90$, $SD = 2.55$). The groups were matched for father's and mother's socioeconomic status. Parental SES was representative of the distribution in the Finnish population.

Children in the LD group had received remedial teaching in addition to regular class instruction before their referral to a clinic specializing in the neuropsychological assessment of learning disabilities (Niilo Mäki Institute, University of Jyväskylä). The goal of the assessment was to provide guidelines for more carefully focused remediation efforts. The very thorough neuropsychological assessment consisted of sensory-perceptual, motor, language, memory, and problem-solving tests (Närhi & Ahonen, 1992). Our definition of learning disability follows that presented by the National Joint Committee on Learning Disabilities (Hammill, Leigh, McNutt, & Larsen, 1981). Each subject was administered the Wechsler Intelligence Scale for Children-Revised (WISC-R) (Wechsler, 1974). Only children who had normal IQ (WISC-R total IQ above 80) and whose learning problems met the diagnostic criteria were included in the LD group.

Most of the children ($n = 27$) manifested language-based learning disabilities. Their difficulties in reading, spelling, or language were identified by teachers and confirmed by achievement testing using local norms for reading (videotaped reading of words, nonwords, and text passages at least 1.5 standard deviations below the age norms) and spelling. Language difficulties were confirmed by the following neuropsychological tests: the Token (DeRenzi & Faglioni, 1978); the PPVT; the Boston Naming Test (Kaplan, Goodglass, & Weintraub, 1983); and rapid naming tests (Denckla & Rudel, 1974; Wolf, 1986). A smaller number of children ($n = 3$) manifested primarily nonverbal learning disabilities, that is, major difficulties in arithmetic or writing. Children who were diagnosed to have primary emotional problems or who had neurological diseases or sensory impairment that may have caused the learning problems were excluded from the LD group.

Procedure

The interactions of the mother-child dyads were videotaped in a laboratory setting while the dyads worked on four structured, interactive tasks. The main focus of this article concerns the teaching task, which was designed to contain features typical of a homework assignment. In the task, the mother and her son sat at a table next to each other. The mother was asked to teach her son a set of five pseudowords and the meanings that were attached to them. The pseudowords were phonologically acceptable letter strings in Finnish, and were easily pronounced. The mother was requested to take the teacher's role, and she was encouraged to do her best in assisting her son in memorizing the new words. The experimenter reminded the pair of the similarity of the situation to times when the child is at home, learning words of a foreign language as homework. They were told that they had 10 minutes to practice the new words. The material consisted of five text cards (with the pseudoword and the object name that it corresponded to in Finnish), picture cards depicting the same objects, and paper and pens. The recordings took place in the video facility in the Department of Psychology, and an S-VHS camera was used, which was situated at 1.5 meters in front of the seated dyad.

Measures

  Maternal Teaching.   Two coders who were blind with respect to the child's group status (LD/NLD) were trained to code the data. Maternal strategies during the teaching session were coded directly from the videotapes by recording percentages of time used for each of the following mutually exclusive categories.

  1. *Looking at the picture card.* Mother asked the child to compare the word and picture cards;
  2. *Repetition of the words.* Mother asked the child to repeat the pseudowords and their Finnish equivalents several times;
  3. *Recognition.* The mother produced the pseudoword and quizzed the child on its Finnish equivalent;
  4. *Production.* The child produced the pseudoword equivalent as a response to the Finnish word presented by the mother;
  5. *Writing.* Mother asked the child to write the pseudowords and their Finnish equivalents on paper;
  6. *Drawing.* Mother asked the child to draw pictures of the pseudowords to aid in memorizing.
  7. *Seeking associative connections.* Mother and child sought associations between the pseudowords and their Finnish equivalents;
  8. *Narrative construction.* Mother and child constructed a narrative that bound the separate pseudowords;
  9. *Word application.* Mother and child attached the pseudowords to a personally motivated context by giving them meanings from the child's own environment;
  10. *Playing a game.* Mother and child constructed a game and played it using their own rules with the available materials.

These 10 teaching strategies used by the mothers can be divided into two main categories, following an adaptation from the criteria set by Sigel (1982) for different levels of distancing strategies. A distinction was made between perceptually based strategies, which relied on information from the ongoing present, and nonperceptually based, or conceptual, strategies, which evoked mental representations of the words to be learned. The first five strategies were considered to represent low- and medium-level distancing as they referred to the present and were based mainly on rote learning. These strategies did not include negotiations between the partners. The last five strategies were considered to include higher cognitive demands. They provided associative connections and representative images for the child that helped him separate the self mentally from the ongoing present. With high-level strategies, the mothers constructed a personally motivated, meaningful context for learning the test words.

The coding consisted of recording the time that the mother used in each of the teaching strategy classes specified above. Percentages were formed by proportioning these times with the total duration of the task. Coding was done using a hand-held data collector that records data elements in terms of frequency and time duration. Total time used in the task and the amount of speech produced by the mother and child during the task were also recorded from the tapes. A measure of the child's performance on the task was reached by summing the number of the words he learned correctly.

*Mother–Child Interactions.*The quality of each mother-child interaction was rated on a Likert-type (5-point) scale. The following variables were used to characterize the behaviors of both mothers and children:

1. *Motivation in the task* indicated how involved both partners were in the task. Motivation was coded separately for mother and child.
2. *Emotionally* referred to the affective tone of the interchange. The atmosphere could vary from negative, nonchalant feelings, to positive, warm feelings expressed toward the partner. This variable was coded separately for mother and child.
3. *Cooperation* indicated each partner's participation in the activity. This variable was coded separately for mother and child. Extent of cooperation varied from acting alone to highest mutual involvement, in which the initiatives of the other partner were taken into consideration and the subjects appeared to strive for a mutual solution of the task.
4. *Dominance* referred to the mother's tendency to control the situation (e.g., objecting to the child's initiatives, presenting demands) and guide it toward the direction of her own wishes. This variable was coded only for mothers.
5. *Initiative* was coded only for the child and it varied from no initiatives by the child or his complete dependence on the mother's suggestions, to the child having lots of ideas and proposals for the solution of the task.
6. *Smiles* were recorded for a 5-minute sample for the mother and child separately.

Interobserver reliability was assessed on 25% of the data by having two assistants independently code the same randomly selected cases. The mean correlation between the ratings of the coders was 0.89 for low- and medium-level strategies and 0.91 for high-level strategies. The correlation for mother interaction ratings was 0.79 and for those of the children was 0.75.

PROCEDURES IN QUALITATIVE RESEARCH

In Chapter 2, the basic nature, types, and characteristics of qualitative research were presented. Chapter 6 contains a discussion of the main instrument for qualitative data collection—the researcher. The discussion here focuses on the specific activities qualitative researchers engage in to record their data. Basically, the data-gathering activities are observing people and events, interviewing people, and examining documents (Wolcott, 1992).

Data Collection

Data in qualitative studies are collected in particular contexts, that is, educational and related settings. The act of collecting contextualized data is commonly called **field-work.** Why a particular site was selected and how permission was obtained for researchers to access the site are important issues. Before entering the site, researchers need to answer questions relating to "What will be done at the site?" and "How will the researcher keep from disrupting the normal routine at the site?"

Researchers need to determine where on the continuum of being a participant/nonparticipant observer they will be. Sometimes this decision is determined by constraints within the fieldwork site, sometimes by the researchers themselves (Bogdan & Biklen, 1998; Maxwell, 1998). They need to determine whether they will act like a teacher or do what the children are doing. Their relationship to students might be influenced by factors such as gender, age, personality, and the way they are perceived by students and teachers under observation. Researchers need to be discreet while being efficient recorders of data. For example, if they openly take notes during class time, students may become curious about what is being written. In the illustrative qualitative research study given in Chapter 2, the researcher took his field notes under the guise of taking class notes.

The question of duration and frequency of observations is critical (Bogdan & Biklen, 1998; Spindler & Spindler, 1992). Valuable qualitative data cannot be obtained without rapport between the subjects and researchers, so there need to be preliminary visits so all participants are comfortable. Researchers want to collect as much information as possible, and that takes time. If they are concerned about the influence of direct note-taking during observations, then they should not observe longer than their memory span. And, they must spend sufficient time at the site so they see events and relationships happening repeatedly.

To ensure representativeness of the collected data, qualitative researchers often use a purposeful sampling technique (Creswell, 1998; Gay & Airasian, 2000; Maxwell, 1998), in which they deliberately select particular settings, persons, and events for the important information they provide. The selection can be (a) *random* when the sample is large, (b) *stratified* when the sample consists of subgroups, (c) *typical* when a normal situation is to be shown, or (d) *extreme* when differences from the typical are to be shown.

While observing people and events, researchers create **field notes.** These notes are written descriptions of people, objects, places, events, activities, and conversations. These notes supplement information from official documents and interviews. An important part of these notes is the researchers' reactions, reflections, and tentative assumptions or hypotheses. Field notes can have two basic aspects, descriptive and reflective (Bogdan & Biklen, 1998). The descriptive aspect might include (a) verbal portraits of individuals, (b) reconstructions of dialogues between the researchers and others, (c) complete descriptions of physical settings, (d) accounts of particular events—who was involved, how, and what was done, (e) details about activities, and (f) the researchers' (observers') behavior. The reflective aspect of field notes might include (a) speculations about the data analysis—emerging themes and patterns,

(b) comments on the research method—accomplishments, problems, and decisions, (c) records of ethical dilemmas and conflicts, (d) analysis of the researchers' frames of mind, and (e) points of clarification.

In recent years, the concept of field notes has been expanded to include the use of photographic and audio and video recording equipment. This can be used to provide records of the physical layout of the setting, artifacts, or details that would be difficult to document verbally. However, use of that equipment can be unproductive if it creates distractions among the subjects.

Field notes are not objective data in the strictest sense of the term; their form and content fully reveal that qualitative research is a subjective process. However, subjectivity should not be considered an undesirable or negative matter. Currently, there is a shift in thinking about the concept and definitions of subjectivity (Jansen & Peshkin, 1992). It no longer is thought of as distortion or bias, but as a unique, useful, personal quality of research. "When subjectivity is seen as distortion and bias, the [research] literature offers more or less prescriptive advice; when seen as an interactional quality, we learn about personal or reflexive, or political and theoretical stands" (p. 682).

Interviewing in qualitative research is used to obtain data in the subjects' own words. The purpose is to gather information from which insights on how the subjects interpret the situation being observed can be obtained (Bogdan & Biklen, 1998; Eisner, 1991). How interviews are conducted and the type of data gathered often depend upon whether the researcher is fulfilling a participant or nonparticipant role. In the latter case, the nature of the data is partly determined by the trust the subject has in the interviewer. In qualitative research, researchers generally use open-ended, informal interview techniques. They do not use fixed-response questionnaires or surveys to guide the talks. They encourage the subjects to talk about their perceptions about what is happening, what they believe about the event, and how they are feeling. Most important, qualitative researchers need to be good listeners. During interviews, researchers may use audio or video recorders and later transcribe the dialogues for analysis.

Another source of data is documents and artifacts (Bogdan & Biklen, 1998; Eisner, 1991). These include materials produced by the subjects (e.g., samples from students' writing portfolios), students' and teachers' personal documents (diaries or letters), school records (memoranda, students' files, minutes of school board meetings, or newsletters), school memorabilia (newspapers, yearbooks, or scrapbooks), and documents and photographs from school and historical society archives. In certain situations, qualitative researchers may include official statistics as data. Such quantitative data can be useful for examining who collected the information and how and why it has been quantified. Quantitative data are not always objective; that is, data are often collected and quantified for social or political reasons, and, as will be explained further in the section "Data Analysis in Qualitative Research" in Chapter 8, there are inherent errors in all statistical analyses.

Reliability of Data

A concern of all researchers, quantitative and qualitative, is the representativeness of the collected data. In Chapter 6, the reliability and validity of instruments was discussed. In qualitative research, since the major instrument is the researcher, it is difficult to establish reliability of the observer. However, the reliability of researchers' data can be ensured through appropriate research procedures in which researchers fully explain their procedures, verify their observations, and cross-check their sources (Bogdan & Biklen, 1998; Creswell, 1998; Eisner, 1991; Hillocks, 1992; Marshall & Rossman, 1995; Pitman & Maxwell, 1992).

Qualitative researchers expect that different researchers will collect different information. In part, that results from different theoretical perspectives and beliefs about the nature and goals of qualitative research (see Chapter 2). Because qualitative researchers' backgrounds and interests may differ, they may collect different information and arrive at different interpretations. However, in all cases, the reliability of the information collected can be seen as a "fit between what they record as data and what actually occurs in the setting under study" (Bogdan & Biklen, 1998, p. 48).

The issue of consistency is also related to the possible replication of a study. Even though qualitative researchers are not usually concerned with replicating a study in the strict sense of the term because of the belief that "the real world changes" (Marshall & Rossman, 1995, p. 146), there are procedures they can follow to ensure the trustworthiness of their data. They can keep thorough notes and records of their activities, and they can keep their data in a well-organized and retrievable form.

Research consumers should look for the following specific evidence of data reliability (Marshall & Rossman, 1995):

1. The researchers' method is detailed so its adequacy and logic can be determined, and there is an abundance of evidence.
2. The researchers provide evidence of their qualifications as participant observers.
3. The researchers' assumptions are clear.
4. The researchers' questions are stated, and the study seeks to answer those questions and generate further questions.
5. The researchers used preliminary days of the study to generate a focus for the study.
6. The researchers were present in the research context for an adequate period of time, and the researchers observed a full range of activities over a full cycle of those activities.
7. The data were collected from multiple sources.
8. The researchers saved their data for reanalysis.

Reading Qualitative Research Procedure Sections

The following method section is from a qualitative descriptive study. Note that the subjects subsection has also been included. In the procedures section, the researcher has provided information about the classroom instructional activity and data collection and analysis procedures.

Purpose of the study: To determine how frequently, when, and for what reasons a group of second-grade writers used their peers' questions to revise their unfinished pieces.

METHOD

Subjects

The study's site was a heterogeneously grouped second-grade classroom of a cooperative teacher in Delaware who was implementing the process approach to teaching writing as described by Graves (1983). Twenty-four students participated in the study, 16 girls and eight boys.

None of the children had participated in a process-oriented writing program previous to this academic year. All had been participating in such a program for three months when this investigation began.

Procedures

[Class activity]
The writing program was implemented two days per week for approximately one hour each session. Data were collected over 25 writing sessions between January and early June, 1985.

Consistent with Graves' recommendations, each writing session began with a mini-lesson, which was followed by the writing workshop, which was followed by a sharing session. The questions raised by peers during these group conferences and the revisions made by these young writers in their texts following the sharing sessions were the focus of this investigation.

During each sharing time, the children were divided randomly into three groups. Those children who wished to share an unfinished draft brought it to the group conference. Approximately one to three children shared their drafts during each sharing session in each small group. While children who had not shared recently were encouraged to share their draft, they were never required to receive their peers' questions.

During the sharing sessions, the writers sat in the author's chair, read their pieces, and called upon their peers for questions about the content of the piece. An adult in each group recorded the peers' questions. At the conclusion of each child's reading of his/her piece and receiving the peers' questions, the adult asked the writer what he/she planned to do next and how he/she planned to do it. At the end of the sharing time, the child attached the shared questions to the draft and returned both papers to his/her writing folder.

[Data collection]
Prior to the next writing session, both papers were photocopied. This photocopy of the draft provided evidence of the text as it existed prior to the insertion of any of the information identified as missing by the peers' questions.

At the conclusion of the following writing session, the previously shared draft was photocopied a second time. This second photocopy provided evidence of the state of the text after the child had one writing workshop to insert the missing information.

Once every two weeks all folders were examined for evidence of the continuation of writing on a previously shared topic. Discovered drafts were photocopied.

[Data Analysis]
To determine how frequently the questions raised were used by these young writers, each question was compared against each appropriate text, by the researcher and a second rater, independently, to determine whether or not the child modified the text in the way suggested by his/her peers' questions. The two raters agreed on all but four revisions. These inconsistencies were discussed until agreement was reached.

To determine how the decision to publish a piece (Hubbard, 1985, had suggested that publishing provides children with a sense of audience and a reason for refining their work) affected the frequency of use of the peers' questions, the number of revisions made as a result of peers' questions in eventually published pieces was compared to the number of such revisions in never-published pieces.

To determine why these writers chose to use only some of the peers' questions, during May each child was questioned at the close of the writing workshop following his/her sharing to determine which peers' questions, if any, were used to revise the piece. If the child had not used all the questions, he/she was asked why he/she had decided not to use some questions. (Vukelich, 1986, pp. 300–301. Reprinted by permission of the National Reading Conference and C. Vukelich)

The next method section is from the qualitative portion of a study that combined qualitative and quantitative research procedures. The subjects section has been included. In the procedures section, the researchers have provided information about the type of data they collected and the specific fieldwork procedures they used.

Purpose of the qualitative portion of the study: To study language arts instruction as it naturally occurred and to categorize the classrooms along a continuum that was based on the teachers' emphasis given to writing extended passages.

SAMPLE

The study was conducted in a large urban school district in the Western United States, which was selected for its racial diversity and considerable variation from school to school in language arts instruction. At the time of the study, 37% of the students in the district were Mexican American; 32% were White, 29% were African American and 2% were Asian American and Native American. Only elementary schools with between 30% and 80% enrollment of Hispanic and African American students and with more than 20% of the students participating in the federal free lunch program were included in the target population. We stratified schools meeting these criteria into categories of either meaning-based or skills-based instruction on the basis of the perceptions expressed in interviews by school district administrators from divisions of instruction, special programs, and student assessment to ensure variation in instructional approach. We randomly selected six schools described by administrators as meaning based or whole language, expecting to find considerable variation among the classrooms in this category, and we selected four schools identified as skills-oriented schools.

Thirty-nine teachers of Grades 4 and 5 in selected schools participated in the study. There were 15 fourth-grade, 14 fifth-grade, and 10 fourth and fifth combined classrooms. Ten of these classrooms were designated as bilingual classrooms by the district, which meant that Spanish was the language used by the teacher to varying degrees during the day. Data were obtained from 931 students; 71% of them were of ethnic minorities (46% Mexican American, 19% African American, 4% Asian, 2% Native American). The selected classrooms ranged from 23% to 100% minority enrollment. Students participating in special programs providing additional instruction in writing were included only if the instruction was provided in the regular classroom where it could be observed.

* * * * *

Data about classroom literacy instruction in each of the 39 classrooms selected for the study were gathered from two major sources: (a) classroom observation of each teacher's reading and writing instruction and (b) interviews with teachers and principals about reading and writing instruction. In addition, we collected samples of student work to augment our observations. Following the advice of Brophy (1990, p. IX16), we used a naturalistic, narrative observational approach rather than a structured coding format, so that we could attend to the sequential flow of classroom events and the purpose and context of student activities. Each researcher received 4 hr of initial training, which consisted of discussion of the focus of observation, video training, and review of exemplary field notes from a pilot observation.

A common set of elements was attended to in all observations. These included (a) the purpose, content, and flow of activities, including the instructions from the teacher that initiated the activity, the roles of the students and the teacher during the activity, and products resulting from the activity; (b) the classroom structure and grouping; (c) the content of the direct instruction; (d) the nature of text written by students, and (e) the level of engagement. Several studies have confirmed the importance of student engagement in tasks as a precondition for learning (e.g., Brophy & Good, 1986; Fisher et al., 1981). We made periodic sweeps of the classroom at 10-min intervals, during which we recorded the number of students engaged in the task designated by the teacher and the number of students not engaged in the task.

In the fall semester of the school year, times designated for reading and writing instruction were observed twice in each classroom by a single observer. All observations took place in mid-October and in the first 3 weeks of November on days mutually agreed on by the teacher and the observer to ensure that writing instruction would occur without interruption by field trips or special programs. Observations averaged 2.24 hr per session. Twenty classrooms (those with high levels of student engagement in tasks) were observed at least twice more in the spring. A total of 285 hr were spent in observation, an average of 7.3 hr per teacher in 3.3 observations. By the close of the school year, field notes that were based on 127 observations had been collected from the 39 classrooms. This amount of time spent in observation compares favorably with other large-scale studies of classrooms (e.g., Durkin, 1979; Wendler, Samuels, & Moore, 1989).

Observers took continuous narrative field notes and in some cases audio tape-recorded the instruction. One classroom was videotaped on several occasions; the teacher and the observer agreed that the students did not behave noticeably differently when the class was videotaped. In addition, the researchers collected representative samples of children's work from the instructional periods that were observed and conducted mini-interviews with teachers, in which the observers asked the teachers about such things as deviations from the general schedule of reading and writing instruction, the activities that had preceded the observation, and the activities planned for the remainder of the week.

One-hour interviews were conducted in the spring of the school year with the teachers and their respective principals. Interview questions focused on demographic information and extensive descriptions of reading and writing instruction, including the teacher's philosophy and goals for language arts instruction, the frequency and types of writing activities assigned in and outside of class, the use of the textbook (if applicable), the integration of writing into other parts of the curriculum, and the process by which written products were produced and assessed (i.e., use of techniques such as individual conferencing, revising, and sharing with peers). Interviews were audio tape-recorded and transcribed for analysis.

From: Davis, A., Clark, M.A., & Rhodes, L.K. (1994). Extended text and the writing proficiency of students in urban elementary schools. *Journal of Educational Psychology* 86(4):556–566. Copyright © 1994 by the American Psychological Association. Reprinted with permission.

OTHER RESEARCH PROCEDURES

Single-subject research, action research, and evaluation research are other ways researchers describe, compare, and draw causative conclusions about educational problems and questions.

Single-Subject Research

Single-subject research is any research in which there is only one subject or one group that is treated as a single entity (e.g., when an entire school is studied without regard to individual students' performances). Single-subject research may be descriptive or experimental. **Case study** is a form of single-subject research. Case studies are undertaken on the premise that someone who is typical of a target population can be located and studied. In case studies, the individual's (a) history within an educational setting can be traced, (b) growth pattern(s) over time can be shown, (c) functioning in one or more situations can be examined, and (d) response(s) to one or more treatments can be measured.

Many insights gained from single-subject and case study research have greatly influenced educational and psychological practice. Classic examples of single-subject

Pretest-Posttest Two-Treatment
   A–B Design
      Pretest
         Treatment A
            Posttest 1
               Treatment B
                  Posttest 2

Pretest-Posttest Counterbalanced Two-Treatment
   A–B–A Design
      Pretest
         Treatment A
            Posttest 1
               Treatment B
                  Posttest 2
                     Treatment A
                        Posttest 3

A–B–A–B Design
   Pretest
      Treatment A
         Posttest 1
            Treatment B
               Posttest 2
                  Treatment A
                     Posttest 3
                        Treatment B
                           Posttest 4

Figure 7.5
Single-Subject Experimental Designs

and case study research that have produced significant hypotheses are those of Jean Piaget and Sigmund Freud. Case study research often follows qualitative research procedures, and it can often be combined with single-subject research (Bisesi & Raphael, 1995). Single-subject experimental designs are variations of pretest-posttest counterbalanced designs. The basic aim of single-subject experimental research is to "establish the effects of an intervention (i.e., an independent variable) on a single individual" (McCormick, 1995, p. 1). Figure 7.5 shows three forms of single-subject experimental designs. In single-subject research, the pretest is called a **baseline measure** and can sometimes take the form of several measurements. Also, each posttest can consist of several measurements because they become the baseline for subsequent treatments. Baselines are the results to which posttest results are compared to determine the effect of each treatment.

Because of the unique relationship that can develop between researcher and subject and because of the possible effect of multiple testing and treatment, single-subject research can have its external and internal validity threatened in several ways. Single-subject research and case study research should have clear, precise descriptions of the subject. This is most important. The results of research with a single subject are not directly generalizable to a target population without replications with other individuals or without follow-up descriptive, comparative, or experimental research with larger samples. The threats to the internal validity of single-subject research include testing, instrumentation, subject-treatment interaction, reactive effects, and research effects. Research consumers should anticipate that research producers will follow the same guidelines as would be used for conducting descriptive and experimental research.

The following method section is from research done with a single subject in a pretest-posttest two-treatment design (referred to as an A–B design in Figure 7.5). The subsections have clarifying headings.

Purpose of the study: To determine the effects of a peer-tutoring procedure on the spelling behavior of a mainstreamed elementary-school student with a learning disability.

METHOD

Subjects and Setting

The subject (tutee) was an 11-year-old learning disabled male student in a regular grade six classroom in a large urban school. Scores on the *Wide Range Achievement Test* (Jastak, Bijou, & Jastak, 1965) ranged from 2.2 to 2.4 grade equivalents for spelling and reading. The subject (S–A) demonstrated a four-year deficiency in at least two academic areas. Subject A had spent five years in and out of special education classes before he was mainstreamed at the request of his mother. Teacher reports indicated that the subject should be academically able to perform well in a lower level spelling group.

The tutor (S–B) was a male student from the same classroom as the above-mentioned subject. He was 11 years old and excelled in all academic areas. Results on the *Wide Range Achievement Test* and *Wechsler Intelligence Scale for Children—Revised* (Wechsler, 1974) indicated superior achievement and intelligence. However, the tutor did not participate in any extracurricular activities and tended to interact with few students.

The classroom was self-contained, equipped with the usual facilities, with 27 students and one certified teacher. The spelling class was divided into two groups according to achievement. Tutoring sessions occurred at a worktable in a corner of the classroom.

Response Definition

The following two dependent variables were employed in the study.

Percent Correct. Data were collected from biweekly spelling tests. The words for the spelling test were obtained from *Basic Goals in Spelling* (Kottmeyer & Claus, 1976). A response was defined as correct if it matched the spelling in the word list. The percent correct was calculated by dividing the number of correct responses by the total number of possible words for each test.

Clinical Significance. During the experimental condition the two subjects were requested to write self-reports. They were asked to indicate whether they liked the program, worked harder in it, and/or performed better than in the regular classroom lesson. In addition, the subjects rated how well they felt they were learning by marking two pluses (++) for very good, one plus (+) for satisfactory (same as in the regular class), and one minus (−) for unsatisfactory. Subjects entered their opinions in small notebooks at the end of each week.

Design Elements and Experimental Conditions

An AB design was employed to examine the effects of peer tutoring (Hersen & Barlow, 1976). A description of the experimental condition follows.

Baseline. During the baseline condition, students were given spelling tests at the middle and end of the week. The tests were corrected upon completion and feedback was communicated in the form of percent correct. This procedure was in effect for two weeks for Subject A. The same procedure was applied to Subject B in order for the experimenter to monitor whether the experimental treatment had any effect on his spelling behavior.

Peer Tutoring.   In this condition, the tutee met with the peer tutor for 15 minutes each day during the regular spelling time. The peer tutor was instructed for two days using a modeling method. The experimenter presented the teaching procedure and the peer tutor was encouraged to emulate it. On the third day, the peer tutor conducted the entire session under the guidance of the experimenter. The tutor represented a good example of academic behavior, and it was anticipated that the tutee would model his behavior. The tutor presented a list of 10 words taken from *Basic Goals in Spelling (Level 5),* which coincided with the lessons of the lower spelling group. The first two word lists were taken from the lesson currently under study in the class. The third word list consisted of difficult words from the previous spelling lesson. The tutor read the words aloud, then asked the tutee to read the word list after which he orally spelled the words. Flashcards and games were used to enhance the teaching process. If the tutee experienced difficulties with a word or words, he was requested to write them out 10 times. The tutor was encouraged to offer assistance, helpful hints, and praise. On Wednesday and Friday the tutor dictated 20 words from the word lists. He checked the completed tests against his word list and tabulated the results before handing back the papers to the tutees. Difficulties and mistakes were discussed at this time. The condition was in effect for five weeks for Subject A.

Reliability

Reliability of measurement as to the percent correct on the spelling tests was assessed biweekly by having the experimenter check the tests prior to having either the peer tutor or the classroom teacher mark them. A third individual who was unaware of the experimental outcomes checked all test papers. An agreement was defined as all graders scoring a word as spelled either correctly or incorrectly. A disagreement was defined as any grader failing to score a word in the same manner as the other two. Intergrader reliability for percent correct was 96.4 percent.

Reliability of measurement as to the use of the peer-tutoring procedure was checked twice during the intervention by the principal and another classroom teacher. Reliability of measurement as to the implementation of the treatment was 100 percent. (Mandoli, Mandoli, & McLaughlin, 1982, pp. 186–187)

Action Research

Action research is quantitative or qualitative research in which results and implications are not generalized beyond the study's specific subjects and educational setting. It is the type of research that exemplifies the work done by teachers-as-researchers (see the section "Teachers as Researchers" in Chapter 1). Action researchers seek answers or solutions to specific questions or problems. Their goal is to create immediate change. Action researchers can use both quantitative and qualitative research methods and either single-subject or case study research.

For quantitative method studies, researchers use the same general plans and procedures as used in more controlled research. However, there are differences in how they select and assign subjects. Also, they do not apply strict procedures to control for the possible influence of extraneous variables. They do identify a problem area and seek out what others have done, create operational definitions, select appropriate instruments, identify possible influencing variables and factors, select appropriate designs for collecting data, and analyze data either qualitatively or quantitatively. Most often, action researchers use convenience samples. Since students are usually assigned to classes before the research begins, random selection and assignment are not possible. Experimental action research is usually done with a simple design such as a pretest-posttest control group(s) design with one or two independent and dependent variables. If the groups are known to differ on important variables, the groups can be equated statistically.

Qualitative educational action research is the collecting of information in order to understand what is happening in particular educational settings; it is an attempt to go beneath the surface to reveal the possible reasons for the situations. As with quantitative action research, qualitative action research begins with a sense that something needs attention and possible change.

Even though action research has only local generalizability, this form of research can be relevant to research consumers. If there are similarities in subject variables, educational setting, or treatment(s), research consumers may wish to replicate the study in searching for answers to their own educational questions. Therefore, research consumers should expect published action research reports to have the same specificity in detail as other research reports.

Action research, especially qualitative action research as described above, is often used in researcher/classroom teacher collaborative projects. When classroom teachers act as teacher researchers, they usually undertake action research.

The following section reports the procedures from a qualitative teacher-as-researcher case study approach. The background portion is included because procedural information is included there. Note that in keeping with the purposes of action research, the researcher focuses on the solving of local instructional problems.

> *Purpose of the study: To determine how the teacher could facilitate students' engagement in literature and critical thinking, and, how students' writing reflects their engagement and thinking.*

After years of watching disheartened as my students' eyes glazed over in English class, I decided I needed to do something dramatic to bring classic American literature to life for them. These young adults could not easily relate to Hester Prynne and Arthur Dimmesdale's guilt in *The Scarlet Letter;* they could not identify with Edwards' methods of persuasion in "Sinners in the Hands of an Angry God"; and *The Autobiography of Benjamin Franklin* seemed to them self-serving and meaningless for today's high-tech, fast-paced world. How could I bridge the gap of time and culture? How could I help my students realize that some of the problems these writers tackle are universal and timeless? How could I help them see that literature and the history it reflects are cyclic and that the solutions to the problems we face today may be available to us in the literature of our ancestors?

At the same time I was puzzling over this problem, I discovered Atwell's *In the Middle* (1987b). Atwell's book opened up for me the idea of student ownership of exploration and learning. Her simple system of providing books, choices, time, and opportunities for response made it possible for her students to become personally involved in literature. I began to mull over how to take her ideas and combine them with the essentials of my district's American literature curriculum. Nothing came into focus for me, but I became convinced that I could not go back to directing study questions and handing down assignments. I was miserable with that approach.

Then I read Fulwiler's *The Journal Book* (1987), and something clicked. Through journals or response logs, my students could track their journeys through literature. I went to our school library to search out contemporary novels that matched by genre or theme the classics in the district's curriculum. The students could choose from among these novels and, I hoped, they would make connections between them and the assigned texts. Personal responses could be made in journals or discussions.

The next item on my agenda was to organize how I would bring students together to discuss, question, and argue about the issues raised in both the contemporary and the classic works. Again Atwell offered a suggestion. In "Building a Dining Room Table" (Atwell,

1987a), she describes how she, her husband, and a few friends gather around her dining room table to discuss books. How could I create a similar atmosphere in my classroom? How could I get students to discuss, care, and become involved?

Class discussions in the past had often been dominated by one or two people who had actually done their homework and were outgoing enough—or who felt sorry enough for me—to risk speaking up. I knew this needed to change. A colleague shared with me *Using Discussion to Promote Reading Comprehension* (Alvermann, Dillon, & O'Brien, 1987). The authors define discussion as differing from simple recitation in three significant ways: (1) participants in a discussion must present multiple points of view and be willing to change their minds; (2) they must interact with one another; and (3) discussions must be more substantive than the typical two- or three-word recitation. I decided to bring discussion into my classroom in the form of a "reading round table." At the outset, to keep discussion alive and interesting, I would give points for questioning, answering, defending, and extending.

I took all these elements—student choice of contemporary literature, assigned classics of American literature, response journals, and seminar-type discussion—and combined them into a program that I hoped would help students connect with literature in a personal way and would lead to an increased level of analytic thinking. Two research questions evolved: (1) How can I facilitate students' engagement in literature and their development of critical thinking? and (2) How does students' writing reflect their engagement and critical thinking?

METHODOLOGY

As my research progressed, I decided to organize my description of it around two case studies. This chapter is the result. Bissex (1990) defines case study as "a reflective story of the unfolding, over time, of a series of events involving particular individuals. . . . The researcher includes . . . intentions and meanings in the meaning she makes of the story and, as interpreter if not also actor, is herself a character in it" (p. 20). That is what I have tried to communicate through these case studies.

The first case study, which focuses on my first research question, describes my own interactions with 120 students in grade 11 in a large suburban high school through one unit of study during the 1989–90 school year. The data sources were my students' response journals and essays, and my evaluations of them at the close of each instructional unit. The student journals included comments from me, which I wrote regularly—sometimes daily, but most often weekly. I also kept records of my observations, particularly observations of students' participation in discussions.

The second case study attempts to address my second research question by presenting Erin's responses over the course of the year. Because I analyzed her response journals during the summer after school was over for the year, Schon (1983) would call this case study "reflection on action," a sort of reflection after the fact. In this analysis, I tried to discover the developmental changes in her levels of thinking from the beginning of the year to the end. I chose Erin because she was typical of the student who did not personally connect with literature at first. When she began to do so, she made startling progress in critical thinking.

At the beginning and end of the study, I talked with a colleague at a nearby university. Those sessions served to focus my questions and to provide a structure for this report. (Hirtle, 1993)

Evaluation Research

Educational **evaluation research** has developed to a great extent because of federal and state mandates to assess the impact (influence) of funded compensatory pro-

grams for students who are educationally disadvantaged, have limited English proficiency, or have special educational needs. It is the systematic study of existing educational programs (treatments). Evaluation researchers wish to know whether a particular instructional program or technique results in improved student performance
or achievement. They can use both quantitative and qualitative research methods.

Qualitative research methods differ from quantitative methods. Qualitative analysis is inductive. Researchers use observed data to draw a conclusion. It emphasizes
an examination and explanation of the processes by which the educational programs
do or do not work. Qualitative analysis focuses on how instruction (teaching and
learning) happens from the point of view of the students, teachers, and administrators. Quantitative research methods are deductive. They begin with predefined
goals—most often the goals of the programs themselves—and focus on whether particular outcomes have been reached (Bogdan & Biklen, 1998).

Evaluation research differs from action research in several ways. These are
(a) the complexity of the research designs, (b) the degree to which the possible effects
of extraneous variables are controlled, and (c) the extent to which the results can be
generalized to other educational settings.

Research consumers can use the following questions to help them judge the appropriateness of the evaluation researchers' statement of the problem, identification of subjects, selection of instruments, collection of data, and analysis of data. Standards for educational evaluation have been established by educational researchers and by a
consortium of educational associations, including the American Educational Research
Association and the American Evaluation Association (Bogdan & Biklen, 1998; Charles,
1995; Sanders & the Joint Committee on Standards for Educational Evaluation, 1994;
see Appendix C). The standards are grouped as (a) *utility standards,* in which an evaluation serves the information needs of intended users; (b) *feasibility standards,* in which an
evaluation is realistic, prudent, diplomatic, and frugal; (c) *propriety standards,* in which
an evaluation is conducted legally, ethically, and with due regard for the welfare of those
involved in the evaluation, as well as those affected by its results; and (d) *accuracy standards,* in which an evaluation reveals and conveys technically adequate information
about the features that determine worth or merit of the program being evaluated. The
following program evaluation questions are based on these standards.

1. In evaluation research using quantitative methods, could the research be useful to the school or agency conducting the study in that its results answer a
   clearly defined question or problem?
2. In evaluation research using qualitative methods, could the research be useful to the school or agency conducting the study in that its results provide
   meanings for and understanding about the processes occurring during teaching and learning?
3. In both quantitative and qualitative designs, was the evaluation research
   appropriate to the educational setting in that it was minimally disruptive to
   the subjects (administrators, teachers, students, and other school personnel)?
4. Were the rights and well-being of the participating administrators, teachers,
   and students protected, and was information about individuals obtained and
   stored in such a way that confidentiality was maintained?
5. Was the evaluation research report clearly written so that the reliability and
   validity of the collected data and the internal and external validity of the study
   could be determined?

ACTIVITIES

Activity 1

Using the Focus Questions at the beginning of the chapter as a guide, summarize the chapter's key ideas.

Activity 2

Read the sections containing research procedures for the two studies in this chapter's Appendix. The researchers' purposes have been included for your information. Using the questions and criteria on page 124, evaluate the studies. For each, list questions and concerns you may have about the following.

   a. The appropriateness of the research design to the researchers' purposes
   b. The research design and data collection procedures
   c. The replicability of the study
   d. The study's internal and external validity

Do not read the Feedback section until you have completed each of the activities.

FEEDBACK

Activity 1

What concerns should research consumers have about research procedures that are common to all research designs?

All research reports should have clear and complete explanations of every step of the research. All instruments should be valid and reliable and administered by trained examiners. Research procedures should be tested in pilot studies.

What concerns should research consumers have about research procedures that are specific to quantitative descriptive research designs?

They need to be sure the data represent a true picture of what occurred and can be generalized to other situations. This process refers to the validity of the research results. Researchers also need to be sure that they are consistent in identifying aspects of a behavior or event and that others working in the same or similar situations would get similar results. This process refers to the reliability of the research results.

What concerns should research consumers have about research procedures that are specific to quantitative comparative research designs?

Research consumers should use the questions for procedures in descriptive research to determine whether the results from comparative research are valid and reliable.

What concerns should research consumers have about research procedures that are specific to experimental research designs?

Research consumers should be concerned about whether variables other than the independent variables caused the observed changes in the dependent variable. Variables that might have an unwanted influence on, or might change, dependent variables are called extraneous variables. One of the best ways to control subject variables is through randomization. When subjects cannot be randomly selected or assigned to groups, researchers can equate them statistically.

How are extraneous variables controlled in experimental research?

Variables that need to be controlled to maintain the internal validity of experimental research are current events, subject growth and development, subject selection, attrition, testing, instrumentation, statistical regression, and interaction. Variables that need to be controlled to maintain the external validity of experimental research are subject-treatment interaction, reactive effects, multiple-treatment interaction, and research effects.

What distinguishes simple and complex experimental research designs?

Simple and complex experimental research designs are distinguished by (a) the number of independent or treatment variables and (b) the extent to which results can be generalized from the immediate subjects to a larger target population. Experimental designs are a continuum from simple to complex plans. Simple experimental plans deal with single independent variables, and complex experimental plans deal with multiple independent variables. Simple experimental designs deal with one independent variable or have subject selection procedures that limit the generalizability of their results. More complex experimental designs deal with two or more experimental and subject variables.

What concerns should research consumers have about research procedures that are specific to causal-comparative research designs?

A major concern for researchers doing causal-comparative research is that the causal effects should be one-way. Since there are no manipulated, or treated, independent variables, the subjects cannot be randomly assigned to groups. For research consumers to generalize the results from causal-comparative studies to other populations and educational situations, they need to be sure that any differences between groups cannot be attributed to one or more important variables that were not accounted for by the researchers. There is always the possibility that these outside variables may be the true causes of the observed differences. Also, they should be sure that the researchers' description of the subjects is clear and that operational definitions are used to identify and distinguish the comparison groups.

What concerns should research consumers have about research procedures that are specific to qualitative research designs?

Qualitative research reports should show how the researchers' method is detailed so its adequacy and logic can be determined, and there should be an abundance of evidence. Research consumers should be sure that the researchers provide evidence of their qualifications as participant observers. They should be sure that the researchers' assumptions are clear, that the researchers' questions are stated, and that the study sought to answer those questions and generate further questions.

The research report should indicate that the researchers used the preliminary days of the study to generate a focus for the study, that the researchers were present in the research context for an adequate period of time, and that the researchers' observations are of a full range of activities over a full cycle of those activities. The research consumer should ascertain that the data were collected from multiple sources. The researchers should have saved their data for reanalysis.

What concerns should research consumers have about research procedures that are specific to single-subject, action, and evaluation research designs?

Single-subject research is any research in which there is only one subject or one group that is treated as a single entity. Single-subject research may be descriptive or experimental. Action research is directed to studying existing educational practice and to producing practical, immediately applicable findings. The questions or problems studied are local in nature. Evaluation research is applying the rigors of experimental research to the judging of the worth or value of educational programs, projects, and instruction. Threats to the internal validity of single-subject research include testing, instrumentation, subject-treatment interaction, reactive effects, and researcher effects. Research consumers should expect research producers to adhere to the same guidelines as used for conducting descriptive and experimental research. Research consumers should expect published action research reports to have the same specificity in detail as other research reports. Research consumers can use several questions to help them judge the appropriateness of the evaluation researchers' statement of the problem, identification of subjects, selection of instruments, and collection and analysis of data.

What questions should be used to evaluate procedure sections?

Are the research design and data collection procedures clearly described? Is the research design appropriate to the researchers' purpose? Can the study be replicated from the information provided? To evaluate qualitative experimental research, the question is Has the researchers' presence influenced the behavior of the subjects? In studies with treatments, Are experimental procedures fully explained? Are examples of special materials included? To determine research validity, Are the procedures free from the influence of extraneous variables? Does the study contain any threats to its internal and external validity?

Activity 2

Extract A: Successful Mainstreaming in Elementary Science Classes. This was a qualitative comparative study in which the researchers observed several classrooms and collected information about mainstreaming practices. Since their purpose was to gather information, their design was appropriate. The research project spanned three years, and, during that time, the researchers were active participants in the school district's plan for creating mainstreaming guidelines. The participants were identified, and the characteristics of each observed classroom were detailed. The instructional program and materials used in the classrooms were also described. In keeping with the generally accepted procedures for qualitative research, the researchers described their research and educational perspectives about special education. The data were analyzed over the three years, and the researchers addressed the issue of the reliability and validity of their data. However, despite the references to trying to control for threats to reliability and validity, the specific procedures were not explicit. For example, they indicate that they "addressed the issue of consistency," yet they do not indicate that this was done by anyone other than themselves.

Extract B: Helping Behaviors and Math Achievement Gain of Students Using Cooperative Learning.   Overall, the design was appropriate to the researcher's purposes. The design used was a 2 (two aspects of gender) × 3 (three ability groups) × 3 (three grade levels) factorial with a pretest-posttest. The experimental variables (no treatments) for the first purpose were these three factors. The experimental variables (treatments) for the second purpose were instruction on helping behavior and cooperative learning instruction. The dependent variable for the second purpose was mathematics performance. Although the researcher took care to balance the groups at each grade level according to gender and ability, there is no indication that the children were assigned randomly. The treatments are explained, and the location of additional information pertaining to the treatments is indicated. The way data were collected and analyzed is detailed. The researcher has included information about establishing interrater reliability. The researcher used a coding system from another researcher, which is appropriate; however, modifications were made to the coding system without any indication of whether those changes altered the validity of the coding. One question left unanswered was "What possible influence did the television cameras have on the subjects' behavior?" Another question pertains to the influence of the researcher: "Since the researcher trained the teachers in conducting cooperative learning procedures and was often present in the classrooms, did his direct involvement have an influence on the subjects?"

Extract A: Successful Mainstreaming in Elementary Science Classes (pp. 208–212)

Purpose of the study: To identify variables meaningfully associated with mainstreaming success in science classes, across grade levels and across categories of disability.

METHOD

Participants

All participants were from a relatively large (about 50,000 students), middle SES school district in a western metropolitan area. This district was one of four with whom we collaborated as part of a larger project to study science and disability. We interviewed district science education administrative personnel, building level administrators, teachers, and special education personnel in that district to identify reputational cases (LeCompte & Preissle, 1993) of mainstreaming success in science (2/18/1–2/22/1; 3/7/2–3/12/2). During these periods, we also observed in identified classrooms. Three classrooms, in three different schools, were identified. During the first and second project years, we worked with these and other district teachers and specialists (along with those of the three other school districts) to develop and refine guidelines for including students with disabilities in science classes. We presented them with draft versions of our guidelines, developed from information from previous literature and previously published guidelines (e.g., Hadary & Cohen, 1978; Hofman & Ricker, 1979), and we solicited and received written feedback. We revised the guidelines based on their feedback on two separate occasions throughout the 2-year period. The final product (Mastropieri & Scruggs, 1994b) contained information on characteristics of specific disability categories, general mainstreaming strategies applied to science classes, and strategies for adapting specific science activities (e.g., electricity units) for students with disabilities. Copies were distributed to all cooperating teachers and administrators. Teachers in the three targeted classrooms were asked to refer to the guidelines when needed, but they were under no obligation to do so. Nevertheless, all teachers reported informally that they had referred to the guidelines frequently. Following is a description of each of these classrooms.

Classroom A. Classroom A was a third grade classroom of 25 students in a regular elementary school containing kindergarten through grade 6 students. The school in which Classroom A was located had enrolled 72 students with hearing impairments and contained special education teachers with specialized training in teaching students with hearing impairments, as well as specialized facilities for students with hearing impairments (e.g., fire alarms that also produced flashing lights). Classroom A included two Caucasian students with hearing impairments in science class. One was a boy with a nearly complete hearing loss, who was provided a sign language interpreter to assist in communication. The other student had a partial hearing loss, and she benefited greatly from an FM phonic ear system. In addition to the two students with hearing impairments, four students with learning disabilities, two students receiving supplementary services for low SES students (Chapter 1), and two students for whom English was a second language were also enrolled. All students who had been classified as learning disabled in these three classrooms were 2 or more years below grade level in reading. In addition, the boy with a severe hearing loss read at an early first grade level, while the girl with the partial hearing loss read at about a second grade level. The teacher, Ms. A, had about 5 years' teaching experience and held no certification in special education.

Students were seated at desks in rows, with adjacent desks touching or nearly touching one another, facing toward the teacher's desk. A wide aisle divided the class laterally into two halves, and the teacher made frequent use of this aisle in moving freely about the classroom. Desks were moved when classroom activities required it. The two students with hearing impairments were seated in the row nearest the teacher, on opposite sides of the room.

Classroom B. Classroom B was a fourth grade class located in a regular elementary school that had enrolled 17 students with visual impairments of varying severity. This school had a special education teacher who was specially trained in teaching students with visual impairments. One Caucasian girl with a nearly total visual impairment was included in this class, in addition to three students with learning disabilities. Although reading achievement is difficult to assess using traditional standardized measures with students who read braille, the girl in this classroom did read more slowly, and at a somewhat lower level, than most of her classmates. The teacher, Ms. B, had about 7 years' teaching experience and held no special education certification.

The classroom was arranged with desks in groups of four that faced one another. The visually impaired student was given additional space to accommodate a braille typewriter (brailler) and braille materials, and her desk was located in a group with two other students near the outside door, at the back of the classroom.

Classroom C. Classroom C was a fifth grade class located in a regular elementary school that had enrolled a number of students with physical disabilities and that included special education teachers who were specially trained in teaching students with physical disabilities. This school was well equipped with wheelchair ramps, adaptable classrooms, and even a playground that could accommodate students in wheelchairs. Classroom C had three Caucasian students with physical disabilities in science class. Two female students, affected by cerebral palsy, employed motorized wheelchairs to assist mobility and also exhibited significant difficulties with motor and speech activities. As a consequence, traditional academic achievement in basic skills areas was very difficult to determine. However, both students exhibited adequate listening comprehension. The third student with physical disabilities was a boy who was affected by arthritis and moved with the aid of arm braces and a motorized walker. He could accomplish, with effort, general pincer-grasp movements. His reading ability was at about grade level, but manual writing presented greater difficulties. Two students with learning disabilities also attended the science class. The teacher, Mr. C., had about 9 years' teaching experience and held no special education certification.

Classroom C was located in a small building near the other school buildings and near the special education classrooms, and it had the most unconventional interior arrangement. Teacher C had asked his students to decide the seating arrangement, and they had elected to place their desks in clusters of three or four, spread around the classroom, facing all different directions

(interview, 11/14/3). Sufficient space was allocated for wheelchairs to pass throughout the classroom. One of the physically handicapped students had elected to have his desk located on the opposite side of the room from the outside door. The outside door was connected to the outside sidewalk by a wheelchair ramp, which all students used to enter and exit the classroom. The teacher's desk and teaching materials were located in a back corner of the room, and Teacher C was never observed seated at this desk during class time.

Curriculum. The cooperating district has a very positive reputation for excellence in science education, and in fact is one of a relatively small number of districts listed by the National Science Resource Center in Washington, DC as "exemplary." This district has created its own science curriculum materials, which are housed in a district distribution center. From this center, science kits for individual units are created, stored, inventoried, and delivered to teacher's classrooms throughout the district on request. Four specific units are targeted for each academic year in the elementary grades, and teachers may elect to request other age-appropriate units. According to personnel from the National Science Resource Center, such a distribution system is strongly associated with the success over time of hands-on science programs in individual school districts (Deputy Director S.G. Shuler, personal communication, 2/1/1).

The curriculum had been based originally on the Elementary Science Study (ESS) and other materials from the 1960s but had been revised on a continuous, ongoing basis, in response to teacher feedback; district needs; local cultural, geographical, and meteorological conditions; and contemporary trends in science education (interview with district science specialist, 2/18/1). The most recent revisions had included integration with other curriculum areas, such as social studies, and included reading passages of differing levels of difficulty to help accommodate diverse reading abilities. District teachers were actively involved in revising these materials on an ongoing basis. Guidelines for accommodating students with disabilities are not specifically included in these materials (they very rarely are in any science curriculum materials, e.g., Parmar & Cawley, 1993), but the materials themselves—focusing on experiential, conceptual learning and de-emphasizing textbook learning—are thought to be potentially accommodating to the needs of students with disabilities (Scruggs & Mastropieri, 1992).

The district materials have a broad, wide scope, covering areas of ecology and life sciences, earth sciences, physical sciences, and scientific method, and are distributed throughout the elementary grades. All include relevant materials for completing activities, and teacher and student editions of activity books that include brief reading passages and recording sheets for relevant activities. For example, one unit entitled "Chemistry" was developed for use in the fifth grade. During this unit, students examine and classify the physical properties of matter; manipulate and observe material changes in a clod of dirt; examine the interactions with solids and liquids in solutions, including food coloring, butyl stearate, ice, and water; measure changes in volume when alcohol and salt are combined with water; observe and measure chemical changes associated with different kinds of oxidation; combine ammonia, water, vinegar, and bromothymol blue in various solutions and record observations; combine vinegar with baking soda or salt and observe reactions; test for acids and bases with litmus paper; and study home safety with chemicals.

Another unit, entitled "Fin and Feather, Tooth and Tail," was developed for use in third grade classrooms. During this unit, students learn about and discuss adaptation; study opposable thumbs; observe and describe which teeth they use to bite and chew various foods; determine eating habits based on pictures of animal skulls; experiment with nonverbal communication and study animal warning signs; act out various types of animal locomotion and identify animals by studying their feet; simulate animal camouflage using different kinds of wallpaper, potatoes, and various art supplies; study and describe adaptation in different vertebrates; study the concept of home range and map out their own home ranges; study animal characteristics using jigsaw activities; and create poster presentations for an animal of their own choice.

RESEARCHER BACKGROUND, DATA COLLECTION, AND ANALYSIS

Researcher Background

We entered this project with extensive backgrounds in special education research and practice (particularly involving students with mild disabilities) but with little experience with, or knowledge of, mainstream science curriculum. If anything, the behavioral influences on the field of special education, and our knowledge of the characteristics of special education students, had made us cautious of discovery or inquiry-based approaches, for fear that students with disabilities might be excluded or fall behind peers who pursued learning more actively and independently. Our special education methods textbook (Mastropieri & Scruggs, 1987, 1994a), based

on instructional research relevant to students with special needs, recommends an approach to teaching that is more structured and teacher directed, particularly in its first edition, than the methods often proposed by science educators (e.g., Abruscato, 1992). Our previous research in science education focused on mnemonic enhancement of science facts, classifications, vocabulary, and verbal concepts with students with learning disabilities and mild mental retardation (e.g., Mastropieri & Scruggs, 1989; Scruggs, Mastropieri, Levin, & Gaffney, 1985). We have made, and have defended, several assumptions relevant to the field of special education—for example, that disabilities are conditions individuals sometimes have (although these conditions can be partly socially determined), that special education practice often can be helpful for such individuals, and that improvement in practice can be influenced by research (Scruggs, 1993; for a critique of such assumptions, see Skrtic, 1991).

During the earliest stages of this project, we first reviewed all available literature on science and students with disabilities (Mastropieri & Scruggs, 1992) and critically examined relevant science curriculum from four school districts across the nation (Mastropieri & Scruggs, 1994c). Our work in this area led us to appreciate the value of hands-on science in providing concrete and meaningful experiences to students who may experience difficulty in deriving meaning from more abstract text presentations or who may have had more limited background experience (Mastropieri & Scruggs, in press; Scruggs & Mastropieri, 1992). As we consulted literature and the expert opinion of teachers, curriculum developers, and national science organizations in developing our guidelines, we began to feel that hands-on science instruction, appropriately implemented, could be highly complementary to the special needs of students with disabilities. We had collected recommendations for adapting science curriculum for students with various disabilities. We were also aware that several other factors might be of critical importance in enhancing mainstreaming. However, we had not systematically preconceptualized all factors that might be necessary for a successful mainstream experience in science.

Data Collection

During the first and second project years, we met with district and building level administrators and collaborated with special education and regular class teachers, including the target teachers, while compiling our guidelines for facilitating mainstreaming. During the third project year, we observed and videotaped in the three science classrooms described previously over a 5-week period in the fall semester and during an additional 3-week period in the spring semester. We also interviewed students, teachers, and administrators and collected examples of student and teacher products. We made follow-up contact during the fourth project year. Overall, we collected data from a number of sources, including observational field notes, videotape and audiotape records, student and teacher products, curriculum materials, and interviews of students, classroom teachers, special education teachers, and building and district-level administrators.

Observations were made during approximately 35 class meetings during the fall semester and approximately 15 class meetings during the spring semester. Two observers were present at least twice in every classroom, so that observers would have familiarity with all settings. We videotaped at least two classes in each of the three settings and took field notes during all classes observed. Additionally, we interviewed the targeted students and peers, the three teachers and cooperating special education teachers, building principals, and district-level personnel in science education and special education. Dialogue with teachers continued throughout the investigation, as the need arose. However, all teachers were asked at least the following questions: (a) What things happen to make mainstreaming successful, and how would you define success in this context? (b) What would you say about [district name] science curriculum versus textbook-based science curriculum? (c) What specific adaptations do you make in science class for students with disabilities? And, (d) do you think administrative support, building or district level, is helpful? These interviews were recorded on audiotape. As described earlier, initial contacts with target teachers began nearly 2 years prior to our classroom observations and included follow-up contact during the year subsequent to our classroom observations.

Data Analysis

After several weeks of interviews and site visits during the third project year, we considered all sources of information collected to date. We then analyzed all data for consistencies and inconsistencies, using analytic induction and the constant comparative method (LeCompte & Preissle, 1993). Divergent cases or instances were also investigated. We then developed a preliminary list of five variables that appeared to be highly relevant to the issue of successful mainstreaming in science. This preliminary list became the basis for future analyses and was revised several times as additional information became available.

At the end of the third year of the project, the list of variables was again reconsidered with respect to all information that had been gathered throughout the project. This analysis yielded a final list of seven variables, which appeared to be consistent and robust with respect to all data sources across the three different classrooms. These variables also were supported by previous research literature, including both convergent and divergent instances. Finally, all final conclusions were re-examined to ensure that they were directly supported by evidence gathered in this investigation, a feature sometimes missing in qualitative research on learning and behavioral disorders (Scruggs & Mastropieri, in press-b).

Although it may have been less appropriate to address concerns of "reliability" and "validity," at least in the more traditional quantitative sense, in this investigation, we nevertheless wished to ensure that our data collection had been accurate and systematic and that our conclusions logically proceeded from the interactions of those data sources with our personal perspectives. We addressed these issues by obtaining multiple sources of evidence in support of each of our conclusions and by planning and implementing extended interaction with the participants. We also addressed the issue of consistency by confirming that all conclusions were supported by evidence from each classroom, considered independently. (Scruggs & Mastropieri, 1994. Copyright 1994 by the American Educational Research Association.)

Extract B: Helping Behaviors and Math Achievement Gain of Students Using Cooperative Learning (pp. 212–216)

Purpose of the study: To examine (a) the effects of learner ability, gender, or grade level on students' performance and (b) the nature of the cooperative group "help" on achievement gains.

METHOD

Subjects

One hundred and one students in three classes participated in the study. They were in grades 3 ($N = 36$), 4 ($N = 34$), and 5 ($N = 31$). There were 54 boys and 47 girls. There was only one class at each grade level. All students in these grades were originally included in the study. Students who moved into or out of the school during the 6 weeks of the study, or who were not able to complete pre- and posttests, were excluded in the final data analysis.

The study was conducted at a school of 290 students in northern Utah that was affiliated with a university and also with the local school district. Although approximately 70% of the population in this area is Mormon, there is a greater degree of heterogeneity at this school because it is attended by children of foreign students and ethnically diverse university faculty, as well as children from the local community.

The faculty at the school were considered exemplary teachers, selected based on their ability to model innovative educational methods. The third-, fourth-, and fifth-grade teachers in this study had taught for 18, 6, and 14 years, respectively. All held master's degrees, had positive attitudes towards math, and enjoyed teaching math.

Procedure

Achievement/Ability. Standardized math scores from the California Test of Basic Skills (CTBS) and Southwest Regional Lab (SWRL) math assessments were utilized to determine students' achievement/ability prior to the treatment. Tests were given 3 months before data collection. Girls were categorized as high-, medium-, or low-achieving students according to whether their scores were in the top quarter, the middle half, or the bottom quarter of the distribution of published standardized scores. I used the same procedure for boys. The two genders were categorized separately so there were almost equal numbers of boys and girls in each

category. Teachers were consulted for confirmation of these placements. I refer to these three categories as ability levels rather than achievement levels so as not to confuse them with the primary variable of achievement gain, although I recognize that these categories may reflect achievement rather than ability.

Assignment of Students to Groups. Heterogeneity within groups, especially in terms of ability/achievement and ethnicity, has been a cornerstone of team formation in cooperative learning as advocated in teacher training and reports of research (Aronson, 1978; Johnson, Johnson, Holubec, & Roy, 1984; Kagan, 1989; Slavin, 1983). Accordingly, in this study, ability was used as basis for group assignments. High-, medium-, and low-ability boys and girls were assigned to groups of five to six students so that each team included students of both genders and the three ability levels. Ethnic variations were also distributed among teams.

Instruction on Helping Behaviors. All students received instruction on helping behaviors for 3 weeks, as Webb (1988) recommended, including the concept that only giving answers was not considered help and was discouraged. Students practiced helping behaviors and received feedback daily during the 3 weeks preceding the data collection and continued doing this during the 3 subsequent weeks of the study as well.

Methods of instruction and reinforcement of helping behaviors included: direct instruction, role play, modeling, calling attention to students and teams engaged in helping behaviors, giving points to teams engaged in helping behaviors, periodic review of what these behaviors entailed, and teacher feedback to students regarding the effectiveness of their use of helping behaviors.

Teachers elicited phrases from students describing what students did and said when giving explanations, asking for help, and receiving explanations. Students responded with statements such as "we put our heads together"; "go through step by step"; "repeat"; "say, 'please help me'"; "shrug shoulders, raise eyebrow, and point to a problem after getting a teammate's attention"; "say 'This is what you do first' "; "say 'You have to find the least common denominator first' "; "smile"; "say thanks"; "pay attention"; "be considerate"; and "don't give up." Teachers put up charts with these words to remind students of examples.

During role plays, one or two pairs of students acted out sample ways in which one student could ask for help and another could give explanations or other useful help. Occasionally, students acted out what not to do. Sometimes teachers read "script starters"; for instance, "Tom is staring at the first problem, $1/2 + 1/4 = $ _____, but he doesn't know what to do and he isn't asking for help. If Darshana says, 'It's three-fourths,' is that helping? What can she do to really help Tom?"

Direct instruction on helping behaviors, role plays, and eliciting phrases from students took only a few minutes on an average of every other day at the beginning of team work time. Modeling of helping behaviors, calling attention to appropriate examples, giving teams points for helping each other, and positive reinforcement were all behaviors in which teachers engaged as they monitored students while they worked in teams. A summary chart of ways in which teachers can help students develop helping behaviors is presented in Appendix A. Further details on these strategies are found in Nattiv (1990).

Students worked in teams daily for under an hour a day during the 3 weeks before videotaping and 3 subsequent weeks. On some days students were in teams for 40-minute periods, but on other days direct instruction lasted for portions of that time. These students and teachers had not been trained previously in cooperative learning or specifically in helping behaviors.

Cooperative Learning Instruction. The cooperative learning format used in this study was Student Teams—Achievement Divisions (STAD) (Slavin, 1986). In this strategy all students were first taught with direct instruction. Then students practiced the concepts in teams rather than doing individual seatwork. Students tutored each other. All students had the same material. Students wanted their teammates to understand the concepts because each student took a test on the concepts and students earned points for their teams. Team total points were determined by combining how much each student on the team improved over her/his average on previous math tests. The ILE Percentile Improvement Scoring System developed by Slavin was used (Kagan, 1989). Students wanted their teams to get as many points as possible. Following the test, teams learned of test results and received recognition.

The STAD format is described in detail in the handbook written by its originator (Slavin, 1986). Components that were added to STAD for this study included (1) initial teambuilding and ongoing skill building as described by Kagan (1986), (2) instruction on helping behaviors as described in the previous section, and (3) greater structure in the implementation of STAD by assigning each student on each team a specific task or role within the team. For instance, in a method labeled by Kagan (1989) as Pairs Check, students worked in pairs (or triads) within their groups. Students alternated roles of solving problems, checking, and coaching. After every few problems each pair of students confirmed solutions with the other pair(s) in the group. Numbered Heads Together and Color Coded Co-op Cards, two other methods described by Kagan (1989), were also used.

Students practiced math concepts in the same teams for 3 weeks prior to data collection. During the portion of the study in which they were tested, the third graders studied multiplication, including story problems; students in the fourth grade studied measurement of distance, area, and volume; and the fifth graders studied complex fractions. In all three grades, most of the cognitive processing involved comprehension, computation, and application. Some lessons included story problems, so problem solving was also expected. Manipulatives were an integrated aspect of the curricula in all grades. Third graders used groups of buttons, sticks, and small objects. Fourth graders measured real items. Fifth graders used paper pies and squares, cut up into eighths, sixteenths, and other fractions. In each class, the teacher used the cooperative learning structure (which included direct instruction and then team practice) for approximately 40 minutes per day, each day of the week.

Data Collection. Each class was videotaped a mean time of 80 minutes per week by one of three hired technicians. Each team was videotaped several times, with approximately 30 minutes per team over the 3 weeks, during team practice on the math content. Each team was videotaped an average of twice a week for 5 minutes each time. Only one team per classroom was videotaped at a time. Three video cameras were used, but never more than one camera per class. Microphone extensions from the video camera recorded all verbal communication, and the camera picked up nonverbal cues as well.

Each student on a team was listed on the observation instrument, and whenever one of the eight helping behaviors occurred, it was coded under the student's name. Behaviors were coded sequentially, as they occurred. Whenever a behavior went on for over 30 seconds, it was recorded again.

Three coders were trained to analyze the tapes using the following behavioral categories for each student: gives explanation, receives explanation, asks for help (and receives it), gives help other than explanation, receives help other than explanation, gives answer only, receives answer only, receives no help (after requesting it). Coders were trained initially in individual sessions with the primary investigator. All coders initially viewed the same sample footage that illustrated the eight behaviors. First they were shown examples, then they verbally compared codings with mine as they went along, and finally they recorded codings independently. The three coders practiced until they reached 85% agreement in all behavioral categories. Agreement was calculated after coding several tapes by dividing the number of behavioral events observed by the coder by the number of behavioral events observed by the primary investigator and later also by the other coders. At that point coders were given tapes to code. Two coders analyzed each tape. Interrater agreement was above 80% on each tape for all categories.

It is important to note that these eight categories are based on a five-category system Webb used in her previous studies. Her categories consisted of "gives explanation," "gives help other than explanation," "receives explanation," "receives help other than explanation," and "receives no help" (Webb, 1987).

To adapt the categories to younger students, I altered some categories. The first two categories, "gives explanation" and "receives explanation," remained the same. They refer to the more complex helping behaviors involving showing or telling how or why. Examples of student behaviors in each of the eight categories are presented in Appendix B.

Webb's categories "gives help other than explanation" and "receives help other than explanation" refer to telling or being told the correct answer. These behaviors do not contribute or could actually be detrimental to achievement because they do not equip the receiving student with any additional learning cues. Likewise a student who gives the answer without explanation is not reprocessing any of the learning. For instance, a student who asks for help with "2/3 minus 1/2" and is told "the answer is 1/6" without any hint about how to arrive at that answer may be just as confused as before. Since such behaviors are actually not helpful, I reclassified them as "gives answer only" and "receives answer only." However, in observing upper-elementary-school students, there was evidence of a middle category of behavior that was helpful but not sophisticated enough to be called an explanation. This included such comments as "look on the other side," "you got the wrong number," "try again," "now it's your turn," as well as helpful gestures such as bringing

math manipulatives to a partner to help him/her work out a solution. I therefore retained the two categories of "giving/receiving help other than an explanation" but gave them new meaning.

I added another category, "asks for help (and receives it)," after a conversation with Noreen Webb during which she made the recommendation. This category was coded when a student asked for help and received either an explanation or other meaningful help. I retained Webb's category "receives no help" and used it when a student asked for help and got no response.

Videotaping was done on a team-by-team basis. Behaviors by individuals other than the team being taped were not coded. If a non-team-member or the teacher asked or answered a question or engaged in one of the helping behaviors, it was not recorded.

Students took weekly pretests and posttests on the specific content covered during the 3 weeks. These tests were part of the published textbook material packets from Harcourt Brace Jovanovich (Mathematics Today, 1987).

Teacher Training. The teachers received nine 2-hour in-service training sessions on components of cooperative learning during 5 months prior to implementation. I conducted the sessions, adapting the training models of Kagan and Slavin that I learned when I became a Certified Cooperative Learning trainer in 1984 at the University of California, Riverside, where Spencer Kagan was my mentor. Topics addressed included philosophical rationale, overview of research findings, step-by-step details of several specific cooperative learning strategies (STAD, Jigsaw, Co-op Co-op Pairs Check, Color Coded Co-op Cards, Numbered Heads Together), team formation, discipline/management, improvement points, charts and record keeping, grading, ways to teach and reinforce helping behaviors, team building, specific application to math, and creative lesson planning. Most training was conducted in experiential cooperative learning groups. All of the teachers used the manual Cooperative Learning Resources for Teachers (Kagan, 1986).

Teachers had not received training in cooperative learning previously. One teacher had tried grouping students, but not according to any consistent framework. Similarly, cooperative learning was new to the students as well.

All of the teachers received additional follow-up assistance. Just before they started using cooperative learning instructional strategies, teachers met with me and/or other colleagues to facilitate a smoother beginning by discussing teaching strategies, lesson plans, and other elements of implementation. These meetings continued throughout the 6 weeks.

All teachers involved in this study implemented cooperative learning competently. Because I was in their classrooms about every 2 days, I was confident that I could correct minor implementation problems before major problems arose, and such was indeed the case. I gave information to teachers as needed regarding the effectiveness of implementation. Also, each teacher met individually with me at least twice to discuss extensively progress, possible problems, and successes and to provide general anecdotal information. (Nattiv, 1994)

From: Nattiv, A. (1994). Helping behaviors and math achievement gain of students using cooperative learning. *The Elementary School Journal* 94:285–297.

Chapter 8

Reading and Interpreting Results Sections

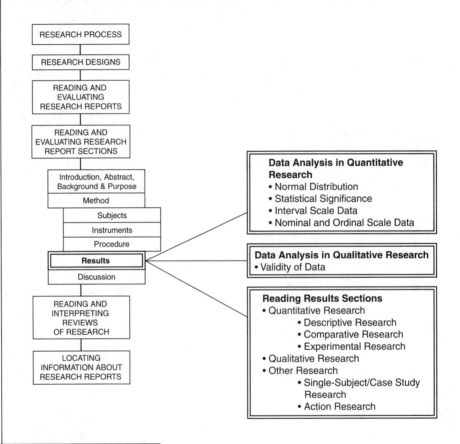

RESEARCH PROCESS

RESEARCH DESIGNS

READING AND EVALUATING RESEARCH REPORTS

READING AND EVALUATING RESEARCH REPORT SECTIONS

Introduction, Abstract, Background & Purpose

Method

Subjects

Instruments

Procedure

Results

Discussion

READING AND INTERPRETING REVIEWS OF RESEARCH

LOCATING INFORMATION ABOUT RESEARCH REPORTS

Data Analysis in Quantitative Research
- Normal Distribution
- Statistical Significance
- Interval Scale Data
- Nominal and Ordinal Scale Data

Data Analysis in Qualitative Research
- Validity of Data

Reading Results Sections
- Quantitative Research
    - Descriptive Research
    - Comparative Research
    - Experimental Research
- Qualitative Research
- Other Research
    - Single-Subject/Case Study Research
    - Action Research

FOCUS QUESTIONS

1. What are the different ways quantitative data are recorded?
2. What is a normal distribution curve?
3. What statistical procedures are used in educational and other behavioral science research?
4. What is statistical significance and effect size?
5. What are the ways data are analyzed in qualitative research?
6. What criteria should be used to read and evaluate results sections?

After collecting data, researchers use several methods to describe, synthesize, analyze, and interpret the information. In all types of quantitative research, statistical procedures facilitate understanding of a vast amount of numerical data. These procedures are the techniques by which researchers summarize and explain quantitative data and determine the existence of relationships and causal effects. In qualitative research, the outcomes of research are the generation of hypotheses and research questions, not the verification of predicted relationships or outcomes. Therefore, qualitative researchers use verbal rather than statistical procedures to analyze data. These inductive analytic procedures involve organizing data, identifying patterns, and synthesizing key ideas as research questions and hypotheses.

Research consumers need to understand (a) the way researchers match data analysis procedures to research designs, (b) the different statistical analyses available to educational and other behavioral and social science researchers, (c) the assumptions researchers make about those analyses to use them effectively, (d) the concept of statistical significance and the criteria generally used to set the point at which results can be considered reliable, (e) the assumptions researchers make about qualitative data analyses, and (f) the way to read and interpret results sections in quantitative and qualitative research reports.

From reading results sections, research consumers should be able to answer the following:

What types of data analysis were used?

What statistical analyses did the researchers use?

Were the statistical analyses appropriate for the researchers' questions, purposes, or hypotheses and for the research design?

What were the research results?

Were the results of quantitative research statistically significant?

Were the qualitative analyses appropriate and logical? Were they meaningful?

Were the results of practical use and importance?

Will the results be applicable to other educational settings, especially the one in which I teach?

Results sections should be evaluated using the following questions, which are from Figure 3.1, page 61.

Evaluating Results Sections

RESULTS SECTION

Data Analysis in Quantitative Research. Are the statistical procedures for data analysis clearly described, and are they appropriate for the type of quantitative research design?
Research Validity in Quantitative Research. Are the procedures free from the influence of extraneous variables? Does the study have any threats to its internal and external validity?
Significance in Quantitative Research. Are statistical significance levels indicated? Does the research have practical significance?
Data Analysis in Qualitative Research. Are the processes for organizing data, identifying patterns, and synthesizing key ideas as hypotheses and research questions clearly described?
Research Validity in Qualitative Research. Are there multiple procedures for corroborating research evidence and researchers' judgments?

DATA ANALYSIS IN QUANTITATIVE RESEARCH

Data analyses in quantitative research involve the use of statistics. **Statistics** are numerical ways to describe, analyze, summarize, and interpret data in a manner that conserves time and space and are precise in nature. Researchers select statistical procedures after they have determined what research designs and types of data will be appropriate for answering their research questions. For example, in answering descriptive research questions, statistics let researchers show the data's central tendencies and variability. In answering comparative and experimental research questions, other statistics allow researchers to draw inferences and make generalizations about target populations. In all three types of research, the specific statistical procedures are determined by the research design and by the type of data that are collected. And, in comparative and experimental research, statistics are tools that let researchers gain two other insights: (a) an estimate of the sampling error, the error (or difference) between the research sample and the target population, and (b) the confidence with which research producers and consumers can accept the results.

The way quantitative data are recorded depends on the instruments (measuring devices) used. Data are recorded as (a) intervals, (b) rankings, (c) categories, and (d) ratios. Each means of recording data requires the use of different statistics. **Interval scales** present data according to preset, equal spans. They are the most common form of data reporting in education and the social sciences, and they are identified by continuous measurement scales: raw scores and derived scores such as IQ scores, standard scores, and normal curve equivalents. They are the way data from most tests are recorded. Rankings, or **ordinal scales**, show the order, from highest to lowest, for a variable. There are no indications about the value or size of differences between or among items in a list; the indications refer only to the relative order of the scores. For instance, subjects can be ranked according to their performance on a set of athletic tasks, and what will be reported is the order in which they scored (e.g., first, second, or third), not their actual accumulation of points. Olympic medal winners are reported using ordinal scales. Data from surveys and observations are sometimes recorded in this manner.

Categories separate data into two or more discrete aspects, such as male-female, red-white-blue, or always-frequently-infrequently-never. The data can be reported as numbers of items or as percentages of a total. Data recorded this way are considered **nominal scales**. Data from surveys and observations are sometimes recorded in this way.

Ratio scales, less frequently used in educational and other behavioral and social science research than the other three, show relative relationships among scores, such as half-as-large or three-times-as-tall. In dealing with educational variables, researchers usually do not have much use for these presentations.

Normal Distribution

Chapter 2 contains an explanation of central tendency and variability. The most common forms of each of these statistics for interval scale data are the mean and the standard deviation. To reiterate, the **mean** is the arithmetical average score, and the **standard deviation** (SD or ; σ) shows how the scores were distributed around the mean. The SD is based on the concept that given a large enough set of scores, they will produce a graph in the shape of a bell. This graph is called the **normal distri-bution curve** and shows a **normal distribution** of scores. In a normal distribution, the scores, or measures, are distributed symmetrically around the mean. In a normal distribution, the mean, median, and mode are identical.

The normal distribution graph, shown in Figure 8.1, represents a theoretical sta-tistical picture of how most human and nonhuman variables are distributed. Using as an example a human variable, such as ability to draw human figures as measured by a test, the curve would show that few people have scores indicating little of the trait (the extreme left end of the graph), that is, an inability to draw human figures, and few people have scores showing a great deal of the trait (the extreme right end of the graph), that is, a great ability to draw human figures. The center of the graph shows that most people have scores indicating some ability to draw human figures. This distribution is commonly called the **norm.**

There is a direct relationship between the SD and the normal distribution curve. Starting at the center, or mean, of the distributed variable, each SD represents a fixed, specific proportion of the population indicated in Figure 8.1 by the vertical lines. For example, the range between the mean and either extreme end of the graph (left or right) equals 50% of the population represented by the graph. The ranges between the mean and +1 SD (the area M↔A) and the mean and −1 SD (the area a↔M) each equal a little more than one-third (34%) of the distributed population. The ranges between +1 SD and +2 SDs (A↔B) and −1 SD and −2 SDs (b↔a) each equal about 14% of the population. Therefore, the range of scores included between −1 and +1 SD (a↔A) equals about 68% of the population, and between −2 and +2 SDs (b↔B) equals slightly over 95%. Most statistical procedures are based on the assumption that data approximate the normal distribution curve. In reality, the graphs produced from the data of many research studies are not as symmetrical as the normal distribution curve.

Frequently, scores used in research are derived from *raw* standardized test scores (the number of items correct). **Derived,** or converted, **scores** are changed to other scores such as *grade equivalents, age equivalents, percentiles, normal curve equivalents, sta-nines, scale scores,* or other *standard scores.* Figure 8.2 illustrates the more common of these derived scores and relates them to the normal distribution curve.

Each of these derived scores is used to describe test performance, and their rela-tion to the normal curve allows the user to compare performance on several mea-sures of performance. The research consumer should note the different derived scores that fall at the mean and the SD points on the normal curve illustrated on Figure 8.1.

Statistical Significance

The normal distribution curve is also called the *normal probability curve* because it is used to estimate the likelihood of an interval score or set of interval scores happen-ing by chance. In comparative and experimental research, researchers want to be sure that the observed differences between the means of two or more groups of sub-jects or two or more variables are truly different. That is, they want to know if the difference is a reliable one. If these means differ, researchers need to know the extent to which the difference could have happened by chance. When the observed differ-ence between these means is large enough to be beyond a predetermined chance level, the difference is considered as significant. **Statistical significance** occurs

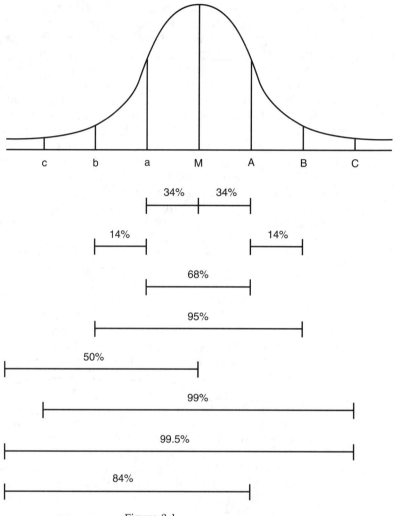

Figure 8.1
The Normal Distribution Curve

when the difference between the means of two sets of results exceeds a predetermined chance level. Researchers can thus know how confident they can be about the conclusions they make from their findings.

Three interrelated factors are usually considered in a statistical analysis: (a) the difference between group means, (b) the variability of the groups, and (c) the number of subjects in each group. All other things being equal, there is an increased likelihood that difference(s) between the means of two or more sets of scores is statistically significant when (a) the difference between the means becomes larger, (b) the variability of each set of scores becomes smaller, or (c) the size of the sample increases. These three relationships can be seen in Figure 8.3.

When researchers statistically conclude if a difference or relationship exists, there is the possibility of error. Two kinds of error can occur: (a) researchers accept the

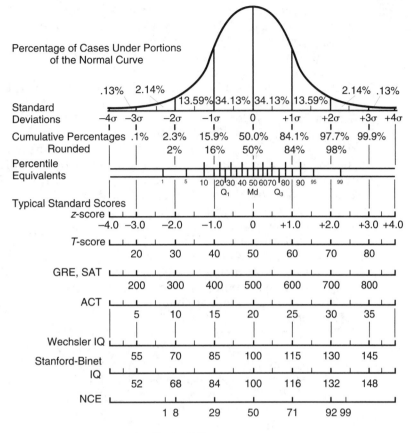

Figure 8.2
Common Derived Scores

The possibility of statistical significance increases as

differences between means	variability	sample size
or		or
↓	↓	↓
get larger	gets smaller	gets larger

Figure 8.3
Factors Affecting Statistical Significance

results as true when they are not and (b) researchers do not accept the results as true when they actually are.

For example, in the first error, researchers find what appears to be a statistically significant difference in student performance over previous performance when using a new instructional program. However, because of imperfections in sampling procedures (subject selection error) and the measuring instruments (reliability estimates), there may not be a true difference in student performance after using the new program, even though it appears as if a difference does exist. In such a case, the researchers will have concluded that the new instructional program is better than the old one when in fact that is not true. In the second error, researchers do not find a significant difference in student learning when actually there is a difference. In this case, there is a change resulting from teachers' use of an instructional technique, but the researchers do not observe it; that is, the change is not large enough to be seen. The second error may also result from imperfections in the sample and instrumentation.

In educational and other behavioral and social science research, researchers try to avoid making the first type of error, but to do this they increase the possibility of making the second. Relative to the discussion of the normal probability curve, researchers have commonly used certain probability levels. These conventional levels correspond to the extreme ends of the curve and designate a very small chance of the first type of error. It is important to realize that research producers and consumers *never* know whether either of these two error types is being made.

Researchers report the probability that the first type of error has occurred as a decimal. The probability level is shown in research reports as $p = .05$. This means that the chances of concluding that differences or relationships exist when they truly do not exist are no more than 5 chances out of 100.

These are odds similar to one's likelihood of winning a state lottery. Sometimes researchers report the probability level as $p < .05$, which is read as "the probability is less than 5 chances out of 100," or as $p \leq .05$, which is read as "the probability is equal to or less than 5 chances out of 100." Of course, when researchers realize that the probability is even less than $p = .05$, they may report it as $p = .01$, or even as $p = .001$.

Research consumers need to be wary of accepting any results (even if they are statistically significant) without considering whether the results are practical or meaningful in educational settings. What is of prime importance to research consumers is the usefulness of the results in terms of improving teacher effectiveness, student learning, and efficient uses of instructional resources. To determine whether research results have **practical significance,** research consumers need to answer the following: How effectively can the results be used in my teaching situation?

In recent years, researchers have begun to add to their findings an indication of the **effect size** of their statistical analyses. Effect size gives the consumer of research an indication of the magnitude (*meaningfulness* or *importance*) of the results by providing an additional measure to the significance level without regard to sample size. Also, reporting effect size is useful in interpreting results of studies with large samples, which might show statistical significance for very small (not practical) differences. It is also recommended that researchers include with the numerical indication of effect size some comments that place those effect sizes in a practical and theoretical context (Wilkinson & APA Task Force on Statistical Inference, 2000). Researchers may use one of several techniques; however, they most often show effect size in relation to the standard deviation of the data gathering instrument. Effect size is reported in several ways, but, most commonly, it is reported as a decimal fraction. Effect sizes of .20 are considered small; .50, medium; and .80, large.

One group of researchers reported their results in the following way:

> The means and standard deviations for the elementary schools showing increasing and decreasing computer use are presented in Table 2, as are the effect sizes for the differences between means. The largest effect size [d] was evident for differences in assault/bat-

tery/robbery. For the decreasing schools, the mean number of incidents was 3.23, while for the increasing schools, the mean was 0.99, a difference of approximately 2/3 of a standard deviation ($d = -0.67$). Similarly, negative effect sizes were evident for disorderly conduct/fighting/harassment ($d = -0.09$) and total conduct violations ($d = -0.14$), but these were much smaller in magnitude. Similarly, increasing schools showed reduced rates of disciplinary action with d values of $-.10$ and $-.13$ for in-school and out-of-school suspensions, respectively. Finally, daily attendance was higher in the increasing schools ($d = 0.25$), while both staff turnover ($d = -0.09$) and dropout prevention enrollment ($d = -0.18$) were lower. (Barron, Hogarty, Kromery, & Lenkway, 1999)

Degrees of Freedom.   Frequently, tables reporting the results of statistical analyses include an entry that identifies the **degrees of freedom** (*df*) used in the analysis. For the purposes of this text, degrees of freedom can be best understood as the number of ways data are *free* to vary in a statistical problem (Gay & Airasian, 2000; Kerlinger, 1973; Wiersma, 1995). In practice, degrees of freedom ordinarily are a function of the number of subjects and groups being analyzed. Usually, degrees of freedom are the total number of subjects or groups minus one. After the frequency of scores has been identified, then the variation remaining equals the number of subjects or groups minus one.

Interval Scale Data

Statistical procedures used with interval scales are based on certain assumptions, all of which are related to the concept of a normal distribution curve. These statistical procedures are called parametric statistics. In using parametric statistics, researchers are trying to draw some conclusion from the differences between the means of sample groups or sets of scores.

The assumptions for using parametric statistics are as follows:

The variables are measured in interval scales.

The score of any subject is not influenced by those of any other subjects; that is, each is an independent phenomenon.

The subjects are selected from and represent a normally distributed population.

When the research involves two or more groups of subjects, each of which represents different populations, the variables that distinguish each population are similarly distributed among each population.

A common parametric statistic is the *t test.* It is used when there are two sets of scores to determine whether the difference between the means of the two sets of scores is significant. It is reported as numbers such as $t = 1.6$ or $t = 3.1$. After determining the value of t, researchers consult a statistical table to determine whether the value is significant at a certain probability level. A t test can be used, for example, to examine the mean scores in reading and mathematics for one group of subjects, or it can be used to examine mean scores in reading for two different groups of subjects. The t test is used frequently in single-variable comparative and experimental research, and its use is limited by the same factors that limit single-variable research.

Another parametric statistic used with interval data in comparative research is the **product-moment correlation,** which refers to the quantified relationship between two sets of scores for the same group of subjects. The result of the arithmetic computation is a correlation coefficient, which is expressed as *r*, a decimal between

Most ~
Common

−1.0 and +1.0. The most common interval scale correlation coefficient is the **Pearson product-moment correlation.** Correlations show whether two or more variables have a systematic relationship of occurrence; that is, whether high scores for one variable occur with high scores of another (a positive relationship) or whether they occur with low scores of that other variable (a negative relationship). The occurrence of low scores for one variable with low scores for another is also an example of a positive relationship. A correlation coefficient of zero indicates that the two variables have no relationship with each other; that is, they are independent of each other.

Correlations can also be used to establish predictions. When a strong relationship has been established between two variables, a correlation can be used to predict the possible occurrence of either variable. The predictive use of correlation is important for such educational endeavors as early intervention programs for students with special needs. For example, certain tests, including tests of basic concepts and cognitive abilities, are appropriate for young children and are highly predictive of students' later school performance.

Table 2.3 (Chapter 2, p. 33) shows how correlation coefficients are reported in table format, from a study about the relationships between topic-specific background knowledge and measures of overall writing quality. When correlation coefficients are statistically significant, they indicate that the variables are probably systematically related beyond a certain level of chance. In other words, the two variables *go together;* significant correlations do not indicate that there are any *causal* effects of one variable on the other. In Table 2.3, the relationship between the holistic scoring method and teachers' marks is positive and significant—high coherence scores were given to the same students' work that received high teacher marks. On the other hand, the relationship between coherence and the number of words and clauses, which is negative, was not significant, and therefore the two scoring methods can be said to be unrelated. Again, no causality is implied, nor should it be assumed.

When research designs call for examining differences among the means of two or more groups of subjects or two or more variables, they frequently use the **analysis of variance** (ANOVA), which is reported in F ratios. The advantage in using an ANOVA is that several independent variables as well as several factors can be examined. In its simplest form, ANOVA can be thought of as a multiple t test. The ANOVA is appropriate for use with some comparative research designs and with experimental research designs, such as the pretest-posttest with multiple control groups, the Solomon four-group design, counterbalanced designs, common factorial designs, and causal-comparative designs. The ANOVA procedure can be used when more than one independent variable is involved. Table 2.4 (Chapter 2, p. 37) shows the ANOVA results for a two-way factorial design from a study using two independent variables: the effect of two levels of reading potential (disabled reader vs. slow learner) and two levels of reading placement (at instructional level vs. above instructional level). Notice that the researchers indicated two significance levels: $p < .05$ and $p < .01$. The results show that there were differences in results (on the dependent variable: vocabulary achievement) based on the subjects' reading potential and for their reading placement. There was no difference in vocabulary achievement when potential and placement were considered (Potential × Placement). On comprehension tests, only Potential showed significant differences ($p < .01$).

An important feature of ANOVA is that it can show the **interaction effects** between and among variables. In Chapter 7, the negative consequence of treatment interaction was discussed, as well as the possibility of measuring the interaction in factorial designs. Interactions are also expressed as F ratios within an ANOVA table, and often the interaction is illustrated in a graph. For research consumers, treatment interactions permit instructional modifications for particular groups of learners. For example, referring again to Table 2.4, there were no significant two-way interactions (Potential × Placement) for achievement in either vocabulary or comprehension. That can be interpreted as indicating that, with this group of subjects, how they are placed for instruction and what their achievement potential is do not *together* influence how they will achieve in vocabulary and comprehension. In this case, there is no interaction effect. Obviously, in other situations an interaction effect may exist. In such situations, an interaction effect may indicate that the two independent variables do affect the dependent variable differently.

In previous chapters, reference was made to situations in which two or more groups of subjects differ on one or more variables, thereby limiting the generalizability of the studies' findings. The differences might have occurred because preexisting groups of subjects were used, instead of randomly selected and assigned groups of subjects. When research producers think these variables might influence the dependent variables under study (and the variables are not features that are used to distinguish between groups, e.g., distinguishing between male and female, or high and low mathematical performance), they use a statistical procedure to equate the groups on these independent variable factors.

One frequently used procedure is known as **analysis of covariance** (ANCOVA). Its use allows researchers to examine differences among the means of groups of subjects as if the means were equal from the start. They do this by adjusting the differences in the means to make them hypothetically equal. The equalizing variable is known as the covariate. The procedure is similar to the use of a "handicap" in bowling or golf leagues to balance out differences among players and teams. In all other ways, ANCOVAs are interpreted like ANOVAs.

When researchers wish to examine the relationships among more than two variables, they can use a **multiple correlation** technique (also called *multiple regression* technique). The procedure is interpreted similarly to a single correlation coefficient. Multiple correlations can also be used to make predictions. Prediction scores are reported as a multiple correlation coefficient, or R, and have the same range as single correlations. Multiple regression is used frequently in causal-comparative experimental research because it combines ANOVA and correlational techniques. Research consumers need to keep in mind that the causality in causal-comparative research is assumed because of a strong, highly predictive relationship. This assumed causality needs to be reconfirmed by further experimental studies.

Nominal and Ordinal Scale Data

When researchers collect data that are measured in nominal and ordinal scales, they must use different types of statistics. These statistics, called **nonparametric statistics,** work on different assumptions. Nonparametric statistics are used when

The populations do not have the characteristics of the normal distribution curve.

Symbols or numbers are used as labels on categories (nominal scales).

An expected or rank order is apparent but the order is not necessarily equally spaced as is the case with interval data.

Table 8.1

Corresponding Parametric and Nonparametric Statistics

Parametric	Nonparametric
t test	Mann-Whitney *U* Test
ANOVA	Friedman two-way analysis of variance
	Kruskal-Wallis one-way analysis of variance
Pearson product-moment correlation	Spearman rank-order correlation

For each parametric statistical procedure there are corresponding nonparametric statistical procedures. In general, nonparametric statistics are less frequently used in educational and other behavioral and social science research than are parametric statistics. Table 8.1 shows corresponding parametric and nonparametric statistics.

One popular nonparametric statistical procedure is the **chi-square test** (χ^2). It is used to test the significance of group differences between observed and expected outcomes when data are reported as frequencies or percentages of a total or as nominal scales. Table 2.2 (Chapter 2, p. 32) shows an example of chi-square reporting from a study that examined how teachers responded when students made miscues (deviant oral reading responses). In their analysis, the researchers found that teachers who dealt with unattempted miscues supplied words more often than they used all other responses combined. Indications of statistical significance are interpreted the same for nonparametric statistics as they are for parametric statistics.

DATA ANALYSIS IN QUALITATIVE RESEARCH

In qualitative studies, researchers verbally analyze data. This involves examining and organizing notes from interviews and observations and reducing the information into smaller segments from which they can see patterns and trends. In addition, researchers interpret the meanings of these patterns and trends and create research hypotheses and questions for verification in further research. Qualitative researchers begin their analyses while still in the research setting and finish it after all data have been collected. An important point about qualitative research is that qualitative researchers often do measure and count; in other words, they quantify some data. However, they do not use statistical analyses to verify or support their results and conclusion, nor do they consider statistical probabilities.

Research consumers should expect qualitative researchers to fully explain their analysis methods so that the logic of their decisions can be followed and evaluated. In Chapter 2, there is a discussion of the features of qualitative research methods, and in Chapter 7 are questions that can be used to determine the reliability of observational research. Research consumers may wish to review those sections before continuing the discussion here, which is a synthesis of the ideas of several scholars who use qualitative research methods (Bogdan & Biklen, 1998; Creswell, 1998; Eisner, 1991; Firestone, 1987; Gay & Airasian, 2000; Guthrie & Hall, 1984; Jacob, 1987, 1988; Lancy, 1993; Lincoln & Guba, 1985; Maxwell, 1998; Putney et al., 1999; Smith, 1987; Smith & Heshusius, 1986; Van Maanen et al., 1982; Wilson, 1977).

In the research setting, commonly called the field, qualitative researchers continually make decisions that narrow their study. They may start out with broad questions and begin looking at an entire educational setting, but as their study proceeds they concentrate on smaller issues and create more specific analytical questions. Data collection is an additive process. New information is looked for and collected on the basis of previous data because the qualitative researchers are interpreting as they assemble additional information. This does not mean they discard or selectively omit information. On the contrary, they maintain extensive on-site field notes. It is the influence of the events in the field and their ongoing interpretation of those events that guide qualitative researchers in their search for additional information. For example, while observing middle-school science lessons to study teachers' use of graphic organizers, a qualitative researcher takes notes in one class about students' collaborative activities in examining and recording the mealworm's life cycle. What the researcher notes is a combination of formalized small-group behaviors and seemingly unstructured, random student interaction. Noting this, the researcher later seeks out information leading to a hypothesis about a possible interrelationship among teachers' teaching style, their development of student collaborations, and students' use of graphic organizers.

One procedure used by qualitative researchers to support their interpretations is **triangulation,** a procedure for cross-validating information. Triangulation is collecting information from several sources about the same event or behavior. For example, in studying parents' attitudes about their involvement in their children's homework activities, data would be collected from interviews with parents, students, siblings, teachers, and from observations of parent-student behaviors during homework activities.

After collecting data in the field, qualitative researchers organize their data by sifting through the information and clustering seemingly similar ideas. These categories of information are labeled for ease of use and cross-referencing. Qualitative researchers start with broad categories:

Settings (*where* teaching and learning occur)

Situations (*when* an activity or behavior occurs)

Activities (*what* teachers and students do)

Behaviors (*how* teachers and students act and respond)

Techniques or methods (*how* and *why* teachers and students respond to an event)

Socializations (*with whom* teachers and students regularly interact)

Depending on the nature of their data, these categories may be expanded, subdivided, eliminated, or renamed. Some notes may be cross-referenced because they contain information relevant to more than one category.

Research consumers need to know the coding categories qualitative researchers use and how the classification systems were developed and revised. Since qualitative analyses are subjective, producers of qualitative research should be explicit about their theoretical formulations and their conceptual positions regarding the topic being investigated. When these are not explicitly stated in research reports, research consumers need to be aware that these formulations and positions usually are reflected in researchers' purpose questions and classification systems.

Validity of Data

An important aspect of quantitative research is its generalizability. In qualitative research, the arguments for generalizability are not particularly strong; that is, qualitative researchers do not presume to be able to generalize from one classroom to another (Erickson, 1986; Firestone, 1993; Maxwell, 1998; Nielsen, 1995).

However, that does not mean that a qualitative study should not have internal and external validity (Creswell, 1998; Maxwell, 1998; Spindler & Spindler, 1992). Research consumers need to be able to identify the *trustworthiness* of the inferences qualitative researchers draw from their data. Nor are qualitative researchers usually concerned with the replicability of their studies or with a broad generalizability of their results.

Research consumers should not ask, "Does the research apply to all individuals within a target population?" Rather, consumers might try to determine whether other researchers have made similar or different conclusions about the instructional implications of the research topic. More important, research consumers should concern themselves with determining whether the researchers' conclusions and instructional implications have meaning for the students with whom they are acquainted, being fully aware that there might be more than one interpretation of the researchers' analyses.

Research consumers should understand that validity in qualitative research is relative to the researchers' purpose and the circumstances under which the data were collected. Each set of qualitative researchers analyzes data differently depending upon their theoretical perspectives, which should be stated explicitly. Research consumers should look for the following specific evidence of data validity in qualitative research reports (Biklen, 1993; Marshall & Rossman, 1995; Maxwell, 1992, 1998):

1. The researchers acknowledge, show sensitivity about, and maintain an ethical stance toward the individuals being researched.
2. The researchers' work and their analyses "in-field" are fully documented, the logic of their data categorizations are evident, and the relationships among those concepts seem accurate within an identified theory of learning and instruction.
3. The researchers' descriptions are factual, and they provide evidence of minimal distortion because of possible errors of omission and commission; they include cases or situations that might challenge their emerging hypotheses or conclusions.
4. The data were collected from more than one source (triangulation), and there is evidence confirming the accuracy of the respondents' accounts.
5. The researchers are tolerant of ambiguity; they have searched out alternative explanations through multiple sources of data and have devised ways for checking the quality of their data.
6. The researchers show evidence of formulating and reformulating their interpretations and analyses of data; there are comparisons of data and checks of hypotheses against new data.
7. The researchers are self-analytical and recognize the limits of their subjectivity; they show evidence of guarding against value judgments in their analyses.
8. The researchers' results are presented in a manner such that others might be able to use them (if deemed appropriate).

9. The study is linked to the larger educational context in which the data were collected.
10. The researchers acknowledge the limitations of their study as far as generalizing to other educational settings.

READING RESULTS SECTIONS

The results sections of research reports are usually the most difficult for research consumers to read and interpret. Often research consumers are intimidated by the statistical procedures and the presentation of numerical data in charts and tables. However, these sections can be read systematically if the reading plan outlined in Chapter 3 is followed. By the time research consumers read the results sections, they should already know the researchers' purpose, questions, and research design; major results and conclusions; target population and subject selection technique; instrumentation; and research method. What is left to understand are the specific results relative to the research questions.

Results sections are read during the third phase of the reading plan, when the research consumer is confirming predictions and knowledge (see p. 60). The goal of this phase for research consumers is to verify that their (not the research producers') purposes have been met and to decide what information supports the researchers' purpose and adds to their (the consumers') knowledge base.

In reports of quantitative research, the results of statistical procedures, such as the *t* test, correlation, and ANOVA, are not always put into table format; the numerical information may be part of the general discourse of the report because of space limitations. Research consumers should expect, however, that the reports' authors give an explanation of the numerical information, whether it is within the text or in tables.

You should review the questions in "Evaluating Results Sections" at the beginning of this chapter before reading the following portions of this chapter, in which the results sections for each of the studies whose method sections were discussed in Chapter 7 are presented.

Quantitative Research

Descriptive Research. The following results section is from a quantitative descriptive study (see Chapter 7, pp. 126–128, to review the method section of this study). Note that the researchers have analyzed the data using a multivariate or factor analysis of variance (MANOVA), which means that the researchers were analyzing data from two or more independent variables at the same time. Research consumers should interpret MANOVA results similar to ANOVA results. The researchers have not presented the results of their statistical analyses in table form.

> *Purpose of the study: To conduct individualized interviews with middle- and high-school students to better understand their perceptions of teachers' adaptations to meet the special learning needs of students in general education classrooms.*

RESULTS

Table 2 summarizes students' responses by achievement level. Tables 3, 4, 5, and 6 provide students' responses by category and rationale with representative supporting comments for selected interview questions.

Table 2 Summary of Students' Responses by Achievement Group (Frequency & Percentages)

Question	LD N	LD %	ESOL N	ESOL %	LA N	LA %	AA N	AA %	HA N	HA %
1. Prefers experiments	15	75	15	75	11	73	16	80	14	70
Prefers textbook	4	20	2	10	2	13	2	10	0	0
Both	1	5	3	15	2	13	2	10	6	30
2. Write summaries	15	75	13	65	13	87	13	65	16	80
No summaries	5	25	7	35	2	13	6	30	4	20
Depends	0	0	0	0	0	0	1	5	0	0
3. Study guides	14	70	18	90	12	80	19	95	16	80
No study guides	6	30	2	10	2	13	0	0	3	15
Depends	0	0	0	0	1	7	1	5	1	5
4. Tell purpose	20	100	19	95	14	93	19	95	20	100
No purpose	0	0	1	5	1	7	1	5	0	0
5. Teach strategies	20	100	20	100	15	100	20	100	20	100
No strategies	0	0	0	0	0	0	0	0	0	0
6. Homogeneous groups	10	50	9	45	10	67	7	35	5	25
Heterogeneous groups	10	50	11	55	5	33	12	60	14	70
Depends	0	0	0	0	0	0	1	5	1	5
7. Stay in same groups	8	40	5	25	1	7	5	25	5	25
Change groups	12	60	12	60	14	93	12	60	15	75
No preference	0	0	3	15	0	0	3	15	0	0
8. Teacher assigns	9	45	8	40	9	60	11	55	11	55
Students choose	11	55	11	55	6	40	8	40	8	40
No preference	0	0	1	5	0	0	1	5	1	5
9. Work alone	4	20	6	30	3	20	5	30	5	25
Work in pairs	12	60	6	30	6	40	9	45	5	25
Work in groups	4	20	7	35	5	33	3	15	5	25
Depends	0	0	1	5	1	7	3	15	5	25
10. Peer tutoring	18	90	20	100	12	80	19	95	17	85
No peer tutoring	2	10	0	0	3	20	1	5	3	15
11. Same test for all	10	50	13	65	11	73	13	65	16	80
Different tests	10	50	7	35	4	27	7	35	4	20
12. Same homework	13	65	15	75	10	67	16	80	16	80
Different homework	7	35	5	25	5	33	4	20	4	20
13. Adapt lesson	18	90	18	90	15	100	20	100	15	75
Do not adapt lesson	1	5	2	10	0	0	0	0	5	25
Depends	1	5	0	0	0	0	0	0	0	0
14. Changes slow class	19	95	14	70	12	80	17	85	19	95
Do not slow class	1	5	6	30	3	20	3	15	1	5

Note. LD = Learning Disabled (*N* = 20); ESOL = English as a Second Language (*N* = 20); LA = Low Achieving (*N* = 15); AA = Average Achieving (*N* = 20); HA = High Achieving (*N* = 20).

Textbook Adaptations vs. No Adaptations (Questions 1–5)

Students in both grade groupings (middle and high school) overwhelmingly agreed that textbook adaptations help them understand difficult content material (see Table 2). However, students differed somewhat on their rationales for selecting adaptations. In general, middle-school students preferred adaptations to promote **interest** whereas high-school students, in general, preferred adaptations to promote **learning.**

Of the textbook adaptations, students were most enthusiastic about learning strategies, with 100% of the sample favoring strategy instruction. Students of all groups commented that strategies make learning more effective. A middle-school student with LD said, "They help students to see, step-by-step, what the material is about." Many students reported that strategies help promote independence as in the case of a HA middle-school student, "I prefer a teacher who will provide techniques and strategies at the beginning and then let students go on their own after that"; and an AA high-school student, "Strategies help prepare students better for studying in college where they're not as likely to receive such help." Thus, a majority of students recognized that strategies can help make learning easier. An AA middle-school student commented, "You don't have to rack your brains to figure out how to do it."

Also highly favored were purpose statements (preferred by 95% of the students), because "they tell you what the point is." As expressed by one HA student, they help you "focus on salient content." Study guides or outlines (preferred by 83%) "tell you what to focus on" and "help you understand better."

Seventy-five percent of the same preferred projects and experiments to textbook reading, because "they are more interesting and fun" and because they facilitate understanding. One LA student explained, "I prefer experiments and projects because the teacher gets more involved in the class, whereas with other assignments the teachers do not get involved." Another LA student commented, "I would love for someone to create a better way to teach chemistry or create a book which would be easier and more interesting to read. It seems every time I try to read a textbook, it's like I'm reading Chinese or something." Fourteen students (15%) advocated the combined use of text and direct experiences as in the case of the HA student who said, "Projects are fun, but the book explains it better."

Although the majority of students felt they learned by writing summaries or answering questions (74% of the total sample, and 65% of the ESOL and AA students), this was not a well-liked learning procedure. Those who favored writing summaries explained that doing so "helps you understand and remember better." However, as noted by one middle-school ESOL student, "Most kids don't like it, but if you don't do it, you won't learn anything." Students who did not like summaries thought they were too much work, and preferred other activities, such as discussions.

Heterogeneous vs. Homogeneous Ability Grouping (Question 6)

Slightly more students preferred heterogeneous to homogeneous grouping (55%). Interesting differences emerged between grade-level groups and among achievement groups regarding grouping (see Tables 2 and 3). Middle-school students tended to be more in favor of homogeneous groups (57%) and high-school students more in favor of heterogeneous groups (67%). Although we had expected to find the opposite, the majority of LA students (67%) favored homogeneous grouping, and the majority of HA students (70%) favored heterogeneous grouping. In fact, the 5 HA students who preferred homogeneous grouping were all middle-school students—100% of the high-school HA students favored mixed ability grouping.

The most common rationale for grouping by ability levels was that "slower students hold back faster students." Most students who favored ability grouping, particularly middle-school and low-achieving students, were concerned about high-achieving students, worrying that "higher students would be bored by easier work." An LA student indicated

Table 3   Frequency of Students' Responses With Breakdown by Rationale and Representative Supporting Comments for Question 6: "Do You Prefer Grouping by Ability Levels or Mixed Groups?"

Categories & Comments	MS	HS
Prefers grouping by ability levels	**27**	**14**
1. Rationale: Faster students learn better "Slower student hold back faster students." "Brighter students get bored with slower students."	19	6
2. Rationale: Slower students learn better "If you put someone slow with people who learn fast, he won't understand and he'll do bad in that class." "The teacher could help those who don't learn fast."	7	7
3. Rationale: Equity "Slower kids might copy from higher kids."	1	1
Prefers mixed groups	**20**	**32**
1. Rationale: Benefits faster students "You learn more when you explain to others."	2	3
2. Rationale: Benefits slower students "Smarter students can help slower students." "It pushes slower kids to do better." "Separate groups by ability level stigmatize the slower learners."	14	31
3. Rationale: Equity "Everyone should learn the same things."	4	4

Note. MS = Middle School; HS = High School.

that it "slows down other students a lot; that's why we should have everyone categorized with people of their same ability." But some students who preferred homogeneous groups were concerned about slower students: "That [ability grouping] gives everyone a chance to learn. If you put someone slow with people who learn fast, he won't understand and he'll do bad in that class."

Students who favored mixed ability grouping noted that "higher kids can help lower kids." Most students who preferred mixed groups demonstrated a concern for slower students though others were also concerned about their own learning. One HA student favored mixed groups, "as long as an individual's grades would not be inhibited by someone else's incompetence." A few students, such as this high-school AA student, noted that "separate groups by ability level stigmatize the slower students." Some students who preferred heterogeneous groups pointed out that there are also benefits for the high-achieving students; for example, "You learn more when you explain it to others."

Same Groups vs. Different Groups (Question 7)

Most students were in favor of sometimes changing groups (68%) (see Table 2), with LA students most strongly favoring this practice (93%). Students conveyed that by switching groups, students can "learn different things" and "get to know other people." By comparison, students who prefer not to switch groups like the familiarity that comes from working in one group and feel they "work better in a constant environment."

Teacher Assignment vs. Student Selection of Groups (Question 8)

Differences were found between the two grade groupings and among ability groups regarding group selection. Whereas most middle-school students (64%) would like to select their own groups, most high-school students (63%) preferred that the teacher assign students to groups. The majority of LD and ESOL students (55%) preferred that students choose their own groups. The majority of LA, AA, and HA students (60%, 55%, and 55%, respectively) preferred that the teacher assign students to groups. Most of the students who would like to select their own groups said that they "don't want to get stuck with kids they don't like" and that they want to work with their friends. Some students favoring student selection were of the opinion that "students know best who they can work with." Students who would rather have the teacher assign groups expressed concerns about task completion and felt they could accomplish more without their friends. Many students said something similar to this comment made by a high-school student with LD, "If I pick my friends I'll just sit and talk and the work won't be done."

Working Alone, in Pairs, in Groups (Question 9)

Forty percent of all students interviewed said they would prefer to work in pairs rather than alone or in larger groups. The preference for pairs was particularly prevalent among students with LD, with 60% selecting this option. Preferences for working alone or in larger groups were equally divided (with 24% and 25% of the students, respectively, selecting each). Middle-school students showed more inclination toward groups, high-school students toward working alone. Eleven percent of all students noted that their preference depended on the assignment. As one student explained, "I prefer to do in-class assignments in a group, but at-home assignments alone so my grade doesn't suffer from someone else's incompetence." Students who preferred to work by themselves noted that there are "fewer distractions" when working alone and that they "do not like to depend on anyone else." Students who preferred working with one other student commented that students in pairs can help one another without the chaos often present in larger groups. Students who prefer working with many students rationalized that "the work is spread out more" and "there are more people to explain things." Some students commented, "Groups are more fun."

Peer Tutoring vs. No Peer Tutoring (Question 10)

The overwhelming majority of students (91%) stated a preference for peer tutoring, with no real differences between grade levels and few differences among achievement groups. Most students supported their preference for tutoring by describing the benefits of tutoring for tutees. As expressed by one HA high-school student, "Students can often explain material better than the teacher. It's better for students to understand a smaller amount of material well [learned from a tutor] than to keep up with teacher lectures through more chapters but not really learning." An ESOL student revealed, "In calculus I don't know what the teacher is talking about, but if someone else explains it to me, I get it." A few students described the benefits of tutoring for tutors; for example, "Sometimes the smarter students learn more when they are teaching it to someone else because they can catch their mistakes." The few students who did not like tutoring remarked that "it was the teacher's job to get them to understand."

Same Tests and Homework vs. Different Tests and Homework (Questions 11 and 12)

The majority of students thought that all students should be administered the same tests (66%) and the same homework (74%). This result is consistent with findings from our previous research (Vaughn, Schumm, Niarhos, & Daugherty, 1993; Vaughn, Schumm, & Kouzekanani, 1993). However, more middle-school than high-school students believed that some students should receive different homework and/or tests (36% and 40% for middle-school students compared with 17% and 27% for high-school students).

Table 4   Frequency of Students' Responses with Breakdown by Rationale and Representative Supporting Comments for Question 10: "Should Students Who Understand Difficult Material Tutor Students Who Do Not Understand?"

Categories & Comments	MS	HS
Prefers tutoring	**44**	**42**
1. Rationale: Tutor learns better "Sometimes the smarter students learn more when they are teaching someone else, because they can catch their mistakes."	3	3
2. Rationale: Tutee learns better "Students can often explain material better than the teacher. It's better for students to understand a smaller amount of material well (learned from a tutor) than to keep up with teacher lectures through more chapters but not really learning."	27	29
3. Rationale: More motivating "I like to help others." "It's easier to relate to another student."	11	7
4. Rationale: Helps teacher "It helps the teacher. She can't go person to person helping each student."	7	6
Prefers no tutoring	**3**	**6**
"Students might make mistakes and make matters worse for the student who doesn't understand." "It's the teacher's responsibility."		

Note. MS = Middle School; HS = High School.

Students with LD were split 50/50 regarding their preference for same vs. different tests, compared to an 80/20 split among HA students. Equity was proffered as the rationale by almost all students, both those who thought all students should receive the same tests and homework and those who felt that tests and homework should be different for some students. Many students exclaimed that it is "not fair to change a test or homework for some students." Other students pointed out that "it's more fair" to give different tests and homework because of students' different ability levels. When students who advocated giving everyone the same tests and homework were asked a follow-up question regarding whether it would be OK to give a different test to a student with LD or an ESOL student, most students said that it would be all right. Some students noted that these students with special needs should be placed in other classes.

Adapt Lesson vs. Do Not Adapt Lesson (Question 13)

Almost all students (91%) felt teachers should slow down or change lessons when some students did not understand the lesson content. No real differences between grade level groups were noted on this issue, but a few differences emerged among achievement groups. In contrast with LA and AA groups (100% of the students favored adaptations), 25% of the students in the HA group opposed adaptations.

As shown in Table 5, the majority of students who favored adaptations did so because changes were perceived as facilitating learning. As expressed by one high-school AA student, "I've been in this position and I found that by making changes, the teacher has made the material more understandable." Some students emphasized that it is the teacher's role to assist all students; for example, "This will help struggling students and show the teacher

Table 5 Frequency of Students' Responses With Breakdown by Rationale and Representative Supporting Comments for Question 13: "Should Teachers Change the Way They Are Teaching (e.g., Slow Down) When Some Students Don't Understand?"

Categories & Comments	MS	HS
Prefers teacher not to change lesson	**4**	**4**
"The teacher should continue the lesson as long as the majority of the class understands it."		
Prefers teacher to change lesson	**40**	**43**
1. Rationale: Better for learning	25	28
"I've been in this position and I found that by changing, the teacher has made the material more understandable."		
"If students are confused and the teacher keeps going, they'll just get more confused. They won't get any better."		
2. Rationale: More motivating	4	1
"Otherwise, students who learn slower say, 'Forget this, I'm never going to get this,' and they give up."		
3. Rationale: Teacher's role	5	9
"This will help struggling students and show the teacher cares about them. Teachers are here to help students learn, not to make it more difficult for them."		
"It's probably the teaching method and not the material that is responsible for the difficulty with understanding the lesson."		
4. Rationale: Equity	3	3
"Everyone has the same right to learn."		
5. Other	3	0

Note. MS = Middle School; HS = High School.

cares about them. Teachers are here to help students learn, not to make it more difficult for them." And one middle-school HA student pointed out, "It's probably the teaching method and not the material that is responsible for the difficulty with understanding the lesson." A few students noted, "Everyone has the same right to learn."

How Much Do Adaptations Slow Down the Rest of the Class? (Question 14)

The majority of students (85%) expressed the opinion that adaptations to assist students who are having difficulty **do** slow down the rest of the class; however, close to half of these students (46%) felt that this is beneficial (see Table 6). Although middle- and high-school students' opinions differed little on this issue, differences were noted among achievement groups. Specifically, 95% of the students in the LD and HA groups felt that adaptations slow down lessons, compared with 70% of the students in the ESOL group.

Fifty-five percent of the total sample felt that adaptations either do not slow down the class or slow down the class a little, but not too much; for example, "I don't think it slows down students who already understand, because practice makes perfect. They might get bored after a while, but they won't forget it." Or, as another student pointed out, "Others can work on assignments during this time so it is sort of a benefit for them."

On the other hand, 44% of all students felt that adaptations inhibit some students too much; for example, "It depends. If the teacher makes changes that are drastically different from what they were doing, it could unfairly slow down the students who already understand. If they make occasional changes until students catch up, however, that would

Table 6   Frequency of Students' Responses With Representative Supporting Comments for Question 14: "Do Adaptations to Assist Students Who Are Having Difficulty Slow Down the Rest of the Class?"

Categories & Comments	MS	HS
Does not slow down the class "I don't think it slows down students who already understand, because practice makes perfect. They might get bored after a while, but they won't forget it."	8	7
A little, but not too much "Others can work on assignments during this time so it is sort of a benefit for them." "Not much. If anything, it gives them a better understanding of the lesson. Most students are courteous and won't complain."	18	19
Somewhat/It depends "It depends. If the teacher makes changes that are drastically different from what they were doing, it could unfairly slow down the students who already understand. If they make occasional changes until students catch up, however, that would be okay."	7	11
A lot "A lot. It is boring for those who understand." "You may get only half the lesson content you're supposed to get."	1	10
Other "The person should go to the teacher other than class time so as not to slow the class, like before or after school."	0	1

Note. MS = Middle School; HS = High School.

be OK." Many students were concerned that changes could slow down some students a lot, limiting content coverage and creating boredom. Several of these students recommended that slower students receive help outside of class or be placed in a different class.

Although many students expressed the view that adaptations slow down some students a great deal, these students still preferred that teachers make adaptations. However, many reported that their teachers did not typically make adaptations. One student stated it this way, "Very few of my teachers abide by these preferences (e.g., textbook adaptations). I believe that it is for this reason that I become bored of school and turn my interests toward out-of-school activities. It is not the text that makes the student, but the method teachers use. Plain and simple, teachers do not teach anymore!" (Vaughn et al., 1995)

Comparative Research.   In quantitative comparative research, researchers examine the descriptions of two or more variables and make decisions about their differences or relationships. They can also make predictions about one variable based on information about another. Research consumers should be concerned that only appropriate generalizations are made from comparative and predictive data. The following results section is from a comparative study of the relationship among several variables (see Chapter 7, pp. 128–130, to review the method section of this study).

Purpose of the study: To examine children's reading difficulties from the perspectives of the children, their parents, and their teachers.

Table 1   Reading Problems Reported by Children, Parents, and Teachers

	Children		Parents		Teachers	
	Gr(1–3) *n* (%)	Gr(4–6) *n* (%)	Gr(1–3) *n* (%)	Gr(4–6) *n* (%)	Gr(1–3) *n* (%)	Gr(4–6) *n* (%)
Word ID	22 (67%)	11 (55%)	10 (29%)	11 (41%)	18 (34%)	8 (32%)
Comprehension	2 (6%)	4 (20%)	8 (23%)	7 (26%)	16 (30%)	9 (36%)
Attitude/Behavior	4 (12%)	4 (20%)	10 (29%)	8 (30%)	13 (25%)	7 (28%)
Other	3 (9%)	0 (0%)	1 (3%)	0 (0%)	5 (9%)	0 (0%)
Don't know/no response	2 (6%)	1 (5%)	6 (17%)	1 (4%)	1 (2%)	1 (4%)

RESULTS

Reading Problems Reported by Children, Parents, and Teachers

The first analysis looked at the difficulties reported by each group by lower elementary (grades 1–3) and by upper elementary (grades 4–6) grade levels (see Table 1). Of the 40 subjects in each group, thirty-seven children, thirty-three parents, and thirty-eight teachers reported at least one reading difficulty, with four children, seventeen parents, and twenty-four teachers reporting 2 or more.

Thirty-three of the forty children in the study reported difficulties with word identification, with lower elementary children expressing more concern about this problem than older children. Few comprehension or attitude/behavior problems were mentioned, and when they occurred, the older children were more likely to report them. Parents' most frequently stated problem was word identification with the older children's parents expressing the most concern. Parents also reported more difficulties with comprehension and attitude/behavior than did children. In addition, they also reported more concern about attitude/behavior problems than their children's comprehension. Teachers reported about the same level of concern for both word identification and comprehension difficulties, and they referred to comprehension problems more frequently than did children and parents.

In addition to the previously described problems, other miscellaneous difficulties were reported for the lower elementary children. Three children mentioned difficulties such as "No problem," "Following lines," and "Losing your place." One parent attributed her third grade child's difficulty to "Poor eyesight in kindergarten." Three teachers reported difficulties with the successful completion of workbook pages and skill sheets. One teacher was concerned about the child, "Being unable to apply skills to reading," and another reported that the child's difficulties were due to, "Speech and hearing patterns."

Agreement Among Child, Parent, and Teacher

Next, we examined the extent to which individual child-parent-teacher triads reported the same problem (see Table 2). At the lower elementary level, there were 26 triads with at least one member reporting a word identification problem, 22 triads with at least one member reporting a comprehension problem, and 18 triads with at least one member reporting an attitude/behavior problem. At the upper elementary level, there were 13 triads with at least one member reporting a word identification problem, 10 triads with at least one member reporting a comprehension problem, and 10 triads with at least one member reporting an attitude/behavior problem.

When child-parent-teacher triads were examined, the most frequently agreed upon problem, regardless of grade level, was word identification. Agreement for all problems

Table 2   Agreement by Reading Problem and Grade Level

	Grades 1–3			Grades4–6		
	Word ID $n=26$ n (%)	Comp $n=22$ n (%)	Att/Beh $n=18$ n (%)	Word ID $n=13$ n (%)	Comp $n=10$ n (%)	Att/Beh $n=10$ n (%)
Child-Parent-Teacher	6 (23%).	1 (5%)	1 (6%)	5 (38%)	2 (20%)	2 (20%)
Parent-Teacher	7 (27%)	5 (23%)	6 (33%)	6 (46%)	7 (70%)	5 (50%)

appeared to increase with age with the actual percentages still being relatively low, ranging from 28% (11 triads) for word identification to 10% (three triads) for attitude/behavior. Across all problem areas, parents and teachers agreed more frequently with each other than with the children, and the pattern of agreement appeared to be different as well. In contrast to the child-parent-teacher agreement which favored word identification, parents and teacher most frequently agreed upon difficulties with attitude/behavior for lower elementary children and comprehension for upper elementary. However, the agreement level for the lower elementary parent-teacher triads was still relatively low, ranging from 33% to attitude/behavior to 23% for comprehension. The upper elementary parent-teacher triads had higher percentages of reported agreement for all three problem areas, ranging from 70% for comprehension to 46% for word identification.

Parents' and Teachers' Assessment of Children's Reading

The comprehension analysis compared teacher's and parents' Likert-scaled ratings of children's text-based and inferential comprehension when listening to a story and when reading independently. A 2 task condition (listening, reading independently) $\times$ 2 respondent (parents, teachers) $\times$ 2 grade (lower elementary, upper elementary) MANOVA, using the two comprehension categories (text-based, inferential) as dependent variables, was performed. Differences were revealed by respondent ($F = 6.681, p = .0139$), task condition ($F = 24.443, p = .001$), and their interaction ($F = 13.335, p = .0008$). Parents rated children's listening comprehension as 4.487 ($SD = 1.36$) and reading comprehension as 3.59 ($SD = 1.37$). Teachers rated children's listening comprehension as 3.66 (SD = 1.34) and reading comprehension as 3.40 ($SD = 1.26$). Differences were found between the parents' ratings ($F = 45.949, p = .0001$) and the parents' and teachers' ratings of the children's listening comprehension ($F = 36.379, p = .0001$). Parents rated listening higher than reading, and they also rated it higher than did teachers. No differences were found between the text-based and inferential categories or between grade levels.

The attitude analysis compared parents' and teachers' scaled ratings of children's attitude when listening to a story and when reading independently. A 2 task condition (listening, reading independently) $\times$ 2 respondent (parents, teachers) $\times$ 2 grade (lower elementary, upper elementary) MANOVA was performed. A significant two-way interaction existed between respondent and task condition ($F = 7.537, p = .0093$). Parents rated attitude when listening as 4.81 ($SD = 1.15$) and when reading as 3.06 ($SD = 1.11$). Teachers rated attitude when listening as 4.5 ($SD = 1.12$) and when reading as 3.39 ($SD = 1.38$). Differences were found between parents' ($F = 94.21, p = .0001$) and teachers' ratings ($F = 33.92, p = .0001$). Both rated listening higher than reading independently. No grade level differences were found.

The word identification analysis compared parents' and teachers' ratings of three word identification categories (letter knowledge, word-based strategies, & meaning-based strategies). A 2 respondent (parents, teachers) $\times$ 2 grade (lower elementary, upper elementary) MANOVA, using the three word identification categories as the dependent variables, was performed. Differences were found between word identification categories

($F = 5.92$, $p = .0048$). Letter knowledge was 3.84 ($SD = 1.22$), word-based strategies was 2.90 ($SD = 1.17$), and meaning-based strategies was 3.04 ($SD = 1.49$). Differences between letter knowledge and word-based strategies ($F = 9.31$, $p = .0036$), and between letter knowledge and meaning-based strategies ($F = 8.43$, $p = .0054$) were significant. Both rated letter knowledge higher than either word-based or meaning-based word identification strategies. (Yochum & Miller, 1993)

Experimental Research.   Researchers use experimental designs when conducting research about the causative effect of one or more variables on other variables. The plans provide researchers with structures for studying one or more independent variables with one or more groups of subjects. Researchers select designs that best fit their purposes, answer questions about causation, and control extraneous variables.

The common experimental designs are discussed in Chapter 7 and illustrated in Figures 7.1 (p. 134), 7.2 (p. 140), 7.3 (p. 141), and 7.4 (p. 142).

The following results section is taken from a pretest-posttest control group design that has one independent variable and three dependent variables. In this section, the results of an analysis of variance (ANOVA) are presented. The subjects did not differ at the start on pretest measures so no analysis of covariance (ANCOVA) was needed. The table shows only the groups' means and standard deviations. (The method section of this report is in Chapter 7, pp. 135–139.)

Purpose of the study: To assess the effects of learning strategy instruction on the completion of job applications by learning-disabled students.

RESULTS

Preliminary analyses indicated that there were nonsignificant differences between the groups on the pretest measures. Posttest measures were analyzed in condition (traditional, strategy) by gender (male, female) analyses of variance (ANOVAs). For every dependent measure, only a significant main effect for condition was obtained. The F values for these effects, along with the means and standard deviations for each of the dependent measures, are presented in Table 2.

The findings indicate that students who received instruction in the learning strategy condition made statistically significant lower numbers of information omission errors and location errors than students under the job application instruction condition. Additionally, these students received statistically significant higher holistic ratings on their job applications than their counterparts. There were statistically nonsignificant main effects for gender and nonsignificant condition by gender interactions for all of the dependent measures.

Confidence in these results is strengthened by the results of the checks for fidelity of implementation conducted under both experimental conditions. These findings showed that the teacher fully completed the teaching functions described above under each condition.

The social validity measure was analyzed in a condition (traditional, strategy) by gender (male, female) ANOVA. A significant main effect for condition was obtained, $F(1,31) = 6.12$, $p < .05$. There were statistically nonsignificant main effects for gender and condition by gender interactions for the social validity measure. The effects of the job application training on the ratings (1 = very unlikely to 5 = very likely) by the supervisor of classified personnel suggest that students under the learning strategy condition (mean = 4.21; SD = 0.46) would be more likely to receive invitations for job interviews after training than those under the traditional condition (mean = 2.88; $SD = 1.02$).

From: Nelson, J. R., Smith, D. J., & Dodd, J. M. (1994). The effects of learning strategy instruction on the completion of job applications by students with learning disabilities. *Journal of Learning Disabilities* 27:104–110. Copyright © 1994 by PRO-ED, Inc. Reprinted with permission.

Table 2   Mean Number of Information Omissions and Location Errors, and Mean Holistic Rating of Overall Application Neatness

Dependent Measure	Group		$F(1, 31)$
	A	B	(Condition)
Omissions	5.35 (2.55)	0.63 (0.63)	15.29*
Location errors	1.35 (0.99)	0.25 (0.25)	5.29**
Neatness rating	3.37 (1.05)	4.46 (0.51)	7.25***

Note. Group A refers to the traditional instruction condition and Group B refers to the strategy instruction condition. Numbers in parentheses are standard deviations.
* $p < .001$,   ** $p < .05$,   *** $p < .01$.

The next results section is from a $2 \times 4 \times 2$ factorial design. The independent variables and their factors are gender (male or female), grade level (3–6), and treatment (experimental or control). (See Chapter 7, pp. 142–144, for the method section of this study.) Notice how the researchers discuss effect size in the subsection "Achievement Gains" from the following article excerpt.

Purpose of the study: To determine the effects of a flexibly paced math program on student achievement.

RESULTS

The achievement gains reported are based solely on results from standardized achievement tests (the STEP and COOP). For comparability, the raw scores on the different forms (pre- and postforms) and levels of the tests were converted to standard scores. All scores and comparisons are from above-level forms (three grade levels higher than the students' school placement) of the STEP, using comparable above-level norm tables (e.g., sixth-grade norms for third graders, seventh-grade norms for fourth graders, and so on).

Achievement Pretest Scores

Although all students in the course had high scores on the quantitative reasoning test (SCAT) administered for eligibility, they varied greatly in mathematics knowledge on entering the course, as assessed by an above-level achievement test (STEP). This variation in pretest achievement scores was found at all grade levels and can be seen in Table 1 with standard scores that ranged across approximately 60 points, or about 60% of the possible range. The standard deviations reported in Table 1 are consistent with those reported for normative samples reported in the STEP manual. It is interesting to consider, however, that highly able students such as these are usually treated as a homogeneous group for instructional purposes, especially since they all scored in the top three percentiles on in-level tests. It is only through above-level testing that the actual variability in their ability and full extent of their knowledge becomes apparent.

Percentile ranks for above-level norm groups, corresponding to the mean STEP scores in Table 1, provide a context for evaluating the precourse knowledge levels of the students. As a group, the students in fourth through sixth grades came into the program with achievement levels higher than 50% of students three grade levels higher than their own. Third graders were only slightly lower at the 35th percentile rank. Because of above-level

Table 1   First Year Achievement: Pre- and Posttest STEP Scores by Grade Level

| Grade Level | *M* | Standard Score | | *SD* |
		Percentile Rank	Range	
3rd (*n* = 51)				
Pretest	427	35th	402–465	12.9
Posttest	450	81st	418–483	15.8
4th (*n* = 92)				
Pretest	438	54th	412–479	11.6
Posttest	466	87th	426–485	14.2
5th (*n* = 101)				
Pretest	448	54th	419–480	12.6
Posttest	474	87th	441–486	8.8
6th (*n* = 62)				
Pretest	461	62nd	426–482	12.1
Posttest	480	86th	437–493	9.4
Total (*n* = 306)				
Pretest	444			16.5
Posttest	469			15.5

Note. Scores are standardized and can range from 400 to 500. All standard scores and percentiles are based on above-grade level testing (students take tests designed for students who are 3 grade levels higher), as well as above-grade-level group norm comparisons (3 grade levels higher).

testing, it was possible to make such comparisons directly without having to use estimates based on an extrapolation of scores to higher grade-level equivalents. Given their high pretest achievement scores, most of these students would be underchallenged and misplaced in a grade-level mathematics program.

Posttest Scores

The mathematics achievement test (STEP) was administered as a posttest (again above-level) when a student completed the arithmetic/prealgebra sequence or at the end of the 7-month course period. Therefore, posttest scores reflect learning over a period of no more than 7 months (approximately 72 instructional hours) and, in some cases, much less time. As shown in Table 1, the range of scores shifted significantly upwards. After exposure to the flexibly paced mathematics class, these academically talented students, on average, performed better than 80% of a normative sample of students three grade levels higher than their own.

Achievement Gains

Arithmetic/Prealgebra. To assess whether or not students who began in the arithmetic/prealgebra portion of the course made significant achievement gains in the math program, their pre- and posttest STEP scores were compared. A 2 × 4 × 2 (Gender × Grade Level × Pre/Post Scores) repeated measures analysis of variance (ANOVA), with pre- and posttest STEP scores as the repeated measures, was conducted. There was no significant interaction between achievement gain and gender or grade level. In other words, both males and females, as well as all grade levels, showed equal pre- to posttest gains in achievement scores. The overall main effect for achievement gain from pretest to posttest was statistically significant ($F(1, 298) = 940.5$, $p < .001$). Effect sizes (*d*), yielding the degree of difference between means in standard deviation units, were calculated for pre/posttest scores at every grade level. Effect sizes were large (Cohen, 1977), ranging from 1.6 standard deviations for third graders to 2.4 standard deviations for fifth graders.

As can be seen from the percentile ranks in Table 1, students at each grade level moved up significantly in percentile rank with third graders displaying the greatest increase, moving from the 35th to the 81st percentile rank (according to 6th grade norms). The largest achievement gain was an increase of 56 standard scale points attained by a fifth grader, with four other students also obtaining gains of 50 points or more. These individual standard-score gains are equivalent to moving from below the fifth percentile rank to above the 90th percentile rank (in comparison to students three grade levels higher). Individually, 87% of third graders, 95% of fourth graders, 94% of fifth graders, and 87% of sixth graders exceeded normative gains as expressed in percentile rank increases. Of those students not showing percentile rank gains, the majority had pretest scores above the 90th percentile, which are subject to the unreliable nature of score distributions at this level.

To appreciate the remarkable nature of the achievement gains made by these students, it is important to consider that normative tables are constructed in such a way that "normal" learning patterns for students at all levels are reflected by maintaining the same percentile rank from the beginning of the school year to the end of the school year (i.e., "normal" pre- to posttest raw score gains are necessary for a student to stay at the same percentile rank relative to other students starting at the same achievement level). For students in this study to make such large gains in their percentile rank, they had to learn a remarkable amount of mathematics content in a short period of time (no more than a 7-month period). This kind of extraordinary gain in learning, however, is only possible when students are allowed to continue learning outside the bounds of a grade-appropriate curriculum. And the magnitude of the gains is only noticeable when above-level testing is done. These remarkable gains are a testament to what highly able students are capable of achieving when they are presented with appropriately challenging instruction and content and allowed to learn at their own pace.

To determine whether the effects of the flexibly paced mathematics program resulted in learning above and beyond that found in students of similar ability without exposure to the program, a "control group" comparison was undertaken. To make such a comparison, students in this study served as their own controls. The STEP pretest achievement scores for beginning fourth-grade students entering the program (after a year in a regular math class and no exposure to the flexibly paced class) were compared with STEP posttest scores from ending third-grade students who had been exposed to the flexibly paced class for one year. Three independent tests showed that third, fourth, and fifth graders' posttest scores were significantly higher ($p < .001$) than pretest scores for entering students ($t(141) = 4.93$, $t(191) = 9.22$, $t(161) = 7.88$, respectively). To be sure, the extra instructional hours these students received should result in some additional increase in achievement scores. The amount of additional learning expected, however, should be judged in relation to the substantially higher percentile rank of the students who had been in the program for one year as compared to students new to the program. This comparison shows a difference of 25 to 33 percentile points.

Algebra

Many students mastered arithmetic and prealgebra material in their first year of the flexibly paced class. However, only a subset of these students returned for a second year to study algebra topics. If they returned the following year, they were pretested to assess retention of their learning. If they again demonstrated mastery of the prerequisite topics, they were placed in the algebra sequence. An examination of these students' progress in the algebra class provided confirmation of their readiness for the subject.

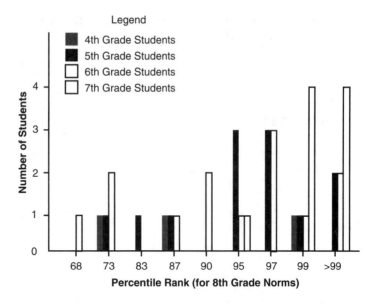

Figure 1 Second year students' algebra performance.
Note. n = 37. Grade level is for students' second year in the program.

Thirty-seven students were placed in the algebra sequence in their second year. They included 3 fourth graders, 12 fifth graders, and 13 sixth graders, and 9 seventh graders. From this group of 37 students, 29 (78%) "mastered" the algebra material by attaining a score at or above the 90th percentile according to eighth-grade norms within the 7-month period of the class. The remaining students scored well above the median score for eighth graders on the Cooperative Mathematics Test (COOP), as can be seen in Figure 1. The lowest score (earned by a sixth-grade student) was at the 68th percentile for eighth-grade norms. What is interesting is that grade level was not highly related to percentile rank on the algebra posttest. Students from the fourth through the sixth grades had scores across the range of percentile ranks from the 73rd to the 99th percentile.

Retention

To address the issue of whether or not students who excel at such a rapid pace retain the knowledge and skills they learn, the scores of 88 students who completed one year of the math program and continued the following year were selected for further study. Retention was measured over a 5-month period by comparing the student's posttest score for the first year with his or her pretest score in the fall of the second year. Means and standard deviations for scores (post- and pretest) by grade level and gender are presented in Table 2.

A 2 × 4 × 2 (Gender × Grade Level × Pre/Post Scores) repeated measures ANOVA, with post- and pretest scores as the repeated measure, was conducted. There was no significant change in scores; scores remained relatively the same over the 5-month interval. The pretest score for the second year was 99 percent of the posttest score for the first year. In addition, there was no interaction between retention and grade level or gender; the amount of retention was the same for males and females, and across all grade levels. (Mills et al., 1994)

Causal-comparative research is ex post facto, or after-the-fact, research, because researchers are trying to establish a causal effect between existing conditions. Researchers want answers to questions but cannot manipulate the independent

Table 2   Retention: Mean STEP Scores and Standard Deviations by Pre- and Posttest, Grade Level, and Gender

| | | Retention Scores | | | |
| | | Year 1 Posttest STEP | | Year 2 Pretest STEP | |
Grade Level	*n*	*M*	*SD*	*M*	*SD*
3rd	26	449	14.4	444	14.7
4th	29	466	11.9	462	14.2
5th	23	472	9.0	472	6.8
6th	10	472	8.6	474	8.3
Gender					
Female	36	462	13.8	458	16.1
Male	52	464	16.2	462	17.5
Total	88	463	15.2	461	16.9

Note. Scores are standardized and can range from 400 to 500.

variable(s) for practical or ethical reasons. They realize a condition exists and sometimes are unsure about what might have been its cause. Causal-comparative designs are built on the posttest-only control group design.

The following results section contains an example of a causal-comparative design (see Chapter 7, pp. 145–146, for the method section of this study). The researchers sought to determine the effect of a preexisting condition (amount of previous mathematics instruction) on mathematics achievement. It should be remembered that researchers using the causal-comparative design are trying to find causal relationships or predictions.

Purpose of the study: To examine the teaching strategies used by mothers of sons with learning disabilities and normally achieving sons.

RESULTS

Mothers' Teaching Strategies

Differences between the LD and NLD groups were tested by using a one-way ANOVA. The mean proportion of the low- and medium-level teaching strategies used by the mothers did not significantly differ between the groups. However, the mothers of NLD children ($M = 19.90$ vs. $M = 9.13$) used more high-level strategies, $F(1,58) = 4.06$, $p < .05$, and the total time they used in teaching ($M = 76.5$ vs. $M = 66.1$) was higher, $F(1,58) = 4.63$, $p < .05$, than that of the mothers of children with LD. No differences between the groups were found in the amount of speech produced by both mothers and children during the task.

Mother-Child Interactions

Maternal motivation in the task did not differentiate the groups. However, the mothers of children with LD showed more dominance ($p < .05$) and expressed less emotionality ($p < .01$) and cooperation ($p < .05$) while teaching their children (see Table 1). Children's lower level of motivation and initiative in the LD group may be one reason for their moth-

Table 1 Differences in the Rated Quality of Mother-Child Interaction

Interaction Variables	LD Group		NLD Group		
	M	*SD*	*M*	*SD*	*F*
Mother					
Motivation in the task	3.47	1.22	3.67	1.03	0.47
Dominance	3.03	1.03	2.50	1.04	3.96*
Emotionality	3.57	0.77	4.17	0.65	10.60**
Cooperation	4.10	0.76	4.57	0.73	5.91*
Child					
Motivation in the task	2.77	1.19	3.80	1.13	11.88***
Initiative	2.67	0.88	3.30	1.02	6.89**
Emotionality	3.37	0.72	4.20	0.71	20.30***
Cooperation	3.46	0.82	4.53	0.63	32.00***

Note. *df* = 1, 58. LD = learning disability; NLD = non-learning disabled.
* *p* < .05, ** *p* < .01, *** *p* < .001.

ers' behavior. Children with and without LD differed significantly in motivation ($p <$ .001), initiative ($p <$ .01), emotionality ($p <$ .001), and cooperation ($p <$ .001). The inactive and noncooperative behavior of the children with LD may partly follow from their earlier experiences with learning tasks.

Correlations indicated that interdependence between mother and child behaviors was stronger in the LD group than in the NLD group. Twelve of the 16 coefficients reached significance in the LD group, whereas only 6 coefficients reached significance in the NLD group (see Table 2). The initiative of the children with LD correlated significantly with their mothers' motivation, emotionality, and cooperation. A significant correlation was also found between cooperation of mother and child. The NLD children's initiative did not correlate with any variable describing the quality of their mothers' interaction. The nondisabled children seemed to be more independent and self-regulated in their task performance. Dominance, which was a prominent feature for mothers of the LD group only, correlated with children's low level of initiative ($p <$ .01). The corresponding correlation was not significant in the NLD group, but dominance in the mothers of nondisabled children correlated negatively with the children's emotionality ($p <$ .01) and cooperation ($p <$ .05).

Children's Task Performance

The children with LD were less successful in learning the words than were the NLD children, $F(1,58) = 37.79$, $p <$ .001, as indicated by the fewer number of words learned (LD group: $M = 2.53$, $SD = 1.17$; NLD group: $M = 4.13$, $SD = 0.82$). The mothers' motivation and emotionality were found to be highly correlated with the children's learning outcome in the LD group (see Table 3). The proportion of high-level strategies used by the mother covaried also with child's performance in the LD group. No corresponding associations between children's performance and mothers' behavior were found in the NLD group, which might partly result from the reduced variance of this group. In addition, child's initiative and emotionality was positively associated with learning of the words in the LD group, although not in the NLD group. However, children's own motivation and cooperation were significantly associated with learning outcome in both groups. Scores on the Raven and the PPVT for children in either group were not related to their performance.

Variation in Maternal Strategies Within the LD Group

Some mothers of children with LD appeared particularly sensitive to their children's skills, used positively motivating teaching strategies, and redirected their children's failing

Table 2   Correlations Between Mother-Child Interaction Variables

		Child			
Mother	Group	Task Motivation	Initiative	Emotionality	Cooperation
Task motivation	LD	.50**	.31*	.46*	.30*
	NLD	.53***	.29	.19	.50**
Dominance	LD	−.18	−.40**	−.11	−.18
	NLD	−.23	−.21	−.42**	−.37*
Emotionality	LD	.44**	.49**	.54**	.27
	NLD	.14	−.08	.52**	.20
Cooperation	LD	.44**	.31*	.31*	.48**
	NLD	.06	−.05	.30*	.14

Note. LD = learning disability; NLD = non-learning disabled.
* $p < .05$, ** $p < .01$, *** $p < .001$.

Table 3   Correlations Among Variables Associated with Children's Performance

	Child's Task Performance	
Interaction Variables	LD Group	NLD Group
Mother		
Task motivation	.47**	.22
Emotionality	.53**	.09
Proportion of high-level strategies	.31*	−.03
Child		
Task motivation	.58***	.48**
Initiative	.38*	.28
Emotionality	.42**	.13
Cooperation	.42**	.32*

Note. LD = learning disability; NLD = non-learning disabled.
* $p < .05$, ** $p < .01$, *** $p < .001$.

attention. These findings demonstrate the relevance of looking at within-group variation of the teaching strategies used by mothers of the LD group. Ten mothers were identified who failed to employ any high-level strategies, and six were identified who used them only randomly (under 8%). These mothers were classified to form the low- and medium-level strategies group ($n = 16$). The proportion of high-level strategies varied between 12% and 72% among the rest of mothers of children with LD. These mothers were classified as belonging to the high-level strategy group ($n = 14$). Comparison of mother-child interactions in these groups revealed that mothers using high-level distancing strategies were more involved in the task, expressed more emotionality and cooperation, and smiled more during the task (see Table 4). Children also learned significantly more test words in the high-level strategy group.

From: Lyytinen, P., Rasku-Puttonen, H., Poikkeus, A. M., Laakso, A. L., & Ahonen, T. (1994). Mother-child teaching strategies and learning disabilities. *Journal of Learning Disabilities* 27:186–192. Copyright © 1994 by PRO-ED, Inc. Reprinted with permission.

Table 4   Level of Teaching Strategies Among Mothers of Group With Learning Disabilities

Interaction Variables	Low- and Medium-Level Strategies Group		High-Level Strategies Group		
	M	*SD*	*M*	*SD*	*F*
Mother					
Task motivation	2.87	0.96	4.14	1.17	10.68**
Emotionality	3.19	0.65	4.00	0.68	11.10**
Cooperation	3.81	0.64	4.43	0.76	5.72*
Smiles	9.56	6.74	19.28	13.67	6.35*
Child					
Task performance	2.06	1.12	3.07	1.00	6.87**

Note. *df* = 1, 28.
* *p* < .05, ** *p* < .01.

Qualitative Research

The following results section is from a qualitative descriptive study (see Chapter 7, pp. 150–151, to review the method section of this study). Note two things about the results section. The researcher has answered specific questions that relate to her data analysis procedures. And, although some quantification was done (percentages of responses), the data were verbally, not statistically, analyzed.

> *Purpose of the study: To determine how frequently, when, and for what reasons a group of second-grade writers used their peers' questions to revise their unfinished pieces.*

RESULTS

How frequently did the children insert the requested information into their texts?

To answer this question the percentage of changes made by each child in his/her texts as a result of the questions raised during the sharing sessions was calculated.

Six of the 24 children (25%) made no changes in their texts as a result of their peers' questions. Three of these six children chose to share only once between January and June.

Eighteen of the 24 children (75%) inserted into their texts, typically at the end, at least some of the information identified as missing by their peers' questions. Six of these 18 children incorporated responses into their texts to more than 50% of the questions they received from their peers. The range of these children's percentage of questions used was from 60 to 100%. Two of these children were nondiscriminating; every question asked was answered by inserting the missing information at the end of their pieces. For one of these two children, the change over the data collection period was from inserting the requested information in phrases (for example, in response to "Why did you have to go to the hospital?" Mathy inserted "Because my eye puffed up" at the end of her text) to inserting the requested information in sentences (for example, in response to "How sunburned did you get?" Mathy inserted "I got a little bit of sunburn."). The other 12 of these 18 children used their peers' questions sometimes, but not often, to modify their text. The range of these 12 children's percentage of changes made as a result of their peers' questions was from 14 to 40%.

Did publishing affect how frequently these writers used their peers' questions for text revisions?

To answer this question the percentage of revisions made in eventually published and in never published drafts by those fourteen children who had shared both kinds of drafts was calculated and compared.

For slightly more than half (57%) of these children, more revisions were made in eventually published than in never published drafts. For five of these children, the decision to publish had a significant effect on their decision to use their peers' questions; they made no revisions based on their peers' questions in never published pieces. Those three children who made some revisions based on their peers' questions in both eventually published and never published drafts made from 15 to 85% more revisions in drafts which were eventually published.

Four of the 14 children (28%) used their peers' questions more frequently to revise never published pieces.

Two children (14%) revised, based on their peers' questions, equally as often in published and never published drafts. One of these children made no changes based on his peers' questions in either eventually published or never published drafts; the other child inserted information based on every question asked by her peers in eventually published and never published drafts.

What reasons did the children provide for their decisions not to use their peers' questions?

During one month (May) the children were asked to provide reasons for their decisions not to use their peers' questions. The most frequently provided reason (30%) was that the child did not know the answer to the question raised by his/her peer. Typically, these rejected questions were requests for specific information, for details, for example, "Why did Baby Anna put her hand in the garbage?" which the writer did not possess. (Roni answered, "I can't answer that! I can't read her mind!")

While the second and third most frequently provided reasons seem similar, the focus of the child's response was different. The focus of the "I didn't want to use the question" response (20%) was the quality of the piece as it existed; the writer liked it as it was. The focus of the "The question wasn't good" (15%) was the value of the question of the peer. In the writer's opinion, the question "What day did that happen?" was unimportant.

Five other reasons were provided by the children. Fifteen percent of their responses were of the "I'm not going to publish this piece" type. This response implied that since the child did not intend to publish the piece no revising to make the meaning clear for others was necessary. "I already answered that question in my piece" was suggested 8% of the time as the reason for rejecting a question. The writer contended that the question-asker had not listened carefully to the reading of the pieces. Six percent of the responses focused on the relationship between the writer and the question-asker. "I didn't like (a child's name)" was typical of the responses in this category. Since the question-asker was not liked, his/her question was not used to guide the piece's revision. Four percent of the responses were of the "I already answered that question during sharing time" type. These responses suggested that the answer to the question had been given orally during the sharing session. Finally, "My parents wouldn't want me to answer that question" was suggested once as the reason for rejecting a question. This response indicated that the answers to some questions were unacceptable.

Every child questioned provided a reason for his/her decision not to insert the requested information into the text. (Vukelich, 1986, pp. 302–303. Reprinted by permission of the National Reading Conference and C. Vukelich)

The next results section is from the qualitative portion of a study that combined qualitative and quantitative research procedures. (See Chapter 7, pp. 152–153, to review the method section of this study.) In their "Qualitative Analysis," the researchers explain the procedures used to categorize the data as well as their interpretations (results). The results of the qualitative portion of their study were used in setting up the quantitative analysis. That is, their categorizations of the "type of text," "exercises," and "extended texts" used in the observed classrooms became the factors that were later statistically analyzed.

Purpose of the qualitative portion of the study: To study language arts instruction as it naturally occurred and to categorize the classrooms along a continuum that was based on the teachers' emphasis given to writing extended passages.

Qualitative Analysis

Coding and Data Reduction. In coding our field notes, we followed procedures described by Miles and Huberman (1984). Codes were derived from the initial foci of research and from the incremental reading of the field notes and were given operational definitions. The codes addressed various aspects of reading and writing instruction: management and student engagement, type of lesson, type of activity, locus of control, and types of assessment. We used Ethnograph qualitative analysis software (Seidel, Kjolseth, & Seymour, 1988) to group episodes from field notes by code within and across classrooms. Using the computer-generated data patterns of the codes and a re-reading of the original field notes, we prepared summaries for each classroom. We used data from the interview transcripts to augment and revise the summaries.

Classification of Classrooms by Level of Engagement. It is apparent that academic learning is not likely to occur when students are not engaged in classroom activities. Nystrand and Gamoran (1991) have broken the construct of student engagement into three levels: (a) disengagement, which can be identified by students declining to undertake assigned tasks and not attending to discussion or instruction; (b) procedural engagement, which can be identified by students' accommodation to classroom regulations through paying attention and completing tasks; and (c) substantive engagement, which involves a "sustained personal commitment" (p. 262) to understanding and exploring the topic of instruction. In our analyses, we distinguished only between the first two levels, disengagement and procedural engagement. Students were coded as engaged if they were either procedurally or substantively engaged. Engagement at the procedural level is associated with achievement (Fisher et al., 1981; Nystrand & Gamoran, 1991, p. 281), and is a proxy measure of classroom management that is distinct from the content of instruction. Substantive engagement, on the other hand, is likely to be associated with a broad pattern of instructional discourse of which the choice and content of writing activities are important elements, along with peer interaction and higher level questioning (Nystrand & Gamoran, 1991, p. 270); substantive engagement is too closely linked to the nature of writing instruction to serve as a control variable.

We coded individual students as engaged or disengaged in sweeps of the classroom conducted at least once in each 10-min interval, according to whether the students were involved in activities directly related to the task designated by the teacher at the time of observation. Thus, if the teacher had designated a period of time for students to write a story, individual students who were looking outside, discussing ideas for math or science problems, or out of the room were coded as not engaged. The data supported classification of classrooms into three levels, on the basis of the average percentage of students coded as engaged across sweeps: high engagement (more than 75% of the students were engaged in the current task), moderate engagement (50% to 75%), and low engagement (fewer than 50%). To check the reliability of the classification, two researchers independently classified each classroom from coded field notes. The percentage of identical classifications across the 39 classrooms was 87%. When discrepancies were obtained, the classroom was placed in the category assigned by the researcher who actually observed in it.

Categorizing Instruction by Type of Text Written by Students. Three approaches to categorizing classrooms according to characteristics of writing instruction were initially explored:

(a) attention to meaning, which we defined as a communicative purpose for writing activities; (b) attention to process, which we defined as modeling the processes used by expert writers, with steps of idea formation, drafting, revising, and editing; and (c) type of text written by students. The first two typologies were of theoretical interest but were not supported by our data. That is, we were unable to arrive at definitions of classroom types on the basis of actual data that could support reliable classification of classrooms by independent analysis on either of these dimensions. The third dimension, type of text written by students, lent itself to clear operational definitions that supported reliable classification of classrooms.

We developed typology of classrooms that was based on the type of text written by students. We were able to categorize the writing products in the 39 classrooms as either "exercise-like" or "extended text." The classification was based on the length of text produced by the student and on the amount of choice exercised by the student in the generation of text. We considered a product to be an exercise (a) if the text produced by students consisted of individual words or single sentences or (b) if student choice and initiative were absent or nearly absent. This meant for example, that stories or paragraphs, which might normally be considered whole texts were considered to be exercises if students were merely inserting sentences or words into a formulaic master. However, if students wrote the text themselves, even though prompted by teacher or textbook, the product was classified extended text.

Exercises.   The most common type of exercise was the workbook or ditto exercise, and these were used to teach a wide variety of content ranging from punctuation and other text mechanics to grammar and vocabulary. These types of exercises were also used in conjunction with reading comprehension and to teach aspects of composition, such as paragraph format or story beginnings and endings. Writing assignments that were focused on grammar, spelling, and vocabulary mastery were also classified as exercises. These typically involved the students' supplying punctuation marks or other short answers, the production of sentences, and other types of focused practice of language or composition skills. Written responses to questions, either teacher-made or from the text, were coded as exercises because students' responses were typically brief and constrained by the preceding text.

Extended Texts.   Extended texts were defined as texts consisting of several lines written by students in which students exercised some autonomy and initiative. This definition included paragraph-length texts in cases where the content could not be easily predicted, that is, in cases where each student was apparently able to write relatively uninhibitedly. The types of extended texts produced in classrooms reflect the broad range of writing that one would expect in society, as well as texts that are common only in classrooms. For example, students wrote letters, stories, obituaries, jokes, journals, and poems in addition to book reports, summaries of reading, and notes on mini-lectures. We were struck by the diversity of writing and the variety of tasks and interactions that occurred in conjunction with the writing.

We classified classrooms according to predominance of writing tasks for students. Two researchers (who were aware of the major hypotheses of the study but unaware of the achievement outcomes for particular classrooms) worked together to classify the classrooms into two categories: those in which writing tasks consisted most of exercises and those in which the writing of extended texts predominated. Each of these categories was further divided into two levels, thus producing four categories that were based on the relative amount of time that students spent working on the two types of tasks: (a) mostly exercises, (b) mixed, mostly exercises, (c) mixed, mostly extended text, and (d) mostly extended text. Three additional researchers, working from descriptions of the characteristics of the different categories, then classified the 39 classrooms. Seven classrooms were classified as emphasizing mostly exercises; 12 as mixed, mostly exercises; 8 as mixed, mostly extended text; and 12 as mostly extended text. Teachers in classrooms categorized as extended text were more likely than teachers in other classrooms to use a process approach to writing (i.e., use of revision, peer editing, etc.). However, some teachers whose students frequently wrote extended texts did not emphasize intermediate stages of writing or vary the process from task to task. There was no consistent relationship between the type of product produced by students and the nature of the process used.

In classrooms classified as mostly exercises, written products consisted primarily of short (word, phrase, or sentence) responses to questions posed by the teacher or appearing on worksheets or in workbooks. The distinguishing characteristic of texts produced by students in the other classrooms was the length of the text and the relative autonomy and initiative allowed to the students in their writing. We found enough variation in the relative production of exercises and extended texts in the two mixed categories to differentiate between ones whose products were predominantly exercises and those whose products were predominately extended texts. However, there was considerable overlap across types of classes. Differences among the classrooms, with the exception of those classified as mostly exercises, consisted of differences in the amount of time devoted to working on extended texts or exercises. One cannot assume that extended text implies a process (i.e., use of revision, peer editing, etc.) approach on the part of the teacher, although there is doubtless some relationship between the type of product and the nature of the process used.

From: Davis, A., Clark, M. A., & Rhodes, L. K. (1994). Extended text and the writing proficiency of students in urban elementary schools. *Journal of Educational Psychology* 86(4):556–566. Copyright © 1994 by the American Psychological Association. Reprinted with permission.

Other Research

Single-subject research, action research, and evaluation research are other ways researchers describe, compare, and draw causative conclusions about educational problems and questions.

Single-Subject and Case Study Research. The following results section is from research done with a single subject in an A–B design. Note that although data were collected and presented in graph form, no tests of statistical significance were performed. Therefore, the research consumer does not know whether the subject's increased spelling scores after tutoring differed significantly from those before tutoring or whether the difference might be attributed to chance or error variations. (See Chapter 7, pp. 155–156, to review the method section of this study.)

Purpose of the study: To determine the effects of a peer-tutoring procedure on the spelling behavior of a mainstreamed elementary school student with a learning disability.

RESULTS

Percent Correct

The overall results indicated that the tutee obtained a greater percent of accuracy on the spelling tests during the peer-tutoring condition than during the baseline condition. As shown in Figure 1, the student increased his mean percent correct from 61.25 percent in baseline to 77.5 percent in the peer-tutoring condition, that is, an improvement of 16.25 percent. The spelling performance of the peer tutor (S–B) did not decrease during either of the experimental conditions; it was 100 percent.

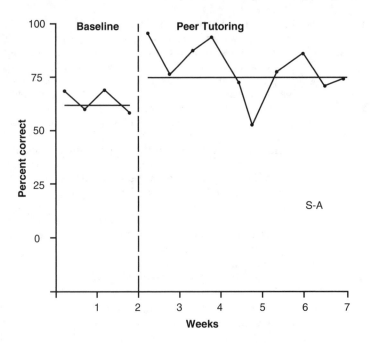

Figure 1 The percent correct on biweekly spelling tests across the duration of the study. Solid horizontal lines indicate condition means.

Table 1   **Weekly Subject Ratings of the Experimental Treatment**

		Rating	
Subjects	Very Good	Satisfactory	Unsatisfactory
A	2	2	1
B	3	2	

Clinical Significance: Student Self-Reports and Ratings

Both the tutee and the tutor rated the peer-tutoring procedure favorably (see Table 1). The program was rated as very good five times, satisfactory on four occasions, and unsatisfactory once. Subject A rated the program as unsatisfactory on the day when he scored 45% on his spelling test. (Mandoli et al., 1982, pp. 187–188)

Action Research.   Action research is descriptive, comparative, or experimental research in which results are not generalized beyond the study's specific subjects and educational setting. Action researchers seek answers to immediate questions or problems.

The following section reports the outcomes from a qualitative teacher-as-researcher project. (See Chapter 7, pp. 157–158, for the method section of this study.) Note that in this action research study no tests of statistical significance were done on the tabulated data. The researcher's purpose was the process of collaboration and its impact on solving a problem of concern to the participating teachers. Action research is useful to research consumers if there are similarities in subject variables, educational setting, or treatment(s). In such cases, research consumers may wish to replicate the study in searching for answers to their own educational questions.

Purpose of the study: To determine how the teacher could facilitate students' engagement in literature and critical thinking, and how students' writing reflects their engagement and thinking.

WHAT CAN I DO? CASE STUDY #1

I was eager to see how my decision to adopt new instructional methods in my classroom would affect students' response to literature. The instructional cycle, which was repeated in each unit throughout the year, included these elements: an assigned text; choice of a contemporary novel connected to the assigned text; response logs with teacher comments; book talks; seminars; critical analysis papers; and evaluation. I hoped that with these elements I would find at least part of the solution to my first research question: How can I help my students become involved in literature and think critically about what they read? The description that follows is based on what happened during one unit that year and shows what I felt was a successful outcome to my research question.

To help them connect with Nathaniel Hawthorne's classic *The Scarlet Letter,* I had my students select a related novel from a list of contemporary fiction. As they read, they were asked to write their reactions to the novel in their response logs. I gave the students what they thought were minimal and far too general instructions:

Each time you finish reading a section, jot down your reactions. What you write will be determined by how you respond. Did you especially like or dislike a section? Why? Do you sympathize with a character? Why? Did a section confuse you or impress you? Why? What would you especially like to remember? Do you see a theme emerging? Does anything seem particularly symbolic? Note any words you don't know and look up the definitions. Write any questions you'd like answered.

I was immediately greeted with a barrage of questions: Do you want all of this for each chapter? How many vocabulary words do we have to have? How many pages does each entry have to be? Does spelling count? What about punctuation? How are you going to grade? I was concerned about words such as "do you want," "have to," and "must be," so I again explained that this was a personal process and that each individual would be in the driver's seat when it came to deciding amount, content, and number of vocabulary words. Spelling and punctuation would not count; those skills would be checked only in papers that had been edited and submitted for evaluation. Grades for the journals themselves would be based on effort. Most of my students were suspicious. Some resented the lack of specific guidelines; others were looking for a trick; a few were delighted because they thought the amount of work would be minimal. I urged them to trust me and told them that they were beginning what I hoped would be an exciting journey toward connecting to *The Scarlet Letter.*

The next day I began reading and responding to what the students were writing in their logs. I was dismayed to discover that almost no one responded in a personal or critical way. What I read were pages and pages of summaries. Instead of repeating the instructions to the whole class, I responded by writing questions in the logs. To one student's summary of the episode in which Louie Banks quits the football team in Chris Crutcher's *Running Loose,* I wrote, "Have you ever heard of anyone being intentionally injured in football? What would you do if you were in Louie's position?" That sparked a dialogue, and it opened the door for this student to write more personal comments in his journal.

Not all the students had problems becoming personally involved with their novels. Alisha found many points of connection in Richard Peck's *Close Enough to Touch.* She first related to the theme of loneliness:

> In the book *Close Enough to Touch*, the main character is very close to his girlfriend Dory. They do a lot of things together and they are in love. Then Matt is left alone because of Dory's tragic death. I have never had anybody close to me die, but I can easily relate to Matt. In grade nine I got really close to a boy and I fell in love. Then that summer he moved away. This was really hard for me because we were like best friends. I felt so alone and sad.

She then mentioned an episode from a television show that related to the guilt Matt was experiencing.

During the time Alisha was reading this book and responding to it in her log, a student at our school committed suicide. Alisha's response to this tragedy was played out in her log:

> Matt tells Linda, "Dory's beginning to fade for me. I can't remember her face. Not missing her is about as bad a feeling as missing her. I'm somewhere between grief and guilt."
>
> I can somewhat relate to Matt's guilty feeling, although my situation is much different. When Stan died I sort of felt guilty for not knowing him. I felt guilty for being so happy while he must have been so very unhappy.

Writing these sorts of journal entries about contemporary novels and personal events seemed to help Alisha have a more personal response to the *The Scarlet Letter*. She began to write descriptively about the book in her log and to give her own opinions about Puritan society:

> The people outside the door start saying Hester Prynne should be put to death. The people watch her come out of the prison with a baby. She holds the baby close to her, to hide the letter "A" sewn on her dress. I get the impression that decorations on clothing are not socially accepted. She is wearing the red "A" so that everyone will know what she has done.
>
> Hester is very beautiful and delicate, but she must feel very bad inside. She will be alienated from everyone else because of the scarlet letter. "It had the effect of a spell, taking her out of the ordinary relations with humanity, and enclosing her in a sphere by herself."
>
> Hester had to show herself and the baby to the people. "The unhappy culprit sustained herself as best a woman might under the heavy weight of unrelenting eyes, all fastened upon her and concentrated on her bosom." Hester must have felt very alone, ailienated [sic] and guilty. She might feel the way I felt when I first moved here. I had no friends and I felt like everyone was judging me. It's not the same exact thing, but maybe she felt the same way.

Alisha was able to transfer the way she responded personally to contemporary novels to her reading of a classic work without any formal lessons.

All the students had been given the same instructions to look for themes from their contemporary novels in the life of Hester Prynne. I encouraged those students who were having trouble making this connection to use a metacognitive strategy: I suggested they go back to an early entry in their log where they had summarized or made an initial comment about a book they were reading. When they found a passage that reflected guilt, alienation, or loneliness, I urged them to make a note in the margin of their response logs and think about those themes in relation to *The Scarlet Letter*.

Kristi was one of the students who complained about the lack of concrete instructions. She did not read for pleasure, but spent hours studying and practicing for the drill team. She was very goal oriented and grade oriented. Following my suggestion, she reread her responses to Ellen White's *Life without Friends*, focusing on the hunt for examples of guilt, loneliness, and alienation. A later journal entry shows her surprise at the personal connections she was able to make:

First, Beverly shows signs of alienation when she says that everyone only took her father's side. Another example is when she asks her stepmother to leave her alone, Beverly is actually choosing to be alienated from others. Beverly's life in some ways reminds me of a friend of mine. This girl always complains that she had no friends but yet it is like she alienates herself from others by not talking and by always staying home, declining invitations to go out. I'm really enjoying this book because it is so different from any other book I've read.

Analysis of *The Scarlet Letter* was not nearly as difficult for her as it would have been had she not first read and responded to an easier-to-relate-to contemporary novel. She easily found examples of guilt and alienation in this classic, commented on Hawthorne's style, and used metaphor to relate to everyday life. She also challenged and encouraged herself as she read:

> Guilt is shown when Hester is thinking about her deed and the effect it will have on Pearl. The phrase is "She knew that her deed had been evil; she could have no faith, therefore, that its result would be for good. Day after day, she looked fearfully into the child's expanding nature; ever dreading to detect some dark and wild peculiarity, that should correspond with the guiltiness to which she owed her being." Loneliness and alienation are described in the following sentences: "Pearl was a born outcast of the infantile world. She was an example of evil and a product of sin, she had no right among christened infants." This goes back to the beginning of my journal when I described Pearl's friends.
>
> The book is really getting interesting, I love it. However, lots of the description is so confusing. I can handle it because I'm in an Honors class! One way of relating this story to school life would be if you have ever noticed when a teacher yells at a student, everyone turns and stares. This is like the emblem that alienates Hester, however this is done with language.

Seminar Discussion

The next step in my instruction was the seminar. I felt strongly that students should determine the points they wanted to discuss. Romano (1987) says that when "searching people interact in a classroom, ideas spark and learning occurs in countless ways" (p. 176). That's what I wanted our seminars to be: not a time when I talked and the students listened and parroted back my words, but a time for student-generated learning.

I set up the seminar as a graded discussion. Points would be awarded for topics raised, expanded on, answered, or extended; points would be deducted for speaking out of turn, interrupting, or insulting another student. I would participate when I felt something was being missed or neglected, but would try to keep my comments to a minimum.

Our first seminar consisted of a lively discussion. The students raised controversial questions about whether Pearl acted as she did because she was possessed or because of the environment in which she was raised; they argued about the point at which evil overcame Roger Chillingworth. Students dragged out books and journals to support the side they chose.

Discussion at first was dominated by the more extroverted students and it took several attempts for the students to rectify that situation. As a group, we finally decided that body language had a great deal to do with who was being called on. Handwavers, grunters, and people who all but fell out of their chairs seemed to command the most attention. At first I acted as moderator, but in the following days we appointed other moderators. We finally settled on appointing a student to raise the first question and call on people until each point was thoroughly discussed; then that person would call on someone else to raise the next question, and that second questioner would act as moderator for the discussion that ensued. With this method, we had several moderators and involved more students in the seminar. However, the people who used body language still seemed to gain more than their fair share of attention. It was a problem we resolved to work on.

The response to the seminars was overwhelmingly positive. I was interested in how students felt these discussions compared to traditional teacher-led discussions so I asked them to make subjective evaluations. Julia wrote as follows:

> I have gotten so much more out of the seminars because, especially with a book that is hard to understand, when everyone pulls together and puts in ideas more things and symbols are clearer. Also, I feel like more of an adult in this situation and I think more mature thinking is encouraged with this kind of an atmosphere.

Stephanie said that she liked the seminars much better than questions:

> I have found out a lot more information in this seminar than I could ever learn from a worksheet. Some of these questions would not have even entered my mind without the seminar. I like hearing other people's views on those questions.

On the negative side, students mentioned that there were so many people in the seminar group that they often did not get a chance to comment. Many times what they wanted to say was expressed by someone else before they could be called on. Overall, however, the class and I felt the seminars were a success, and we looked forward to continuing these discussions.

Analytic Papers

The next step for me was to prepare my students for writing analytic papers. I felt students should choose their own topics so they could explore issues that were meaningful to them. As a class we brainstormed for issues or questions that were of interest. Many of the points that were raised had been discussed but not fully resolved in seminars; these were issues that seemed to depend on each reader's interpretation. One of the most popular issues was the question of who had committed the greater sin— Hester and Arthur or Roger Chillingworth. Scott chose this issue for his paper. In it he argued as follows:

> The sin of Chillingworth is far worse than that of Hester or Dimmesdale. He committed not only one sin, but two. His first one was against nature. He committed the first sin the day he married Hester. He knew she didn't love him and that he wasn't the man to marry her. Chillingworth's second sin is far worse than any other one. His sin is the subordination of the heart to the mind. He becomes willing to satisfy his fellow man for his own selfish interests.

Scott chose with this paper to take some risks. He made some assumptions about moral values and degrees of right and wrong. As a reader, I responded emotionally to his sensitive, idealistic assertion that Chillingworth's "subordination of the heart to the mind" was the far greater sin. As a teacher, I was delighted with his personal involvement with this composition. He was actively involved from the beginning to the end in a book that in years past had seemed so dry, sterile, and incomprehensible to students.

Marie also displayed a great depth of understanding and feeling in her analysis of symbols in *The Scarlet Letter*:

> A common object that many people see may mean nothing to most; yet to another person, it may serve as a reminder of his or her most sinful or regretted act. The sight of a playing child brings a smile to most faces along

with thoughts of younger, happier days; in Nathaniel Hawthorne's novel, Pearl serves to remind Hester of her shame. . . . Pearl's attire reminds us of Hester first emerging from prison, when the letter was described as being "surrounded with an elaborate embroidery and fantastic flourishes of gold thread."

Marie clearly demonstrates her analytic skills in this passage. This was made easier for her because of the pool of resources she had available in her response journal. The relationships between the characters in the book and real-life situations that were mentioned in other papers were also inspired by the journals. (Hirtle, 1993)

SUMMARY

What are the different ways quantitative data are recorded?

Statistics are numerical ways to describe, analyze, summarize, and interpret data in a manner that conserves time and space. Researchers select statistical procedures after they have determined what research designs and types of data will be appropriate for answering their research questions.

In answering descriptive research questions, statistics let researchers show the data's central tendencies and variability. In answering comparative and experimental research questions, other statistics allow researchers to draw inferences from samples and make generalizations about target populations. In all three types of research, the specific statistical procedures are determined by the research design and the type of data that are collected. And, in comparative and experimental research, statistics are tools that let researchers gain two other insights: (a) an estimate of the error (or difference) between the research sample and the target population and (b) the confidence with which research producers and consumers can accept the results.

Data are recorded as (a) categories, (b) rankings, (c) intervals, and (d) ratios. Each requires the use of different statistics. Interval scales present data according to preset, equal spans. They are the most common form of data reporting in education and social science, and they are identified by continuous measurement scales: raw scores and derived scores such as IQ scores, standard scores, scaled scores, and normal curve equivalents. Interval scores are the form in which data from most tests are recorded. Rankings, or ordinal scales, show the order, from highest to lowest, for a variable. There are no indications as to the value or size of differences between or among items in a list; the indications refer only to the relative order of the scores. Subjects can be ranked according to their performance on a set of athletic tasks, and what will be reported is the order in which they scored (e.g., first, second, or third), not their actual accumulation of points. Data from surveys and observations are often recorded in this manner. Categories separate data into two or more discrete aspects, such as male-female, red-white-blue, or always-frequently-infrequently-never. The data can be reported as numbers of items or as percentages of a total. Data recorded in that way, often from surveys and observations, are considered nominal scales. Ratio scales, less frequently used in educational and other behavioral and social science research than the other three statistical procedures, show relative relationships among scores, such as half-as-large or three-times-as-tall.

What is a normal distribution curve?

Parametric statistics are based on the concept that if a set of scores is large enough, the scores will be distributed systematically and predictably. They will produce a graph in the shape of a bell, which is called the normal distribution curve. There is a direct relationship between the standard deviation (*SD*) and the normal distribution curve. Starting at the center, or mean, of the distributed variable, each *SD* represents a fixed, specific proportion of the population.

What statistical procedures are used in educational and other behavioral science research?

A common parametric statistic is the *t* test. It is used when the difference between two sets of scores is being tested. It is reported as numbers such as $t = 1.6$ or $t = 3.1$. Another parametric statistic used with interval data in comparative research is the product-moment correlation, which refers to the quantified relationship between two sets of scores for the same groups of subjects. The result of the arithmetic computation is a coefficient of correlation which is expressed as *r*, a decimal between -1.0 and $+1.0$. When research designs call for examining differences among the means of two or more groups of subjects or two or more variables, they frequently use the analysis of variance (ANOVA), which is reported in *F* ratios. The advantage in using an ANOVA is that two or more variables as well as two or more factors can be examined. In its simplest form, ANOVA can be thought of as a multiple *t* test. The ANOVA is appropriate for use with some comparative research designs and with experimental research designs, such as the pretest-posttest with multiple control groups, the Solomon four-group design, counterbalanced designs, common factorial designs, and causal-comparative designs. Analysis of covariance (ANCOVA) allows researchers to examine differences among the means of groups of subjects as if the means were statistically equal from the start. They do this by adjusting the differences in the means to make them hypothetically equal. In all other ways, ANCOVAs are interpreted like ANOVAs. When researchers wish to examine the relationships among more than two variables, they can use multiple or partial correlation techniques. These procedures are interpreted similarly to a single correlation coefficient.

For each parametric statistical procedure there are corresponding nonparametric procedures. In general, nonparametric statistics, which utilize nominal or ordinal data, are less frequently used in educational and other behavioral and social science research than are parametric statistics.

What is statistical significance and effect size?

In comparative and experimental research, researchers want to be sure that the differences between the means of two or more groups of subjects or two or more variables are truly different. If the means differ, researchers need to know whether the difference happened by chance. When the difference between the means is large enough that it cannot be attributed to chance, the difference is considered as significant and, therefore, reliable. Statistical significance occurs when results exceed a particular *p, probability* or *chance*, level and researchers are confident about the conclusions they make from their findings. When researchers determine whether a difference or relationship exists, there is the possibility of error. Two kinds of error can occur: (a) researchers accept the results as true when they are not and (b) researchers do not accept the results as true when they actually are.

The effect size gives the consumer of research an indication of the *meaningfulness* or *importance* of the results by providing an additional measure to the significance level. Researchers may use one of several techniques; however, they most often show effect size in relation to the standard deviation of the data gathering instrument. Effect size is reported in several ways, but, most commonly, it is reported as a decimal fraction of the standard deviation.

What are the ways data are analyzed in qualitative research?

In qualitative studies, researchers analyze data by examining and organizing notes from interviews and observations and reducing the information into smaller segments from which they can see patterns and trends. In addition, they interpret the meanings of these patterns and trends and create research hypotheses and questions for verification in further research. Qualitative researchers begin their analyses while still in the field and finish it after all data have been collected. An important point about qualitative research is that qualitative researchers often do measure and count; in other words, they quantify some data. However, they do not use statistical analyses to verify or support their results and conclusions, nor do they consider statistical probabilities. In the field, qualitative researchers continually make decisions that narrow their study. They may start out with broad questions and begin looking at an entire educational setting, but as their study proceeds they concentrate on smaller issues and create more specific analytical questions. Data collection is an additive process: New information is sought and collected on the basis of previous data, because the qualitative researchers are interpreting as they assemble additional information. One procedure used by qualitative researchers to support their interpretations is triangulation, a procedure for cross-validating information. Triangulation is collecting information from several different sources about the same event or behavior.

What criteria should be used to read and evaluate results sections?

Research consumers need to be able to answer these questions about research reports: What types of data analyses were used? What statistical analyses did the researchers use? Were the statistical analyses appropriate for the researchers' questions, purposes, or hypotheses and for the research design? What were the research results? Were the results of quantitative research statistically significant? Were the qualitative analyses appropriate and logical? Were the results of practical use and importance and educationally meaningful? Will the results be applicable to other educational settings, especially the one in which I teach?

ACTIVITY

Read the results sections in Extracts A and B that are found in this chapter's Appendix beginning on p. 217. They are from the same studies as the method sections presented in the Appendix portion of Chapter 7, pages 164–171. Using the questions and criteria discussed in this chapter, evaluate the studies. For each, list questions and concerns you may have about

    a. The appropriateness of the statistical procedures to the researchers' purposes and designs

    b. The indicated statistical significance levels

    c. The practical significance of the research

    d. If it is a qualitative study, the processes for organizing data, identifying patterns, and synthesizing key ideas as hypotheses and research questions

Do not read the Feedback section until you have completed each of the activities.

FEEDBACK

Extract A: Successful Mainstreaming in Elementary Science Classes.   In qualitative observational studies, researchers should identify the categories for organizing their data. Although the researchers do not identify the initial categories for sorting their data, they clearly identify the seven trends that seem to characterize successful mainstreaming. Each trend, or variable, is supported by descriptive examples. The main question research consumers need to consider is How much of the success that was seen is due to the researchers' close involvement with establishing the curriculum and professional development of the teachers? Surely, they were more than participant observers. It is to the researchers' credit that they clearly detail their background (see Chapter 7, pp. 166–167), and it seems it was their intent to let the research consumer judge the validity and reliability of their data collection and analysis. Overall, the researchers have taken care to document their ideas and to relate them to other research results.

Extract B: Helping Behaviors and Math Achievement Gain of Students Using Cooperative Learning.   The researcher used several statistical procedures to analyze the data—analysis of covariance (ANCOVA) and multiple regression analysis. The ANCOVA was used instead of analysis of variance (ANOVA) because of differences in the pretest scores of the three ability groups. Without that correction, it would not be possible to determine whether any changes in the subjects' behavior were due to the treatments or their ability. The results indicate that the subjects' mathematics achievement on posttests was significantly influenced by the pretest, their ability, and whether they received no help, gave explanations, received explanation, or received help from others. The results can be questioned for practical significance because of the strong influence of the pretest on the subjects' final mathematics achievement. It may be that the treatments had no real effect, but the taking of the pretest influences the subjects as to what to expect on the posttest.

Extract A: Successful Mainstreaming in Elementary Science Classes

Purpose of the study: To identify variables meaningfully associated with mainstreaming success in science classes, across grade levels and across categories of disability.

RESULTS AND DISCUSSION

Our first consideration was: Were the three science classrooms successful in mainstreaming students with visual, physical, auditory, and learning disabilities? Our conclusion, based on all available evidence, was that these classrooms had been successful. Teachers (interviews, 2/5/3; 2/10/3) stated that mainstreaming efforts were successful and that they defined success in this context as meaningful participation, throughout the school year, in classroom science activities and classroom discussion and as completion of (possibly adapted) classroom assignments. Administrators generally concurred with these statements (e.g., 11/13/3).

Our analysis of field notes and videotapes suggested that all students did in fact participate meaningfully in science activities and class discussion and that they completed relevant classroom assignments. For example, the girl with a mild hearing impairment in Classroom A led the class in a data collection and recording activity (videotape record, 11/20/3); the student with a visual impairment in Classroom B took her regular turn in a "Simon Says" communication activity (videotape record 2/10/3), and children with physical and learning disabilities participated fully in an activity involving testing for the presence of chemical acids and bases in Classroom C (field notes, 11/16/3; 11/20/3). Teacher B reported that her student with a visual impairment completed assignments throughout the year, using the brailler and/or peer recorders, although sometimes additional prompting was needed to ensure task completion (interview, 2/10/3).

We did observe a negative instance of successful mainstreaming, using the same definition, in a school in a small village in northern Italy, in which inclusive practices were being undertaken as part of Italy's national education policy (Organisation for Economic Co-Operation and Development, 1985). In one such classroom, we observed one student with disabilities independently coloring a coloring book while all other students were participating in class discussion and relevant activities (videotape record, 3/15/4). Such practices would not be considered to be successful mainstreaming by the standards employed in this investigation, because the student was simply physically present in the classroom, without actively participating in relevant classroom activities.

Analysis of all data collected for this investigation revealed seven variables which appeared to be meaningfully associated with observed mainstreaming success, across categories of disability and grade level. These seven variables included administrative support; support from special education personnel; an accepting, positive classroom atmosphere; appropriate curriculum; effective general teaching skills; peer assistance; and disability-specific teaching skills. Each is now described in detail.

Variable 1: Administrative Support

All classrooms clearly benefited from administrative support for the mainstreaming effort, provided both at the district and the building level. Interviews with science education and special education district personnel confirmed that integration of students with disabilities had a high priority in the district and that an active, problem-solving approach was used to facilitate such mainstreaming efforts. In interviews, all building administrators also voiced strong support for mainstreaming efforts and were well informed about mainstreaming activities being undertaken in their buildings. Further, all administrators took apparent pride in mainstreaming successes at their schools. The principal of School C, for example, openly praised Teacher C for his work on developing the mainstreaming guidelines and his work with physically handicapped children (field notes, teacher meeting, School C, 11/12/3). Principals of all three schools could readily identify by name the teachers who were most facilitative in mainstreaming (interviews with principals, 2/18/1–2/20/1; 11/12/2; 11/13/2; 11/13/3). In turn, teachers in interviews in this investigation spoke positively of their administrative support and administrative arrangements and underlined the importance of this variable. Research literature has also underlined the importance of administrative support in promoting mainstreaming (e.g., Center, Ward, Parmenter, & Nash, 1985).

District and local administration had also provided excellent physical facilities for meeting the needs of students with disabilities. All buildings were single story and provided very easy access between class-rooms. More specifically, School A included fire alarms with flashing lights and distributed FM systems when needed to all teachers interacting with students with hearing impairments. School B offered braillers, closed-circuit televisions, and adapted computer systems. School C had single-story construction and ramps whenever needed (e.g., to make portable buildings accessible), in addition to a wheelchair-accessible playground.

Variable 2: Support From Special Education Personnel

The direct assistance of special education teachers and staff was very much in evidence in all three class-rooms. Teacher A communicated regularly with special education teachers about her students with hearing impairments and learning disabilities (Teacher A interview, 2/5/3); a licensed sign language interpreter provided a necessary communication link. Teacher B relied on the special education teacher and aide to provide braille curriculum materials and interlining (writing in between braille lines), braillers, and methods and materials for reducing stereotypic behaviors and other special problems (Teacher B interview, 2/10/3). Teacher C received regular assistance and support from special education teachers regarding the needs of his students with physical disabilities. In addition, a special education undergraduate student from a local university was employed to assist students with physical disabilities in the classroom (Teacher C interview, 2/5/3).

All teachers acknowledged the necessary assistance of special education staff in interviews, and observational records and interviews with principals supported the critical role played by special education personnel. These teachers and staff were seen to assume responsibility in several critical areas, including assisting students with disabilities to and from class, monitoring and adjusting class procedures and assignments, preparing regular education students for students with disabilities prior to mainstreaming, conferring with classroom teachers, recommending teaching strategies, and providing social support for their mainstreaming efforts. These roles follow very closely those identified in a major mainstreaming text (Wood, 1993, p. 51).

Overall, the ongoing support of special education personnel appeared to play a critical role in the continued presence of students with disabilities in regular classrooms. Teacher B, for example, commented,

[Special education teacher] is really great to work with. I know she's busy, but she's always got a moment for me when I need to talk to her about [name], or if I am having a problem, or if I am not sure of something. She is always there for me, which I think is very important. (Interview, 2/10/3)

Similarly, Teacher C commented,

[Special education teacher] came in and talked specifically about my children and my classroom. She was very supportive. She wanted to know exactly what we were doing and how we were doing it—how we were making it so this child could be mainstreamed into my class-room. I just felt like whatever I asked for they [special education staff] were going to see if it's feasible and work with me to get it that way. I feel like they trust me, too. (Interview, 2/5/3)

Investigations by others have also underlined the important role of special education personnel in supporting mainstreaming efforts. Glang, Gersten, and Morvant (in press), for example, described the critical role of special education personnel working in a consultant capacity in improving basic skills functioning of students with disabilities in the regular education classroom.

Variable 3: Accepting, Positive Classroom Atmosphere

All teachers not only accepted the idea of diverse learning needs in their classrooms but voiced opinions that all students benefited from the atmosphere created by such diversity. Teacher A remarked to her class (videotape record, 2/10/3),

We're all different in some ways. Even [name] wears glasses. And the twins, they were different, weren't they? You have to expect that kind of difference; it's sometimes fun and happy to work with someone who is a little bit different. You don't always want to work with the same kinds of people, do you? It makes life more exciting to work with different kinds of people.

Teacher B commented, "I think it is something I have set up. Everybody belongs here . . . I work very hard to make all my kids feel accepted" (interview, 2/10/3). Teacher C concurred, "I think if a teacher puts some effort into it, everything can be adapted so that [students with disabilities] can do it" (interview, 2/5/3).

Evidence for positive classroom atmosphere was also obtained in observations of all classrooms. All three teachers were seen to be very accepting of divergent answers and other unexpected responses from all students. This open environment was also perceived by students with and without disabilities as positive and accommodating, as expressed in student interviews. For example, when asked how it feels to come to science class, the boy with hearing impairments in Classroom A signed, "Fine, I like to come to Room #—" (field notes, 2/10/3).

One specific way in which this open classroom atmosphere was expressed across classrooms was in teacher responses to incorrect answers or statements. Each of the three teachers responded positively to both correct and incorrect statements, reinforcing correct answers and following incorrect statements with further questioning, and expressing approval for the student volunteering a response (field notes, all classes). For another example, all three teachers took a very personal view of the teaching process, knew all their students well, and interacted with them in a friendly, positive manner.

Interviews with students suggested that students were aware of, and appreciative of, this personal approach to teaching.

In contrast, a negative or hostile atmosphere can hinder mainstreaming efforts. Centra (1990) described the accounts of several students with learning disabilities who had encountered a lack of acceptance in mainstream environments and the resulting negative effects. For instance, one female student reported,

I was put in Mr. Sheldon's class to see if I could do the work. He found out that I was having a hard time. I was supposed to go to resource to take tests and all that. He would always say, "You can't go." You know, he was always sticking his nose up at me. He never said anything to me; he would just be failing me. . . . He was like—he wanted nothing to do with me whatsoever. It hurt really bad. I finally went down to guidance and told them I couldn't take it any more. (p. 151)

Variable 4: Appropriate Curriculum

Scruggs and Mastropieri (1992) argued that science curriculum that deemphasized textbook and vocabulary learning and emphasized active exploration of scientific phenomena would be likely to be associated with mainstreaming success. This hypothesis was partially supported by previous research—such as, that of Bay et al. (1992), MacDougall et al. (1981), Linn et al. (1979), Putnam et al. (1989), and Morocco et al. (1990)—all of which demonstrated to some extent the facilitative effects of activities-oriented curricula on mainstreaming outcomes. Further support is evidenced by an experiment by Scruggs, Mastropieri, Bakken, and Brigham (1993), who demonstrated that students with learning disabilities in self-contained classes learned and applied more science information from activities-oriented lessons than from textbook/lecture lessons. More recent research has supported the value of more inquiry-based teaching methods in promoting science learning of students with learning disabilities and mild mental retardation (Scruggs, Mastropieri, and Sullivan, 1994).

In the present investigation, students with disabilities were typically performing markedly below grade level in reading and writing skills. Further, many of them lacked experiences or prior knowledge relevant to the areas being studied. In this context, activities-oriented lessons allowed all students to experience, explore, and investigate new phenomena for themselves, without reliance on literacy skills. Finally, the nature of the curriculum allowed them to interact freely with peers, who could lend assistance or support when needed. All the teachers expressed appreciation for the facilitative effects of the science curriculum. For example, Teacher C remarked,

Science curriculum is easily adaptable if you work with cooperative groups. . . . I am not a textbook person. I think it makes it easier if they have a hands-on experience; they can actually see what's going on. That's not just for handicapped children, but for every child. . . . Some of these kids that have come from [classrooms for students with physical disabilities] to a regular classroom have never seen things like this before [science materials]. If you explain it they have no concept, no idea, of what's going on. When you actually go ahead and show them, they're just as fascinated [as nondisabled students] and they can come up with their own ideas of "Why did it happen?" and "How did it happen?" and so forth. (Interview, 2/5/3)

Teacher A expressed a similar opinion:

[Students are successful] because science is so hands-on, and that's exactly what our special needs children need. They need the hands-on activities to help them understand and learn. . . . There's no way that these kids can't learn something because they don't have to sit and read a book. They might not catch on to . . . one part of our activity that day, but there are so many activities. . . . I think each and every one of them learns something. (Interview, 2/5/3)

Teacher B also agreed, "The hands-on science is nice . . . the kids have a good time using it . . . " (interview, 2/10/3).

Interviews with classroom teachers revealed that all appreciated the value of concreteness and meaningfulness in teaching science to students with disabilities. These two variables have been considered extremely important in special education methods textbooks (e.g., Mastropieri & Scruggs, 1994a).

Teachers also remarked positively about the role of the district administration in making hands-on science activities easily available to teachers, thus ensuring that such activities are more likely to take place. Teacher B commented,

> Most of the [materials] are included in the kit, which makes it very nice, and very easy to use, and the kids . . . have a good time using it too, because we can do all the experiments and we don't have to worry about if we've got enough of this. They've experimented to make sure they have enough of everything. (2/10/3)

Variable 5: Effective General Teaching Skills

Teachers in all classrooms employed many, if not most, of the effective teaching skills described by—for example, Brophy and Good (1986) and Rosenshine and Stevens (1986). Mastropieri and Scruggs (1994a) summarized many of these as the SCREAM variables: structure, clarity, redundancy, enthusiasm, appropriate pace, and maximized student engagement. Structure and clarity were employed in shaping the purpose and focus of overall lessons, but they were not used to stifle or suppress student divergent thinking. Redundancy was applied as needed, typically in summarizing or reinforcing lesson content. Enthusiasm was expressed by all teachers toward the content of each lesson, in order to focus attention and model positive attitudes toward science. Finally, appropriate pace and maximized student engagement were employed to maintain a positive learning atmosphere (all field notes).

In addition, all teachers employed well-established and systematic behavior management programs, although the structure appeared more concrete in the lower grades and less so in the higher grades. For example, all elementary teachers posted class rules; the third grade teacher also posted possible rewards and penalties. Teacher A used a number of tangible rewards and prizes to keep her third grade class attentive and appropriately engaged; Teacher B used goldfish crackers to reinforce task engagement, but she discontinued this during the year and later relied more on direct appeals for cooperation:

> First, I would do it just on behavior. If they were working together well, then they would get the goldfish. And then I slowly progressed into looking at the outcomes . . . then I wean them off of it, because I want it to become more intrinsic, instead of extrinsic and always wanting that food reward. (Interview, 2/10/3)

Teacher C used more abstract cues, such as "E.O.M." (for "Eyes on me"), when he felt the need to refocus his fifth grade students' attention. He also used longer term rewards (e.g., class party, field notes, 11/19/3) for cooperation and task engagement. Nevertheless, all teachers effectively enlisted the cooperation and task engagement of their respective classes. Finally, all teachers were seen to use the positive, personal relations they had established with students to engage their support and cooperation with classroom activities.

These effective teaching procedures did not appear to serve as an inhibiting effect on students' efforts to construct scientific knowledge; on the contrary, these procedures appeared to create an atmosphere that was conducive to, and respectful for, scientific learning (see also Scruggs & Mastropieri, in press-a; Mastropieri, Scruggs & Bohs, 1994). In all classes, the overall structure of the lessons was maintained, while students were encouraged to express divergent thoughts regarding particular lessons. The open acceptance of different ideas appeared to be related to the open acceptance of diversity in the classrooms, described previously.

Overall, the structure and order of the classrooms, within the context of free inquiry, served to establish and maintain an overall environment that was safe, predictable, and facilitative of the needs of students with disabilities, who appeared to benefit greatly from these environments. Such environments also appeared to be facilitative of peers' appropriate interaction with students with disabilities. The present observations are further supported by one of the few teacher effectiveness studies to include mainstreamed handicapped students (Larrivee, 1985). Teacher behaviors said to be facilitative of mainstreaming included positive feedback, ensuring a positive success rate, using time efficiently, and reducing off-task behavior.

Variable 6: Peer Assistance

In all classrooms, nondisabled student peers were also employed to assist students with disabilities. For instance, Teacher A employed students to provide social and communicative support for the hearing impaired children; Teacher B employed student peers to assist the blind girl's movements through the classroom, and Teacher C employed peers to assist and encourage physically handicapped students with science activities. All teachers employed peer assistance for students with learning disabilities (field notes, videotape records, interviews with teachers).

Classroom observations and interviews suggested that nondisabled peers generally felt positively about lending assistance to students with disabilities and felt that they learned from the interactions. Questioned by Teacher A about working with "extra special" people in the room (field notes, 2/10/3), students replied, "helpful," "great," "I feel happy and fun and different," "I'm surprised at how I learned to make signs like that."

One student reported that working with students with disabilities was "frustrating," a response which was also openly accepted by Teacher A.

In the present investigation, peer assistance, commonly described as an important mainstreaming strategy in the literature (e.g., Lewis & Doorlag, 1991; Wood, 1993), seemed clearly necessary. These three classrooms, while not excessive in class size, were nevertheless large enough to render it impossible for the teacher to provide all necessary individual assistance. The use of small groups for many of the classroom activities provided opportunities for classroom peers to provide necessary support for students with special needs. Typically, students enjoyed helping other students, as evidenced by interviews and observational records, and appeared to gain additional insight and focus on relevant tasks as a consequence of lending assistance. Teacher B, commented,

> The kids are real good with her . . . but I'm not sure if that's because they are just used to having blind kids on campus. [Name] has always been in their classroom, so she is just one of the persons there . . . They really try to help her. In fact, to the point they are sometimes too helpful, and I have to stop them. . . . They do too much for her. (Interview, 2/10/3)

Teacher C, referring to a student with physical disabilities, commented (interview, 2/5/3), "She's put with kids who'll work with her. They work directly with her all the time. . . . " Referring to students with learning disabilities, Teacher C commented,

> There's a lot of peer tutoring that goes on with those children. They have to be with kids who grab the concepts. [They can] explain it to them in terms they can understand. I usually put my LD children with somebody that is a higher achiever. They usually are successful that way. (Interview, 2/5/3)

These teacher observations have been supported to some extent by neo-Piagetian researchers (e.g., Perret-Clermont, 1980), who have suggested that higher functioning students can be helpful in leading lower functioning students in constructing scientific knowledge.

Interestingly, the idea of students helping other students as a normal class function appears to have been accepted by students with disabilities. One student with hearing impairments remarked, "[I'm] sort of happy [to come to the mainstream class] because I get to help other people out" (field notes, 2/10/3). This supports the results of a previous meta-analysis, which found that students with disabilities could serve as tutors and that they benefited socially and academically when they did so (Cook, Scruggs, Mastropieri, & Casto, 1985–1986).

Variable 7: Disability-Specific Teaching Skills

Although all three teachers lacked formal special education certification, all exhibited skill in adapting their instruction to the special needs of specific disability areas. These skills went beyond the general teacher effectiveness skills and were acquired through previous experience with students with similar disabilities, interaction with the special education teachers, and consultation with the guidelines for mainstreaming in science (Mastropieri & Scruggs, 1994b), which we provided to all participating teachers. As Teacher A commented, "When you work with these children, you learn that if you explain something to them and they don't understand it, you have to take another route" (interview, 2/10/3).

These diverse skills impacted directly on the disability areas of the students being mainstreamed. For example, Teacher A moved her students with hearing impairments to the front row; used a clear, direct speaking voice; did not stand in front of light sources; used pantomime when necessary; and carefully repeated important information. Periodically, she checked for understanding and comprehension (field notes and videotape records). Such procedures also appeared to be helpful for others in the class, including her nonnative English speaking students. When relevant, she openly discussed the special needs of her students. In a communication activity ("Telephone"), she allowed classroom peers to hold hands in a circle and send a tactual, rather than a vocal, message around the group (field notes, 11/12/3). At another time, she allowed classroom peers to use her own microphone to communicate with the hearing impaired girl. She then used this example to discuss diverse communication needs (field notes, 11/16/3). In a lesson on opposable thumbs of primates, she adapted an activity which involved taping students' thumbs, so that manual signing would not be inhibited (field notes, 11/9/3).

Similar to the activities of special education teachers in the Linn, Hadary, Rosenberg, and Haushalter (1979) study, Teacher A promoted the acquisition of language in her science teaching:

> Lots of visual—Any new words, we draw pictures of the new words, we put them on the board, the kids interact with those new words, act out new words, to learn vocabulary. With the kind of kids I work with, it's really the main focus, because they don't know vocabulary, they don't hear it like other kids hear it, and [vocabulary enhancement] reinforces [their learning]. (Interview, 2/10/3)

Such enhancement was also thought to be helpful for her students served by Chapter 1, nonnative English-speaking students, and students with learning disabilities—which suggests that even disability-specific interventions can have positive applications with other students. Teacher A also carefully monitored data recording tasks with her students with learning disabilities who appeared to exhibit literacy problems, blackboard copying problems, or other perceptual-motor problems (videotape record, 11/20/3).

Teacher B also adapted her instruction for the special needs of her visually impaired student, as shown throughout in field notes, videotape records, and interview data. She used careful, concrete descriptions, avoiding vague referents, and was careful to note when more visually oriented tasks were being employed:

> There are more concrete models I have to provide. . . . If she can feel it, she'll understand it better that way. . . . [If she doesn't understand the vocabulary] she says, "Let me see it," and that is her way of seeing it—holding it and touching it. (Interview, 2/10/3)

Teacher B trained classroom peers to offer an arm to the visually impaired girl, rather than push or pull her into position. Teacher B provided additional space and furniture for a brailler and braille reading materials. Teacher B also implemented a self-monitoring strategy to control stereotypic head movements:

> We just put a bean bag on top of her head. [Special education teacher] did it for walking back and forth to her classroom, because we have to improve her posture, because she has a gait to her walk and she has nothing physically wrong. It is just not being able to see what she is doing and get reinforcement by watching how other kids walk. . . . So I saw her walk into the classroom one day with it on, and she put it on her desk, and her head started moving around as soon as she took it off and set it down. And I said, "[name], put that bean bag back on your head." And the kids are real accepting—which really helps. And when we start something new like that—wearing a bean bag is not your ordinary, normal, everyday thing. And I could see [other students] weren't going to say anything, but . . . it is different from the rest. [So I said], "Boy, [name], this is really going to improve your posture. And, that is what models do to improve their posture." So the rest of the kids kind of think it is neat, too. (Interview, 2/10/3)

Teacher B also noted when the student's disability appeared to impact positively in classroom activities. For instance, in a "Simon Says" activity used as part of a communication unit, she told the class that the student appeared to have an advantage in not being distracted by irrelevant or contradictory visual cures (videotape record and field notes, 2/10/3).

Teacher C also used several specific techniques for accommodating students with physical disabilities. He consulted his class about their preferences for seating arrangements and, using their input, arranged his classroom in clusters of desks that left larger open spaces to facilitate the movement of wheelchairs. He used Velcro bindings to help one student keep his braces attached to his desk, yet easily disengage them manually when needed. He also arranged for this student to have a lower desk than other students and for the other two students with physical disabilities to have large desks to accommodate their wheelchairs (interview, Teacher C, 2/5/3). When engaged in lessons that involved a good deal of fine motor control—for example, mixing chemicals and solutions—peers provided necessary assistance (field notes, 11/16/3). When conducting a reaction time experiment, in which all students were to be tested individually, he adapted relevant apparatus to be engaged manually rather than with the feet for one student who was unable to use her feet for this purpose (videotape record, 2/14/3). When introducing reaction time, he used as an example his own reaction time in avoiding the path of an electrically driven wheelchair. When working in cooperative groups, students were periodically required to be the group "getter," which meant collecting/obtaining relevant materials from a centrally designated space. Students with physical disabilities also played the role of getter when it was their turn, and Teacher C signaled them when it was easiest to acquire group materials and provided assistance as needed (e.g., field notes, 2/14/3). Overall, disability-specific teaching skills appeared to play an essential role in the successful inclusion of students with disabilities in all three science classes.

In contrast, inappropriate adaptations can result in learning failures. Centra (1990), for example, cited a student's recollections of inappropriate learning adaptations: "When the rest of the class did their reading work, the teachers took me and a few others who had trouble reading and had us do puzzles in the corner. I didn't learn anything!" (p. 147). Although such an example seems extreme, Parmar and Cawley (1993) reported that many currently available science textbooks recommend "adaptations" that are not far removed from this example. (Scruggs & Mastropieri, 1994)

Extract B: Helping Behaviors and Math Achievement Gain of Students Using Cooperative Learning

Purpose of the study: To examine (a) the effects of learner ability, gender, or grade level on students' performance and (b) the nature of the cooperative group "help" on achievement gains.

RESULTS

The first part of the analysis was conducted to see if gender, grade, or ability was related to achievement gain. Gain scores were used in order to measure how much students learned, since pretest performance varied from 3% to 89%. A major factor in determining the method of analysis was the need to correct for the ceiling effect as much as possible. The use of the pretest as the covariate appears to have corrected for this fairly well, because the slope is close to -1 ($-.889$), so that there is almost a full unit of decrease in the gain score for every unit increase in the pretest score. The high-ability group began with higher pretest scores ($x = 67\%$), so their gain scores could not be as high as those of low-ability students, who began with lower pretest scores ($S = 22\%$). Therefore, a three-way factorial analysis of covariance (ANCOVA) (gender $\times$ grade $\times$ ability) was conducted with the pretest as the covariate. Achievement gain was the dependent variable.

The ANCOVA was conducted primarily to determine whether students in different grades (3, 4, 5), of different gender (male, female), or of varying ability levels (low, middle, high) showed different achievement gains. Table 1 shows that there were no statistically significant differences on any of these three independent variables, nor were there any statistically significant interactions.

Table 1 ANCOVA Tests of Significance for Achievement Gains ($N = 101$)

Independent Variable	df	MS	F	Significance of F
Pretest (covariate)	1	15,624.74	139.72	.000
Ability	2	247.39	2.21	.116
Gender	1	41.06	.37	.545
Grade	2	26.25	.23	.791
Ability $\times$ gender	2	2.67	.02	.976
Ability $\times$ grade	4	18.76	.17	.954
Gender $\times$ grade	4	19.51	.17	.840
Ability $\times$ gender $\times$ grade	4	76.61	.69	.604
Within cells	80			

The extreme significance of the pretest showed the importance of using it as a covariate. The assumption in using the pretest as the covariate in order to correct for the ceiling effect is that as the pretest score increased, the gain would decrease. Such was indeed the case. The slope was $-.889$ with a standard error of 0.75 and a T value of -11.82 ($p < .000$).

A stepwise multiple regression was next conducted, with the helping behaviors and the pretest as the nine independent variables and achievement gain as the dependent variable. This was done to determine the unique contribution of each behavior after accounting for the contribution of the pretest. As expected, the pretest accounted for the greatest amount of variance (75.5%). Following that, "receiving no help after requesting it" accounted for over 9.4% of the variance. The next largest unique contribution (3.9%) was made by the variable "gives explanation," followed by "receives explanation" (2.6%). These variables all made significant contributions to achievement gains ($p = .000$, $p = .000$, and $p = .003$, respectively), as did "receives other help" ($p = .02$) and "gives other help" ($p = .03$). The other three variables ("asks for help and receives it," "gives answer only," and "receives answer only") did not make significant contributions to the regression equation, although "asks for help" approaches significance ($p = .06$). Table 2 shows the results of this analysis in more detail.

Table 3 shows that "receiving no help after requesting it" related negatively to gains. The other helping behaviors in the equation related positively to the gain scores.

Subsequently, a forced-entry multiple regression analysis was conducted to confirm the findings. The same variables emerged as significant contributors to achievement gains. The three nonsignificant contributors remained nonsignificant.

A final research question dealt with whether students of different ability levels, grades, or gender engaged in significantly different helping behaviors. A three-way factorial analysis of variance (all gender

Table 2 Coefficients of Multiple Determination (N = 101) Dependent Variable = Achievement Gain

Step and Variable Entered	R^2	R^2 Change	F Change	Significance of Change
1 Pretest	.7546	.7546	304.4672	.0000
2 Receives no help	.8485	.0939	60.7473	.0000
3 Gives explanation	.8874	.0388	33.4280	.0000
4 Receives explanation	.9138	.0264	29.3987	.0000
5 Receives other help	.9192	.0055	6.4138	.0000
6 Gives other help	.9231	.0039	4.7941	.0310

Table 3 Multiple Regression Table of Coefficients (N = 101) Dependent Variable = Achievement Gain

Variable in Equation	B	SE B	Beta	T	Significance of T
Pretest	−.827	.034	−.907	−24.38	.0000
Receives no help	−7.999	1.382	−.184	−5.78	.0000
Gives explanation	1.194	.265	.184	4.51	.0000
Receives explanation	.795	.256	.125	3.11	.0025
Receives other help	.994	.388	.098	2.56	.0019
Gives other help	.749	.342	.092	2.19	.0310
Constant	70.172	2.175		32.26	.0000

and ability levels) was conducted for this purpose. There were significant effects of ability on all behaviors. There were no significant gender effects on any of the behaviors, nor were there any statistically significant interactions between gender and ability regarding the behaviors. In fact, gender and gender interactions were far from approaching significance (p = .546, .976, .840, .604; see Table 1). Thee were two cases where grade was significant. These were for the behaviors of "gives answer only" and "receives answer only." Table 4 shows all the significant effects on all behaviors.

Since there was a violation of the assumption of homogeneity of variance underling the ANOVA test for some of the behaviors ("receives explanation," "asks for help and receives it," "gives answer only," and "receives no help after requesting it"), a Kruskal-Wallis test was also conducted to confirm the results of the factorial ANOVa. This is a nonparametric test that does not require that assumption of homoscedasticity. Table 5 shows the results of the Kruskal-Wallis test. due to the robustness of the factorial ANOVAs it was assumed that those effects that were highly nonsignificant in the ANOVA would remain nonsignificant in the nonparametric test since nonparametric tests are less powerful.

Table 5 shows the chi-square values and significance levels for these behaviors.

High-ability students gave far more explanations, more "other help," and more answers than low-ability students, with middle-ability students engaging in these behaviors at a frequency between the other two groups. Correspondingly, low-ability students received the most explanations, other help, and answers and also asked for help most often.

Figure 1 shows the interaction effect of ability and grade level on the behavior "receives answer only." This was the only statistically significant interaction found in the analysis. Low-ability third graders received more answers than low-ability fourth or fifth graders, or than any other low-, middle-, or high-ability students in any grades.

Table 6 presents the means and standard deviations for the number of occurrences of helping behaviors on which ability and/or grade had significant effects. The frequencies of each behavior refer to the total observational period.

From: Nattiv, A. (1994). Helping behaviors and math achievement gain of students using cooperative learning. *The Elementary School Journal* 94:285–297.

Table 4 ANOVA Tables of Significant Effects on Helping Behaviors ($N = 101$)

Variables	df	MS	Significance F	of F
Gives explanation:				
Ability	2	155.99	20.84	.000
Error	83	7.49		
Receives explanation:				
Ability	2	179.17	25.88	.000
Error	83	6.92		
Asks for help (and receives it):				
Ability	2	351.86	35.72	.000
Error	83	9.85		
Gives other help:				
Ability	2	70.66	13.73	.000
Error	83	5.15		
Receives other help:				
Ability	2	45.66	12.70	.000
Error	83	3.60		
Gives answer only:				
Ability	2	3.20	5.77	.005
Grade	2	2.52	4.54	.014
Error	83	.56		
Receives answer only:				
Ability	2	2.05	5.91	.004
Grade	2	1.16	3.34	.040
Ability $\times$ Grade	4	1.23	3.55	.010
Error	83	.35		
Receives no help (after requesting it):				
Ability	2	.85	3.71	.029
Error	83	.23		

Table 5 Kruskal-Wallis Test Showing Significant Effects of Ability and Grade on Helping Behaviors ($N = 101$)

Helping Behaviors	Chi-Squares Corrected for Ties	Significance Level
Receives explanation—Ability	45.901	.0000
Asks for help (and receives it)—Ability	52.085	.0000
Gives answer only:		
Ability	6.753	.0342
Grade	6.397	.0408
Receives no help (after requesting it)—Ability levels	9.032	.0109

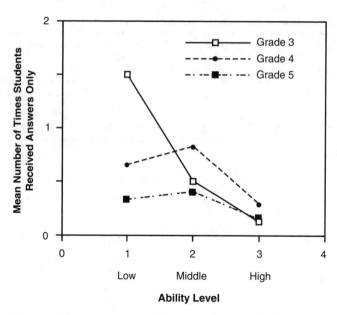

Figure 1 Interaction between grade and ability on helping behavior "receives answer only."

Table 6 Mean (and Standard Deviation) of Occurrences of Helping Behaviors That Showed Significant Effects by Ability and Grade (*N* = 101)

Behavior	Ability			
	Low	Medium	High	Total
Gives explanation	.720 (.936)	3.333 (2.917)	5.920 (3.108)	3.327 (3.188)
Gives other help	1.120 (1.013)	2.588 (2.539)	4.520 (2.452)	2.703 (2.524)
Receives explanation	5.800 (3.240)	4.196 (2.926)	.640 (.638)	3.713 (3.235)
Receives other help	3.400 (2.381)	2.177 (1.862)	.720 (.678)	2.118 (2.026)
Asks for help	8.040 (3.835)	6.216 (3.460)	.920 (.954)	5.356 (4.103)
Gives answer only:	.320 (.476)	.490 (.704)	1.000 (1.118)	.574 (.817)
Grade 3	.333 (.500)	.667 (.840)	1.333 (1.414)	
Grade 4	.250 (.463)	.556 (.705)	1.375 (.916)	
Grade 5	.375 (.518)	.200 (.414)	.250 (.463)	
Receives answer only:	.800 (.764)	.529 (.644)	.160 (.374)	.505 (.658)
Grade 3	1.444 (.727)	.500 (.618)	.111 (.333)	
Grade 4	.625 (.518)	.667 (.767)	.250 (.463)	
Grade 5	.250 (.463)	.400 (.507)	.125 (.354)	
Receives no help after requesting it	.400 (.646)	.216 (.461)	.000 (.000)	.208 (.476)

Chapter 9

Reading and Evaluating Discussion Sections

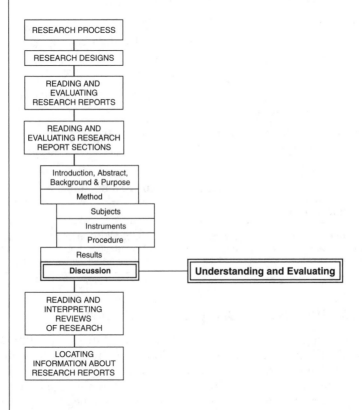

FOCUS QUESTIONS

1. What information should research consumers get from discussion sections of research reports?
2. What criteria should be used to evaluate discussion sections?
3. What is the plan for reading discussion sections?

In Chapter 3, a plan for reading research reports is set out. The plan calls for the reading of the discussion section as part of the second stage of the plan. The demonstrations of the plan show that discussion sections usually contain several types of information: (a) a restatement of the researchers' purposes (or research questions or hypotheses), (b) a summary of the results, (c) a discussion or interpretation of those results, and (d) recommendations based on those results. By reading the discussion section together with the abstract, research consumers have an overview of the research project.

From reading discussion sections, research consumers should be able to answer the following:

What were the researchers' purposes for the study?

What were the researchers' major results?

How did the researchers interpret their results?

What recommendations did the researchers make for applying the results to instructional situations or for future research projects?

Are the researchers' issues and concerns relevant to me as a professional or to my teaching situation?

Discussion sections should be evaluated using the following questions, which are from Figure 3.1, page 61:

Evaluating Discussion Sections

DISCUSSION SECTION

Discussion (Conclusions, Recommendations). Are conclusions related to answering the research question(s), and are they appropriate to the results? Is the report free from inappropriate generalizations and implications? If inappropriate, are suggestions for additional research provided?

UNDERSTANDING AND EVALUATING DISCUSSION SECTIONS

Some researchers label the discussion sections as conclusions, summary, or implications, and they may subdivide the section to highlight specific information. As a research consumer, you will have determined the specific format of research producers' discussion sections during the first, or preview, phase of the reading plan.

A common procedure for research producers is to begin discussion sections with a statement of the research purpose and then to follow that with a statement of their results and, in the case of quantitative studies, whether the results were statistically significant. In the remainder of the section, the researchers usually explain (a) whether the results answered their research questions, (b) how their results relate to related literature presented in the introduction, and (c) what implications the results have for practitioners and other researchers.

The following section, called "Conclusions" by the researchers, has all the elements of a discussion section in a quantitative research report.

Purpose of the study: To investigate a broad-based program to foster children's social development that includes supportive teacher-student relationships and opportunities for students to interact and collaborate in cooperative groups.

CONCLUSIONS

[Purpose]

The goal of the present project was to devise, implement, and assess the effectiveness of a comprehensive school-based program designed to enhance children's prosocial orientations. In this paper we have demonstrated, through quasi-experimental analyses, that the program was implemented by classroom teachers and that it had substantial positive effects on children's interpersonal behavior in the classroom (without impeding their achievement).

[General Results]

Children in the first-cohort classrooms participating in the program over 5 years of program implementation were observed to be more supportive, friendly, and helpful, and to display more spontaneous prosocial behavior toward one another than children in a group of comparison classrooms. A replication with a second cohort, in kindergarten and grade 1, produced similar results. Outcomes such as these have not often been investigated in classroom observational studies, despite a growing concern with problems relating to students' interpersonal behavior in classrooms and recent calls for schools to renew their emphasis on preparing students for responsible roles in our democratic society (e.g., Bastian, 1985; Honig, 1985). If social development is a legitimate goal of elementary education, then research identifying factors that can serve to promote it is essential. The project described in this paper is one such effort.

[Specific Results]

When the program developed in this project is being fully implemented, students exercise considerable autonomy and self control: they help make decisions about their classrooms, participate in rule-development and revision, discuss and help solve classroom problems, and in general develop a shared sense of membership in, and responsibility for, their community. It is our expectation, as Dewey (1916) suggested long ago and others have more recently (e.g., Wood, 1986), that engaged participation in activities such as the ones used should help to prepare students for adult democratic responsibilities.

[Relation to other research]

The approach to classroom organization and activity embodied in this program, particularly its attempt to minimize the use of extrinsic incentives, represents a fairly radical departure from some of the classroom management systems currently in vogue (e.g., Canter's, 1976, "assertive discipline"). It is however, quite consistent with the ideas and findings of much recent research concerning the conditions that enhance intrinsic motivation. Several researchers (see Lepper, 1983) have investigated the deleterious effect on intrinsic motivation of the use of external incentives (rewards in particular), often from an attributional perspective. Ryan, Connell, and Deci (1985), in a discussion of classroom factors that influence the development of students' self-regulation and intrinsic motivation for learning, emphasize teachers' provision of autonomy and decision-making opportunities, and the minimization of external control "in a context of adequate structure and guidance" (p. 44). The present findings suggest that these factors may also play a role in enhancing students' social orientations and behavior.

[Significance]

The two general aspects of classroom life that have been found to be related to children's social development in prior research—establishment of supportive teacher-student relationships and provision of opportunities for collaborative interstudent interaction—are incorporated in our Positive Discipline and Cooperative Activities program components, respectively. These aspects have previously been investigated separately. Our approach has been to combine these, along with other consistent elements (providing experiences in helping and understanding others; exposure to and discussion of examples of prosocial behavior, motives and attitudes) into a general, pervasive, and coherent whole. We believe that the data reported in this paper indicate that the total program has had clear and strong effects on children's classroom behavior. We do not know whether these results could have been obtained with less than the total program (for example, with Developmental Discipline alone, or Developmental Discipline combined with Cooperative Activities). Because these elements are designed to be mutually supportive and interrelated (and are in fact intercorrelated), it is somewhat arbitrary and perhaps somewhat misleading to describe them as separate "components." We do intend, however, to conduct a series of natural variation analyses to try to assess the relative influence on student social behavior of various combinations of teacher behavior and classroom activity measures.

[Implications]   It is our hope and expectation that through participating in an environment in which certain central values of the society are both discussed and exemplified (e.g., mutual concern and respect, responsibility, helpfulness), such values and behaviors consistent with them will become more deeply ingrained in the children. While the present data, indicating substantial effects on students' behavior in the classroom, reflect only some surface aspects of the kinds of change we hope to engender, including a long-range commitment to democratic values, they do suggest that such changes may result from participating in this program. In other papers, we will be describing effects outside the classroom and on other areas of children's functioning. (Solomon, Watson, Delucchi, Schaps, & Battistich, 1988, pp. 545–546)

Research consumers need to evaluate research producers' interpretations of results carefully for unwarranted or overgeneralized conclusions. They need to examine four aspects of research producers' conclusions: (a) predicted results (in the case of quantitative research), (b) unpredicted results, (c) statistical and practical significance, and (d) further research or replications of the studies.

Researchers should explain whether results logically answer their research purposes or questions. Also, they need to indicate whether results are consistent with results of other researchers. As stated in Chapter 4, background sections provide three major kinds of information: problem areas and their educational importance, related literature, and research purposes. Research consumers need to compare research producers' conclusions about anticipated or predicted results with the information provided in background sections. Also, research consumers need to determine whether research producers have drawn appropriate conclusions from the research designs and statistical procedures they used. For example, quantitative research producers should not conclude causality from descriptive or comparative research, and they should not generalize beyond the target population in any category of research.

Since comparative studies provide information about the existence of relationships (similarities and differences), it is not appropriate for research producers and consumers to infer a causal effect among variables. Most research producers avoid making this error, as did the researchers of a spelling program who found the existence of strong relationships and appropriately indicated that "the results support the idea of a common conceptual base for varying aspects of word knowledge" (Zutell & Rasinski, 1986, p. 111). This is not a statement of causation but of coexistence.

Nevertheless, the error of inferring causality from relationship studies is common. In the following passage, taken from a newspaper article about educational television and young children, note the italicized portions. Those statements imply causation, an inappropriate conclusion based on correlation data.

In the 25 years since "Sesame Street" was created, assorted studies have shown that it helps preschool children learn about numbers and the alphabet, and thus helps prepare them for school.

A new study, being released today, takes that conclusion two steps further. It found that preschoolers in low-income areas around Kansas City who had watched educational television programming, including "Sesame Street," not only were better prepared for school but actually performed better on verbal and math tests as late as age 7 than would have been expected otherwise.

Conversely, it found that preschoolers who had watched primarily adult programming and entertainment cartoons performed worse on those later tests than would have been expected.

"This study shows that terrific television causes kids to be more receptive to learning, more receptive to reading, more receptive in school," said Peggy Charren, founder of the now-inactive advocacy group Action for Children's Television and now a visiting scholar at Harvard University's School of Education, who has read the new study.

The study was done by a research team at the Center for Research on the Influences of Television on Children at the University of Kansas. It was unusual in both length and depth. In all, 250 children were followed for three years, some from age 2 to 5, others from age 4 to 7. In that period, each child was assessed four times in the researchers' office and four times in the child's home. Each assessment session lasted two hours and included the child's parents. Between visits, the parents were interviewed by telephone every two months, and kept a diary of the child's activities.

The families were mostly low-income, with some moderate-income. Statistical controls were applied to family income, parents' education, preschool attendance, the child's first language, the home environment and other factors that could affect test scores and school readiness measurements.

The study also found that among these children, those who had watched children's educational programs in general and "Sesame Street" in particular spent more time reading than those who had watched more adult programming or noneducational cartoons.

"Most other studies have looked at television generally in its effect on kids and their intellectual development, but not at specific different types of television," said Dr. Aletha C. Huston, who performed the study with her husband, Dr. John C. Wright. Both are professors of human development at Kansas.

Dr. Huston also said she believed that the study was *the first to assess television's effect on children* as young as 2, "at least with this extensive a form of measurement." (Mifflin, 1995)

The researchers' statements are inappropriate because factors other than educational television might have resulted in the children knowing "numbers and the alphabet" and spending "more time reading." The cause of watching educational television, learning about numbers and letters, and reading books might be an undisclosed factor reflecting special aspects in the children's upbringing—that is, certain family dynamics that lead to these school-linked behaviors.

In the next example, taken from a newspaper article about the relationship between television viewing and school achievement, a more appropriate statement is made. (It has been italicized for emphasis.)

A team of social scientists in California is not prepared to say that watching "B. J. and the Bear" made students do poorly in school, but the researchers do maintain that children who watched the show regularly were the students most likely to have low scores on standard achievement tests. The next most likely shows to have been viewed by low-achieving students were "The Incredible Hulk" and "Dance Fever."

New results such as these are providing fresh insight into the possible links between television viewing and classroom achievement. Several such studies from around the country were discussed publicly for the first time last week at the annual meeting of the American Educational Research Association in New York City.

It is widely believed that children who spend more time watching the popular programs on commercial television tend to be lower achievers in school, but researchers have yet to show that television causes that poor performance. (Maeroff, 1982. Copyright © 1995 by the New York Times Co. Reprinted by permission.)

Researchers sometimes need to explain results that they did not expect. For example, one research team found that one of their treatments produced an unusual outcome. The following discussion section shows how those researchers put forth a possible reason for the unexpected finding.

Purpose of the study: To examine the effects on students' comprehension of voiced versions (i.e., prose that invites reading) of more and less coherent texts.

DISCUSSION

In this study, students were presented with one of four versions of a passage, either its original form taken directly from a textbook, a version of the textbook passage with features of voice added, a more coherent version of the original textbook passage, or a version that exhibited both coherence and voice. Given that the present study worked with four versions of one base text, the study should be viewed as an initial exploration of whether text that appears to be more engaging can provide advantage for readers. There has been a long-standing assumption that more lively text language will lead to better reader outcomes, but heretofore there was no empirical evidence to back up those intuitions. Thus we felt that it was important to delve into the area of the value of "vivid language," "liveliness," and other such qualities of text that are attributed to tradebooks and tend to be lacking in textbooks. Given the findings, further research is now warranted for fleshing out the effects of these more elusive text qualities.

The results showed the strongest advantage for the passage that exhibited both coherence and voice, with the coherent passage showing advantage over the other two in performance on questions, and over the original textbook version in recall. These results pertained to students' responses on recall and questions immediately after reading. The same results were obtained on the questions after a week's delay, yet differences in recall after delay did not reach significance.

As mentioned earlier, the study unfortunately provided for a somewhat flawed test of how much text content was retained after delay. A problem apparently arose because some of the students in the study were given a tradebook to read that was about the Revolutionary War period. The book is a lively and interestingly written one, and it seemed to have left an impression on at least some of the students. We saw this effect, particularly in recalls of students who read the textbook and voiced textbook versions, because some of their recalls included information that was accurate about the period, but had not been contained in the passages they read for this study. Additionally, some of the students in both textbook conditions improved in the quality of recall after a week's delay.

The effect of the tradebook was not noticed in the coherent and voiced coherent conditions, probably for two reasons. First, fewer students in these conditions had read the tradebook (8 vs. 12). But more importantly, it seems that these students were less in a position to benefit from additional information or another exposure to engaging text, since they had already developed higher quality representations of the events portrayed in the texts. Thus the same potential for enhancing comprehension did not exist for readers of the coherent passages as for readers of the textbook passages.

Interestingly, exposure to the tradebook did not have the same effect on question performance. Perhaps that is because, although students who had read the tradebook account were able to add some of that information to their retelling, they seemed unable to enhance their responses to the questions that required them to understand the role of certain information within the chain of events (i.e., the three issue questions). Thus, although we cannot be as definitive as we would like about the retention effects from a coherent text with features of voice, there is a suggestion that positive potential exists for lasting effects. This suggestion is based on the results of the question measure and the trend in the recall data.

The present study focused on the understanding that students can get from working independently with texts that exhibit various characteristics. Yet when texts are used in classrooms, instructional and social factors mediate the text interaction. For example, teachers may provide background, add explanations, or question students about their understanding. Additionally, other students may question or comment on the text and provide responses to teacher questions. The ways in which these influences may interact with text features is an issue for further study. The results of this study do not speak directly to that issue, but consideration of the pattern of results may provide some basis for pursuing the interaction of classroom factors with text characteristics.

The overall pattern of results in this study indicates that comprehension is promoted when text is written to exhibit some of the features of oral language, to communicate the immediacy of events and emotional reactions of agents, and to vitalize relationships among agents. The pattern of results adds to our understanding of the relationship between interesting or engaging features of text and comprehension. Previous research pointed out problems in adding isolated pieces of engaging information to text, finding that such information was well remembered, but to the detriment of central information in a text (Britton et al., 1989; Duffy et al., 1989; Garner et al., 1989; Graves et al., 1991; Hidi & Baird, 1988; Wade & Adams, 1990). The present study indicates that, when engaging features are used to enhance central information, comprehension of that central material can be improved.

The present findings also extend caveats about the role of interesting or engaging text features, however. That is, the results of this study suggest that such features may not have effect when added to a text that lacks coherence. The voiced version of the textbook passage did not enhance comprehension. This finding highlights our notion that the role of voice is to engage students in a text. Potential for engagement, however, is not productive if the content of the text is not accessible. In the case of the textbook versions, the information provided seems just too far beyond the reach for most young students to make sense of it on their own, even when the language of the text promotes engagement.

Potential for increasing comprehension through voice may be better realized under certain text circumstances. One such circumstance involves situations that are pivotal to making sense of a text. That is, students who received the voiced coherent passage were better able to recall the concepts of representation and the colonists' protests, which were central to the conflict between Britain and the colonies. On the other hand, voice features did not improve recall of Britain's reaction of removing the taxes. The role of this information was made less crucial to comprehension of the passage because another, simpler and more general, statement of resolution existed—that "things quieted down." Students were apparently able to substitute this information to satisfy the need for closure to the events, rather than using the more specified information about Britain's action. Thus students seemed to fill in the needed information in the most accessible way.

Another circumstance that may optimize the potential for the effects of voice is situations that can portray emotion and active response. These qualities characterized the segments of text that showed a difference in recall between the coherent and voiced coherent passages. However, the better remembered concepts—representation and protest—were also central to the situation portrayed in the text, so it cannot be determined whether the enhancement was due to the voicing of those specific concepts or to a general effect of voicing that interacted with their role in the text.

A more general consideration of the circumstances under which features of voice enhance understanding is the extent to which the concept of voicing texts can be implemented. One direction to explore is whether voicing is appropriate for text content other than history. Our results allow us to speculate that voicing may be more widely applicable. Consider the three voicing themes used here—orality, activity, and connectivity. Certainly, features of oral language can be brought to bear on text presentations of a wide range of phenomena and need not be restricted to sequences of human action. The theme of activity was used here in relation to human events in a causal sequence. Yet, one component of activity, the notion of immediacy of events, could apply to sequences of events in the natural world as well. Connectivity pertains to relationships both among text agents and between the text and the reader. Although the first type may be limited for some content, features of text that provide for relationship between reader and text, such as directly addressing the reader, have wide applicability.

The essential concept is that, for understanding to be developed from encounters with text, readers need to engage with the text. Engagement should be possible for an almost endless assortment of text types and topics. The key is to discover elements through which engagement can be promoted. Creating texts so that they exhibit features of voice is certainly one of those elements, and the extent of its applicability is an interesting question for further study.

In the meantime, how can insights about engaging texts be applied to classroom instruction? A ready resource of engaging material exists in tradebooks. Tradebooks on historical topics can bring the past alive for young readers, and may help to reinforce the motivations and principles that drove people to action.

In focusing on bringing engagement to encounters with text, however, one must not lose sight of other text aspects that may need to be present to promote understanding. Our results suggest that engaging features can contribute to understanding when such features coincide with a coherent presentation of ideas. Engaging text might invite a reader's participation, focus attention within a text, and place emphasis on certain ideas. But once a reader's engagement and attention are activated, the text ideas that are attended to must have adequate connection and explanation to allow the building of meaning. (Beck, McKeown, & Worthy, 1995, pp. 232–234)

For some reason, quantitative research reports published in journals all seem to have statistically significant results. Less often published are studies with nonsignificant results. Reports of this kind sometimes occur when one set of researchers attempts to show that particular treatments do not produce results that other researchers have previously produced. It is important that professionals examine each others' work and that researchers be able to replicate their work. In fact, many journals will ask for "responses" from researchers when publishing studies that seem to refute their position. Research consumers need to examine both sets of reports for biases, and they need to determine the practical significance of all research. For example, the July/August/September 1994 issue of *Reading Research Quarterly* contains an exchange of ideas:

> McCarthy, S. J. Authors, text, and talk: The internalization of dialogue from social interaction during writing.
>
> Bloome, D. Response to McCarthy: On the nature of language in classroom literacy research.
>
> Rowe, D. W. Response to McCarthy: The limitations of eclecticism in research.
>
> McCarthy, S. J. Response to Bloome: Violence, risk, and the indeterminacy of language.
>
> McCarthy, S. J. Response to Rowe: Aligning methods to assumptions.

Consumers need to be concerned with the applicability of researchers' results to their own educational situation: "Are the results generalizable to my local educational setting and can the treatment, when there is one, be implemented with practical considerations given to time, effort, money, and personnel?"

Researchers often cite questions that their research has left unanswered. These questions can, and often do, become the research purposes in future studies by the researchers themselves or by other researchers. The questions might be about research design, research procedures, subject selection, instrumentation, data analysis, or research results. Research consumers need to examine the logic of these recommendations.

ACTIVITY

Read the discussion and conclusion sections in this chapter's Appendix beginning on p. 236. Using the questions and criteria discussed in this chapter, evaluate the discussion sections. Using the limited information available to you, list questions and concerns you may have about

a. The applicability of the results to your teaching situation
b. The researchers' purposes for the study
c. Major results
d. Recommendations for applying the results to instructional situations and future research projects

Do not read the Feedback section until you have completed the activity.

FEEDBACK

Extract A: Grade Retention: Prevalence, Timing, and Effects.   The section begins with a restatement of the problem area with a general conclusion (paragraph 1). Although it is not stated, this conclusion is based on a review of literature. The next two paragraphs (2 and 3) discuss problems that exist in that research. Next (paragraph 4), the researcher restates the purpose of the study using the term *effect* to indicate that one purpose is to determine a causal relationship between retention and student performance. However, that term is preceded by "to investigate the practice," which implies the researcher will indicate what things are associated or related with retention (comparative research). The researcher presents these major findings in paragraphs 5 through 10. Then, the researcher indicates the effect of retention (causality) on student achievement (paragraphs 11 through 15). In the next two paragraphs (16 and 17), additional comparative results are discussed. Then, the researcher sets out a conclusion as an answer to his purpose question (paragraph 17), emphasizing the possible effect of retention of student performance.

Overall, the researcher's discussion can be judged as appropriate because she provides the expected information. Whether research consumers can extend or generalize the results to their educational situation depends upon how closely their first-grade-retained students are representative of the cohort first-grade students (the target population).

Extract B: Implementing Standards With English Language Learners.   Although it is not apparent from the information provided in these final report sections, this is an experimental study. The researchers begin with a statement about the importance of the research and a reference to related literature (paragraph 1). Then, they set out a conclusion from the study interspersed with results from the study and reference to other research (paragraphs 2 through 9). The Conclusion section contains what seem to be the researchers' feelings as a result of the study and additional questions that seem to need answering.

The purpose statement preceding the extract indicates these are preliminary findings, that is, the first part of a three-year study. As such, the researchers' discussion can be judged as generally appropriate. They do not overgeneralize from the preliminary data.

Extract A: Grade Retention: Prevalence, Timing, and Effects

Purpose: The study investigates the correlates and consequences of grade repetition on student academic progress and social and emotional development using the first-grade cohort data from Prospects, *a nationally representative longitudinal database, which permit comparisons of students who were in and who were not in Chapter 1.*

SUMMARY

(1) The benefits and disadvantages of holding children back a year in school have been debated for years in the scholarly and popular press. Despite the wealth of studies addressing this topic, little consensus has emerged on the effectiveness of grade retention as a practice.

(2) Several factors have contributed to the conflicting results. The choice of study design and the types of comparisons made tend to favor retention or promotion in a systematic way. For example, studies that compare retained and promoted students when they are the same age, but in a different grade, tend to favor the promoted students, who are, after all, studying more advanced material. At the same time, studies that compare retained and promoted students in the same grade, after retention, favor the retained students, who have spent twice as long on the same material.

(3) In addition, there are differences in the reasons for and practices of retention. In some cases, retention is undertaken primarily because of academic difficulties; in others, students are retained due to immaturity or pauses in their social and emotional development. These differences in the reasons for retention may be related to differences in effects. Similarly, differences in populations (e.g., suburban vs rural vs urban or students in 1980 vs students today) may contribute to differences in conclusions.

(4) The present study deals with these issues as it addresses the question of the effects of retention. The purpose of the present study is to investigate the practice and effects of grade repetition using a nationally representative sample of early elementary children coupled with a methodologically adequate approach. We utilize the first grade cohort in the *Prospects* data. We focus on the first grade cohort because most retentions take place before or in the early grades. The timing of retention in the first grade cohort allows us to look at the students before, during, and after retention, an important analysis strategy.

(5) The paper addresses four topics: the measurement, prevalence and demographics of retention (Chapters 1 and 2), the timing of retention (Chapters 2 and 3), the achievement (Chapter 4) and behavioral (Chapter 5) effects of retention, and the context and content of retention (Chapter 6).

(6) The major findings from Chapter 1 include the fact that most children (81.6%) in grades K–3 in the *Prospects* study never repeat a grade. Of the children who do repeat, most (90.5%) repeat a grade only one time. First grade is the most frequent grade for retention. Of the retentions that take place in K–3, 51.8% take place in grade 1.

(7) In Chapter 2, we look at the question of who is retained. Several background and demographic factors substantially increase the chances of being retained in grade. In particular, the following characteristics increase the likelihood of being retained in grade: gender (male), race/ethnicity (other), mobility, disability and health status, family size, living in the South, attending a high poverty school, and being a Title I student.

(8) By the same token, there are background and other factors that serve to protect children from being retained in grade. These include being of Hispanic origin, attending preschool, living in an urban area, having a more educated mother with a higher income, and being rated by the teacher as more motivated and not having trouble paying attention.

(9) Factors that were not associated in this sample with being retained in grade included attending Head Start before first grade, the number of items in the home, living in a household headed by a single parent, being Black, and initial reading vocabulary score.

(10) The timing of grade retention, the topic of Chapter 3, is related to child, family, and school characteristics. White children in rural and Western states who attend medium poverty schools are much more likely to be held back in kindergarten and in pre-first programs than they are at first grade or later. Children who are Black, who participate in Title I and who attend urban

and high poverty schools in the South are much more likely to be retained in first grade or later than they are in kindergarten. Parents of children who are retained before first grade see immaturity as the major reason for retention while parents of children who are retained in first grade or later see academic difficulties as the main reason for retention.

⑪ In Chapter 4, we address the question of the academic achievement effects of retention. Keeping in mind that same-age and same-grade comparisons provide different information, both sets of analyses were carried out. Same grade comparisons of regularly promoted and retained children indicate positive academic achievement effects for retention in the year of retention, with decreasing effectiveness in subsequent years. Before retention, the average standardized difference between these two groups was 1.21; at the end of the year of retention, the difference was .38. In the next years, the difference between these two groups averaged about .60 of a standard deviation.

⑫ When these comparisons are adjusted for family background factors and prior test scores, the differences shrink appreciably. However, the general pattern of large differences between retained and never-retained students prior to retention, followed by smaller differences after retention, was found as well. Prior to retention, the adjusted effect size was .50 of a standard deviation, at the end of the year of retention the effect size was .19. In the following years, the effect size became .21.

⑬ Same grade comparisons of low performing students who are and are not retained indicated a strong positive effect for retention in the year of retention which was substantially reduced in the year following. The same-age comparisons generally did not yield positive results for retention. Therefore, the effects of retention vary with the basis of comparison utilized.

⑭ The relationship between retention and social and emotional development was discussed in Chapter 5. Retained and promoted children differed in teacher ratings of attention, cooperation, and participation. Same-grade and same-age comparisons were presented for three comparison groups: never-retained children in comparison to first grade repeaters, never-retained

children compared to first grade repeaters after adjusting for differences in background characteristics, and never-retained low performing children compared to first grade repeaters with comparable low performance.

⑮ Patterns of differences between retained and promoted children varied somewhat with the sample used and whether same-age or same-grade comparisons were being made. Differences in ratings of attention/motivation to learn, however, were consistently observed prior to retention. These differences were also consistently reduced after retention across the various samples and comparisons made. The difference between ratings of cooperation and participation prior to and following retention were not as striking or as consistent as those for attention/motivation.

⑯ Finally in Chapter 6, we compared the children's experiences in the first grade and in the retained grade. Due to differences in questionnaire construction at the different years, there were not many items which were directly comparable. However, the available data do suggest that students who are retained in fact do repeat first grade, in that the experiences, classroom organization, instructional content, and approaches do not seem to differ significantly between the regular and the retained year.

⑰ Is retention beneficial to students? The comparison strategies (same age or same grade), and comparison groups (comparable or not-matched children) used influence the answer to this question. In same grade comparisons, retention does appear to consistently shrink the before-retention achievement gap between retained and promoted children. In this sense, retention may be said to be beneficial. At the same time, retention does not close the gap, nor does it leave retained children performing at an acceptably high level. Even after the gains from retention, the retained children are still not performing adequately. Given these results, whether retention is seen as effective or a waste of time largely depends upon the outcome expected. Yes, retained children do catch up somewhat to their same grade peers after retention, but in many instances, they are still not performing adequately. (Karweit, 1999, pp. 66–68)

Extract B: Implementing Standards With English Language Learners

Purpose: To describe the first phase of a three-year applied research project on professional development for teaching to high standards in culturally diverse middle schools.

IMPLICATIONS

(1) These preliminary research findings have implications for other districts that are instituting standards-based reform with English language learners. Some of the points have been made previously in the professional development literature but have not yet been translated into practice (Clair, 1998).

(2) The research the [The Northeast and Islands Regional Educational Laboratory] has conducted suggests that implementing standards will require significant investments of time. Teachers need time to understand what a document listing goals for student learning implies about the teaching and learning dynamic in culturally diverse classrooms.

(3) They need to examine and discuss their own beliefs and attitudes about teaching, student learning, and assessment. They need to develop a shared vision of what students should know and be able to do in a particular subject area at a particular grade level and how teachers can share responsibility for ensuring that students meet these standards. For teachers to engage in each of these processes takes more time than might be anticipated.

(4) Implementation of standards-based reform also requires significant investment by school districts. The failure of teacher education programs to adequately prepare regular elementary and secondary classroom teachers to instruct linguistically and culturally diverse students (Clair, 1995; Crawford, 1993; National Commission on Teaching and America's Future, 1996; Zeichner, 1993) increases the burden on districts to offer in-service training to teachers who are implementing standards with these students. Even students who have exited from language support programs need additional assistance in mainstream classes to complete the assignments and continue their English language development. Raising the standards implies helping teachers redouble their efforts to support these students.

(5) To create successful in-service professional development, administrators and professional developers must recognize the importance of letting adults set their own learning goals and participate in the design of their learning (Renyi, 1996). Teachers have deep understandings of the teaching and learning process in their classrooms in cases where outside observers may only scratch the surface. Therefore, teacher involvement in planning professional development is critical. Effective professional development must be a two-way process with both parties—the outside technical assistance providers and the teachers—bringing knowledge to the sessions and learning from one another.

(6) This project was designed to counter typical professional development that brings in outside experts for a day or two to train teachers in certain "recipes" that may have little relationship to the school's needs.

(7) Not surprisingly in those cases, teachers may try out a recipe or two for a few days and then revert to their habitual practices. Instead, the long term nature of the professional development allowed the lab staff to learn about the district, the schools, and the teachers and then use that knowledge constructively with teachers to help them implement standards-based instruction with English language learners.

(8) To implement standards effectively, districts must also utilize all the professional resources they possess. Our data revealed that teachers were not turning to their colleagues to ask for information about cultural phenomena, linguistic patterns, effective reading techniques, and so forth. This project helped to rectify that. Joint productive activity involving collaborative inquiry among ESL, bilingual, and content area teachers seems crucial to spreading the knowledge that already exists in schools. Furthermore, because the bureaucratic nature of schools and school districts favors fragmentation (Darling-Hammond, 1997), projects that are born in different departments tend not to work well together although they may complement each other conceptually.

(9) When engaged in several projects at once, even highly competent personnel and professionally active schools sometimes become drained. Because it stands at the heart of the schools' mission to educate students,

standards implementation can shape the running of schools on a daily basis, and it can serve as a foundation for other school reform activities. Yet for standards to play a powerful role, strong district leadership is needed to weave reform projects together and create conditions that encourage flexibility in the ongoing work of the system. Policy and practice must be linked in a reciprocal relationship that is reviewed regularly.

CONCLUSION

(10) Standards-based reform involves students, teachers, administrators, parents, and policy makers in ways that can not be fully specified in advance. Lowell teachers have investigated a previously unexplored domain: the union of standards, instructional practice, and the educational needs of English language learners. Clearly, those most directly involved—teachers, schools, and districts—need professional support as they initiate reform, but what kind of support they need is not fully known.

In Lowell a self-discovery process has been initiated in which participants have begun to reveal their beliefs and practices and to examine ways of working with English language learners. To begin this work, researchers and district personnel have had to establish trust in each other and develop ways of working and learning together. The first year's work helped some teachers to refine their instructional practice so that it more directly addresses the goal of including English language learners in standards implementation. The implications for instruction across disciplines remain unclear, however. Does enhanced cultural and linguistic knowledge affect teachers' attitudes in ways that improve their relationships with students? Does this knowledge lead naturally to more appropriate instruction? If not, what supports would be required? These questions remain to be investigated. Nonetheless, the primary accomplishment of this project was developing the conditions for growth that may quite possibly be a prerequisite for change in practice. (Clair, Adger, Short, & Millen, 1998, pp. 26–29)

Chapter 10

Reading and Interpreting Reviews of Research

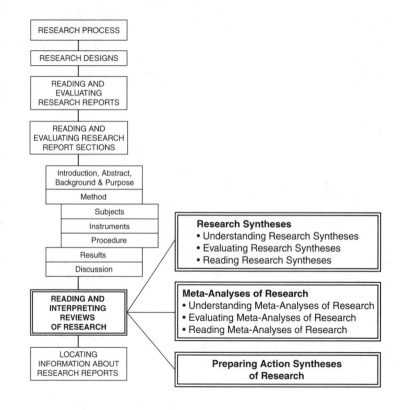

RESEARCH PROCESS

RESEARCH DESIGNS

READING AND EVALUATING RESEARCH REPORTS

READING AND EVALUATING RESEARCH REPORT SECTIONS

Introduction, Abstract, Background & Purpose

Method

Subjects

Instruments

Procedure

Results

Discussion

READING AND INTERPRETING REVIEWS OF RESEARCH

LOCATING INFORMATION ABOUT RESEARCH REPORTS

Research Syntheses
• Understanding Research Syntheses
• Evaluating Research Syntheses
• Reading Research Syntheses

Meta-Analyses of Research
• Understanding Meta-Analyses of Research
• Evaluating Meta-Analyses of Research
• Reading Meta-Analyses of Research

Preparing Action Syntheses of Research

FOCUS QUESTIONS

1. What are research syntheses?
2. What criteria are used to evaluate research syntheses?
3. What are meta-analyses?
4. What criteria are used to evaluate meta-analyses?
5. How are action research syntheses prepared?

In Chapter 4, part of the discussion about introductory sections dealt with researchers' brief summaries of other researchers' results that were related to a research problem area. In these limited reviews, called **literature reviews**, researchers indicate strengths from reviewed research that they used in their own research and weaknesses or limitations in the reviewed research that were changed. A set of questions was given in Chapter 4 so that research consumers could evaluate how critically researchers analyzed related research. These limited literature searches, however, are not intended to be comprehensive, or in-depth, reports of research related to a problem area. When researchers report comprehensive reviews of research related to problem areas, they do so in research syntheses or in meta-analyses of research.

Comprehensive reviews of research are important to educators—both research producers and research consumers. First, preparers of research reviews provide overviews of the research related to a particular problem area. They explain why the problem area is important as a research concern and also report the extent to which the problem area has been researched. Second, research reviewers provide information about the types of research designs used to study the problem, and they may show methodological changes over time in how research producers approached the problem. Third, they identify and define key terms related to the problem area, and they may discover differences in the operational definitions researchers used. Fourth, research reviewers can provide insights about the appropriateness of research producers' methodology. This is important for research consumers when they wish to determine the generalizability of results from various research situations to other teaching and learning situations. Fifth, and possibly the most important reason for these reviews, reviewers join together and interpret the results from a group of research studies dealing with a research problem area. Through their interpretation of the collective results and their general commentary, research reviewers in education indicate trends in the development of concepts about learning and instruction. These ideas help research producers understand possible areas for future research and help research consumers gain insight about education-related issues.

Research consumers need to understand (a) researchers' reason(s) for preparing reviews of research, (b) the way research reviewers prepare research syntheses, (c) the rationale underlying meta-analyses of research and the procedures for doing meta-analyses, and (d) the way to read and interpret syntheses and meta-analyses of research.

From reading a synthesis or meta-analysis of research, research consumers should be able to answer the following:

How did the research reviewer define the problem area?

What questions did the research reviewer seek to answer and why did he or she think the answers would be important for educators to know?

How did the research reviewer locate relevant research reports?

How did the research reviewer determine what studies to include in the review?

What procedures did the research reviewer use to analyze and interpret the results of the research?

What conclusions did the research reviewer make from the research?

Research consumers should keep in mind that research related to any educational problem can be summarized, interpreted, and reported for different purposes and for different consumers (Ladas, 1980). For example, research can be summarized to provide educators with an overview of the type of research being conducted and the results of that research. Or, research can be reviewed to point out weaknesses or limitations in instruction and make recommendations for improvement in teaching practices. Or, it can be reviewed to establish the improvement of research practices. Or, it can be reviewed to influence broad educational policy and provide conclusions for applied use. The reviews can be directed at audiences such as researchers, those in powerful or influential positions, practitioners, or the public at large. Research consumers, then, need to identify the intended audience(s) of research syntheses and meta-analytic reviews of educational research.

RESEARCH SYNTHESES

A research synthesis is undertaken as a research project in which the sources of data are the primary research reports of other researchers. These reviews are more than summaries of research; **research syntheses** are critical examinations of research producers' methods and conclusions and of the generalizability of their combined results.

What are now considered *research syntheses* have in the past been called *integrative reviews of research*. Research syntheses, integrative reviews of research, and *research integration* can be considered synonyms. The newer term is used because it is felt that *synthesis* more clearly describes how the results of primary research are combined so that the knowledge constructed from those results is applied to issues of instructional practice and policymaking (Shanahan, 2000).

Understanding Research Syntheses

Research syntheses consist of five stages (Cooper, 1982; Cooper & Lindsay, 1998; Jackson, 1980): (1) problem formation, (2) data collection, (3) evaluation of data quality, (4) data analysis and interpretation, and (5) presentation of results.

The stages of research synthesis are summarized in Table 10.1. The table includes the characteristics of each stage of the review process and the issues research reviewers need to address. For each stage, these include (a) a research question that needs to be asked, (b) the activities that need to be done, (c) the sources of differences among reviewers that can cause variations in their conclusions, and (d) the possible sources of threats to the validity of the review. The discussion that follows is based on ideas expressed in several sources (Abrami, Cohen, & d'Apollonia, 1988; Cooper, 1982; Cooper & Lindsay, 1998; Eisenhart, 1999; Jackson, 1980; Schwandt, 1999; Shanahan, 2000).

Problem Formulation.   The first stage begins with a search of existing research syntheses for ideas about questions or hypotheses. Ideas are sought for questions about the phenomenon being researched and variations in methods that might account for variations in results. In addition, questions might be formulated from available theory and the reviewers' own insights. Research reviewers then set out operational definitions for key concepts within the problem area. These definitions may reflect those used by primary researchers or may be created for the research review. Research reviewers use the operational definitions to identify relevant primary research stud-

Table 10.1

Research Synthesis Conceptualized as a Research Process

Stage Characteristics	Stages of Research				
	Problem Formulation	Data Collection	Data Evaluation	Analysis and Interpretation	Public Presentation
Research question asked	What evidence should be included in the review?	What procedures should be used to find relevant evidence?	What retrieved evidence should be included in the review?	What procedures should be used to make inferences about the literature as a whole?	What information should be included in the review report?
Primary function in review	Constructing definitions that distinguish relevant from irrelevant studies	Determining which of potentially relevant studies to examine	Applying criteria to separate "valid" from "invalid" studies	Synthesizing valid retrieved studies	Applying editorial criteria to separate important from unimportant information
Procedural differences that create variation in review conclusions	1. Differences in included operational definitions 2. Differences in operational detail	Differences in the research contained in sources of information	1. Differences in quality criteria 2. Differences in the influence of nonquality criteria	Differences in rules of inference	Differences in guidelines for editorial judgment
Sources of potential invalidity in review conclusions	1. Narrow concepts might make review conclusions less definitive and robust. 2. Superficial operational detail might obscure interacting variables.	1. Accessed studies might be qualitatively different from the target population of studies 2. People sample in accessible studies might be different from target population	1. Nonquality factors might cause improper weighting of study 2. Omissions in study reports might make conclusions unreliable	1. Rules for distinguishing patterns from noise might be inappropriate 2. Review-based evidence might be used to infer causality	1. Omission of review procedures might make conclusions irreproducible 2. Omissions of review findings and study procedures might make conclusions obsolete

Source: Cooper, H. M. & Lindsay, J. J., "Research Synthesis and Meta-Analysis." In L. Bickman & D. J. Rog (Eds.), *Handbook of Applied Social Research Methods*, pp. 315–341. Copyright © 1998 by Sage Publications, Thousand Oaks, CA. Reprinted by permission of Sage Publications.

ies for inclusion in the research synthesis. For example, the following is how one team of research reviewers operationally defined key concepts such as linear and nonlinear texts. Note that the reviewers indicate the references upon which they based their operational definitions.

> *Purpose of the review: To examine empirical investigations that related to subject-matter information and interest and that involved connected discourse presented either in traditional written form or on computer.*
>
> We use the term *linear text* to designate connected discourse presented in written form where decisions relative to processing are left solely to the reader. Defined in this manner, linear text is text of a more traditional nature—that is, the writings students are apt to encounter in textbooks, journals, and magazines. *Nonlinear text* is also connected discourse; however, it is discourse accompanied by some type of data base management system. This system guides or prompts readers to reaccess or extend the main text through associative computer-based links to other informational screens (see Gillingham, Young, & Kulikowich, in press, for an extensive discussion of the nature of nonlinear text). One category of nonlinear texts that we will inspect in this review, for example, is hypertext. With the evolution of situated theories of learning that emphasize rich and unique learning environments (e.g., Brown, Collins, & Duguid, 1989; Greeno, 1989; Resinick, Levine, & Teasley, 1991), nonlinear texts, such as hypertext, have gained in popularity. Many of these hypertexts are part of extensive multimedia systems that include not only nonlinear texts but also supporting videos, maps, and commercial movie clips (Christense, Giamo, & Jones, 1993; Trumbull, Gay, & Mazur, 1992). Therefore, it is important to consider the impact of these more nontraditional texts on the acquisition of subject-matter knowledge (Bolter, 1991b). (Alexander, Kulikowich, & Jetton, 1994, pp. 202–203).

In some cases, researchers synthesize the research that has been reviewed or synthesized in other researchers' studies. Such syntheses might be considered as syntheses of syntheses.

Data Collection.   In collecting, organizing, and summarizing data, research reviewers try to use as many information sources as possible. An important responsibility of research reviewers is to identify the target population, accessible population, and sample population of primary research reports. The target population of primary research reports is the total body of research reports about which generalizations can be made. Therefore, accessible populations of research reports may be determined by the availability to researchers of library holdings and electronic databases. The sample population of research reports is the specific research reports the reviewers select for review. Practical considerations for reviewers about selection relate to the resources for locating primary research reports (see Chapter 11, Locating Information About Research Reports) and the time period(s) to be covered (e.g., only research published between 1980 and 1990). Also, research reviewers cluster research reports by research designs, since each type of research must be judged by separate criteria.

Data Evaluation.   In evaluating data quality, research reviewers set up evaluation criteria before they search the literature. As a rule, research reviewers use critical questions about research that are similar to those about primary research reports included in this text (see Figure 3.1, p. 61, and Chapters 4 to 9).

Analysis and Interpretation.   In analyzing and interpreting data, the research reviewers should explicitly state how they made inferences, and they should distinguish between inferences they made on the basis of individual studies and those they made as a result of their review of a group of studies.

Public Presentation. In presenting their results, authors of research syntheses try to avoid omitting details and evidence. In other words, in making a research synthesis comprehensible, they attend to the same factors that make a primary research report understandable. The article "English-as-a-Second-Language Learners' Cognitive Reading Processes" in this chapter's Appendix A, pages 258–274, is taken from a research synthesis about the cognitive processes used by English-as-a-second-language learners. It includes the general background and introduction, the procedures for locating and selecting research reports, the categorization of the studies and the general findings of the primary researchers, and a summary and discussion of the combined findings. What has not been included here, for reasons of space, is the table containing brief summaries of the primary reports and the references.

Before reading the article, you may want to refer to the following section, "Reading Research Syntheses," on page 246. When reading the article, note that in "Methods," the researcher detailed how the studies were located and selected, and in "Limitations of the Studies," she critically evaluated the research methodology of the studies. Compare the limitations she notes with the criteria for evaluating research in Figure 3.1, page 61.

Evaluating Research Syntheses

Research consumers need to determine whether research reviewers have critically analyzed and interpreted the data they present. The information in Table 10.1 and the following discussion indicate characteristics in research reviews that may lead them to be invalid. Research consumers need to identify whether research reviewers controlled variables that could threaten the internal and external validity of their reviews. If the researcher has synthesized information from other researchers' syntheses, research consumers can use the information in Table 10.1 to determine the effectiveness of the synthesis of research syntheses.

Procedural Differences That Create Variation in Review Conclusions and Sources of Potential Invalidity in Review Conclusions. In the problem formulation stage, research reviewers should identify differences that exist among their operational definitions, those of other reviewers, and those found in the sampled research. Reviewers should indicate how the specific details of the reviewed studies differ. Research consumers should be able to distinguish precisely between aspects of primary researchers' methods that research reviewers believe are relevant to their critique and those that are not.

In the data collection stage, research reviewers should identify differences that exist between the target population of available studies, their sample of studies, and studies used in other reviews. The target population of research studies consists of all published research reports related to the problem area. The studies selected for analysis constitute the review sample. Research consumers need an understanding of the target population of studies and the representativeness of the reviewers' sample of studies. Also, research reviewers determine their own criteria for including or excluding primary research reports from their reviews, so it is possible for research reviewers to select different samples of studies for analysis. (This limitation is similar to the one discussed in Chapter 5 about the need for research consumers to be sensitive to primary researchers' identification of their target populations and subject selection techniques.) Research reviewers should explain the time span covered by the research and the type of research designs used. And, research consumers need assurance that there was no selection bias. Differences in conclusions by different research reviewers can result from differences in their samples.

Also, research consumers need to understand subject sampling procedures used by primary researchers. It is possible for several primary researchers to use similar labels for their subject while actually dealing with different target populations. Research consumers should expect research reviewers to delineate the operational definitions used in primary researchers' subject selection.

In the data evaluation stage, research reviewers should indicate what differences exist between the criteria they used for evaluating the research and those used by other reviewers. Research reviewers should indicate whether their critical evaluations were limited by the absence of information in the primary studies. Also, if more than one evaluator is used in reviewing the primary studies, interevaluator agreements should be reported.

In the analysis and interpretation stage, research reviewers should indicate how their method of interpretation and their conclusions differ from those of other research reviewers. They need to indicate how they distinguished between relevant information (patterns of results) and extraneous information (noise). Research consumers need to identify whether reviewers effectively synthesized results and noted trends, or whether they made inaccurate inferences, such as basing causality on relationship results or drawing conclusions not directly related to their purpose questions or extending beyond the data.

In the public presentation stage, research reviewers might not be responsible for differences in editorial guidelines; however, research consumers should be critical of research review reports that are not complete. Omissions restrict the replicability of a research synthesis, thereby limiting the effective use of the reviewers' results and conclusions.

Research consumers can use these questions when evaluating research syntheses:

Are there differences in operational definitions among the synthesis reviewers, other reviewers, and the primary researchers? Are those differences explained?

Has the target population of research been identified? Are there differences between the samples of studies in the review and other reviews? What is the nature of those differences?

Are there explicit evaluation criteria? Do they differ from those of other reviewers? Have the synthesis researchers cited studies with methodological limitations? Have those limitations been explained?

Have the reviewers drawn conclusions that are different from those of other reviewers? Are those differences discussed?

Does the review report present information in a standard research format? Is the report complete?

Reading Research Syntheses

Research syntheses can be read using the plan for reading research reports discussed in Chapter 3, with some slight modifications. The idea is to understand the purposes and conclusions of the research reviewers before reading their data collection and data analyses. As you read, keep in mind the evaluative questions.

The first phase of reading the Fitzgerald (1995) article on pages 258–274 is to *preview and predict*. Briefly, list answers to these questions: "What do I know about the topic?" "What do I know about the authors?" "What information would I expect to gain from this review?" Read the major headings and subheadings and answer, "Is the review organized logically and is the location of information clearly identified?"

The second phase, reading the research synthesis, is to find information suggested by your expectations and to confirm or modify the information you know about the topic.

> Read the report title, the abstract, the background section, the method section, the theoretical frameworks section, and the summary and discussion sections.
>
> Note as you read (a) the identification of a target population, (b) the discussion of reliability of data interpretations, and (c) the operational definitions presented in paragraph 3.
>
> Read any of the remaining sections that might help you better understand the reviewers' conclusions.

The third phase, confirming predictions and knowledge, is to verify that the purpose has been met and to immediately recall key information. You should decide which information supports the reviewers' purpose and adds to your knowledge base. Answer the question "Can the instructional implications presented in this review be used in my teaching situation?"

Write a short (two- to three-sentence) statement that applies to the purpose for reading the review and contains the review's key points.

META-ANALYSES OF RESEARCH

Meta-analyses of research are ways of critically examining primary research studies that use quantitative data analyses. Research reviewers use meta-analysis as "analysis of analyses" (Glass, 1976, p. 3), that is, statistical data analysis of already completed statistical data analyses. In them, the reviewers convert the statistical results of the individual studies into a common measurement so that they can obtain an overall, combined result. Research reviewers convert primary researchers' statistical results into standard numerical forms, and then they analyze those measures by traditional statistical procedures. A key assumption of this analysis is that by putting together results from various studies, a more accurate representation of the target population is provided than by the individual studies.

The following discussions about understanding and evaluating meta-analyses are synthesized from several sources (Abrami et al., 1988; Bangert-Drowns & Rudner, 1991; Carlberg et al., 1984; Cooper & Lindsay, 1998; Glass, 1976; Joyce, 1987; MacColl & White, 1998; Moore, 1999; Slavin, 1984a, 1984b, 1986, 1987b; Stock et al., 1982; Thompson, 1999).

Understanding Meta-Analyses of Research

The meta-analysis approach was devised as an attempt to eliminate reviewer biases in synthesizing results from primary quantitative research reports. Some researchers

wished to reduce the possible influence of reviewers' biases in the selection and interpretation of research reports. To do this, they designed several quantitative procedures for tabulating and comparing research results from a large number of primary
research reports, especially experimental research. A simple quantitative tabulation
for estimating the effectiveness of a treatment is called vote counting. *Vote counting*
consists of tabulating the number of positive significant results (+), the number of
negative significant results—those in which the control results exceed the treatment
(−), and the number of studies without significant results (0). Vote counting, however, can provide misleading ideas about the effectiveness of a treatment or the relationship among variables because vote counting does not take into account the magnitude of the effect or relationship. *Magnitude* can be thought of as the size of the
difference between two or more variables.

Meta-analysis is a quantitative procedure that research reviewers use to
account for the magnitude of an effect or relationship. The meta-analysis procedure
has become increasingly popular with research reviewers because it is systematic and
easily replicable. Given the same set of research reports (selected by the same set of
criteria) and using the same statistical procedures, all research reviewers should get
the same results. Also, its users say meta-analysis can be used with the results of
research projects with varying methodological quality, with similar but not exactly
the same statistical procedures, and with different sample sizes. And, it allows
research reviewers to concurrently examine the degree of influence or relationship
among the methods, subjects, treatments, duration of treatments, and results of primary research (regardless of whether they are significant).

Meta-analyses have stages similar to those of research syntheses. In meta-analyses, (1) problems are formed, (2) research studies are collected, (3) pertinent data
are identified, (4) analyses and interpretations are made of the data, and (5) results
and conclusions are presented to the public. Meta-analyses begin with reviewers
doing an exhaustive, or complete, search to locate previous research syntheses and
meta-analyses and all primary research studies relating to the education questions or
problems under review.

Problem Formulation.   The first stage of a meta-analysis is the same as that in a
research synthesis. The purpose and scope of the review are set and key concepts are
defined. The theoretical framework of the problem area is discussed, operational definitions are presented, and specific research questions are posed.

Data Collection and Coding of Studies.   In the second stage, the meta-analysts survey
the existing primary research and indicate how they located and selected the studies
for review. Meta-analysts usually indicate the procedures used (a) to obtain studies,
(b) to identify those for inclusion in the review, and (c) to select the variables for
analysis. These procedures are similar to those used in research syntheses. To ensure
accurate coding, meta-analysis researchers use multiple raters and report interrater
reliability. Summaries of the coding are sometimes, but not always, reported in tables
that list characteristics of the research studies and the computed effect size of each
study (see the next paragraph for an explanation of effect size).

Reporting Results.   In the third stage, the reviewers describe the results of their analyses. After coding, meta-analysis reviewers use statistical procedures to examine the
combined research results. They group the research according to their research designs.

Most often, meta-analyses are done with research using experimental designs. Meta-analysts create an effect size for each experimental study. **Effect sizes** are standard scores created from a ratio derived from the mean scores of the experimental and control groups and the standard deviation of the control group. Effect size scores are based on the number of subjects in the primary studies and show the extent of the difference between the mean scores of the experimental and control groups in relation to the standard deviation. For example, an effect size of +.50 would mean that the experimental group scored about .5 *SD* above the control group, and an effect size of −.50 would mean that the experimental group scored about .5 *SD* below the control group.

These effect sizes can be averaged, and significant differences (e.g., *t* or *F* ratios) can be determined between treatment and control groups or among several other independent variables.

Public Presentation.   In presenting their results, authors of meta-analyses try to avoid omitting details and evidence. Their approach to reporting is no less stringent than that of primary researchers and synthesis reviewers in making their analyses understandable.

The article in this chapter's Appendix A, pages 248–274, is taken from a meta-analysis about the effects of students' cooperative and competitive learning on their problem-solving achievement. All sections are included except the references section.

Evaluating Meta-Analyses of Research

Research consumers need to determine whether research reviewers using meta-analytic techniques have critically analyzed and interpreted the data they present. Research consumers need to know how research reviewers using meta-analyses controlled variables that could threaten the internal and external validity of their reviews.

Although meta-analyses are systematic and their results may be replicable, several major limitations affect the usability and generalizability of their results. Some of these limitations are common to both synthesis and meta-analytic research reviews. Research consumers need to understand what these limitations are and how to critically evaluate meta-analytic reviews of research.

In evaluating meta-analyses, research consumers need to have the same understanding about the stages of problem formulation, data collection, data evaluation, analysis and interpretation, and public presentation as they have about these stages in research syntheses.

A limitation specific to evaluating meta-analyses in the data evaluation stage is the possible lack of appropriate data in the primary studies. Meta-analysis reviewers must have the means, standard deviations, and sample sizes for all subject groups. When data are insufficient, primary studies are excluded; therefore, meta-analyses are only effective in examining the results of well-reported research.

And, meta-analyses involve the specific coding of primary research reports on several factors. The coding procedures involve rational or subjective, not statistical or objective, judgments. Therefore, meta-analysis reviewers should use more than one coder, and they need to report the consistency, or reliability, factors among coders.

Another limitation of meta-analyses is that they can examine only primary research with direct quantitative evidence. Direct evidence comes from the examination of explicit variables and specific defined subjects. However, one benefit of a research synthesis is that reviewers can provide indications of indirect evidence that might give research producers and consumers insight about possible effects or relationships. And, research synthesizers can analyze and combine results from qualitative research.

Also, meta-analyses include only primary research studies with complete data in the analyses. Primary research studies that have major methodological weaknesses or problems are not excluded. Consequently, poorly designed and implemented research studies are given equal status with well-designed and implemented studies. Thus, important qualitative information may be hidden by the statistical averaging of simple numerical data.

And, meta-analyses may seem to indicate a greater precision or accuracy than syntheses of research because they may appear more scientific. If the researchers have demonstrated that their selection of studies is representative of the research in the area, then consumers of research can have more confidence in accepting the results. Also, in interpreting effect sizes, researchers undertaking meta-analyses need to interpret for research consumers the meaning of the relative magnitude of those effect sizes. What constitutes a small, average, or large effect size seems to be different in different educational and psychological disciplines (Cooper & Lindsay, 1998).

These problems have been highlighted by some researchers who reviewed meta-analyses of research. One review team did a synthesis critique and comparison of six meta-analyses of research concerning the validity of college students' rating of instruction (Abrami et al., 1988). These reviewers found that all six meta-analyses resulted in different conclusions about students' rating of instruction. They concluded that they, the synthesis researchers,

> found differences at each of five steps in the quantitative syntheses which contributed to the discrepant conclusions reached by the [six meta-analytic] reviewers. The [six] reviewers had dissimilar inclusion criteria; thus the operational definitions of the problems were not the same, making the questions addressed somewhat incomparable. . . . Only one reviewer coded study features. This suggests an undue emphasis on single summary judgments of the literature without attempts to analyze thoroughly factors contributing to variability in the main relationship[s]. Agreement among the reviewers in reported effect magnitudes were low . . . [so] extracting data from reports and then calculating individual study outcomes appears more difficult than was initially envisioned. Finally, methods of analysis differed, most noticeably with regard to variability in effect magnitudes where opposite conclusions about the importance of outcome variability were reached.
>
> Overall, the differences uncovered [by the reviewers of the meta-analyses] were in both conception and execution, not limited to technical details of quantification. Clearly, computing effect magnitudes or sizes provided no assurance of an objective review. Thus the enterprise of quantitative synthesis must be conceived broadly by reviewers to include both statistical and substantive [or problem-related] issues. Attention must be paid to the procedures used and decisions reached at each step in a quantitative synthesis. (pp. 162–163)

Research consumers can use these questions when evaluating meta-analytic reviews of research:

> Are there differences in operational definitions among the meta-analysis reviewers, other reviewers (synthesis and meta-analysis), and the primary researchers? Are those differences explained?
>
> Have the target populations of studies been identified? Are there differences between the samples of studies in the meta-analysis and other reviews?
>
> Are there explicit coding and evaluation criteria? Do they differ from those of other meta-analysis reviewers? Have the meta-analysis reviewers produced

separate results for methodologically strong and weak studies? Has more than one coder been used and are interrater reliability coefficients provided?

Have the meta-analysis reviewers drawn conclusions that differ from those of other reviewers? Are those differences discussed?

Do the meta-analysis reports present information in a standard research format? Are the reports complete?

Reading Meta-Analyses of Research

Meta-analyses of research can be read using a plan similar to that used for reading research syntheses. Again, the idea is to understand the purposes and conclusions of the meta-analysts before reading their data collection and analyses. As you read, keep in mind the evaluative questions given above.

The first phase of reading the meta-analysis by Xin & Jitendra (1999) in this chapter's Appendix B, pages 274–292, is to *preview and predict.* Note that the report is presented without the References section. Briefly, list answers to these questions: "What do I know about the topic (i.e., mathematical work problems and students with learning problems)?" "What do I know about the authors?" "What information would I expect to gain from this meta-analysis (i.e., how might the results help me in developing effective classroom instruction)?"

Read the major headings and subheadings and answer, "Is the meta-analysis organized logically and is the location of information clearly identified?"

Note that the researchers have included sections about (a) locating the studies, (b) computing the statistical analysis, (c) coding the studies for "features" and "characteristics," (d) determining the rater reliability, and (e) presenting the results.

The second phase, reading the meta-analysis report, is to find information suggested by your expectations and to confirm or modify the information you know about the topic. Read the report title, the abstract, the introductory section with the theoretical frameworks and specific research questions, and the discussion and implications sections.

Note as you read (a) the discussion about the problems the meta-analysts believe their analysis will solve, (b) the operational definitions used, and (c) the discussion of why their results may be different than other researchers'.

Read any of the remaining sections that might help you better understand the authors' conclusions.

The third phase, confirming predictions and knowledge, is to verify that the purpose has been met and to immediately recall key information. You should decide which information supports the authors' purpose and adds to your knowledge base. Answer the question "Can the instructional implications presented in this meta-analysis be used in my teaching situation?"

Finally, write a short (two- to three-sentence) statement that applies to the purpose for reading the meta-analysis and contains the authors' key points.

PREPARING ACTION SYNTHESES OF RESEARCH REVIEWS

Research consumers may need to synthesize, or bring together, the results of research concerning a school-related organizational, learning, or instructional issue. For example, teachers and supervisors in a middle school may wish to examine the research relating to alternative ways to integrate or include special education students into general education classes. Or, the members of a high-school English department may wish to examine research related to the holistic scoring of students' writing. Or, the staff of an early childhood center may wish to gain additional insights about the development of children's self-concept during structured and spontaneous play.

Research syntheses are prepared by going through stages similar to those shown in Table 10.1. However, research reviews produced for local use can be considered **action research syntheses** rather than full synthesis reviews. Action research reviews are to synthesis reviews what action research is to comparative and experimental research (see Chapters 7 and 8).

To prepare action synthesis reviews, research consumers can use the concept of best evidence (Slavin, 1986, 1987a), by which they select and review only studies that (a) have purposes specifically related to an immediate issue or concern, (b) are methodologically adequate, and (c) are generalizable to the local situation. In selecting studies specifically related to an immediate issue, research consumers would include only studies that have explicit descriptions of independent and dependent variables. The early childhood staff, for example, would only select studies that clearly define "self-concept," "structured play," and "spontaneous play." Since no research project is without some methodological limitation, research consumers need to determine what aspects in the primary research they would expect to have been rigidly controlled and for what aspects they could tolerate less rigorous controls. That is, studies without complete information about instrument reliability or subject selection procedures might be included, but studies without full documentation of structured play as a treatment would not be. And, primary studies in which the subjects are not representative of local students and those containing apparent research biases or influences should be excluded.

The first steps in conducting action research reviews are to locate, summarize, and interpret the most recent synthesis and meta-analytic reviews of research. (Chapter 11 contains discussion about locating primary research reports and research reviews.) Then, using the principle of best evidence, you should locate, summarize, and interpret the most recent primary research, working back to studies published in the previous five to eight years.

As an aid to organizing information from these two steps, you can use forms such as those in Figures 10.1, 10.2, and 10.3. Figure 10.1 contains a form for summarizing information from synthesis reviews of research and meta-analyses. Figure 10.2 contains a form for summarizing information from primary research. Figure 10.3 contains a form for synthesizing the major results from the reviews and primary research reports. These forms should be used in conjunction with the evaluation questions in Figure 3.1, page 61, and those in this chapter for evaluating synthesis reviews and meta-analyses.

To complete Figure 10.1

> Enter the appropriate information in the heading; on the Location line, indicate the place (i.e., the specific library) where the original research review is located—in case it has to be reexamined.

> Summarize the pertinent information about the type of review and the stated purposes, definitions, and conclusions of the reviewers.

> Enter your decisions about the generalizability of the reviewers' conclusions to your local situation.

Authors: _____

Date: _____

Title: _____

Journal: _____

Volume: _____ Pages: _____

Location: _____

Type of review: _____ Synthesis _____ Meta-analysis

Purpose(s): _____
_____
_____

Operational definitions: _____
_____
_____

Conclusions: _____
_____
_____

Generalizability of conclusions to local issue: _____
_____
_____

Evaluaton:

Appropriateness of reviewers' evaluation criteria: _____
_____
_____

Appropriateness of reviewers' explanation of differences in definitions or selecton criteria/coding with other reviewers: ___
_____
_____
_____

Appropriateness of reviewers' explanation of differences in conclusions with other reviewers: _____
_____
_____
_____

Figure 10.1
Summarizing Information From Research Syntheses and Meta-Analyses

Enter your evaluative comments about the appropriateness of the reviewers' evaluation criteria, definitions, coding procedures, and conclusions.

To complete Figure 10.2

Enter the appropriate information in the heading; on the Location line, indicate the place (i.e., the specific library) where the primary research report is located.

Summarize pertinent information about the primary research.

Indicate the generalizability of the primary researchers' results and conclusions to your local situation.

Enter your evaluative comments about the appropriateness of the primary researchers' methodology.

Figure 10.3 is a prototype of a form for synthesizing information from several primary research reports. It is shown foreshortened and should be drawn to accommo-

Authors: _____

Date: _____

Title: _____

Journal: _____

Volume: _____ Pages: _____

Location: _____

Type of research: _____ Descriptive   _____ Comparative   _____ Experimental

_____ Quantitative   _____ Qualitative

Purpose(s): _____

_____

_____

Instruments: _____

_____

Operational definitions:

Subjects: _____

Treatments: _____

Special materials: _____

Results and conclusions: _____

_____

_____

Generalizability of results and conclusions to local issue: _____

_____

_____

Evaluation:

Validity and reliability and appropriateness of instruments: _____

_____

Possible influence of extraneous variables: _____

_____

Possible threats to internal and external validity: _____

_____

_____

Figure 10.2

Summarizing Information From Primary Research

date the number of primary research studies obtained. The last column, Synthesis, should remain the same.

To complete Figure 10.3

List the citations for the selected research reviews in the spaces along the top of the form; use the authors' last names and the dates of publication. For example, the research synthesis about the cognitive reading processes of ESL readers would be listed as "Fitzgerald (1995)" and the primary research study about whether boys and girls equally share in performing science-related activities (discussed in Chapter 4) would be listed as "Jovanovic & King, (1998)."

Place pertinent information about each synthesis review, meta-analysis, and primary study in the appropriate box for each of the evaluative topics; your comments should be taken from the information you entered on the summary forms shown in Figures 10.1 and 10.2.

	Citation:	Citation:	Citation:	Synthesis
Purpose				
Design				
Subjects				
Instruments				
Procedures Treatment Materials				
Results				
Generalizability				
Weaknesses				

Figure 10.3
Synthesizing Information About Primary Research

Synthesize the results, generalizability to your local situation, and weaknesses of the reviews and primary research; appropriate synthesizing comments reflect a conclusion you have drawn about the research result as a whole and not just a repeat of individual results. These sentences would become key or main ideas when preparing action reports; each could be used as a main idea for paragraphs or subsections.

SUMMARY

What are synthesis reviews of research?

Research syntheses are undertaken as research projects in which the sources of data are the primary research reports of other researchers. These are critical examinations of research producers' methods and conclusions and of the generalizability of their combined results. They consist of five stages: (1) problem formulation, (2) data collection, (3) evaluation of data quality, (4) data analysis and interpretation, and (5) presentation of results.

What criteria are used to evaluate research syntheses?

These questions can be used to evaluate research syntheses:

> Are there differences in operational definitions among the synthesis reviewers, other reviewers, and the primary researchers? Are those differences explained?

> Has the target population of research been identified? Are there differences between the samples of studies in the review and other reviews? What is the nature of those differences?

> Are there explicit evaluation criteria? Do they differ from those of other reviewers? Have the synthesis reviewers cited studies with methodological limitations? Have those limitations been explained?

> Have the reviewers drawn conclusions that are different from those of other reviewers? Are those differences discussed?

> Does the review report present information in a standard research format? Is the report complete?

What are meta-analyses?

Meta-analyses of research are ways to critically examine primary research studies that used quantitative data analysis. Research reviewers use meta-analyses as analyses of analyses (data analyses of data analyses already done). In them, they convert the statistical results of the individual studies into a common measurement so they can obtain an overall, combined result. Meta-analyses have stages similar to those of synthesis research reviews. In meta-analyses, (1) problems are formulated and research studies are collected, (2) pertinent data are identified, (3) analyses and interpretations are made of the data, and (4) results are presented to the public. Meta-analyses begin with reviewers doing an exhaustive, or complete, search to locate previous synthesis research reviews and meta-analyses and all primary research studies relating to the education question or problem under review.

What criteria are used to evaluate meta-analyses?

In addition to the questions for evaluating synthesis research reviews, these questions can be used:

> Are there differences in operational definitions among the meta-analysis reviewers, other reviewers (synthesis and meta-analysis), and the primary researchers? Are those differences explained?

> Have the target populations of studies been identified? Are there differences between the samples of studies in the meta-analysis and other reviews?

> Are there explicit coding and evaluation criteria? Do they differ from those of other meta-analysis reviewers? Have the meta-analysis reviewers produced separate results for methodologically strong and weak studies? Has more than one coder been used and are interrater reliability coefficients provided?

Have the meta-analysis reviewers drawn conclusions that differ from those of other reviewers? Are those differences discussed?

Do the meta-analysis reports present information in a standard research format? Are the reports complete?

How are action research syntheses prepared?

Action research syntheses are prepared by going through stages similar to those for preparing research syntheses. Research reviews produced for local consumption can be considered action research reviews rather than full synthesis reviews. To prepare action research reviews, research consumers can use the concept of best evidence. Best evidence is an idea about selecting and reviewing studies that (a) have purposes specifically related to an immediate issue or concern, (b) are methodologically adequate, and (c) are generalizable to the local situation.

ACTIVITY

Read the research synthesis article (Lloyd, 1999) in this chapter's Appendix C on pages 293–307. Use the plan for reading research syntheses presented in this chapter.

Read the title and abstract.

Determine a purpose for reading the review.

Survey the subheadings.

Locate and read the conclusion section(s).

Read the entire review.

As you survey and read the review, check for the stages of (1) problem formulation, (2) data collection, (3) evaluation of data quality, and (4) data analysis and interpretation. Then judge the completeness of the report using the questions on page 246 to evaluate the research synthesis.

Do not read the Feedback section until you have completed the activity.

FEEDBACK

Lloyd (1999)

In the introductory section, the author of the research synthesis sets out the scope of the problem area. At the end of the section, in the last sentence, he states the specific research question for the synthesis. In the second section, "Terminology," the researcher presents operational definitions of key terms related to the problem area as they appear in the research and some problems related to problems related to interpreting the different terms. In the introductory part to the next section, "Reviews of Research Relation to Multi-Age Classes," he sets out some general observations about the studies to be reviewed. From information in the last two paragraphs, it becomes apparent that the author is reviewing other reviews and syntheses of research about multi-age classes. Then, in the next five subsections, the researcher presents the reviews and syntheses of other researchers and critiques them. In the last sections, "Discussion" and "Conclusion," the researcher draws generalizations about multi-age classes and offers his opinion as to whether they provide any educational advantage for high-ability children—thereby answering his research question. Overall, the reviewer does not overgeneralize his conclusions and even cautions the research consumer about the conditions under which his findings may apply.

However, this synthesis of research syntheses has limitations. First, the researcher does not clearly identify for the research consumer that this is a synthesis of *other* syntheses. In fact, both research syntheses and meta-analyses are discussed. There is no problem in undertaking this type of synthesis, but the researcher should be explicit at the outset of the article. Second, even though the researcher has evaluated the other researchers' syntheses, he has not indicated the criteria, other than an examination of terminology differences, by which those syntheses are evaluated. The criteria are implicit in his critiques, especially since he is evaluating and creating generalizations from both research syntheses and meta-analyses. In that regard, no attention is given to interpreting the different effect sizes reported in the meta-analyses. Third, the researcher states, "Other studies were selected according to whether they specifically referred to high ability children. Library and internet searches were used to locate potential material." However, there is no explanation about the specific search methods used (e.g., ERIC descriptors), nor are there any criteria for the actual selection of those studies. Furthermore, the additional studies are not labeled for easy identification.

Chapter 10 Appendix A

Fitzgerald, J. (1995). English-as-a-second-language learners' cognitive reading processes: A review of research in the United States. *Review of Educational Research, 65*(2), 145–190. Copyright 1995 by the American Educational Research Association. Reprinted by permission of the publisher.

English-as-a-Second-Language Learners' Cognitive Reading Processes: A Review of Research in the United States

Jill Fitzgerald

The University of North Carolina at Chapel Hill

An integrative review of United States research on English-as-a-second-language (ESL) learners' cognitive reading processes suggested that, on the whole, ESL readers recognized cognate vocabulary fairly well, monitored their comprehension and used many metacognitive strategies, used schema and prior knowledge to affect comprehension and recall, and were affected differently by different types of text structures. In the main, where United States ESL readers' processes appeared to be used differently from those of native English readers, the differences were in speed and depressed activation of selected processes. Significantly, overall, the findings from the studies suggested a relatively good fit to preexisting reading theories and views generally thought to describe native-language readers. However, the quantitative differences between processes of ESL readers and those of native English readers indicated that the preexisting theories and views might need to be revisited and elaborated to address a subset of factors special to ESL learners.

Ethnic and racial diversification in the United States is growing, particularly among school-age children. In our schools there are currently about 2.3 million students identified as having "limited English proficiency" (United States Department of Education, 1992). About 50% of all Californian students speak a language other than English as their primary, or only, language, and it is predicted that by 2030 that percentage will increase to about 70% (E. Garcia, 1992a). As non-White Hispanic and Asian/Pacific Islander presence in schools increased considerably from 1976 to 1986 (by 6% and 116%, respectively), Caucasian and non-Hispanic enrollment decreased (by 13%) (E. Garcia, 1992a). However, the educational achievement, including reading achievement, of language minorities has not kept pace with that of English-speaking Caucasians. For example, among Hispanics there is a 40% high school dropout rate, a 35% grade retention rate, and a two- to four-grade-level achievement gap (E. Garcia, 1992b).

As our population has become more diverse, educators' concerns about English-as-a-second-language (ESL) literacy have also increased. Perhaps as an outgrowth of such concerns, more and more research has been conducted on ESL reading issues over the last decade or so. Many facets of ESL reading have been studied, ranging from instructional evaluations to sociocultural issues to cognitive processes. The purpose of this article is to characterize United States research and integrate findings in one area of ESL reading, namely, cognitive processes.

For the purposes of this review, ESL learners in the United States were considered to be individuals living in the United States who meet the federal government's definition of "limited English proficient" (Public Law 100–297 [1988]). These individuals (a) were not born in the United States, (b) have native languages other than English, (c) come from environments where English is not dominant, or (d) are American Indians or Alaskan natives from environments where languages other than English impact their English proficiency levels. The term *ESL learner* is used as a special case of the more general term *language minority,* which refers to individuals who are living in a place where they do not speak the majority's language. *Cognitive reading processes* refers to any internal or mental aspects of reading— that is, aspects of the brain's activity during reading (q.v. Bernhardt, 1991; Just & Carpenter, 1987).

By focusing solely on cognitive reading processes, I do not in any way wish to imply that other aspects of ESL reading are unimportant. To the contrary, some other aspects, such as the social setting in which students learn to read English, the classroom instructional

method, and congruence between learners' native-language culture and the target-language culture, may be as important, if not more important, than ESL readers' cognitive processes. Further, there may be interactions of cognitive processes with other aspects of ESL reading. Notably, researchers investigating cognition in ESL reading have tended not to explore such complex interrelations, highlighting instead isolated cognitive features.

Also, I do not want to imply that this article reflects an English-only position. It does not. Research suggests that many benefits may accrue from the development and maintenance of bilingualism, and some long-term benefits of bilingual education might outweigh those gained from English-only approaches (Hakuta, 1986; Hakuta & Gould, 1987; Snow, 1987; Wong, Fillmore & Valadez, 1986).

There are several reasons why an in-depth integration of research findings on United States ESL learners' cognitive reading processes is needed. First, there are currently countless situations in our country where ESL programs are offered in lieu of bilingual education programs (Hakuta & Gould, 1987; U.S. Department of Education, 1991, 1992). Also, ESL reading is a significant component of bilingual education programs. Further, there are situations where ESL learners do not have the benefit of teachers trained in ESL issues. More ESL students are served by Chapter I reading programs (about 1.2 million) than by Title VII programs (about 251,000), which are specially designed for ESL learners (U.S. Department of Education, 1992). It is highly likely that many Chapter I reading teachers have little background in ESL issues. Equally important, many ESL learners spend the majority of their school hours in regular classroom settings with teachers who also often have little background in ESL issues. A better understanding of the reading processes used by ESL learners could benefit virtually all teachers—ESL, bilingual, reading, and regular classroom teachers alike—as well as their students.

Second, to my knowledge no prior in-depth synthesis of reading-process research done solely with ESL learners either in the United States or in general has been conducted. A few selective reviews (e.g., Grabe, 1991; Hatch, 1974; Swaffar, 1988) and at least one comprehensive review (Bernhardt, 1991) of research in the broad area of second-language reading have been done. Both selective and comprehensive broad-based reviews of second-language reading research can certainly make significant contributions to our understanding of second-language reading processes. For example, Bernhardt used her review to begin to build a model of second-language reading.

However, it is not clear to what extent selective or broad-based reviews of second-language reading research deeply inform on specific issues such as cognitive processes, or to what extent conclusions drawn from such reviews apply to specific second languages and/or to specific settings in which a second language is learned. Indeed, authors of selective reviews generally do not intend to reveal details about a wide array of specific issues (and sometimes about any specific issues), and authors of broad-based reviews may not intend to imply that any generalizations drawn hold for any and all specific target languages. At the very least, drawing both general and specific conclusions from selective or sweeping reviews of second-language reading research is arduous. For example, after reviewing second-language data-based studies dating back to 1974, ranging from text analyses and reader factors to instruction and assessment, Bernhardt (1991) concluded that it was "extremely difficult" (p. 20) and "tantamount to impossible" (p. 68) to synthesize the information, largely due to "the wide array of subject groups studied [later referring to wide variability in language groups and language-proficiency levels], experimental tasks, and methodologies employed" (p. 20).

At least two factors might critically affect second-language reading processes (q.v. Grabe, 1991) and therefore impede generalizations about selected second-language cognitions across certain target languages and certain language-learning settings. A first factor is the target language to be learned. For example, there is some evidence that the target language may be relevant to any conclusion about the difficulty of various genres in second-language reading (Allen, Bernhardt, Berry, & Demel, 1988) and that the magnitudes of correlations between first- and second-language reading achievement may be different depending upon the languages involved (Bernhardt & Kamil, 1993; Bossers, 1991; Brisbois, 1992; Carrell, 1991).

A second factor which might potentially affect second-language learners' reading is the sociopolitical context in which the second language is learned. For example, elective bilinguals, such as students in their home cultures who are learning a foreign language, can be distinguished from circumstantial bilinguals, such as immigrants to a new country who more or less must learn a new language (Valdes, 1991). These groups are often quite different, not only in motivations for learning English, but also in educational background and socioeconomic status (Krashen, 1985a; Valdes, 1991). Any of these variables could impact how individual learners approach texts in the target language, how rapidly they advance, and ultimately, how well and how much they read.

Because the target language to be learned and the sociopolitical context in which second-language learning occurs may affect language minorities' learning about reading, reading development, reading achievement, and reading processes, it may be important to control for, or consider, these contexts when reviewing studies of second-language reading. One way (though not the only way) to do this is to select a particular target language in a particular type of setting and to review research done under those circumstances in order to see if an in-depth characterization would emerge for each particular group. This could be done for different languages and types of setting, and ultimately, comparisons could be made across the successive, highly detailed, particular characterizations. The comparative benefits and problems associated with such an approach as compared to sweeping reviews remain to be detailed.

The present review is a modest first step in such a programmatic approach; it scrutinizes research done on one target language group in one particular setting. Specifically, it attempts an in-depth integration of findings from research on cognitive reading processes of ESL learners in the United States. A characterization of this research might inform us on several issues, such as the particular strengths and/or weaknesses of United States ESL readers, the extent to which their cognitive reading processes are similar to those of native English speakers, and helpful directions for future research.

METHOD

To locate research, a broad search was initially done with few limiting criteria. The following computer searches were done to locate studies for this review: ERIC documents back to 1980, using the limiters (a) literacy (reading and writing) and ESL, (b) literacy and ESL students, (c) literacy and bilingual education, (d) literacy and language-minority learners, and (e) literacy and limited-English proficiency; *Dissertation Abstracts International* back to 1989 with the limiters (a) literacy (reading and writing) and language-minority learners, (b) literacy and limited-English proficiency, (c) literacy and ESL, and (d) literacy and bilingual education; and *Linguistics and Language Behavior Abstracts* with the limiters (a) English as a foreign language, (b) English as a second language, and (c) bilingualism. Additionally, indexes from the following journals were searched back to 1980: *Reading Research Quarterly, JRB: A Journal of Literacy,* and *TESOL Quarterly.* The sections on "Teaching Bilingual and Other Learners" in the *Annual Summary of Investigations in Reading* were searched back to 1980. Further, program books for the following annual conferences were scanned for the years 1991 to date, and papers were requested from authors: International Reading Association, National Reading Conference, Teachers of English to Speakers of Other Languages, National Association of Bilingual Education, and American Educational Research Association. Finally, a "network" approach was used. That is, all reference lists of retrieved documents were checked for additional research pieces, and an effort was made to obtain those pieces.

Later, after much of the research had been read, the review was restricted to all published, data-based research (with no date restriction) and all recent data-based conference papers, technical reports, and dissertations dating back to 1989 which dealt with ESL reading processes in studies conducted in the United States. Unpublished reports of work prior to 1989 were excluded on the grounds that such reports had not undergone rigorous peer review. Additionally, for inclusion, reports had to be complete enough to determine important factors, such as what the outcome measures were, where the study was conducted, and what the study's procedures were. In a handful of cases, studies were excluded due to incompleteness with regard to one or more of these factors.

I analyzed studies reviewed for this project using a systematic interpretive procedure (similar to a constant-comparative method often used in qualitative research [Glaser, 1978]). The following steps were taken. First, I tried to detail all the data available to me. All studies were read and reviewed, and for each study notes were taken to reflect the number of, and any identifying information about, participants; procedures; instruments, and their reliabilities, if given; and main outcomes. Sometimes key words were written along with the notes to describe the main topics investigated. Second, I perused all of the notes on the studies to see if there were patterns and themes in research issues that were addressed. As these emerged, labels were given to tentative topic clusters. Third, I again perused the notes and sorted studies into the tentative clusters. Some studies fell into more than one cluster. Fourth, I worked within each cluster, one at a time, to discern themes by looking for similarities and differences in studies and their results. This pass through the data was highly detailed, and I often returned to the original pieces to reread for clarification, confirmation, or disconfirmation of emerging hypotheses. During this period, charts and lists were made to sort studies according to developing hypotheses. For example, a list was made of all schema studies—and their salient features, including results—done with younger participants and then with older participants. In this way,

patterns and themes could be compared across ages. When hypotheses were confirmed (e.g., all studies with older participants suggested "x," while all studies with younger participants suggested "y"), at least one counterexplanation was entertained (e.g., is there a feature "z" correlated with age which is likely to be a mediating variable?). Also, at this stage, I further refined the clusters by moving some studies from one cluster to another and collapsing one to two others. As I worked through this process within each cluster, I also made separate notes about general problems with methods as they seemed to emerge. Fifth, as themes from a given section solidified, I wrote about that section. Sixth, after all clusters of studies had been analyzed, I read what had been written about each, considered the results as a whole, and, when any discrepancies occurred, reread original pieces. Seventh, to summarize across clusters, a chart was made of the main themes from each cluster of studies.

The issue of reliability of my interpretations centered on the extent to which the themes and images drawn from the review were fairly generalizable from the available data (q.v. Moss, 1994, p. 7). Reliability was clearly an aspect of validity defined as "consonance among multiple lines of evidence supporting the intended interpretation[s] over alternative interpretations" (Moss, 1994, p. 7). The criteria for reliability for this interpretive review were not quantitative. Rather, reliability should be assessed by the extent to which my interpretations were warranted using criteria such as these, given by Moss (1994, p. 7): the extent of my knowledge of the range of existing work on the topic (called "context" by Moss), the existence of "multiple and varied sources of evidence" (i.e., in this case, studies, and data and method contained in the studies), and the "transparency of the trail of evidence leading to the interpretations . . . [allowing others] to evaluate the conclusions for themselves." I worked to meet each of these criteria to the fullest extent possible. A further possible criterion suggested by Moss (1994, p. 7), the application of which I invite as response to this article, is that there might be an "ethic of disciplined, collaborative inquiry that encourages challenges and revisions to initial interpretations."

THE STUDIES

Theoretical Frameworks Used to Study ESL Readers'
Processes in the United States

How researchers in the United States have situated investigations in ESL reading processes is in itself informative. Some reports did not provide a theoretical basis for the investigations, and in some of those instances, a theoretical basis was not easily inferred. (These reports were still included in the review because they might provide informative evidence to corroborate or to call into question conclusions drawn from other studies.) However, in general, the studies were seated in two sets of theories or views: (a) *native-language reading* theories, models, or views widely known and accepted in the reading research community at large; and (b) theories or views related to *second-language acquisition* and widely known in the second-language acquisition research community.

In particular, four preexisting theories, models or views of reading, originally formed for readers in general and presumably for individuals reading in their native languages, were relied on: (a) a psycholinguistic view of reading, (b) schema theory, (c) an interactive view of reading, and (d) views of metacognition in reading. In some studies, investigators were specifically "testing" the applicability of aspects of a preexisting reading theory, model, or view in ESL reading situations. Occasionally they hypothesized easy applicability; sometimes they hypothesized how the theory, model, or view would need to be modified for ESL learners.

In brief, a psycholinguistic view of reading holds that reading is not a linear process, but that readers sample texts and make and test hypotheses and predictions, relying on their own background knowledge of the text's content as well as background knowledge about how language works (Goodman, 1970). In the sampling process, readers use three cueing systems: graphophonics, syntax, and semantics.

Schema theory postulates that knowledge is systematically organized (Rumelhart, 1980). A schema can be defined as having elements or components which can be delineated and which are ordered in specific ways. Readers are thought to use schemata to anticipate text content and structures, to guide understanding during reading, and to aid recall after reading.

An interactive view of reading holds that reading is both "top-down" and "bottom-up" (Rumelhart, 1985). That is, stated in a very oversimplified way, part of the reading process entails interpreting graphic information from the page (bottom-up), and part involves using knowledge already present in the mind (top-down). The term interactive also refers to the interactions that can occur between and among "higher-level" and "lower-level" information, such as the influence of surrounding context (higher-level) on perception of individual letters or words (lower-level).

Finally, in reading, metacognition refers to awareness of one's own reading processes (Brown, 1980). Principally, it entails awareness of one's own under-

standing and nonunderstanding, of reading strategies, and of monitoring comprehension during reading.

The investigators' use of these reading views and theories is interesting because they were designed to explain reading processes in general, and presumably of individuals reading in their native languages. Some scholars have begun to detail why certain preexisting reading theories are particularly applicable to second-language learners (e.g., see Carrell, Devine, & Eskey, 1988, on interactive models of reading for second-language learners). It might also be argued, however, that by working from preexisting theories of reading, research on ESL reading might be limited. That is, questions that need to be asked about specific aspects of second-language reading might not be addressed, and therefore, advances in knowledge might be slowed (q.v. Bernhardt, 1991).

Because the investigators relied heavily on preexisting views of reading, it was possible, in a broad sense, to assess in the present review the extent to which findings from the studies, taken collectively, were good fits to those preexisting views. Such an assessment will be made in the discussion section of this article.

Some ESL reading-process researchers situated their work in one or more theoretical positions predominant in the field of second-language acquisition. One position was that significant components of orality and literacy transfer from one language to another. This position was generally used as a foundation for studies which investigated various aspects of individuals' transfer of knowledge and skills from native-language orality or literacy to ESL literacy (or which investigated similarities in reading processes across languages). The Common Underlying Proficiency (CUP) model of how two languages are related is perhaps the most widely known model espousing this position (Cummins, 1981). Basically, it holds that a common set of proficiencies underlies both the first and second languages. What is learned in one language will transfer to another language. Also, using a skill or strategy in one language will transfer to another language. Also, using a skill or strategy in one language is pretty much the same process as in another. A significant feature of the CUP model is that major literacy skills thought to be the same in both languages have been identified, including conceptual knowledge, subject-matter knowledge, higher-order thinking skills, and reading strategies. A related refinement of the basic notion of CUP is Cummins's (1979) developmental interdependence hypothesis, which states that the development of second-language competence is partially a function of the competence already developed in the native language at the time when intensive exposure to the second language begins.

The other position was that second-language literacy and second-language orality are highly related. ESL reading-process researchers in the United States sometimes used this position to ground correlational studies of the relationship between ESL reading and ESL oral proficiency. This position has at least two forms in the second-language literature. In one form, the relationship is directional; second-language reading is dependent upon second-language oral proficiency (q.v. Clarke & Silberstein, 1977). That is, second-language orality must precede second-language literacy. In the other form, not only is the relationship directional, but there is a "threshhold of linguistic competence" necessary for successful second-language reading (Clarke, 1980; Cummins, 1979). As originally discussed by Cummins (1979), the threshold hypothesis referred to the need for optimal competence—presumably *oral* proficiency, though this was not specified—in *both* the native language and the second language in order for higher-level cognitive growth to occur. However, the threshold hypothesis has also been interpreted to mean that unless second-language orality is developed to some optimal level, second-language reading-process development and, consequently, reading and other academic achievement will be stunted. The most significant reading-instructional implication of the threshold hypothesis as originally presented was that students who have not developed native-language reading abilities to some optimal level should initially be taught to read in their native language. With respect to English learning, a significant instructional implication that has been extracted from these views is that second-language learners should develop their English oral abilities first, and then later, when oral proficiency is more developed, second-language reading should be introduced (see, for example, Krashen, 1985b; Wong Fillmore & Valadez, 1986).

Because some have interpreted positions such as the "threshold of linguistic competence" position as having dramatic implications for when and how reading should be introduced to ESL learners in the United States, a global assessment will be made in the summary of this article regarding the fit of the findings from the ESL reading-process studies reviewed to views such as the CUP model and the "threshold of linguistic competence" position.

Limitations of the Studies

Some limitations posed difficulties and/or constraints on the interpretation of the studies and their results. It may be helpful to readers to keep these limitations in mind as the following sections are read. First, many authors failed to report what might have been salient features of participants—most importantly, the participants' extent of literacy in their native language and their ESL oral proficiency level. Such features may affect ESL learners' reading (McLaughlin, 1987). Also, inadequate information about participants sometimes made it difficult to determine whether participants met the required criteria for being ESL learners as defined in this review. Occasionally, studies were excluded because it could not be determined whether participants did meet the criteria. Second, in many instances, even when authors reported important related participant characteristics, such as native language background or ESL oral proficiency level, participants were not sorted by those variables for analyses. If such characteristics interact with ESL reading, then failure to account for them could lead to confounded results. Third, even when ESL proficiency level was mentioned, there was a widespread lack of clarity as to what authors meant by that phrase. For example, the phrase could refer to ESL oral, ESL reading, or ESL writing proficiency. As another example of difficulties in interpreting what authors meant by ESL proficiency, some authors referred to particular test scores as representing an intermediate ESL proficiency level, while at least one investigator said the same test scores meant that the participants could read college-level materials about as well as their average college-level native-English-speaking counterparts. A further problem was that some authors mentioned standardized tests, but did not provide complete references for them. Fourth, measures were not always given in conjunction with authors' labels of ESL proficiency level, and evidence given at times did not clarify. In these cases, interpretation of participants' actual ESL oral and/or reading proficiency was impossible. For example, some authors stated the length of time participants had lived in the United States as evidence of proficiency level, but because individuals acquire English at differing rates, it would be helpful to have more clearly defined evidence. Fifth, a widespread lack of attention to reporting reliability and validity estimates of measures used in the quantitative studies considerably weakened interpretations of results at times.

What Has Been Asked and What Has Been Learned?

The final sources of data were 67 research reports. A summary of key aspects of the studies reported is shown in Table 1. Six clusters were formed according to the main areas addressed in the studies: (a) vocabulary knowledge, (b) strategies (psycholinguistic and metacognitive), (c) schema and prior-knowledge utilization (reader-based and text-based), (d) the relationship between ESL reading and ESL oral proficiency, (e) the relationship between ESL reading proficiency and variables other than ESL oral proficiency, and (f) issues about similarities in cognitive reading processes across United States ESL learners and native English learners, as well as across United States ESL learners' native language and English. There was also a seventh cluster for miscellaneous studies. The two most researched areas (as gauged by the number of studies conducted) were strategies and schema use.

In each of the following sections, (a) typical paradigms are explained (where there were typical ones), (b) participants' ages, grade levels, ESL proficiency levels (as given by authors), and native language backgrounds are described, and (c) themes are presented. For some clusters, special issues are also discussed.

ESL Readers' Vocabulary Knowledge. Paradigms varied in the eight reports of studies on vocabulary. For example, in one, participants took a standardized reading test and were interviewed, and then test items were analyzed. In another, participants read silently, circling all cognates (English-Spanish look-alike words with similar meanings), and also took vocabulary tests. Most participants were young (second through seventh grade), though there were 4 college students in one study and 12 in another. ESL proficiency levels, where reported, ranged from beginning to advanced. Participants were mainly Hispanic, though other ethnicities were represented.

One of the most important themes in this cluster was that vocabulary knowledge may be a highly significant variable in United States ESL readers' success. Unknown vocabulary in questions and answer choices on tests was a main linguistic factor adversely affecting the reading test performance of beginning-level and relatively proficient Hispanic and Cantonese third, fifth, and sixth graders (Ammon, 1987; G. E. Garcia, 1991). In one study, oral vocabulary production was a very strong correlate, and the only oral proficiency correlate, of English reading achievement (Saville-Troike, 1984). In another, vocabulary knowledge was even more important for test performance than was prior knowledge of content (G.E. Garcia, 1991).

Other studies looked at fourth- through seventh-grade Hispanic United States ESL learners' ability to recognize and use cognate relationships. Although cognates were fairly well recognized on the whole, the ability to recognize cognates was not fully developed; that is, there was substantial variability in cognate

recognition (G.E. Garcia & Nagy, 1993; Jimenez, Garcia, & Pearson, 1991; Nagy, Garcia, Durgunoglu, & Hancin-Bhatt, 1992).

An additional finding was that there was considerable individual variability in approaches to learning English vocabulary for four United States ESL college students (Parry, 1991). Also, advanced ESL college students in the United States used first-language vocabulary knowledge to read idioms, with idioms that were identical in Spanish and English being easiest, similar idioms being almost as easy (but showing the most native-language interference), and different idioms being most difficult (Irujo, 1986).

ESL Readers' Strategies. Two sorts of ESL readers' strategies have been studied in the United States. In one group of studies, here called *psycholinguistic-strategy* studies, researchers investigated the psycholinguistic cueing systems (graphophonics, syntax, and semantics) that readers used to recognize and comprehend words. In another, here called *metacognitive-strategy* studies, researchers tried to determine the systematic ways in which readers approached texts, and how readers tried to repair miscomprehension.

Psycholinguistic Strategies. In 12 of the 13 psycholinguistic-strategy studies, participants read orally and then retold the text without looking back. Either an examiner listened to the oral reading and simultaneously made marks on a copy of the text to record all deviations the participant made from the printed words, or the oral readings were tape recorded so the examiner could later listen and mark a protocol. In the 13th study, participants read (apparently silently), told what they understood, identified words they had found difficult, and guessed orally what the words might mean. In some studies only one text was read, and in others multiple texts were read. At least some participants in every study read in English, but some also read at least one passage in their native language. Twelve sets of investigators used miscue analysis. Basically, this means that each text deviation was assessed for whether it (a) looked and/or sounded like the text word (was graphophonically similar), (b) was syntactically acceptable, and (c) was semantically acceptable. Other details were also assessed, such as reader regressions and self-corrections. The main purpose of the analysis was to determine how readers approach text. For example, when readers made many graphophonic substitutions, made few syntactically and semantically acceptable substitutions, and rarely self-corrected, their strategies might have been characterized as overreliant on the graphic aspects of text, with little attention to text meaning.

Most of the studies in this group were done with children in elementary school grades, as low as second grade, but a few were done with participants covering the range from seventh grade to adult. Many authors identified English oral and/or reading proficiency level, and these levels covered the full range from beginner to advanced. By and large, in the studies dealing with psycholinguistic strategies, native language groups were not as mixed as in some other research clusters in this review. When there were individuals of diverse native languages within studies, several authors sorted results accordingly.

It was very difficult to arrive at pointed and highly meaningful themes across this group of studies. On the whole, the studies did not shed much light on the psycholinguistic strategies of ESL readers in the United States, at least not for ESL readers as a group. Even sorting studies by participants' English oral and/or reading proficiency, age, and whether or not investigators mixed native language groups did not reveal clear patterns leading to grand generalizations for subgroups of readers.

Following are statements about findings from the studies; most of these are either about mixed findings or supported by only one or two studies. First, the most pointed statement that can be made is that there was no single pattern in the use of psycholinguistic strategies across ESL readers. That is, there was no general reliance on a particular cue system, such as graphophonics, nor was there a general balanced reliance across the cueing systems. To the contrary, there was variability in ESL readers' psycholinguistic strategies. For example, some studies (covering participants from elementary school to high school and from beginning to intermediate English proficiency) showed that ESL readers' substitutions tended to be graphically similar (Rigg, 1976; Romatowski, 1981) and syntactically (Rigg, 1976; Romatowski, 1981) and semantically acceptable (Rigg, 1977, 1988; Romatowski, 1981). Also, adult ESL readers used graphophonic, syntactic, and semantic cueing systems to guess at word meanings after reading passages (Haynes, 1984). These results would suggest that ESL readers had a balanced set of psycholinguistic strategies; that is, it would seem that they did focus on meaning while reading English, but that they also took into account the graphic aspects of print. However, opposite results also emerged, sometimes with participants at the same age and proficiency level and/or with the same native language background. For example, Rigg's (1986) beginning ESL readers and McLeod and McLaughlin's (1986) beginning and advanced ESL readers tended to overrely on graphophonics. Participants in Haddad's (1981)

study made many syntactically unacceptable miscues, and participants in Connor's (1981) and McLeod and McLaughlin's (1986) studies made many semantically unacceptable miscues.

Second, it was not clear whether language dominance and/or native language background affected ESL readers' psycholinguistic strategies. On the one hand, in at least three studies, strategies differed according to language dominance (Barrera, Valdes, & Cardenes, 1986; Miramontes, 1987, 1990); in another, participants' miscues reflected negative transfer from their native language (Romatowski, 1981). For example, Miramontes (1990) found complex and significant differences between three groups of Mexican American readers in numbers of miscues in various categories. The three groups were (a) good English readers (whose first language was considered English), (b) good Spanish (ESL) readers, and (c) mixed-dominant ESL readers who spoke only Spanish at home and only English at school. One major conclusion of the study was that, on the whole, the mixed-dominant group seemed to focus less on meaning than did the good Spanish readers. On the other hand, however, at least two investigators found more variation in miscue patterns within language groups than between them (Connor, 1981; Rigg, 1977).

Finally, there was some evidence that the number and/or rate of miscues, and of meaning-change miscues in particular, was negatively associated with retelling scores (Connor, 1981; Devine, 1988). That is, making fewer miscues (most notably, fewer meaning-change miscues) was aligned with better comprehension. But in one study, the pattern was reversed (Romatowski, 1981).

One set of possible reasons why more pointed thematic statements cannot be garnered from the psycholinguistic studies is related to the way the studies were conducted. First, in many studies, the research issues did not always seem precise. I often had a vague sense that a study was meant to reveal something about ESL readers' miscue patterns, but specific research questions were elusive.

Second, the analyses and/or interpretations of data sometimes tended to meander, probably because research issues regarding the use of strategies were not clearly specified. Authors infrequently moved past descriptions of the actual percentages of various types of miscues made to make inferences about readers' strategies or ways of thinking about comprehending while reading.

Third, two major methodological drawbacks in this group of studies may have contributed to the inability to infer pointed themes. In many cases, reports did not provide information about the match between readers' English reading levels and the texts' readability levels. A basic principle of miscue analysis is that participants should be reading texts which are slightly difficult for them so that there is enough contextual information to build on but also some opportunity to apply strategies in hard spots. Lack of information about the extent of adherence to that principle strained the interpretation of results.

Another methodological difficulty was that in ESL research, it may be difficult to characterize how closely miscues match text because the readers' oral pronunciations may be in transition from their native language to English (Bernhardt, 1987; Brown & Haynes, 1985). It is impossible to know how different researchers handled this problem.

Another reason for the inability to draw very pointed statements simply may have been that individual differences among ESL readers in the use of psycholinguistic strategies obviate overall statements. While factors such as native language background, extent of native language literacy, extent of homeland schooling, and age of entry into the United States may mediate ESL readers' strategies, individuals' own particular ways of using psycholinguistic text cues may outweigh, or interact with, any such factors.

Metacognitive Strategies. The paradigm used in the 10 studies (in 11 reports) on United States ESL readers' metacognitive strategies was usually some variation on a typical paradigm used in studies with native English speakers. Participants read texts, always in English and sometimes additionally in Spanish, generally stopping at selected points to "think aloud," telling whatever was on their minds. Sometimes the texts had catalysts to miscomprehension, such as incoherent sentences. In at least one study, participants could do the "think aloud" in Spanish. The "think aloud" sessions were taped and later analyzed primarily to determine readers' metacognitive strategies and/or methods of monitoring their own comprehension.

All but three of the studies were done with individuals at the high school level or higher; the remaining three were done with third through fifth graders. Investigators rarely explored metacognitive strategies of individuals at beginning English proficiency levels; they favored instead intermediate or advanced learners. Two studies incorporated beginners, and a few authors did not report proficiency levels. All studies but one were done with Hispanic individuals; the remaining one was done with Chinese as well as Hispanic individuals.

Three main themes emerged. First, ESL readers in the United States did tend to monitor their comprehension (Block, 1992; Mikulecky, 1991; Padron, Knight, & Waxman, 1986; Pritchard, 1990). The monitoring process was described by one author as "evaluate, act, and check" (Block, 1992). That is, readers recognized problems and identified problem sources, they established strategic plans and attempted to solve the problems, and they checked and revised throughout problem recognition and solution.

Second, a myriad (probably over 50) of ESL readers' metacognitive strategies was commonly reported across seven studies (in eight reports). The following nine strategies all appeared in at least three of the seven studies: asking questions, rereading, imaging, using a dictionary, anticipating or predicting, reading fast or changing speed, thinking about something else while reading or associating, skipping, and summarizing or paraphrasing (Anderson, 1991; Anderson, Bachman, Perkins, & Cohen, 1991; Block, 1986a, 1986b; Knight, Padron, & Waxman, 1985; Padron et al., 1986; Padron & Waxman, 1988; Walker, 1983).

Third, at least one study supported the belief that language background did not influence the types of strategies used by ESL readers (Block, 1986a, 1986b).

Schema and Prior Knowledge Utilization. Studies on the use of schemata by ESL readers in the United States tended to fall into two subtly different groups. Although in all instances the investigators were interested in the interaction of readers' schemata or prior knowledge with text content and/or structure, some researchers focused more on *readers'* schemata or prior knowledge, whereas others tended to emphasize the schemata or structures embodied in *texts.*

Studies Emphasizing Readers' Schemata or Prior Knowledge. The methodologies of studies which emphasized *readers'* schemata or prior knowledge were typically patterned after what may now be termed classic reading studies in schema theory with native English speakers. Though exceptions can be identified, the methodologies used in the 10 reports of studies in this group were, by and large, variations on a paradigm exemplified by Carrell (1987). In this study, participants were 28 Muslim Arabs and 24 Catholic Hispanics who were ESL students of high-intermediate proficiency enrolled in an intensive English program at a midwestern university. The students each read two texts, one with Muslim-oriented content and one with Catholic-oriented content. Further, each text was presented in either a well-organized rhetorical format or an unfamiliar, altered rhetorical format. After reading each text, students recalled the text in writing and answered multiple-choice comprehension questions about the text. All aspects of data collection were conducted in English. Recall protocols were analyzed for quantity of idea units recalled from the original texts as well as whether recalled ideas were from various levels of the text hierarchy (e.g., main ideas versus details). The protocols were also scored for features such as elaborations and distortions. Answers to the multiple-choice questions were scored for number correct.

The studies were done mainly with university-age participants; only three explored schema issues at seventh grade or below. Most participants were reported to be of intermediate- to advanced-level ESL proficiency, but at least two studies included participants with beginning-level proficiency. Many language groups were represented.

The results of studies in this area resoundingly suggested that schemata affected United States ESL readers' comprehension and recall. In most studies, participants better comprehended and/or remembered passages that either were more consonant with their native cultures or were deemed more familiar (Ammon, 1987; Carrell, 1981, 1987; G.E. Garcia, 1991; Johnson, 1981, 1982; Langer, Bartolome, Vasquez, & Lucas, 1990). There was some further evidence that ESL readers' schemata for content affected comprehension and/or remembering more than did their formal schemata for text organization (Carrell, 1987; Johnson, 1981). For example, in the Carrell (1987) study described in the beginning of this section, participants remembered the most when both the text content and the rhetorical form were familiar. They remembered the least when both the text content and the rhetorical form were unfamiliar. However, when only content or only form was unfamiliar, unfamiliar content presented more difficulty than did unfamiliar form.

No common reasons could be discerned for the lack of schema effects in three studies (Barnitz & Speaker, 1991; Carrell, 1983; Carrell & Wallace, 1983). All were done with older, intermediate- to advanced-level ESL learners, except that Barnitz and Speaker (1991) also included seventh graders (whose ESL level was not stated). All had mixed native language groups. One explanation might be that although the participants were generally designated as intermediate to advanced in ESL proficiency, no evidence was reported that they could read the words in the passages with little difficulty. Inadequate recognition of the passage words could confound results. Another explanation in the Carrell (1983) study might be that the novel passage, "Balloon Serenade" (from Bransford & Johnson, 1973), was simply overwhelmingly bizarre for ESL students. Roller and Matambo (1992), in an English-as-a-foreign-language study (conducted in Zimbabwe),

replicated Carrell's (1983) effect and then went on to analyze the "Balloon" passage. They suggested that perhaps the results were contaminated due to a confounding of familiarity (of passage) with other factors, such as difficulty level of the formal structure and noun concreteness. That is, they believed the "Balloon Serenade" passage was more formally consistent and had more concrete nouns than the so-called familiar passage, "Washing Clothes."

Studies Emphasizing Text Schemata. Paradigms used in the seven reports of studies in this group were variations on what might now be termed classic reading studies on text structure done with English-speaking participants. Participants read texts and then recalled information, for the most part in writing. The structures in texts (e.g., compare-contrast and problem-solving structures in expository text, and standard versus structurally interleaved versions of stories) were identified, and the recalled information was analyzed for variables such as number of propositions recalled, number of high- versus low-level propositions recalled, and recall of temporal sequence of story components. All aspects of the studies were conducted in English.

All the participants in these studies were in ESL-intensive college or precollege matriculation programs, except that there were fourth and fifth graders in one study. All were labeled intermediate- to advanced-level ESL learners. In all studies except one, there were mixed native language groups.

The main overall theme was that different types of text structure affected comprehension and recall—most specifically, quantity of recall (Bean, Potter, & Clark, 1980; Carrell, 1984a, 1984b, though this was not true in Carrell, 1992), type of information recalled (high- versus low-level information) (Carrell, 1984a, 1992), and temporal sequence of recall (Carrell, 1984b).

Another theme was that there may have been differences among language groups as to which text structures facilitated recall better (Carrell, 1984a). For example, Arabs remembered best from expository texts with comparison structures, next best from problem-solution structures and collections of descriptions, and least well from causation structures. Asians, however, remembered best from texts with either problem-solution or causation structures and least well from either comparison structures or collections of descriptions. It remains to be seen whether this interaction of language background with text structure was due to interference/facilitation from known native-language rhetorical patterns (Carrell, 1984a; Hinds, 1983). For example, some have documented a preferred rhetorical Arabic pattern, called "coordinate parallelism"

(Kaplan, 1966). Arabs' better performance on texts with comparison structures may have been related to familiarity with "coordinate parallelism" patterns in their native-language texts. However, some other recent work also suggests that culture-specific rhetorical patterns do not transfer to a new language (Connor & McCagg, 1983).

A third theme was that although type of text structure affected the information recalled by ESL students, the students were not highly able to name the organizational plans in the texts they read (Carrell, 1984a, 1992). Finally, there was some minimal evidence that ESL readers with a greater ability to extract nonverbal schemata (on shape-classification tasks) were more able to use text structure to comprehend and recall (Perkins, 1987; Perkins & Angelis, 1985).

Relationship Between ESL Reading Proficiency and ESL Oral Proficiency. Seven studies aimed specifically to address the relationship between ESL reading proficiency and ESL oral proficiency for individuals in the United States. With minor exceptions, investigators in this group typically gave participants several tests (standardized, informal, and/or self-devised) once, or sometimes more than once over a year or so. Occasionally, participants were videotaped conversing in natural settings. Intercorrelations among measures were then examined to determine the extent of relationships. Participants were mainly young (kindergarten through eighth grade in three studies, age 16 through adult in two others). Because both reading and oral language proficiency were main research issues, each was measured, and wide ranges of ability levels were represented. Many different languages were also represented.

These studies produced quite mixed results. Thus, it is not possible to make a simple statement about the relationship between ESL reading proficiency and ESL oral proficiency. Rather, the relationship may have depended on at least three factors: native language, age or grade level, and the type of English oral proficiency measure used. First, native language background mediated the relationship between ESL reading proficiency and ESL oral proficiency (Brown & Haynes, 1985; Tragar & Wong, 1984). Tragar and Wong and Brown and Haynes were the only investigators in this cluster of studies who parsed results by both native language background and grade level. Tragar and Wong worked with 200 Cantonese students and 200 Hispanic students, all of whom had bilingual education in Boston for 1 to 2.5 years. They found a strong positive relationship for Hispanic sixth through eighth graders, and a strong negative relationship for

Cantonese sixth through eighth graders. Brown and Haynes found moderately strong positive correlations for adult Arabs and Spaniards, but a negligible correlation for Japanese.

Second, the relationship between ESL reading proficiency and ESL oral proficiency may have been stronger at higher grade levels. Although there was a positive relationship in one study with first-grade Hispanic ESL students (Lara, 1991), there was no significant relationship in two other studies with young children. In contrast to the overall strong correlations just cited for sixth through eighth graders and for adults, as well as in one additional study with adults (Carrell, 1991), no relationship emerged for either Hispanic or Cantonese ESL learners at Grades 3 through 5 (Tragar & Wong, 1984). Likewise, Saville-Troike (1984) found mainly no relationships between ESL reading and ESL oral proficiency (excepting primarily oral English vocabulary) for second through sixth graders with little prior English experience. Even amount of time spent using English orally (with peers and adults) was not related to English reading achievement (Saville-Troike, 1984).

If native language background and ESL-learner age or grade level do mediate the relationship between ESL reading proficiency and ESL oral proficiency, these factors might help to explain mixed results from two other studies. Snow (1991) found mainly positive relationships, and Devine (1987) found some positive and some negative correlations. Only Snow had a large sample; the Devine study had 20 participants. Snow covered kindergarten through eighth grade and two languages. Devine covered 16- to 38-year-olds and five different languages. Results were not reported by age or language background in interpretable ways. It is highly possible that overall false correlations resulted from the combining of subgroups which might have had different correlations.

Third, it may be that a greater number of lower correlations surfaced when less formal and more naturalistic oral proficiency measures were used. For example, where scores were obtained from measures such as interviews, videotapes of natural classroom situations, and conversation tasks (Saville-Troike, 1984; Snow, 1991), a preponderance of, or at least some, near-zero correlations emerged. However, formal, isolated measures of grammar and vocabulary tended to yield strong negative correlations (Devine, 1987).

The Relationship Between ESL Reading Proficiency and Variables Other Than English Oral Proficiency. Results in this section were from studies which were designed primarily to investigate the relationship between ESL learners' English reading proficiency and selected other variables, or which secondarily provided information pertinent to these issues. Most of these compared good ESL readers and poor ESL readers, some gave correlational tendencies, and one solely investigated poor ESL readers. A variety of tasks and analyses were used—nearly as wide a variety as is represented by all of the topics in this review. Most of the studies were done with elementary school students, but four were done with college-age or older participants. Most were done with Hispanics, but four studies also included participants from other language backgrounds. Several investigators reported English oral language proficiency levels in addition to English reading proficiencies. Where mentioned, English oral proficiencies ranged from beginning to advanced.

On the whole, results from 14 reports were robust across ages and grade levels, language backgrounds, and oral proficiency levels. There tended to be a positive relationship between English reading proficiency and the variables investigated. The following thematic conclusions were drawn. ESL learners who were more proficient in English reading and those who were less proficient tended to be different in the following ways. The more proficient readers tended to (a) use more schema knowledge (Ammon, 1987); (b) use strategies that were more meaning-oriented (e.g., make more miscues that were syntactically and semantically acceptable [Devine, 1988; Langer et al., 1990] and be more global or top-down in perceiving effective and difficulty-causing strategies [Carrell, 1989]); (c) use a greater variety of metacognitive strategies and use metacognitive strategies more frequently (Anderson, 1991); (d) take more action on plans to solve miscomprehension problems and check their solutions more often (Block, 1992); (e) persist more in the application of metacognitive strategies (Carrell, 1989); (f) make better use of cognates between languages and have more vocabulary knowledge (Ammon, 1987; Garcia & Nagy, 1993; Jimenez et al., 1991; Nagy et al., 1992); (g) make better and/or more inferences (Ammon, 1987; G.E. Garcia, 1991); (h) do better on social studies and science achievement tests (taken in English) (Saville-Troike, 1984); (i) be better readers in their native languages (Carson, Carrell, Silberstein, Kroll, & Kuehn, 1990; Tragar & Wong, 1984), with native-language reading scores best predicting English reading achievement at Grades 3 through 5, but oral English best predicting it at Grades 6 through 8 (Tragar & Wong, 1984); (j) be more proficient in English writing (Carson et al., 1990); and (k) have parents who perceived education to be highly important (Lara, 1991). One study (Carson et al., 1990) suggested that the strength of the relationships between ESL reading achievement and both native-language reading and ESL writing achievement might have been mediated by what the native language was (Chinese vs. Japanese).

However, although the variety and amount of metacognitive-strategy use varied according to English reading proficiency, both more and less proficient ESL readers applied the same most-frequent metacognitive strategies to answer test questions (Anderson, 1991), and identified problems and their sources equally well (Block, 1992). Also, there was no relationship between English reading and (a) math achievement, when tested in English (Saville-Troike, 1984); (b) language background (Saville-Troike, 1984); (c) the extent to which individuals used code switching in oral language (Lara, 1991); (d) a variety of written measures of English language knowledge (excepting one positive correlation) (Saville-Troike, 1984); or, surprisingly, (e) amount of time spent interacting with English text (Saville-Troike, 1984).

Similarities Across Learners and Languages. In this section, two issues are examined: similarities in cognitive reading processes (a) across United States ESL learners and native English learners and (b) across United States ESL learners' native language and English. To address these two issues, I analyzed only studies which either included and compared both ESL readers and native English readers, or had research designs which allowed inferences about whether the ESL readers used native-language knowledge while they read in English. That is, I analyzed only studies which had data available within the reports to arrive at comparative conclusions. Studies were not included if investigators drew conclusions about similarities or differences in results solely by comparing their results to their (or others') assessments of collective prior work on the given topic.

ESL Readers' Processes Compared to Those of Native English Speakers. A variety of paradigms was used in this group of 17 reports. Only two studies involved young children (third and fifth graders); one study involved ninth graders; the remainder included college-age participants. When given, ESL proficiency levels reportedly ranged from beginning to advanced. A variety of native language backgrounds was represented.

The results tentatively suggested that there were some similarities and some differences in aspects of United States ESL readers' processes as compared to those of native English speakers. Qualitatively, or substantively, on the whole, many facets of the processes appeared similar. For the most part, differences tended to be associated with quantitative aspects of using the processes, that is, with the extent to which particular processes were used or with processing speed. No differences in outcomes due to the native language backgrounds of the participants were discernible. One study revealed different outcomes according to proficiency level, and one according to grade level.

Both groups of readers (a) used metacognitive strategies and monitored their reading (Block, 1986a, 1986b, 1992; Padron et al., 1986), (b) generally drew correct inferences from sentences with implicative and factive predicates (Carrell, 1984c), (c) recalled superordinate ideas (Connor, 1984) and propositions in general (Barrera et al., 1986), and (d) identified antecedents and other cohesive signals when reading (Demel, 1990; Duran & Revlin, 1994). (In one study involving antecedents, anaphora was equally difficult for Hispanic ESL fourth-grade readers and for monolingual English-speaking fourth-grade readers [Robbins, 1985].) Like native-English-speaking college students, advanced ESL college learners focused more on content than on function words and appeared to use acoustic scanning (Hatch, Polin, & Part, 1974).

However, with reference to qualitative differences, ESL readers did not use context as well as native English speakers (Carrell, 1983; Carrell & Wallace, 1983). Also, unlike native-English-speaking college students, beginning and intermediate ESL readers relied more on visual cues than on acoustic cues for reading, and focused equally on function and content words (Hatch et al., 1974). Further, at the ninth-grade level, although fluent ESL readers identified cohesive signals as well as native English speakers, they were less able to make use of the information—for example, to make inferences—than were the native English speakers (Duran & Revlin, 1994). However, with college-age participants, there was no difference between groups (Duran & Revlin, 1994).

Quantitatively, compared to native English speakers, the ESL readers tended to (a) use fewer metacognitive strategies (Knight et al., 1985; Padron et al., 1986), (b) use selected metacognitive strategies with different relative frequencies (Knight et al., 1985; Padron et al., 1986), (c) verbalize their metacognitive strategies less (Block, 1992), (d) make proportionately fewer meaningful miscues (Barrera et al., 1986; McLeod & McLaughlin, 1986), (e) have higher error rates for making inferences (Carrell, 1984c), and (f) recall fewer subordinate ideas from text (Connor, 1984). They also tended to monitor their comprehension more slowly (Block, 1992) and perform reading tasks more slowly (Mestre, 1984; Oller, 1972). Further, eye-movement photography revealed that as compared to norms of approximately 12,000 college-level native English readers, ESL college-level readers,

though they tended to make about the same number of regressions, differed somewhat in making more fixations with narrower word spans, and differed significantly in that duration of fixation was much longer—about as long as for typical native-English-speaking third or fourth graders (Oller, 1972). This led to the conclusion that a main contrast between the two groups was the speed with which they processed verbal information in short-term memory.

Native-Language Transfer to ESL Reading. The 17 reports in this group covered a variety of paradigms, with second graders through adults and, where reported, beginning to advanced ESL proficiency levels. The majority of studies involved Hispanic participants, though several other language backgrounds were represented in the remaining studies.

Overwhelmingly, results showed a transfer of native-language knowledge to ESL reading. Six statements supporting native-language transfer can be made. First, there was a positive relationship between ESL and native-language reading ability for readers in the United States (Carrell, 1991; Carson et al., 1990; Saville-Troike, 1984; Tragar & Wong, 1984). Interestingly, for college-age ESL learners in one study (Carrell, 1991), native Spanish reading ability accounted for more variance in English reading than did English oral proficiency. Second, knowledge used to guide comprehension in native-language reading was also used in ESL reading (Carrell, 1984a; Goldman, Reyes, & Varnhagen, 1984; Langer et al., 1990). Third, knowledge of Spanish vocabulary and idioms transferred to ESL reading (Garcia & Nagy, 1993; Irujo, 1986; Jimenez et al., 1991; Nagy et al., 1992). Fourth, participants used the same metacognitive strategies in ESL reading as in their own Spanish reading (Pritchard, 1990). Fifth, at least a minimal number of miscues in ESL oral reading could be attributed to native-language syntactical knowledge (Gonzalez & Elijah, 1979; Romatowski, 1981). And sixth, some participants apparently phonologically recorded their ESL reading into their native language (Muchisky, 1983).

Notably, some transfer could be considered negative, such as omission of articles in English reading when the articles could be omitted in the reader's native language, or such as interference caused by Spanish idioms when the reader came across similar, but not identical, English idioms (Irujo, 1986). On the other hand, much could be considered positive, as in one study where some participants' miscue patterns were the same in ESL and in Spanish reading, but one feature was different: the participants made more miscues on function words than on nouns in Spanish and vice versa in ESL reading (Clarke, 1981).

Only two studies suggested quantitative differences, and these were in the use of comprehension-monitoring and metacognitive strategies in ESL reading as compared to native-language reading. One showed less monitoring in ESL reading (Pritchard, 1990); the other showed more strategy use in ESL reading (Mikulecky, 1991).

Miscellaneous. I located a handful of studies covering a variety of additional topics. There was some limited evidence that college-age ESL readers used phonological recoding when they read English silently (Muchisky, 1983; see also similar findings on acoustic scanning in Hatch et al., 1974). However, two other studies suggested significant variability in adult beginning and intermediate ESL learners' perceptions of the reading process as sound- versus meaning-centered; this influenced the way they read (Define, 1984, 1988). Also, in the phonological recoding study done by Muchisky (1983), ESL students were able to comprehend well without using phonological recoding. Finally, for adults with intermediate to advanced ESL proficiency, awareness of parts of speech was positively related to reading comprehension (Guarino & Perkins, 1986).

SUMMARY AND DISCUSSION

A partial image of United States ESL readers' cognitive processes emerged. Most notably, there was substantial individual variability in at least two areas: vocabulary knowledge and psycholinguistic strategies. However, on the whole, ESL readers (a) recognized cognate vocabulary fairly well, (b) monitored their comprehension and used many metacognitive strategies, (c) used schemata and prior knowledge to affect their comprehension and recall, and (d) were affected differently by different types of text structures.

Further, tentative images of more proficient versus less proficient ESL readers in the United States were formed. On the whole, more proficient ESL readers (a) made better use of vocabulary knowledge, (b) used a greater variety of metacognitive strategies and used selected strategies more frequently, (c) took more action to solve miscomprehension and checked solutions to problems more often, (d) used psycholinguistic strategies that were more meaning-oriented, (e) used more schema knowledge, and (f) made better and/or more inferences.

Theoretical Issues

On the whole, the studies reviewed in this article support the contention that the cognitive reading processes of ESL learners are substantively the same as those of native English speakers. At least, they are more alike than they are different. At the same time, some of the studies reviewed suggested that while the same basic processes may be used, a few selected facets of those processes may be used less or may operate more slowly for ESL learners than for native English readers. Let me first point to two forms of evidence from the present review which support the contention of essential sameness, and then I will summarize the evidence supporting the suggestion that selected facets of cognitive processes may be used less or more slowly by ESL learners.

Findings from a broad array of studies pointed to an image of the cognitive processes of ESL readers (just summarized at the beginning of this section) which was highly similar to portraits of the cognitive processes of native English readers that abound in the more general reading literature. On the whole, the statements made about ESL readers in general and about more proficient ESL readers in the opening to this section could well be made about native English readers.

Also, the results of studies in which United States ESL readers and native English readers were compared indicated that the two groups' cognitive processes were substantively more alike than different. They used similar metacognitive strategies and monitored their comprehension when reading, and identified antecedents in text equally well.

Collectively, these forms of evidence along with other specific findings from the studies, suggested a relatively good fit to the preexisting native-language reading theories, models, and views many of the studies were grounded in, most specifically to a psycholinguistic view, schema theory, an interactive view of reading, and views of metacognition in reading.

On the other hand, the evidence for the specialness of ESL readers' processes was mainly the amount of use and the length of time to use certain processes. That is, in some instances, ESL readers seemed to use a given process or aspects of it less often, less well, and/or more slowly. On the whole, they used fewer metacognitive strategies and favored some different ones, verbalized metacognitive strategies less, recalled subordinate ideas less well, monitored comprehension more slowly, and did reading tasks more slowly. Less proficient ESL readers did less acoustic scanning and focused more on function words than did others. An additional important specialness was that language background may have affected preferred text structures.

These areas of specialness suggest that the preexisting theories, models, and views might be revisited and modified to account for these data and to specifically allow for explanation of ESL learners' processes.

Explorations of the preexisting native-language reading theories, models, and views might address areas such as (a) reasons for decreased use of specific strategies, (b) reasons for depressed recall of subordinate ideas, and (c) what factors account for slower rates of reading for ESL learners as compared to native English speakers.

Whether or not there is a need for a theory of reading specific to ESL or second-language learners is a highly controversial issue. Some second-language researchers believe that second-language reading is "a different phenomenon" from first-language reading (Bernhardt, 1991, p. 226) and, consequently, that a reading theory specific to second-language learners is needed. Others, however, believe that second-language reading is highly similar to first-language reading. For example, Heath's (1986) notion of transferable generic literacies and Krashen's (1984, 1988) reading hypothesis both reveal an underlying assumption that second-language literacy entails the same basic processes as first-language literacy (q.v. Hedgcock & Atkinson, 1993). Another example is the previously mentioned work of Carrell, Devine, and Eskey (1988) on the application of an interactive model of reading to ESL reading. Though the results of the present review on United States ESL readers provide more support for the view that second-language cognitive reading processes are highly similar to those involved in first-language reading, it must be remembered that studies from only one second language and only one country were assessed in this review. It is still possible that quite different results could occur for other second languages or in other situations.

Recall that two second-language acquisition positions tended to be used to ground some of the studies in this review. These were positions widely known in the second-language education community and ones which were not, in themselves, complete theories of the reading process. The findings from studies and the themes in this review indicated a fit to one of the positions, but insufficient information was available to inform about the remaining position. That is, considerable evidence emerged to support the CUP model. United States ESL readers used knowledge of their native language as they read in English. This supports a prominent current view that native-language development can enhance ESL reading.

However, the data were unclear on the separate issue of whether ESL oral proficiency is a prerequisite for ESL reading. The relationship between ESL reading proficiency and ESL oral proficiency may have varied according to age and/or grade level (the relationship may have been stronger at higher grades) as well as according to native language background. Further, the

studies were correlational and provided virtually no information about the causal direction of the relationship. Consequently, what their results mean is not clear with regard to the position that English orality must be developed to an optimal level in order for English literacy to fully develop.

Research Directions

Earlier comments on the limitations of the research, combined with the images and themes gleaned from the findings, suggest several research directions which can be considered in four areas: research issues to focus on, methodological issues, specific aspects of modifying existing reading theories, and cross-specialty collaboration.

Several factors lead to the belief that a new agenda of research issues might advance the field. First, both the research questions and the methodologies have tended to follow major trends in reading research done with native English speakers, but selectively and 5 to 10 years later. Applying or replicating native-language reading research has been helpful in that it has sometimes enabled comparisons across groups. However, while the questions posed to date have helped us to know something about what United States readers' cognitive processes are, they have provided little insight as to how they happen. Notably absent were studies designed to trace the cognitive development of ESL readers in the United States. Also, reasons for differences between ESL and native-English-speaking readers' use of particular processes, such as why ESL readers' cognitive processing was sometimes slower, were underexplored. Second, the occasional emergence of interactions among reading processes and ESL readers' native language background, age or grade level, and/or ESL proficiency level suggest considerable complexity in some areas of cognitive activity. Third, individual variability in vocabulary knowledge and in the use of psycholinguistic strategies also suggests that pursuing average effects across readers may not be enlightening in some areas of cognitive activity.

It would appear helpful now for researchers to pursue ESL reading research centering around the issues of how and why ESL readers in the United States acquire, deploy, and change their cognitive processes. Such research might examine the following questions. How do ESL readers learn (or fail to learn) about cognates? How do they use cognates when reading? How do beginning ESL readers at various age levels approach text? What accounts for quantitative differences (such as processing speed) in ESL and native-English-speaking readers' processes?

Another important set of neglected research issues centers around the age of participants. There has been very little attention to how cognitive reading processes emerge and develop for preschool through second-grade students in the United States. This is probably due to prior oral primacy beliefs. That is, perhaps United States researchers have tended to think that ESL learners at these young ages cannot or should not acquire ESL literacy, and therefore have not chosen to study children at these ages. However, most literacy researchers would probably agree that we need to know much more now about the early emergence and development of ESL reading. For example, how do ESL cognitive reading processes develop over time, from the inception of learning English onward to some relatively high level of proficiency, and how are the early ESL reading processes similar to, and different from, those of early native English literacy?

Further, we need to know much more about how, when, and why ESL reading and ESL oral processes interact, rather than continuing to pursue the more general question of whether they are related. Along similar lines, only one study of United States ESL reading and writing relationships was located. It would also be interesting to pursue "how," "when," and "why" questions about the interchange between ESL reading and writing.

A second suggested area to consider as future research is conducted has to do with methodology. Virtually all of the methodological limitations noted earlier in this review could be addressed in future studies. That is, all investigators should report important characteristics of participants, especially characteristics that might potentially mediate results, including extent of literacy in a native language and ESL oral proficiency level. When participants have mixed backgrounds and/or language/literacy levels, findings should be sorted according to the differences, or analyses should at least account for the differences. Definitions of ESL proficiency should be given, and procedures for determining proficiency should be well-documented. Complete references should be reported for all standardized measures used. Reliabilities and, where possible, validity indexes should be given for all measures.

The agenda of issues given above brings to mind several types of research methods which might be useful. As an example of a way to get at the "howness" of processes, researchers might use a tracking technique similar to "think aloud" protocol analysis, such as that done by Hayes and Flower (1983), to track writers' problem solving. Participants could be videotaped talking aloud while reading, and they could give retrospective interviews. Though "think alouds" have been used in ESL reading research, they have not been used very much, if at all, in conjunction with other methods such as interviews or with videotapes, and they have not been used to actually track or describe the intricacies of how reading processes are used or when they vary.

Alongside tracking techniques, other designs could be formulated to help sort out, or to at least take into account, complexities in reading processes such as native language background. An example is interpretive work in which investigators visit classrooms and follow selected children over a year or longer. Through observation, interviews, and collection of reading samples, and so on, much could be learned about how and when cognitive reading processes develop and are used.

Also, where researchers still wish to pursue questions that involve comparison to native English readers in prior research, it seems imperative that extremely close replications be conducted on selected studies with rigorous designs. If close replications are done, we can more easily compare outcomes across studies.

A third direction is that it would be very useful for theoreticians to select some of the current views on reading and to detail hypothetical points of adaptation for ESL learners. Then a program of research could be conducted to address each of the hypothetical points.

Fourth, and perhaps most importantly, the United States research on ESL reading has tended to be isolated somewhat to the ESL community. Most of the ESL reading research has been published in journals associated with the ESL profession—journals on language, ESL, and/or linguistics. Few ESL cognitive reading research pieces were located in journals known primarily as reading or literacy research journals. This suggests that researchers whose primary specialty is reading might not be doing much work with ESL learners; that if they are studying ESL readers, they are not seeking the audiences of reading research journals; or that ESL reading research, on the whole, has been submitted to literacy journals but has not passed the review process. In any case, if the many communities interested in reading and issues of diversity could cross boundaries and learn and teach with each other, the potential for progress might increase.

Instructional Implications

As for instruction, the images drawn from the findings in this review strongly imply that for the most part, as least with regard to the cognitive aspects of reading, United States teachers of ESL students could follow sound principles of reading instruction based on current cognitive research done with native English speakers. There was virtually no evidence that ESL learners need notably divergent forms of instruction to guide or develop their cognitive reading processes. This finding runs parallel to results of a recent review of United States research on ESL reading instruction (Fitzgerald, in press). A main conclusion of that review was that results of instructional studies with ESL learners were positive and highly consistent with findings generally reported for native-language participants. Evidence in the present review did suggest, though, that teachers need to be aware of some cognitive processing areas that might deserve extra consideration in

ESL learning settings in the United States. For example, ESL learners' slower reading and fewer responses in reading situations, on average, suggest mainly that teachers might display even more than normal patience with ESL learners and that they take extra care when wording questions and making interactive comments in order to maximize the opportunity for activation of thought processes. Another example is that the potential effects of background knowledge suggest that the development of readers' topic knowledge for specific reading selections warrants even more attention from teachers than in other situations.

Chapter 10 Appendix B

Xin, Y. P., & Jitendra, A. K. (1999). The effects of instruction in solving mathematical word problems for students with learning problems: A meta-analysis. *The Journal of Special Education 32*(4), 207–225. Copyright © 1999 by PRO-ED, Inc. Reprinted with permission.

The Effects of Instruction in Solving Mathematical Word Problems for Students With Learning Problems: A Meta-Analysis

Yan Ping Xin and Asha K. Jitendra

Lehigh University

ABSTRACT

This article provides a synthesis of word-problem-solving intervention research with samples of students with learning problems (i.e., mild disabilities and at risk for mathematics failure). The effectiveness of word-problem-solving instruction in 25 outcome studies was examined across student characteristics (e.g., grade, IQ); instructional features (e.g., intervention approach, treatment length); methodological features; skill maintenance; and generalization components. Separate analyses were performed for group-design studies and single-subject studies using standardized mean change and percentage of nonoverlapping data (PND), respectively. The overall mean weighted effect size (d) and PND for word-problem-solving instruction were positive across the group-design studies (ES = +.89) and single-subject studies (PND = 89%). In addition, positive effects for skill maintenance and generalization were found for group design (ES = +.78 and +.84, respectively) and single-subject studies (PND = 100%). Computer-assisted instruction was found to be most effective for group-design studies. Effects for representation techniques and strategy training were found to be significantly higher than the "other" approach for both group-design and single-subject studies. Long-term (>1 month) intervention effects were significantly higher than short- or intermediate-term interventions for group-design studies, whereas both long-term and intermediate treatments were seen to be more effective than short-term treatments for single-subject studies. Other significant effects found for group-design studies only in terms of student characteristics, instructional features, and methodological features are reported. Finally, implications of the current analysis for future research in the area of word-problem solving are discussed.

Problems of mathematics underachievement are greatest for students with mild disabilities and those at risk for mathematics failure (Carnine, Jones, & Dixon, 1994; Nuzum, 1987; Parmar, Cawley, & Frazita, 1996; Zentall & Ferkis, 1993). The term *mild disabilities* refers to students with learning disabilities, mild mental retardation, and emotional disabilities, who are often placed together in classrooms and receive similar curricula. Increasingly, reports point to the difficulties that students with mild disabilities experience in several aspects of mathematics (for reviews see Jitendra & Xin, 1997; Mastropieri, Bakken, & Scruggs, 1991; Mastropieri, Scruggs, & Shiah, 1991; Pereira & Winton, 1991; and Rivera, 1997). Cawley and Miller (1989) reported that the mathematical performance of 8- and 9-year-old students with learning disabilities was equivalent to the first-grade level and that the performance of 16- and 17-year-old students with learning disabilities was equivalent to about the fifth-grade level. In addition, students with mild mental retardation scored significantly lower than age-equivalent students with learning disabilities on four mathematics domains (basic concepts, listening vocabulary, problem solving, and fractions; Parmar, Cawley, & Miller, 1994). Specifically, word-problem solving is difficult for students with disabilities who evidence problems in reading, computation, or both (Dunlap, 1982). As a result, some of these students reportedly spend more than one third of their resource room time studying mathematics (Carpenter, 1985).

The poor problem-solving performance by students with mild disabilities seems to follow the pattern of lackluster mathematics performance of general education students across the nation. That is, U.S. students are often placed last or next to last in international mathematics comparisons (Anrig & LaPointe, 1989; Gray & Kemp, 1993; LaPointe, Mead, & Phillips, 1989; Stedman, 1994). They have ranked lower than students in other countries in many mathematical areas (e.g., measurement, geometry, data organization), particularly word-problem solving (National Center for Education Statistics [NCES], 1991, 1992). In sum, word-problem solving presents difficulties for students of all ability and age levels (National Assessment of Educational Progress, 1992) and has received considerable attention from the National Council of Teachers of Mathematics (Miller & Mercer, 1993).

Given the relevance of problem solving in today's technologically advanced society, Patton, Cronin, Bassett, and Koppel (1997) recommended teaching students with learning problems to be proficient problem solvers in dealing with everyday situations and work settings. The importance of providing quality word-problem-solving instruction for students with mild disabilities and at-risk students is clear. Although mathematics instruction in general, and word-problem solving in particular, has not received as much in-depth study and analysis as reading (Bender, 1992), a reasonable number of mathematics word-problem-solving intervention studies with samples of students with learning problems is now available. A recent narrative review of word-problem-solving research (Jitendra & Xin, 1997) provided information of practical importance but was limited by its reliance on published studies only, and by a lack of quantitative techniques for analyzing the magnitude of intervention effectiveness. The present review uses a meta-analytic technique to aggregate intervention studies on solving word problems and examine the relationship between study characteristics and intervention outcomes.

Meta-analysis is a statistical analysis technique that provides a quantitative summary of the findings and characteristics of many empirical studies (Glass, 1977). Unlike more traditional narrative and vote-count research syntheses, meta-analysis has the potential to compare the magnitude of different treatment effects across studies to address more macroscopic research questions or high-order interactions on a specified topic. Thus, this technique increases the effective translation of research findings into practice (Kavale, 1984; Kavale & Glass, 1984; Sindelar & Wilson, cited in Mostert, 1996). The present meta-analysis study was designed to answer the following questions.

1. What is the general effectiveness of word-problem-solving interventions (e.g., representation, strategy training, CAI) for teaching students?
2. Is intervention effectiveness related to important student characteristics (i.e., grade/age, IQ level, or classification label)?
3. Are treatment outcomes related to instructional features, such as (a) setting, (b) length of treatment, (c) instructional arrangement, (d) implementation of instruction, (e) word-problem task, and (f) student-directed intervention?
4. Is there a relationship between methodological features (publication bias, group assignment) and effect size?
5. What is the effectiveness of word-problem-solving instruction in fostering skill maintenance and generalization? Are skill maintenance and generalization functions of instructional features (e.g., treatment length)?

METHOD

Literature Search

We first conducted a computer search of the Educational Resources Information Clearinghouse (ERIC), 1986 to June 1996, *Psychological Abstracts* (PsycLIT), 1986 to 1996, and *Dissertation Abstracts International* (DAI), 1960 to 1996, databases using the keywords problem solving, word problems, disabilities, remedial, and at risk. Following the identification of various articles involving mathematics word-problem-solving instruction designed for students with mild disabilities and those at risk, we searched the references cited in them for more studies. In addition, we hand-searched recent issues (1995–1996) of particular journals (i.e., *Exceptional Children, Exceptionality, Journal of Learning Disabilities, Learning Disabilities Research & Practice, Learning Disability Quarterly, Remedial and Special Education,* and *The Journal of Special Education*) for studies that met the inclusion criteria. The criteria for including a study were as follows: (a) The participants were diagnosed or described as having a disability (e.g., learning disabilities, mental retardation, emotional disturbance) or receiving remedial mathematics instruction, and therefore were deemed to be at-risk; (b) the study investigated the effects of specific word-problem-solving instructional strategies; (c) the study included baseline or pre- and posttreatment assessment data; (d) if of group design, the study reported enough quantitative information (e.g., means, standard deviations, t tests or F tests) regarding performance outcomes that effect sizes could be calculated; and (e) the study was available in English and either was published in a peer-reviewed journal or was an unpublished research report (e.g., doctoral dissertation).

The studies excluded from this review were those that were descriptive or did not include instruction in solving mathematical word problems. Specifically, studies were excluded when they identified or analyzed the characteristics of difficult-problem solvers (e.g., Liedtke, 1984; Montague, Bos, & Doucette, 1991; Zentall, 1990), assessed learners' mathematics abilities (Parmar, 1992), or examined the influence of task features (e.g., syntax, relevant and/or irrelevant information in word problems) on students' word-problem-solving performance (Englert, Culatta, & Horn, 1987; Wheeler & McNutt, 1983). Two studies had to be excluded from the sample of studies because, although they met most criteria, they did not provide pretreatment assessment data (e.g., Darch, 1982; Miller & Mercer, 1993).

The literature search and selection procedures identified 15 published studies and 10 unpublished doctoral dissertations. All published studies were located in journals between 1986 and 1996, whereas unpublished doctoral dissertations were identified to be from 1980 to 1996. The final sample of 25 studies yielded 14 group-design studies and 12 single-subject studies. The study by Hutchinson (1993) included both a group design and a single-subject design. Tables 1 and 6 present the summary of information from the group and single-subject studies, respectively.

Computation and Analysis of Treatment Effectiveness

Group Design Studies. The standardized mean change was used to calculate the intervention effect (Becker, 1988). Because a majority of the studies compared the effects of two or more intervention approaches, rather than the effects of one type of intervention versus no intervention, the standardized mean change computed for each sample (experimental or comparison) was deemed to be an appropriate measure of effect size (ES) for within-subject comparisons. As Becker noted, the standardized mean change has several advantages over Glass's effect size: It allows for the direct comparison of data from studies using different designs; in addition, studies without true control groups need not be omitted (Becker, 1988). Another advantage is that because the standardized mean change technique does not entail comparing several intervention conditions to the same control group, such as when numerous intervention conditions are examined in a single study, the violation of independence is not a concern (Becker, 1988; Hunter & Schmidt, 1990). According to Becker, "mean changes from separate samples could be considered independent data points and analyzed using methods of meta-analysis devised for effect-size data" (p. 264). In addition, Becker argued that one could aggregate standardized change measures across studies within treatment or comparison populations and examine the relation of "relevant predictors to the standardized mean changes" (p. 264) by analyzing the independent treatment effects.

The effect size (g) in this study was computed as the difference between the posttest and pretest means for a single sample, divided by the pretest standard deviation. This computation allowed us to treat the pretreatment status as the control group, because the assumption was that the treated group members' pretreatment status was a good estimate of their hypothetical posttreatment status in the absence of a treatment (Glass, 1977). The gs in this study were converted to unbiased ds by correcting them for sampling error artifacts (Hedges & Olkin, 1985).

The dependent measure used to calculate effect sizes was either the correct answer in word-problem solving (i.e., operation and computation) or the correct operation chosen. In the event that a study reported both correct answer and correct operation (or correct calculation) scores, only the correct answer was used to calculate the effect size. Effect sizes were calculated for each intervention sample independently within a study, with positive signs given to the ES when the posttreatment was attributed to higher performance. A total of 35 effect sizes were obtained.

In addition to the overall main effect size for the mathematics instruction variable, we calculated effect sizes for the study characteristics (e.g., IQ, label, intervention approach, length of treatment). Furthermore, we tested the homogeneity of effect sizes using Hedges and Olkin's homogeneity statistics Q. The Q statistic has an approximate chi-square distribution with $k-1$ degrees of freedom, where k is the number of effect sizes (Hedges & Olkin, 1985). Using the DSTAT (Johnson, 1989) program, we calculated Q_B and Q_W to estimate the homogeneity of effect sizes between and within classes, respectively. In addition, we used the homogeneity statistics to identify statistical outliers (those that were much larger or smaller than the other effect sizes) that "would result in the largest reduction to the homogeneity statistics" (Johnson, 1989, p. 81). The DSTAT program allows for the stepwise removal of outliers until homogeneity is reached. Such an approach would allow for "stronger conclusions regarding a research literature" (Johnson, 1989, p. 4). In this study, we conducted tests with and without the outliers to examine their influence on the mean effect size. Alpha levels for all analyses of homogeneity of effect sizes in this meta-analysis were set at the .01 level of significance.

Single-Subject Design Studies. Problems associated with the application of parametric statistical procedures in the estimation and analysis of single-subject research effect sizes make it difficult to directly compare group and single-subject research effect sizes (Scruggs, Mastropieri, & Casto, 1987; White, Rusch, Kazdin, & Hartmann, 1989). Effect sizes have been computed from single-subject studies (Busk & Serlin, 1992) by treating the baseline data points as pretreatment scores and the treatment data points as posttreatment scores. However, the lack of sufficient baseline data points (as few as 3) in the single-subject research on word-problem solving presented problems in terms of the reliability of the effect size procedures and interpretation (Scruggs et al., 1987; White et al., 1989). Instead, we used percentage of nonoverlapping

data (PND), a nonparametric approach for synthesizing findings from single-subject design studies (Scruggs et al., 1987). This approach presents a promising alternative to standardized mean difference effect size for quantifying single-subject time series data (Busse, Kratochwill, & Elliott, 1995).

PND between treatment and baseline phases of single-subject studies was used to determine treatment effectiveness. PND was computed as the number of treatment data points that exceeded the highest baseline data point in an expected direction, divided by the total number of points in the treatment phase. A positive PND indicated that the intervention scores were higher than the baseline scores. Again, the dependent measure was either the correct answer in word-problem solving (i.e., operation and computation) or the correct operation chosen. We calculated PND scores for each intervention sample independently within a study. When a multiple baseline design across participants was used, individual PND scores were aggregated across participants in a study to obtain an overall treatment effect. Thus, PND scores were aggregated across studies in this review for the main variable of mathematics instruction and for the study characteristics (e.g., IQ, label, intervention approach, length of treatment). A total of 15 PND scores were obtained from the 12 single-subject design studies. One single-subject study (Montague, 1992) involved two groups and the sequential componential analysis of cognitive and metacognitive strategies. Therefore, four treatment effects came from that one study. We also tested for significant differences among variables using Kruskal-Wallis, a nonparametric statistic.

Coding Study Features

The following information was coded from each article to describe the main characteristics of the individual study.

Grade and Age. This variable refers to three levels: elementary (Grades 1–6, ages 6–12); secondary (Grades 7–12, ages 13–18); and postsecondary (college, ages 19 and above).

IQ. Two levels of IQ were recorded: IQ lower than 85 and IQ equal to or above 85 (i.e., more than 1 standard deviation above the mean). Given the discrepancy among states in specifying IQ cutoff scores (Frankenberger & Fronzaglio, 1991), especially when describing and identifying students with learning disabilities, we deemed that the criteria of 1 standard deviation below the mean as the cutoff score would help to distinguish the population identified as learning disabled from other categories of disabilities (e.g., mild mental retardation, emotional disturbance).

Classification Label. Three classes were assigned to this variable: learning disabilities (LD), mixed disabilities (i.e., learning disabilities, mild mental retardation, and emotional disabilities), and at risk (i.e., those in remedial programs).

Intervention Approach. The orientation of each intervention approach was coded into one of the four categories described below. This grouping of interventions into separate categories does not necessarily indicate mutually exclusive interventions. Instead, it is more likely that approaches overlap or share many similar components. For example, a representational technique or CAI might employ a strategy-training procedure or vice versa. Thus, our classification was based on the primary orientation of the study as determined by the following descriptions.

Representation Techniques. This approach refers to the interpretation or representation of ideas or information given in a word problem. Representation approaches to solving mathematical problems include pictorial (e.g., diagramming); concrete (e.g., manipulatives); verbal (linguistic training); and mapping instruction (schema-based) (Lesh, Post, & Behr, 1987; Resnick & Omanson, 1987; Swing, Stoiber, & Peterson, 1988).

Strategy Training. This category refers to any explicit problem-solving heuristic procedures (e.g., direct instruction, cognitive and metacognitive) that lead to the solution of the problem. These may involve explicit teaching or self-regulation of a strategy in isolation or together with other elements (e.g., paraphrasing, visualizing, hypothesizing, estimating the answer) (Montague & Bos, 1986). Direct instruction and cognitive strategies relate to how to solve a problem, whereas metacognitive strategies relate to knowing how to solve a problem and may include self-instruction, self-questioning, and self-regulation procedures (Kameenui & Griffin, 1989; Montague, 1992).

Computer-Aided Instruction (CAI). This variable refers to an intervention that employs CAI tutorial or interactive videodisc programs.

Other. This category refers to no instruction (e.g., attention only, use of calculators) or any type of task instruction not included in the above categories (e.g., key word, problem sequence).

Setting. This variable refers to whether instruction was provided in pull-out settings or classrooms (i.e., resource, self-contained, or remedial). For the purpose of this review, pull-out referred to instruction outside of the special education or remedial classroom in which regularly scheduled mathematics instruction occurred.

Length of Treatment. Three levels were assigned to this category: short (equal to or less than 1 week, 1 to 7 training sessions); intermediate (equal to or less than 1 month, more than seven sessions); and long-term (more than 1 month) interventions. It must be noted that this categorization was arbitrary, in that the mathematics intervention literature does not provide any direction for defining length of treatment.

Implementation of Intervention. This variable refers to the person (i.e., teacher, researcher, or both) implementing the instruction.

Instructional Arrangement. This variable refers to whether instruction occurred in groups or individually.

Word-Problem Task. The word problems used in the reviewed studies were coded into one of three categories: (a) one-step word problems, which required a single mathematical operation to arrive at the correct solution; (b) multistep word problems, which required two or more mathematical operations; and (c) mixed, in which both one-step and multistep word problems were used.

Student Directed. This category was created to classify studies according to whether or not students were actively involved in strategy regulation. That is, interventions that taught students self-instruction, self-questioning, and/or self-monitoring "to gain access to strategy knowledge, guide execution of strategies, and regulate use of strategies and problem solving performance" (Montague, 1992, p. 231) were coded as high student directed. Those studies that involved teacher-directed instruction only were coded as low student directed.

Publication Bias. This variable indicates whether the identified study was a published journal article or an unpublished research report.

Group Assignment. Studies were classified according to the way in which participants were assigned to treatment and comparison conditions. A procedure in which students were randomly assigned to treatment and comparison conditions was coded as "random," a matching technique whereby students were matched on variables and assigned to the treatment and comparison conditions was coded as "matched," and a study that used previously formed groups of students was coded as "intact."

Treatment Integrity. This variable refers to the presence or absence of treatment integrity information.

Length of Follow-up. Three categories were identified to disclose when the maintenance tests were given, on the basis of the elapsed time between the termination of the training and the time when follow-up probing was conducted (i.e., 1 to 4 weeks; more than 4 weeks but no more than 10 weeks; and more than 10 weeks).

Type of Generalization. This category refers to near transfer (similar task transfer or setting generalization) and far transfer (different task transfer). When a study used two different measures at immediate posttesting to compare group performances (e.g., paper and pencil or online in Shiah, Mastropieri, Scruggs, & Fulk, 1995; typical word problems or contextualized problems in Bottge & Hasselbring, 1993), we used the posttest that was dissimilar to the instructional task as the transfer measure.

Study Characteristics

Group Design Studies. The 14 group design studies included 9 published studies (64%) and 5 unpublished studies (36%). All published studies were located in journals between 1986 and 1995 (median = 1993), whereas unpublished doctoral dissertations were from 1980 to 1992 (median = 1987). The total number of participants was 581, ranging in age from 8 to 65 years (mean = 14.7). Sample size of the treatment conditions varied from 9 to 37, with a mean sample size of 18.66 and a standard deviation of 7.13. Studies included participants from elementary (34%), secondary (49%), and postsecondary (17%) grades. Only 6 of the 14 studies reported IQ scores; those scores varied from 84.17 to 99.30, with a mean of 92.19 and a standard deviation of 4.94. Of the 35 effect sizes, 444 (76%) of the students were described as having a learning disability, 19 (3%) were identified as having mild disabilities (mixed), and the remaining 118 (20%) were students at risk.

Of the interventions identified in the studies, the most frequent approach was strategy training (46%). Representation techniques constituted 23% of the 35 effect sizes, while CAI and the "other" category constituted 17% and 14%, respectively. In terms of setting, the typical setting for the research intervention was the resource or remedial classroom (71%), whereas instruction in pull-out settings occurred 29% of the time. No instruction was conducted in the general education classroom. The length of interventions varied from 2 days to 4 months, and each session ranged from 30 to 50 minutes. The majority of instruction occurred in small groups (86%); 14% of the instruction was provided individually. The most commonly employed measures were criterion-referenced tests (86%) developed by researchers. Only two studies (14%; Gleason, Carnine, & Boriero, 1990, and

Hutchinson, 1993) employed items from standardized tests in addition to criterion-referenced tests. Researcher-implemented treatment (63%) was the most common; studies that reported instruction implemented by the teacher constituted 26% and both teacher and researcher constituted 11%. The most frequent type of word problem tasks used in the studies was one-step tasks (57%), followed by mixed (36%) and multistep problems (7%). In terms of student-directed interventions, the majority of studies reported infrequent student involvement (80%); high student involvement was noted only 20% of the time. For group assignment, most studies involved random assignment (54%), whereas matched and intact group assignments entailed 15% and 31% of the studies, respectively. Seven (50%) of the 14 studies did not report treatment integrity information, and therefore these results were excluded from the analysis.

Single-Subject Design Studies. The 12 single-subject studies included 7 published (58%) and 5 unpublished (42%) studies. All published studies were located in journals between 1986 and 1996 (median = 1993), whereas unpublished doctoral dissertations were from 1981 to 1994 (median = 1987). The total number of participants was 63, ranging in age from 8 to 18 years (mean = 13). Studies included participants from elementary (33%) and secondary (67%) grades. Ten of the 12 studies reported IQ scores; of those, Hutchinson (1993) did not provide individual IQ scores for the 12 students. The IQ scores varied from 70 to 115, with a mean of 93 and a standard deviation of 8.2. The sample included 55 (87%) students with learning disabilities and 8 (13%) identified as mildly disabled.

The two intervention approaches identified from the 15 PND were strategy training (80%) and representation techniques (20%). The length of interventions varied from 5 days to 4 months, and each session ranged from 20 to 55 minutes. Only one study (Hutchinson, 1993) employed items from standardized tests in addition to criterion-referenced tests developed by researchers. Researcher-implemented treatment (87%) was the most common; studies that reported instruction implemented by the teacher constituted 13% and both teacher and researcher constituted 7%. The most frequent type of word-problem tasks used in the studies was one-step (50%), followed by mixed (33%) and multistep problems (17%). In terms of student-directed interventions, the majority of studies reported high student involvement (67%); low student involvement was noted only 33% of the time.

Nine (75%) of the 12 studies reported treatment integrity information.

Interrater Agreement

The first author coded all studies and calculated effect sizes. A second rater (a doctoral student) independently coded 30% of all selected studies and calculated 30% of all effect sizes. The interrater agreement was defined as the total number of agreements divided by the total number of agreements plus disagreements and multiplied by 100. The interrater agreements for effect size calculation and coding of study features were 100% and 94%, respectively. The disagreements primarily involved coding of the intervention approaches. Therefore, a discussion was held between the author and the second rater, and all discrepancies were resolved following further clarification of the coding definitions.

RESULTS: GROUP DESIGN STUDIES

Overall Effect of Mathematics Word-Problem-Solving Instruction

All effect sizes in the reviewed studies were calculated from the reported mean and standard deviation scores; no effect sizes had to be calculated from t or F ratios. Table 1 reports the unbiased effect sizes (d). The mean effect size before correction for sample size (g) was +.92, with a range of -0.43 to $+7.23$, whereas the unbiased d was +.89, with a range of -0.42 to $+6.77$. An examination of Table 1 indicates that the largest effect size ($d = 6.77$) was from the Moore and Carnine (1989) study, and that the only two negative effect sizes were from the one study by Walker and Poteet (1989). The homogeneity test for the detection of outliers using the DSTAT statistical software program

Table 1 Summary of Group Design Studies Included in the Meta-Analysis

Author	Date	Grade	IQ	Label	TrtA	Setting	InstrA
Published studies							
Bottge & Hasselbring	1993	Sec	NA	At-risk	CAI	Class	Group
Hutchinson	1993	Sec	[greater or equal] 85	LD	Strat	CI	
Gleason, Carnine, & Boriero	1990	Sec	NA	Mixed	CAI Strat	Class	Group
Montague, Applegate, & Marquard	1993	Sec	[greater or equal] 85	LD	Strat Strat Strat Strat Strat Strat	PU	
Moore & Carnine	1989	Sec	NA	At-risk	CAI Strat	Class	Group
Shiah, Mastropieri, Scruggs, & Fulk	1995	Elem	<85	LD	CAI CAI CAI	Class	Group
Walker & Poteet	1988–89	Sec	[greater or equal] 85	LD	Repres	CI	
Wilson & Sindelar	1991	Elem	[greater or equal] 85	LD	Strat Strat Other	Pu	
Zawaiza & Gerber	1993	Postsec	[greater or equal] 85	LD	Repres Repres Other	CL	
Unpublished studies							
Bennett	1980	Sec	NA	LD	Strat	NA	Group
Baker	1992	Elem	NA	LD	Repres Strat	Pull-out	Group
Lee	1992	Elem	[greater or equal]85	LD	Strat	CI	
Marzola	1987	Elem	NA	LD	Strat	Class	Group
Noll	1983	Postsec	NA	At-risk	Repres Repres Repres Repres	Class	Indiv

280

Table 1 (Continued)

Author	WPT	StD	GrA	TrtF	Maint (FNa)	Gen.	n	
Published studies								
Bottge & Hasselbring	Mixed	Low	Matched	Yes	NA	Far	15	+
							14	+
Hutchinson	Mixed	High	Random	Yes	2	Far	12	+
Gleason, Carnine, & Boriero	One-step	Low	Random	NA	NA	Near, Far	9	+
						Near, Far	10	+
Montague, Applegate, & Marquard	Mixed	Low	Random	Yes	NA	NA	25	+
		High			NA	NA	23	+
		High			Na	NA	24	+
		High			1, 2, 3	Near	25	+
		High			1, 2, 3	Near	23	+
		High			1, 2, 3	Near	24	+
Moore & Carnine	One-step	Low	Matched	Yes	1	NA	13	+
							16	+
Shiah, Mastropieri, Scruggs, & Fulk	One-step	Low	Random	NA	1	Far	10	+
						Far	10	+
						Far	10	+
Walker & Poteet	One-step	Low	Intact	Yes	NA	NA	33	−
							37	−
Wilson & Sindelar	One-step	Low	Random	Yes	1	NA	21	+
							21	+
							20	+
Zawaiza & Gerber	Multi	Low	Intact	NA	NA	NA	12	+
							13	+
Unpublished Studies								
Bennett	Mixed	High	NA	NA	NA	NA	21	+
Baker	One-step	Low	Random	NA	NA	NA	25	+
							21	+
Lee	One-step	Low	Intact	Yes	1	NA	18	+
						NA	15	+
Marzola	Mixed	High	Intact	NA	NA	NA	30	+
		Low					30	+
Noll	One-step	Low	Random	NA	NA	NA	15	+
							15	+
							15	+
							15	+

Note. TrtA = treatment approach; InstrA = instructional arrangement; TrL = treatment length; Inter = intermediate; TrtI = treatment implemented; TrtF = treatment fidelity; GrA = Group assignment; WPT = word problem task; StD = student directed; n = sample size; d = unbiased effect size; CI = confidence interval; NA = not available.
a 1 = [less or equal] 4 weeks; 2 => 4 weeks but < 10 weeks; 3 = > 10 weeks.
*95% confidence interval contains d = .00.

identified the largest outlier as the one effect size from the Bottge and Hasselbring (1993) study.

When the homogeneity test for the detection of outliers was conducted on the entire set of selected studies, it resulted in an attrition of approximately 43% of the effect sizes to obtain homogeneity of samples. Because we started with only 35 effect sizes for our analysis and removal of such a large number of outliers would "[defeat] the purpose of metaanalysis which is to draw on the commonality across diverse studies" (Swanson, Carson, & Saches-Lee, 1996, p. 375), we retained the original data set. Instead, we conducted categorical model testing for the rest of the analyses both before and after the outliers were removed within each categorical class to determine the relation between the study characteristics and the magnitude of the effect sizes (B. Johnson, personal communication, January 9, 1997).

Effect of Intervention Approaches on Word-Problem Solving

The mean effect size as a function of the intervention approach is shown in Tables 2 and 3 before and after outliers were removed. Results were essentially the same for trimmed data ($k = 27$) and untrimmed data

Table 2 Summary of Effect Sizes Before Outliers Were Removed

Variable and class	Q[subB]	k	d+	95% CI Lower	95% CI Upper	Q[su
Sample characteristics						
Grade/age	8.34					
Elementary		12	+1.00	+0.80	+1.20	66.05
Secondary		16	+0.73	+0.56	+0.90	165.28
Postsecondary		7	+1.20	+0.88	+1.51	27.15
IQ	19.47 (FN*)					
< 85		3	+1.87	+1.26	+2.49	2.43
>/= 85		17	+0.45	+0.30	+0.60	63.12
Label	74.10 (FN*)					
LD		25	+0.68	+0.55	+0.81	140.04
Mixed		2	+1.96	+1.18	+2.74	1.06
At-risk		8	+2.22	+1.88	+2.56	51.61
Instructional features						
Intervention approach	87.83 (FN*)					
Representation		8	+1.05	+0.79	+1.31	53.55
Strategy		16	+1.01	+0.85	+1.18	78.53
CAI		6	+2.46	+1.97	+2.94	41.19
Other		5	+0.00	−0.26	+0.26	5.72
Setting	1.07					
Pull-out		11	+0.84	+0.66	+1.06	37.24
Classroom		23	+0.97	+0.81	+1.14	225.50
Length of treatment	18.05 (FN*)					
Short		18	+1.10	+0.92	+1.29	101.09
Intermediate		14	+0.62	+0.44	+0.79	110.56
Long		3	+1.25	+0.87	+1.63	37.12
Instructional arrangement	38.26 (FN*)					
Individual		5	+2.18	+1.76	+2.61	9.00
Group		30	+0.78	+0.66	+0.91	219.56
Instr. implemented	48.45 (FN*)					
Teacher		9	+0.50	+0.28	+0.72	70.91
Researcher		22	+0.95	+0.80	+1.10	100.14
Both		4	+2.58	+2.02	+3.13	47.32
Word problem task	5.56					
One-step problems		20	+0.96	+0.80	+1.13	173.48
Multistep problems		3	+0.38	−0.08	+0.83	0.94
Mixed problems		12	+0.89	+0.71	+1.08	67.17
Student directed	0.36					
Low		27	+0.87	+0.73	+1.01	219.61
High		8	+0.95	+0.73	+1.18	46.85
Methodological features						
Publicaton bias	12.72 (FN*)					
Published		24	+0.74	+0.60	+0.89	188.92
Unpublished		11	+1.21	+1.00	+1.42	65.17
Group assignment	76.72 (FN*)					
Random		21	+1.15	+0.99	+1.31	92.41
Matched		4	+2.58	+2.02	+3.13	47.32
Intact		9	+0.31	+0.11	+0.52	47.35

Note. k = number of effect sizes; d+ = effect size corrected for sample size; CI = confidence interval.
Significance of d+ was assessed by the z distribution, and nonsignificant Q reflects homogeneity within category. Q[subB] = homogeneity between-class effect, and Q[subW] = homogeneity within each class.
* p [less or equal] .01.

Table 3. Summary of Effect Sizes After Outliers Were Removed

Variable and class	Q_B	k	d+	95% CI Lower	95% CI Upper	Q_W
Sample characteristics						
Grade/age	26.25 (FN*)					
Elementary		7	+0.47	+0.23	+0.72	9.73
Secondary		10	+0.78	+0.58	+0.99	20.04
Postsecondary		5	+1.68	+1.29	+2.07	9.82
IQ	17.75 (FN*)					
< 85		3	+1.87	+1.26	+2.49	2.43
>/= 85		15	+0.51	+0.35	+0.67	23.65
Label	58.70 (FN*)					
LD		18	+0.50	+0.35	+0.65	27.08
Mixed		2	+1.96	+1.18	+2.74	1.06
At-risk		6	+1.90	+1.54	+2.26	11.52
Instructional features						
Intervention approach	81.37 (FN*)					
Representation		6	+1.77	+1.43	+2.12	10.72
Strategy		12	+0.74	+0.56	+0.93	19.24
CAI		4	+1.80	+1.27	+2.33	2.66
Other		5	+0.00	−0.26	+0.26	5.72
Setting	51.03					
Pull-out		9	+0.66	+0.46	+0.86	13.48
Classroom		13	+1.83	+1.58	+2.08	24.67
Length of treatment	52.14 (FN*)					
Short		11	+1.72	+1.46	+1.98	17.32
Intermediate		9	+0.73	+0.51	+0.95	16.30
16.30						
Long		2	+2.51	+1.93	+3.09	5.41
Instructional arrangement	51.45 (FN*)					
Individual		5	+2.18	+1.76	+2.61	9.00
Group		20	+0.54	+0.39	+0.68	32.19
Instr. implemented	98.41 (FN*)					
Teacher		5	+1.93	+1.52	+2.34	2.17
Researcher		16	+0.65	+0.49	+0.82	26.24
Both		2	+6.01	+4.77	+7.24	0.91
Word problem task	87.87 (FN*)					
One-step problems		13	+1.89	+1.64	+2.13	16.75
Multistep problems		3	+0.38	−0.08	+0.83	0.94
Mixed problems		9	+0.63	+0.43	+0.83	11.67
Student directed	0.34					
Low		14	+0.59	+0.40	+0.78	21.65
High		6	+0.68	+0.44	+0.92	9.07
Methodological features						
Publication bias	45.02 (FN*)					
Published		16	+0.71	+0.54	+0.88	28.46
Unpublished		8	+1.81	+1.54	+2.08	15.80
Group assignment	157.60 (FN*)					
Random		15	+1.55	+1.35	+1.76	26.13
Matched		2	+6.01	+4.77	+7.24	0.91
Intact		8	+0.11	−0.11	+0.32	10.73

Note. k = number of effect sizes; d+ = effect size corrected for sample size; CI = confidence interval.
Significance of d+ was assessed by the z distribution, and nonsignificant Q reflects homogeneity within category. Q_B = homogeneity between-class effect, and Q_W = homogeneity within each class.
* p [less or equal] .01.

(*k* = 35). CAI yielded the highest effect size (*d* = +1.80), followed by representation (*d* = +1.77), strategy (*d* = + .74), and "other" (*d* = .00) approaches. With the exception of the "other" category, the magnitude of mean effect sizes for all approaches was moderate to large for the trimmed data (range = +.74 to +1.8). Further simple contrasts indicated significant differences between CAI and strategy training and between CAI and the "other" approach (*p* < .01). Differences between the representation technique and CAI, however, were not significant. In addition, significant differences existed between the representation technique and strategy training (*p* < .01); and the differences between the "other" category and all approaches were significant (*p* < .01).

Mediator Influences on the Effect of Word-Problem Solving

The mediator variables related to sample characteristics (e.g., grade/age, IQ, classification label) and instructional features (setting, length of treatment, instructional arrangement, implementation of instruction, word-problem type, and student direction) were analyzed to explore their influence on math-problem-solving instruction. Again, all categorical model testing was conducted both before and after outliers were removed. The results from both analyses are presented in Tables 2 and 3. Most of the results from the trimmed data in Table 3 yielded an amount of significant results similar to that of the untrimmed data in Table 2. For all categories, the removal of outliers yielded a more homogeneous within-categories effect size.

Grade/Age. Tables 2 and 3 present the results for the category of grade/age before and after outliers were removed. Results of the untrimmed data in Table 2 indicate no significant differences among groups. However, an analysis of the trimmed data in Table 3 reveals a large effect size for the postsecondary group (*d* = +1.68) followed by a moderate effect size for the secondary group (*d* = +.78) and a low effect size for the elementary group (*d* = +.47). Apparently, intervention effects were pronounced with an increase in age. Further simple contrasts revealed that the effect size for the postsecondary group was significantly different from that for the other two groups (*p* < .01). No significant differences were found between elementary and secondary groups. In sum, the inconsistent findings from the two analyses fail to indicate whether this category mediated the intervention effect size.

IQ. Table 2 reports the results for the category IQ, in which only 20 effects sizes were reportedly calculated for the studies. Results of the trimmed data (see Table 3) indicated that the effect size for participants with IQ < 85 was significantly greater (*d* = + 1.87) than that for those with IQ ≤ 85 (*d* = +.51, *p* < .01). It seems that IQ did mediate the effect size of the intervention.

Classification Label. An examination of Table 3 indicates that the effect size for students with LD (*d* = +.50) was less than that for students with mixed disabilities (*d* = + 1.96) and those at risk (*d* = + 1.90). Further post hoc simple contrasts revealed significant differences between the LD and mixed groups and between LD and at-risk groups only (*p* < .01), indicating a mediating influence of this variable on effect size.

Setting. Tables 2 and 3 report the results for the variable of setting, in which 34 effect sizes were calculated. The categorical model testing for differences before outliers were removed indicated no differences between pull-out and classroom settings. However, the effect size for the classroom setting was significantly greater than that for the pull-out setting (*p* < .01) when outliers were removed. Thus, setting may not have mediated the effect size of the intervention, given the different findings for the trimmed and untrimmed data.

Treatment Length. Table 3 presents the results for the category of treatment length. The effect sizes for short-term (≥ 7 sessions) interventions were seen to be more effective than intermediate (> 7 sessions, ≥ 1 month) interventions, but less effective than long-term (> 1 month) interventions. Further simple contrasts indicated that these differences were significant (*p* < .02). Treatment duration seemed to mediate the effect size of the intervention.

Instructional Arrangement. Table 3 reports the results for the category of instructional arrangement. The effect size for individually provided instruction was greater than that for small-group instruction. The categorical model testing revealed significant differences between the two groups (*p* < .01). Thus, instructional arrangement seemed to have a mediating influence on the effect size of the intervention.

Implementation of Instruction. Tables 2 and 3 present the results before and after outliers were removed for interventions implemented by the teacher, researcher, or both. In general, results from trimmed and untrimmed data seem to indicate that interventions implemented by both teachers and researchers were the most effective. However, these results are based on a small number of effect sizes. Results for interventions implemented by teachers were inconsistent for trimmed and untrimmed data. It seems that teacher-implemented interventions were less effective than those implemented by researchers before outliers were removed (see Table 2). In contrast, results of the trimmed data in Table 3 indicate that interventions conducted by teachers were more effective than those implemented by researchers. Although further simple contrasts showed that the differences among the three groups were significant, we cannot determine whether this category did mediate the effect size of the intervention, given the inconsistent findings before and after outliers were removed.

Word-Problem Task. Results in Table 3 indicate that the effectiveness of interventions involving one-step word problems was greater than that for multistep and mixed word problems. Also, the effect size of mixed word problems was greater than that of multistep problems. Further simple contrasts revealed that the differences between one-step and multistep problems only were significant ($p < .01$). This variable seemed to mediate the effect size of the intervention.

Student Direction. Table 3 presents the results for studies categorized by the presence or absence of instruction that was student regulated (e.g., self-instruction, self-questioning). Results indicate that the effect size for student-directed interventions was slightly higher than that for interventions with low student regulation. However, no statistically significant differences were found between these two categories, indicating that this category did not mediate the effect size.

Other Influences on the Effect of Word-Problem Solving

Publication Bias. Tables 2 and 3 provide the results for published and unpublished studies. The removal of outliers yielded a more homogeneous outcome for this category. Both untrimmed and trimmed data analyses indicated that unpublished studies entailed greater effect sizes than published studies, and the differences between them were significant ($p < .01$). The category of publication bias did mediate the effect size of the intervention.

Group Assignment. Table 3 reports the results for group assignment. The removal of outliers indicated homogeneous within-class effect sizes. For this category of group assignment, both random and matched assignments yielded greater effect sizes when compared with intact group assignment. The differences between the three groups were found to be significant ($p < .01$). Group assignment did mediate the effect size of the intervention.

Effect of Word-Problem-Solving Instruction on Maintenance and Generalization

Table 4 presents the results for follow-up length and generalization type. Thirteen of 35 cases (37%) pro-

Table 4 Mean Effect Sizes for Maintenance and Generalization

	n	*d*	95% CI Lower	95% CI Upper
Maintenance				
< 4 weeks	12	+0.78	+0.58	+0.99
> 4 wks–10 wks	4	+0.89	+0.89	+1.22
> 10 wks	3	+1.12	+0.77	+1.48
Generalization				
Near	5	+1.03	+0.71	+1.34
Far	8	+0.65	+0.34	+0.96

Note. *n* = number of effect sizes; *d* = effect size corrected for sample size; CI = confidence interval.

vided follow-up data that allowed for the calculation of effect sizes, and 11 of the 35 cases (31%) included generalization data. The overall unbiased mean effect sizes for maintenance and generalization were +.78 and +.84, respectively. No significant differences for maintenance effects were found in terms of different elapsed time between training and follow-up testing. Also, no significant differences were found between near-transfer generalization (i.e., applying an acquired skill to similar tasks or to different settings) and far-transfer generalization (i.e., applying acquired skills to different tasks). For the remaining analyses of maintenance and generalization by instructional features, we report only the effect sizes because we did not conduct significance tests for differences, given the small sample size in each category.

Maintenance and generalization effect sizes for selected mediator variables related to instructional features (e.g., intervention approach, implementation of instruction, student direction) were computed. Table 5 provides a summary of these results. In terms of intervention approaches, CAI was seen to be more effective in promoting maintenance ($d = +1.53$) than generalization ($d = +.44$). Strategy training was seen to be effective for both maintenance ($d = +.77$) and generalization ($d = +1.09$) of word-problem solving. The category "other" approach included only one sample for maintenance and none for generalization. This class yielded a negative effect size ($d = -.29$) for maintenance. For the representation technique, no data were available for either maintenance or generalization.

Long-term interventions (more than 1 month) were most effective in promoting both maintenance ($d = +3.85$) and generalization ($d = +2.10$). However, the data were limited by only one observation from one study (Hutchinson, 1993). Although short-term

Table 5 Summary of Effect Sizes for Maintenance and Generalization by Instructional Parameters

			95% CI					
			Maintenance				Generalize	
Variable and class	n	d+	Lower	Upper	n	d+	Lower	U
Intervention approach								
Strategy	8	+0.77	+0.54	+1.01	6	+1.09	+0.80	+
CAI	4	+1.53	+1.03	+2.04	5	+0.44	+0.05	+
Other	1	−0.29	−0.92	+0.33	NA	NA	NA	
Length of treatment								
Short	3	+2.29	+1.63	+2.95	5	+0.64	+0.25	+
Intermediate	9	+0.55	+0.33	+0.76	5	+0.86	+0.58	+
Long	1	+3.85	+2.50	+5.20	1	+2.10	+1.10	+
Instr. implementation								
Teacher	NA	NA	NA	NA	1	+0.94	−0.03	+
Researcher	11	+.86	+0.64	+1.07	8	+0.84	+0.57	+
Both	2	+.36	−0.16	+0.88	2	+0.93	+0.37	+
Student directed								
Low	9	+0.54	+0.29	+0.79	7	+0.76	+0.43	+
High	4	+1.21	+0.87	+1.56	4	+0.95	+0.63	+

Note. NA = not available; n = number of effect sizes; d+ = effect size corrected for sample size; CI = confidence interval.

(fewer than 7 sessions) interventions were seen to be effective in promoting maintenance ($d = +2.29$), they were less effective than intermediate and long-term interventions of instruction, no data were available on teacher-implemented instruction for maintenance, whereas the results for researcher-implemented instruction ($d = +.86$) indicated a higher effect size when compared with that for instruction implemented by both ($d = +.36$). For skill generalization, teacher-implemented ($d = +.94$) or both teacher- and researcher-implemented instruction ($d = .93$) yielded larger effect sizes than researcher-delivered ($d = +.84$) teaching. For the category student direction, student self-regulated instruction was seen to be more effective than teacher-directed instruction in promoting both maintenance and generalization.

RESULTS: SINGLE-SUBJECT STUDIES

Table 6 summarizes and Table 7 presents the categorical comparisons of single-subject studies. Overall, the median PND score for interventions was 89%, with a range of 11% to 100%. Because PND scores are not always normally distributed, we reported median scores, which are less likely to be affected by outliers than mean scores (Scruggs et al., 1986). An analysis of mediator variables indicated significant differences for intervention approach and treatment length only ($p < .05$). Representational techniques (PND = +100; $n = 3$) were found to be more effective than strategy training (PND = +87; $n = 12$). Intermediate (PND = +97;

$n = 10$) and long-term treatments (PND = +100; $n = 1$) were seen to be more effective than short-term (PND = +49; $n = 4$) treatment. All other categorical comparisons were not statistically significant. Ten of 15 cases (67%) provided follow-up data that allowed for the calculation of PND scores, and 7 of the 15 cases (47%) included generalization data. The overall median PND scores for both skill maintenance and generalization were 100%. Given the small sample size, we did not do further significance tests for differences among instructional features in terms of maintenance and generalization.

DISCUSSION AND IMPLICATIONS

Results of the meta-analysis indicated that word-problem-solving instruction improved the performance of students with learning problems and promoted the maintenance and generalization of the skill. The overall mean effect size after correction for sample size in the group design studies was +.89, while the treatment effect for single-subject studies was 89%. However, the present synthesis is limited in several ways. The effect size measure used in this review was the standardized mean change from preintervention to postintervention test scores. This effect size is a scale-free index of the amount of change due to history, growth, retesting, and treatment (Becker, 1988). As a result, the effect size scores in this study may have been larger than Glass's (1977) traditional effect size, which is the standardized mean difference between

Table 6 Summary Characteristics of Single-Subject Design Studies

Author	Date	Grade	IQ	Label	TrtA	TrtL	TrtI	W
Published studies								
Case, Harris, & Graham	1992	Elem	<85	LD	Strat	Short	Res	On
Cassel & Reid	1996	Elem	>/=85	Mixed	Strat	Inter	Res	On
Hutchinson	1993	Sec	>/=85	LD	Strat	Long	Res	Mi
Jitendra & Hoff	1996	Elem	>85	LD	Repres	Inter	Res	On
Marsch & Cooke	1996	Elem	>85	LD	Repres	Inter	Res	On
Montague	1992	Sec	>85	LD	Strat	Short	Res	Mi
		Sec	>85	LD	Strat	Short	Res	Mi
		Sec	>85	LD	Strat	Inter	Res	MI
		Sec	>85	LD	Strat	inter	Res	Mi
Montague & Bos	1986	Sec	>85	LD	Strat	Short	Res	Mu
Unpublished studies								
Huntington	1994	Sec	>85	LD	Repres	Inter	Both	Mu
Nuzum	1983	Elem	NA	LD	Strat	Inter	Res	Mi
Smith	1981	Elem	NA	LD	Strat	Inter	Res	On
Tippins	1987	Sec	>85	LD	Strat	inter	Teacher	Mi
Watanabe	1991	Sec	>85	Mixed	Strat	Inter	Teacher	On

Author	Maint (FNa)	Gen.	n	PND (%)
Published studies				
Case, Harris, & Graham	2	Near	4	39
Cassel & Reid	2	NA	4	95
Hutchinson	NA	NA	12	100
Jitendra & Hoff	1	NA	3	100
Marsch & Cooke	NA	NA	3	100
Montague	NA	NA	3	11
	NA	NA	3	58
	1, 2	Near	3	88
	1, 2	Near	3	89
Montague & Bos	1, 2	Far	6	87
Unpublished Studies				
Huntington	2	Near, Far	3	100
Nuzum	NA	NA	4	100
Smith	1	NA	3	100
Tippins	2	Near	5	86
Watanabe	1	Far	10	73

Note. TrtA = treatment approach; TrtL = treatment length; Inter = intermediate; TrtI = treatment implemented; TrtF = treatment fidelity; WPT = word problem task; StD = student directed; n = sample size; PND = percentage of nonoverlapping data; NA = not available.
a1 = [less or equal] 4 weeks; 2 = > 4 weeks but [less or equal] 10 weeks; 3 = > 10 weeks.

the experimental and control group divided by the control group's standard deviation. Moreover, the use of the standardized mean change as an effect size measure may have been one of several factors contributing to the very heterogeneity of effect sizes obtained from the present sample. However, these limitations of the standardized mean change measure do not negate its potential for exploring the relationship between mediating variables and treatment effectiveness. Several limitations of the PND measure used in this review to synthesize single-subject research also are present (Allison & Gorman, 1993). For example, the PND measure can result in a ceiling effect, because the largest possible treatment effect defined by PND is +1.00 (i.e., 100%). Also, a PND measure counts only the percentage of data points in the intervention condition that either exceeds or overlaps with the highest data point in the baseline. Therefore, the measure may not be

Table 7 Summary of Categorical Comparisons for Single-Subject Studies

Variable and class	n	PND+ (%)	Range
Sample characteristics			
Grade/age			
Elementary	6	+100	+39 to +100
Secondary	9	+87	+11 to +100
IQ			
< 85	1	+39	NA
>/= 85	11	+88	+11 to +100
Label			
LD	13	+89	+11 to +100
Mixed	2	+84	+73 to +95
Instructional features			
Intervention approach (FN*)			
Representation	3	+100	+100 to +100
Strategy	12	+87	+11 to +100
Length of treatment (FN*)			
Short	4	+49	+11 to +100
Intermediate	10	+97	+73 to +100
Long	1	+100	NA
Instr. implementation			
Teacher	2	+80	+73 to +86
Researcher	12	+92	+11 to +100
Both	1	+100	NA
Word problem task			
One-step	6	+97	+39 to +100
Multistep	2	+94	+87 to +100
Mixed	7	+88	+11 to +100
Student directed			
Low	5	+87	+11 to +100
High	10	+92	+39 to +100
Methodological features			
Publication bias			
Published	10	+88	+11 to +100
Unpublished	5	+100	+73 to +100

Note. NA = not available; n = number of PND scores; PND+ = median percentage of nonoverlapping data.
* $p < .05$.

sensitive to the magnitude of treatment effectiveness and may account for the insignificant findings from the single-subject studies.

Another limitation of the present analysis is that approximately 30% (range: 10%–43%) of the effect sizes had to be removed to establish homogeneity within each class of all categories, resulting in a substantial attrition of data. Due to the heterogeneity within each categorized class, it was necessary to conduct model testing or categorical analyses both before and after outliers were excluded. When the homogeneity within a model's categories is lacking, we cannot interpret the results accurately (Hedges & Olkin, 1985; Johnson, 1989). Therefore, when sum-

marizing the results, we presented the findings both before and after data were trimmed, and for most categories the analyses seemed to yield consistent results (see Tables 2 and 3). At the same time, we exercised caution in interpreting the effects of instruction, because the overall sample size and the number of effect sizes in each class were small. The small number of effect sizes was particularly difficult to interpret when effect sizes were analyzed for the mediator variables and for skill maintenance and generalization components. Given these limitations, the following section presents a discussion of each research question raised in this study. In general, we discuss the findings for group design studies and note only the relevant findings from the single-subject studies.

1. *What is the general effectiveness of word-problem-solving interventions (e.g., representation, strategy training) for teaching students?*

All intervention approaches, with the exception of the "other" approach, yielded moderate to large mean effect sizes (range = .74 to 1.80). The largest effect size was obtained from the samples coded as CAI intervention. The effect size of 1.8 for CAI is greater than effect sizes (ES = .30 to .53) reported in previous meta-analyses on CAI in general (J. Kulik & C. Kulik, 1987; C. Kulik & J. Kulik, 1991; Niemiec & Walberg, 1987; Schmidt, Weinstein, Niemic, & Walberg, 1985–1986). These differences in effect sizes may be a function of the differences in the manner in which effect sizes were calculated (between-subject vs. within-subject comparisons), content domains (basic skills vs. word-problem solving), type of CAI (e.g., drill and practice vs. tutorial), and population (general education or special education students vs. students with mild disabilities and at-risk students). In the present study, CAI mostly entailed strategy or representation techniques presented via tutorial or videodisc programs. These findings are consistent with those in the literature suggesting that computer-assisted instruction is especially effective when empirically validated strategies and curriculum design principles are incorporated (Carnine, 1994; Jitendra & Xin, 1997; Shiah, Mastropieri, & Scruggs, 1995).

It must be noted that the CAI category included the largest effect size obtained from the Moore and Carnine (1989) study and the largest outlier effect size from the Bottge and Hasselbring (1993) study. One explanation for the large effect sizes may be that these studies combined principles of effective curriculum design with interactive videodisc programs. For example, in the Moore and Carnine study, students were taught ratio and proportion word problems either via an interactive video disc program that used principles of active teaching with curriculum design (ATCD), or by teachers whose instruction was based on active teaching with basals (ATB). Although both groups made significant gains from the pre- to posttest, students in the ATCD group performed significantly higher ($d = +6.77$) than students in the ATB group ($d = +2.95$) on the posttest. In the study by Bottge and Hasselbring, students were taught to solve one-step and multistep addition and subtraction fraction word problems using either contextualized word problems presented on videodiscs (CP) or problems typically found in many basal mathematics textbooks (WP) pre-

sented by the instructor. Results indicated that the CP group scored significantly higher ($d = +5.5$) on the contextualized problem posttest than the WP group ($d = +.97$). However, differences between groups on the typical word problem posttest following the intervention were not significant.

Representation technique was seen to be the next most effective approach in facilitating word-problem-solving performance. This finding was supported by the review of single-subject studies that also found it to be the most effective intervention when compared with strategy training. However, the effect sizes for the representation approach were found to be heterogeneous, which, in turn, resulted in substantial differences in effect sizes before and after outliers were excluded (see Tables 2 and 3). The representation technique in one study (e.g., Walker & Poteet, 1989) yielded a negative effect size ($d = -.04$). One plausible explanation is that the strategy in this study was as simple as having students draw a diagram to represent the problem and failed to make explicit, or teach them to identify, important relationships among key components of the word problem. Clearly, it is important that students develop conceptual understanding in making representational links to be successful problem solvers (Lesh et al., 1987; Prawat, 1989; Resnick & Omanson, 1987; Swing et al., 1988).

In addition, strategy training was found to be moderately effective in facilitating acquisition of problem-solving skills. The single-subject data also indicated strategy training to be an effective intervention. Most strategy training procedures across synthesized studies were similar in that they incorporated explicit instruction and/or metacognitive strategies (e.g., self-instruction, self-questioning, or self-regulation). The present findings seem to support the use of direct instruction, cognitive, and goal-directed strategies to promote student learning (Mercer, Jordan, & Miller, 1994; Pressley, Harris, & Marks, 1992). In this meta-analysis, we did not separate direct instruction from cognitive strategies, as they share many instructional features (Swanson et al., 1996). At the same time, given the limited number of studies, we did not believe that separating them at present would be meaningful. Perhaps with increasing research in problem solving, future investigations should isolate the individual effects of direct instruction and cognitive strategies on student learning.

In contrast, studies classified as "other" (e.g., key word, attention only) were the least effective in improving word-problem-solving performance. In fact, one study (Walker & Poteet, 1989) resulted in a negative effect size ($d = -.42$) for the key word method typically found in basal mathematics programs. These results support the call for a comprehensive analysis of word-problem-solving instruction in basal mathematics curricula (Carnine, Jitendra, & Silbert, 1997; Carnine et al., 1994; Jitendra, Carnine, & Silbert, 1996; Kameenui & Griffin, 1989; Stein, Silbert, & Carnine, 1997).

2. *Is intervention effectiveness related to important student characteristics (i.e., grade/age, IQ level, or classification label)?*

It seemed that the variable grade/age did not mediate the effect size of the intervention, whereas the variables IQ and label had a mediating influence on the effect size. Students who had IQ scores below 85 scored higher than students with IQ scores above 85, a finding that is contraintuitive. One reason for the present findings is the limited number of effect sizes: Of the 35 effect sizes, only 20 could be computed for this category because many studies in the sample did not report IQ scores. Additionally, a limited number of observations (i.e., three) were used to calculate the effect size for IQ lower than 85, and the three effect sizes were obtained from one study (Shiah et al., 1995). This study used simple one-step problems, which may explain the benefits associated with the treatment outcomes.

For the variable label, students with LD seemed to benefit less from the intervention than students with mixed disabilities or those at risk. This finding may be explained in terms of instructional arrangement. With the exception of the one study (Hutchinson, 1993) that provided instruction individually and yielded a large effect size ($d = +4.00$), all other studies provided word-problem-solving instruction in small groups for students with LD. Given the heterogeneous nature of LD, it may be that teachers who use group instruction should consider carefully the manner in which these students' individual needs are met (Goldman, 1989; Mercer et al., 1994; Montague, 1993, 1997). However, the treatment effects from the single-subject studies for the various study features did not indicate a mediating influence on effect size.

3. *Are treatment outcomes related to instructional features, such as (a) setting, (b) length of treatment, (c) instructional arrangement, (d) implementation of instruction, (e) word-problem task, and (f) student-directed intervention?*

Our study seems to indicate that the mediator variables of length of treatment, instructional grouping, and word-problem task did mediate the effect size. The results for treatment length suggest that long-term interventions are more effective than short-term interventions, a finding consistent with the results from the single-subject studies. However, the most short-term interventions (no more than seven sessions) were seen to be more effective than the intermediate-term interventions (more than seven sessions, but no more than 1 month). This finding was different for the single-subject studies, in which intermediate treatment length was seen to be more effective than short-term treatment. It is possible that in the group design studies, some effective interventions, such as the CAI (Shiah, Mastropieri, Scruggs, & Fulk, 1995), resulted in immediate gains after a relatively short period of training, due to the unique, visualized presentation of word-problem-solving instruction. None of the single-subject studies included CAI.

In addition, from the results of this study it would seem that individually provided instruction is more effective than group instruction—a finding that is generally supported in the literature (Mercer et al., 1994; Montague, 1997). However, it must be noted that only five observations were used to calculate the effect size for individual instruction, and they were obtained from two studies (Hutchinson, 1993; Noll, 1983). Thus, interpretation of the present findings may be limited by the small number of effect sizes. Finally, interventions involving simple one-step problems yielded larger effect sizes than multistep word problems or mixed problem types. This finding is consistent with previous research indicating that one-step problems are easier than multistep problems (Stein et al., 1997).

For the variable instructional setting, we cannot at present make the explicit statement that instruction provided in classroom settings is more effective than that provided in pullout settings, given the inconsistent results before and after outliers were removed. In terms of implementation of treatment, joint researcher- and teacher-implemented interventions were seen to be more effective than either researcher-only or teacher-only interventions. The results of the analysis, after four outliers from three studies (Lee, 1992; Marzola, 1987; Walker & Poteet, 1989) were excluded, yielded more homogeneous within-category effect sizes but altered the findings for teacher- and researcher-implemented instruction in isolation. It seems that interventions implemented by teachers were more effective than the researcher-implemented instruction after outliers were removed, whereas the results were the reverse before outliers were removed. The present finding is not consistent with research results in this area suggesting that when implemented by teachers, intervention effectiveness is questionable on the basis of poor treatment integrity (Allinder, 1996; Fuchs, 1988). One explanation for the inconsistent finding in this study is that the large effect size (d

= +1.93) was obtained from five observations in two studies (Gleason et al., 1990; Noll, 1983). Of the five observations, four were from the study by Noll, in which all instruction was administered individually. Furthermore, neither study reported any treatment integrity data, which makes it difficult to accurately assess the effectiveness of treatments implemented by teachers.

Instruction involving student self-regulation of strategy did not have a mediating influence on the effect size for word-problem-solving interventions. This finding is not consistent with previous relevant literature suggesting that self-instruction training directly assists students with the process of internalizing the solution sequence and enhances students' word-problem-solving skills (Goldman, 1989; Mercer et al., 1994). One explanation for this finding may be that three of the observations from two studies (Bennett, 1981; Montague, Applegate, & Marquard, 1993) coded as high in student-directed strategy instruction involved a metacognitive strategy only, or a cognitive strategy plus a metacognitive strategy. On the one hand, the emphasis on a metacognitive strategy that regulated students' performance but lacked problem-solving-strategy specificity was not sufficient to promote learning. On the other hand, the length of the treatment for cognitive plus metacognitive strategy in the first cycle of strategy training in the Montague et al. study was too short (i.e., seven sessions) for students to internalize the strategy and apply it to effectively solve problems. Again, results of treatment effects from the single-subject studies for the various instructional features, with the exception of treatment length, did not indicate a mediating influence on the PND score.

4. *Is there a relationship between methodological features (i.e., publication bias, group assignment) and effect size?*
On the basis of results after outliers were removed, it seems that the variables publication bias and group assignment did moderate the effect size. Unpublished studies in this meta-analysis yielded larger overall effect sizes than published studies. This finding seems to be at odds with the popular assumption that published studies generally reflect more positive results. It may be that various factors (e.g., treatment integrity, experimental control) related to the overall quality of a study are critical criteria for publishing a study. For example, whereas 67% of the published studies showed high treatment integrity, only 20% of the unpublished studies reported assessment for treatment integrity. In this meta-analysis, we also examined group assignment, and these results revealed signifi-

cantly higher effect size scores for matched and randomly assigned groups than for intact groups, thus strengthening the conclusions about the effects of word-problem-solving instruction on student learning. In addition, the findings of single-subject design studies do not indicate a mediating influence of publication bias on the PND score.

5. *What is the effectiveness of word-problem-solving instruction in fostering skill maintenance and generalization? Are skill maintenance and generalization functions of instructional features (e.g., treatment length)?*
In general, word-problem-solving instruction seemed to positively affect skill maintenance ($d = +.78$) and generalization ($d = +.84$). These findings suggest that students may benefit from specific word-problem-solving instruction for skill maintenance and generalization (Goldman, 1989; Mercer et al., 1994; Pressley et al., 1992) and are supported by the results of maintenance (PND = 100%) and generalization (PND = 100%) effects in single-subject studies.

For the group design studies, with the exception of the "other" category, CAI and strategy training were seen to be effective in promoting skill maintenance and generalization. Although CAI was found to be most effective in promoting maintenance of the skill, it was not as effective when compared to strategy training in promoting generalization (e.g., from online to paper-and-pencil tasks). As Shiah, Mastropieri, Scruggs, and Fulk (1995) noted, it may be that the connection between the online CAI and paper-and-pencil tasks was not well established by students with special needs. Further research in computer-assisted instruction needs to explore and clarify the conditions under which the transfer of acquired skills from online to paper-and-pencil tasks can be achieved. For single-subject studies, although both representation and strategy training approaches were seen to promote skill maintenance and generalization, the database is too limited for the representation category (only two treatment effects) to provide meaningful comparisons.

In the group design studies, generalization was promoted, whether instruction was implemented by teacher, researcher, or both. For single-subject studies, although researcher-implemented instruction (PND = 92%) was seen to be more effective than teacher-implemented instruction (PND = 80%) in improving performance during or after the training, the former was less effective in fostering skill generalization (PND = 69%). It could be that the initial individualized attention provided by the researcher during the study resulted in improved performance on the immediate posttest, but when the researcher's presence in the setting was reduced following the completion of instruction, students' generalization performance was adversely affected. In addition, student performance may have been influenced by various competing factors involved in the generalization setting (i.e., distractions) or the task (e.g., problem complexity, vocabulary, etc.). Results of both group and single-subject studies indicate that maintenance and generalization were influenced by treatment length, in that relatively longer term interventions led to greater benefits than shorter term treatments, indicating the need for students to internalize the strategy steps needed for problem solution. Finally, a high level of student-directed intervention was seen to result in greater levels of maintenance and generalization—a finding supported in the literature (Mercer et al., 1994; Montague, 1997); this finding was supported by generalization effects found in single-subject studies.

IMPLICATIONS FOR RESEARCH

In summary, the effects of varied instructional approaches on student learning are encouraging. Several implications of our analysis for future research in the area of word-problem solving are presented. Our analysis showed that many studies failed to report critical information needed to accurately interpret the study findings. It is important that future research studies provide detailed information of study characteristics that would allow for accurate inferences. This would include identifying data, such as IQ and achievement scores. In addition, clearly defining the population (e.g., LD, mildly disabled, at risk) and providing detailed descriptions of the intervention and comparison conditions are seen as critical to interpreting study findings. Without a description of the comparison group (e.g., Hutchinson, 1993), it is difficult to determine the equivalency of the experimental and comparison groups. It could be that the findings were affected by factors other than the intervention effectiveness. At the same time, details of instructional (e.g., setting, treatment length, task) and methodological features (group assignment, treatment integrity) can be informative. We cannot be certain that many of the approaches implemented by researchers in settings outside of the classroom would be effective in the natural contexts with the existing word-problem-solving database. Furthermore, future studies in this area should address how acceptable interventions are to teachers and students.

This review was further limited by the small number of studies that addressed maintenance and generalizations skills. Future research should continue to assess skill maintenance on an ongoing basis (a few weeks to more than a month). The practice of teaching and assessing for generalization of word-problem solving is important. Presenting opportunities to apply the learned skills in new situations and contexts is especially important for students with learning problems. In addition, although different approaches were found to be useful in mathematics word-problem solving, it is important to note that limitations imposed by students' insufficient background or prerequisite skill knowledge can undermine the effectiveness of these approaches. Therefore, future research should assess students' understanding of concepts and skills needed to solve word problems, so as to inform instruction in this area.

Finally, further examination of the area of word-problem solving may be warranted when a larger database of primary studies is available. At the same time, future research should explore measures that would allow for a direct comparison of treatment effects from both group and single-subject design studies in order to make a generalized statement about a specific body of research and to effectively translate the research findings into practice.

Lloyd, L. (1999). Multi-age classes and high ability students. *Review of Educational Research, 69*(2), 187–212.

Multi-Age Classes and High Ability Students

Linley Lloyd

University of New England

This article reviews research on multi-age classroom organization as an option for high ability students. Studies of both cognitive and affective factors in multi-age contexts have consistently shown positive, sometimes significant, effect sizes. Studies of different types of ability grouping have shown that arrangements most likely to have positive and significant results are those where the curriculum is differentiated. Teachers of multi-age classes may be more likely to see their students as diverse than as similar and to provide developmentally appropriate (that is, differentiated) curricula. Multi-age classes are discussed as an alternative to self-contained classes and pullout programs for high ability children.

If the explosion in recent decades of theories about intelligence, language, and culture has been nothing short of exciting it has also contained a core of despair—for, given the forces of inertia and vested interest plus constraints on resources, how can we possibly ensure that all our children are educated in a stimulating environment which will allow development of all facets of their being, including their multiple intelligences and their social/emotional selves (whatever the circumstances of their home life)? Arguments about what it means to promote "equality" and "equity" have changed to emphasize the crucial fact of diversity, and "positive discrimination" has entered our language as a description of a means of trying to reduce the less desirable effects of diversity. Thus we no longer believe that everyone should be treated the same, thereby being given an equal chance to succeed. The idea that to encourage equality (of opportunity) we need to treat children unequally is no longer a foreign concept. Diversity is now actively promoted and officially sanctioned. "Appropriate" education has become a banner under which different types of schooling provision are evaluated.

Talented and Gifted (TAG) programs exist in various guises; examples include full-time self-contained classes, pullout programs (within-grade and cross-grade), within-class clusters, after-school provision, various enrichment options, acceleration and grade skipping, early entry, dual programs (such as high school and college), and mentor schemes. In many schools, however—and for reasons as diverse as population density, unease about identification, concerns relating to equity, community opinion, and resource difficulties—whole class or within-class provisions are seen as the only acceptable options. In these cases, emphasis on differentiating the curriculum is necessary, with the possible adjuncts of curriculum compacting (Reis & Renzulli, 1992) and individual educational programs (IEPs).

Multi-age classes could be a low-cost, mainstream restructuring particularly advantageous to such schools and their high ability students. Multi-age classes are not a new idea (see, e.g., Pratt, 1986). Is a call for an increase in such classes just another example of the swinging educational pendulum? The pendulum model of viewing change is a familiar but not, arguably, an accurate one. "Revisiting" of old ideas is never an exact repetition. More often, an idea is resurrected because some circumstance has changed and the potential appropriateness of the old idea in the new situation is recognized. Perhaps a zigzag metaphor is more appropriate than that of a pendulum—the ideas of "revisiting" things from the past, of returning always to the present/future, and at the same time of movement forward are all implied in the image, whereas a pendulum stays in the same place, slowly dying perhaps but not venturing forward. In the same way, the move between "black" and "white" views implied by a pendulum is not as powerfully suggested by a zigzag motion which allows for movement forward as well as from side to side, into "gray" areas rather than simply between the "black" and "white" poles. So having "zigged" from multi-age classes to an age-grade determination, why consider a "zag" back to multi-age?

The lock-step progression of children, sometimes solely on chronological grounds, is easy to attack from many vantage points yet, as one writer expressed it, "the awful truth is this—what is mostly wrong . . . is an old fashioned mindset; a notion that links classes strictly with ages" (Parker, 1994). The explosion of theories and research studies related to "advanced," "talented," "high ability," "extraordinary," "above average," "gifted," and "high achieving" children has been extremely influential in emphasizing the lack of any necessary correlation between chronological age and "mental" or intellectual age. A classroom organization that openly breaks such a nexus and focuses instead on children as individuals should, on the face of it, be an attractive option for parents and teachers of high ability children who are dissatisfied with the "appropriateness" of the educational experiences of these children. Does the published research on multi-age schooling provide any evidence to suggest that such a classroom organization would be advantageous for high ability children?

TERMINOLOGY

In education nothing is ever clear-cut and multi-age schooling is no exception. In my part of the world, Australia, very little has been published at all; in America there have been many studies but not always of the same thing or, just as relevantly, of the same time period. There was, in both countries, a "zig" in the early 1970s, with a proliferation of "open" schools; there is currently a "zag" of nongraded schools. In-between, in both countries, there has been an increase in the number of combination classes (called composite classes in Australia) and some nostalgic yearnings for the warm and simple one- or two-teacher "rural school." Differences in terminology, usually (but not always) reflecting differences in organization, and differences in time make comparisons and conclusions tenuous. In spite of all this, there do seem to be some consistent findings, and these will be reported below. First, it may be useful to look briefly at the different arrangements reported in the various studies.

Combination Class/Composite Class/Split Class/Mixed-Age Class. Students from two or more grades are housed in the same classroom but taught, at least some of the time and commonly for most of the time, as separate grades. The classes are usually formed on a yearly basis to cope with uneven grade enrolments, that is,

for administrative rather than educational reasons. Class members are often chosen on the basis of their mature work habits, most commonly the ability to work independently.

Multi-Grade Class. Children from different grades form one class. Whereas combination classes are commonly two-grade classes, multi-grade classes are commonly three or more. The term implies nothing definite about classroom organization, that is, whether or not the teacher primarily teaches each grade separately, but the most common situation is one resembling a combination class. The children are seen as members of a particular grade and are separately taught grade-specific curricula. Some authors use the terms "combination class" and "multi-grade class" interchangeably. The common defining characteristic of both terms is that they describe classes formed for administrative and/or economic reasons rather than because of philosophical preference.

Multi-Age Class. Children of different ages form one class. The range is commonly three or more years. The teacher does not see the children as members of a particular grade though for administrative reasons the classes are usually referred to as, for example, K-1-2, 2-3, 3-4, 5-6-7. Some grade-specific teaching may occur because of State-mandated curricula and testing but crossgrade teaching is the norm, based on the teacher's judgement of the developmental level of each child. Children usually stay with the same teacher or teachers for several years (team teaching is also common). This term is used to describe a class formed by choice, not necessity, though it is also sometimes used (especially in older references) as an umbrella term to cover all classes that are not age-segregated.

Nongraded. Children of different ages form one class and are seen as members of that class, not as members of a particular grade. Progress is dependent on development, not time—children take as little or as long as is necessary and work at different levels in different subjects. The focus is on a 'developmentally appropriate' curriculum. It is common for children to stay in the class for several years with the same teacher. The term "multi-age" is commonly but not universally used to refer to a nongraded setup.

Family Group or Class. A multi-age arrangement, often with siblings in the same class. Children usually stay in the same class for several years. The class may be formed to house all the "leftovers" after classes have been formed for each grade or because a particular teacher does not desire to teach within the grade structure of the rest of the school. The teacher may or may not divide the children along grade lines for much of their learning.

Open Education. The arrangement which was popular in the 1970s where large numbers of children (several classes under previous arrangements) were team-taught in spaces that could be partitioned or opened up as necessary. The underlying philosophy of open education is quite similar to that of nongradedness.

Horizontal Groups. Children are put into classes on chronological (age) grounds. Thus, for example, 9-year-olds are in 3rd grade.

Vertical Groups. Children of different ages/grades are put into a single class. Sometimes this is done for pragmatic reasons, such as better utilization of resources. At the secondary level, some subject areas have been designed to fit a 'core plus electives' model and students choose their preferred electives after having completed the core. Depending upon when they did the core, students in any particular elective may, for example, be nominally in 8th, 9th, or 10th grades.

When trying to make sense of the literature, then, a reader first has to make sense of the terminology, a task which is frequently difficult (see Goodlad & Anderson, 1987, p. xiv). The situation is complicated by the fact that most classrooms are not static and most teachers not entirely rigid in their approach. Thus a teacher of a multi-age class may separate the children along grade lines for some subjects and teach them as a single group for others; s/he may form within-grade small groups for some activities and across-grade groups for others (and for reasons of either homogeneity or heterogeneity); and s/he may or may not vary the process demands (i.e. what is expected) for each child doing a common activity. While such flexibility is commendable in educational terms, it makes any causal relationship between "multi-age" and achievement, development, contentedness, or any other variable difficult to promote, though the existence of correlations raises tantalizing questions.

In this review the broader term "multi-age" is generally used and should be interpreted as follows: classes which are formed deliberately because of a philosophical commitment that such classes are educationally preferable. The acceptance of "philosophical commitment" in turn implies that at least some cross-grade grouping and whole-class teaching (i.e. cross-grade instruction) occur, with a focus on individual progress through a developmentally appropriate curriculum. If the studies discussed use clearly defined terms such as "nongraded," then these terms are maintained in the discussion. "Multi-grade" should be interpreted to mean the classes were formed for some sort of necessity rather than philosophical commitment—a necessity related to fluctuations in enrolment or more efficient use of resources (including the available number of teachers and classrooms).

Reviews of Research Relating to Multi-Age Classes

In spite of the difficulties mentioned above, many good studies have been done and many conclusions offered. Perhaps the least controversial way of expressing any overall tendency is that there is no evidence of any disadvantage to a child who is a member of a multi-age class. Tests of academic achievement consistently show either the same or slightly improved scores from children in multi-age classes (Goodlad & Anderson, 1987; Guiterrez & Slavin, 1992; Milburn, 1981; Miller, 1991; Pavan, 1992; Slavin, 1992; Veenman, 1995). In addition, there seems to be a benign positive (though small) effect in terms of social emotional development—children seem to like school better and be more advanced in "interpersonal intelligence" than their peers in age-segregated or 'straight' classes (Anderson & Pavan, 1993; Goodlad & Anderson, 1987; Pratt, 1986; Veenman, 1995). Results are more clear-cut for nongraded programs, and are more likely the longer a child has been in such a class.

A common reason proffered as an advantage of a multi-age class, using the definition above, is the teacher's ability to respond to individual differences, especially to children at both ends of any particular spectrum, without having to resort to "remediation" or "acceleration" in their conventional sense. (Any proponent of nongradedness would proclaim this view. Three examples are American Association of School Administrators, 1992; Anderson & Pavan, 1993; and Goodlad & Anderson, 1987.) The focus of this discussion is what the multi-age literature says about high ability children. Note that "gifted," "talented," "high ability" or any other such term suffers from the same difficulties of not having a precise and universally accepted definition as do the various descriptors of class organization. "High ability" has been selected here because it is somewhat less rigid, covering underachievers and others whose talents may not always be exposed. Where authors of the various studies have defined such children as "the top 5%" or "the top third," then their terminology has been retained but the question of a precise definition of "high ability" is one which is beyond the scope of this review.

The lack of precision in relation to use of these terms adds another layer of complication. Therefore there can be no necessary comparability across studies and many studies need to be examined for even tenuous conclusions to be drawn. But in recent years several authors have tried to control for such difficulties by preparing overviews of research findings using one of two methodologies—either a meta-analysis or a best-evidence synthesis. These overviews provided the starting point for this review. Other studies were selected according to whether they added any new element to the current knowledge base or whether they specifically referred to high ability children. Library and internet searches were used to locate potential material.

Most of the overviews published using meta-analysis or best-evidence synthesis have been concerned with looking at ability grouping as a criterion for class formation. Any relevant results for multi-age are thus frequently contained within other categories. For example, a multi-age group may be formed for reading or mathematics only, but formed on the basis of perceived homogeneous ability and consisting of children from several different "home" classes. Any group so formed is thus an ability group and also a multi-age group.

Reviews by Slavin

An early synthesis of studies on ability grouping and achievement in elementary schools was carried out by Robert Slavin (1987). His conclusion was that the evidence did not support assignment of students to classes on the basis of ability—that is, streaming or tracking. In relation to high ability students, he reported one study which specifically grouped children across a range of ability groupings, including homogeneous IQ (1-decile classes) and heterogeneous IQ (5-decile classes). He concluded that the patterns of findings in the study "consistently favor broad, heterogeneous grouping plans for all students except for the most gifted (130+), who did equally well in broad- or narrow-range classes" (1987, p. 305).

Slavin concluded that the studies reported "unequivocally refute" (1987, p. 307) any relationship between ability-grouped classes and achievement in the elementary grades. He did find, however, that forming multi-age, cross-grade groups for one subject (usually reading or mathematics) was particularly supported in terms of achievement. This arrangement is called the Joplin Plan, and was an innovation of the 1950s/early 1960s in Joplin, Missouri. It requires constant reviewing of the groups and reassignment where necessary to maintain as much homogeneity in the groups as possible. One consequence of this is that each temporarily formed "class" (for reading or math) consists of only one or two different groups or levels, allowing the teacher more time with each group than in a more heterogeneous class. (Slavin, 1987, p. 295)

If the claim is accepted that high ability children benefit from ability grouping (Hannon, 1995; and see

next section), then this arrangement would seem to have obvious applicability to high ability students, especially those who are talented in the area of language development or mathematics. A concern of many teachers, and some parents, is that a child may not be socially or emotionally ready to join with older children, especially only for some lessons (since joining the class only for mathematics, say, denies any opportunity to settle in and feel accepted as a member of the class). Although the research on acceleration and grade skipping is on the whole positive (Southern & Jones, 1991), many children are never given the option because of expressed fears relating to "immaturity" in some form other than a specific intellectual capacity. Often such temporary promotion is difficult because of timetabling difficulties (with different grades having, say, mathematics at different times). If the acceleration is done by the child joining a higher-grade class, the intellectual benefits may be minimal anyway, or at least short-term. A cross-grade, multi-age, ability-grouped class formed for reading or mathematics (the most common options) could help high ability children, who would be amongst the youngest members of the class, feel less like the isolated intruder (since the whole class is formed temporarily).

Slavin did not review special classes for high achievers, such as TAG classes, because the formation of such classes implies significant changes in curriculum, teacher approach, and resources, thus making it difficult to attribute any changes to the ability grouping per se. One reason for the success of the Joplin Plan may also be related to such factors as change in curriculum and teacher approach (there was less likely to have been any significant change in resources), and the delivery of appropriate instruction could easily be a significant factor in the success of the arrangement. Wherever there is little likelihood of expansion of special classes for high ability children, implementation of cross-grade groups for one or perhaps two subjects could be a low-cost but beneficial initiative, especially for children with high ability in the particular subjects. Such an arrangement does, however, require whole-school support with regard to timetabling, a difficulty which can potentially be overcome by the alternative of a more autonomous multi-age class (with, perhaps, a cluster group of high ability children) and within-class ability groups for math or reading.

The positive results of Joplin Plan arrangements led to an interest in "crossgrade" classes, that is, multi-age classes, and in nongradedness as a form of organization. A teacher of a multi-age class, it was believed, had increased flexibility in terms of forming appropriate, homogeneous groups based on performance or demonstrated outcomes rather than on age. Thus since the early 1960s studies of achievement related to (ability) grouping practices in the elementary school have included nongraded programs. A retrospective review of nongraded elementary schools and achievement was published by Guiterrez and Slavin in 1992.

This review, another best-evidence synthesis, in general confirmed the positive findings for multi-age cross-grade classes hinted at in Slavin's earlier review of different forms of ability grouping in the elementary school. Four categories of nongraded programs were distinguished, programs which form a temporal sequence in terms of median publication date of the various studies (p. 10):

Nongraded programs involving only one subject (Joplin-like programs)
The subject was most commonly reading; in one study it was mathematics. Median publication date for these programs is 1962.

Nongraded programs involving multiple subjects (comprehensive programs)
These programs emphasized individual progress and flexible, multi-age groupings but without a major emphasis on individualized instruction. These programs are not as clearly limited to a particular time-frame, with studies reported from the late 1960s to the early 1980s.

Nongraded programs incorporating individualized instruction
These programs emphasized individualized instruction, learning centers, learning activity packages, programmed instruction, and/or tutoring. Median publication date for these programs is 1969.

Individually Guided Education (IGE)
This program grew out of the emphasis on individualized instruction but its implementation had effects that were more far-reaching because they went beyond flexible groupings and included as well preparation of individualized plans for each student, development of comprehensive instructional models, and organization of students and a team of teachers into instruction and research units of 100–150 students. Most studies of IGE programs were reported in the 1970s.

Results from the first category of Joplin-like nongraded programs consistently showed "substantial positive results in favor of the nongraded program. The median effect size (ES) for the four best-quality studies is +.50; for all studies from which effect sizes could be estimated, it is +.46" (p. 13). Most of the reported studies compared nongraded children's achievement with that of their chronological peers in graded classes. One study of third graders who had spent three years in a nongraded program, however, specifically mentioned results for different IQs, stating that the increased achievement in reading of students with IQs of 125 or higher was particularly large, with an ES = .91.

In the second category of nongraded program, comprehensive nongradedness, results also consistently favored the nongraded program, with higher positive differences correlated to increase in duration of the program. A crucial factor in the success of these programs seems to be the change in instructional practice of the teacher. Frequent and flexible regrouping in order to reduce the heterogeneity of the groups, particularly where sequential learning was relevant and important, was a feature of the nongraded programs, a feature with obvious advantages for an "advanced" student (as suggested by other studies which confirm that those students with most talent/ability need to be grouped at least some of the time with their intellectual peers; e.g. Rogers, 1991).

In the third category of nongraded programs, those incorporating individualized instruction, results were remarkably consistent but showed no significant differences in academic achievement between these programs and ordinary graded programs. "As the nongraded plans became more complicated in their grouping arrangements, they apparently lost the comparative advantage Joplinlike or comprehensive nongraded programs had" (Guiterrez & Slavin, 1992, p. 18). Two other trends in the data, however, are notable. Firstly, the longer the duration of the nongraded program, the better the results were in terms of higher academic achievement. Secondly, in these programs with individualized instruction, more positive effects were obtained with older than with younger children. "It may be that students need a certain level of maturity or self-organizational skills to profit from a continuous program which includes a good deal of independent work" (1992, p. 18).

There seem to be implications here for the success of individual education programs (at least those which assume a significant amount of independent work by the student) and mentoring schemes, two arrangements commonly advocated for those children with advanced development in at least one area of intelligence. Development of a child's intrapersonal or "emotional" intelligence, which includes self-motivation, needs to reach a certain level if an individual (independent) program has a chance to succeed. Whereas with most children the ability to set goals, work alone, and monitor progress develops over time, with exceptionally high ability children such abilities may already be well-developed, at least in relation to their area of expertise. In such cases, an individual education program may indeed be suitable. Where such abilities are immature a mentoring scheme may be a better alternative. Successful adults commonly had supportive relationships when they were young and some sort of expert tuition or guidance (Bloom in Alvino, 1985, pp. 137–8; Csikszentmihalyi, 1996). When development in the "personal intelligences" has not kept pace with development of an intellectual ability, a mentor might succeed where "individualized instruction" (where this means independent work) in an otherwise large-group situation rarely can, as suggested by these findings of Gutierrez and Slavin.

Studies in the last category of nongraded programs, those incorporating Individually Guided Education (IGE), generally support these conclusions. Whereas overall results do not support individualized instruction, it should be noted that the degree of implementation of IGE varied across studies and in fact must always do so, since IGE emphasizes individual differences and specialized curriculum programs. Several studies did report significant differences in favor of IGE schools, one with an ES of +0.80. All studies which did report significant differences were evaluations of schools with clear differences from each other. Gutierrez and Slavin conclude:

> It seems that schools which are closer to a full implementation of IGE concepts supply students with a wider range of instructional possibilities for their specific needs: small groups, one-to-one tutoring, or independent work. This finding supports the argument that selective use of individualized instruction can yield positive results for children's academic performance. (1992, p. 20)

It is clear from this best-evidence synthesis that "nongradedness" may be too broad a term and that studies of multi-age classrooms need to be categorized by the type of instruction used. The studies analyzed supported other research which shows that student learning is enhanced by interaction with teachers (see, e.g., Brophy & Good, 1986). Flexible cross-age groupings, which are a feature of multi-age programs, may work because they allow the teacher to teach a small group rather than one individual, as is often the case with the "misfit" in a more narrowly age-defined class; alternatively, multi-age arrangements may increase the number of possible "teachers" in the class. In this latter arrangement, both the "teacher" and the taught benefit. Peer tutoring can be a favorable influence on high ability children both intellectually and socially (Lou et al., 1996, p. 449). For either or both reasons, placing a high ability child in a multi-age classroom could increase the opportunities for that child to be part of a group learning situation rather than being condemned either to inappropriate instruction or isolation.

As hinted above, one difficulty which should not be ignored in trying to make sense of studies of multi-age classrooms is the difficulty of imputing any positive effects to the multi-age organization rather than to some other variable, such as the change in instructional approach which so often accompanies such an organizational change (Gamoran, 1992, p. 11; Wheelock, 1992, p. 9). Teachers of TAG classes typically have a different approach to teaching from that of traditional teachers (for an interesting vignette, see Brown, 1993, pp. 104–11). Similarly, most teachers who are committed to a multi-age setting are certainly not committed to a hierarchical structure of learning related to age or grade level. In other words, they are more likely to see the children in their class as individuals with different developmental needs rather than with similarities based on age. To this extent they are more likely to provide developmentally appropriate learning situations. And to this extent, high ability children are more likely to have satisfying learning experiences. "Multi-age" may not be a cause in any identifiable way, but it may be a strong enabling factor.

Slavin's conclusions have sometimes been dismissed, especially by those whose research interests focus on high-achieving students. Statements such as "Research clearly shows that gifted students learn best in a homogeneous class setting" (Hannon, 1995, p. 13) are certainly not uncommon in the TAG literature. Yet in all his syntheses covering elementary, middle, and secondary schools—Slavin concluded that full-time ability grouping is not supported by research studies. In his synthesis of secondary schools, for example, he found that "overall achievement effects were found to be essentially zero at all grade levels . . . This finding contrasts with those of studies comparing the achievement of students in different tracks, which generally find positive effects of ability grouping for high achievers . . . " (1990, p. 471).

One critic of this "secondary school" synthesis claimed a bias in terms of selection of experimental studies and the ignoring of survey and case studies (Hallinan, 1990, p. 502). What such qualitative studies show, according to Hallinan, is "distinct differences in instructional techniques, teacher interactions, reward systems, student motivation, effort and self-esteem, student behavior, disciplinary measures, administrative load, role modeling, and peer influences by level of ability group" (p. 503).

The enormous growth in qualitative research in recent decades has underlined the complexity of all cultural processes, including education. Dissatisfaction with purely quantitative measures, which often seem to acquire statistical credibility at the expense of intuitive credibility (because they only tell part of the story), is likely to increase rather than decrease. Quantitative test scores, for example, which are used in experimental studies as the criterion for measuring change or the effectiveness of an intervention, will only ever tell (within the ceiling imposed by the test) what happened under controlled conditions of instruction (see Allan, 1991, pp. 60–1).

Slavin seems to have taken this point, at least, to heart. In an adaptation of his synthesis related to secondary schools, "Ability Grouping in the Middle Grades" (1993–4), he concluded that "there is a need for descriptive studies of schools" (p. 548) and "there is a need to study tracked and untracked classes using a variety of affective and cognitive measures, including measures more sensitive to curriculum and instruction than standardized tests" (p. 549). Such descriptive approaches would, of course, focus on the sorts of variables discussed above in relation to multi-age classes, that is, change in instructional approach, differentiated curriculum, developmentally appropriate education; and would provide a means of comparing, for example, multi-age classrooms with TAG classes with graded classes whose teacher used differentiated curriculum.

One could add that more descriptive studies should also help overcome the problem of definition which can make interpretation of research studies so nebulous. In this context, the perennial problem of how to define "high ability" or "talented" or "high achievers" is relevant. For in his "middle school" adaptation of the synthesis of research on secondary schools Slavin admits: "Few if any benefits of ability grouping have been found for the top 33% of students, but for the very highest achievers the evidence is less clearcut" (1993–4, p. 548).

Review by Rogers and Survey by Marshall et al.

Karen Rogers has also published (1991) an overview of studies of grouping practices but with a specific focus on their suitability for high ability learners K–12. Her analysis is more encompassing because it includes secondary students and also focuses on social and psychological effects of various practices, not merely on their academic effects.

According to Rogers, high ability learners benefit from ability grouping—full-time ability grouping, cross-grade grouping (both across the school for a single subject or as can occur across subjects in a non-

graded classroom), cluster grouping and pullout enrichment grouping all produced substantial academic gains and a moderate gain in attitude towards subject (pp. vii, x, 11–18). As well, high ability students in nongraded classrooms showed substantial academic gains when grouped for acceleration (pp. vii, xi, 21–24). These findings can be interpreted as (qualified) support for multi-age settings since:

Cross-grade grouping is by definition multi-age and pullout enrichment grouping is commonly multi-age (when only a small number of students from each grade are withdrawn for a common enrichment experience).

Full-time ability grouping is often not an option in schools for several reasons, including a small number of similar ability students (as must be the case with those of very high ability), the uneven distribution of talents in any student (making a global assessment meaningless and continual regrouping essential), and concerns relating to equity (classes of low achievers are not usually seen as desirable, either for teachers or the students themselves). Other ways of short-term grouping must therefore be found. The least disruptive option is multi-age classes.

Cross-grade grouping and cluster groupings are more likely to be effective if appropriate groupings can be formed, however "appropriate" is defined. A multi-age pool enlarges the number of possibilities, or it should if there is any credence at all to the opposite argument that children of a particular age are more likely to be similar in their development. A multi-age setting should have a wider range of development on any particular variable, thus increasing the possibility that any particular child, with any "non-standard" profile, can find another child who "matches" in terms of some characteristic relevant to the particular learning situation.

"Mixed-ability co-operative learning should be used sparingly for students who are gifted and talented, perhaps only for social skills development programs" (p. xiii). Since schools are not concerned only with academic development, grouping high ability students by academic achievement or potential is not likely to be universally accepted as a desirable option. In a multi-age setting, there can be opportunities for both grouping on the basis of ability and grouping on the basis of mixed-ability or mixed development.

Any conclusion of support for multi-age or nongraded programs per se should again be tempered by the acknowledgement that teachers who are committed to such an organization are likely to change their way of teaching. Rogers also recognizes this:

> The major benefit of each grouping strategy for students who are gifted and talented is its provision of the format for enriching or accelerating the curriculum they are offered . . . It is unlikely that grouping itself causes academic gains; rather, what goes on in the group does (p. x).

Other authors have made this point: "how teachers teach and how they work with children is more important than any single feature of organization" (Otto, quoted in Goodlad & Anderson, 1987, pp. xxii–xxiii) and "these studies suggest that the form of grouping itself does not significantly affect student achievement either positively or negatively" (Veenman, 1996, p. 335).

One widely perceived benefit of multi-age classes is the opportunity to accelerate students without the disruption implied by changing classes and being the "odd one out" in the new class of older students. Rogers herself carried out a study of the effects of various acceleration options for high ability students, and one such option was the nongraded classroom. For the studies she analyzed, she reported a significant effect size of +0.38 for academic achievement, an insignificant but positive effect size of +0.02 for socialization, and a larger positive but still insignificant effect size of +0.11 for psychological adjustment (Rogers, 1991, p. 23). These results clearly show an academic advantage of a nongraded classroom and no negative social and emotional effects. One common objection to acceleration is perceived negative consequences related to social and emotional adjustment. Rogers' analysis suggests that a nongraded class is unlikely to cause such problems—indeed, since an accelerated child would change groups, perhaps, but not change classes, this suggestion is unremarkable, especially if the teacher regularly reformed the small groups.

Among the recommendations drawn from her synthesis of research studies were several of direct relevance to a multi-age setting. Guideline Three is worth quoting:

> In the absence of full-time gifted program enrollment, gifted and talented students might be offered specific group instruction across grade levels, according to their individual knowledge acquisition in school subjects, either in conjunction with cluster grouping or in its stead. . . . Full-time 'cross-grading' might also be considered Nongraded Classroom experiences, which for the gifted have been found to produce a mean academic Effect Size of +.38. . . . Putting these sets of findings together makes a good case for the strength of this form

of educational provision for the gifted. (Rogers, 1991, p. 28)

Other guidelines can also be interpreted as support for multi-age classrooms. Guideline One recommended that students "who are academically or intellectually gifted and talented should spend the majority of their school day with others of similar abilities and interests" (p. 27). Since the number of such children in any school may be small, and since full-time ability grouping is fraught with problems relating both to classification and ethical convictions, a more acceptable option could be a multi-age classroom with judicious selection of members. Guideline Two recommended cluster grouping as a "second choice" option. The same comments apply—there is more likelihood of being able to select a particular proportion of the class (say, one-third) to be of similar ability in some domain if the available pool includes children across the school. Guideline Four suggested giving high ability children a variety of acceleration-based options. The five options which gave substantial gains were nongraded classrooms (ES = +.38), curriculum compaction (ES = +.45), grade telescoping (ES = +.56), subject acceleration (ES = +.49), and early admission to college (+.44). Curriculum compaction, grade telescoping and subject acceleration are the norm for high ability students in a nongraded classroom where developmentally appropriate curriculum is the focus, and are easy to provide in a multi-age setting by having a high ability child work with (usually) older classmates or by adapting work from a higher grade. Once again, a potential reason for the encouraging findings from multi-age is probably related to other changes which occur, apart from the simple regrouping—a teacher committed to a multi-age setting is likely to approach learning and teaching in a way which includes focus on each child as an individual, flexible and frequent regrouping for the specific task in hand, and selection of activities which can be completed at different levels of complexity by the different children in the class. All these features should benefit a high ability child.

Although Rogers' synthesis of studies of acceleration covered both elementary and secondary, she did not distinguish between the levels when reporting on the nongraded classroom as an acceleration option. Since such an arrangement is most common up to and including 8th grade, it is likely that the studies covered elementary and junior high/middle schools. Studies reporting results of some sort of multi-age arrangement at secondary level are less common than studies at primary or elementary level but one Australian study suggests that a multi-age organization might be beneficial for high ability secondary students as well (Marshall, Walton, Maxwell, & Laird, 1988). The study investigated two patterns of curriculum organization in New South Wales secondary schools, Years (Grades) 7–10: (a) vertical grouping and (b) alternative length courses (i.e. full-year courses which have been repackaged into two or more semester-length courses). A significant number of schools (about one-third) reported using one or both organizations, with 15% overall involved in vertical grouping (p. 14).

The reasons for introducing vertical grouping were ranked by frequency of response. The second-highest ranking was the reason "respond to students' expression of interest in particular areas" (92% rated this reason "high or very high" in importance); the reason ranked fifth was "meet the needs of students with special talents" (70% rated this reason "high or very high" in importance). Schools were then asked to judge the effects of introducing vertical grouping. Of particular interest to advocates for high ability children is the result that 100% of responding schools with vertical grouping alone reported an increase in their ability to meet the needs of more able students (pp. 29, 33). Total endorsement is a rare result and is thus suggestive that vertical grouping, that is, a multi-age option, should be seriously considered as an arrangement which could benefit high ability students. Seventy-one per cent of schools with both vertical grouping and alternative length courses also reported an increase in their ability to meet the needs of more able students.

Effects reported more frequently by schools with vertical grouping were a decrease in discipline problems, both in the classroom and schoolwide; an increase in the quality of pastoral care (the arrangements made to support student welfare); an increase in academic standards; and an increase in application to schoolwork (p. 38). All these effects are encouraging for all students but their relevance to high ability students in particular should be obvious.

Review by Kulik and Kulik

Several other meta-analytic reviews have appeared since Rogers examined the literature for her 1991 summary. In 1992 Kulik and Kulik investigated the findings from published studies of different grouping programs. Their conclusions generally support those of Slavin discussed above; that is, that putting children in any particular grade into supposedly homogeneous classes on the basis of a general categorization of their ability (streaming or tracking) has little or no effect on student achievement. Crossgrade grouping, however, produced clear positive effects, as did within-class grouping when adjustment of curriculum to ability was made. Similarly, enrichment

and acceleration options produced moderate to large effect sizes. Their conclusion was "that effects of grouping are a function of program type" (p. 74) and "that the key factor is the degree to which course content is adjusted to group ability in the programs" (p. 76).

Review by Lou, Abrami, Spence, Poulsen, Chambers, and d'Apollonia

Lou et al. (1996) conducted a meta-analysis of the effects of within-class grouping on both achievement and noncognitive variables such as self concept and liking for school. Their general conclusion was that 'there are small but positive effects of placing students in groups within the classroom for learning. On average, students placed in small groups achieved more, held more positive attitudes, and reported higher general self-concept than students in nongrouped classes' (p. 446).

Their conclusions in relation to achievement were in agreement with those of Kulik and Kulik; that is, that instructional methods and materials need to be adapted for different groups if significant differences in achievement are to be realized. They also analyzed the effects of small group instruction for students of different ability, concluding that, in relation to achievement, students of low ability benefit from heterogeneous groups, students of middle ability benefit from homogeneous groups, and for students of high ability, group composition makes no significant difference. Two tendencies probably contribute to this finding for high ability students: "High ability students may benefit from being placed in heterogeneous groups to the extent that they are often called upon to provide elaborated explanations by their less able peers" and "high ability students may especially benefit [from homogeneous grouping] without compromising their aspirations or pace of learning to accommodate the lower ability students" (Lou et al., 1996, p. 449).

If the type of grouping for high ability students needs to be varied in relation to instructional objectives, then the classroom structure must facilitate such regrouping. Although the authors did not specifically isolate studies of multi-age classrooms in their analysis, their findings certainly do not detract from the benefits perceived by advocates of multi-age for the simple reason that frequent and flexible groupings are fundamental to the multi-age approach.

Review by Veenman

In 1995, Veenman published a best-evidence synthesis of the cognitive and noncognitive effects of multi-grade (usually combination) classes and multi-age classes in elementary schools. His definition of multi-age was not "nongraded"; rather, in these classes the children maintained their grade identity but spent several years in the same classroom with older and younger classmates. Multi-grade classes are usually formed on a temporary basis, for economic and administrative reasons, whereas multi-age classes are deliberately formed for perceived educational benefits. In his review, Veenman generally excluded studies of nongraded classes on the grounds that nongradedness "involves more than the vertical grouping of students for learning" (p. 325) and implies a whole-school philosophy of education.

Although he excluded studies which specifically focused on "gifted students", Veenman did report studies where some assessment of the students' ability was made. For example, in one study published in 1981 a reported result was that students with high intelligence scores in multi-grade classes performed as well as students with high intelligence scores in single-grade classrooms (ES = +.08).

Unlike other authors, Veenman included information from around the world, including from developing countries. The breadth of his review makes it worth examining in some detail. A wide range of studies was reported, but a description of the conditions operating in the various countries gives the impression that comparisons should be treated with caution. For example:

studies from two African countries included classes with up to 150 students

a study from the USA (Virginia) included the information that more than half the principals had selected their better teachers to teach the multi-grade classes

a study in The Netherlands mentioned that students in the multi-grade classes were not grouped on the basis of similar ability for any of their work

a study in rural Colombian schools compared multi-grade classes where attempts were made to integrate the schools into their communities with traditional classes where little effort was made to differentiate instruction according to the interests and abilities of the students

a study from Pakistan included teachers who were assigned to teach outside their ethnic or linguistic area

another study from the USA (California) included the information that parents had volunteered their children for the multi-grade classes.

These examples alone indicate that, even after careful examination of every study and exclusion of those which do not meet the prespecified criteria (which are usually to do with validity and reliability), a best-evidence synthesis can be fraught with uncertainty. [Veenman himself admitted, in a "reconsideration" (1996) prompted by a critique of his article (Mason & Burns, 1996), that such factors "need the attention of investigators in future research"; p. 323.] An umbrella label such as "multi-grade" can be used to control for obvious organizational features but it will not necessarily lead to comparisons of like with like. What goes on inside the classrooms (and at home) is at least as important as how the classes were formed.

As much as possible, Veenman took note of such differences by categorizing the studies by quality (and calculating effect sizes for each category) and by taking account (in an unspecified way) of differences between developing and Western countries and of location effects (e.g. between urban and rural schools). The results across all categories were quite consistent with respect to achievement (i.e. cognitive effects) of both the multi-grade and the multi-age classroom and led him to conclude that "students in multi-grade classes learn as much as their counterparts in single-grade classes" (1995, p. 350) and "multi-age classes appear to be generally equivalent to single-age classes" (1995, p. 362).

Results for noncognitive effects were similar though effect sizes were slightly higher. In the case of multi-grade classes, they were "so small that they did not translate into higher academic achievement scores" (Veenman, p. 357) but were high enough to suggest "that in affective areas such as attitudes towards school, self-concept, and personal and social adjustment, students are sometimes better off in multi-grade classes than in single-grade classes" (p. 367). Effect sizes for multi-age classes in relation to self-concept and attitudes towards school were higher, suggesting "a small positive effect for students in multi-age classes" (p. 366).

Veenman's results are, on the face of it, less supportive of multi-age classes than those discussed earlier, though he did not look specifically at multi-grade or multi-age from the point of view of their suitability for high ability children and he did not include nongraded examples. The review was interesting because it was broader than previous reviews have been. In this case, however, more was not necessarily better because including studies from countries with widely varying approaches to teaching and learning within the classroom does detract from any conclusions that can be drawn about the relevance of the class organization itself, whether multi-grade, multi-age, single-grade, or single-age. And this point is crucial even when looking at schools which are matched on a wide range of variables. It is unlikely that the way classes are formed will be, by itself, a determining factor in influencing a student's achievement or self-concept. In the case of individual students the class organization may indeed have far-reaching effects—a common claim by proponents of multi-age classes is that the "misfits" are not so obvious and find it easier to be accepted into a class with pronounced and acknowledged diversity. Overall, however, the studies did not provide evidence that multi-age grouping is sufficient to affect either achievement or social-emotional development.

Within each of Veenman's categories there was some disparity amongst the results of individual studies, and the more interesting question becomes one of explaining why some results could give such positive effect sizes for multi-age or multi-grade classes. There is little evidence provided in the studies but it is relatively easy to speculate on reasons why, especially when the conclusions of Slavin, Gutierrez and Slavin, Rogers, and Kulik and Kulik are considered. Recall that, collectively, they concluded that there was a definite advantage to cross-age grouping and that achievement effects were a function of program type. The more successfully a teacher grouped children into homogeneous groups, the more likely was the effect size to be significant. In Veenman's studies there is almost no discussion of how the teachers arranged the children—"most studies provide no information whatsoever on the instructional practices employed in the classroom" (p. 370). It was clear from some studies, however, that teachers of a multi-grade (combination) class were likely to see the children as members of a particular grade and to teach them separately. In this case any potential benefits of a multi-age grouping are lost and it is not surprising that the results did not favor a multi-grade arrangement over a single-grade one. If anything, it is surprising that the effect sizes were not negative, that is, did not favor the single-grade arrangement.

In relation to this last remark, other authors have, in fact, concluded that multi-grade classes do lead to at least small negative effects. In a response to Veenman's review, Mason and Bums (1996) have suggested that the result of "no achievement difference" between multi-grade and single-grade classes is a zero sum result which occurs because positive and negative factors balance each other out. The positive effects result from selection bias in the formation of the classes: "There is considerable evidence that principals, in an effort to reduce the burden on multigrade teachers, place more able, more independent, and more cooperative students in multigrade classes" (p. 311) and "In addition to evidence that principals create favorable class compositions in multigrade classes, there is evidence, though more sketchy, that better teachers are assigned to these classes" (p. 312). The negative effects result from the lower quality of instruction which the authors claim is a feature of multi-grade classes:

> . . . the two curricula that are part and parcel of these classes require more preparation, more grouped instruction, and more teaching time on the part of teachers. With grouped instruction, teachers generally provide less instruction (per grade-level group) and less attention to individual students than in single-grade classes, and they contend with greater classroom management demands. Consequently, teacher stress is exacerbated, and curriculum coverage and adaptive assistance are diminished, with negative outcomes. (Mason & Bums, 1996, pp. 313, 315)

In his rejoinder to Mason and Burns, Veenman summarizes the findings of a reanalysis of the data and claims the results "provide little support for the assumption that the quality of instruction in multigrade classes is lower than in single-grade classes" (1996, p. 323). Significantly, Veenman also emphasized that "the students in the multigrade classes and the students in the single-grade classes did not spend their learning time differently" (p. 324). This comment is tantalizing because it is somewhat at odds with (a) the statement quoted above (from p. 370) about the lack of information on instructional practices employed, and (b) the conclusion offered by Veenman when discussing the between-study analyses in relation to various ways of comparing the studies—such as by country of publication, (sub)urban/rural location, socioeconomic status of the students, number of years students spent in multi-grade classes, and grade levels studied. Veenman states that the "studies concerned with lower grades (K–2) show a small positive effect for multigrade grouping; the effect for intermediate grades (3–4) is essentially zero; and the studies directed at higher grades (5–6) show a small negative effect" (p. 333). What is arresting is not this finding itself, interesting as it is, but Veenman's interpretation of it:

> It can be hypothesized that the intellectual abilities of the students grow further apart as the students enter the higher elementary grades, and that the teachers in single-grade classes can deal with these differences better than teachers in multigrade classes (p. 333).

Both the premise and the conclusion are arresting (and questionable) but what is not arguable, as Veenman recognizes, is that the influence of factors such as grade level of the students (as well as location effects, socioeconomic status, and number of years spent in multi-grade classes) "need the attention of investigators" (p. 323). Until that happens, the conclusion that institutional practices might differ from grade to grade is at least as valid an hypothesis as that of changing intellectual abilities.

The situation with multi-age classes is less clear but almost all the studies reviewed were carried out in America at a time when individualized instruction was in vogue. The lack of significant positive effects for multi-age classes in Veenman's review could be explained by this fact alone, if the findings of Gutierrez and Slavin have validity. In sum, then, although Veenman's review is not proselytizing in its support for a multi-age arrangement, it can nevertheless be interpreted as indirect support for the earlier reviews.

Individual studies continue to be published and the results continue to support multi-age programs, especially nongraded developmentally appropriate programs at the K–3 level (see, e.g., Cantrell, 1994; Shaeffer & Hook, 1996; Tanner & Decotis, 1995). Despite all the problems associated with extrapolating from research studies (see, e.g., Rogers, 1991, p. 25), authors continue to see value in the multi-age concept and to find compelling reasons why effect sizes were not even more favorable.

DISCUSSION

Many authors have expended an enormous amount of effort in conducting meta-analyses of studies related to some form of mixed-age (multi-age or multi-grade) schooling. Some of these reviews have been examined here with particular reference to multi-age classes and high ability students. No author has drawn negative conclusions about the value of a multi-age organization. All have recognized the difficulties of making comparisons when little was known about what went on in the actual classroom. Yet the findings have been remarkably consistent, ranging from (qualified) support to the avuncular statements of Veenman:

> In conclusion, parents, teachers and administrators need not worry about the academic progress or social-emotional adjustment of students in multigrade or multi-age classes. These classes are simply no worse, and simply no better, than single-grade or single-age classes (1995, p. 367).

The question remains as to whether a multi-age arrangement is a neutral option for high ability students or whether it might have real benefits.

There are too many consistently positive studies for the option to be dismissed but the advice that "oversell should be avoided" (Tanner & Decotis, 1995, p. 142) is apposite. The lack of overall negative conclusions for multi-age classes is encouraging in this regard, and the studies which did report conclusions specifically related to high ability students tended to be positive. The following discussion is offered to draw the various threads together.

In view of the earlier reference to "black" and "white" options, "multi-age" should not be seen as a panacea. Any radical reorganization of the structure of schooling is not a practical option without within-school agreement as well as community and government support, financial as well as ideological and/or legislative (see, e.g., Sarason, 1996). But multi-age classes should be seen as one potentially effective option, especially where they are formed as a permanent option and taught by teachers committed to and able to support each other in this form of organization. If such teachers are a subset of the total number in any school and if the school is large enough, then an option is to structure classes into a graded stream and a multi-age stream. If a particular child seemed not to be thriving in the multi-age arrangement, s/he could be moved into the graded stream. The existence of a graded stream and a multi-age stream opens up the number of choices for all stakeholders—teachers, students, and parents. The amount of reorganization required to set up two streams in a school would not, perhaps, be minimal but it would not necessarily be highly stressful either and there would be few, if any, insurmountable resource implications. The existence of choice implies flexibility and less reluctance caused by feelings of "imposition". No teacher should be forced to teach a multi-age class (just as no teacher should be forced to teach a single-grade class).

It is interesting to note here that a recurring complaint by practicing multi-age teachers who air their views on a *listserv* subscribed to by the author [multi-age@mail.connect.more.net] is that single-grade teachers in their schools are hostile to the multi-age teachers, for various reasons but commonly including their perceived amount of parental support. Such problems are perhaps inescapable in a school where conflicting philosophies are openly practiced; nevertheless many schools do exist with only a proportion of the classes structured in a multi-age format.

One school which introduced elements of choice and flexibility by structuring into two streams is the Germantown Friends School in Pennsylvania. Writing in the early 1980s, the Principal of the Lower School discussed the evolution over a ten-year period of the school's present structure, from graded classes to a combination of graded and vertically grouped, so that at every level parents and teachers can choose their preferred option. By increasing the choices available, the school increased its flexibility—children and teachers can be moved to a different structure as and when the need arises. Thus some children progress through their elementary (K–6) schooling entirely in graded classes, some entirely in a "multi-age" setting, and some moving between the two, in both directions, on one or more occasions.

Introducing an element of choice should mean that only teachers with some commitment to or interest in the concept of 'multi-age' would volunteer to teach such a class. (In one state in Australia, Queensland, teachers who apply to the Department of Education for employment in a government school are specifically asked to indicate their willingness or otherwise to teach in a multi-age school. This item was added to the application form following pressure from principals of multi-age schools who had found that employing teachers without a commitment to the multi-age philosophy was an untenable situation.) Under normal circumstances this commitment would suggest either a particular approach to learning, such as a developmentally appropriate approach, or at least an openness to such an approach. This fact alone is enough to explain why many multi-age classes, including here combination classes or multi-grade classes, are so successful. The experience of a school which did introduce multi-age classes is relevant in this regard:

> What became increasingly evident was that introducing multiage classrooms was more than an organizational innovation. It provided an agenda for reconsidering the nature of teaching and learning processes. In a real sense, the organizational change was not really important; what was significant was the fact that it presented new challenges, produced new thinking, and gave an opportunity for putting theory into practice (Maehr & Midgley, 1996, p. 147).

These changes are what Blount (1995) calls genuine restructuring as opposed to mere cosmetic changes.

By extension from this point, a teacher of a multi-age class cannot, by definition, have similar expectations of all the students in the class. Thus a focus on individual differences is more likely in practice rather than simply in theory. Such a focus would imply that the teacher would be much more likely to use small groups in his/her teaching and to form and reform these groups on a regular (and probably frequent) basis.

An approach which was based on frequent regrouping would imply some thought on the teacher's part as to whether a homogeneous or heterogeneous group would be more suitable for the particular activity or desired learning. In a multi-age set-ting, the opportunities for both types of grouping should, on average, increase because of the increased range of development/diversity in the class. A talented child is therefore much more likely to be able to find a classmate who "matches" on some variable or in one of Gardner's intelligences. Although many authors support the claim that full-time ability grouping produces substantial academic gains for high ability students (e.g., Hannon, 1995, p. 13; Rogers, 1991, p. x), there have been many studies which also support heterogeneous grouping, as one part of a flexible arrangement if not as a stand-alone alternative. One Australian study, for example, reported the results of an Academic Enrichment Initiative developed by a consortium of five elementary schools. The Initiative included some ability-grouped activities and some mixed-ability (chronologically grouped) activities, and the advantages of both forms of grouping were confirmed (Varley & Vialle, 1994).

The research literature, in general, suggests that high ability children should spend at least part of every day with their intellectual peers. The probability of being able to provide in this way for such a child may be increased in a multi-age class. There is little chance of an exact match, or of a match across a range of variables, but there is more chance on average of a match in some area than there would be in a same-age class, especially if the high ability child is amongst the youngest.

Although many authors recommend multi-age classes because of their increased options for homogeneous grouping, there are strong arguments for heterogeneous groups as well. A reviewer of doctoral research in 1993 concluded that co-operative learning "is generally useful as a strategy for gifted students to advance their studies" (Geffen, 1993, p. 298) and is viable in both homogeneous and heterogeneous settings provided appropriate learning tasks are the focus. Anderson and Pavan (1993) reviewed the literature on grouping and disagreed that "gifted children . . . are best served in special, separate classes" (p. 25 and passim). All children, no matter how they are classified in terms of intelligence, need to learn to work productively with others (Australian Commission for the Future). The evidence of social/emotional development in a multi-age class, which is anecdotally extremely strong and in the literature suggestive of being strong, would seem intuitively to be of particular relevance to high ability children who often have problems with self-esteem and with feelings of "not fitting in." Again, "flexibility" and "choice" are the watchwords, and a multi-age class provides many opportunities for both types of grouping, and for cognitive as well as affective reasons. When special classes for high ability children are either not feasible or not thought to be desirable, a multi-age class might be a more readily acceptable option.

A multi-age mixed-ability class may also have decided advantages, in relation to self-concept, over a class organized on the grounds of similar ability (Goodlad & Anderson, 1987, pp. xxiii–xxiv). The role of affective experiences in relation to learning has not been studied to the same extent as the role of perceptual and psychomotor development. It has long been known that children will not learn effectively if they are unhappy but research into "emotions" has only recently shed new physiological light on the interplay between emotional regulation and cognitive processes (see, e.g., Blakeslee, 1996; Brunt, 1996; Cytowic, 1995; Goleman, 1995). Vygotsky (1962) and Sacks (1990) have written persuasively of the fundamental importance of social conditions in stimulating learning. One educational psychologist, writing of the importance of the affective domain to good learning experiences, has called for teachers to be more aware of affective taxonomies as well as cognitive ones: "Unless teachers begin to understand this affective domain associated with teaching the gifted, and indeed all children, it will be extremely difficult to establish successful programs that can be said to meet the needs of gifted children" (Smee, 1996, p. 25; see also Brunt, 1996). To the extent that children have a broader social experience in a multi-age class, and to the extent that they feel more contented and have a liking for school, then their cognitive experiences should also be enhanced.

Some studies have focused on affective outcomes, such as on the effect on self-esteem of moving a student from a traditional school to a selective school (i.e. a school where students are offered enrolment on the basis of a competitive examination). The results have not always been encouraging, with many students suffering a loss of self-esteem, and therefore an increase in negative emotions, because of what has been labeled the Big-Fish-Little-Pond Effect (BFLPE); that is, an individual student moves from being a top student to being perhaps only average or below in terms of the immediate context in the selective school (Craven & Marsh, 1994, pp. 13–14; see also Allan, 1991, p. 64). And the effects of being only average have been shown "to have implications for other academic outcomes such as selection of less demanding coursework, lower academic self-concepts, lower grade point averages, and lower educational aspirations" (Craven & Marsh, 1994, p. 13). These results have been observed for students across the spectrum of ability, leading these authors to conclude that

Even though the disadvantages of attending higher-ability schools may not generalize to all higher-ability schools and to all individual students, the results of BFLPE studies demonstrate that it is unjustifiable to assume that attending higher ability schools will necessarily result in any academic advantages (Craven & Marsh, 1994, p. 13).

If affective factors are also felt to be important, then further judgements need to be made about the desirability for any particular student of a permanent, supposedly homogeneous grouping as opposed to an alternative such as a multi-age class.

In addition, the diversity in a multi-age class could prove beneficial to an underachiever. There are many reasons why a child chooses to underachieve in terms of someone else's assessment of potential, but one common reason is inappropriate curriculum. A teacher committed to a multi-age class is more likely to have different expectations of different students and consequently to be less rigid in his/her approach to activities. The freedom to explore in ways which might be different from the ways of others could encourage underachievers to be more motivated.

The existence of multi-age classes in a school, and the individual-centered philosophy that multi-age implies, would mean that a high ability child could move through the curriculum at an appropriate pace. Parents are commonly reported as being happier when their child is one of the younger members of the class (see, e.g., Harkins, 1982; Lloyd, 1996) because of the increased opportunities for stimulation from the older students, even where the teacher is fairly rigid in keeping to grade placement. (A bright child has no trouble keeping one ear on the other grade.) In a multi-age arrangement, when a child has achieved the desired outcomes, say for primary level, s/he can simply move up to the next multi-age class (for an interesting proposal along these lines, see Osin & Lesgold, 1996). Some problems can be foreseen under this arrangement because there must come a time when the child has achieved all the desired outcomes for the particular level of institution. If acceleration to the next level of schooling is not an option, some comfort can be taken from the finding by Gutierrez and Slavin that older children cope better with individualized programs. A good teacher can find many ways to extend and enrich, one of which might be individual research projects which are presented ("taught") to the rest of the class.

CONCLUSION

All the above reasons suggest that a multi-age class could well be a desirable option for any particular high ability child. If the class is formed by choice and the teacher is committed to the concept, it is likely that the sorts of activities which are carried out in the class are different from those in a single-grade class or multi-grade class where the teacher approaches the students as members of a particular grade and with expectations of similarity rather than difference. Commonly, continuous-progress approaches emphasize "individual progress and higher-order thinking skills" (Tanner & Decotis, 1995, p. 141), qualities too often lacking in traditional classrooms. For parents and students who are frustrated with their current options, a multi-age arrangement could prove rewarding. Indeed, with a genuine focus on developmentally appropriate curriculum, why would any parent hesitate?

This conclusion begs the question of whether the multi-age structure is a necessary condition for delivery of developmentally appropriate curriculum or whether a more fruitful approach would be to ensure teachers of single-grade classrooms adopted the practices of good multi-age teachers, such as a focus on diversity/individual differences and continuous progress, differentiated instruction and developmentally appropriate curriculum, curriculum which can be engaged in at different levels of complexity, flexible grouping, and collaborative learning. While there is some evidence from published resources, professional development courses and changes in government mandates that teachers are more aware of the importance of not relying exclusively on whole-class teaching and sameness or equivalence of curriculum delivery and assessment, there is little likelihood that such changes will become widespread quickly enough to be the norm for contemporary students. As well, the mindset of age-related assumptions about development is likely to prove resistant to widespread change. Unless this happens—that is, unless there is a zigzag of lightning speed—multi-age classes are probably more likely to offer the perceived benefits discussed above. There is no guarantee but the odds do seem, on present evidence, to be worth serious consideration.

Chapter 11

Locating Information About Research Reports

with
Suzanne Li
City University of New York/Queens College

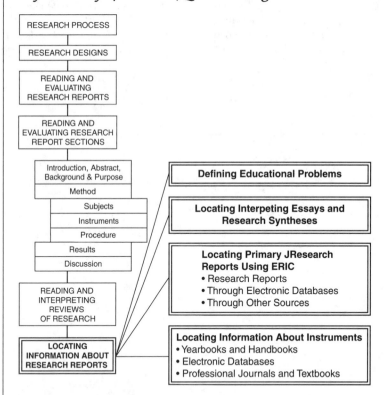

FOCUS QUESTIONS

1. How is an educational problem defined before primary research reports are located?
2. How are research syntheses and essays about research located?
3. How are primary research reports located?
4. Where can information about instruments be located?

To reiterate from Chapter 1, educators, whether they are college or university instructors, school practitioners, administrators, or researchers, are continually making decisions about curriculum, teaching, classroom management, and learning. These decisions are based on their experiences, others' experiences, and their understanding of accumulated knowledge about education. Much of this accumulated knowledge is in the form of research reports and interpretations of research. The sign of a productive profession, such as education, is that its members systematically examine the knowledge base upon which it functions. The chapters in this text are aimed at helping educators examine and interpret research from education, psychology, and related areas in the social sciences.

This chapter provides research consumers with some guidance for locating primary research reports and research syntheses and meta-analyses, as well as evaluations of instruments used in research. Most of the resources for locating these reports, and the reports themselves, can be found in college and university libraries. Some of these resources can be found in public libraries. Research consumers need to know (a) what resources exist for locating reports and reviews of instruments and (b) how to locate research syntheses, primary research reports, and reviews of instruments.

Initially, a research consumer needs to identify an educational question or problem. Then, the consumer must decide what kind of information is required to answer the question. To illustrate, a representative educational question is used here. In the following sections, the question's subject area (or topic) is used with the different kinds of resources available to research consumers.

DEFINING THE EDUCATIONAL PROBLEM

The general subject area to be used for illustration in this chapter of the text is **authentic assessment.** The educational questions are "How is authentic assessment used in elementary and middle schools, grades 1–8, for evaluating students' reading and writing?" and "How does authentic assessment provide for more effective student evaluations in reading and writing?" The first step in answering these questions is to be clear about the definitions of key terms. Precise definitions allow research consumers to pose answerable questions and locate relevant studies. Since the target population is defined—first through eighth graders—a key term remains to be defined, that is, *authentic assessment.*

Possible sources of definitions, in addition to definitions that may appear within primary research articles, are textbooks on the subject, dictionaries of educational terms, and educational encyclopedias. Textbooks can be found through libraries' online catalogs under the appropriate subject heading (i.e., *assessment* or *authentic assessment*). Although textbooks may not be a source of research, their authors often include references to and syntheses of primary studies. For example, a search of one university library's online catalog did not uncover the subject heading *authentic assessment,* but a keyword search did show several books with the term in their titles. Among them were the following:

Tombari, M. L. (1999). *Authentic assessment in the classroom: Applications and practice.* Upper Saddle River, NJ: Merrill.

Collins, M. D., & Moss, B. G. (Eds.) (1996). *Literacy assessment for today's schools: Monograph of the College Reading Association.* Harrisonburg, VA: College Reading Association.

Valencia, S. W., Hiebert, E. H., & Afflerbach, P. P. (Eds.). (1993). *Authentic reading assessment: Practices and possibilities.* Newark, DE: International Reading Association.

In Valencia, Hiebert, and Afflerback (1993), the aim of authentic assessment of reading and writing is "to assess many different kinds of literacy abilities in contexts that closely resemble the actual situations in which those abilities are used" (p. 9). The online catalog showed as subject headings for these books *educational tests and measurements, case studies,* and *portfolios in education.* These subject headings were noted as possible sources of other materials related to the educational question.

Educational and psychological dictionaries, usually found in libraries' reference sections, contain definitions of technical and professional terms used in these fields. Dictionaries that are important to educators are

The Literacy Dictionary: The Vocabulary of Reading and Writing

A Comprehensive Dictionary of Psychological and Psychoanalytic Terms: A Guide to Usage

Dictionary of Education, Third Edition

Dictionary of Multicultural Education

Dictionary of Philosophy and Psychology

Encyclopedic Dictionary of Psychology

International Dictionary of Education

Longman Dictionary of Psychology and Psychiatry

The Concise Dictionary of Education

In *The Literacy Dictionary,* listed previously, the following definition appears:

authentic assessment   A type of assessment that seeks to address widespread concerns about standardized, norm-referenced testing by representing "literacy behavior of the community and workplace" and reflecting "the actual learning and instructional activities of the classroom and out-of-school worlds" (Hiebert et al., 1994), as with the use of portfolios; naturalistic assessment. See also **alternative assessment; assessment.** *Cp.* **classroom-based assessment.** (Harris & Hodges, 1995, p. 15)

Obtaining these definitions and insights from information about authentic assessment, which might be found under headings such as *alternative assessment* and *classroom-based assessment,* is preparatory to seeking summaries and interpretations of the research related to authentic assessment.

LOCATING INTERPRETIVE ESSAYS AND RESEARCH SYNTHESES

Several sources provide interpretive reviews and essays about educational, psychological, and other related social science topics. These sources include the following:

American Educators' Encyclopedia

Encyclopedia of Bilingualism and Bilingual Education

Encyclopedia of Special Education

Handbook of Reading Research, Volumes I, II, III

Handbook of Research on Teaching Literacy Through the Communicative and Visual Arts

Handbook of Research on Teaching the English Language Arts

Handbook of Research on Teaching, Third Edition

Review of Research in Education

The Encyclopedia of Education

The Encyclopedia of Educational Research, Sixth Edition

The International Encyclopedia of Education

The International Encyclopedia of Education: Research and Studies

The International Encyclopedia of Teaching and Teacher Education

A sampling of the indexes of these handbooks and encyclopedias yields references to the following, among other subject headings (the numbers after the entries refer to the volume and pages in the particular encyclopedia):

In *The International Encyclopedia of Education, second edition*, there was no entry for authentic assessment, but there was the following:

Assessment

    criterion-referenced

      see criterion-referenced tests

    early childhood education **1:** 355

    and learning **1:** 370–374

    performance

      and educational assessment **1:** 369

    grading **10:** 5855

    special needs students

      cultural differences **2:** 717

    See also

      Evaluation

      Measurement

      Testing

Portfolio assessment

    and cognitive strategy instruction **2:** 866

    effects on instruction **7:** 3724

Portfolios (background materials) **8:** 4617–4623

    and student evaluation **8:** 4621

In the essay on page 4622, it was indicated that "portfolios are flexible and well-suited for 'authentic' or 'performance' assessment" (*International Encyclopedia of Education*, Vol. 12).

The Encyclopedia of Educational Research, (Sixth Edition) contained the following index entries:

Authentic assessment, in state assessment programs 1262

Portfolio assessment

    in state assessment programs 1262

    of writing 450

Upon referring to the pages noted in the indexes, several interpretive essays are found. In one essay about authentic assessment, it was noted that

> The innovation in state assessment that is currently garnering the most attention goes under several different rubrics, including performance assessment and authentic assessment. These terms subsume a variety of different efforts to substantially expand the tasks students perform beyond multiple-choice and similar (such as short-answer and cloze) formats. (Alkin, 1992, p. 1264)

Each of the interpretive essays contains a bibliography of all references discussed within the essay. These are excellent sources of additional interpretive essays and research syntheses.

The journal *Review of Educational Research* (*RER*) is published quarterly by the American Educational Research Association. It is an excellent source of research syntheses and meta-analyses. Research consumers can locate research syntheses in *RER* through the sources discussed in the next section.

LOCATING PRIMARY RESEARCH REPORTS USING ERIC

Educational, psychological, and other social science journals containing primary research reports are usually located in the periodicals sections of libraries. To locate specific research reports—and, for the discussion here, reports about authentic assessment—research consumers need to use sources that index all journal articles (research and nonresearch) and other relevant documents. The *Current Index to Journals in Education* (*CIJE*) is a monthly print publication with semiannual compilations that indexes and abstracts articles from almost 900 educational journals. To locate primary research reports and other professional materials that are not published in journals, such as federal and state department of education reports, papers presented at conferences, yearbooks, and even some commercially published books, *Resources in Education* (*RIE*) offers the same services as *CIJE*. Most of these documents are unpublished and noncopyrighted materials that would otherwise be hard to find. *CIJE* and *RIE* together make up the **ERIC** (Educational Resources Information Center) database, which is available in print, CD-ROM, and on the Internet. Material is referenced in the ERIC system with an accession, or catalog, number. Each accession number has a prefix. The prefix **EJ** indicates the material is published in a journal. The prefix **ED** indicates the material is a document, i.e., it is either an unpublished paper (e.g., a conference presentation) or material published by a private or public agency (e.g., a government report).

ERIC is a national network supported by the Office of Education Research and Improvement (OERI) of the U.S. Department of Education. The purpose of ERIC is to provide access to current research results and related information in the field of education. It is a decentralized system composed of about 16 clearinghouses, each specializing in a major educational area, as well as additional adjunct clearinghouses. For example, some of the clearinghouses within the ERIC network are Elementary and Early Childhood Education; Disabilities and Gifted Education; Reading, English, and Communication; Science, Mathematics, and Environmental Education; Social Studies/Social Science Education; and Teaching and Teacher Education. Adjunct clearinghouses include Child Care, ESL Literacy Education, School Counseling Services, and Test Collection, among others. The clearinghouses collect, index, abstract, and disseminate information that is available through a central computerized facility. This information appears monthly in *CIJE, RIE,* and ERIC-sponsored Internet Web sites. Most CD-ROM versions of ERIC are updated quarterly.

All formats of the ERIC database, whether print, CD-ROM, or Internet, offer the same information; only the presentation and accessibility vary. ERIC-sponsored Web sites offer direct, free public access to the database, but searching is not as efficient or thorough as with the CD-ROM formats. They are available, however, when a research consumer with a home computer and Internet access cannot get to a library to use the print or CD-ROM formats. They can be accessed at *http://accesseric. org/searchdb/dbchart.html.* E-mail messages and educational questions can be sent to *askeric@askeric.org* if assistance is required. The individual specialized ERIC clearinghouses also respond to educational questions and provide access to the ERIC database. For example, to obtain information about authentic assessment, the ERIC Clearinghouse on Assessment and Evaluation can be accessed at *http://ericae.net.* Various clearinghouses have also developed interactive tutorials to help researchers learn to use ERIC more effectively, such as the one developed by the ERIC Clearinghouse on Higher Education at *http://www.eriche.org/Workshops/searching2. html.* (Note that all Internet Web sites and e-mail addresses are current for Fall of 2000.)

Locating Research Reports

To use any format of ERIC, research consumers refer first to a guide for determining appropriate subject headings. To maintain uniformity of subject listings, the ERIC system publishes a *Thesaurus of ERIC Descriptors*, which is updated periodically. **Descriptors** are keywords used in indexing documents. The *Thesaurus* indicates the subject terms that are used to index a topic. For example, checking the 13th edition of the *Thesaurus*, published in 1995, there is no listing for *authentic assessment*. When the listing for assessment is checked, the following is noted:

Assessment

Use Evaluation

The entry for *evaluation* is shown in Figure 11.1.

The Scope Note (SN) for *evaluation* shows a definition of the term. The Related Terms (RT) list does not include several terms that have appeared in dictionaries and encyclopedias—*alternative assessment, authentic assessment*—because these terms entered educational vocabulary after this printing of the *Thesaurus*. To keep the database current, other terms that are not yet represented as descriptors in the *Thesaurus* are used in the ERIC subject indexes. They are called **identifiers.**

When a specific subject listing is not in the *ERIC Thesaurus,* research consumers can use a researcher's name to locate references in the *CIJE.* For example, the name Linda Darling-Hammond appears several times in the card catalog, encyclopedic essays, and *Education Index (EI).* That name is located in the author index of *CIJE.* The entry for Linda Darling-Hammond in the April 1995 issue is shown in Figure 11.2.

Using the EJ-prefixed accession number appearing after the title, the entry is found in the main entry section. It is shown in Figure 11.3. Note the separate listing of descriptors and identifiers.

The journal article by Darling-Hammond, "Setting Standards for Students: The Case for Authentic Assessment," is listed in the subject index of *CIJE* under all subject headings listed as descriptors and marked with an asterisk. That is, it is found in the subject index under the headings "Student Evaluation" and "Testing Problems." It is also listed under the headings listed as identifiers, which are headings that reflect

EVALUATION *JUL. 1966*
CIJE: 3,559 RIE: 4,720 GC: 820

SCOPE NOTE   A definition ⟶ SN Appraising or judging persons,
of the term.   organizations, or things in relation
                                          to stated objectives, standards, or
                                          criteria (note: use a more specific
                                          term if possible—see also "testing"
                                          and measurement")

USED FOR   The terms ⟶ UF Appraisal
here are not used in ERIC.   NT Course Evaluation
To locate entries, use the   Curriculum Evaluation
subject heading or another   Educational Assessment
term.   Equipment Evaluation
                                         Formative Evaluation
NARROWER TERM   Holistic Evaluation
More specific descriptors   Informal Assessment
that can be used to locate   Institutional Evaluation
entries.   Medical Care Evaluation
                                         Medical Evaluation
                                         Needs Assessment
                                         Peer Evaluation
                                         Personnel Evaluation
                                         Preschool Evaluation
                                         Program Evaluation
                                         Property Appraisal
                                         Psychological Evaluation
                                         Recognition (Achievement)
                                         Self Evaluation (Groups)
                                         Self Evaluation (Individuals)
                                         Student Evaluation
                                         Summative Evaluation
                                         Test Interpretation
                                         Textbook Evaluation
                                         Writing Evaluation

RELATED TERMS   Other ⟶ RT Achievement
descriptors possibly related to   Credentials
entries listed under the   Differences
main descriptor.   Evaluation Criteria
                                         Evaluation Methods
                                         Evaluation Needs
                                         Evaluation Thinking
                                         Evaluators
                                         Expectation
                                         Failure
                                         Inspection
                                         Literary Criticism
                                         Measurement
                                         Measures (Individuals)
                                         Objectives
                                         Observation
                                         Participant Satisfaction
                                         Performance Factors
                                         Quality of Life
                                         Research
                                         Specifications
                                         Standards
                                         Success
                                         Testing
                                         Tests
                                         User Satisfaction (Information)
                                         Validity

Figure 11.1

Sample From the Thesaurus of ERIC Descriptors, *13th edition, 1995, p. 108.*
Published by the Oryx Press. Reprinted with permission.

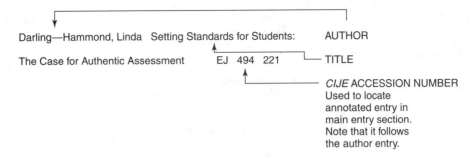

Figure 11.2
Sample CIJE *Author Entry (From* CIJE, *1995).*

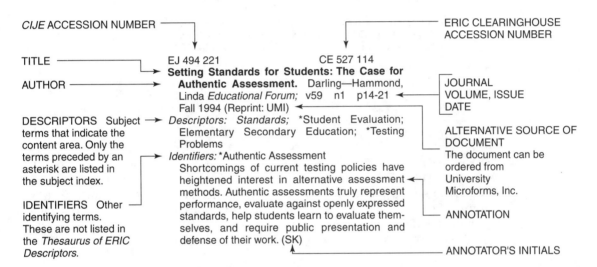

Figure 11.3
Sample CIJE *Document Resume (From* CIJE, *1995). ERIC EJ 494 22.*

terms currently used by researchers and other authors that have not been officially recognized as ERIC descriptors. By going to the subject heading "Authentic Assessment" in the subject index, one finds the entries as shown in Figure 11.4. Note that authors' names are not listed in the subject index.

Each of the entries under "Authentic Assessment" in the *CIJE* subject index can be located in the main entry section. After reading the annotations, the user selects a journal article. The full text of the selected article can be found in the periodicals section of the library or on microfilm in the library's microform section.

Locating an entry in *RIE* is similar to finding one in *CIJE*. That is, both use the same system of descriptors and identifiers, list entries under subject and author indexes, and use a similar accession number system. However, *RIE* accession numbers are prefixed with ED instead of EJ.

After an item listed in *RIE* has been determined to fit the problem area being searched, the full text of the document can usually be found on small sheets of microfilm called **microfiche,** which can be read only on special microfiche readers. ERIC

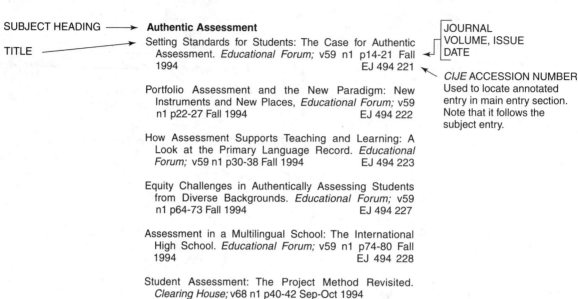

Figure 11.4.
Sample CIJE *Subject Entry (From* CIJE, *1995) ERIC EJ 494 221.*

microfiche collections and microfiche readers can be found in college and university libraries and some public libraries. *RIE* contains information for ordering a document on microfiche or in printed-copy form. In some cases, documents are not available from the ERIC document reproduction service.

The steps for using *RIE* are as follows:

1. Refer to the *Thesaurus of ERIC Descriptors.*
2. Select an appropriate monthly, semiannual, or annual edition of *RIE.*
3. Go to the subject or author index to locate entries and ED accession numbers.
4. Locate abstracts of the entries in the document resume section.
5. Locate the full text of the document in the microfiche collection.

The following is an example of a manual search of the ERIC system using *RIE* for entries related to the problem area *authentic assessment.*

Since the *Thesaurus* has already been examined, the research consumer goes directly to *RIE*. The entries for *authentic assessment* found in the subject index of the January 1995 issue of *RIE* are shown in Figure 11.5.

The first entry, "Authentic Assessment of Self-Concept through Portfolios: Building a Model with Public Schools," with the accession number ED 374 085, is noted. The author entry for this document is shown in Figure 11.6.

The noted research project is located in the document resume section. The entry for ED 374 085 is shown in Figure 11.7. Note the separate listing of descriptors and identifiers.

Since the information in the abstract indicates that this is a study to "investigate the viability of the portfolio model for authentic assessment," the user can tell that

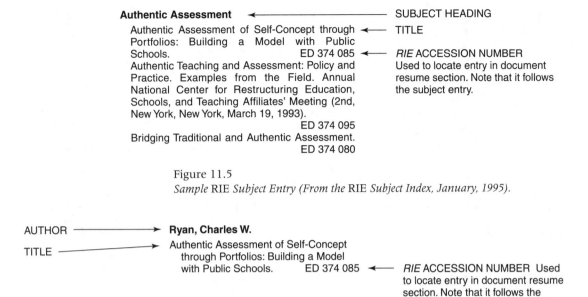

Figure 11.5
Sample RIE *Subject Entry (From the* RIE *Subject Index, January, 1995).*

Figure 11.6
Sample RIE *Author Entry (From the* RIE, *Author Index, January, 1995) ERIC ED 374 085.*

this is a relevant document to his or her purpose and will locate the full text of the document in the library's ERIC microfiche collection.

Locating Research Reports Through Electronic Databases

The ERIC system in electronic format is in two versions: One is found on the Internet; the other is available in libraries on CD-ROMS. Accessing ERIC electronically allows research consumers to search the database more efficiently, since the Internet version and CD-ROMs contain all the terms found in the *Thesaurus of ERIC Descriptors* (see p. 313). By combining terms and modifying preliminary searches, the labor of examining compilations of *RIE* and *CIJE* and cross-referencing is eliminated. Whereas the print format can only be searched one subject at a time, for either journal articles or other documents, the CD-ROM and Internet formats can be searched for either articles or documents or both. Also, searches can include other specifications, such as educational level (early childhood, elementary, secondary, etc.) or publication type (journal articles, research reports, curriculum guides, etc.).

When a subject is not listed in the *ERIC Thesaurus* and no alternate descriptor is suggested, research consumers can use a CD-ROM or Internet version of ERIC to find references in which the term is used in other parts of the ERIC entry, for example, in the title or abstract of the reference. Figure 11.8 contains an example from a search using the *SilverPlatter* ERIC CD-ROM (*SilverPlatter* is the registered trademark of SilverPlatter Information, Inc.). Note that *authentic assessment* appears both as a major identifier and a phrase in the abstract. If the abstract describes the kind of information desired by the research consumer, then one or more of the other descriptors used in

ERIC CLEARING HOUSE ACCESSION NUMBER

RIE ACCESSION NUMBER

AUTHOR

TITLE

DATE PUBLISHED

DESCRIPTIVE NOTE The number of pages in the document and other information.

PUBLICATION TYPE These are broad categories showing the type or organization of the document. The number after the name is the ERIC category code. These are not subject headings.

ERIC DOCUMENT REPRODUCTION SERVICE (EDRS) AVAILABILITY "MF" means microfiche, "PC" means reproduced paper copy. When the listing here says "Document Not Available from EDRS," use the source cited in note.

DESCRIPTORS Subject terms that indicate the content area. Only the terms preceded by an asterisk are listed in the subject index.

IDENTIFIERS Other identifying terms. These are not listed in the *Thesaurus of ERIC Descriptors.*

ABSTRACT

ABSTRACTOR'S INITIALS

ED 374 085   SP 035 353

Ryan, Charles W.

Authentic Assessment of Self-Concept through Portfolios: Building a Model with Public Schools.

Pub Date—94

Note—16p.; Paper presented at the Annual Meeting of the American Association of Colleges for Teacher Education (Chicago, IL, February 16-19, 1994). Printed on colored paper.

Pub Type—Speeches/Meeting Papers (150) —Reports-Research (143)

EDRS Price-MF01/PC01 Plus Postage.

Descriptors—College School Cooperation, Elementary Education, Elementary School Students, Elementary School Teachers, *Evaluation Methods, Evaluation Research Higher Education, Learning Activities, *Portfolios (Background Materials), Public Schools, *Self Concept Measures, *Student Evaluation

Identifiers—*Authentic Assessment, *Reflection Process, Wright State University OH

Teachers commonly use only two types of assessment-written examinations that test basic skills and direct observation of student learning. Both assessment procedures have been the subject of intense criticism. This study was conducted to investigate the viability of the portfolio model for authentic assessment of student growth, to analyze self-concept related teaching activities, and to develop the reflective abilities of students in grades K-6. Data were gathered from three selected public schools and teachers who implemented portfolios as part of a drug education effort. All subject areas were included in the portfolios along with accompanying documentation in the areas of self-concept growth and drug education curriculum activities. Analysis of 40 portfolios revealed that the majority of students' materials included self-concept activities and some drug education information, and that student worksheets showed completion of both drug education and self-concept learning activities. However, findings provided little evidence of student-based reflection on what the portfolio entries meant to them. Student portfolio evaluations are summarized in tabular form. (LL)

Figure 11.7
Sample RIE *Document Resume (From* RIE, *Main Entry Section, 1995). ERIC ED 374 085.*

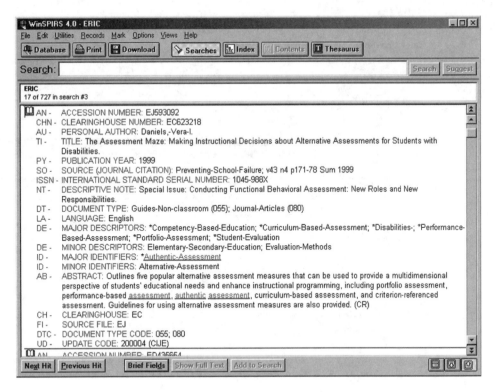

Figure 11.8
SilverPlatter *CD-ROM Entry.*

that record, for example, *portfolio assessment,* might be used in extending the search. (In Figure 11.8, note the "Thesaurus" button in the upper menu bar.)

Using *authentic assessment* and *portfolio-approach,* a cross-referenced search brings up the information shown in Figure 11.9. Notice that *authentic assessment* appears in the title of the first entry, but neither *authentic assessment* nor *portfolio-approach* appear in the second or third. Since those records were identified in the cross-referenced search, the terms will appear elsewhere, most probably in the abstract. To access the abstract, click on the "All Fields" button in the lower menu bar.

The search of the key terms (which include descriptors and identifiers) used in one university's *SilverPlatter* CD-ROM system revealed that *authentic assessment* and *portfolio assessment* had 162 common entries. One of those entries, as follows, was the full text of an *ERIC Digest,* which itself had references to five additional ERIC documents.

ED369075

Theory Meets Practice in Language Arts Assessment. ERIC Digest. Farr, Roger; Tone, Bruce. ERIC Clearinghouse on Reading, English, and Communication, Bloomington, IN, 1994, 3p.

Using *educational research,* one of 86 related terms for "research" in the *ERIC Thesaurus* and *authentic assessment* together showed 12 entries, but only three of these were primary research studies and only one dealt with students in grades 1–8.

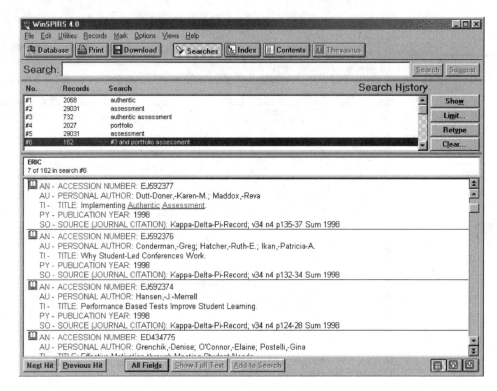

Figure 11.9
Cross-Referenced Search of the SilverPlatter *CD-ROM.*

However, using *portfolio assessment* and *action research* (a related term for "research") together showed a journal article (EJ) as follows:

EJ489228
Literacy Portfolios in Third Grade: A School-College Collaboration. Cirincione, Karen M.; Michael, Denise. *Reading Horizons,* v34 n5 p443–64 Jun 1994

Using *authentic assessment* and *action research* together showed an educational document (ED) as follows:

ED371013
A Qualitative Look at Kentucky's Primary Program: Interim Findings From a Five-Year Study. Aagaard, Lola; and Others. Apr 1994, 31p.; Paper presented at the Annual Meeting of the American Educational Research Association (New Orleans, LA, April 4–8, 1994)

An important detail to note concerns the different way ERIC identification numbers are listed in print and *SilverPlatter* CD-ROM and Internet versions. The six-digit identification number is labeled "accession number" in print and on *SilverPlatter* CD-ROM. In Internet versions, the identification number may be labeled "ERIC No." or "ERIC Identifier."

Remember that ERIC identification numbers, whatever their label, prefixed with ED are documents and usually are available on microfiche. Those prefixed with EJ are articles in journals. (Note that some university and college libraries subscribe to electronic databases containing full-text versions of selected journals. Check with your institution's reference librarian about availability.) Information about "Descriptors" and "Identifiers" is laid out similarly in versions of ERIC.

Locating Research Reports Through Other Sources

There are other, specialized, abstract compilations and indexes (both in print and electronic formats and not connected with the ERIC system) that research consumers might wish to examine for information related to educational problems or questions. Each of these abstract compilations and indexes uses its own format for subject and author indexes; a full explanation of those systems is contained in each. Several that might be of most interest to educators are *Sociological Abstracts, Psychological Abstracts, State Education Journal Index, Business Education Index, Educational Administration Abstracts, Physical Education Index,* and *Child Development Abstracts and Bibliography.*

If a research consumer requires in-depth educational information published prior to 1995, especially in regard to special education issues, *Exceptional Child Education Resources (ECER)* could complement information found in ERIC. *Education Index* is another source useful for earlier research, when it covered some journals that were not indexed in ERIC. (Its current electronic version, *Education Abstracts,* now includes abstracts and some full text articles as well, but still not as many as ERIC.)

Dissertation Abstracts International contains abstracts of doctoral dissertations from about 400 participating universities. It is published monthly in two sections. Section A contains dissertations in the humanities and social sciences, which includes education. Section B covers the science areas, which includes psychology. The dissertations themselves are usually not available, but research consumers should check with reference librarians to see whether copies of selected dissertations are available in the universities' microform sections. The index is arranged alphabetically by keyword and alphabetically by title for keywords. The location of abstracts is indicated by page numbers.

LOCATING INFORMATION ABOUT INSTRUMENTS

Information about instruments' format, content, and administration procedures, together with reliability and validity estimates, can be found in yearbooks, handbooks, and professional journals.

Yearbooks and Handbooks

The major source of information on standardized tests is the *Mental Measurements Yearbooks (MMY).* These have been published since 1938. The most recent are the *Eleventh Mental Measurements Yearbook (11th MMY;* Kramer & Conoley, 1992), the *Supplement to the Eleventh Mental Measurements Yearbook (11th MMY-S;* Conoley & Impara, 1994), the *Twelfth Mental Measurements Yearbook (12th MMY;* Conoley & Impara, 1995), the *Supplement to the Twelfth Mental Measurements Yearbook (12th MMY-S;* Conoley, Impara, & Murphy, 1996), the *Thirteenth Mental Measurements Yearbook (13th MMY;* Impara & Plake, 1998), the *Supplement to the Thirteenth Mental Measurements Yearbook (13th MMY-S;* Plake & Impara, 1999) . They contain reviews of tests and selected bibliographies of related books and journal articles for each instrument.

The purposes of the latest *MMY*s are to provide (a) factual information on all known new or reviewed tests in the English-speaking world, (b) objective test reviews written specifically for the *MMY*s, and (c) comprehensive bibliographies, for specific tests, of related references from published literature. Each volume of the *MMY*s contains information on tests that have been published or significantly revised since a previous edition.

The *11th MMY, 12th MMY,* and *13th MMY* each provide six indexes. The index of titles is an alphabetical listing of test titles. The classified subject index lists tests alphabetically under one or more classification headings, for example, Achievement, Intelligence, Mathematics, Personality, and Reading. This index is of great help to those wishing to locate tests in a particular curriculum area. The publisher's directory and index give the names and addresses of the publishers of all the tests included in the *MMY,* as well as a list of test numbers for each publisher. The index of names includes the names of test developers and test reviewers, as well as authors of related references. The index of acronyms gives full titles for commonly used abbreviations. For example, someone may not know that *DRP* stands for *Degrees of Reading Power.* Each entry also gives the population for which the test is intended. The score index gives the subtest scores and their associated labels for each test. These labels are operational definitions of the tests' variables.

The organization of the *MMY*s is encyclopedic: All the test descriptions and reviews are presented alphabetically by test title. To find a particular test, the reader can go right to it without using any index. All test entries are given index numbers that are used in place of page numbers in the indexes.

Entries for new or significantly revised tests in the tests and reviews section, the main body of the volume, include information such as title, author (developer), publisher, cost, a brief description, a description of groups for whom the test is intended, norming information, validity and reliability data, whether the test is a group or individual test, time requirements, test references, and critical reviews by qualified reviewers. Among other things, the reviews generally cite any special requirements or problems involved in test administration, scoring, or interpretation.

The classified subject index is a quick way to determine whether an instrument is reviewed within a particular volume of *MMY.* For example, in the classified subject index of the *11th MMY* under achievement (p.1079), the following entry (among others) is found:

> **Comprehensive Tests of Basic Skills,** Fourth Edition, grades K.0–K.9, K.6–1.6, 1.0–2.2, 1.6–3.2, 2.6–4.2, 3.6–5.2, 4.6–6.2, 5.6–7.2, 6.6–9.2, 8.6–11.2, 10.6–12.9, *see* 81.

Remember, the 81 means that the description of the *Comprehensive Tests of Basic Skills* is entry 81 in the main body of the volume; it does not mean that it is on page 81. Page numbers are used only for table of contents purposes.

However, the *Degrees of Reading Power* cannot be found under either achievement or reading in the classified subject index of the *10th MMY* or *11th MMY* because it has not been significantly revised since its original publication. It is found under "reading" in the classified subject index of the *12th MMY* as

> **Degrees of Reading Power,** Primary: Grades 1–3; Standard: Grades 3–5, 5–8, 8–12 and over; Advanced: Grades 6–9, 9–12 and over, *see* 101.

A companion source of information about instruments is *Tests in Print* (*TIP*), which contains comprehensive bibliographies of instruments that have been reviewed in *MMY*s. The latest two-volume edition, *TIP V* (Murphy, Conoley, Impara, & Plake, 1999) is structured in the same way as the classified subject index of *MMY*s. Its value comes not from its reviews of instruments, but from its listings of all tests that were in print at the time of publication, the location of test reviews in *MMY*s 1 through 13, and other writings about the instruments.

There are specialized volumes that contain information about instruments in various curriculum areas. These duplicate *MMY* information and reviews; their value comes from having test information for a particular discipline in a single volume. These monographs are as follows:

English Tests and Reviews

Foreign Language Tests and Reviews

Intelligence Tests and Reviews

Mathematics Tests and Reviews

Personality Tests and Reviews

Reading Tests and Reviews

Science Tests and Reviews

Social Studies Tests and Reviews

Vocational Tests and Reviews

Additional specialized sources of test information reviews are as follows:

A Sourcebook for Mental Health Measures

Advances in Psychological Assessment

Assessment in Gifted Children

Assessment Instruments in Bilingual Education

Bilingual Education Resource Guide

CSE Elementary School Test Evaluations

Directory of Unpublished Experimental Mental Measures

Evaluating Classroom Instruction: A Sourcebook of Instruments

Handbook for Measurement and Evaluation in Early Childhood Education

Instruments That Measure Self-Concept

Language Assessment Instruments for Limited English-Speaking Students

Measures for Psychological Assessment: A Guide to 3,000 Sources and Their Applications

Mirrors for Behavior III

Oral Language Tests for Bilingual Students

Preschool Test Descriptions

Psychological Testing and Assessment

Psychological Testing and Assessment of the Mentally Retarded

Reading Tests for Secondary Grades

Review of Tests and Assessments in Early Education

Scales for the Measurement of Attitudes

Screening and Evaluating the Young Child

Socioemotional Measures for Preschool and Kindergarten Children

Sociological Measurement

Tests and Measurements in Child Development

Tests Used With Exceptional Children

Testing Children: A Reference Guide for Effective Clinical and Psychological Assessments

Valuable companions to the *11th MMY, 12th MMY,* and *13th MMY* are *Tests: A Comprehensive Reference for Assessment in Psychology, Education, and Business, Third Edition.* (Sweetland & Geyser, 1991) and *Test Critiques* (Geyser & Sweetland, 1991). These volumes contain listings and critical reviews of instruments by specialty area.

Electronic Databases

Research consumers can also access electronic databases of test collections, test reviews, and test publishers. Each record provides the title, author, publication date, relevant population, subject terms, *ERIC Thesaurus* terms, availability, and a short abstract about the test's content and form. The test review databases provide index information of volume and test review number for reviews in the *MMY*s and *Tests in Print* (TIP; the Buros Test Review Locator), and *Test Critiques* (the Pro-Ed Test Review Locator).

The ERIC Clearinghouse on Assessment and Evaluation with its Test Locator hyperlink can be accessed through the Internet at *http://ericae.net.*

Some academic libraries also provide CD-ROM versions of the recent *MMY*s that offer much easier searching and full text of the test reviews. Figure 11.10 shows the result of a search for the *Degrees of Reading Power* test. By typing "tn = test name" in the search box, basic information for the test appears. Clicking on the menu choice "Show Full Text" on the bottom menu bar brings up the full text available in the print version of the *MMY,* as shown in Figure 11.11. The menu frame on the left of the figure shows the range of information about the test available on the CD-ROM.

Professional Journals and Textbooks

A number of professional journals and textbooks contain information and reviews of instruments. Journals such as the *Journal of Educational Measurement, Journal of Reading,* and *The Reading Teacher* regularly contain reviews of new and revised instruments. Other journals published by professional associations often contain information about newly published instruments.

Several professional textbooks dealing with educational assessment and evaluation contain information and critiques about various types of instruments. Although the title suggests that the book is intended only for special education, the following textbook is an excellent reference about instruments commonly used in research for measuring academic school performance, learning attributes, classroom behavior, academic areas, and career and vocational interests:

McLoughlin, J. A., & Lewis, R. B. (2001). *Assessing students with special needs* (5th ed.). Upper Saddle River, NJ: Prentice-Hall/Merrill.

Figure 11.10
Result of Search of CD-ROM Version of MMY.

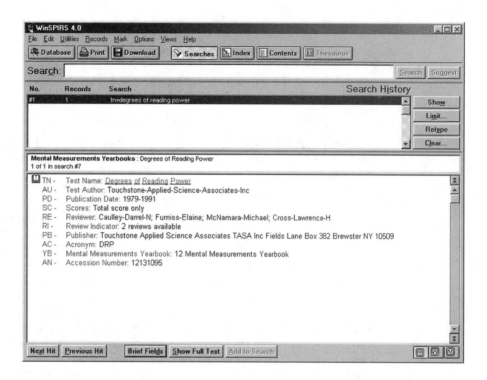

Figure 11.11
Full-Text CD-ROM Information.

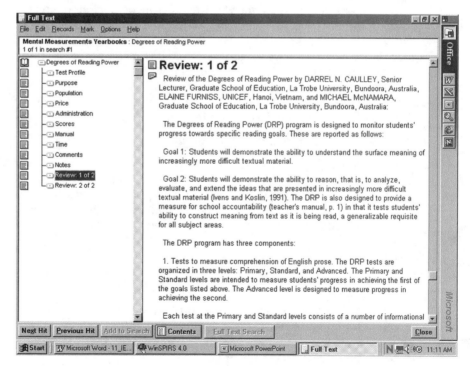

SUMMARY

How is an educational problem defined before primary research reports are located?

After considering an educational problem, research consumers should refer to educational dictionaries for specific technical definitions.

How are syntheses of research and essays about research located?

Research consumers can locate an educational question in educational encyclopedias and journals specializing in only research syntheses, integrative reviews, and meta-analyses.

How are primary research reports located?

Primary research reports are published in journals or issued by federal, state, and other organizations. They can be located through the print and electronic versions of the ERIC database, which supplies record items for journal articles containing the article's title, the author's name, the journal's title and volume number, the article's number of pages, the date of publication, document type, and a brief annotation of the contents. Similar information is supplied for nonjournal reports. Using ERIC necessitates several steps: (1) referring to the *Thesaurus of ERIC Descriptors*, (2) combining appropriate subject terms, educational level, and document type, (3) determining whether the ERIC record refers to a journal article (EJ accession number) or other document (ED accession number). The journals containing the selected articles are then located with the library's online catalog. Most of the other documents can be located in the library's ERIC microfiche document collection using the ED accession numbers. A companion ERIC resource, *Exceptional Child Education Resources (ECER)* and *Education Index* can be used to complement searches in ERIC for older research. Other abstracts produced by specialty areas and for doctoral dissertations in education can also be examined.

These databases can be accessed electronically through CD-ROM formats or by personal computer through the Internet. Electronic access lets the consumer search the databases by using multiple search terms.

Where can information about instruments be located?

Research consumers can find descriptive information and critical reviews about instruments in yearbooks, handbooks, professional journals, and textbooks. The major sources of this information are the *Mental Measurements Yearbooks*, available in print and sometimes CD-ROM. Searching ERIC can locate information published later than the most currently available *MMY*.

ACTIVITIES

Activity 1.
Using either the CD-ROM or print versions of the *Mental Measurements Yearbook* and one or more other sources discussed in the section "Locating Information About Instruments," determine the appropriateness of the following instruments for the indicated research purposes.

   a.   *Slosson Intelligence Test for Children and Adults, Revised, 1991 edition,* ages 4–0 and over

Research purpose: To identify the learning potential and establish profiles of learning strengths and weaknesses for students with limited English proficiency.

b. *Test of Early Language Development, second edition,* 1991, ages 2–0 to 7–11
Research purpose: To compare the language proficiency of primary-grade students with and without language disabilities and to determine the relationship between their language proficiency and beginning reading achievement.

c. *Family Environment Scale, second edition,* family members
Research purpose: To determine family characteristics that might contribute to children's success in kindergarten and first grade.

Activity 2

a. Select an education topic related to your teaching situation and locate (a) the definition of at least one key term in an educational dictionary; (b) one interpretive essay or synthesis of research; (c) one primary research report in an educational, psychological, or other social science journal; and (d) one primary research report reproduced on microfiche in the ERIC system, or one downloaded and printed from an ERIC clearinghouse Web site, if available.

b. Using the questions and criteria for evaluating primary research reports, research syntheses, or meta-analyses presented in this text (Chapters 3–10), evaluate the selected essays, reviews, and reports.

FEEDBACK

Activity 1

a. Cultural minorities were significantly underrepresented in the sample of the norming group for the revised Slosson Intelligence Test. Therefore, it might not be appropriate to use the test in a study with individuals with limited English proficiency.

b. The Test of Early Language Development, or TELD-2, was developed for use with normal students, but with certain adjustments in administering and establishing separate forms, the test might be used with special populations. Since it does not contain any reading sections, it might be used in a correlational study with a reading test. However, there is some question about the procedures used to obtain the norming sample and the validity of the test results when used with students with mild language impairments. So, the test should be used with caution.

c. The Family Environment Scale (FES) is a norm-referenced instrument with fixed responses. If, in the study, researchers used quantitative research procedures, the instrument might be appropriate. The instrument seems to have appropriate content validity. Whether the FES has construct validity for the study could be determined by checking the study's sample against the norming group used for the test. FES might not be appropriate to use in a study with qualitative research procedures.

Activity 2

Feedback will be provided by your course instructor.

Appendix A

Glossary

abstract A summary of a research report.

accessible population A group that is convenient to the researchers and representative of the target population. Practical considerations that lead to the use of an accessible population include time, money, and physical accessibility.

action research Research directed to studying existing educational practice and to producing practical, immediately applicable findings. The questions or problems studied are local in nature (e.g., a specific class) and generalizability to other educational situations is not important to the researchers. Often action research is a collaboration between classroom teachers without research expertise and trained researchers.

action research review A review of research produced for local consumption.

analysis of covariance (ANCOVA) A statistical procedure based on analysis of variance (ANOVA) allowing researchers to examine the means of groups of subjects as if they were equal from the start. They do this by adjusting the differences in the means to make the means hypothetically equal.

analysis of variance (ANOVA) A statistical procedure used to show differences among the means of two or more groups of subjects or two or more variables. It is reported in F ratios. The advantage in using an ANOVA is that several variables as well as several factors can be examined. In its simplest form, ANOVA can be thought of as a multiple t test.

authentic assessment Assessment of students' work and the products of their learning by comparing their performance and products (e.g., oral reading, writing samples, art or other creative output, and curriculum-related projects) to specified levels of performance. The materials and instruction used are true representations of students' actual learning and their activities in the classroom and out-of-school worlds. (See *criterion-referenced tests.*)

background section The section of the research report that contains (a) an explanation of the researchers' problem area, (b) its educational

importance, (c) summaries of other researchers' results that are related to the problem (called a *literature review*), and (d) strengths from the related research that were used and weaknesses or limitations that were changed.

baseline measure The pretest in single-subject research; it can take the form of one or several measurements. It is the result to which the posttest result is compared to determine the effect of each treatment.

best evidence A concept by which research consumers can select and review studies for inclusion in research reviews only if they are specifically related to the topic, are methodologically adequate, and are generalizable to a specific situation.

case study A form of single-subject research, undertaken on the premise that someone who is typical of a target population can be located and studied. In case studies, the individual's (a) history within an educational setting can be traced, (b) growth pattern(s) over time can be shown, (c) functioning in one or more situations can be examined, and (d) response(s) to one or more treatments can be measured.

causal-comparative research Research that seeks to establish causation based on preexisting independent variables. Researchers do not induce differences in an experimental situation; instead they seek to identify one or more preexisting conditions (independent variables) in one group that exist to a lesser degree in the other. When one or more conditions are identified, they can attribute causality. (Also called *ex post facto research.*)

causative research See *experimental research.*

central tendency, measure of The middle or average score in a group of scores. The middle score is called the *median;* the arithmetic average score is called the *mean.* The most common score is called the *mode.*

chi-square test A nonparametric statistic used to test the significance of group differences between observed and expected outcomes when data are reported as frequencies or percentages of a total or as nominal scales.

cluster sampling   The procedure by which intact groups are selected because of convenience or accessibility. This procedure is especially common in *causal-comparative research.*

comparative research   Research that seeks to provide an explanation about the extent of the relationship between two or more variables or examines differences or relationships among several variables. These variables might represent characteristics of the same group of subjects or those of separate groups.

concurrent validity   The extent to which the results show that subjects' scores correlate, or are similar, on two instruments administered during the same time period.

construct validity   The quality obtained when an instrument's creator demonstrates the instrument as representing a supportable theory.

content validity   The quality obtained when an instrument's creator demonstrates that the specific items or questions used in the instrument represent an accurate sampling of specific bodies of knowledge (i.e., curricula or courses of study).

control   Use of procedures by researchers to limit or account for the possible influence of variables not being studied.

control group   The group of subjects in experimental research not receiving the experimental condition or treatment (sometimes called the *comparison group*).

correlation   A measure of the extent to which two or more variables have a systematic relationship. (See *product-moment correlation*.)

correlation of coefficient   The result of an arithmetic computation done as part of a product-moment correlation. It is expressed as *r,* a decimal between -1.0 and $+1.0$. (See *product-moment correlation* and *Pearson product-moment correlation.*)

counterbalanced design   The research design in which two or more groups get the same treatment; however, the order of the treatments for each group is different and is usually randomly determined. For this type of design to work, the number of treatments and groups must match. Although the groups may be randomly selected and assigned, researchers often use this design with already existing groups of subjects, such as all classes in a grade level.

criterion-referenced test   An instrument that measures students' performances in terms of expected learner behaviors or to specified expected levels of performance. Scores show students' abilities and performances in relation to sets of goals or to what students are able to do. They do not show subjects' rankings compared with others, as norm-referenced tests do. A *standardized criterion-referenced test* is one for which the administration and scoring procedures are uniform but the scoring is in relation to the established goals, not to a norm group. (See *authentic assessment*.)

cross-validation   The procedure in which researchers investigate using the same purpose, method, and data analysis procedure but use subjects from a different population.

data   The information obtained through the use of instruments.

degrees of freedom   The number of ways data can vary in a statistical problem.

dependent variable   The variable researchers make the acted-upon variable. It is the variable whose value may change as the result of the experimental treatment (the *independent variable*).

derived scores   Test scores that are converted from raw scores into other scores, such as grade equivalents, normal curve equivalents, percentiles, or stanines.

descriptive research   Research that seeks to provide information about one or more variables. It is used to answer the question "What exists?" This question can be answered in one of two ways: using *quantitative methods* or *qualitative methods.*

descriptors   Key words found in the *Thesaurus of ERIC Descriptors* and used in such indexing documents as *Resources in Education* and *Current Index to Journals in Education.*

direct observation   The research procedure in which researchers take extensive field notes or use observation forms to record information. They categorize information on forms in response to questions about subjects' actions or categories of actions. Or, they tally subjects' actions within some predetermined categories during a time period.

directional hypothesis   A statement of the specific way one variable will affect another variable when previous research evidence supports it (also called a *one-tailed hypothesis*).

discussion section   A section of the research report that contains the researchers' ideas about the educational implications of the research results (also called *conclusions section*).

effect   The influence of one variable on another.

effect size   An indication of the magnitude (meaningfulness or importance) of statistical results by providing a measure in relation to the standard deviation of the data gathering instrument. Effect size is commonly reported as a decimal fraction of the standard deviation. In meta-analyses, it is shown as a ratio derived from the combined mean scores of the experimental and control groups and the standard deviations of the control groups. It shows the size of the difference between the mean scores of the experimental and control groups in relation to the standard deviations.

equivalent forms reliability Reliability determined by correlating the scores from two forms of an instrument given to the same subjects. The instruments differ only in the specific nature of the items. (Sometimes called *parallel forms reliability*.)

ERIC or Educational Resources Information Center A national network supported by the Office of Education Research and Improvement of the U.S. Department of Education. Its purpose is to provide access to current research results and related information in the field of education. It is a decentralized system composed of about 16 clearinghouses, each specializing in a major educational area.

ethnographic research A term often used synonymously with *qualitative research,* although some researchers consider ethnography a subtype of qualitative research.

evaluation research The application of the rigors of research to the judging of the worth or value of educational programs, projects, and instruction. It extends the principle of action research, which is primarily of local interest, so that generalizations may be made to other educational situations. And, although undertaken for different reasons than is experimental research, the quantitative research method used in evaluation research is based on that of experimental research.

experimental condition The condition whereby the independent variable is manipulated, varied, or subcategorized by the researcher in experimental research. (Also called *treatment*.)

experimental group The group of subjects in experimental research receiving the experimental condition or treatment.

experimental research Research that seeks to answer questions about causation. Researchers wish to attribute the change in one variable to the effect of one or more other variables. The variables causing changes in subjects' responses or performance are the *independent variables*. The variables whose measurements may change are the *dependent variables*. The measurements can be made with any instrument type: survey, test, or observation.

external validity Validity based on researchers' assurance that results can be generalized to other persons and other settings.

extraneous variables Variables that might have an unwanted influence on, or might change, the dependent variable. Researchers can restrict the influence of extraneous variables by controlling subject variables and situational variables.

F ratio The way in which analysis of variance (ANOVA) and analysis of covariance (ANCOVA) are reported.

face validity The extent to which an instrument *appears* to measure a specific body of information. In other words, "Does the instrument look as if it would measure what it intends to measure?"

factorial designs Research designs in which there are multiple variables and each is subcategorized into two or more levels, or factors. The simplest factorial design involves two independent variables, each of which has two factors. This is called a 2×2 factorial design. Factorial designs can have any combination of variables and factors.

field notes Written narratives describing subjects' behaviors or performances during an instructional activity. These notes are then analyzed and the information categorized for reporting. The analysis can start with predetermined categories, and information from the notes is recorded accordingly. Or, the analysis can be open-ended in that the researchers cluster similar information and then create a label for each cluster.

fieldwork The collection of data during qualitative studies in particular educational settings.

generalizability The ability of results to be extended to other students or the target population. That means a research consumer in a different place can have confidence in applying the research producers' results.

hypothesis A tentative statement about how two or more variables are related. A hypothesis is the researchers' conjectural statement of the relationship between the research variables and is created after the investigators have examined the related literature but before they undertake their study. It is a tentative explanation for certain behaviors, phenomena, or events that have occurred or will occur. It can be either directional or nondirectional.

identifiers Key words used in indexing documents that are not yet represented as descriptors in the ERIC *Thesaurus of ERIC Descriptors.*

independent variable The influencing variable in experimental research, the one to which researchers wish to attribute causation. (Sometimes called the *experimental variable*.) When the independent variable is an activity of the researcher, it is called a treatment variable.

instruments A broad range of specific devices and procedures for collecting, sorting, and categorizing information about subjects and research questions.

instruments section   A subsection of the method section of a research report, containing a description of the data collection instruments: observation forms, standardized and researcher-made tests, and surveys.

integrative review of research   See *research synthesis.*

interaction effect   The effect in experimental studies of two or more variables acting together. Interactions are expressed as *F* ratios within ANOVA or ANCOVA tables and can be shown in a graph.

internal consistency reliability   Reliability determined by statistically comparing the subjects' scores on individual items with their scores on each of the other items and with their scores on the instrument as a whole. (Sometimes called *rationale equivalence reliability.*)

internal validity   Validity based on researchers' assurance that changes to dependent variables can be attributed to independent variables.

interrater/interjudge reliability.   See *scorer reliability.*

interval scale   The statistical form presenting data according to preset, equal spans and identified by continuous measurement scales: raw scores and derived scores such as IQ scores, percentiles, stanines, standard scores, and normal curve equivalents. It is the most common form of data reporting in educational and social science research and is the way data from most tests are recorded.

interview   An instrument used to obtain structured or open-ended responses from subjects. It differs from a questionnaire in that the researcher can modify the data-collection situation to fit the respondent's responses.

inventory   A questionnaire that requires subjects to respond to statements, questions, or category labels with a "yes" or "no" or asks subjects to check off appropriate information within a category.

Likert-type scale   A scale that uses forced choices of response to statements or questions; for example, "Always," "Sometimes," or "Never." Each response is assigned a value; a value of 1 represents the least positive response.

literature review   A subsection of the background section of a research report, containing summaries of related research; in it, researchers indicate strengths from the related research that were used in their study and weaknesses or limitations that were changed.

matched groups design   The research design in which the experimental and control groups are selected or assigned to groups on the basis of a single-subject variable, such as reading ability, grade level, ethnicity, or special disabling condition.

mean   The arithmetical average score.

median   The middle score in a group of scores.

meta-analysis   A critical examination of primary research studies in which quantitative data analyses were used. Research reviewers use meta-analysis as "analysis of analyses" (statistical data analysis of already completed statistical data analyses). In them, the reviewers convert the statistical results of the individual studies into a common measurement so they can obtain an overall, combined result.

method section   The section of the research report usually composed of three subsections: *subjects, instruments,* and *procedure.*

microfiche   Small sheets of microfilm containing images of documents that can be read only on special microfiche readers.

mode   The most frequent (common) score in a distribution of scores.

multiple correlation   A statistical technique used to examine the relationships among more than two variables. The procedure is interpreted similarly to a single correlation coefficient. It can also be used to make predictions. The technique is used frequently in causal-comparative experimental research. (Also called *multiple regression.*)

nominal scale   The statistical form reporting as numbers of items or as percentages of a total. Data from surveys and observations are often recorded in this way.

nondirectional hypothesis   A statement used when researchers have strong evidence from examining previous research that a relationship or influence exists but the evidence does not provide indications about the direction (positive or negative) of the influence.

nonequivalent control group design   The research design in which the groups are not randomly selected or assigned, and no effort is made to equate them statistically.

nonparametric statistics   Statistical procedures used with data that are measured in nominal and ordinal scales. These statistics work on different assumptions than do parametric statistics and are used for populations that do not have the characteristics of the normal distribution curve.

norm   See *normal distribution curve.*

norm-referenced test   An instrument that measures an individual's performance compared with a standardization, or *norming*, group.

normal curve equivalent (NCE)   A normalized standard score with a mean of 50 and a standard deviation of 21.06. NCEs of 1 and 99 are equivalent to percentiles 1 and 99.

normal distribution   A distribution of scores or other measures that in graphic form present a distinct bell-shaped appearance. In a normal distribution, the measures are distributed symetrically around the mean. In a normal distribution, the mean, median, and mode are identical.

norming group   The individuals used in researching the standardization of the administration and scoring of norm-referenced tests.

one-tailed hypothesis   See *directional hypothesis.*

operational definition   A definition of a variable that gives the precise way an occurrence of that variable is viewed by researchers.

ordinal scale   The statistical form showing the order, from highest to lowest, for a variable ranking. There is no indication as to the value or size of differences between or among items in a list; the indication is only to the relative order of the scores.

parallel forms reliability   See *equivalent forms reliability.*

parametric statistics   Statistical procedures used with data measured in interval scales and based on certain assumptions, all of which are related to the concept of a normal distribution curve.

participant observer   A qualitative researcher who goes to the particular setting being studied and participates in the activities of the people in that setting. Researchers functioning in this role try to maintain a middle position on a continuum of complete independence as an observer to complete involvement in the people's activities.

Pearson product-moment correlation   The most common correlation coefficient. (See *product-moment correlation* and *correlation coefficient.*)

pilot study   A limited research project, usually with a few subjects, that follows the original research plan in every respect. By analyzing the results, research producers can identify potential problems.

population   A group of individuals having at least one characteristic that distinguishes them from other groups. A population can be any size and can include people from any place in the world.

posttest   The second and subsequent measurements after a pretest.

posttest-only control group design   The research design in which the experimental and control groups are not pretested. An example of this design is two or more randomized groups being engaged in comparison activities without being given a pretest.

practical significance   A determination about how useful research results are. To determine this, research consumers need to answer: How effectively can the results be used in my teaching situation?

predictive validity   The extent to which an instrument can predict a target population's performance after some future situation. It is determined by comparing a sample's results on the instrument to their results after some other activity.

pretest   The test given to the subjects to collect initial, or baseline, data.

pretest-posttest control group design   The research design in which all groups are given the same pretest and posttest (survey, observation, or test).

procedure section   A subsection of the method section of a research report, containing a detailed explanation of how the researchers conducted their study.

product-moment correlation   Refers to the quantified relationship between two sets of scores for the same group of subjects. The result of the arithmetic computation is a *correlation coefficient,* which is expressed as *r,* a decimal between −1.0 and +1.0. The most common interval scale correlation coefficient is the Pearson product-moment correlation. Correlations show whether two or more variables have a systematic relationship of occurrence—that is, whether high scores for one variable occur with high scores of another (a positive relationship) or whether they occur with low scores of that other variable (a negative relationship). The occurrence of low scores for one variable with low scores for another is also an example of a positive relationship. A correlation coefficient of zero indicates that the two variables have no relationship with each other, that is, are independent of each other.

purpose section   The section of the research report that contains the specific goal or goals of the research project. A goal may be expressed as a statement of purpose, a question, or a hypothesis.

qualitative research   Research using a broad range of strategies that have roots in the field research of anthropology and sociology. It involves collecting data within natural settings, and the key data collection instruments are the researchers themselves. Qualitative research data are verbal, not numerical. Since qualitative researchers are equally concerned with the process of activities and events as they are with results from those activities or events, they analyze data through inductive reasoning rather than by statistical procedures.

quantitative research   Research using procedures involving the assignment of numerical values to variables. The most common quantitative descriptive measures researchers use are the *mean* (a measure of central tendency) and the *standard deviation* (a measure of the variability of the data around the mean).

questionnaire   An instrument which necessitates the respondent either writing or orally providing answers to questions about a topic. The answer form may be structured in that there are fixed choices, or the form may be open-ended in that respondents can use their own words. Fixed-choice questionnaires may be called *inventories.*

random sampling   Based on the principle of randomization, whereby all members of the target population have an equal chance of being selected for the sample. The subjects that are finally selected should reflect the distribution of relevant variables found in the target population.

randomization   An unbiased, systematic selection or assignment of subjects. When randomization is used, researchers assume that all members of the target population have an equal chance of being selected for the sample and that most human characteristics are evenly distributed among the groups.

ratio scale   The statistical form showing relative relationships among scores, such as half-as-large or three-times-as-tall. In dealing with educational variables, researchers do not have much use for these scales.

rationale equivalence reliability   See *internal consistency reliability.*

research synthesis   A critical examination of research producers' methods and conclusions in primary studies and of the generalizability of their combined findings. Also referred to as *integrative review of research* and *research integration.*

reference section   The section of the research report that contains an alphabetical listing of the books, journal articles, other research reports, instructional materials, and instruments cited in the report.

reliability   The extent to which tests scores are consistent; that is, the degree to which the test scores are dependable or relatively free from random errors of measurement. Reliability is usually expressed in the form of a reliability coefficient. Or, it is expressed as the standard error of measurement derived from the reliability coefficient. The higher the reliability coefficient, the better. A test (or set of test scores) with a reliability of 1.00 would have a standard error measurement of 0 and thus it would be perfectly reliable. The reliability coefficient (usually expressed as *r*) can range from .00 to 1.00.

reliability coefficient   The number expressing an instrument's reliability, expressed in decimal form, ranging from .00 to 1.00. The higher the coefficient, the higher the instrument's reliability.

replication   The procedure in which researchers repeat an investigation of a previous study's purpose, question, or hypothesis.

representative   The quality of a sample in which the researchers' results are generalizable from the sample to the target population.

research   A process of systematically collecting information about an identified problem or question, analyzing the data, and, on the basis of the evidence, confirming or refuting a prior prediction or statement.

research design   The structure for researchers' methods of answering research questions and conducting studies. Three basic research designs are descriptive, comparative, and causative or experimental.

research report   A summary of researchers' activities and findings.

results section   The section of the research report that contains the results of the researchers' data analyses; it contains not only the numerical results (often presented in tables and charts) but an explanation of the significance of those results.

sample   A representative group of subjects; it is a miniature target population. Ideally, the sample has the same distribution of relevant variables as found in the target population.

sampling error   Any mismatch between the sample and the target population.

scales   Methods of measurement that measure variables related to attitudes, interests, and personality and social adjustment. Usually, data are quantified in predetermined categories representing the degree or intensity of the subjects' responses to each of the statements or questions. Unlike data from tests, which are measured in continuous measurements (e.g., stanines 1 through 9, or percentiles 1 through 99), data from scales are discrete measurements, forcing respondents to indicate their level of reaction; common forced choices are "Always," "Sometimes," or "Never." This type of data quantification is called a *Likert-type scale.*

scorer or rater reliability   Reliability determined by comparing the results of two or more scorers, raters, or judges. Sometimes presented as a percentage of agreement or as a coefficient. (Sometimes called *interrater* or *interjudge reliability.*)

simple experimental design   An experimental design with one independent variable or using a subject selection procedure that limits the generalizability of its results. (See *experimental research.*)

single-subject research   Any research in which there is only one subject or one group that is treated as a single entity (e.g., when an entire school is studied without regard to individual students' performances). Single-subject research may be descriptive or experimental. *Case study* is a form of single-subject research.

situational variable   A variable related to the experimental condition (i.e., a variable outside the subjects) that might cause changes in their responses relating to the dependent variable.

Solomon four-group design The research design in which four groups are formed using random selection and random assignment. All four groups are posttested, but only two groups are pretested. One pretested group and one nonpretested group are then given the experimental condition.

split-half reliability A form of *internal consistency reliability* determined by dividing the instrument in half and statistically comparing the subjects' results on both parts. The most common way to split a test is into odd- and even-numbered items.

standard deviation A measure of the variability of the data around the mean. It is based on the normal curve. It shows how scores were distributed around the mean. It is the way variability is usually reported.

standardized test An instrument that has been experimentally constructed. The test constructor uses accepted procedures and researches the test's (a) content, (b) procedures for administering, (c) system for recording and scoring answers, and (d) method of turning the results into a usable form. A standardized test is one for which the methods of administering, recording, scoring, and interpreting have been made uniform. Everything about the test has been standardized so that if all its directions are correctly followed, the results can be interpreted in the same manner, regardless of where in the country the test was given.

statistical regression The tendency of extreme high and low standardized test scores to move toward the group arithmetic mean.

statistical significance The probability of results being caused by something other than mere chance; this occurs when the difference between the means of two sets of results exceeds a predetermined chance level. When results are significant, researchers know how confident they can be about the conclusions they may make from their findings.

statistics Numerical ways to describe, analyze, summarize, and interpret data in a manner that conserves time and space. Researchers select statistical procedures after they have determined what research design and types of data will be appropriate for answering their research question.

stratified random sample A sample whose subjects are randomly selected by relevant variables in the same proportion as those variables appear in the target population.

subject variable A variable on which humans are naturally different and that might influence their responses in regard to the dependent variable.

subjects The particular individuals or objects used in the research.

subjects section A subsection of the method section of a research report, containing a description of the individuals or objects used in the study. The section gives general information about age, sex, grade level, intellectual and academic abilities, socioeconomic level, and so on. It also contains the number of subjects and an account of how the subjects were selected and assigned to groups.

***t* test** A statistical procedure used when there are two sets of scores to determine whether the difference between the means of the two sets of scores is significant. It is reported as numbers such as $t = 1.6$ or $t = 3.1$. After determining the value of t, researchers consult a statistical table to determine whether the value is a significant one.

target population The specific group to which the researchers would like to apply their findings. It is from the target population that the researchers select the sample, which become the subjects of their study.

test-retest reliability Reliability as determined by administering the same instrument again to the same subjects after a time period has elapsed (also referred to as *test stability*).

treatment See *experimental condition* and *independent variable*.

triangulation A procedure of collecting information from several different sources about the same event or behavior; it is used in qualitative research for cross-validating information.

two-tailed hypothesis See *nondirectional hypothesis*.

validity The extent to which an instrument measures what it is intended to measure. (See *concurrent validity, construct validity, content validity, external validity, face validity, internal validity,* and *predictive validity*).

validity generalization The procedure in which researchers use the same purpose, method, and data analysis procedure, but they use subjects from a unique population.

variability The extent to which scores cluster about the mean. The variability of a normal distribution is usually reported as the *standard deviation (SD)*.

variable Anything in a research situation that varies and can be measured. It can be human characteristics (of students or teachers) or it can be characteristics of classrooms, groups, schools and school districts, instructional materials, and so on.

volunteer subjects Different by nature from nonvolunteers because of some inherent motivational factor. Results from the use of volunteer subjects might not be directly generalizable to the target population containing seemingly similar, but nonvolunteer, individuals or groups.

Appendix B

Research Reports and Reviews for Analysis

Darch, C., Soobang, K., Johnson, S., & James, H. (2000). The strategic spelling skills of students with learning disabilities: The results of two studies. *Journal of Instructional Psychology, 27*(1), 15–27.

The Strategic Spelling Skills of Students With Learning Disabilities: The Results of Two Studies

Craig Darch

Soobang Kim

Auburn University, AL

Susan Johnson

Columbus State University, AL

Hollis James

Tuskegee University

ABSTRACT

This study reports the results of two experiments which focused on the use of spelling strategies by students with learning disabilities and the relative effectiveness of two different approaches for teaching spelling. In experiment 1, qualitative research method was employed with four elementary students with learning disabilities to document the spelling strategies used during a structured interview, a formal spelling test and an informal writing activity. The data revealed 4 categories of spelling strategies: (1) rule-based, (2) multiple, (3) resource-based, and (4) brute force. Patterns that emerged from the data suggested that students with learning disabilities mostly used inappropriate spelling strategies (e.g., brute force, multiple, resource-based). Based on the results of experiment 1, experiment 2 compared the effectiveness of two highly dissimilar spelling instructional approaches (i.e., rule-based strategy and traditional method) to 30 elementary students with learning disabilities. The results of the experiment 2 showed that students with learning disabilities learned spelling words more effectively when the rule-based teaching and correction procedures were employed in three different probes and one post-test. This study concludes with a discussion of the instructional implications for students with learning disabilities in spelling.

Although most students with learning disabilities have difficulty with all forms of written expression, spelling problems rank as some of the most difficult to remediate and are common (Cone, Wilson, Bradley, & Reese, 1985; Bruck, 1988). One explanation for why students with learning disabilities have difficulties in spelling is that they are less adept than students in general education in devising and utilizing spelling strategies that allow for the systematic application of spelling rules. As Bailet and Lyon suggest (1985), deficient rule application "either alone or in combination with other processing difficulties, can cause spelling difficulties" (p. 164). Similarly, Bruck (1988) has argued that disabled spellers "do not use their knowledge of sound-letter correspondence rules when spelling unfamiliar words" (p. 66).

To better understand why students with learning disabilities have spelling problems, it is important to identify the strategy use when they attempt to spell words. It is equally important to find the most effective approaches for teaching spelling. There is a growing awareness that for instructional models to be effective with students with learning disabilities, academic programs must be tailored specifically to meet the needs of those students (Darch & Simpson, 1990). Unfortunately, many students in the United States receive very little formal instruction in spelling (Gerber & Hall, 1987) nor has there been extensive empirical research with students with learning disabilities that have investigated and compared different approaches to teach spelling (Seda, 1989; Vallecorsa, Zigmond, & Henderson, 1985).

Presently, very few studies exist that focus on the strategy use in spelling of students with learning disabilities. Horn, O'Donnell, and Leicht (1988) found that high school students with learning disabilities had difficulties correctly using soundletter correspondence rules in spelling when compared to young adults without disabilities. Among the sample of this study, 50% of the adults with learning disabilities made 60% or more of their spelling errors as phonetically inaccurate errors. Similarly, Carlisle (1987) found that ninth-grade students with learning disabilities were less apt to use morphological spelling rules relative to the fourth-, sixth-, and eighth-grade general education students. For the general education students, knowledge of the morphemic components of words appeared to be used in spelling dictated words. For example, knowing how to spell the base form (e.g., equal) preceded and aided in learning to spell the derived form (e.g., equality). In contrast, ninth-graders with learning disabilities were more apt to spell only one of the pair correctly, be it the base form or the derived form.

This indicated that, in some cases, the base word was spelled incorrectly (e.g., glorry), but the derived word was spelled correctly (e.g., glorious). This suggested that students with learning disabilities were more apt to learn derived forms as whole words, without regard for the relationship to the base form or the morphemic transformation. They appeared to lack awareness of the presence of base forms within derived counterparts, and they lacked specific knowledge about how to spell suffixes and how to attach suffixes to base words correctly.

Similarly, Bailet (1990) compared phonemic and morphemic spelling rule usage of sixth-grade students with learning disabilities with that of same-age normally achieving students. Two dictation spelling tasks requiring a written response were developed to assess application of soundletter correspondence rules and morphemic rules (e.g., suffix-adding rules). The results showed that normally achieving students' performance was superior to that of students with learning disabilities on the sound-letter correspondence rule task and the suffix-adding task.

There are few studies that investigated the effectiveness of strategy instruction to teach application of spelling rules. Bailet and Lyon (1985) have reported that a 37-year-old adult with a learning disability displayed initial deficits in suffix rule usage (e.g., -ing, -ion, -al, -ily), and significant improvement after task structure was modified to provide an implicit cue to the critical morphological spelling principle. This showed that increased structure may enable a speller with learning disability to demonstrate rule knowledge that was not readily apparent in performance on a less structured word list. Darch and Simpson (1990) compared rule-based strategy and visual imagery mnemonic method for teaching spelling to elementary students with learning disabilities. Results of the study indicated that students with learning disabilities who received instruction based on a rule-based strategy approach displayed significant spelling achievement gains when compared to visual imagery method.

The purpose of this paper is to report the results of two studies which focused on the use of spelling strategy by students with learning disabilities and the relative effectiveness of two, very different approaches for teaching spelling. Specifically, two research questions guided this study. First, we investigated the use of spelling strategies by elementary students with learning disabilities. We did this with the use of qualitative research methods by conducting intensive interviews with four students with learning disabilities. We felt that this research methodology would not only provide a picture of the type of spelling strategies used by these students but also, would provide insight as to why these students approached spelling as they did. Our second question was to determine effective spelling instructional approaches by comparing two highly dissimilar commercial spelling programs to see if one approach was superior. One method, rule-based strategy instruction, focused on teaching students spelling rules in which they utilized phonemic and morphemic strategies to spell words. The other method, traditional instruction, provided an array of spelling activities (e.g., introducing the words in the context of story, defining the meaning of the words, sentence writing, and dictionary skill training) to teach spelling words.

Our approaches (e.g., qualitative and quantitative study) are supported by Borg, Gall, & Gall (1993) who stated "many educational phenomena are best studied through a combination of qualitative and quantitative research designs. Qualitative research is best suited for initial investigation of a problem. Qualitative studies can produce thick description of an interesting phenomenon, discover relevant variables, and generate hypotheses about cause-and-effect relationships between them. Quantitative research then can make rigorous measurements of these variables and test for the presence of the hypothesized relationships" (p. 202).

EXPERIMENT 1: THE STRATEGIC SPELLING SKILLS OF STUDENTS WITH LEARNING DISABILITIES

The purpose of this descriptive study was to use qualitative research methods to determine the strategies students with learning disabilities use when they are attempting to spell different word types. Intensive interviews were conducted with four students with learning disabilities to identify the strategies they used in spelling. Elementary students with learning disabilities were selected based on recommendations from their teachers. Our interest was also to better understand how these students attempted to make adjustments in their approaches to spelling during observed spelling activities.

METHOD

Research Design

Qualitative research method (Patton, 1990) designed to identify the spelling strategy skills of the students as well as their perceptions on spelling instruction they received in their classrooms was used in this study. Qualitative data included audio tapes of interviews with

the students, written spellings that students produced, and field notes documenting informal conversations with the students' teachers and classroom observations. Qualitative research methods were appropriate for focusing on the primary question for this study which was to find out or understand the strategic spelling skills of students with learning disabilities and their perceptions of instruction they received.

Subjects

The four second grade students with learning disabilities who served as subjects for this study were interviewed in a group and individually to determine their use of spelling strategies and their perceptions about spelling. An "intensity sampling technique," discussed by Patton (1990), was the method to select subjects for this study. In this sampling procedure, teachers were asked to identify students who would be able to provide "information rich examples." That is, teachers identified students who were having difficulty with spelling, both in writing activities and testing situations. Our interest was to conduct interviews with these four subjects to gain a better understanding of (a) students' use of spelling strategies, (b) students' perceptions on the spelling instruction they had received during the school year, and (c) students' attempts to make adjustments in their approach to spelling during observed spelling activities.

The four students with learning disabilities had a mean age of 8.6 years and were completing the second grade. The sample consisted of two males and two females. Each of the four subjects met state and federal guidelines for placement into programs for students with learning disabilities. The mean full-scale IQ (Wechsler Intelligence Scale for Children–Revised) was 91. All students had been placed in a classroom for students with learning disabilities for at least one year. All subjects were identified by their teachers as having spelling difficulties as compared to their general education peers.

Instrumentation Interviews, Stimulus Materials and Testing

The questions that were developed for the structured and activity-based interviews were patterned after a study by Rabren and Darch (1996). Data were collected by the authors over six weeks. Two types of interviews were conducted with these students. Structured interviews were conducted as a group and occurred before the students were asked to complete specified spelling activities. The senior author conducted the structured 45-minute interviews. The activity-based interviews, which were conducted individually with the four students, were completed at the conclusion of the assigned spelling activities. The

Table 1 Questions Used for Structured and Activity-Based Interviews

Structured Interview	Activity-Based Interviews
1. When you spell words, what kind of things do you do to help you spell correctly?	1. Tell me the words you had trouble in spelling.
2. If you are having trouble with a word, what do you do to try and spell it correctly?	2. Why did you spell this word like that (experimenter points to a misspelled word)?
3. Why do you think some kids have trouble with spelling?	3. How did you come up with this word? (experimenter points to a respelled word)?
4. How do you feel if you can't spell words when you are writing?	4. If a teacher asks you to correct a misspelled word, what kinds of things do you do to spell it correctly?
5. Tell me how your teachers teach you to spell.	

activity-based interviews helped us to determine specific strategies these students used while they were completing a series of writing tasks. All interviews, structured and activity-based, were audio taped and transcribed for the analysis.

Structured Interview

The four subjects met as a group in a room adjacent to their classroom. This group interview lasted approximately 45 minutes. The structured interview was designed to foster general discussion among the students and the experimenter about students' use of spelling strategies and their perceptions about the importance of spelling and the type of spelling instruction they had received in school. The students were prompted to discuss in as much detail as possible the strategies they used to spell words, and whether they used strategies whenever they were engaged in writing activities. Our interest was to determine if these students used spelling strategies in all of their writing activities regardless of the content area. Table 1 provides questions that the authors used to guide the structured interview. As can be seen from Table 1, students were probed as to their use of strategies when they were spelling, how they attempted to correct spelling mistakes, and their personal feelings about their spelling difficulties.

Activity-Based Interviews

To explore the task specificity of spelling strategies, we used two spelling tasks, a spelling test and a writing activity. The spelling test was a formal assessment of spelling skills. The senior author met individually with each student on consecutive days to conduct activity-based interviews. After a short introduction and explanation as to our intent, the activity-based interviews began with the experimenter asking the student to complete a 15 word spelling test. The words chosen for this test represented words from 4 different word

types. The word types tested were (a) phonetically regular words (e.g., did, fast, cup), (b) words with a final e and a long vowel sound (e.g., gave, ride), (c) words comprised of two morphographs (e.g., reteach), and (d) phonetically irregular words in which one or more letters do not represent their most common sound (e.g., was, your, tall). We were interested in determining the strategies these students used for spelling different words types. The purpose of this activity was to discuss with the students the strategies they used to spell words during this activity.

Next, after a 5 minute break, the senior author administered the writing activity individually to the four children. The subjects were presented with a picture taken from an elementary reading text which depicted several animals playing in a field. After presenting the picture, the experimenter began a discussion with the student about what was happening in the picture. After this discussion, which usually lasted about 5–10 minutes, the student was asked to write as many sentences as they could that described what they saw in the picture. The purpose of this activity was to determine whether, when writing sentences, students used spelling strategies and what types of spelling errors they made during this writing activity. For example, after a student completed writing a sentence, the experimenter would point to a word that was misspelled and asked the subject what way he/she used to spell that particular word. Next, the student was told that the word was spelled incorrectly and asked to try and respell it. After the student completed the respelling, the student was asked to describe how he/she came up with the new spelling of the word. Table 1 provides a list of the questions that the experimenter used to identify the strategies used by the students.

Data Analysis

In analyzing individual questions, students' responses were divided into idea units. An idea unit was defined

Table 2   Spelling Strategy Categories

Strategies	Examples of Students' Comments
Rule-based Comments made that referenced appropriate rule-based strategies	"I thought of the letter in the word and tried to spell it." "If you don't know the word, you sound it out."
Multiple Comments made indicating the use of more than one strategy during spelling	"I tried to look for other words like the one I though hard."
Resource-based Indications of the use of prior learning experience	"I would get a piece of paper, and ask teacher to write down the word I didn't know."
Brute force Reports of less sophisticated procedures and recall information. These methods indicate tenacity rather than the use of systematic strategies.	"I keep on trying. I keep thinking about the word. Sometimes I guess if I don't know." "I just spelled it and did the best I could."

as a unit of comments during which the student described spelling strategy. Our goal was to examine the students with learning disabilities' use of spelling 11 strategies as well as the perceptions of spelling instruction they received. Verbal descriptions of spelling strategies were divided into units for each spelling task. We read the data record of each student several times as different kinds of spelling strategies emerged. We developed and refined a coding system to categorize the kinds of spelling strategies described in the units.

This process yielded four major categories: (1) rule-based, (2) multiple, (3) resource-based, and (4) brute force. Table 2 presents the four categories along with their definition and examples of some of the students' responses to interview questions. Using the transcribed data from the structured and activity-based interviews, we documented the number of times students stated that they used any of the four spelling strategies (e.g., rule-based, multiple, resource-based, and brute force).

RESULTS AND DISCUSSION

The results of this study provide a framework for understanding how students with learning disabilities attempt to spell words. These findings are consistent with other content instruction research (e.g., Simmons, Kameenui, & Darch, 1988; Rabren & Darch, 1996) which shows that students with learning disabilities often fail to use appropriate strategies.

Reported Use of Spelling Strategies: Activity-Based and Structured Interviews

While one of the students discussed using a rule based strategy, almost all of the other comments students

made regarding how they attempted to spell words and how they tried to correct misspelled words showed that they used inappropriate strategies almost exclusively. Jean, one of our female subjects almost always used multiple strategies. For example, when asked how she tried to spell words she did not know, she responded "I tried to look for other words like that one and thought hard." Most of the student comments about how they attempted to spell unknown words were categorized as "brute force" strategies. As can be noted from the sample comments from Table 2, students who used the brute force strategy often became impatient during the spelling and writing activities. In fact, we noticed that three of the students who used the brute force strategy almost often showed high levels of frustration while engaged in the writing activities. When we probed one student on how they tried to respell a word if their first strategy was not effective, one student replied, "I guess I'll just stop, I probably won't get it right anyway."

It was also interesting to note that students were most articulate about how they attempted to spell words during the activity-based interviews when discussing the spelling test. Even though they often identified strategies that were inappropriate, we found that they often discussed several attempts using strategies. One of the students said "it was easy for me to spell 'hand'. I just sounded out, /hhaanndd/, it's how to spell it." However, most students tried to sound out during spelling for irregular words too (e.g., wus for was, tol for tall).

They made fewer comments about spelling strategy use during the sentence writing activity. Their responses were much more vague about their using strategies during the sentence writing activity. There may be two reasons for this outcome. First, the students may have been more motivated when taking the spelling test and the students may have been less motivated when they were writing sentences that described the stimulus picture. The other reason may be that writing sentences for students with learning disabilities is such a difficult process for them, one that includes handwriting, composition, and grammar, that correct spelling was the least of their concerns. This analysis is supported by some of the comments students made during the writing activity: "I don't get a sentence, the problem is I can't write a sentence good, you know I don't know where to put period, question marks, that's the problem." Only one of the four subjects discussed using a rule-based spelling strategy when asked how they tried to spell words correctly during writing assignments.

In addition to determining how students with learning disabilities identified strategy use in spelling, we were further interested in their perception on the spelling instruction they received. For the question designed to tap their spelling instruction (e.g., tell me how your teachers teach you to spell), their comments placed greater emphasis on superficial form involved in the instruction than they did on the specific instructional contents. For example, one of the students described the spelling instruction like this: "It was, we did reading, then write. And had extra hard work. We learned from the book, we go back at the back table and had spelling test." Overall, the students failed to pick up details of spelling instruction.

IMPLICATIONS FOR DEVELOPING SPELLING INTERVENTION

The results from study 1 have important implications for teaching spelling to students with learning disabilities. This study is consistent with the results of other researchers who have shown that students with learning disabilities have strategy deficits (e.g., Gerber & Hall, 1987). The present study extends these results and provides examples of the types of inappropriate spelling strategies students with learning disabilities use when taking tests and writing text. These results suggest that effective spelling programs must teach students to use strategies systematically, across a variety of word types. It is important to point out here that these students were no better applying spelling strategies to easy word types (e.g., phonetically regular words) than they were with difficult word types (e.g., words comprised of two morphographs and irregular words). This suggests that students must be taught specific spelling strategies for various word types. In addition, it seems reasonable to assume that students will require intensive instruction to learn to apply spelling strategies.

Students in this study rarely attempted any type of systematic spelling strategies when they were writing sentences during the activity-based interviews. These students seemed overwhelmed with the mechanics of writing sentences and this led to almost no attempt to use strategic methods when spelling individual words. One possible implication is that when teachers first introduce spelling strategies to students with learning disabilities, instruction should occur with carefully sequenced words in an academic context that does not initially require students to write lengthy sentences.

EXPERIMENT 2: TEACHING SPELLING TO STUDENTS WITH LEARNING DISABILITIES: THE DIFFERENTIAL EFFECTS OF TWO SPELLING PROGRAMS

The purpose of this experiment was to evaluate the relative effectiveness of two spelling instructional approaches that were quite different. Based on the results of Experiment 1, we were interested in determining which of two spelling instructional programs, Spelling Mastery Program (Dixon & Engelmann, 1990), a program that teaches students to use spelling rules in a direct, uncompromising way, and the Laidlaw Spelling Program (Roser, 1987), a traditional program that utilized writing activities based on word families, practice in spelling words, and motivational activities. We were interested in determining the relative effectiveness of each of these programs for teaching effective spelling to children with learning disabilities. The spelling words were selected on the basis of different word types and level of difficulty (2nd grade) from Spelling Mastery and Laidlaw Spelling Programs.

METHOD

Subjects and Setting

The subjects for this study were 30 students with learning disabilities. Each of the students who participated in this study were placed in classrooms for students with learning disabilities located in a school system in the Southeastern part of the United States. Five of the students who participated in this study were African-American and 14 of the students of the total sample were female. The mean IQ for the entire sample of subjects was 89. The subjects had been placed in learning disabilities programs based on federal guidelines for the identification of learning disabilities programs. These guidelines required that students demonstrate at least average potential as measured by their performance on a standardized intelligence test and a measured severe discrepancy in one of the major academic areas. In addition, all students who participated in this study were identified by their respective teachers as having spelling difficulties.

Two graduate students who were completing a masters' training program in learning disabilities served as experimental teachers for this study. The experimental teachers were randomly assigned to one of the treatment conditions. Each experimental teacher was trained to use the spelling intervention program that they were assigned to teach. The authors demonstrated the appropriate lessons from each of the instructional interventions to each of the teachers and then requested that the experimental teachers practice implementing lessons in role-playing situations with the authors. The experimental teachers learned to follow the semiscripted lessons for their assigned treatment group. Training sessions for the teachers was completed individually and was completed in three, one-hour practice sessions. One experimental teacher was 28 years old and the other was 26. Both were female and each had practicum experience teaching students with learning disabilities as part of their graduate program.

Instructional Materials and Procedures

In order to determine the relative effectiveness of two different approaches for teaching spelling to students with learning disabilities, subjects were randomly assigned to either a group who received instruction in using rule-based strategies for spelling or another group who received instruction in a commercial program that implemented activities centered around word practice, exposure to spelling rules, and sentence and story writing. The program used to teach students rule-based spelling strategies was the Spelling Mastery Level C

(Dixon & Engelmann, 1990). The students who were assigned to the alternative treatment group were taught from activities taken from the Laidlaw Spelling Program. Table 3 provides a comparison of the two treatment groups on six critical instructional features.

To increase the internal validity of this study, critical features of the instructional programs were controlled. Students in both treatment groups received instruction for 12 instructional sessions. The length of these daily instructional lessons was the same for both instructional groups, about 20 minutes. The same spelling words were used in both treatment groups. In addition, lessons for both treatment groups were semiscripted which ensured that the lessons from each treatment group were taught as they were designed.

Spelling Mastery Program: A Rule-Based Approach. The Spelling Mastery Program Level C (Dixon & Engelmann, 1990) served as one of the instructional programs evaluated in this study. This commercial spelling program contains 137 lessons and is designed to teach students spelling rules in an intensive fashion. Students assigned to this treatment group received instruction based on activities taken from the first 50 lessons of the program. This direct instruction program (Gersten, Woodward, & Darch, 1986) has scripted lessons with scripts that provide to the teacher specific teaching activities. The critical aspect of this program is that it teaches students spelling using carefully sequenced rule-based strategies. Figure 2 provides an example of one of the scripts from this treatment group which is designed to teach students a morphographic analysis.

Students are taught the morphographic units of a series of words. The students are asked to identify these units, learn the meaning and spelling of the presented morphograph. The two other spelling strategies, phonemic analysis and final e rule were presented to students in this group in a similar fashion. For

Table 3   Means, Standard Deviations, and Percentage Correct on Spelling Words on Three Probe Measures

	Treatment						
	Spelling Master			Traditional			
Test	*M*	*SD*	% Correct	*M*	*SD*	% Correct	*t*-Test
Probe 1	8.7	1.3	87	6.3	3.1	63	*p* < .01
Probe 2	8.3	1.4	83	5.0	2.2	50	*p* < 0.1
Probe 3	7.0	1.8	70	4.2	3.1	42	*p* < .01
Posttest	22	2.2	73	16	4.3	53	*p* < .01

Probe contained 10 items. Posttest contained 30 items.

example, when students were taught phonemic analysis, students were taught how to sound out the individual letters in words that were phonetically regular (e.g., cat). Next students practiced using this strategy on a carefully selected group of words.

Laidlaw Spelling Program: An Activity-Based Approach. The alternative instructional approach was based on activities taken from Laidlaw Spelling Program (1990), a popular commercial spelling program used in many classrooms. Students in this treatment group received instruction on the same three word types that were taught in the Spelling Mastery program. However, the teaching procedures for this group differed from the procedures in the Spelling Mastery group. This program contained 3 primary spelling activities. The first feature was that practice words were organized around word pairs (e.g., make, making) with several word types presented at the same time. Students were instructed to look carefully at the various word endings. Next the students were asked to write each word with the ending (e.g., making) and without the ending (e.g., make). Next, the students used the spelling words to complete a story that was presented by filling in blanks with the correct spelling word. Finally, the students were asked to complete a dictionary and sentence writing activities for selected spelling words. All spelling lessons, regardless of the word type introduced were organized around these general spelling activities.

Dependent Measures

Probes. Ten-item probe spelling tests were administered to students in each of the instructional groups after they had been taught for four consecutive days for each of the three word types evaluated in this study. Probe 1, administered on day 5 of the study, contained 10 phonetically regular words that the students were taught in the four-day lesson sequence. Probe 2 focused on words that were taught using a morphographic analysis, while Probe 3 contained only words that ended in "e" and contained a long vowel sound (e.g., skate). Probe 2 was administered on day 10 of the experiment and probe 3 was administered on day 15. All probes were administered by the senior author and took approximately 20 minutes to complete. Probes were administered in groups for students in each instructional condition.

Post Test. A 30-item post test was administered the day following the completion of all other experimental activities. This test contained 10 words for each of the three word types taught in this study. No help was provided to any student during post testing. If a student asked for help with spelling a word, the experimenter told the student to just do the best they could. Post testing was completed in groups as lasted approximately 45–50 minutes.

RESULTS AND DISCUSSION

Table 3 provides the means, standard deviations, and percent correct for the students in each of the two treatment groups, the rule-based approach (Spelling Mastery) and the traditional approach (Laidlaw Spelling Program). As can be seen from Table 3, there are differences favoring the Spelling Mastery group on each of the three probe measures and the post test. While the range of percentage correct for the Reading Mastery group was 87% correct on Probe 1 (phonetically regular words) to 70% correct on Probe 3 (spelling rule words), the scores for students in the Laidlaw Spelling programs were significantly lower on each of the three measures ($p < .01$). For example on Probe 1, these students scored 63% correct, and on Probe 3, they scored only 42% correct. Even though the students scored lower on the post test measure (73% correct) than they did on Probe 1 and Probe 2, they significantly performed higher than the students who were taught with the Laidlaw Program (53% correct).

These results demonstrate the superiority of a rule-based spelling instructional program (Spelling Mastery Program) when compared to the effectiveness of an instructional program that relies on the use of motivational spelling activities and intensive practice writing words and sentences without systematic introduction of spelling rules with carefully sequenced practice. The students taught with the rule-based program became more proficient spelling words representing each of the three word types.

The results of both experiments provide information regarding students' use of appropriate spelling strategies as well as curriculum designed to teach spelling. The purpose of both experiments was to examine the strategies students use to spell words and the programs designed to teach them. The results of each study provide support for the other. Students with learning disabilities do not use appropriate strategies when spelling words, so they need curricula which provide an intense, systematic method for teaching specific spelling strategies.

CONCLUSIONS AND IMPLICATIONS

The purpose of the first study was to determine the types of strategies that students with learning disabilities use when they are trying to spell words that they find difficult. As these results show, students with learning disabilities are not effective in using appropriate, rule-based spelling strategies. When these students discussed the methods that they used to spell words, they rarely discussed rule-based strategies, and instead discussed using strategies that were either characterized as brute force, individualized, or multiple approaches, all of which are considered to be ineffective spelling strategies.

The purpose of the second study reported in this paper was to determine which of two highly dissimilar programs for teaching spelling was the most effective in teaching elementary aged students with learning disabilities how to spell three classifications of words. Table 3 provides comparison of the rule-based approach (Spelling Mastery) with a traditional approach (Laidlaw Spelling Program). The results of the intervention study reported here suggest that rule-based programs that are skill-directed intensive, with specified corrections and practice are most effective for children with learning disabilities.

Each experiment has important implications regarding students with learning disabilities and instructional programs designed to teach spelling. Moreover, the findings of the first experiment, which suggests that students with disabilities do not use appropriate strategy (i.e., rule-based strategy), offer support to the second study which favors using rule-based programs to teach students with learning disabilities. These results suggest that students with learning disabilities who frequently experience problems with spelling, benefit from programs that incorporate rule-based strategies that are intensive and skill-directed, and provide specified correction and practice procedures. School administrators and teachers can use the results when planning instruction for students with learning disabilities. Students with learning disabilities often experience difficulty in spelling and oftentimes use inappropriate strategies when engaging in spelling tasks. These studies suggest that rule-based curricula provide teachers with strategies to teach students who experience difficulty in spelling.

REFERENCES

Bailet, L. L. (1990). Spelling rule usage among students with learning disabilities and normally achieving students. *Journal of Learning Disabilities, 23*(2), 121–128.

Bailet, L. L., & Lyon, R. L. (1985). Deficient linguistic rule application in a learning disabled speller: A case study. *Journal of Learning Disabilities, 18*(3), 162–164.

Borg, W. R., Gall, J. P., & Gall, M. D. (1993). *Applying educational research: A practical guide.* (3rd ed.) New York: Longman.

Bruck, M. (1988). The word recognition and spelling of dyslexic children. *Reading Research Quarterly, 23,* 51–69.

Carlisle, J. (1987). The use of morphological knowledge in spelling derived forms by LD and normal students. *Annals of Dyslexia, 37,* 90–108.

Cone, T., Wilson, L., Bradley, & Reese. (1985). Characteristics of LD students in Iowa: An empirical investigation. *Learning Disability Quarterly, 8* (3), 211–220.

Darch, C., & Simpson, R. G. (1990). Effectiveness of visual imagery versus rule-based strategies in teaching spelling to learning disabled students. *Research in Rural Education, 7*(1), 61–70.

Dixon, R., & Englemann, S. (1990). *Spelling mastery* (teacher's book). Chicago, IL: Science Research Associates.

Gerber, M. M., & Hall, R. (1987). Cognitive-behavioral training in spelling for learning handicapped students. *Learning Disability Quarterly, 12,* 159–171.

Gersten, R., Woodward, J., & Darch, C. (1986). Direct instruction: Designing successful curriculum for the handicapped. *Exceptional Children, 53,* 17–31.

Horn, I, O'Donnell, J., & Leicht, D. (1988). Phonetically inaccurate spelling among learning disabled, head-injured, and nondisabled young adults. *Brain and Language, 33,* 55–64.

Patton, M. (1990). *Qualitative evaluation and research methods.* Newbury Park, CA: Sage Publications.

Rabren, K., & Darch, C. (1996). The strategic comprehension behavior of students with learning disabilities and general education students: Teachers' and students' perspectives. *Journal of Research and Development in Education, 29,* 172–180.

Roser, N. L. (1987). *Laidlaw spelling.* River Forest, IL: Laidlaw Brothers.

Seda, M. M. (1989). Examining the proverbial gap between spelling research and the practice of spelling in American classrooms. *Reading Improvement, 26*(4), 315–322.

Simmons, D., Kameenui, E., & Darch, C. (1988). The effect of textual proximity on fourth and fifth-grade students' metacognitive awareness and strategic comprehension behavior. *Learning Disability Quarterly, 11,* 380–395.

Vallecorsa, A. L., Zigmond, N., & Henderson, L. M. (1985). Spelling instruction in special education classrooms: A survey of practices. *Exceptional Children, 52*(1), 19–24.

Scott, B. N., & Hannafin, R. D. (2000). How teachers and parents view classroom learning environments: An exploratory study. *Journal of Research on Computing in Education, 32*(3), 401–416. Copyright © 2000 ISTE (International Society for Technology in Education), 800.336.5191 (U.S. & Canada) or 541.302.3777 (International), iste@iste.org, www.iste.org. All rights reserved. Reprint permission does not constitute an endorsement by ISTE.

How Teachers and Parents View Classroom Learning Environments: An Exploratory Study

Barry N. Scott

Robert D. Hannafin

The College of William & Mary

ABSTRACT

The purpose of this investigation was to examine teachers' and parents' beliefs across several dimensions of the classroom learning environment (CLE). The sample consisted of 132 teachers and 809 parents in a public school district in a southeastern suburban university town. Participants responded to a survey that was designed to measure beliefs along a continuum from "consistent with the traditional classroom" to "consistent with the reformed classroom" about four components of the school learning environment: assessment, knowledge, student role, and pedagogy. Results indicated that parents held more traditional views than teachers about all four of the components, significantly in regard to knowledge and content. Among teachers, a separate analysis revealed that significant differences existed among grade-level groups on the pedagogy and student role components, while no differences existed among experience levels. These findings have important implications for instructional designers, curriculum developers, and school reformers.

Efforts to change schools have taken various forms throughout the 20th century, but recent educational and other media reports seem to have fueled an increase in the urgency and vigor with which educators and other stakeholders pursue reform programs. Combined with concerns about the state of education in the United States have come efforts to increase and improve the use of computer technology in schools. In some cases, reformers have explicitly pointed to technology as an important link to the creation of more efficient and effective learning environments (Means, 1994). However, previous efforts by educators to integrate new technologies into educational practices have typically fallen short of lofty expectations (Cuban, 1986). Likewise, a myriad of reform efforts in general appear to have been met with resistance by teachers and other school stakeholders. Fullan (1993) proposed that:

> It is probably closer to the truth to say that the main problem in public education is not resistance to change, but the presence of too many innovations mandated or adopted uncritically and superficially on an ad hoc fragmented basis. (p. 23)

Recent reform efforts have emphasized reflective, continuous processes that see schools redefined as learning organizations (Senge, 1990) and that involve a variety of stakeholders in the school and local community (Fullan, 1993; Henderson & Hawthorne, 1995) including students, parents, educators, and local leaders. An important aspect of these processes is the identification of core beliefs held by those involved. In the foreword to *Teaching With Technology* (Sandholtz, Ringstaff, & Dwyer, 1996), Cuban acknowledged the importance of considering teachers' beliefs about teaching and learning as well as the difficulty in altering those beliefs as related to the use of technology. Similarly, Tobin and Dawson (1992) argued that curriculum reform required of both teachers and students a reconceptualization of their respective roles in the learning environment, a difficult process at best. As reformers bring other stakeholders into the mix, identifying attitudes and beliefs about teaching and learning may become even more critical. And although teacher beliefs about education-related matters have been studied (e.g., Bennett, Jordan, Long, & Wade,

1976), little is known about the belief systems of other stakeholders. Our study examines beliefs about the classroom learning environment held by teachers and parents and explores some important issues related to these beliefs.

Determining technology's role in K–12 education is critical for teachers, administrators, educational technologists, curriculum developers, and school reformers. A more fundamental issue, however, is identifying and understanding the teacher's role in technology-supported learning environments (Cuban, 1986; Hannafin & Freeman, 1995). If technology is to assist educators in improving teaching and learning processes, then how precisely is that to occur?

The use of computers in schools has been linked to a shift from traditional, didactic educational practices to more student-centered, interactive learning activities (Means, 1994; Sandholtz, et al., 1996). Recently, several notable innovative projects have been developed that exemplify how technology can support these types of activities. The Jasper Woodbury series (Cognition and Technology Group at Vanderbilt [CTGV], 1992), the Computer-Supported Intentional Learning Environments (CSILE) project (Scardamalia, Bereiter, & Lamon, 1994), and multimedia environments that organize and support learning through teaching (MOST) (CTGV, 1994) use technology as a tool to enable students to explore problem situations in authentic learning environments while stressing higher-order thinking skills and collaborative problem-solving strategies.

Encouraged, in part, by the success of these programs, it has been suggested that technology, in particular computer technology, should play a vital role in the school reform movement because of its ability to extend traditional classroom practices and support student-centered, open-ended learning environments (Means, 1994). Learning in such environments, Means argued, differs from traditional educational practices in a number of ways. Learning in a reformed classroom might be characterized by a high level of student exploration, highly interactive instruction, student collaboration for extended periods of time on authentic and multidisciplinary projects, the teacher acting as facilitator and coach, and predominantly performance-based assessment strategies.

Brown et al. (1993) contrasted classroom "activity patterns" likely experienced in traditional public school classrooms with those they found in communities of learners, or intentional (nontraditional) learning environments (Bereiter & Scardamalia, 1989). In an intentional learning environment, students are engaged in active research and become managers of their own learning. Central to this model is the belief that expertise is distributed among people, tools, and other contextual artifacts found in the learning environment. To illustrate the differences between their communities of learners and traditional classrooms, Brown and her colleagues contrasted the two classroom philosophies in terms of five roles: students, teachers, curriculum, computers, and assessment.

In the intentional learning environment, the student becomes an active researcher and a teacher to other students instead of a receptacle into which information is deposited. The teacher becomes more of a facilitator, not just the provider of knowledge and manager of the classroom. The focus of the curriculum, according to Brown et al. (1993) is on understanding of content rather than fragmented fact retention. The role of the computer in the intentional learning environment is as a tool to support and extend learning opportunities, as opposed to delivering drill-and-practice activities. Finally, assessment focuses on the process of learning, through portfolios and projects, rather than on recall of factual content. Heller and Gordon (1992), co-investigators in the community of learners research project, described six roles: curriculum and content are listed as distinct categories along with the student, teacher, computer, and assessment roles described previously. Curriculum in an intentional learning environment, for Heller and Gordon, focuses on "learning to learn" or thinking skills and process of learning as opposed to basic skill acquisition and focus on content knowledge in the traditional classroom. Regarding the role of content in the nontraditional learning environment, emphasis is placed on depth of instructional content rather than broad coverage of subjects and on integration of skills across curricula rather than on a fragmented curriculum. The tenets of intentional learning environments parallel those advocated by Means (1994) and other school reformers.

The design of open-ended learning environments, including intentional learning environments described previously and the technology-integration projects cited earlier, are to varying degrees consistent with a constructivist philosophy. Von Glasersfeld (1989) described constructivism in very broad terms as the belief that knowledge exists in each individual's mind and is developed and altered by individual experiences and interactions with different phenomena. In contrast, most traditional instructional programs are grounded in an objectivist philosophy, which holds that knowledge exists outside the mind and must be transmitted to the learner by some means, primarily a teacher, for learning to occur (Lakoff, 1987). The authenticity of learning outcomes in the objectivist learning environment, that has been dominant in most public schools, has been questioned by advocates of school reform (e.g., Means, 1994). However, though there is general agreement that a dramatic shift in the teacher's role is essential for a successful conversion to more open-ended learning environments, few have measured the degree of teacher support or resistance they may encounter toward those ideas (Tobin & Dawson, 1992). It is quite possible, even likely, that teachers and others who maintain a teacher- and content-centered view of teaching and learning will resist implementing instructional programs that require them to relinquish to the student control of his or her learning (Hannafin & Freeman, 1995). Though technology can help create and support student-centered learning environments, cultural values rooted in school tradition may prohibit, or significantly delay, their adoption (Hawisher & Selfe, 1993; Papert, 1980; Tobin & Dawson, 1992).

Consideration needs to be given not only to those ultimately responsible for implementing change, namely teachers, but also to others being asked to support the reform, namely parents. What parents think and believe about various reform components could certainly affect adoption of an instructional program (Konzal, 1997; Prawat, 1992; Tobin & Dawson, 1992). Gaining the support of these stakeholders may be a critical factor in building and sustaining a viable technology presence in a school district (Davidson & Ritchie, 1993). At least tacit approval from parents is required to sustain any reform initiative. Davidson and Ritchie found that, in general, parents held positive attitudes about computers and their use in the classroom. However, very little investigation has been conducted to determine parents' beliefs about individual reform components, like those identified by Heller and Gordon (1992) and Means (1994), within classroom learning environments. Though parents may have positive attitudes about the use of computers in the classroom, how do they believe computers should be used in the classroom? What do parents believe about teaching and learning in general? A key task for school reformers, including those interested in the use of technology to support reform, is to determine what educators and other school stakeholders believe about the classroom learning environment.

Age is a factor possibly related to how teachers and parents view classroom learning environments. What little is known about parents' views pertains to opinions about teaching styles. Bennett et al. (1976) found that older teachers held more traditional views about teaching styles, while younger teachers held more progressive views. Eiken (1974) found that older teachers favored more traditional instructional content goals for social studies education than their younger colleagues. Older teachers, then, and possibly older parents as well, may be more likely than younger teachers and younger parents to hold more traditional beliefs about the classroom learning environment.

Several other factors that may influence teachers' attitudes and beliefs about classroom learning environments have been investigated. It has been hypothesized that years of teaching experience may influence teachers' views of school practices. For example, Hannafin and Freeman (1995) found that experienced teachers held more objectivist views toward knowledge acquisition than those with fewer years of teaching experience. McCoy and Haggard (1989) found that years of teaching experience correlated positively with amount of computer use. In terms of the classroom learning environment, perhaps more experienced teachers hold beliefs that are more traditional as they are more likely to be entrenched in the school culture. Conversely, teachers with less experience are influenced less by school traditions and perhaps more by teacher education programs that may advocate current and emerging theories of teaching and learning.

Another factor that may be related to teachers' beliefs about the nature of classroom learning environments is the grade level taught. McCoy and Haggard (1989) found that elementary school teachers were more likely to use computers in the classroom than were secondary school teachers. This pattern was also detected by Becker (1991), who reported that high school teachers were less likely to be computer users than teachers of lower grades. However, less is known about how a teacher's grade level may influence his or her attitudes about the overall classroom environment and the components within the environment. It is reasonable to believe that elementary, especially early childhood, teachers, whose pedagogical practices are by nature often student centered and activity oriented, would hold different views about the nature of learning than their content-focused secondary education counterparts. For example, elementary teachers have long been encouraged to adopt instructional strategies that are holistic and multidisciplinary in nature—such as those exemplified by whole-language reading programs—and are arguably more aligned with the Brown et al. (1993) intentional learning environment. Meanwhile, secondary teachers have generally remained focused on their students gaining discipline-specific knowledge typically using instructional strategies, such as lecture, that are consistent with the traditional classroom.

The purpose of this study was to determine teachers' and parents' beliefs and attitudes about the classroom learning environment in terms of the roles described by Brown et al. (1993) and Heller and Gordon (1992) and to identify factors that influenced these attitudes. Our research grew from an initiative by a school district's technology committee to develop a long-range technology plan. It was believed that efforts to improve the use of technology in the district should involve various parties in the school community, especially parents. Identifying core beliefs about teaching and learning was seen as a fundamental part of this process. The remainder of this article focuses on teacher and parent beliefs and attitudes about the classroom learning environment in general. Specific questions related to computer use are examined in another report.

In the present study, the following questions were addressed:

1. Do teachers' and parents' beliefs about different aspects of the classroom learning environment differ significantly? If so, is age a factor that helps explain the differences?
2. Among teachers, are there significant differences in beliefs about different aspects of the classroom learning environment? Does grade level taught or years of experience influence teachers' beliefs?

METHOD

Sample

Participants were 809 parents and 132 teachers of students in a middle-class public school district. The district is located in a suburban southeastern university town. Approximately 4,015 students attended the seven schools in the district, which included a high school (Grades 9–12), a junior high school (Grades 7–8), a middle school (Grades 5–6), three elementary schools (Grades 1–4), and one early childhood school (kindergarten).

The teacher sample included 10 males and 116 females (six teachers did not provide gender information). Teachers varied fairly evenly in number of years of teaching experience: 16.7% of the respondents had more than 20 years of experience, 18.2% had 15–20 years, 18.2% had 9–14 years, 25.8% had 3–8 years, and 21.2% had fewer than 3 years. Out of the seven schools in the district, 16.7% of the respondents were from the high school, 18.2% were from the junior high school, 14.4% were from the middle school, 37.1% were from the elementary schools, and 13.6% were

from the early childhood school. The highest participation rate occurred with the early childhood school, where 18 of 25 (72%) teachers responded, while the high school had the lowest participation rate with 23 of 73 (31.5%) teachers returning surveys. Response rates among the other schools ranged from 47.5% to 67.6%. Overall, 52% of teachers in the district participated. More than half of these teachers held master's degrees or higher (59.1%). In terms of age, 3.2% of parents were older than 55, 10.8% were from 46–55, 52.8% were from 36–45, 30.4% were from 26–35, and 2.3% were younger than 26. The median annual income of parents in the district was approximately $25,500. The parent sample included respondents who identified themselves as African American (24.5% of the parent sample), White (64.4%), and other (8.7%). Twenty respondents (2.4%) did not provide information about ethnicity.

Survey Instrument

The questionnaire consisted of three primary components: demographics; items concerning computer use, availability, and experience; and a 13-item scale developed to measure theoretical beliefs about the classroom learning environment.

The 13-item scale was developed collaboratively by us and the district's technology committee to measure teacher and parent beliefs about components of the classroom learning environment (Table 1). The scale, hereafter referred to as the classroom learning environment (CLE) scale, was originally constructed as follows: 11 items were developed to roughly correspond to five of the six areas of change in traditional classroom philosophy described by Heller and Gordon (1992) (two each for assessment, content, student role, and curriculum; three for teacher role); two additional items measured beliefs about the nature of knowledge, or epistemology (Hannafin & Freeman, 1995). The sixth area described by Heller and Gordon—computer use—was measured elsewhere in the survey and is not addressed in this article. Although we had intended to design the survey items to measure the six components listed previously, results of a factor analysis (varimax rotation, listwise deletion) revealed that only four factors explained all 13 items. Results of the analysis are provided in Table 2. Following is a description of the four new factors (see Table 1) examined in the present study.

Factor 1—Pedagogy The four survey items that loaded on factor 1 (items 1–4), though related to Heller and Gordon's (1992) teacher's role component, seemed better explained by teachers' pedagogy. The items seemed to be a general measure of respondents'

Table 1 Classroom Learning Environment Item Mean Scores by Group

Survey Items	Group	
	Parent	Teacher
Students are able to effectively manage their own instruction. (P)	3.85	3.94
Teachers should not identify student "errors"; rather, they should allow students to "work it out themselves." (P)	3.79	3.64
Projects and portfolios are better than tests as a measure of student performance. (P)	2.95	2.59
A textbook includes only the author's opinions at the time it was written. (P)	3.29	3.15
Standardized tests (like SAT) really show how well a student can do in school. (K)	3.02	2.38
Most of the time, there is really only one right answer to a problem. (K)	2.69	2.13
Once a scientific fact is discovered, it remains part of that science from then on. (K)	3.08	2.73
Students should learn at their own pace and in a way that suits them, even if it means somewhat lower standardized test scores. (K)	2.67	2.38
Depth of student knowledge rather than breadth of student knowledge should be stressed in schools. (Teacher version.) (Co)	3.06	2.70
It is better for students to know at least a little about a lot of subjects than to know a lot about a few subjects. (Co)	3.27	2.89
If left alone, many students will waste a lot of time approaching a problem from a completely wrong direction. (SR)	3.24	2.76
If given the choice during an instructional lesson, students will most often choose the easiest path, not the best path for their learning. (SR)	3.67	3.73
It is not productive to give students problems if they don't have the necessary skills to solve them. (SR)	3.34	3.42

P = Pedagogy. K = Knowledge/epistemology. Co = Content. SR = Student/Role.

Table 2 Classroom Learning Environment Factors (VARIMAX Rotated Common Factor Matrix)

Variables	Factor 1 (P)	Factor 2 (K)	Factor 3 (Co)	Factor 4 (SR)	h^2
Item 1	.641	−.222	.009	.137	.478
Item 2	.513	.058	.006	−.015	.267
Item 3	.438	.327	.036	−.055	.303
Item 4	.326	.048	−.013	−.324	.213
Item 5	.051	.533	.032	.080	.295
Item 6	.057	.474	−.048	.286	.312
Item 7	−.101	.407	.041	.188	.213
Item 8	.287	.324	.018	−.122	.203
Item 9	.163	−.052	.712	−.224	.587
Item 10	−.112	.099	.682	.155	.512
Item 11	.017	.255	.039	.472	.289
Item 12	.088	.190	.075	.468	.269
Item 13	−.046	.003	−.072	.271	.081
Eigenvalue	1.120	1.055	.991	.855	4.021
% trace (common variance)	27.9	26.2	24.7	21.3	100.0

P = Pedagogy; K = Knowledge/epistemology; Co = Content; SR = Student/Role.

views about creating a student-centered classroom and how teachers should teach in that classroom. Teacher use of portfolios as an assessment tool (item 1), allowing students to struggle a bit (item 2), students' ability to effectively manage their own instruction (item 3), and the belief that truth and knowledge are negotiated and relative (item 4) are probably related to how much respondents believe, or do not believe, that the teacher should adopt a pedagogical style consistent with a student-centered, reformed classroom.

Factor 2—Knowledge or Epistemology. Responses to items 5–8 seemed to be consistent with respondents' views about knowledge structure and how it is acquired. The degree to which respondents believe that knowledge exists in discrete chunks and is transferable from teacher to students would seem to predict whether they agreed that standardized tests show how well a student can do (item 5), that there is only one right answer to a given problem, and that a scientific "fact" remains so forever. It also seemed reasonable to assume that a view of knowledge structure would also influence whether students should work at their own pace even at the detriment of standardized test scores as the scores may be viewed as measures of objective knowledge.

Factor 3—Content. The two survey items (items 9–10) originally designed to measure Heller and Gordon's content component did in fact load, by themselves, on factor 3.

Factor 4—Student Role. The three survey items (items 11–13) that loaded on factor 4 all seemed to measure beliefs about students' ability to perform in unstructured environments where they are expected to efficiently manage their learning. Twelve of the 13 items comprising the CLE scale were identical on both teacher and parent surveys. Item 9, "Depth of student knowledge rather than breadth of student knowledge should be stressed in classrooms," was simplified to "It is better for students to know a few subjects really well than to know a little about a lot of subjects," on the parent survey to reduce confusion over educational jargon. All items were written using a Likert-type scale that ranged from 1 (Strongly Agree) to 5 (Strongly Disagree). Six survey items expressed a view in agreement with a reformed classroom environment; the other seven expressed a view in agreement with a traditional classroom environment. Responses to the latter items were reverse-coded before analysis. Composite scores for each of the four CLE components were then calculated by averaging the adjusted item responses based on their factor loadings (e.g., items 1–4 for the pedagogy component, 5–8 for the knowl-

edge component, etc.). These composite scores represented a measure of respondents' views on a continuum from consistent with a reformed classroom to consistent with a traditional classroom.

A measure of internal consistency of the 13 CLE items, as measured by Cronbach's coefficient alpha, was a moderate 0.51. That the items did not correlate highly with each other was not altogether surprising considering that each of the component areas (the four factors described earlier) represented different dimensions of the classroom learning environment. This result was similar to a previous study of teachers' attitudes and beliefs about "the educative process," in which Wehling and Charters (1969) identified eight dimensions of beliefs that were statistically independent of one another. It is realistic, therefore, to expect a moderate, or even low, measure of internal consistency in this study. This statistic is perhaps not the most informative in this case but does seem to support the notion that beliefs and attitudes about issues represented by the 13 CLE items may be independent of one another. In other words, participant responses to a given survey item would not be highly correlated to their responses to other items.

Procedures

Approximately 270 teachers and 2,500 parents (or legal guardians) were asked to complete and return the survey. To increase the likelihood of return, the surveys were hand delivered: parent surveys were taken home by students, and teacher surveys were distributed during weekly faculty meetings at each school. Parent survey instructions requested that only one parent per household complete a survey and that parents with more than one child in the school system return only one survey for their youngest child. Participants were given one week to complete and return their questionnaires.

Teachers and parents provided survey information about the range of their age. They categorized their age as younger than 25 years old, 26–35, 36–45, 46–55, or older than 55. Because of the uneven distribution of the resulting cell sizes, these five categories were collapsed into three categories for analysis purposes— younger than 36, 36–45, and older than 45. Teachers reported the grade level taught and their number of years of teaching experience. Teachers categorized the number of years of teaching experience fewer than 2 years, 3–5 years, 6–10 years, 11–20 years, or more than 20 years. Again to even the cell size distributions and to simplify analysis, these categories were later collapsed into two categories, eight years or fewer and more than eight years.

Design & Data Analysis

Multivariate analysis of variance (MANOVA) was used to analyze mean CLE scores for each of the four component measures (pedagogy, knowledge, content, and student role) in a 2-group (parents, teachers) × 3 age (> 45, 36–45, and < 36) factorial design. In a separate test, teachers' component mean CLE scores were examined using MANOVA in a 2 (number of years of teaching experience) × 5 (grade level taught) factorial design. MANOVA was selected because multiple independent and dependent variables (with both categorical and metric data) were involved and because it is a comparably conservative statistic, thus reducing the risk of spurious results. Follow-up univariate tests were examined wherever significant multivariate effects were found. For significant univariate effects, the least significant differences post hoc tests were conducted where necessary to identify group differences.

RESULTS

Parents' and Teachers' Views Toward CLE Components

CLE component mean scores and standard deviations for group (teacher and parent) and age level are displayed in Table 3. As described earlier, higher mean CLE component scores indicate agreement with a more traditional viewpoint, while lower scores indicate agreement with a more reformed viewpoint. MANOVA revealed a multivariate main effect for group, as indicated by a Hotelling's trace value of .071, $F(4, 932) = 16.504$, $p < .001$. This result indicates that teachers reported beliefs about the classroom learning environment that were significantly different than parents. No group-by-age interaction across all CLE components was detected, Hotelling's trace value = .011, $F(8, 1862) = 1.260$, $p = .260$. And there was no main effect for age, Hotelling's trace value of .010, $F(8, 1862) = 1.210$, $p = .289$. Age, then, was not a significant factor in identifying espoused beliefs.

Because a significant multivariate effect was found, components of the classroom learning environment were then examined individually. Univariate tests revealed that parent and teacher responses differed significantly on two of the four CLE components; in each case, parents held more traditional views than teachers did. Parent responses ($M = 2.88$) were significantly more traditional than teacher responses ($M = 2.41$) to the knowledge component, $F(1, 935) = 50.359$, $p < .001$, and to the content component, $M = 3.17$ vs. $M = 2.80$, $F(1, 935) = 15.926$, $p < .001$. Parent ($M = 3.47$) and teacher ($M = 3.33$) responses did not differ significantly regarding the pedagogy component, $F(1, 935) = 2.595$, $p = .108$. Finally, parent responses ($M = 3.42$) to the fourth component, student role, did not differ from teacher responses ($M = 3.31$), $F(1, 935) = 2.559$, $p = .110$.

Table 3 Component Mean Scores and Standard Deviations by Group and Age Level Classroom Learning Environment

	Age							
	<36		36–45		>45		Total	
	M	SD	M	SD	M	SD	M	SD
Parents	(n = 268)		(n = 427)		(n = 114)		(n = 809)	
Pedagogy	3.38	0.60	3.54	0.60	3.40	0.70	3.47	0.62
Knowledge	2.96	0.71	2.81	0.75	3.00	0.73	2.88	0.73
Content	3.16	0.94	3.20	0.95	3.10	0.89	3.17	0.94
Student role	3.45	0.69	3.38	0.71	3.47	0.77	3.42	0.81
Teachers	(n = 56)		(n = 38)		(n = 38)		(n = 132)	
Pedagogy	3.22	0.63	3.40	0.65	3.42	0.61	3.33	0.63
Knowledge	2.33	0.63	2.52	0.66	2.41	0.66	2.41	0.69
Content	2.81	0.74	2.70	0.77	2.87	0.89	2.80	0.79
Student role	3.21	0.82	3.29	0.79	3.46	0.67	3.31	0.77
Total	(n = 324)		(n = 465)		(n = 152)		(n = 941)	
Pedagogy	3.36	0.61	3.53	0.60	3.41	0.68	3.45	0.62
Knowledge	2.85	0.73	2.78	0.75	2.85	0.75	2.82	0.74
Content	3.10	0.92	3.15	0.95	3.04	0.89	3.12	0.93
Student role	3.41	0.72	3.38	0.72	3.47	0.74	3.40	0.72

Teachers' CLE component mean scores for grade level taught and number of years of teaching experience are shown in Table 4. A significant difference was detected across grade level, Hotelling's trace = .280, $F(16, 470)$ = 2.059, p = .009, indicating that teachers in at least one grade level differed in their views from teachers in one or more grade levels. However, no multivariate effect was detected for years of experience, Hotelling's trace = .007, $F(4, 119)$ = .201, p = .938, which indicated that teachers with fewer years of experience did not report significantly different views on the CLE scale than teachers with more years of experience. Likewise, no effect was found when examining the grade-level-by-years-of-experience multivariate interaction, Hotelling's trace = .117, $F(16, 470)$ = .862, p = .614. Thus, teachers with differing years of experience within each grade level reported statistically similar beliefs about the classroom learning environment.

Univariate tests for the grade level main effect indicated that of the four CLE components, pedagogy, $F(4, 122)$ = 3.445, p = .011, and student role, $F(4, 122)$ = 2.648, p = .037, had significant relationships with teachers' grade level taught. Post hoc analyses were conducted to determine the nature of the relationships. The LSD test identified kindergarten teachers' (M = 2.72) pedagogical beliefs to be more consistent with a reformed classroom than elementary (M = 3.44), middle school (M = 3.39), junior high (M = 3.31), and high school (M = 3.55) teachers' responses.

Regarding the student role component, kindergarten teachers (M = 2.78) reported views more consistent with a reformed classroom environment than did all other grade levels: elementary (M = 3.24), middle school (M = 3.35), junior high (M = 3.47), and high school (M = 3.65). In addition, the difference between elementary and high school teachers was significant, consistent with the trend toward more traditional views as the grade level taught increases. No other significant relationships were identified.

DISCUSSION

Teachers' and Parents' Beliefs

The present findings indicate that teachers and parents hold differing views about the classroom learning environment. In particular, teachers' beliefs about how knowledge is constructed and how content should be covered are more consistent with a successful reformed classroom environment than parents' beliefs. Parents were also found to hold more traditional views, though not significantly so, regarding pedagogy and the student's role in the classroom.

That parents' views of the classroom learning environment, at least as they pertain to content coverage and knowledge acquisition, differed from those of teachers, indicating a need for greater communication with parents as partners in school reform efforts. The majority of parents are typically far removed from

Table 4   Teacher Classroom Learning Environment Component Mean Scores and Standard Deviations by Grade Taught and Years Experience

	Grade											
	K		1–4		5–6		7–8		9–12		Total	
	M	*SD*	*M*	*SD*	*M*	*SD*	*M*	*SD*	*M*	*SD*	*M*	*SD*
Years Exp > 8	(n = 3)		(n = 26)		(n = 10)		(n = 15)		(n = 16)		(n = 70)	
Pedagogy	2.67	0.29	3.41	0.48	3.48	0.53	3.28	0.76	3.64	0.59	3.33	0.63
Knowledge	2.25	0.25	2.49	0.68	2.58	0.94	2.52	0.72	2.63	0.63	2.53	0.69
Content	2.83	0.29	3.02	0.71	2.55	0.69	3.10	0.95	2.47	0.83	2.84	0.81
Student role	2.67	0.33	3.44	0.63	3.13	0.71	3.56	0.67	3.69	0.74	3.44	0.69
Years Exp ≤ 8	(n = 15)		(n = 23)		(n = 9)		(n = 9)		(n = 6)		(n = 62)	
Pedagogy	2.73	0.57	3.47	0.71	3.31	0.65	3.36	0.40	3.29	0.53	3.23	0.66
Knowledge	1.83	0.50	2.23	0.48	2.42	0.38	2.64	0.63	2.79	0.68	2.27	0.59
Content	2.70	0.82	2.83	0.85	2.67	0.79	2.78	0.57	2.67	0.88	2.75	0.78
Student role	2.80	0.89	3.03	0.93	3.59	0.62	3.33	0.50	3.56	0.66	3.15	0.77
Total	(n = 18)		(n = 49)		(n = 19)		(n = 24)		(n = 22)		(n = 132)	
Pedagogy	2.72	0.53	3.44	0.59	3.39	.058	3.31	0.64	3.55	0.59	3.33	0.63
Knowledge	1.90	0.49	2.37	0.60	2.50	0.71	2.56	0.68	2.67	0.63	2.41	0.66
Content	2.72	0.75	2.93	0.78	2.61	0.72	2.98	0.83	2.52	0.82	2.80	0.79
Student role	2.78	0.82	3.24	0.80	3.35	0.69	3.47	0.61	3.65	0.70	3.31	0.77

news of the "latest" trends or developments in education. If schools and school districts are to gain community support for new programs that are grounded in nontraditional instructional methods, surely parents must be kept informed and educated about proposed programs and curricula and, further, encouraged to learn and think about the programs alongside educators (Konzal, 1997).

A less optimistic, for educational reformers at least, interpretation of the divide between parents' and teachers' beliefs is that parents value the traditional view of the classroom learning environment and will resist reform efforts. For example, most reform initiatives require a shift in curricular content emphasis from breadth to depth (Heller & Gordon, 1992; Means, 1994) where more time is spent exploring fewer topics. The present finding about the content effect may be discouraging in this regard. Parents reported that they were more in favor of wide coverage of topics (consistent with the traditional CLE) than were teachers.

A more fundamental issue regards how teachers and parents view the nature of knowledge and how knowledge is acquired. As with their view of content coverage, parents held more traditional views about knowledge. Parents, who for the most part have only their own school experiences as a guide, may believe that the model of teacher as professor and dispenser of discrete knowledge is the best one. Though teachers are also heavily influenced by their own schooling experiences, they also have had the benefit of courses in learning theories and educational philosophy, which also affect their beliefs. Many curriculum reformers advocate the critical analysis of content being studied, but parents may be less comfortable with this approach and more in favor of programs that emphasize learning facts about a discipline, as espoused by experts.

Different age groups, between and within teacher and parent groups, might also have been expected to reflect different sets of beliefs. However, age was not a significant factor in the beliefs espoused by these groups. Though it is encouraging, in this case at least, that differences in viewpoints are not reduced to a "generation gap" effect, this finding also points to the need for a more complex study into the factors that might affect belief systems.

Teachers' Beliefs

In this study, grade level taught was a significant factor in how two aspects of the classroom learning environment were viewed: pedagogy and the student's role. That kindergarten teachers differed significantly from each of the other grade levels (elementary, middle school, junior high, and high school) and that elementary teachers differed from high school teachers on their responses to the student role component is in accord with what one would expect to find when considering the different curriculum frameworks guiding each grade level. Kindergarten and elementary teachers, for example, typically use projects and portfolios for assessment and, in some cases, have received specialized training in how to use these assessment methods. Teachers in higher grades, who emphasize objective testing and who often feel external pressures to meet standardized objectives, may feel less comfortable with alternative forms of assessment, practices that are advocated by many school reformers.

For similar reasons, it is not surprising that kindergarten teachers differed from teachers in the other grade levels in their beliefs about the student's role. The kindergarten curriculum tends to be grounded in a tradition that emphasizes student activity, exploration, and play. This, arguably, is more in line with a child's natural learning processes; perhaps because of this, kindergarten teachers may hold a more positive view about the responsibility a student can handle in his or her own learning. It may also be true that classroom activities that reflect a constructivist philosophy provide students with more natural learning contexts, ones that students choose to engage in rather than circumvent. Teachers who do not believe students can be effective managers of their learning most assuredly represent a hurdle to school reformers who advocate student-centered learning environments.

Within schools, teachers are in the best position to be change agents. Therefore, it is important to determine which teachers are more likely to embrace change and hold views that are consistent with school reform efforts. As Means (1994) and others have pointed out, use of technology in the reformed classroom requires a significant shift in the teacher's traditional classroom role. For many teachers, it requires that they embrace a new way of thinking about the learning process. In traditional school environments, this may not be easy for teachers to accomplish. Even if teachers profess a belief in a particular philosophy of teaching, it may be difficult for them to carry out their beliefs in practice. Teachers face many outside pressures each day that may prohibit, or at least discourage, fully embracing new methods of instruction. For example, even with encouragement from administrators to consider alternative teaching methods, teachers, particularly those in higher grades, are still expected to prepare students to meet objectives of standardized achievement tests, to teach a certain amount of content to students to meet state or school curriculum guidelines or both. The cumulative effect of these external pressures surely affects the degree to which teachers adopt nontraditional teaching styles. Further, these other ongoing pressures may limit the likelihood that teachers may integrate technology into their curriculum.

Limitations

Examining a school district with a different socioeconomic and demographic mix of parents and teachers may yield somewhat different results. At the time the survey was conducted, the district would not be considered "technology rich." Teachers in school districts further along in reform efforts or fortunate to have had technology in place for some time—or both—may differ from those represented in this study. Finally, although the present teacher sample was adequate, teacher research should examine larger samples with a more systematic distribution across grade levels.

CONCLUSION

Our research suggests that teachers hold beliefs about classroom learning environments that are more aligned with reformed classrooms than those held by parents. These findings have important implications for school administrators, curriculum developers, and others interested in educational reform, as well as those engaged in designing learning environments rooted in constructivism. As school systems attempt to embrace student-centered, open-ended learning environments across their curricula, school administrators should be aware not only of teachers' beliefs concerning such environments, but also those of parents.

If technology's role in the reformed classroom is critical, it would seem that more needs to be done to examine teachers' and parents' attitudes about proposed changes and technology initiatives. Considerable research has been done about how teachers and, to some extent, parents feel about computers and computer use; however, less is known about how these groups feel about the way technology can and should affect teaching and learning processes. This exploratory study indicated that parents and teachers held different beliefs about certain aspects of the classroom learning environment. These gaps may indicate potential barriers to successful reform efforts. However, knowledge that teachers and parents hold similar viewpoints about some components of the classroom learning environment may also prove useful because these areas could provide a starting point for collaborative dialogue about reform efforts.

REFERENCES

Becker, H. (1991). How computers are used in United States schools: Basic data from the 1989 I.E.A. computers in education survey. *Journal of Educational Computing Research, 7*(4), 385–406.

Bennett, N., Jordan, J., Long, G., & Wade, B. (1976). *Teaching styles and pupil progress.* Cambridge, MA: Harvard University Press.

Bereiter, C., & Scardamalia, M. (1989). Intentional learning as a goal of instruction. In L. B. Resnick (Ed.) *Knowing, learning, and instruction: Essays in honor of Robert Glaser* (pp. 361–392). Hillsdale, NJ: Erlbaum.

Brown, A., Ash, D., Rutherford, M., Nakagawa, K., Gordon, A., & Campione, J. (1993). Distributed expertise in the classroom. In G. Salomon (Ed.), *Distributed cognitions* (pp. 188–228). New York: Cambridge.

Cognition and Technology Group at Vanderbilt. (1992). The Jasper experiment: An exploration of issues in learning and instructional design. *Educational Technology Research and Development, 40*(1), 65–80.

Cognition and Technology Group at Vanderbilt. (1994). Multimedia environments for developing literacy in at-risk students. In B. Means (Ed.), *Technology and education reform: The reality behind the promise* (pp. 23–56). San Francisco: Jossey-Bass.

Cuban, L. (1986). *Teachers and machines: The classroom use of technology since 1920.* New York: Teachers College Press.

Davidson, G., & Ritchie, S. (1993, April). How do attitudes of parents, teachers, and students affect the integration of technology into schools? A case study. Paper presented at the annual meeting of the American Educational Research Association, Atlanta, GA.

Eiken, K. (1974). Beliefs of teachers, students, and parents about social studies goals in senior high school United States history. Unpublished doctoral dissertation, Indiana University, Bloomington.

Fullan, M. (1993). *Change forces: Probing the depths of educational reform.* London: Falmer Press.

Hannafin, R., & Freeman, D. (1995). An exploratory study of teachers' views of knowledge acquisition. *Educational Technology, 35*(1), 49–56.

Hawisher, G., & Selfe, C. (1993). Tradition and change in computer-supported writing environments: A call for action. In P. Kahaney, L. Perry, & J. Janagelo (Ed.), *Theoretical and critical perspectives on teacher change* (pp. 155–186). Norwood, NJ: Ablex.

Henderson, J. G., & Hawthorne, R. D. (1995). *Transformative curriculum leadership.* Englewood Cliffs, NJ: Merrill.

Heller, J., & Gordon, A. (1992). Lifelong learning: A unique school-university collaboration is preparing students for the future. *Educator, 6*(1), 4–19.

Konzal, J. (1997, March). Attitudes: How parental attitudes may influence classroom instructional practices. Paper presented at the annual meeting of the American Educational Research Association, Chicago.

Lakoff, G. (1987). *Women, fire, and dangerous things: What categories reveal about the mind.* Chicago: University of Chicago Press.

McCoy, L., & Haggard, C. (1989, February). Determinants of computer use by teachers. Paper presented at the annual meeting of the Eastern Educational Research Association, Savannah, GA.

Means, B. (1994). Introduction: Using technology to advance educational goals. In B. Means (Ed.), *Technology and education reform: The reality behind the promise* (pp. 1–21). San Francisco: Jossey-Bass.

Papert, S. (1980). *Mindstorms: Children, computers, and powerful ideas.* New York: Basic Books.

Prawat, R. (1992). Teachers' beliefs about teaching and learning: A constructivist perspective. *American Journal of Education, 100,* 354–395.

Sandholtz, J., Ringstaff, C., & Dwyer, D. (1996). *Teaching with technology: Creating student-centered classrooms.* New York: Teacher's College Press.

Scardamalia, M., Bereiter, C., & Lamon, M. (1994). The CSILE project: Trying to bring the classroom into World 3. In K. McGilly (Ed.), *Classroom lessons* (pp. 201–228). Cambridge, MA: MIT Press.

Senge, P. (1990). *The fifth discipline: The art and practice of the learning organization.* New York: Doubleday.

Tobin, K., & Dawson, G. (1992). Constraints to curriculum reform: Teachers and the myths of schooling. *Educational Technology Research and Development, 40*(1), 81–92.

von Glasersfeld, E. (1989). Cognition, construction of knowledge, and teaching. *Syntheses, 80*(1), 121–140.

Wehling, L., & Charters, W. (1969). Dimensions of teacher beliefs about the teaching process. *American Educational Research Journal, 6*(1), 3–7.

Gutman, L. M., & Sulzby, E. (2000). The role of autonomy-support versus control in the emergent writing behaviors of African-American kindergarten children. *Reading Research and Instruction 39*(2), 170–184.

The Role of Autonomy-Support Versus Control in the Emergent Writing Behaviors of African-American Kindergarten Children

Leslie Morrison Gutman

Elizabeth Sulzby

University of Michigan

ABSTRACT

This study examined children's intrinsic motivation during an emergent letter writing task in both controlling and autonomy-supportive adult-child interactions. Using a repeated measures design, 20 African-American kindergartners from a predominately low-income elementary school were randomly assigned to experience either the autonomy-supportive followed by the controlling interaction or the controlling followed by the autonomy-supportive interaction. Using videotapes of the interactions, children's motivation was coded according to categories based on Harter's (1981, 1982) Scale of Intrinsic-Extrinsic Orientation in the Classroom and Perceived Competence Scale for Children. Childrens' letters were assessed using categories based on Sulzby's (1990) Forms of Writing and Rereading Checklist. Results revealed that the autonomy-supportive versus controlling context of the task and the order of the interactions influenced children's motivation. Childrens' use of emergent literacy was also influenced by the context of the interaction. Implications for literacy learning and teaching are discussed.

Children begin life with intrinsic motivation to explore, master, and manipulate their surroundings. However, as children grow older, features of the environment influence their intrinsic motivation. In particular, the autonomy-supportive versus controlling context in which children learn new skills may affect their intrinsic motivation in that skill domain in the future (Boggiano, Main, & Katz, 1988; Deci & Ryan, 1985). Controlling events and contexts undermine motivation by removing choice and pressuring children toward particular outcomes. Autonomy-supportive events and contexts, on the other hand, encourage motivation by allowing self-determination, or behaviors initiated and regulated through choice (Deci & Ryan, 1985). When controlled, children may lack a true sense of choice and are "pawns" to desired outcomes even though they may intend to achieve those outcomes (deCharms, 1976; Deci & Ryan, 1987). However, although autonomy-supportive environments and interpersonal contexts may allow individuals the freedom of choice or the opportunity to choose

what they wish to do, choice is not equivalent to "permissiveness." Instead, choice means providing guidance that is informational rather than controlling (Ryan, Connell, & Deci, 1985).

Previous studies have demonstrated that autonomy-supportive versus controlling interactions with others such as teachers and parents can have a profound impact on childrens' motivation for particular tasks (Deci, Nezlek, & Sheinman, 1981; Deci, Schwartz, Sheinman, & Ryan, 1981; Swann & Pittman, 1977; Zuckerman, Porac, Lathin, Smith, and Deci, 1978). More recent studies, in particular, have focused on the importance of autonomy-supportive interactions for children's motivated literacy behaviors. For example, Grolnick and Ryan (1987) assigned fifth grade students to read a social studies text under three conditions. The first group was instructed to read in order to answer questions that they thought were important, the second group was instructed to read on their own, and the third group was instructed to read in order to remember the content for a graded test. Although the third group was highest in rote learning, interest in the topic and conceptual learning were highest for the first group. The authors concluded that the students' motivation was influenced by the perception of an external locus of causality in the reading assignment. The importance of autonomy in students' motivated reading has also been shown in other studies of elementary school students, such as Gambrell (1995) and Morrow (1992), who found that the books that third to fifth-graders enjoyed the most were the ones they had the most freedom in selecting.

Other studies have also demonstrated the importance of autonomy-support for motivated reading and writing in elementary school classrooms. For example, Ng and her colleagues (1998) videotaped third and fifth-grade classrooms and then interviewed the students to determine their motivations and perceptions of the classroom context. Students who perceived freedom of choice in reading, writing, and interpreting texts reported more involvement, curiosity, and challenge than did students who did not perceive such freedom (Ng, Guthrie, Van Meter, McCann, & Alao, 1998). In another study of third to fifth graders, Skinner and Belmont (1993) found that when students believed that teachers were providing meaningful choices for them, students showed an increase in effort, attention, and interest in classroom reading and writing tasks.

These studies provide substantial evidence for the value of autonomy-support in children's motivated literacy behaviors. However, they have focused primarily on how the classroom context influences the literacy behaviors of older elementary school students (third to fifth graders). There is less information regarding how autonomy-supportive versus controlling interactions influence children's early literacy learning. Yet, according to Teale (1982), early literacy development often depends upon the experiences the child has in reading and writing activities that are mediated by literate adults, older siblings, or events in the child's everyday life. Depending on the context, these early experiences may either encourage or hinder children's emergent reading and writing. For instance, autonomy-supportive experiences may support children's gradual progression from emergent to conventional reading and writing, whereas controlling experiences may not only limit children's opportunities to read and write emergently but also undermine their motivation to do so. Clearly, an examination of both autonomy-supportive and controlling environments seems essential in understanding the contextual influences on children's early engagements with literacy. The present study examined kindergartners'

intrinsic motivation in the context of an emergent writing task in both autonomy-supportive and controlling interactions. As kindergartners, these children are in the process of becoming literate—emerging as young readers and writers (Sulzby, 1990).

EMERGENT LITERACY

Emergent literacy is the reading and writing behaviors of young children (birth through age 6–7) that precede and develop into conventional reading and writing (Sulzby, 1990). According to this perspective, young children engage in meaningful literacy events long before they receive direct, school-based literacy instruction (Bissex, 1980; Clay, 1975; Schickendanz, 1986; Sulzby, 1990; Teale, 1982). Research has found that much literacy learning and teaching has gone on in the home setting well before kindergarten in the homes of both middle- and low-income children (Heath, 1982; Sulzby & Teale, 1987; Taylor, 1983; Teale, 1987).

The focus on young children's literacy development has brought more attention to the social context in which young children learn about literacy. As a result, numerous studies have documented the importance of parent-child and teacher-child interactions on children's early literacy development (for example; McMahon, Richmond, & Reeves-Kazelskies, 1998; Ninio, 1980; Pellegrini, Brody, and Sigel, 1985; Snow, 1983; Snow & Ninio, 1986). However, only a few studies have explored the role of autonomy versus control in such interactions (Burns & Casbergue, 1992; Turner, 1995). In one study, Burns and Casberque (1992) examined the degree of parental control in parent-child interactions during a letter-writing task. In a sample of middle-income European American families, they found that a higher degree of parental control was associated with the parent demonstrating how to complete at least one step of the task, correcting the child's performance, or verbally commanding the child to pursue a given course of action. A lower degree of parental control was associated with the parent asking the child more open-ended questions, giving the child more choices, repeating what the child said, or commenting on the child's work. They also found that lower levels of parental control were associated with a more emergent-looking letter (e.g., scribbles, drawings, invented spellings, and letter-strings), while higher levels of parental control were associated with more conventional spelling and writing. This may be due to the fact that controlling parents often wrote the letter for their children, while less controlling parents allowed their children to write their own letter.

Furthermore, higher levels of parental control were associated with children who passively responded more than initiated conversation, whereas lower levels of control were associated with more verbal input and initiation from the child.

In an observational study of the classroom context, Turner (1995) demonstrated similar findings for first graders in a predominantly middle-income European American school district. Turner (1995) found that when children were given a reasonable amount of freedom and responsibility for literacy activities, such as choosing their own books to read and deciding whether to write or draw, they demonstrated more motivated literacy behaviors. Turner (1995) concluded that motivation for early literacy learning is situated in children's encounters with reading and writing; however, she suggested that future research investigate the applicability of her results to other cultural and ethnic groups.

RESEARCH QUESTIONS

Despite some evidence that autonomy-support is an important consideration for motivated literacy behaviors, there has been little empirical attention to how autonomy-supportive versus controlling interactions influence young children's motivation for emergent literacy. Additionally, there has been little work on the motivation of African-American children from low-income communities (Graham, 1994), especially the contextual influences on their motivation to engage in early literacy behaviors.

The present study addressed these issues by examining children's intrinsic motivation during an emergent writing task in both controlling and autonomy-supportive interactions. There were three main hypotheses. First, we examined whether the same child's intrinsic motivation changed over qualitatively different adult-child interactions. We hypothesized that children would make more statements of independent-mastery, interest, and competence in the autonomy-supportive context than in the controlling context. This prediction was based on numerous studies demonstrating that autonomy-supportive interpersonal contexts are positively correlated with independent mastery, perceived competence, and interest (Deci, Nezlek, et al., 1981; Deci, Schwartz, et al., 1981; Ryan & Grolnick, 1986).

Second, the order of the autonomy-supportive and controlling interaction was considered. We hypothesized that children experiencing the controlling interaction first would demonstrate less interest and competence, and more dependent mastery in the subsequent autonomy-supportive context than children who experience the autonomy-supportive interaction first. This prediction was based on research demonstrating that when controlled, children display less intrinsic motivation in similar, subsequent activities (Swann & Pittman, 1977; Zuckerman et al., 1978).

Third, we examined the quality of children's writing product in both autonomy-supportive and controlling interactions. It was expected that children's written products in the autonomy-supportive context would be more emergent-looking than their written products in the controlling context. This was based on previous research suggesting that children in autonomy-supportive contexts engage in more emergent literacy behaviors (e.g., scribbles, invented spellings, and letter-strings), whereas children in controlling contexts use more conventional spelling and writing dictated by adults (Burns & Casberque, 1992).

METHOD

Sample and Context

The sample consisted of 20 African-American kindergarten-age children (10 boys and 10 girls). The children were recruited from a kindergarten class in a public elementary school in a low-income suburb of Detroit. There was both a morning class and an afternoon class with approximately 25 children each. Ten children from the morning class and 10 children from the afternoon class participated in the study. These children were randomly selected from the African-American children in both classes.

The kindergarten class had one teacher and an aide. The teacher frequently interacted with the children, while the aide organized the classroom materials. The teacher followed a routine, but was flexible in her approach. She frequently read to the children and many of her lessons incorporated writing. The classroom was organized around centers that included a writing and computer center.

Materials

All the interactions took place in a small conference room in the children's school. The first researcher and a child sat together in front of a table. The researcher sat on the right-hand side of all the children. Writing materials that were used in the activity were placed on the table, including primary color markers and white paper.

The researcher used a set of guidelines or a script for both the controlling and autonomy-supportive interactions. In order to simulate parent-child interactions, the framework for both the controlling and autonomy-supportive contexts was developed with transcripts of parents and their children from the Burns and Casbergue (1992) study. In particular, the framework for both contexts was based on one or two transcripts that exemplified either a controlling or autonomy-supportive context.

A video camera was in the room and visible to the child. The video camera was placed directly in front of and focused on the faces of the researcher and the child in order to record their affect. The second researcher videotaped and took notes on the interactions. She also rechecked the first researcher for consistency in following the interaction guidelines.

Procedure

Data collection occurred during a two-week period in March. Using a repeated measures design, the first researcher wrote a letter with each of the 20 children in both the controlling and autonomy-supportive interactions. Writing a letter was chosen as an authentic task since it is an activity that young children are likely to have knowledge of, both from emergent literacy activities prior to school and in school through activities such as notes that are regularly sent to and from school. This task was also chosen because of the different ways in which a letter can be written, from an adult-controlled perspective that does not necessarily honor the child's emerging literacy to an adult autonomy-supportive perspective that accepts and supports the child's concepts.

Order effects were controlled by random assignment of children to either the controlling followed by autonomy-supportive interaction or the reverse order. The first researcher interacted with all of the children on the letter-writing task in both the controlling and autonomy-supportive contexts.

The adult took one child at a time and walked with him or her to the room where the videotaping was to take place. During that time, she talked with the child and often held the child's hand. Once the child and the adult were in the room, the adult interacted with the child according to the following guidelines.

Autonomy-Supportive Guidelines. In autonomy-supportive contexts, the adult allows the child to make his/her own choices; asks the child a where, when, who, tell me about or why question; uses phatics (e.g. yes, uh-huh, okay) to indicate that he/she understands the child, is listening and perhaps interested; and provides guidance that is informational rather than controlling (Deci & Ryan, 1987; Hess & Shipman, 1965; Laosa, 1980; Ryan et al., 1985; Tizard, Hughes, Pinkerton, & Carmichael, 1982; Wood, 1980).

In the autonomy-supportive context of the study, the researcher first provided information about the task to the child. The adult then asked the child whom he or she was going to write to, what he or she was going to write about, and what color marker he or she was going use to write the letter. The adult used phatics and repeated what the child said in order to indicate that she understood and was listening to the child. The adult did not offer unsolicited help to the child; however, the adult answered the child's questions if the child specifically asked for help. The adult also allowed the child to write autonomously without disturbing the child.

Writing-Controlling Guidelines. In controlling contexts, the adult demonstrates how to complete at least one step of the task, corrects the child's performance, limits the child's choices, or verbally commands the child to pursue a given course of action (Deci & Ryan, 1987; Hess & Shipman, 1965; Laosa, 1980; Tizard et al., 1982; Wood, 1980). The adult uses directives (e.g., "put," "place," "take," etc.) and statements of "should," "must," and so forth (Ryan, Mims, & Koestner, 1983). The adult decides what is right and utilizes highly controlling sanctions to produce the desired behavior (Deci, Nezlek, et al., 1981).

In the controlling context of the study, the adult first told the child about the task. The child was then told whom to write to and what to write about. The researchers told the child that he or she should write a letter to his/her mother and tell her what she/he did in school yesterday. In order to demonstrate the task, the researcher had queried the classroom teacher about a recent event that the child would have taken part in. In the session, the researcher asked the child a series of yes/no questions about that event which would be the content of the letter. The adult then asked the child whether he/she wanted the adult to write the letter. If the adult wrote the letter, she wrote several sentences and then told the child to sign his or her name and draw a small picture. If the child wrote the letter, the adult told the child what to write, where to write it, and how to spell it. The adult also demonstrated how to write certain letters and words by placing her hand over the child's hand.

Coding System

Children's intrinsic motivation was assessed using categories based on Harter's (1981) Scale of Intrinsic-Extrinsic Orientation in the Classroom and Harter's (1982) Perceived Competence Scale for Children. Harter's (1981) Scale of Intrinsic-Extrinsic Orientation in the Classroom taps five separate dimensions defined by an intrinsic and extrinsic pole including preference for challenge versus preference for easy work, interest versus teacher approval, independent mastery versus dependence on the teacher, independent judgment versus reliance on the teacher's judgment, and internal versus external criteria for success/failure. Harter's (1982) Perceived Competence Scale for Children defines three discreet domains of self-evaluation specific to various types of competence as well as general satisfaction with the self. The three domains of perceived competence include cognitive (or academic), social (competence in relation to peers), and physical (mostly sports related), as well as children's general self-esteem (i.e., the degree to which one likes oneself as a person). In this study, the motivational categories were based on two of Harter's (1981) intrinsic dimensions (independent mastery and interest) and one of Harter's (1982) perceived competence domains (cognitive). The other categories were not considered since preliminary analyses revealed that the children did not verbalize these dimensions. Children's written products were assessed using categories based on the Forms of Writing and Rereading Checklist developed by Sulzby (1990).

Intrinsic Motivation. Children's intrinsic motivation was coded with the videotapes through examination of children's statements. From the videotapes, transcripts were made of all the children's statements along with a description of their context. Children's statements were defined as those statements that were not direct answers to the adult's questions or repetitions of the adult's comments. Statements were defined according to adult-child turns. Reliability was assessed between the first and second researchers on five children in both interactions. There was perfect agreement for the number of children's statements.

The children's statements were coded using categories based on Harter's scales (1981, 1982). These categories are mutually exclusive categories, that is, all comments were coded into one category, and no comments overlapped into more than one category.

The motivational categories included:

1. Mastery—The child comments or asks a question about his/her letter.
   a. Independent—The child tells the adult how to write or spell a word or letter, what he/she is going to write about or what he/she already wrote, when he/she wants to begin or finish writing, where he/she is going to write, or what color marker he/she wants to write with.

   b. Dependent—The child asks the adult how to write or spell a word or letter, what he/she should write about or what he/she already wrote, when he/she should begin or finish writing, or where he/she should write.
2. Interest—The child comments about his/her interest in writing the letter.
   a. Claim—The child comments that he/she had fun writing the letter, that he/she wants to write another one, or that he/she wants to write more.
   b. Deny—The child comments that writing the letter is boring or that he/she is tired of writing the letter.
3. Competence—The child comments specifically on his/her cognitive ability in writing the letter.
   a. Claim—The child comments that he/she knows how to write or spell a word, wrote a word or letter correctly, or wrote a good letter.
   b. Deny—The child comments that he/she does not know how to write or spell a word, wrote a letter or word incorrectly, or does not know what to write.

The other verbal categories included:

1. Comment—The child comments about his/her class, superficial aspects of task itself, or his/her personal life. The child asks the adult what she said.
2. Completion—The child completes the adult's statement.

Reliability was also assessed between the first and second researchers on five children in both interactions for each of the motivational categories. Mean reliability for the motivational categories was .98. The reliability was .88 for independent mastery and 1.00 for dependent mastery, claimed competence, denied competence, claimed interest, and denied interest.

Forms of Writing. Children's forms of writing were coded using the children's written product from both the autonomy-supportive and controlling contexts. The children's written products were divided into several categories based on their relative level of emergent versus conventional writing. These categories were based on Sulzby's (1990) Forms of Writing and Rereading Checklist. For each written product, the categories were evaluated as present or absent. All forms of writing on the children's letters were coded. The categories included:

1. Drawing
2. Letter-like units—These resemble manuscript letters but they appear to be forms the child has created.
3. Nonphonemic Letter-strings
   Random—Letters that appear to be generated at random.
   Patterned—Letters that have reoccurring patterns, particularly in alternating vowels and consonants.
   Name-elements—The letters of the child's name are recombined in numerous ways.
4. Invented Spelling—The creative or invented spelling of words.
   Conventional—Words that approximate dictionary or "correct" spelling.
   Adult Produced—Words written or dictated by adult.
   Child Produced—Words written and composed by child.

Reliability between the first and second researcher was assessed on five children in both interactions. Mean reliability for the forms of writing was .94.

RESULTS

Intrinsic Motivation

Multivariate analyses of variance including Order (2) as the between-subjects variable and Context (2) as the within-subjects variable were performed on eight dependent variables including independent mastery, dependent mastery, claimed competence, denied competence, claimed interest, denied interest, comment, and completion. As evident in Table 1, there was a significant main effect of Context for interest $F (1, 18) =$ 8.32, $(p < .01)$. Children in the autonomy-supportive context made more statements of interest than children in the controlling context (see Table 1). There was also a significant main effect of Order for dependent mastery $F(1, 18) = 4.82$, $(p < .05)$. Means indicated that children in the controlling followed by autonomy-supportive interaction made more statements of dependent mastery than children in the autonomy-supportive followed by controlling interaction (see Table 1).

There was also a significant interaction between Order and Context for the dependent variable independent mastery $F (1, 18) = 4.58$, $(p < .05)$. In fact, the differences between the levels of independent mastery obtained in the autonomy-supportive context and the controlling context differed according to which context came first (Order). As shown in Figure 1, when the autonomy-supportive context was first, the mean of independent mastery was 5.7 statements, but this value declined to 2.5 in the immediately following controlling context. The pattern was very different when the controlling context was first: the level of independent mastery began at the negligible level of .5 statements, but climbed steeply to 31.3 in the following autonomy-supportive context.

Forms of Writing

Multiple analysis of variance including Order (2) as the between-subjects variable and Context (2) as the within-subjects variable were performed on eight dependent variables including drawing, letter-like units, random letter-strings, patterned letter-strings, name-elements, invented spelling, adult produced conventional words, and child produced conventional

Table 1 Mean Numbers of Children's Statements in the Controlling Followed by Autonomy-Supportive Context and Autonomy-Supportive Followed by Controlling Context

Categories	Context			
	C followed by A-S $n = 10$		A-S followed by C $n = 10$	
	Control	A-S	A-S	Control
Mastery				
Independent	.5	31.3	2.8	5.7
Dependent	2.8	11.1	1.2	1.2
Competence				
Claim	.7	1.3	.3	.4
Deny	1.0	4.4	.3	1.2
Interest				
Claim	0.0	1.2	.1	0.0
Deny	0.0	0.0	0.0	0.0
Comment	.5	11.9	.9	1.7
Completion	.5	0.0	.9	1.5

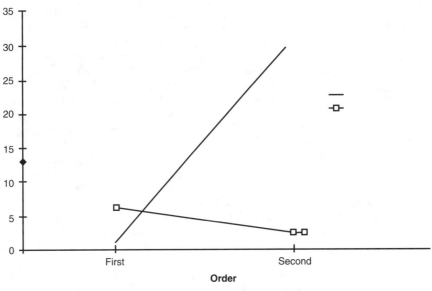

Number of Independent Mastery Statements

C followed by A-S
A-S followed by C

Figure 1 Interaction between context and order for independent mastery.

words. There were significant main effects of Context for drawing $F (1, 18) = 18.00$, $p < .0001$, letter-like units $F (1, 18) = 6.08$, $p < .03$, random letter-strings $F (1, 18) = 10.76$, $p < .01$, patterned letter-strings $F (1, 18) = 14.40$, $p < .001$, name-elements $F (1, 18) = 22.22$, $p < .0001$, adult produced conventional words $F (1, 18) = 61.36$, $p < .0001$, and child produced conventional words $F (1, 18) = 4.8$, $p < .05$. Children in the autonomy-supportive context included more drawings, letter-like units, random letter-strings, patterned letter-strings, name-elements, and child produced conventional words than in the controlling context (see Table 2). Moreover, the adult produced more conventional words in the controlling context than in the autonomy-supportive context (see Table 2). Although children in the autonomy-supportive context included more invented spelling than in the controlling context (see Table 2), the difference was not statistically significant.

DISCUSSION

This study revealed three major findings. First, children's motivation was influenced by the context of the letter writing task. In the autonomy-supportive context, children demonstrated more interest in the letter writing task than in the controlling context. Second,

the order of the interactions affected children's motivation. Children in the controlling followed by autonomy-supportive interaction made more statements of dependent mastery than children in the autonomy-supportive followed by controlling interaction. However, children in the controlling followed by autonomy-supportive interaction also made more statements of independent mastery in the autonomy-supportive context than children in the autonomy-supportive followed by controlling interaction. Third, children used more emergent literacy in the autonomy-supportive context than in the controlling context. When children were in the autonomy-supportive context, they included more drawings, more letter-like units, more random and patterned letter-strings, more name-elements, more child produced conventional words and less adult produced conventional words in their letter than when they were in the controlling context. Each of these findings will be discussed below.

The present study supports previous research indicating that autonomy-support has a positive influence on children's motivation for literacy. This study also expands past research by demonstrating this association in the framework of an emergent literacy task and, in particular, for low-income African-American children. Our study found that the same children demonstrated more interest in the autonomy-supportive context than

Table 2 Mean Numbers of Children's Forms of Writing in Both the Controlling and Autonomy-Supportive Context

Categories	Context	
	Controlling	Autonomy-Supportive
Drawing	.2	1.0
Letter-like units	0.0	.5
Nonphonemic letter-strings		
Random	0.0	.7
Patterned	0.0	.8
Name-elements	0.0	1.1
Invented spelling	0.0	.1
Conventional		
Adult produced	1.9	0.0
Child produced	0.0	.4

in controlling context. This finding is especially important since few studies have examined the motivational influences on African-American children (Graham, 1994). In support of Turner's (1995) findings with middle-income European American children, our results suggest that low-income African-American children's motivation to engage in literacy tasks are not determined solely by a general orientation toward extrinsic versus intrinsic motivation, but rather may also be situated in their encounters with reading and writing.

Our study also supports previous research indicating that the context in which a child learns new skills may affect their intrinsic motivation in that skill domain in the future (Boggiano et al., 1988; Deci & Ryan, 1985). In particular, our study suggests that the controlling nature of the context in which a child engages in an emergent literacy task may undermine their subsequent motivation for that task. As predicted, we found that children in the controlling followed by the autonomy-supportive interaction demonstrated more dependent mastery in both the controlling and autonomy-supportive contexts than children in the autonomy-supportive followed by the controlling interaction. However, we also found that children in the controlling followed by autonomy-supportive interaction made more statements of independent mastery in the autonomy-supportive context than children in the autonomy-supportive followed by controlling interaction. These unexpected findings may be explained, in part, by the children's prior knowledge of letter writing. As kindergartners, these children are likely to have had few experiences with letter writing. Indeed, when visiting their classroom, we did not evidence any classroom lessons on writing a letter. Since research in emergent literacy clearly indicates that many facets of children's literacy development are facilitated through adult guidance, these children may have been more receptive to instruction when first learning how to write a letter. Therefore, although children in the controlling followed by autonomy-supportive interaction elicited more adult help, they also demonstrated more independent mastery since they had more previous adult guidance concerning how to write a letter.

Our study also highlights the importance of autonomy-supportive contexts for children's literacy productions. As expected, the controlling context discouraged emergent literacy behaviors and limited children's opportunities to engage in natural literacy practices. In contrast, the autonomy-supportive context allowed children to write in their own way. As a result, in the autonomy-supportive context, children used many forms of emergent writing such as drawing, scribbling, and invented spellings and wrote for relatively long periods of time without soliciting adult help. These children showed such behaviors as maintaining a flow of writing while changing colors of markers, keeping an attentive eye on the paper, occasionally sounding out words or saying letters aloud. This suggests that autonomy-supportive environments are important in encouraging children's gradual and natural literacy development.

IMPLICATIONS

This study has important, practical implications concerning the context in which literacy occurs. According to Teale (1982), children's literacy environments do not have independent existence, but rather they are constructed in the interactions between children and the persons around them. Our findings support Teale's (1982) contention by suggesting that children's motivation for emergent literacy is situated in their encounters with others and the environment. And, as our data indicate, the autonomy-supportive versus controlling context in which children learn literacy tasks may not only affect their present motivation but may also influence their subsequent motivation for that task. Practically, teachers may allow children more freedom in daily literacy instruction and be more open to children's emergent literacy behaviors. Both teachers and parents may also be more aware of how their language may affect children's motivation for literacy. Whereas controlling language such as verbal commands or criticisms and statements of "should" may undermine children's motivation, open-ended questions, the use of phatics, and repeating what children say may encourage children's motivation for emergent literacy.

Our study also highlights the importance of scaffolding for emergent literacy. In particular, our data suggest that children's literacy development is facilitated through adult guidance especially when learning a new task such as writing a letter. As Teale (1982) asserted, literacy learning is not an independent and purely autonomous activity. In addition to autonomy-support, emergent writers also need guidance, involvement, and structure. What seems important is the right match of structure in a warm and supportive environment with positively motivated role models (Grolnick & Ryan, 1992). In order to encourage natural literacy learning, teachers and parents need to give children the freedom of choice, encourage expressiveness and initiation, and provide guidance and structure that is informational rather than controlling.

CONCLUSIONS

This study provides both theoretical and practical insights into children's motivated literacy learning; however, much research remains to be done. First, although we chose an authentic task for our study, this work was not embedded in the social context of children's everyday lives. Interactions in children's home and classroom environments have an important influence on their intrinsic motivation. For example, in our study, the children's motivation may have been affected by previous writing interactions with the teacher. However, since our study was limited to one classroom, we could not determine how classroom interactions influenced the children's motivated literacy behaviors beyond the effects of our study. Future research may collect data from several classrooms to determine how past writing interactions with teachers influence students' motivation. Future research may also examine the effects of the classroom environment in interaction with the effects of the home environment. For example, can a more autonomy-supportive

context in the home compensate for a more controlling context in the classroom?

Second, although we used a repeated measures design, our study examined only a small time frame for these children. Further research may investigate the longitudinal effects of context on children's motivation for literacy. For example, how does autonomy-supportive versus controlling nature of the context in which children engage in early literacy learning influence their literacy behaviors as they grow older? Moreover, can more autonomy-supportive contexts in children's later literacy experiences facilitate increased motivated engagements with literacy?

In conclusion, motivation is clearly an important factor in children's early engagements with literacy. As our data suggest, the controlling nature of the context in which children learn literacy may not only limit children's opportunities to use emergent literacy, they may also undermine their motivation to do so. Evidently, researchers and educators need to place sharper attention on how the nature of the context influences children's motivation for emergent literacy.

REFERENCES

Bissex, G. L. (1980). *GNYS AT WORK: A child learns to write and read.* Cambridge, MA: Harvard University Press.

Boggiano, A. K., Main, D. S., & Katz, P. A. (1988). Children's preferences for challenge: The role of perceived competence and control. *Journal of Personality and Social Psychology, 54,* 134–142.

Burns, M. S., & Casbergue, R. M. (1992). Parent-child interaction in a writing context. *Journal of Reading Behavior, 20,* 289–312.

Clay, M. M. (1975). *What did I write?* Portsmouth, New Hampshire: Heinemann Press. deCharms, R. (1976). *Enhancing motivation: Change in the classroom.* New York: Irvington.

Deci, E. L., Nezlek, J., & Sheinman, L. (1981). Characteristics of the rewarder and the intrinsic motivation of the rewardee. *Journal of Personality and Social Psychology, 40,* 1–10.

Deci, E. L., & Ryan, R. M. (1985). *Intrinsic motivation and self-determination in human behavior.* New York: Plenum.

Deci, E. L., & Ryan, R. M. (1987). The support of autonomy and the control of behavior. *Journal of Personality and Social Psychology, 53,* 1024–1037.

Deci, E. L., Schwartz, A. J., Sheinman, L., & Ryan, R. M. (1981). An instrument to assess adults' orientations toward control versus autonomy with children: Reflections on intrinsic motivation and perceived competence. *Journal of Educational Psychology, 73*, 642–650.

Gambrell, L. B. (1995). Motivation matters. In W. M. Linek (Ed.), *Generations of literacy: The seventeenth yearbook of the College Reading Association 1995.* Harrisonburg, VA: College Reading Association.

Graham, S. (1994). Motivation in African-Americans. *Review of Educational Research, 64*, 55–117.

Grolnick, W. S., & Ryan, R. M. (1987). Autonomy in children's learning: An experimental and individual difference investigation. *Journal of Personality and Social Psychology, 52*, 273–288.

Grolnick, W. S., & Ryan, R. M. (1992). Parental resources and the developing child in school. In M. E. Procidano (Ed.), *Contemporary families: A handbook for school professionals.* New York: Teachers College Press.

Harter, S. (1981). A new self-report scale of intrinsic versus extrinsic orientation in the classroom: Motivational and informational components. *Developmental Psychology, 17*(3), 300–312.

Harter, S. (1982). The perceived competence scale for children. *Child Development, 53*, 87–97.

Heath, S. B. (1982). What no bedtime story means: Narrative skills at home and at school. *Language in Society, 11*, 49–76.

Hess, R., & Shipman, V. (1965). Early experiences and socialization of cognitive models in children. *Child Development, 34*, 869–886.

Laosa, L. M. (1980). Maternal teaching strategies in Chicano and Anglo-American families: The influence of culture and education on maternal behavior. *Child Development, 51*, 759–765.

McMahon, R., Richmond, M. G., & Reeves-Kazelskies, C. (1998). Relationships between kindergartner teachers' perceptions of literacy acquisition and children's literacy involvement and classroom materials. *Journal of Educational Research, 91*, 173–182.

Morrow, L. M. (1992). The impact of a literature-based program on literacy achievement, use of literature and attitudes of children from minority backgrounds. *Reading Research Quarterly, 27*, 250–275.

Ninio, A. (1980). Picture-book reading in mother-infant dyad belonging to two subgroups in Israel. *Child Development, 51*, 587–590.

Ng, M. M., Guthrie, J. T., Van Meter, P., McCann, A., & Alao, S. (1998). How do classroom characteristics influence intrinsic motivation for literacy? *Reading Psychology, 19*, 319–398.

Pellegrini, A. D., Brody, G. H., & Sigel, I. E. (1985). Parents' book-reading habits with their children. *Journal of Educational Psychology, 77*, 332–340.

Ryan, R. M., Connell, J. P., & Deci, E. L. (1985). A motivational analysis of self-determination and self-regulation in education. In C. Ames and R. Ames (Eds.), *Research on motivation in education: Vol. 2. The classroom milieu.* New York: Academic Press.

Ryan, R. M., & Grolnick, W. (1986). Origins and pawns in the classroom: Self-report and projective assessments of individual differences in children's perceptions. *Journal of Personality and Social Psychology, 50*, 550–558.

Ryan, R. M., Mims, V., & Koestner, R. (1983). Relation of reward contingency and interpersonal context to intrinsic motivation: A review and test using cognitive evaluation theory. *Journal of Personality and Social Psychology, 45*, 736–750.

Schickedanz, J. A. (1986). *More than ABCs: The early stages of reading and writing.* Washington, D.C.: National Association for the Education of Young Children.

Skinner, E. A., & Belmont, M. J. (1993). Motivation in the classroom: Reciprocal effects of teacher behavior and student engagement across the school year. *Journal of Educational Psychology, 85*, 571–581.

Snow, C. E. (1983). Literacy and language: Relationships during the preschool years. *Harvard Educational Review, 53*, 165–189.

Snow, C. E., & Ninio, A. (1986). The contracts of literacy: What children learn from learning to read books. In W. H. Teale and E. Sulzby (Eds.), *Emergent literacy: Writing and reading.* Norwood, New Jersey: Ablex.

Sulzby, E. (1990). Assessment of writing and children's language while writing. In L. M. Morrow and J. K. Smith (Eds.), *Assessment for instruction in early literacy.* Englewood Cliff, New Jersey: Prentice Hall.

Sulzby, E., & Teale, W. H. (1987). *Young children's storybook reading: Longitudinal study of parent-child interaction and children's independent functioning.* Final report to the Spencer Foundation. Ann Arbor, MI: University of Michigan.

Swann, W. B., & Pittman, T. S. (1977). Initiating play activity of children: The moderating influence of verbal cues on intrinsic motivation. *Child Development, 48*, 1128–1132.

Taylor, D. (1983). *Family literacy: Young children learning to read.* Portsmouth, NH: Heinemann.

Teale, W. H. (1982). Toward a theory of how children learn to read and write naturally. *Language Arts, 59*, 555–570.

Teale, W. H. (1987). Emergent literacy: Reading and writing development in early childhood. *National Reading Conference Yearbook, 36*, 45–74.

Turner, J. C. (1995). The influence of classroom contexts on young children's motivation for literacy. *Reading Research Quarterly, 30,* 410–441.

Tizard, B., Hughes, M., Pinkerton, G., & Carmichael, H. (1982). Adult's cognitive demands at home and at nursery school. *Journal of Child Psychology and Psychiatry, 23,* 105–116.

Wood, D. J. (1980). Teaching young children: Some relationships between social interaction, language, and thought. In D. R. Olson (Ed.), *The social foundation of language and thought.* New York: W. W. Norton.

Zuckerman, M., Porac, J., Lathin, D., Smith, R., & Deci, E. L. (1978). On the importance of self-determination for intrinsically motivated behavior. *Personality and Social Psychology Bulletin, 4,* 443–466.

Williams, C. L. (1999). Preschool deaf children's use of signed language during writing events. *Journal of Literacy Research, 31*(2), 183–212.

Preschool Deaf Children's Use of Signed Language During Writing Events

Cheri Lynn Williams

University of Cincinnati

This research examined young deaf children's social interaction during free-choice writing time in their preschool classroom. The study examined the ways in which five deaf children used signed language as they wrote. Results of the study indicated that the children used both signed language and nonverbal expression to engage in representational, directive, interactional, personal, and heuristic use of language to support their writing endeavors. The study raises the question of whether nonverbal expression might also be salient among emergent writers who are not deaf.

In her extensive research on young children's writing development, Dyson (1981, 1983, 1989, 1993) has demonstrated the importance of social interaction in young children's learning to write. In each of her investigations, Dyson has illustrated how children's verbal interaction with one another, and with adults, supports their growth as young writers. For example, in a recent study of the early writing development of young African American children, Dyson (1993) found that the children used oral folk traditions learned in their homes and their talk about popular culture to compose written texts and social places for themselves in their urban primary school. Dyson portrayed the children's writing development as a social process in a complex social world. In an earlier work, Dyson (1989) illustrated how kindergarten, first-grade, and second-grade children used talk, drawing, and dramatic play to represent their worlds and to build relationships with one another. The children's actual writing was only a part of ongoing literacy events,[1] and it was dependent on other symbolic media and other friends' learning to write. The children's social relationships with one another helped to nurture their growth as writers. In another study,

Dyson (1983) examined the role of oral language in kindergarten children's writing development and found the children's talk with one another to be an integral part of the early writing process. The children used oral language to give their writing meaning, to get that meaning into print, and to elaborate on the meaning of the written text. For these children, oral language served a variety of functions and permeated the writing process.

In a recent investigation of the language and emergent literacy experiences of young deaf children (Williams, 1994), I too observed children interacting socially while they wrote in school. Specifically, I noticed that several children interacted with one another a great deal at the writing table of their preschool classroom. I undertook the analysis reported here to examine the children's social interaction and to explicate the role of that interaction in their writing development. I was particularly interested in how the children used signed language as they participated in these writing events. Did these children use signed language in ways that supported their writing development? Was the social interaction related to the writing? Were these children's uses for signed language similar to, or different from, hearing children's uses of oral language as documented in Dyson' studies?

Challenging the once popular belief that "writing begins as written down speech" (Britton, 1970, p. 164), Dyson (1981, 1983, 1989, 1993) has suggested that children's early writing "develops from a form of

---

[1] I am defining *literacy event* as any activity or interaction that involves reading, writing, and drawing (Dyson, 1989). I include drawing because the theoretical position of this paper is that young children's writing develops from a form of drawing (Vygotsky, 1978). The social talk and dramatic play that surrounds and supports the reading, writing, or drawing is part of the literacy event.

drawing" and moves toward "a form of language" (Dyson, 1983, p. 18). That is, young children's writing develops as a direct, or first-order, symbolism. Written language is not merely a written version of spoken language; it is a symbolic system with its own integrity that children explore as part of their total symbolic development (Dyson, 1991).

When children begin to write, they first draw, and from their perspective, these drawings directly represent objects, actions, or people—the drawing does not represent the oral utterance. Young children also scribble as a precursor to writing. Their scribbles, like their drawings, represent specific objects, actions, or people rather than spoken language. In fact, Ferreiro and Teberosky (1982) found that when young children used scribbling or letter-like shapes (i.e., a series of small circles or vertical lines) to represent objects or individuals, the children's graphic representations reflected characteristics (e.g., size, height) of the object or person (see also Schickedanz, 1990; Temple, Nathan, & Burris, 1982). At this point in their development, children are not translating oral language into written language. They are representing their ideas and experiences in graphic form, and these graphics directly represent their intended meaning. Thus, as Vygotsky (1978) suggested, writing is initially a first-order symbolism.

Gradually, children come to understand that they can also "draw their speech" (Vygotsky, 1978, p. 115), and at this point, they begin to use written language as a designation for oral language. Writing then becomes a second-order symbolism as children move toward conventional literacy. Eventually, children come to understand that written language directly represents meanings, and writing becomes, again, a first-order symbolism.

As young children begin to write, they weave together scribbles, drawing, talk, dramatic play, and gradually, written letters and words—instantiating all their symbolic powers to express meaning in written form. The bulk of their meaning is often in the talk and the actions they use to participate in the writing event (Dyson, 1983, 1989; Luria, 1983; Newkirk, 1987). As children move toward conventional literacy, however, they gradually negotiate the boundaries between symbol systems. They differentiate written symbols from those that are drawn, spoken, or dramatized, and eventually, they come to understand that writing can fulfill the functions served by their talk, drawing, and dramatic play. Dyson (1991) suggested that such development occurs through social dialogue as children interact with one another during literacy events that have meaning to their lives. In fact, she argued

that a child's ways of interacting with people and with symbolic materials is an organizing force in the child's written language development (Dyson, 1987).

This theoretical perspective on young children's writing development focuses attention on and acknowledges the various symbolic media and social experiences children rely on as they learn to write. To understand written language development, then, such a perspective requires not only an exploration of children's written texts, but of the social interaction that permeates their earliest attempts at writing (Sulzby, 1990).

THE WRITING DEVELOPMENT OF PRESCHOOL DEAF CHILDREN

Little research has examined the writing development of preschool deaf children. Researchers have focused on young deaf children's language acquisition and development, with little attention to emergent literacy learning. The few studies available examine aspects of deaf children's writing development, and the researchers typically have related their findings to research on young hearing children's writing development.

For example, Ewoldt (1985) examined the patterns of development and the strategies that 4- and 5-year-old deaf children employed in learning to write. Ewoldt related her findings to the major patterns of the literacy process identified by Harste, Woodward, and Burke (1984). As Ewoldt observed the children participating in free-writing time in preschool, she found that, like the hearing children in the Harste et al. project, the deaf children used the principles of organization, generativeness, flexibility, and intentionality as they created their drawn and written texts (see Clay, 1975). Further, Ewoldt noticed that the children interacted socially as they worked. The children made comments about each other's work, which demonstrated their interest in their peers' writing. They offered and received input from one another, often in the form of evaluative statements. Ewoldt concluded that social interaction was important to the children's developing literacy.

Rottenberg and Searfoss (1992) also explored the literacy development of preschool deaf children. They were primarily interested in documenting what young deaf children knew and learned about reading and writing in a preschool setting. Results of the study indicated that the deaf children used drawing and writing as a primary form of communication and as an interactional tool. Most of the children in this study lacked a strong oral or signed language, and throughout the course of the school year, the children came to understand that drawing and writing could be used to communicate specific information and to initiate and maintain social interaction with classmates and teachers. Thus, written language became a primary mode of communication for these children. Further, the children learned a great deal about written language despite their lack of a strong oral or signed language. The authors argued, with other researchers of hearing children's early literacy learning (Baghban, 1984; Y. Goodman, 1986; Sulzby, 1986), that proficiency in oral or signed language is not a prerequisite for learning to read and write.

Conway (1985) explored the free writing of deaf kindergarten children. The primary goal of his study was to examine the purposes for which the deaf children wrote. Results of the study indicated that the children used writing to serve message-related purposes and nonmessage-related purposes. Message-related purposes included using writing to preserve or recall experiences, convey personal information, organize general information, interact with a specific audience, and to entertain. Children used nonmessage-related writing to practice skills (e.g., letter formation) and to explore the mechanics of writing (e.g., how writing implements can be used, how content can be expressed). Conway noted that the purposes for which these deaf kindergarten children used writing were similar to those identified by Dyson (1983) in her study of kindergarten children learning to write.

Andrews and Gonzales (1991) also investigated the free writing of deaf children in kindergarten. They used the children's written products to document and evaluate the children's emerging knowledge about print, particularly their understanding of how the alphabet system works. Results of the study indicated that all six children created drawings labeled with print, which they "read" to their classmates and teachers. Like many hearing children, the deaf children progressed from scribbling, to printing a single random letter, to printing a series of random letters, to printing whole words, and for some of the children, to printing phrases and sentences. The researchers concluded that free writing provided an authentic and meaningful literacy event through which the deaf children discovered "on their own" (p. 72) how the alphabet system works.

In a recent investigation, Ruiz (1995) examined her young deaf daughter Elena's hypotheses about writing. She collected Elena's written products from the home setting from age 3 to 7. Ruiz found that Elena developed many hypotheses about writing, some of which were similar to those of hearing children as documented in the research literature. For example, Elena demonstrated her understanding that writing "stands for things" (p. 209), that there should be correspondence between the size or age of the referent and the written word (Ferreiro & Teberosky, 1982; Schickedanz, 1990), and that sound has something to do with writing. Ruiz also described hypotheses that were unique to Elena, and possibly other deaf children. For example, Elena hypothesized that "the shape of your hand when you sign a word tells you its first letter" (p. 213; see also Mayer, 1995; Padden, 1993; Schleper, 1992), and "sound-based strategies don't help much with real, independent writing when you're deaf" (p. 214). Ruiz argued that although sound played a role in Elena's writing development, Elena did not need a well-developed phonemic awareness to become a successful reader and writer. Like other researchers of hearing children's literacy development (K. Goodman, 1993; Sulzby, 1992), Ruiz questioned whether deaf children could also forego this path in learning to read and write.

Collectively, these studies suggest that preschool deaf children's early writing development may be similar to that of hearing children. Additional documentation of these similarities would provide support for the patterns of writing development researchers have already identified. Exploring the similarities and differences between the ways in which deaf and hearing children learn to read and write may allow theories of literacy development to identify what is fundamental to becoming literate and what may be superfluous. Moreover, describing the ways in which young deaf children learn to read and write may offer important information about the various paths and strategies available to all children in becoming literate. None of the existing research on young deaf children's writing development investigates the specific role of social interaction in that development. Rather, the studies were exploratory in nature, examining deaf children's emerging hypotheses and knowledge about print and the purposes for which they wrote. The previous research was not specifically designed to investigate the ways in which deaf children used signed language to support their writing endeavors. This study aimed at filling that gap. Thus, it has the potential for contributing to our understanding of deaf children's early writing development in particular and to our theories of emergent writing in general.

BACKGROUND OF THE STUDY

The present study is an extension of a qualitative investigation of the language and literacy experiences of young deaf children (Williams, 1994). In the larger study, I examined reading and writing activities in three classrooms of an urban day-school program for preschool children who were deaf or hard of hearing: Preschool I (ages 3–4), Preschool II (ages 4–5), and Kindergarten (ages 5–7). Results of the study indicated that the children learned a great deal about written language despite severe language delay. The findings corroborated those of other emergent literacy studies in suggesting that language acquisition and written language development occur simultaneously and "mutually reinforce one another in development" (Teale & Sulzby, 1989, p. 4).

An extension of the larger study, the analysis reported in this article is based on data I collected in the Preschool II classroom during "writing time," an open-ended composing period that occurred first each morning. Anna, the classroom teacher, permitted the children to interact socially as they worked. To investigate systematically the children's social dialogue during writing events, I used the data collected at the writing table in this classroom as the corpus for the present analysis.

All five children in the Preschool II class were profoundly deaf, and each child had hearing parents. All of the children's parents knew some signs, but none were fluent signers. In fact, several visits to one child's home indicated that signed communication was very limited (Williams, 1991). The children were from different ethnic backgrounds, but they all lived in working-class communities. The children's ages, degree of hearing loss, and ethnicity are provided in Table 1.

The children used signed language as their primary mode of communication, although spoken language, gesture, pantomime, body movement, and facial expression often accompanied their signs. Sometimes the children used American Sign Language (ASL) to communicate. American Sign Language is not derived from any spoken language. It is a visual-gestural language with a grammar and modality different from that of standard English (Liddell, 1980), and thus, it does not have a one-to-one correspondence with spoken English. In fact, the linguistic structure of ASL differs so greatly from that of spoken English that simultaneous communication in ASL and spoken English is very difficult to achieve (Wilbur, 1987). Linguists have described ASL as having the regularity and rule-governedness of a true language with its own mechanisms for relating visual form with meaning (Bellugi, 1988; Lane & Grosjean, 1980).

The children also used Pidgin Sign English (PSE) to communicate. Pidgin Sign English is a contact language in which an individual typically uses ASL signs in English-like word order with some inclusion of English morphemes (Luetke-Stahlman & Luckner, 1991; Schirmer, 1994). Thus, PSE may be referred to as "English-like signing" (Paul & Quigley, 1990). It is often used simultaneously with speech, but it does not consistently maintain a one-to-one correspondence with spoken English.

Pidgin Sign English was used for instructional purposes by most teachers in the preschool, although some teachers also used ASL, particularly when interacting with the children on a personal level. Anna, the classroom teacher in the current study, was a proficient signer, fluent in both ASL and PSE. For the most part, Anna used PSE for instructional purposes, and she approximated English syntax as much as possible. Unlike other teachers in the preschool, Anna was able to sign a majority of the words she spoke (Williams, 1991). Anna sometimes used ASL to communicate, particularly in instances where the children did not understand the concepts she was teaching or when there was a breakdown in communication. Anna made language communication choices based on her ongoing assessment of the children's construction of meaning.

Table 1 Age, Degree of Hearing Loss, and Ethnicity of the Children

| | | PTA (unaided) | | | |
	Age	Right ear	Left ear	SAT (aided)	Ethnicity
Leona	5 yr 7 mo	102	107	50	African American
Marta	5 yr 6 mo	117	112	70	Asian Indian
Carita	5 yr 3 mo	115	75	55	African American
Andrew	5 yr	112	111	45	European American
Kyle	4 yr 11 mo	100	105	60	African American

PTA = pure tone average.
SAT = speech awareness threshold in sound field.

METHODS

Data for the current study were drawn from 18 observations at the writing table in the Preschool II classroom. Although the data included handwritten field notes that described the children's participation at the writing table throughout the study, and particularly during the months of September and October, the primary data were 10 videotapes of the children (and occasionally an adult) participating at the writing table during the months of November through February. The videotapes ranged in length from 14 to 26 minutes, the mean time being 17 minutes. Photocopies of the children's written products that corresponded to the field notes and video tapes were also reviewed in conjunction with videotape transcription.

During the first week of school, Anna told the children that when they arrived each morning, they were to put away their book bags and jackets and go directly to the table to write. There was only one table in Anna's classroom, and it was used for writing time, snack time, and group-work time. The rectangular table was surrounded by six chairs, including one for Anna, and the children had assigned seats, which Anna rotated throughout the year. Each child would get a piece of paper from a nearby shelf and his or her crayon bucket and sit in the appropriate seat at the writing table. Anna gave no further directive about the writing activity. As the children worked, Anna marked attendance, read notes from the children's parents and attended to other school-related business. When she finished these tasks, writing period typically ended. In the early months of the study, Anna seldom interacted with the children during writing time. Later in the investigation, however, when Anna began to witness the children's growing interest in written language (Williams, 1995), she ended writing time by asking the children to tell her about their work. For the purpose of data collection and analysis, I defined a writing event as beginning when the first child came to the table and ending when the last child handed Anna his or her paper.

For the most part, I sat near the video camera during writing time so that I could monitor its functioning. I observed all six children and wrote field notes about their participation in the writing event. Later, these notes were used to annotate the videotape transcriptions. When the children showed me their work, I always commented or asked a question in response. At the end of writing time, I typically asked one or two children to tell me about their writing, and across the 10 videotaped observations, I spoke with each child at least once. During data analysis, these interactions, and all interactions initiated by other adults, were marked with an asterisk.

Data analysis proceeded in several phases and made use of Dyson's two-tiered classification system, which was an adaptation of Halliday's (1973) categories of the functions of language. The five language function categories (interactional, representational, directive, personal, and heuristic) described how the children used language during writing time. The strategy codes described the language devices the children used to carry out each function (Tough, 1977). Dyson provides definitions for each language function and strategy (see Table 2). As an example, she defines directive language as language that is used to direct the actions of self and/or others. Children sometimes use the monitoring strategy to accomplish the directive function of language. Dyson defines monitoring as the use of language to control and direct ongoing writing actions. A child can also direct his or her writing through the accessing strategy, rereading what has been written in order to remember what word needs to be written next. I used Dyson's language function categories, strategy codes, and definitions as a guiding framework throughout data analysis.

The first step in data analysis was the transcription of the videotaped data.[2] I then conducted an ethnographic microanalysis of the transcriptions and my handwritten field notes to identify the children's utterances and social interaction occurring at the writing table (Erickson, 1991). An utterance was defined as any use of signed language during a writing event. I identified 242 signed utterances across the data set. Some utterances were directed at self. Other utterances were directed at peers or adults, and I defined these as social interaction.

For ease of manipulation and organization purposes, the children's utterances were transferred onto individual records in the FileMaker Pro database computer program. I kept the children's social interactions whole so as not to lose meaningful context. Then, I examined each of the 242 signed utterances to identify the various functions for which the children used signed language. Using Dyson's categories, I coded each signed utterance as an interactional, representational, directive, personal, or heuristic use of language.

---

[2]The VCR I used for transcription was equipped with a remote control, which allowed me to pause for still-picture viewing during playback, advance frame-by-frame in still mode, and view in slow motion. These features facilitated detailed transcription. I transcribed the children's signs directly without adding English grammatical markers (e.g., "No play" rather than "Don't play with my crayons."), and I described the children's gestures, body movements, and facial expressions in detail.

Table 2 Categories and Coding System

	Language Functions and Strategies

Interactional language: used to manage social relationships. Strategies include:

Initiating friendship	child asks peer if he/she want to be "the same"
Maintaining friendship	child signs "the same" to a peer indicating a continued friendship
Terminating friendship	child indicates that he/she no longer wants to be "the same" with a classmate
Sharing experiences	child shares personal experience with classmate
Teasing	child teases/jests with classmate
Arguing	child argues with classmate over crayons, friendships, information, etc.
Name calling	child calls classmate a name (e.g., "big mouth")
Establishing status	child establishes his/her status in the group by telling how many crayons he/she possesses

Representational language: provides information about events and situations (real or imagined, past or present) related to the current writing project. Strategies include:

Labeling or naming	child labels or provides a name for object/person drawn
Elaborating or detailing	child provides details about or elaborates on written work
Associating or comparing	child relates current written work to earlier experiences
Reporting	child reports an action or event related to written work
Narrating	child narrates a series of actions or events related to written work
Dramatizing	child acts out a series of actions related to written work
Reasoning	child reasons with self/others about written work to be done

Directive language: used to direct the actions of self and/or others. Strategies include:

Monitoring	child uses language to control and direct ongoing writing actions
Planning	child uses language to control and direct future writing actions
Encoding	child uses language to transfer oral/signed words and phrases into written language (e.g., pronounces sounds, signs specific words)
Decoding	child uses language to read, transferring written symbols into the oral/signed channel
Accession	child rereads what has been written to remember what word needs to be written next
Instructing	child conveys information, teaches peer
Requesting	child asks for needed materials, assistance
Commanding	child directs peer to behave in specific ways
Offering	child offers materials, assistance

Personal language: used to express one's feeling and attitudes. Strategies include:

Evaluating others	child make evaluative comment about peer's work (e.g., "That's a good drawing!")
Evaluating self	child makes evaluative comment regarding his or her own work
Playing with language	child plays with language, including the sounds of language and unique words

Heuristic language: used to explore, or to seek information, or learn about reality. Strategies include:

Seeking confirmation	child asks for confirmation about spelling, mechanical formation, etc.
Seeking fact	child asks for specific information (e.g., "What's that?")
Seeking demonstration	child asks for specific demonstration (e.g., "Will you make the *R* for me?")
Seeking to test	child asks information of peers that he or she already knows

Note. Adapted from Dyson (1983, 1989).

Because many of the children's social interactions included utterances in several categories, I duplicated the records as many times as necessary to permit appropriate categorization by language function. For example, when a child used signed language to label her drawing for a peer (representational function), and that peer responded with an evaluative comment (per-sonal function), the interaction was duplicated and placed in the two broad categories. On one record, the child utterance that was coded representational was highlighted in bold print; on the other record, the personal use of language was highlighted.

Using this process, 8 of the 242 signed utterances fell into the heuristic category, 16 served the personal function of language, 57 were categorized as representational, and 72 were directive. The majority, 89, of the children's signed utterances were interactional in nature.

Then, using Dyson's strategy codes, I analyzed all of the records a second time to identify the strategies the children used to accomplish each language function (see Table 2). For example, children used the strategies of labeling, elaborating, and/or dramatizing to give information about their writing (representational function).

As Dyson (1989) has indicated, the categories of language function are not mutually exclusive; that is, a child's utterance may serve more than one language function at a time (Tough, 1977). Consequently, in some instances, I found that the children's utterances warranted coding in more than one category. This was especially true when the children used facial expression along with their signed communication. For example, when the children labeled their work for peers or adults (representational function), their facial expressions often communicated their own pleasure and satisfaction (personal function). When the children requested help from their peers (directive function), they were often, in essence, seeking demonstration (heuristic function), and this heuristic request was frequently signaled by their facial expression. Facial expression was a significant part of these children's face-to-face communication, which was not surprising, given the nature of signed language, especially ASL. In ASL, facial expression and body position is often integral to the signed communication. In fact, sometimes the children used facial expression and gesture without signs to communicate. For example, it was common for a child to push his or her paper toward a peer and with raised eyebrows and a tilt of the head request assistance (heuristic function) in forming specific letters of the alphabet.

In the initial phase of data analysis, I coded each utterance in only one category based specifically on the signed language the child used. Later, however, feeling that I may have limited the children's intentions, I performed a third phase of analysis and attended to nonverbal communication, particularly facial expression, in conjunction with the signed utterances. In most instances, transcribing the children's signed language was a straightforward task. Transcribing nonverbal expression was another matter. I approached the task conservatively. I only transcribed nonverbal communication when the child's face was clearly in view on the videotape. In some instances, the children's subsequent actions strengthened the intent of their nonverbal communication. Yet, this phase of data analysis was necessarily impres-

sionistic. In essence, I coded my interpretation of the children's facial expressions, gestures, and pantomime, which yielded an additional 41 records.

Using this approach, then, the final analysis produced 283 individual records that documented instances of the children using signed language and nonverbal expression to serve all five language functions. The sections that follow describe the children's use of signed language and non-verbal expression during writing time and demonstrate that social interaction permeated writing events in this preschool classroom.

DRAWING, WRITING, AND SOCIAL INTERACTION

For the five children in this preschool classroom, free-choice writing period was a time for drawing, writing, and social interaction. Although Anna directed the children to write, she permitted them to talk[3] as they worked and so the children engaged in a great deal of social dialogue during writing time. Andrew, Carita, and Leona talked frequently and as much as, if not more than, they drew or wrote. Marta talked less frequently than these three, and Kyle talked the least of all. Yet, the writing table was a place for work and for social interaction, and the children engaged in these activities with interest and enthusiasm.

The children used signed language to serve a variety of functions as they participated at the writing table. As noted above, all five language functions (interactional, representational, directive, personal, and heuristic) were observed over the course of the investigation. Andrew, Carita, and Leona primarily used signed language at the writing table to initiate, maintain, or terminate relationships (interactional function) and to instruct one another (directive function). Marta's most frequent use of language was representational as she provided information about her drawings and written texts. Kyle seldom signed, but through his facial expressions (e.g., smiles) and gestures, he let us know when he was pleased with his work (personal function).[4] Throughout the study, these children used signed language and facial expression in sophisticated ways to support their writing and in ways that were similar to the ways hearing children used oral language as emergent writers.

---

[3]The children's "talk" or face-to-face interaction consisted primarily of signed language. The influence of both ASL and PSE was evident in their communication. Sometimes spoken language accompanied the children's signs, and on occasion, the children spoke without signing. When they interacted with the teacher, spoken language accompanied the children's signs, because the teacher required simultaneous communication.

Interactional Function

Vygotsky (1978) argued that young children's developmental understandings are interpersonal before intrapersonal. Children accomplish developmental work as they interact and cooperate with their peers and other people in the environment who support their endeavors. Dyson (1989) suggested that children's growth as writers is set "firmly within the broad context of children's growth as symbolizers and socializers" (p. 14). The children in the present investigation socialized a great deal during writing time. They shared personal experiences ("Me birthday party."), talked about upcoming events ("Zoo, Friday!"), teased and argued with one another ("Bad, you!"), called each other names ("Big mouth!" "Tattletale!"), and almost on a daily basis, reprimanded one another for inappropriate behavior ("Stop hit!").

The children frequently counted the shades of colored crayons (red, red violet, reddish blue, reddish orange, etc.) in each child's crayon bucket, which established a kind of authority among them. Apparently, having many shades of a colored crayon was noteworthy and cause for attention and respect from one's classmates. Consequently, the children spent a great deal of time socializing in this way ("Blue, me, many! You, one! Ha, ha, ha!"). Elgas (1988) and Kantor, Elgas, and Fernie (1993) also found that certain objects (red rhythm sticks and superhero capes) wielded authority and were used by preschool children as social markers that signaled membership within, and identification with, specific play groups.

On occasion, the children's interactions and arguments over crayon ownership led them to check the print on the sides of the crayons to make sure they were shades of the same color. In these instances, the children's dialogue led to experiences with print that were relevant to the children's ongoing social worlds. Moreover, through these peer interactions, the children demonstrated for one another their shared cultural understanding that written language has authority. For example, if the print on the side of a crayon indicated that the crayon was a shade of red, the children accepted it as so, even if the crayon looked more like orange or pink.

Throughout the study, the children used interactional language to initiate, maintain, and terminate social relationships. They used one sign in particular to indicate the person with whom they would be friends that day (or, more often, that hour). The sign is often translated "same," and is executed by moving the y handshape from one point to another, indicating that the two objects or persons are "the same." The children consistently used this sign to indicate friendships. One child would be "the same" with another child, indicating that the two of them were friends. The children often used this sign to exclude a classmate, and its use frequently resulted in hurt feelings. The classroom teacher, Anna, strictly prohibited use of the sign in this fashion; nevertheless, the children frequently used it as they interacted at the writing table. The following vignette is illustrative:

Videotape Analysis (VT 1, #58), 11/12

Andrew:	(signing to Carita) Same, Leona. [i.e., I'm friends with Leona.] (He has a "smug" look on his face.)
	. . .
Andrew:	(signing to Carita) Same, Leona. (Andrew pulls a red crayon from his bucket.)
Andrew	(signing to Carita) Ha, ha, ha! Red! [i.e., I have a red crayon!] (Leona hands Andrew another crayon. They compare shades to see if both of the crayons are red. They are. They smile at one another, almost conspiratorially.)
Andrew:	(signing to Leona) Same. [i.e., I'm your friend.]
Andrew:	(signing to Carita) Sorry. [i.e., Sorry, I'm not your friend.] (Again, Andrew has a "smug" look on his face. He snaps his finger as if to say "too bad for you" and then signs "Sorry" again, but his facial expression and body language clearly indicate that he is not sorry.)
	. . .
Andrew:	(signing to Leona) Same. Good. [i.e., "We're friends. Good."] (After this, Carita looks away, which effectively terminates Andrew's taunting. Carita's facial expression and body language clearly indicate that she is upset.)

The children made their alliances quite clear. On almost any day I observed, it was easy to determine which children were "the same." These friendships were short lived, however, changing frequently throughout the day. Corsaro (1981) also found that preschool children's friendships were fluid and transitory, being temporally and contextually bound to the immediate situation. Children typically remained friends "for the duration of the interactive episode" (p. 138), and peers who sought access were often

---

[4]Kyle was absent from school on 2 of the 10 days I videotaped. He was a shy child who seldom interacted with peers or adults. From September through February, Kyle contributed only 21 utterances to the entire data corpus, 15 of which involved no signed language. For the most part, Kyle would vocalize to gain attention, hold up his paper for a peer or an adult to see, point to it, and then smile brightly. Kyle's three, one-word utterances consisted of the signs "stop," "finish," and "home." The other three signed utterances were unintelligible to both the classroom teacher and to me.

excluded because they were not a part of the original activity. In fact, children went so far as to deny their earlier friendships as a basis for exclusion, for example, "You're not our friend today" (Corsaro, 1985, p. 164). For these children, friendships served specific functions (e.g., protecting the dynamics of ongoing play) and were rarely based on the personal characteristics of playmates (see also Kantor et al., 1993; Fernie, Davies, Kantor, & McMurray, 1993).

Britton (1970) suggested that young children's talk is the "recruiting area" for their writing. In this study, the children's social lives often interacted with their symbolic lives as their dialogue made its way into their drawing and writing. For example, when Andrew shared the gory details of loosing his front tooth—"Dad, slow, cut"—Carita drew a picture of his snaggletoothed face. On a day when Leona was discussing her upcoming birthday party and the balloons she would be giving each child who attended, Carita drew pictures of different colored balloons. When Marta was absent for several days, the children filled their writing paper with her name, commenting to one another and to adults, "Marta sick. Bed. Home." On this day (and others like it), the children's talk included the naming of individual letters (e.g., *M-A-R-T-A* to spell Marta) and direct instruction in mechanical formation to encode specific messages. The children shared with, or taught, one another what they knew about letter names and how specific letters are formed. For example, Leona showed Andrew how to write the letter *m* by drawing one in the air and exaggerating the two curves. Because the children's knowledge about letter names and how to write the letters varied, these interactions were important to the children's emerging concepts about print. Thus, in some instances, the children's interpersonal communication had the potential for supporting their movement toward conventional literacy.

Representational Function

Representational language serves to give information about real, imagined, past, or present events and situations. Children use the strategies of labeling, elaborating or detailing, associating or comparing, reporting, narrating, dramatizing, and reasoning to carry out this language function. Dyson (1981) found that the kindergarten children in her study initially labeled their drawings only after they had completed them. The drawing activity preceded and determined what was said. This was also true for the deaf children in the current study, particularly in the early months of the investigation.

Field Notes, 10/4

> Andrew is using many different crayons in his drawing. He holds up his paper for me to see. "What is that?" I ask, but he does not answer—he just looks at me and smiles, clearly pleased with his work.
> . . .
> The teacher's aide joins the children at the writing table. Andrew has finished his drawing and is now writing his name on the bottom of the paper. I ask the teacher's aide to ask Andrew what he has drawn. She does so, and Andrew signs, "Dinosaur stamp."

The deaf children primarily used the representational function of language to label their written products for one another and for adults who joined them at the writing table or asked them about their work.

Videotape Analysis (VT 1, #1743), 11/13

> The teacher's aide is sitting at the writing table with the children. Marta taps the aide on the arm, points to her drawing, and signs "Santa Claus." She smiles, clearly pleased with her accomplishment.

Videotape Analysis (VT 2, #1230), 11/28

> Kyle is absent, and I am sitting in his chair, next to Andrew. Andrew calls my attention to what he has written. He is smiling brightly, clearly pleased with his writing.
>
> Researcher: What does that say?
> Andrew: Name, Leona. [i.e., It's Leona's name.]

The children also used signed language, facial expression, gesture, and pantomime to elaborate on what they had drawn or written.

Videotape Analysis (VT 1, #553), 11/12

> Leona leans over and looks intently at Andrew's drawing. She raises her eyebrows as if to ask "What's that?" or "Who's that?" He responds with a sign name I do not recognize, but Leona nods in recognition. Then, Andrew elaborates by signing "Strong, loud, big."
> . . .
> Anna comes to the table and tells the children that it is time to stop writing. Marta holds up her paper for Anna to see.
>
> Anna: Who is that?
> Marta: Woman.
> Anna: It's a woman?
> Marta: (elaborating) Big woman!
> Anna: Oh, it's a big woman. All right.

Videotape Analysis (VT 2, #502), 11/28

> Leona vocalizes to get my attention. Pointing to her drawing, she signs and voices, "Bag. Look. Santa Claus's bag."

Researcher: Are you drawing Santa's bag?
(Leona stands up and pantomimes Santa Claus pulling a heavy bag onto his shoulder. Her movements are deliberate and exaggerated.)

Researcher: Yeah, you're drawing Santa Claus's bag. I see.

Although less frequently, the children also reported on specific actions or events, dramatized or acted out a series of actions related to their drawing, or reasoned with one another during the writing endeavor. They also made associations with previous experiences or people they knew.

Videotape Analysis (VT 8, #4040), 2/26

Andrew has drawn a monster-type creature on his paper. He picks up the paper, and pretends to bite Carita with it. She ignores him and continues writing. Andrew makes monster noises. He pretends to bite Leona as well. Leona tells him to stop. Her facial expression signals her irritation with him. Andrew then walks around the table as his monster "flies" through the air. He continues to make monster noises.

Field Notes, 10/29

Andrew and Carita are talking about Andrew's new tennis shoes. They've noticed that the shoes have letters on them, a *B* and a *K*. (He's wearing British Knights tennis shoes.) Carita points to the *B* and tells Andrew that it is the same as the letter for her sister, Brenda. She smiles. Andrew touches the *K* and says that it is the same as the letter for Kyle's name.

Interestingly, there were no instances in the data of the children narrating a series of actions or events while they wrote, as did the hearing children in Dyson's studies.

Directive Function

As mentioned above, the kindergarten children in Dyson's (1981) investigation and the deaf children in this study initially labeled their drawings only after completion. Later in their development, however, the children decided what they would draw before they began: Language preceded the activity and took on a directive function. Here, the children used "regulatory language" (Halliday, 1973) to organize the writing activity. Thus, language not only assisted the children in representing their world, language also increased their control over it. Specifically, directive language serves to direct the actions of self and others. Children use the strategies of monitoring, planning, encoding, decoding, accessing, instructing, requesting, commanding, and offering to accomplish this language function.

On a regular basis, the children in this investigation used language in directive ways. They frequently signed to themselves, using language as a strategy for planning which crayons they would use and the letters or words they would write. They also used signed language to monitor their ongoing writing process.

Field Notes, 10/4

Andrew is writing his name. Without looking up from his paper, he signs, "Wrong." He marks over the apparent mistake, rewrites the letter, and then signs "Fine." He doesn't look up from his work. He is clearly self-monitoring—signing to himself.

Videotape Analysis (VT 1, #1504), 11/13

The children are busy writing. Today they are writing with markers instead of crayons. Without looking up from her paper, Leona signs "purple" and reaches for the purple marker.
. . .
Everyone seems really into writing with markers. Andrew signs "Marta, me" [i.e., I'm writing Marta's name] and then makes a letter-like shape on his paper. He doesn't look up—clearly signing to himself.

. . .

Marta signs "red" to herself and reaches for a red marker.

Videotape Analysis (VT 7, #3410), 2/19

The children are busy writing. Andrew is using a variety of crayons. Before he pulls a crayon out of his bucket, he signs the color. That is, he signs "red" then searches for the red crayon. He seems to be talking to himself. He writes with the red crayon. After a few seconds, without looking up from his paper, he signs, "Fine, know" [i.e., This is fine; I know what I'm doing]. Then, he signs "blue" and searches for a blue crayon. He pulls out a blue crayon and then checks the print on the side of the crayon. Then he writes with the blue crayon.

This self-directing language is more than an accompaniment to the child's actions; it is part of the action, promoting or supporting the child's activity (Vygotsky, 1962).

Just as frequently, the children used "other-directing" language (Tough, 1977, p. 50) to request help from one another, to offer help, or to instruct one another, conveying information deemed necessary for the writing task at hand.

Videotape Analysis (VT 3, #253 ff.), 12/7

Carita has just responded to Andrew's request for help in encoding Marta's name, and now Carita offers to write Marta's name for Leona. As she writes the name, Leona and Andrew intently watch the demonstration. Their facial expressions reflect their keen interest. After Carita has completed the writing, she touches and immediately fingerspells the *a* and the *r*, making connections between the written form and the signed form. All three children smile, apparently pleased with their work.

. . .

Leona tells Carita and Andrew that she is going to write the word "Mommy." She signs *y* and then tells them that there are two *m*'s in the word. With sign and voice, she directs her classmates to "Watch! Watch!" as she writes.

. . .

Andrew asks Carita to help him write Leona's name, "Leona, help." His facial expression signals the heuristic nature of his request. Carita turns Leona's crayon bucket so that Andrew can see the name tag with Leona's name printed on it. Andrew begins to copy the name, but Carita stops him, signing "wrong," and points emphatically to the model. Andrew touches the letter in question on the name tag and intently studies it. Then, he rewrites the letter.

When the children talked about their writing in this fashion, they transformed written language into a visual object—a thing—which they manipulated and reflected on, developmental tasks essential to their growth as emergent writers (Vygotsky, 1962).

The children frequently used directive language to reprimand one another for what they believed to be inappropriate behavior at the writing table, and, in turn, they commanded one another to behave in ways that were more acceptable for young authors.

Videotape Analysis (VT 1, #1152), 11/12

Leona has placed a pile of crayons near her writing paper. These crayons are all shades of the same color. Apparently, she plans to write with each shade. Anna tells Leona it is time to put on her Phonic Ear [i.e., an auditory assistance device]. As Leona leaves the table, she speaks and signs emphatically to Andrew: "No touch! Stay!" [i.e., Don't touch these crayons! Leave them here!] Her stern facial expression demonstrates the seriousness of her command.

Videotape Analysis (VT 5, #5375), 1/31

Leona has just taken a clean sheet of paper from the shelf. Signing very emphatically, Andrew reprimands her, "Wrong! Forgot!" Then, with slow exaggerated movements, Andrew picks up Leona's first sheet, points to the back, and, pantomiming, he indicates that she must turn the paper over and write on the back before she is permitted to get a second sheet of paper. His face is flushed, as if he is exasperated with her.

The children used both spoken language and signed language to encode. Because the children's speech was (for the most part) unintelligible, it was very difficult to tell whether a child was overtly saying a specific sound to encode a particular letter (as Dyson's children frequently did), or if the oral utterance was the whole word to be encoded. Recent research has indicated that some deaf children frequently use visual strategies for producing their texts rather than, or in addition to, sound-based strategies (Haydon, 1987; Romig, 1985; Ruiz, 1995). For example, some deaf children often use signs as the basis for inventing the spelling of a word. Mayer (1995) explains:

> For some signs the handshape used to make the sign also happens to be a letter from the manual alphabet. For instance, the signs for both "apple" and "onion" are formed using the "x" handshape. The signs for "class" and "concept" use the "c" handshape. As well, the signs given for proper names often incorporate the letter shape into the formation of the sign. A child named "John" or "Jim" would quite likely have their name sign formed using the "j" handshape. The children bring this information to bear on their efforts to invent spellings for words they already know how to sign. (p. 5)

Mayer then gives an example of a child using this strategy in spelling the word *drink*. The sign for the word *drink* has a *c* handshape, so the child wrote *c* as the first letter of the word. Nevertheless, in the present study the videotaped data are not definitive on this point. More clear was the children's common practice of signing the letter or the word (especially names) they were about to write, thus demonstrating the use of signed language to encode.

I did not observe these preschool deaf children using the accessing strategy. Dyson (1989) defined accessing as a "strategy used to seek or to retrieve letters or words from memory; in written language situations, this strategy involves rereading" (p. 285). For example, when children use the accessing strategy while writing, they reread their text to help them remember what word needs to be written next. Because the children in this study wrote individual words and not sentences, this finding was not surprising. Importantly, however, the accessing strategy was documented among the older, kindergarten children as part of the larger investigation. For example, I observed a 6-year-old child in the kindergarten class using the accessing strategy as he composed a story. After he wrote a word, the child reread what he had written, then he signed (and/or said) what he would write next:

Kindergarten Videotaped Data (JVT 6, #4638 ff.), 2/7

> John is writing the story of the three little pigs. I am sitting at the table across from him. John writes *The Three little*, and then he rereads his text and says, "pig." He looks up from his paper and scans the

room, apparently looking for the spelling of the word *pig*. This room is devoid of any print, so when he does not find the word, he asks me for the spelling. John writes *PiG* and then rereads his text. He looks up at me and asks for the spelling of the word *paint*. I fingerspell the word and he writes *Paint*. Then, he rereads the word *paint*, signs/says the word "a" and writes it. At this point, John rereads his text from the beginning, pointing to each word as he reads, "The three little pig paint a" and then he asks me to spell the word *house*. I fingerspell it for him and he writes *House*. He rereads "paint a house" and then says "to." He writes the word *to* and then asks me how to spell *show*. I fingerspell it for him and he writes it. Then he signs/says the word "how" and writes it. He rereads "show how" and then says "to" and writes it. Then, pointing to each word with his pencil, he rereads his entire text in sign and voice. Then he asks me to spell the word *build*. . . .

Sulzby (1990) suggested that developmental tracing of young children's composing and accessing (i.e., rereading) behaviors can provide researchers and educators important information on how young children become conventionally literate.

Personal Function

Dyson (1989) has suggested that personal language is used to "express one's feelings and attitudes" (p. 286). Children use the strategies of evaluating self, evaluating others, and playing with language to accomplish this broad language function. The children in this study frequently used the personal function of language to evaluate their own work. Andrew frequently told himself and others that his written work was "good." He also demonstrated the personal function of language when he signed to himself "Like, yummy," as he added icing to the birthday cake he was drawing. As mentioned earlier, Kyle primarily used facial expression (e.g., smiles) along with his vocalizations, gestures (e.g., pointing), and, presumably, his signs to demonstrate how pleased he was with the pictures he had drawn.

Videotape Analysis (VT 1, #421), 11/12

Kyle vocalizes to get my attention. I am sitting beside the camera. When I look over at him, he holds up his paper and smiles. "What is that?" I ask, but he does not respond. He then walks over to Anna's desk. He does not sign or say anything to her; he just stands beside her desk holding the paper and smiling, clearly pleased with his work. "Oh wow, I like your picture, Kyle. What is that? What did you make?" Anna asks. Kyle vocalizes unintelligibly, presumably in response to Anna's question, and then without waiting for fur-

ther comment, he walks back to the table, sits down, and goes back to his work. He is still smiling.

Like Kyle, all of the children used facial expression, particularly smiles, to demonstrate personal pleasure and satisfaction with their drawn and written accomplishments.

The children also used the personal function of language to evaluate their classmates' written work, regardless of whether or not the critique had been invited.

Videotape Analysis (VT 3, #811), 12/7

Andrew has written Leona's name. He taps her on the arm, and as he runs his finger along the print from left to right, he signs/voices "Leona." Leona immediately picks up her crayon bucket and points to her name tag. She signs "Wrong, one" [i.e., telling Andrew that he made a mistake on one of the letters]. This angers Andrew who yells and signs "No!" But, then he leans forward and intently studies his writing. He looks at Leona and again signs "No," but less emphatically. A few minutes later, Andrew makes the change Leona has suggested.

Videotape Analysis (VT 7, #3550), 2/20

Anna walks by the writing table, and Andrew holds up his paper so that she can see his work. He is smiling, pleased with his work.

Andrew: (signing and speaking) Careful me. [i.e., "I'm working carefully."]
Anna: Yes, that's beautiful.
(Andrew then turns to Leona, looks at her paper, and signs: "Fine. Not." [i.e., "My work is fine, but yours is not."] His facial expression signals a kind of superiority. Leona covers her paper with her arm and looks away.)

As indicated above, the children's facial expressions often demonstrated the evaluative nature of their signed comments. Moreover, sometimes the children used facial expression or gestures without signs to signal approval or disapproval of a classmate's work.

Videotape Analysis (VT 4, #1876), 1/14

Marta is writing letter-like shapes and scribbles on her paper. She taps Andrew on the arm to get his attention and points to her work. He looks at her paper, and then at her. He furrows his brow and makes a face as if to say, "So what." He quickly goes back to his own writing, as if to dismiss her.

Videotape Analysis (VT 5, #5035), 1/31

Andrew has drawn several yellow balloons on his paper. He shows his work to Carita. Carita looks at his paper, and then she places her hand over her eyes and shakes her head disapprovingly.

Dyson (1989) gave the following example of children playing with language: "For some reason, I just made a bubble car. Sounds fun. Bubble car" (p. 286). There were no instances in the data corpus of the deaf children playing with language.

Heuristic Function

Halliday (1973) has suggested that the heuristic function of language is "the use of language to learn" (p. 9). In reference to written language, Dyson (1989) has explained that heuristic language may be used to seek information or learn about encoding, decoding, mechanical formation, or content. The strategies children use to accomplish this language function include seeking confirmation, seeking fact, seeking demonstration, and seeking to test. The deaf children in the present study frequently used heuristic language to ask for specific information about a peer's drawn or written text.

Videotape Analysis (VT 8, #3770), 2/26

Andrew holds up his paper so that Leona can see what he has written. His facial expression clearly indicates that he is pleased with his work. The writing includes letters and letter-like shapes, but there are no conventionally spelled words. Leona points to one of the letters and, raising her eyebrows, she signs, "Who?" [i.e., "Who is that?"]. Andrew answers with a sign name that I do not recognize. Leona nods in recognition, smiles approvingly, and the two return to their writing.

As well, the children often asked for demonstrations of how to write specific letters or words, and they sought confirmation on what they had written. As mentioned earlier, based on their facial expressions, body language, and gestures (i.e., the total context of the videotaped interaction), I argue here that child utterances that requested help (directive function) were also heuristic in nature. Often the children handed their crayons and paper to Carita, who, apparently, was considered the expert writer, and requested that she make a specific letter or word for them. As Carita formed the letters, the children intently watched the demonstration, sometimes leaning completely across the table to follow the mechanical formation. As well, the children frequently asked if they could see Carita's paper, perhaps seeking information for their own endeavors. Moreover, it is interesting to note that, as the expert writer, only Carita tested her classmates' knowledge, for example, "Me *m*. You?" [i.e., "I can make an *m*. Can you?"].

Summary

The data analysis revealed then that the children used signed language and nonverbal expression during writing events to accomplish a wide range of language functions—interactional, representational, directive, personal, and heuristic. The children's social interaction permeated the writing process and assisted them in accomplishing their writing goals.

LANGUAGE USE AND SIGNED COMMUNICATION

Several other patterns emerged during data analysis. First, it was clear that the deaf children's uses for signed language were similar to hearing children's uses of oral language as documented in Dyson's (1983, 1989) studies. Both groups of children talked about their friendships with one another. They discussed past experiences, and through their dramatic play, created new ones to share. Both groups argued over materials; the deaf children disputed crayon ownership, whereas the hearing children "ripped each other off" by taking the "whole tin can" of colored pencils from one another (Dyson, 1989, p. 53). Both groups of children talked about writing competence; the deaf children focused on the ability to form letters and write their classmates' names, whereas the hearing children emphasized the ability to correctly spell specific words. Both groups of children critiqued their classmates' work, focusing on form as well as content. Indeed, the functions for which the deaf children in this study used signed language were similar to the functions for which Dyson's children used oral language as they participated in classroom writing events.

Differences were noted, however, in the children's use of specific strategies to accomplish the language functions. Although Dyson's children used oral language to narrate a series of actions or events, this strategy was not observed among the preschool deaf children. Nor were the deaf children observed playing with language or using the accessing strategy to support encoding (i.e., rereading what they had written in order to remember what word was to be written next). These findings may be related to differences between the hearing and deaf children's ages and experiences with literacy. This explanation seems logical, because, as noted earlier, I have observed kindergarten deaf children using the accessing strategy while writing (Williams, 1994). The children in Dyson's (1983, 1989) studies ranged in age from 5 years to 7 years, 3 months at the beginning of the investigations. The preschool deaf children were younger, ranging in age from 4 years, 11 months to 5 years, 7 months when the study began.

Second, data analysis indicated that the deaf children primarily used ASL to interact with one another and to self-monitor their endeavors at the writing table. Interestingly, the children used both ASL and English-like signing to interact with Anna and other adults who joined them during writing time. It is important to note, however, that the children did not use ASL to accomplish specific language functions and PSE to accomplish others. Rather, these young deaf children demonstrated their ability to code-switch based on their interlocutor's typical mode of communication.

Finally, another interesting pattern that emerged was the children's use of facial expression, gesture, and pantomime to accomplish specific language functions during free-choice writing time. In particular, the children used gesture and pantomime to elaborate on their drawn and written texts (representational function). They often used facial expression to demonstrate satisfaction with their work (personal function), to request assistance from peers (heuristic function), and to signal approval or disapproval of a classmate's writing (personal function). If I had not attended to the children's nonverbal expression during videotape transcription and data analysis, I would have missed much of the meaning the children intended.

CONCLUSIONS AND IMPLICATIONS

The results of this study have several important implications for educators and researchers in the field of literacy and the education of deaf children. This study corroborates Dyson's finding that social interaction is important to young children's writing development. The deaf children in this study engaged in a great deal of social interaction as they worked at the writing table of their preschool classroom, and the talk was often directly related to their writing. As they interacted socially around their evolving texts, the children talked about the spelling of specific words, the names of the letters of the alphabet and how they are formed, the relationship of written letters to fingerspelling, and the relationship of written words to signed words. Metalinguistic conversations such as these had the potential for supporting the children's emerging concepts about print (Andrews & Akamatsu, 1993; Clay, 1975). This finding highlights the importance of an instructional context that provides opportunities for young children to interact with other people as they move from the familiar terrain of talk, drawing, and dramatic play to the less familiar terrain of conventional written language (Clay, 1979; Harste et al., 1984; Rowe, 1989).

The findings of this study also address the current controversy among educators of deaf children concerning the language of instruction in school. For the past 20 years or so, various forms of English signing systems have been used for instructional purposes in classrooms for deaf children and in mainstreaming situations. In recent years, the success of this English-based approach has been questioned, because deaf students have generally failed to achieve the competence in English that this approach was designed to effect (Allen, 1986; Commission on Education of the Deaf, 1988). Consequently, many educators and researchers are now calling for the use of ASL as both the language of instruction and communication (Bouvet, 1990; Israelite, Ewoldt, & Hoffmeister, 1992; Livingston, 1997; Ramsey, 1997). In the study reported here, the deaf children primarily used ASL as they interacted with one another and as they self-directed their own endeavors at the writing table. Their preference for ASL over English signs may be noteworthy. Vernon (1987) argued that ASL hand configurations are easier for deaf children to learn and that ASL is easier to read because its "structure is ideally suited to sight and to the motor and visual functions of human beings" (p. 159). However, I do not want to oversimplify this issue. The children also purposefully used English-like signing to engage hearing adults in conversations about their drawing and writing. This is noteworthy, too, because most deaf children are born into hearing families, who—if they learn to sign—typically use English-like signs. The point is this: These deaf children maneuvered between two forms of signed communication that were visually accessible, intelligible, and meaningful to them. Even as preschoolers, the children were developing knowledge about, and competence navigating within, the complicated linguistic world that was theirs. These children were focused on their written compositions, and they strategically used all the social and symbolic resources available to them to accomplish their goals as young authors. Perhaps in our debates over ASL and English signing systems, we are underestimating the ability of deaf children to make sense of the complex linguistic worlds in which they live, to be the meaning makers that they are (Wells, 1986).

Finally, the results of this study highlight the importance of nonverbal expression to deaf children's emergent writing development. The deaf children not only used signed language to accomplish a full range of language functions related to their writing, they also frequently used facial expression, gesture, and pantomime. In fact, nonverbal expression was used without signing. Our theories of deaf children's writing development must account for the saliency of this emotive communication. Further, this finding begs the question of whether nonverbal expression might also be salient for emergent writers in general. Although we have attended to young children's oral language during composing events (Dyson, 1989; Rowe, 1989), we have yet to incorporate facial expression and body gesture into accounts of early writing development across populations of children (for notable exceptions, see Bloome, 1989, 1991; Woolfolk & Galloway, 1985). But these are, in fact, elements of young children's writing. A child scrunches up his face to accompany the mention of a bad guy's name; it is as much a part of the meaning as is the orthography. Another child gracefully waves her hand over her head to accompany a fairy flying away, and that hand waving is also code for that particular literacy event. Young children perform their early writings, and we miss much of the meaning potential of those performances unless we attend to nonverbal expression. Doing so may contribute significantly to our understanding of emergent writing development for all young children.

REFERENCES

Allen, T. (1986). Patterns of academic achievement among hearing impaired students: 1974 and 1983. In A. Schildroth & M. Karchmer (Eds.), *Deaf children in America* (pp. 161–206). San Diego, CA: College-Hill Press.

Andrews, J. F., & Akamatsu, C. T. (1993). Building blocks for literacy: Getting the signs right. *Perspectives in Education and Deafness, 11*(3), 5–9.

Andrews, J. F., & Gonzales, K. (1991). Free writing of deaf children in kindergarten. *Sign Language Studies, 73*, 63–78.

Baghban, M. (1984). *Our daughter learns to read and write.* Newark, DE: International Reading Association.

Bellugi, U. (1988). The acquisition of a spatial language. In F. Kessel (Ed.), *The development of language and language researchers: Essays in honor of Roger Brown* (pp. 153–185). Hillsdale, NJ: Erlbaum.

Bloome, D. (1989). *Classrooms and literacy.* Norwood, NJ: Ablex.

Bloome, D. (1991, June). *Interaction and intertextuality in the study of classroom reading and writing events: Microanalysis as a theoretical enterprise.* Paper presented at the Second InterAmerican Conference on Classroom Ethnography, Mexico City.

Bouvet, D. (1990). *The path to language: Bilingual education for deaf children.* Bristol, PA: Multilingual Matters.

Britton, J. (1970). The student's writing. In E. Everts (Ed.), *Explorations in children's writing* (pp. 21–32). Urbana, IL: National Council of Teachers of English.

Clay, M. M. (1975). *What did I write? Beginning writing behaviour.* Portsmouth, NH: Heinemann.

Clay, M. M. (1979). *The early detection of reading disabilities* (3rd ed.). Auckland, New Zealand: Heinemann.

Commission on Education of the Deaf. (1988). *Toward equality: Education of the deaf.* Washington, DC: U.S. Government Printing Office.

Conway, D. (1985). Children (re)creating writing: A preliminary look at the purposes of free-choice writing of hearing-impaired kindergartners. *The Volta Review, 87*(5), 91–107.

Corsaro, W. (1981). Entering the children's world—research strategies for field entry and data collection in a preschool setting. In J. Green & C. Wallat (Eds.), *Ethnography and language in educational settings* (pp. 117–146). Norwood, NJ: Ablex.

Corsaro, W. (1985). *Friendship and peer culture in the early years.* Norwood, NJ: Ablex.

Dyson, A. H. (1981). *A case study examination of the role of oral language in the writing process of kindergartners.* Unpublished doctoral dissertation, University of Texas at Austin.

Dyson, A. H. (1983). The role of oral language in early writing processes. *Research in the Teaching of English, 17*, 1–30.

Dyson, A. H. (1987). Individual differences in beginning composing: An orchestral vision of learning to compose. *Written Communication, 4*, 411–442.

Dyson, A. H. (1989). *Multiple worlds of child writers: Friends learning to write.* New York: Teachers College Press.

Dyson, A. H. (1991). The word and the world: Reconceptualizing written language development or, Do rainbows mean a lot to little girls? *Research in the Teaching of English, 25*, 97–123.

Dyson, A. H. (1993). *Social worlds of children learning to write in an urban primary school.* New York: Teachers College Press.

Elgas, P. (1988). *The construction of a preschool culture: The role of objects and play styles.* Unpublished doctoral dissertation, The Ohio State University, Columbus.

Erickson, F. (1991). Ethnographic microanalysis of interaction. In M. LeCompte, W. Millroy, & J. Preissle (Eds.), *Qualitative research in education* (pp. 201–225). San Diego, CA: Academic Press.

Ewoldt, C. (1985). A descriptive study of the developing literacy of young hearing-impaired children. *The Volta Review, 87*(5), 109–126.

Fernie, D., Davies, B., Kantor, R., & McMurray, P. (1993). Becoming a person in the preschool: Creating integrated gender, school culture, and peer culture positionings. *Qualitative Studies in Education, 6*,(2), 95–110.

Ferreiro, E., & Teberosky, A. (1982). *Literacy before schooling.* Exeter, NH: Heinemann.

FileMaker Pro 4.1 [Computer software]. (1998). Santa Clara, CA: FileMaker, Inc.

Goodman, K. (1993). *Phonics phacts*. Portsmouth, NH: Heinemann.

Goodman, Y. (1986). Children coming to know literacy. In W. H. Teale & E. Sulzby (Eds.), *Emergent literacy: Writing and reading* (pp. 1–14). Norwood, NJ: Ablex.

Halliday, M. A. K. (1973). *Explorations in the functions of language*. London: Edward Arnold.

Harste, J., Woodward, V., & Burke, C. (1984). *Language stories and literacy lessons*. Portsmouth, NH: Heinemann.

Haydon, D. M. (1987). *An interpretation of the writing process and written language strategies used by a selected group of hearing impaired children*. Unpublished doctoral dissertation, University of Missouri, Columbia.

Israelite, N., Ewoldt, C., & Hoffmeister, R. (1992). *Bilingual-bicultural education for deaf and hard-of-hearing students*. Toronto, Ontario: MGS Publications Services.

Kantor, R., Elgas, P., & Fernie, D. (1993). Cultural knowledge and social competence within a preschool peer culture group. *Early Childhood Research Quarterly, 8*(2), 125–147.

Lane, H., & Grosjean, F. (1980). *Recent perspectives on American Sign Language*. Hillsdale, NJ: Erlbaum.

Liddell, S. (1980). *American Sign Language syntax*. The Hague, The Netherlands: Mouton.

Livingston, S. (1997). *Rethinking the education of deaf students: Theory and practice from a teacher's perspective*. Portsmouth, NH: Heinemann.

Luetke-Stahlman, B., & Luckner, J. (1991). *Effectively educating students with hearing impairments*. New York: Longman.

Luria, A. (1983). The development of writing in the child. In M. Martlew (Ed.), *The psychology of written language* (pp. 237–277). New York: Wiley.

Mayer, C. (1995). *Further lessons to be learned from the young deaf orthographer*. Paper presented at the meeting of the American Educational Research Association, San Francisco.

Newkirk, T. (1987). The non-narrative writing of young children. *Research in the Teaching of English, 21*, 121–145.

Padden, C. A. (1993). Lessons to be learned from the young deaf orthographer. *Linguistics and Education, 5*, 71–86.

Paul, P., & Quigley, S. (1990). *Education and deafness*. New York: Longman.

Ramsey, C. (1997). Tom, Robbie, and Paul: Deaf children as literacy learners. In J. Flood, S. B. Heath, & D. Lapp (Eds.), *Handbook of research on teaching literacy through the communicative and visual arts* (pp. 314–322). New York: Macmillan.

Romig, L. G. (1985). *The cognitive processing and cueing systems used by young hearing impaired children when spelling*. Unpublished doctoral dissertation, University of Missouri, Columbia.

Rottenberg, C., & Searfoss, L. (1992). Becoming literate in a preschool class: Literacy development of hearing-impaired children. *Journal of Reading Behavior, 24*, 463–479.

Rowe, D. W. (1989). Author/audience interaction in the preschool: The role of social interaction in literacy lessons. *Journal of Reading Behavior, 21*, 311–349.

Ruiz, N. T. (1995). A young deaf child learns to write: Implications for literacy development. *Reading Teacher, 49*, 206–217.

Schickedanz, J. (1990). *Adam's righting revolutions: One child's literacy development from infancy through grade one*. Portsmouth, NH: Heinemann.

Schirmer, B. R. (1994). *Language and literacy development in children who are deaf*. New York: Macmillan.

Schleper, D. R. (1992). When F spells cat: Spelling in a whole language program. *Perspectives in Education and Deafness, 11*, 11–14.

Sulzby, E. (1986). Writing and reading: Signs of oral and written language organization in the young child. In W. H. Teale & E. Sulzby (Eds.), *Emergent literacy: Writing and reading* (pp. 50–89). Norwood, NJ: Ablex.

Sulzby, E. (1990). Assessment of emergent writing and children's language while writing. In L. Morrow & J. Smith (Eds.), *Assessment for instruction in early literacy* (pp. 83–109). Englewood Cliffs, NJ: Prentice-Hall.

Sulzby, E. (1992). Transitions from emergent to conventional writing. *Language Arts, 69*, 290–297.

Teale, W., & Sulzby, E. (1989). Emergent literacy: New perspectives. In D. Strickland & L. Morrow (Eds.), *Emerging literacy: Young children learn to read and write* (pp. 1–15). Newark, DE: International Reading Association.

Temple, C., Nathan, R., & Burris, N. (1982). *The beginning of writing*. Boston: Allyn & Bacon.

Tough, J. (1977). *The development of meaning: A study of children's use of language*. New York: Wiley.

Vernon, M. (1987). Controversy within sign language. *ACEHI Journal, 12*(3), 155–164.

Vygotsky, L. S. (1962). *Thought and language*. Cambridge, MA: Massachusetts Institute of Technology Press.

Vygotsky, L. S. (1978). *Mind in society*. Cambridge, MA: Harvard University Press.

Wells, G. (1986). *The meaning makers: Children learning language and using language to learn.* Portsmouth, NH: Heinemann.

Wilbur, R. (1987). *American Sign Language: Linguistic and applied dimensions* (2nd ed.). Boston: Little, Brown, & Co.

Williams, C. L. (1991). *The verbal language worlds and early childhood literacy development of three profoundly deaf preschool children.* Unpublished doctoral dissertation. The Ohio State University, Columbus.

Williams, C. L. (1994). The language and literacy worlds of three profoundly deaf preschool children. *Reading Research Quarterly, 29,* 125–155.

Williams, C. L. (1995). Preschool teachers' theoretical and pedagogical stances on the language and literacy development of deaf and hard-of-hearing children: Implications for teacher preparation and in-service programs. *American Annals of the Deaf, 140*(1), 56–64.

Woolfolk, A., & Galloway, C. (1985). Nonverbal communication and the study of teaching. *Theory into Practice, 24*(1), 77–84.

Fuson, K. C., Carroll, W. M., & Drueck, J. V. (2000). Achievement results for second and third graders using the standards-based curriculum everyday mathematics. *Journal for Research in Mathematics Education 31* (3), 277–295.

Achievement Results for Second and Third Graders Using the Standards-Based Curriculum Everyday Mathematics

Karen C. Fuson, William M. Carroll, and Jane V. Drueck

Northwestern University

ABSTRACT

Students using Everyday Mathematics (EM), developed to incorporate ideas from the NCTM Standards, were at normative U.S. levels on multidigit addition and subtraction symbolic computation on traditional, reform-based, and EM-specific test items. Heterogeneous EM 2nd graders scored higher than middle- to upper-middle-class U.S. traditional students on 2 number sense items, matched them on others, and were equivalent to a middle-class Japanese group. On a computation test, the EM 2nd graders outperformed the U.S. traditional students on 3 items involving 3-digit numbers and were outperformed on the 6 most difficult test items by the Japanese children. EM 3rd graders outscored traditional U.S. students on place value and numeration, reasoning, geometry, data, and number-story items.

The mathematics education community, stimulated by new economic and technological contexts and by research on students' mathematical thinking, has called for substantial changes in the nature of elementary school mathematics classroom instruction (National Council of Teachers of Mathematics [NCTM], 1989, 1991, 1995). In contrast to traditional textbook instruction focused primarily on rote learning and practice of skills, instruction is envisioned through which students construct meaning for the mathematical concepts and procedures they are investigating and engage in meaningful problem-solving activities (e.g., Cobb & Bauersfeld, 1995; Hiebert et al., 1996; Lampert, 1991). This student construction of mathematical knowledge is facilitated by teachers who elicit, support, and extend children's mathematical thinking (Fraivillig, Murphy, & Fuson, 1999); promote discussions (e.g., Schifter & O'Brien, 1997); use meaningful representations of mathematical concepts (Fuson, Smith, & Lo Cicero, 1997; Fuson, Wearne, et al., 1997); and encourage use of alternative solution methods (Carpenter & Fennema, 1991; Hiebert & Carpenter, 1992). However, results from the recent Third

International Mathematics and Science Study (TIMSS) indicate that the U.S. curriculum continues to be an "underachieving curriculum" compared to the mathematics curricula in higher achieving nations and that instruction in the United States is still more likely to focus on practice of skills than on understanding (McKnight et al., 1989; Peak, 1996; Stigler, 1997).

A number of U.S. researchers investigating the progress of students experiencing meaning-based instruction have reported positive effects on students' understanding and achievement (Carpenter, Franke, Jacobs, Fennema, & Empson, 1998; Cobb, Wood, Yackel, & Perlwitz, 1992; Fuson, Smith, & Lo Cicero, 1997; Fuson, Wearne, et al., 1997). For example, when compared with students in traditional textbook-based classes, students in Cobb et al.'s Problem-Centered Mathematics Project scored significantly higher on measures of conceptual understanding as well as on standardized tests (Wood & Sellers, 1997). These students also saw mathematics as a more purposeful and understandable activity than did students using traditional approaches. Carpenter, Fennema, and colleagues have reported similar gains for Cognitively

Guided Instruction in problem solving and conceptual understanding (Carpenter et al., 1998). Others have reported strong gains in students' conceptual understanding and use of calculation methods when students are actively involved in activities that make mathematics meaningful (Fuson, Smith, & Lo Cicero, 1997; Fuson, Wearne, et al., 1997; Hiebert & Wearne, 1993).

With support from the National Science Foundation and other sources, a number of mathematics educators have developed elementary mathematics programs to attempt to incorporate this research on learning and teaching into a full-scale curriculum. Although these new curricula differ in design and in details, they all were developed to incorporate the ideas of the NCTM Standards (1989, 1991, 1995). One of these curricula in wide use around the country is the University of Chicago School Mathematics Project's elementary curriculum Everyday Mathematics (EM). The design of this curriculum generally reflects constructivist theories of learning (Steffe & Cobb, 1988; Steffe & Gale, 1995). Students, frequently working in small groups or pairs, actively explore mathematical ideas. Lessons are designed so that students build upon their substantial informal knowledge by making connections to everyday experiences. To scaffold students' thinking during problem solving and discussions, teachers are advised to use manipulatives such as pattern blocks or the hundreds grid for many lessons. By frequently generating and solving story problems, students build conceptual understanding of number and operations. With respect to computational proficiency, both paper-and-pencil and mental activities are designed to allow students to develop conceptual understandings of the operations, and the standard multidigit algorithms are omitted from the curriculum (in accordance with Kamii, 1989). Students are encouraged to invent and discuss their own solution methods. Research from mathematics education and cognitive science regarding the development of conceptual structures and solution methods has also guided the sequence of topics in the curriculum (e.g., see the literature reviewed in Fuson, 1992).

Along with an emphasis on active learning and conceptual understanding, a guiding principle in the development of EM is that developers of the traditional elementary curricula have seriously underestimated the capabilities of children (Bell, 1974; Bell & Bell, 1988). The EM curriculum was based on the belief that children can learn far more mathematics, with deeper understanding, than has been expected in more traditional programs. Along with whole number concepts and operations, topics that are usually delayed until the upper elementary grades—such as uses of negative numbers, functions, fractions, mental computation, and geometry—are explored beginning in kindergarten. Calculators, rulers, and other mathematical tools are used throughout the curriculum. Because of the breadth of the mathematics covered, developers have taken a spiral approach through which ideas are continuously reviewed and are practiced frequently in different contexts and with increasing complexity. For example, kindergartners and first graders investigate the properties of polygons using geoboards or shapes constructed with plastic straws, and fourth graders make compass and straight-edge constructions and investigate relationships among geometric properties. Games are frequently used to review and practice skills as well as to introduce new concepts.

Although the EM curriculum was extensively field tested and information from classroom observation, teacher feedback, and student tests was incorporated into the revisions (Hedges & Stodolsky, 1987), no study had followed students for multiple years. In conjunction with their funding of development of the EM 4–6 curriculum, the National Science Foundation funded such a longitudinal study of students in the EM curriculum by an outside investigator familiar with the curricular approach (the first author of this study). During the 1994–1995 school year, first graders ($n = 496$) in six school districts using the EM curriculum were tested and interviewed (Drueck, Fuson, & Carroll, 1999). On a broad range of questions, the performance of EM students exceeded that of U.S. students receiving traditional instruction and matched or exceeded performance of one or both of the East Asian (Taiwanese and Japanese) samples on many of the questions (comparison samples were from Stigler, Lee, & Stevenson, 1990).

In the two studies reported here, these same students are followed in second and third grades. Because whole districts often opt for the adoption of a new curriculum, it was difficult to match EM schools to comparable schools for a 5-year longitudinal study. Therefore, existing studies in relevant areas of mathematics were chosen to provide comparisons. For example, during the first year of the study, items from Stigler et al.'s cross-national study (1990) were used (Drueck et al., 1999). A similar design was used in the two studies here (i.e., items were selected because they are considered important in new mathematics curricula, they were taken from tests like the National Assessment of Educational Progress [NAEP] that reflect some consensus about the type of mathematics that students should know, or they were chosen from cross-national comparisons).

In Study 1 we followed the progress of EM second graders on developing concepts related to whole numbers and to multidigit computation. For comparison, assessment items were drawn from a study of U.S. and Japanese second graders (Okamoto, Miura, & Tajika, 1995; Okamoto, Miura, Tajika, & Takeuchi, 1995). In Okamoto et al.'s study, two subtests were constructed, one to assess number sense and the other to assess mathematics achievement, chiefly in computation. Given the "invented algorithm" approach taken by EM, student achievement in each of these areas was of interest. The cross-national nature of the Okamoto et al. study also provided a follow-up to the cross-national aspect of our first-grade study.

In Study 2 we followed the progress of EM third graders in their understandings and uses of whole number concepts and computation together with other mathematical topics, such as geometry and measurement. Results from the fourth NAEP as well as test data from Wood and Cobb (1989) provided a basis for comparing EM students to other U.S. students in several mathematical areas. Although the EM longitudinal sample was not a random sample as was the NAEP sample, the EM sample was selected to represent students and schools from a wide range of backgrounds. Items from the Wood and Cobb Cognitively Based Elementary School Mathematics Test were selected because this test was devised to assess conceptual understanding. It was developed as part of a meaning-focused research project, the Problem-Centered Mathematics Project, and thus reflects mathematical performance valued in those project classes. Assessments in both Study 1 and Study 2 included additional items, including some performance-based questions, that represent other aspects of the EM curriculum.

Formal and informal interactions with the Grade 2 and Grade 3 teachers involved in the study, their principals, and school or district mathematics coordinators indicated that all teachers in each grade used the EM curriculum as their only curriculum—with the exception of one teacher who also used material from a textbook. Data of students from this teacher were included because many teachers supplement any given curriculum, and these data would be biased against the main direction of the results. In these and all interactions, we made clear that we were outside researchers examining strengths and weaknesses of EM and were not representatives for the curriculum itself. Determining how teachers were using the curriculum is a complex issue and would have required more substantial classroom observation and teacher interviews than were allowed for in these studies. We were able to make only one videotaped classroom observation and to hold one teacher post-observation interview for each teacher. Observed lessons were selected to be ones of central importance for the grade level and to permit the display of EM practices (such as discussing children's solution methods) in the lesson. Teachers were randomly assigned to be observed while they taught the selected five lessons on word-problem solving and multidigit addition and subtraction in Grade 2 and the six lessons on addition, subtraction, multiplication, division, and decimals in Grade 3.

The whole-class portions of the classroom observations were coded on a scale of meaning-based classroom practices constructed in consultation with prominent researchers. The most striking strengths identified were the degree to which children were engaged in the learning process and the extent to which teachers established a safe environment in which students could explore and discuss their mathematical thinking (Mills, 1996; Mills, Wolfe, & Brown, 1997). Almost all teachers established classrooms that appeared to have safe and supportive climates. Most children were actively engaged in the learning process and appeared to enjoy learning mathematics. In most classrooms, at least a few children made contributions to the class on their own initiatives. These aspects all relate to recent results concerning aspects of classroom practices that support learning. Stipek et al. (1998) reported that children who enjoyed mathematics learned more than those who did not and that students of teachers who supported learning and effort and encouraged autonomy showed more gains in conceptual understanding than children whose teachers did not engage in these practices.

Additional informal evidence validating the above characteristics in EM classrooms came from extensive conversations with several Grade 3 teachers. They reported conversations among Grade 3 teachers in their buildings concerning differences they all noticed in children who had used EM in Grades 1 and 2. They found that children entered their classes liking mathematics more than in previous years (e.g., "The EM children really look forward to math class"). The children also expected teachers to ask them how they solved a problem, not just to report their answers ("If we don't ask how children solved a problem, they'll just volunteer their method").

STUDY 1

METHOD

Participants

At the end of the school year, 392 second graders in 22 classes were tested. Of these students, 343 students had been in the original first-grade longitudinal sample. Because we were evaluating the longitudinal effect of the EM curriculum, only the scores of these original 343 students are discussed in this analysis. The 11 schools included urban, suburban, and rural or small-town schools, and the student populations ranged from low-income to affluent. Two classes were Spanish-speaking bilingual classes.

Test, Items, and Procedure

Whole-class tests were administered by a researcher from the Northwestern University Longitudinal Study in April or May of second grade. Each question on the 45-item test was read aloud while students followed along in their test books. Questions were read twice and repeated as necessary, and students were allowed sufficient time to complete each item. Test administration took approximately 60 minutes.

For comparative purposes, a subset of the questions was taken from the Okamoto et al. study (Okamoto, Miura, & Tajika, 1995; Okamoto, Miura, Tajika, & Takeuchi, 1995); 10 items were taken from their number-sense subtest and 14 from their mathematics-achievement subtest. These questions were presented in the same order as in the original study as part of our class test. Okamoto et al.'s study included 29 U.S. second graders attending a middle- to upper-middle-class school in the San Francisco area and 33 Japanese second-grade students attending a middle-class public school in Tokyo. Because the questions were drawn from the

texts at both schools, the test was considered to be "curriculum fair." Although these questions covered only a portion of the mathematics in the EM curriculum (e.g., no geometry or data items were included), all were on topics that were covered in the second-grade EM curriculum. One caveat is that although symbolic computation was tested, this topic had not been given much emphasis in the EM curriculum. Instead, students were more likely to have carried out computations in solving a story problem or as part of a larger activity. Furthermore, Okamoto et al.'s students were middle class to upper-middle class whereas the EM sample was more heterogeneous. Although these differences somewhat complicated direct comparisons, both were biased against EM. Because X^2 tests were done for the individual items, a more conservative .01 level of significance (instead of .05) was used, $X^2(1) \geq 6.64$.

RESULTS AND DISCUSSION

Table 1 shows the results on the number-sense test for U.S. and Japanese students in Okamoto et al.'s study and for EM students in this study. EM students scored significantly better than the U.S. traditional students on two items and lower than both the U.S. and Japanese students on one item. No other differences were significant. EM students were outscored on the question "How many numbers are there between 6 and 2?" However, the question is somewhat ambiguous;

Table 1   Grade 2: Percentages Correct on Number-Sense Test

Item	Okamoto et al. Samples[a]		
	EM $n = 343$	U.S. $n = 29$	Japanese $n = 30$
1. Which number is closer to 28: 31 or 22?	88	69*	87
2. How many numbers are between 2 and 6?	35	66*	60*
3. What number comes 4 numbers before 60?	72	66	93
4. What is the smallest 2-digit number?	62	79	47
5. What number comes 10 after 99?	64	59	43
6. What number comes 9 after 999?	41	14*	27
7. Which difference is bigger: between 6 and 2 or between 8 and 5?	46	62	47
8. Which difference is smaller: between 99 and 92 or between 25 and 11?	48	55	40
9. What is the smallest 5-digit number?	43	28	27
10. How much is 301 take away 7?	39	17	33
Mean	54	52	50

[a] These samples are from Okamoto, Miura, & Tajika (1995). The U.S. students were middle class to upper-middle class and used a traditional textbook approach.
* On the chi-square test, significantly different from the EM sample with $p \leq .01$.

Table 2   Grade 2: Percentages Correct on Mathematics Achievement Test

Item	Okamoto et al. Samples[a]		
	EM $n = 343$	U.S. $n = 29$	Japanese $n = 30$
1. Fill in the missing numbers: ___ , 630, 640, 650, ___ , ___ , 680			
1a. 620	95	59*	100
1b. 660	96	55*	100
1c. 670	94	55*	100
2. 67 + 5	87	66*	96
3. 80 − 7	67	76	96*
4. 600 + 100	94	35*	92
5. 110 − 40	50	21*	84*
6. 2 × 3	78	79	100
7. 4 × 1	78	76	100
8. 6 × 4	53	52	92*
9. 1 × 5	77	72	100
10. 296 + 604	54	69	88*
11. 536 − 127	26	41	88*
12. How long is the shaded area?	24	10	56*
Mean	70	55	92

[a]   U.S. and Japanese samples are from Okamoto, Miura, & Tajika, 1995.
*   On the chi-square test, significantly different from the EM sample with $p \leq .01$.

EM students perhaps interpreted it as "How many steps are there between 2 and 6?" or "What is the difference between 6 and 2?" An error analysis showed that 51% of EM students gave the answer four, indicating that they had interpreted the question in one of these ways. The only other question answered correctly by fewer than 40% of the EM students was "How much is 301 − 7?" However, this percentage correct was higher than for either the U.S. comparison or Japanese students. Results on the mathematics-achievement test showed a pattern different from the number-sense results, with the Japanese students scoring near ceiling on most items and the EM students scoring between the Japanese and the U.S. comparison students (see Table 2). The Japanese students scored significantly higher than the EM students on the six most advanced items. EM students scored significantly higher than the traditional U.S. students on six problems (four if problems 1a, 1b, and 1c are counted as a single problem); these six items involved knowledge of patterns, addition, and subtraction of tens.

Results on other items given to the EM students are shown in Table 3. More than three fourths of the EM second graders correctly wrote 3- and 4-digit numbers, and even when place values were given out of order, as on Problems 5 and 6, two thirds of the students correctly wrote the 3-digit number (the 5-digit number in

Item 6 is advanced for second graders but was still answered correctly by 38% of the EM second graders).

Because Okamoto et al.'s U.S. students were of higher socioeconomic status than those in the heterogeneous EM sample, EM performance on the 2-digit computation items was compared to that of national norms for comparable individual items on a standardized test (Stanford Achievement Test, Psychological Corporation, 1992). The EM students were above national norms for multidigit addition (65% vs. 50%) and at the norm for multidigit subtraction (38%).

EM first graders had demonstrated strong conceptual knowledge of the fraction one half. The item requiring circling half of 12 stars in an uneven array was correctly answered by 32% of the EM first graders compared to 11% of U.S. students in traditional instruction (Drueck et al., 1999). By second grade, the proportion of EM students correctly answering this question more than doubled (to 65%), approaching the 71% of U.S. fifth graders in traditional instruction (Stigler et al., 1990) who answered this question correctly.

The strength of EM students seems to be related to the intended curriculum. Compared to time allotted in a traditional curriculum, more time in the EM curriculum was allotted to discussion of students' strategies, such as various counting strategies. These ideas and skills also were reinforced and practiced through

Table 3 Grade 2: Percentages Correct on Additional Items From EM Test

Question	EM $n = 343$
Place value	
1. Write the number five thousand four.	76
2. Write the number three hundred twenty-six.	85
3. Write the number that is 10 more than 57.	85
4. Write the number that is 100 less than 465.	71
5. Write the number that has 6 tens, 3 ones, 5 hundreds.	66
6. Write the number that has 7 thousands, 8 tens, 5 ten thousands, 1 one, 0 hundreds.	38
7. What is the number that is the same as ten tens?	62

8. Complete the number grid:
    "Here is a piece of the hundreds grid,
    Fill in the missing numbers on the grid,"
	84

Computation	
9. 36 + 47 (vertical format, no context)	65
10. 72 − 26 (vertical format, no context)	38
11. At the water park, the Loop Slide is 65 feet high. The Tower Slide is 28 feet high. How much shorter is the Tower Slide?	30

12. Jim had 63 crayons. He put 10 in each box.
     a. How many boxes did he fill?
     b. How many crayons were left over?
	56
	65

13. There are 264 children at school. How many teams of 10 could you make with these 264 children?	29
Fractions	
14. Circle 1/4 of the dots.	23
15. Draw a circle around one half of the stars.	65

counting exercises (e.g., "Write 10 more than 43") and regular activities involving computation and number comparisons on number lines and number grids. EM students also explored fractions in everyday situations from kindergarten onward. In contrast, the EM curriculum had fewer examples of vertical context-free symbolic computations, items on which the EM students did not outperform traditional U.S. samples.

STUDY 2

Comparison computation problems in Study 1 were largely symbolic because the comparison items were originally presented in that way. However, computation in the EM curriculum is usually embedded in a context such as a story problem or a larger problem-solving activity, so the Grade 2 symbolic items did not present a complete picture of the computational abilities of EM students. Study 2 included both symbolic and contextualized computation problems as well as questions in geometry, data, and reasoning.

Third-grade items from the fourth NAEP (Brown & Silver, 1989; Kouba, Carpenter, & Swafford, 1989; Lindquist & Kouba, 1989a, 1989b) and from a cognitively based test for Grade 3 (Wood & Cobb, 1989) were used for comparative purposes. Because of the nature of the tests and their construction by experts in the field, they provided items considered to be important both in new and in traditional U.S. mathematics curricula.

METHOD

Participants

A whole-class test was administered to 620 third graders in 29 classes. These were in the same districts described in Study 1, with additional students and classes due to the mixing of classes and the influx of students new to the schools. Of this group, 236 were part of the original first-grade sample, and their scores are the focus of this study.

Whole-class tests were administered during the month of May by a researcher from the Northwestern University Longitudinal Study staff. Each test consisted of 33 questions and took approximately 50 minutes to administer. The first questions, taken from the Wood and Cobb test (1989), were administered orally, as they had been on the original test; on the remaining items, students worked independently, although, upon request, questions were read to an individual. Four forms of the test were constructed to increase the number of questions without increasing the test time, and two forms were used in each class. All students answered four of the items, and the remaining questions were each answered by about half the EM students. Testing was planned so that each question was given to students from the whole range of achievement levels and SES backgrounds.

Of the total 64 questions, 22 were taken from the fourth NAEP for the purpose of comparison. Nine were taken from a third-grade cognitively based mathematics test (Wood & Cobb, 1989) given at the same time of the school year. The results for the Wood and Cobb sample are for traditional and problem-centered students combined, as reported by Wood and Cobb. Additional questions were follow-ups to the second-grade tests or were taken from the third-grade EM curriculum. Several performance-based items reflective of the curriculum were included (e.g., drawing or measuring a line segment of a given length).

The 22 NAEP questions were divided into two subtests for analysis: a Number Concepts and Computation subtest and a Geometry, Data, and Reasoning subtest. Each of these subtests contained 11 questions. These questions were presented in the same format as on the NAEP, either multiple choice or open-ended. Chi-square tests were used to compare performance on all NAEP and Wood and Cobb (1989) items. Because of the number of tests, the more conservative .01 level of significance was used (instead of .05), $X^2(1) \geq 6.64$. Because between 10% and 15% of the 18,033 students were tested on each NAEP item (Carpenter, 1989), the NAEP sample was assumed to be 1,800 on each question.

RESULTS AND DISCUSSION

Number and Computation

As shown in Table 4, the EM third graders scored higher overall than did third graders in the NAEP comparison group on the Number and Computation test (mean 65% vs. 52%). The difference between groups

was significant on six of the items, in each case favoring the EM students (by a mean percentage of 25%). EM students outscored the NAEP group on the two questions that involved place-value knowledge (e.g., "What number is 100 more than 498?"), on all three story problems, and on Item 8, which assessed understanding of the connection between addition and subtraction. Thus, EM students did better on problems that were more conceptual or that involved a context.

On eight of the nine items, EM students scored significantly higher than the Wood and Cobb (1989) students (an economically heterogeneous sample comprised of some students receiving a traditional approach and some students receiving the Wood and Cobb meaning-based approach) (see Table 5). The EM students scored about 20% higher on each of the six number stories (addition, subtraction, multiplication, and division story problems), on a numerical problem with an unknown factor (3 * _____ = 27), and on the unknown-added problem in the context of base-ten blocks.

To assess progress of EM students in computation, we repeated three symbolic computation questions from the second-grade test (Study 1) on the third-grade test and gave a comparable 2-digit subtraction problem (54 − 37). As the results in Table 6 indicate, EM students made progress on both multidigit addition and subtraction. Along with better performance on subtraction, the incidence of the common error of "subtracting the smaller digit from the larger in each column" decreased from 31% for the students in Grade 2 (50% of the 62% incorrect) to only 12% for the students in Grade 3 (43% of the 28% incorrect).

Geometry, Data, and Reasoning

The EM students significantly outperformed the NAEP students on the four geometry items, half the data and graphing items, and the reasoning item (see Table 7). Differences were especially large for the following items: finding the perimeter of a rectangle with length and width shown (50% higher), showing a conceptual understanding of area (36% higher), and using reasoning (35% higher). In fact, EM third graders did as well as or outperformed the seventh graders in the NAEP sample on three of the questions: finding the area of a 6-by-5 rectangle with square units shown (56% of students in both groups correct), finding the perimeter of a 4-by-7 rectangle with the dimensions given (67% of EM third graders correct vs. 46% of seventh graders), and the reasoning question (64% of EM third graders correct vs. 45% of the seventh graders). EM students scored a mean of 23% higher on the three significant data and graphing items.

Table 4　EM Grade 3 and NAEP Grade 4: Percentages Correct on NAEP Number and Computation Items

Question	EM Grade 3 n = 107 to 119[a]	NAEP Grade 4 n = 1,800[b]
Place value		
1. What digit is in the thousands place in the number 43,486?	67*	45
2. What number is 100 more than 498?	80*	43
Symbolic computation (Vertical form except Question 8, which was horizontal)		
3. 57 + 35	79	84
4. 49 + 56 + 62 + 88	60	48
5. 54 − 37	72	70
6. 504 − 306	38	45
7. 242 − 178	62	50
8. If 49 + 83 = 132, which of the following is true? (132 − 49 = 83 is the answer)	56*	29
Computation in number stories		
9. Robert spends 94 cents. How much change should he get back from $1.00?	85*	68
10. Chris buys a pencil for 35 cents and a soda for 59 cents. How much change does she get back from $1.00?	59*	29
11. At the store, a package of screws costs 30 cents, a role of tape costs 35 cents, and a box of nails costs 20 cents. What is the cost of a roll of tape and a package of screws?	77*	58
Mean	65	52

[a]　From a total of 236, EM samples varied across various subsamples of 107, 117, and 119. Item samples are available from the authors.

[b]　A total of 18,033 third graders participated in the fourth NAEP. Only 10% to 15% of these students answered each item (Carpenter, 1989). On Chi-square tests, the NAEP subsample was assumed to be 1,800 on each item.

*　On the chi-square test, the EM sample was significantly higher than the NAEP sample, $p \leq .01$.

Although these problems were presented separately from computation, some of the geometry and data problems obviously involved computation (e.g., finding the perimeter of a rectangle or adding data from a table). Thus, the emphasis of the EM program on problem solving, applications, and computation in a context seems to be effective in reducing the consistent complaint about students in traditional curricula—that even when they master algorithms, they can have difficulty using these algorithms in applied situations (Kouba et al., 1989).

The high scores on the area and perimeter questions indicate that the EM emphasis on meaningful concrete exploration of traditionally underrepresented topics like geometry and measure is effective. Perhaps because EM students use tools (e.g., rulers, tape measures, and pattern-block geometry templates) and manipulatives (e.g., using geoboards to construct rectangles and counting the distance around) that involve area and perimeter, these students are less likely to confuse the two concepts.

SUMMARY

Various efforts are underway nationally to improve the mathematics achievement of U.S. students. The approach taken in the University of Chicago School Mathematics Project and similar meaning-based projects and curricula is an attempt to replace the "underachieving curriculum" (McKnight et al., 1989) with a more ambitious and meaningful mathematics program grounded in solving problems in contexts (rather than mostly symbolic problems), using manipulatives and tools to facilitate children's thinking, and fostering children's mathematical thinking by teachers. Whereas traditional U.S. primary programs have focused on practice of facts and of whole number algorithms, the EM curriculum and other reform programs also include a wider range of mathematical topics as envisioned by the NCTM Standards (1989).

Results from the two studies here show positive results for this approach. EM students at Grades 2 and 3 were at normative U.S. levels on multidigit addition

Table 5   Grade 3: Percentages Correct on Items From Wood and Cobb Test

Question	EM n = 107 to 119[a]	Wood & Cobb n = 191
Number stories		
1. Paul planted 46 tulips. His dog dug up some of them. Now there are 27 tulips left. How many tulips did Paul's dog dig up?	68*	49
2. Sue had some crayons. Then her mother gave her 14 more crayons. Now Sue has 33 crayons. How many crayons did Sue have in the beginning?	76*	50
3. Ann and Stacy picked 31 roses altogether. Ann picked 17 roses. How many roses did Stacy pick?	79*	52
4. Mary, Sue, and Ann sold 12 boxes of candy each. How many boxes of candy did they sell in all?	74*	49
5. There were 48 birds in a tree. Then, 14 flew away and 8 more arrived. How many birds are in the tree?	70*	51
6. In school, 24 children play soccer. Each soccer team has 6 players. How many teams are there?	88*	60
Place value and conceptual addition/subtraction		
1. There are 12 cubes hidden in the box. How many cubes are there altogether? (Drawing shows 4 ten-longs, 7 unit-cubes [base-10 blocks], and a box.)	77	67
2. Some cubes are hidden in the box. There are 57 cubes altogether. How many cubes are hidden? (Drawing shows 2 ten-longs, 2 unit-cubes [base-10 blocks], and a box.)	73*	50
Multiplication and division computation		
1. 3*___ = 27	80*	59

[a]   Because different forms of the test were given, the number of EM students varied from a total sample of 236 across subsamples of 107, 117, and 119. Item samples are available from the authors.
*   On the chi-square test, the EM sample was significantly higher than the Wood and Cobb (1989) sample with $p \le .01$.

Table 6   Second- and Third-Grade EM: Percentages Correct on Longitudinal Symbolic Computation

Question	End of second grade n = 343	End of third grade n = 236
80 − 7	67	82
110 − 40	50	80
296 + 604	54	78
72 − 26	38	—
54 − 37	—	72

Note. Comparable but different 2-digit subtraction problems were used in the two tests.

and subtraction symbolic computation. On a test of number sense, the heterogeneous EM Grade 2 students scored higher than middle-class to upper-middle-class U.S. traditional-textbook students on two items and matched them on the remaining items, and their scores were equivalent to those of middle-class Japanese students. On a computation test, the Grade 2 EM students outperformed the same U.S. students on

three items involving 3-digit numbers. They were, however, outperformed on the six most difficult test items by the Japanese children. Compared to other heterogeneous groups of U.S. students using traditional approaches, EM Grade 3 students scored higher on items assessing knowledge of place value and numeration, reasoning, geometry, data, and solving number stories. EM third graders even showed performance equivalent to or stronger than NAEP seventh graders on a few questions in these areas. Given the generally poor performance of U.S. students in geometry and measurement, such as on the recent TIMSS and sixth NAEP (Kenney & Silver, 1997), these results show the improvements in both understanding and achievement that can be attained with a more ambitious elementary curriculum.

Stipek et al. (1998) found that teachers' practices promoted by motivation researchers and mathematics education reformers (focusing on learning and effort and encouraging autonomy) enhanced students' conceptual understanding. They related this finding to experimental motivation studies in which focusing subjects' attention on mastery (as opposed to performance)

Table 7 EM Grade 3 and NAEP Grade 4: Percentages Correct on Geometry, Data, and Reasoning Items

Question	EM Grade 3 $n = 107$[a]	NAEP Grade 4 $n = 1,800$[b]
Geometry		
1. What is the area of this rectangle?		
a. 6-by-5 rectangle with square units shown	56*	20
b. With length and width shown (6 by 5)	19*	5
2. What is the perimeter of this rectangle?		
a. What is the distance around a 4-by-7 rectangle?	23*	15
b. With length and width shown (4 by 7)	67*	17
Data and graphing		
3. Using a graph		
a. Reading bar graph	80	67
b. Comparing information from bar graph	54*	29
c. Combining information from bar graph	46	44
4. Using a table		
a. Reading a table	87*	70
b. Comparing information in a table	60*	34
c. Combining information in a table	63	58
Reasoning		
5. Four cars wait in a single line at a traffic light. The red car is first in line. The blue car is next to the red. The green car is between the white car and the blue car. Which car is at the end of the line?	64*	29
Subtest mean	56	35

[a] Because different forms of the test were given, slightly different numbers of students were tested on different items (EM n = 129 or 107).

[b] Nationwide, a total of 18,033 third graders participated in the fourth NAEP. Only 10% to 15% of these students answered each question (Carpenter, 1989). A sample of 1,800 was assumed for the chi-square tests.

* On the chi-square test, the EM sample was significantly higher than the NAEP sample, $p \leq .01$.

contributed to "deep" as opposed to "shallow" processing. Performance on some of the tasks on which EM students outperformed other students provides indirect support for the interpretation that EM students were approaching tasks in a deeper, more engaged way. For example, the reasoning task (Table 7, Item 5) on which the Grade 3 EM students outperformed NAEP Grade 7 students (64% to 45%) is simple if students draw a picture, a deeper form of engagement with the problem. Similarly, number stories are more accessible if students try to understand the underlying situation instead of focusing on key words or on the sizes of numbers (shallow strategies frequently used by students using traditional textbooks).

Children's opportunity to learn was an important issue in interpreting the results of this study. However, several other issues relate to opportunity to learn. EM developers recommend 60 minutes of class time a day, and schools in the study reported scheduling that much time for math—exceeding the more common 45-minute mathematics period. However, this greater time for learning was accompanied by two other important changes: the inclusion of more ambitious topics and the support of learning in the new ways discussed in this report. Topics generally underrepresented or delayed in traditional curricula, such as geometry, fractions, and algebra, were explored at all grades in the EM curriculum. To assist students, mathematical ideas were often presented in real-life contexts and in problem-solving activities. Alternative solution methods were to be elicited and discussed. In brief, a greater opportunity to learn, in terms of both total time and the inclusion of more ambitious topics, was accompanied by activities that made the mathematics meaningful to the students.

Some caveats are also important in interpreting these results. First, we do not claim or show that Everyday Mathematics is the only or the best of the new curricula approaches. We suggest only that children learning from the EM curriculum can learn more than children learning from teachers using a traditional curriculum. Second, we are not arguing for the inclusion of any particular topic at any grade. We are concluding only that U.S. children can learn more advanced topics not ordinarily covered in traditional textbooks.

Third, we are not saying that the EM teachers were exemplary teachers but only that their classrooms showed certain characteristics described above. In fact, the classroom coding indicated some areas of relative weakness. Almost all whole-class discourse was teacher-to-student instead of student-to-student; the majority of student responses were brief; descriptions and discussion of solution methods were largely superficial; and few teachers extended student thinking (see Fraivillig et al., 1999; Mills, 1996; Mills et al., 1997, for more details).

Fourth, although EM student computation was at normative levels (i.e., it was as good as performance of students using traditional textbooks), this normative level was not as high as the level in East Asian countries and not as high as one would wish (e.g., at Grade 2, only 38% correct on 2-digit subtraction with regrouping). EM did not "fix" this national computation problem as well as it "fixed" learning in other areas. The reasons for this finding are complex and cannot be summarized briefly (see Mills & Fuson, 1998, for a discussion and more data).

Fifth, and related to all the above, is the issue of breadth versus depth in the topics covered in a given year. This issue is one that needs to be addressed in future research and in discussion within the research community. EM developers deliberately chose a spiral approach in which topics were repeated within a year and across years. Many teachers reported difficulty with this approach because they did not know when to seek mastery of a particular topic by all children. Furthermore, in the first three grades, the one or two teachers in whose classrooms we saw indepth discussion of student thinking articulated their vision of the curriculum as consisting of a progression or range of solution methods through which they helped all children move (what Simon, 1995, called a "learning trajectory"); they did not view the curriculum as being composed just of the content of the EM lessons. These teachers looked for ways to help children move along throughout the year rather than just in the EM lessons focused on these topics, and they felt comfortable stopping on a given day to follow up on student thinking. Other teachers said that they felt considerable pressure to "cover" or "get through" the EM curriculum because there were so many lessons; in fact, no teacher taught all lessons in any year. Thus, there is conflict resulting from at the same time increased breadth of a curriculum that includes more advanced new topics and the depth required in allowing time for children to discuss their thinking. The trade-offs need to be examined in future research.

One alternative that might be explored in such research is the approach taken in the Children's Math Worlds project: Concentrate on more ambitious grade-level goals that are connected to the usual grade-level goals instead of including new topics such as fractions. Teachers can help urban children from poverty backgrounds if the teachers are supported by a curriculum that has ambitious computational goals more in line with East Asian curricula (e.g., 2-digit addition with regrouping in Grade 1) and enables teachers to support children through a learning progression of single-digit (Fuson, Perry, & Ron, 1998) and multidigit methods (e.g., Fuson, 1998). In this project, urban children from poverty backgrounds outperform U.S. children from an economic range of backgrounds and look more like East Asian children in their performance and conceptual understanding (Fuson, 1996; Fuson, Smith, & Lo Cicero, 1997).

The reform movement is under attack nationally as promoting "fuzzy mathematics" and as failing to support traditional grade-level calculation performance. Our results from the most widely used elementary reform curriculum (at the time of the research) do not support such critics. On traditional vertical symbolic multidigit addition and subtraction, EM students performed as well as students using traditional approaches. On a wide range of other mathematically and conceptually demanding tasks, EM students outperformed other groups. Thus, this study provides an existence proof that U.S. students can perform considerably better than they ordinarily do when learning from traditional approaches and that teachers can learn to support such learning through use of a carefully developed curriculum.

REFERENCES

Bell, M. S. (1974). What does "Everyman" really need from school mathematics? *Mathematics Teacher, 67,* 196–202.

Bell, M. S., & Bell, J. B. (1988). Assessing and enhancing the counting and numeration capabilities and basic operation concepts of primary school children. Unpublished manuscript, University of Chicago.

Brown, C. A., & Silver, E. A. (1989). Data organization and interpretation. In M. M. Lindquist (Ed.), *Results from the fourth mathematics assessment of the National Assessment of Educational Progress* (pp. 28–34). Reston, VA: National Council of Teachers of Mathematics.

Carpenter, T. P. (1989). Introduction. In M. M. Lindquist (Ed.), *Results from the fourth mathematics assessment of the National Assessment of Educational Progress* (pp. 1–9). Reston, VA: National Council of Teachers of Mathematics.

Carpenter, T. P., & Fennema, E. (1991). Research and cognitively guided instruction. In E. Fennema, T. P. Carpenter, & S. J. Lamon (Eds.), *Integrating research on teaching and learning mathematics* (pp. 1–16). Albany: State University of New York Press.

Carpenter, T. P., Franke, M. L., Jacobs, V. R., Fennema, E., & Empson, S. B. (1998). A longitudinal study of invention and understanding in children's multidigit addition and subtraction. *Journal for Research in Mathematics Education, 29,* 3–20.

Cobb, P., & Bauersfeld, H. (Eds.). (1995). *The emergence of mathematical meaning: Interaction in classroom cultures.* Hillsdale, NJ: Erlbaum.

Cobb, P., Wood, T., Yackel, E., & Perlwitz, M. (1992). A follow-up assessment of a second-grade problem-centered mathematics project. *Educational Studies in Mathematics, 23,* 483–504.

Drueck, J. V., Fuson, K. C., & Carroll, W. M. (1999). Performance of U.S. first graders in a reform math curriculum compared to Japanese, Chinese, and traditionally taught U.S. students. Manuscript submitted for publication.

Fraivillig, J. L., Murphy, L. A., & Fuson, K. C. (1999). Advancing children's mathematical thinking in Everyday Mathematics classrooms. *Journal for Research in Mathematics Education, 30,* 148–170.

Fuson, K. C. (1992). Research on whole number addition and subtraction. In D. A. Grouws (Ed.), *Handbook of research on mathematics teaching and learning* (pp. 243–275). New York: Macmillan.

Fuson, K. C. (1996, April). Latino children's construction of arithmetic understanding in urban classrooms that support thinking. Paper presented at the annual meeting of the American Educational Research Association, New York.

Fuson, K. C. (1998). Pedagogical, mathematical, and real-world conceptual-support nets: A model for building children's mathematical domain knowledge. *Mathematical Cognition, 4,* 147–186.

Fuson, K. C., Perry, T., & Ron, P. (1996). Developmental levels in culturally-different finger methods: Anglo and Latino children's finger methods of addition. In E. Jakubowski, D. Watkins, & H. Biske (Eds.), *Proceedings of the eighteenth annual meeting of the North American Chapter of the International Group for the Psychology of Mathematics Education* (Vol. 2, pp. 347–352). Columbus, OH: ERIC Clearinghouse for Science, Mathematics, and Environmental Education.

Fuson, K. C., Smith, S. T., & Lo Cicero, A. M. (1997). Supporting Latino first graders' ten-structured thinking in urban classrooms. *Journal for Research in Mathematics Education, 28,* 738–760.

Fuson, K. C., Wearne, D., Hiebert, J. C., Murray, H. G., Human, P. G., Olivier, A. I., Carpenter, T. P., & Fennema, E. (1997). Children's conceptual structures for multidigit numbers and methods of multidigit addition and subtraction. *Journal for Research in Mathematics Education, 28,* 130–162.

Hedges, L. V., & Stodolsky, S. S. (1987). *A formative evaluation of Kindergarten Everyday Mathematics* (Evaluation report #86/87-KEM-1). Chicago: University of Chicago School Mathematics Project.

Hiebert, J., & Carpenter, T. P. (1992). Learning and teaching with understanding. In D. A. Grouws (Ed.), *Handbook of research on mathematics teaching and learning* (pp. 65–97). New York: Macmillan.

Hiebert, J., Carpenter, T. P., Fennema, E., Fuson, K., Human, P., Murray, H., Olivier, A., & Wearne, D. (1996). Problem solving as a basis for reform in curriculum and instruction: The case of mathematics. *Educational Researcher, 25*(4), 12–21.

Hiebert, J., & Wearne, D. (1993). Instructional tasks, classroom discourse, and students' learning in second-grade arithmetic. *American Educational Research Journal, 30,* 393–425.

Kamii, C. (with Joseph, L. L.). (1989). *Young children continue to reinvent arithmetic—2nd grade: Implications of Piaget's theory.* New York: Teachers College Press.

Kenney, P. A., & Silver, E. A. (1997). *Results from the sixth mathematics assessment of the National Assessment of Educational Progress.* Reston, VA: National Council of Teachers of Mathematics.

Kouba, V. L., Carpenter, T. P., & Swafford, J. O. (1989). Number and operations. In M. M. Lindquist (Ed.), *Results from the fourth mathematics assessment of the National Assessment of Educational Progress* (pp. 64–93). Reston, VA: National Council of Teachers of Mathematics.

Lampert, M. (1991). Connecting mathematical teaching and learning. In E. Fennema, T. P. Carpenter, & S. J. Lamon (Eds.), *Integrating research on teaching and learning mathematics* (pp. 121–152). Albany: State University of New York Press.

Lindquist, M. M., & Kouba, V. L. (1989a). Geometry. In M. M. Lindquist (Ed.), *Results from the fourth mathematics assessment of the National Assessment of Educational Progress* (pp. 44–54). Reston, VA: National Council of Teachers of Mathematics.

Lindquist, M. M., & Kouba, V. L. (1989b). Measurement. In M. M. Lindquist (Ed.), *Results from* the fourth mathematics assessment of the National Assessment of Educational Progress (pp. 35–43). Reston, VA: National Council of Teachers of Mathematics.

McKnight, C. C., Crosswhite, F. J., Dossey, J. A., Kifer, E., Swafford, J. O., Travers, K. J., & Cooney, T. J. (1989). The underachieving curriculum: Assessing U.S. school mathematics from an international perspective. Champaign, IL: Stipes.

Mills, V. L. (1996, April). Observing second-grade classrooms implementing Everyday Mathematics: What do we see of reform goals? Paper presented at the annual meeting of the American Educational Research Association, New York.

Mills, V. L., & Fuson, K. C. (1998). Issues surrounding reform-curriculum computational performance. Manuscript in preparation.

Mills, V. L., Wolfe, R., & Brown, R. (1997, March). Supporting reform goals through a reform curriculum: Observing second- and third-grade teachers implementing Everyday Mathematics. Paper presented at the annual meeting of the American Educational Research Association, Chicago.

National Council of Teachers of Mathematics. (1989). Curriculum and evaluation standards for school mathematics. Reston, VA: Author.

National Council of Teachers of Mathematics. (1991). Professional standards for teaching mathematics. Reston, VA: Author.

National Council of Teachers of Mathematics. (1995). Assessment standards for school mathematics. Reston, VA: Author.

Okamoto, Y., Miura, I. T., & Tajika, H. (1995, April). Children's intuitive understanding of number and formal mathematics learning: A cross-national comparison. Paper presented at the annual meeting of the American Educational Research Association, San Francisco.

Okamoto, Y., Miura, I. T., Tajika, H., & Takeuchi, Y. (1995, April). A developmental study of U.S. and Japanese children's representations of number, place value understanding, and mathematics achievement. Paper presented at the annual meeting of the American Educational Research Association, San Francisco.

Peak, L. (1996). Pursuing excellence: A study of the U.S. eighth-grade mathematics and science teaching, learning, curriculum, and achievement in an international context. Washington, DC: National Center for Educational Statistics.

Psychological Corporation. (1992). Stanford Achievement Test, Primary 2, Form L. Harcourt Brace Jovanovich.

Schifter, D. E., & O'Brien, D. C. (1997). Interpreting the standards: Translating principles into practice. Teaching Children Mathematics, 4, 202–205.

Simon, M. A. (1995). Reconstructing mathematics pedagogy from a constructivist perspective. Journal for Research in Mathematics Education, 26, 114–145.

Steffe, L. P., & Cobb, P. (1988). Construction of arithmetical meanings and strategies. New York: Springer-Verlag.

Steffe, L. P., & Gale, J. (1995). Constructivism in education. Hillsdale, NJ: Erlbaum.

Stigler, J. W. (1997, April). Classroom mathematics instruction in Germany, Japan, and the United States: An introduction to the TIMSS videotape classroom study. Paper presented at the annual meeting of the American Educational Research Association, Chicago.

Stigler, J. W., Lee, S., & Stevenson, H. W. (1990). Mathematical knowledge of Japanese, Chinese, and American elementary school children. Reston, VA: National Council of Teachers of Mathematics.

Stipek, D., Salmon, J. M, Givvin, K. B., Kazemi, E., Saxe, G., & MacGyvers, V. L. (1998). The value (and convergence) of practices suggested by motivation research and promoted by mathematics education reformers. Journal for Research in Mathematics Education, 29, 465–488.

Wood, T., & Cobb, P. (1989). The development of a cognitively-based elementary school mathematics test: Final report. West Lafayette, IN: Purdue University, School Mathematics and Science Center.

Wood, T., & Sellers, P. (1997). Deepening the analysis: Longitudinal assessment of a problem-centered mathematics program. Journal for Research in Mathematics Education, 28, 163–186.

de Jong, T., & van Joolingen, W. R. (1998). Scientific discovery learning with computer simulations of conceptual domains. *Review of Educational Research, 68*(2), 179–201.

Scientific Discovery Learning with Computer Simulations of Conceptual Domains

Ton de Jong and Wouter R. van Joolingen

University of Twente

Scientific discovery learning is a highly self-directed and constructivistic form of learning. A computer simulation is a type of computer-based environment that is well suited for discovery learning, the main task of the learner being to infer, through experimentation, characteristics of the model underlying the simulation. In this article we give a review of the observed effectiveness and efficiency of discovery learning in simulation environments together with problems that learners may encounter in discovery learning, and we discuss how simulations may be combined with instructional support in order to overcome these problems.

In the field of learning and instruction we now see an impressive influence of the so-called constructivistic approach. In this approach a strong emphasis is placed on the learner as an active agent in the process of knowledge acquisition. As in the objectivistic tradition, where developments were followed and encouraged by computer-based learning environments such as programmed instruction, tutorials, and drill-and-practice programs (Alessi & Trollip, 1985), computer learning environments help to advance developments. Examples are *hypertext environments* (see, e.g., Gall & Hannafin, 1994), *concept mapping environments* (see e.g., Novak & Wandersee, 1990), *simulations* (De Jong, 1991; Reigeluth & Schwartz, 1989; Towne, 1995), and *modeling environments* (e.g., diSessa & Abelson, 1986; Riley, 1990; Smith, 1986).

In this article we concentrate on the use of *computer simulations* for learning because learning with simulations is closely related to a specific form of constructivistic learning, namely, *scientific discovery learning*. First, we give a short introduction to the

two key terms in this article (computer simulation and scientific discovery learning) followed by a short overview of studies that compared unsupported simulation-based discovery learning to some form of expository teaching. These studies show that the advantages of simulation-based learning are not always evident and suggest that one of the reasons for this is that learners have problems with discovery learning. This conclusion brings us to the main questions discussed in this article: What are the problems that learners have in discovery learning, and how can we design simulation environments that support learners in overcoming these problems?

A *computer simulation* is a program that contains a model of a system (natural or artificial; e.g., equipment) or a process. Computer simulations can broadly be divided into two types: simulations containing *conceptual* models, and those based on *operational* models. Conceptual models hold principles, concepts, and facts related to the (class of) system(s) being simulated. Operational models include sequences of cognitive and noncognitive operations (procedures) that can be applied to the (class of) simulated system(s). Examples of conceptual models can be found in economics (Shute & Glaser, 1990) and in physics (e.g., electrical circuits; White & Frederiksen, 1989, 1990). Operational models can, for example, be found in radar control tasks (Munro, Fehling, & Towne, 1985).

In discovery learning contexts we generally find conceptual rather than operational simulations. (The latter are mainly used for experiential learning.) As a class,

Part of the work presented here was carried out within the SAFE/SIMULATE, the SMISLE, and the SERVIVE projects. These projects were partially sponsored by the European Commission in its Telematics programs. We appreciate the contributions of our colleagues from these projects to the work presented here, especially Jules Pieters and Janine Swaak (University of Twente), Melanie Njoo (now at Origin/Instruction Technology), Anja van der Hulst (now at TNO Physics and Electronics Laboratory), and Robert de Hoog (University of Amsterdam). Jules Pieters, Jeroen van Merriënboer (University of Twente), Patricia Alexander (University of Maryland), and Simon King (EDS-Ingévision) provided us with helpful comments on a draft of this article. Please address correspondence concerning this article to the first author.

conceptual models encompass a wide range of model types—for instance, qualitative versus quantitative models, continuous versus discrete models, and static versus dynamic models (see Van Joolingen & De Jong, 1991a). Models may also differ considerably in complexity. They range from very simple, straightforward models—for example, simple Mendelian genetics (Brant, Hooper, & Sugrue, 1991)—to very complex models—for example, the medical simulation HUMAN (Coleman & Randall, 1986), in which 200 variables and parameters can be changed. Also, specific characteristics, like the place of variables in the model or the distance between theoretical and operational variables, can help to define a conceptual model (Glaser, Schauble, Raghavan, & Zeitz, 1992). In scientific discovery learning the main task of the learner is to infer the characteristics of the model underlying the simulation. The learners' basic actions are changing values of input variables and observing the resulting changes in values of output variables (De Jong, 1991; Reigeluth & Schwartz, 1989). Originally, the means of giving input and receiving output of simulation environments were rather limited, but now increasingly sophisticated interfaces using direct manipulation for input and graphics and animations as outputs are emerging (e.g., Härtel, 1994; Kozma, Russell, Jones, Marx, & Davis, 1996; Teodoro, 1992); virtual reality environments are the latest development (see e.g., Thurman & Mattoon, 1994).

Discovery learning has its roots in Gestalt psychology and the work of Bruner (1961). The study of discovery learning has, over the last few decades, moved away from concept discovery (as in Bruner's studies) toward what has been called *scientific discovery learning* (Klahr & Dunbar, 1988; Reimann, 1991). Theories of scientific discovery learning are usually based on theories of scientific discovery. Rivers and Vockell (1987), for example, described a cycle that involves planning (designing an experiment), executing (carrying out the experiment and collecting data), and evaluating (analyzing the data and developing a hypothesis). Friedler, Nachmias, and Linn (1990) said that scientific reasoning comprises the following steps: "(a) define a scientific problem; (b) state a hypothesis; (c) design an experiment; (d) observe, collect, analyze, and interpret data; (e) apply the results; and (f) make predictions on the basis of the results" (p. 173). De Jong and Njoo (1992) added the distinction between *transformative processes*—that is, processes that yield knowledge directly (for example, the ones mentioned by Friedler et al. and Rivers and Vockell)—and *regulative processes*—that is, processes that are necessary to manage the discovery process (for example, planning and monitoring). A second group of theories on scientific discovery

learning finds its inspiration in the work of Simon (e.g., Kulkarni & Simon, 1988; Qin & Simon, 1990; Simon & Lea, 1974). A major contribution in this field is Klahr and Dunbar's theory of scientific discovery as dual search (SDDS), which takes as central concepts two spaces: *hypothesis space* and *experiment space*. In SDDS theory, hypothesis space is a search space consisting of all rules possibly describing the phenomena that can be observed within a domain. Experiment space consists of experiments that can be performed with the domain and the outcomes of these experiments. Although the first emphasis in SDDS theory is on the structure of the search spaces, Klahr and Dunbar have paid considerable attention to discovery processes.

In an early overview of computer-based education, Bangert-Drowns, Kulik, and Kulik (1985) reported that simulation-based learning does not raise examination scores. Later studies that contrasted (sometimes as part of a larger set of comparisons) learning from "pure" simulation (containing conceptual models) with learning from some form of expository instruction (computer tutorial, classroom) covered a variety of domains, such as biology (Rivers & Vockell, 1987), economics (Grimes & Willey, 1990), Newtonian mechanics (Rieber, Boyce, & Assad, 1990; Rieber & Parmley, 1995), and electrical circuits (Carlsen & Andre, 1992; Chambers et al., 1994). Sometimes a single simulation is compared to expository instruction (Rieber & Parmley, 1995), but quite often a comparison is made between (a) a simulation embedded in a curriculum or expository instruction and (b) the curriculum or expository instruction as such (Carlsen & Andre, 1992; Chambers et al., 1994; Grimes & Willey, 1990; Rieber et al., 1990; Rivers & Vockell, 1987). Also, in some cases the expository instruction to which the simulation is compared is "enhanced"—for example, by "conceptual change features" (Chambers et al., 1994) or by questions (in one condition of Rieber et al., 1990). As an overall picture, favorable results for simulation-based learning were reported by Grimes and Willey (1990), and no difference between simulation-based learning and expository teaching was reported by Carlsen and Andre (1992) and Chambers et al. (1994). A mixture of favorable and no-difference results was found in several substudies by Rivers and Vockell (1987). In Rieber et al. (1990) the group of students receiving a simulation in addition to a tutorial scored higher on a test measuring "application of rules" than the tutorial-only group, but scored at the same level as a tutorial group that received additional questions while learning. In Rieber and Parmley (1995) subjects who received only an unstructured (pure) simulation fell short of the performance of subjects who received a tutorial.

The general conclusion that emerges from these studies is that there is no clear and univocal outcome in favor of simulations. An explanation of why simulation-based learning does not improve learning results can be found in the intrinsic problems that learners may have with discovery learning. Chambers et al. (1994), for example, analyzed videotapes of students working with a simulation and noticed that the students were unable to deal with unexpected results and that the students did not utilize all the experimenting possibilities that were available. Also, studies that have compared the learning behaviors of successful and unsuccessful learners in simulation learning environments (e.g., Schauble, Glaser, Raghavan, & Reiner, 1991) have pointed to specific shortcomings of learners. For this reason, authors of a number of studies have suggested additional instructional measures to help learners overcome the problems that they may have with scientific discovery learning.

In the discussion that follows we provide an overview of potential problems with simulation-based scientific discovery learning and search for guidance in dealing with these problems. In addition, we examine studies that have looked at the effect of combining simulations with various instructional support measures for learners.

The literature that serves as the framework for this discussion comes from several sources. First, we began with documents from two relevant research programs: the Learning Research and Development Center and Carnegie Mellon (e.g., Klahr & Dunbar, 1988; Reimann, 1991; Schauble, Glaser, et al., 1991; Shute & Glaser, 1990). Not only were these documents useful in organizing this review, but they were valuable resources in locating additional studies of scientific discovery learning with computer simulations. Next, we searched on-line retrieval systems (e.g., the ERIC database) using the main descriptor *computer simulation(s)*. This yielded (in the June 1997 version of the ERIC database) 2,073 writings. Because limiting this initial search with the additional descriptor *discovery (learning or processes)* gave a set of papers that did not contain some relevant papers we knew of, we examined the ERIC descriptions of all 2,073 papers. We also solicited papers presented at national and international conferences (e.g., American Educational Research Association, European Association for Research on Learning and Instruction, World Conference on Artificial Intelligence in Education, and the International Conference on Intelligent Tutoring Systems) that addressed the topic of computer simulations, and we examined the contents of edited volumes published over the last five years. Furthermore,

we engaged in a physical search of selected research journals likely to publish studies dealing with computer simulations. These journals included the *Journal of Research in Science Teaching, Computers and Education,* the *Journal of Computer-Based Instruction, Instructional Science,* and *The Journal of the Learning Sciences.*

On the topic of discovery learning with computer simulations we found four types of papers. First, we found papers that we call engineering studies, in which a learning environment is merely described. The second type is conceptual papers that deal with theoretical issues related to discovery learning and simulations. Third, we found papers in which empirical data were gathered (through, for example, log files or thinking-aloud procedures) on discovery learning processes. In the fourth type of paper, experimental studies are described in which simulation environments are evaluated against expository teaching, or in which different versions of basically the same simulation environment are compared. Our selection process was guided by the following criteria. First, we excluded experimental papers if they did not use carefully controlled experimental designs and/or did not have well defined performance measures. Second, we targeted original studies for this review and excluded subsequent writings that merely recast a previous study or repeated the same argumentation.

PROBLEMS THAT LEARNERS ENCOUNTER IN DISCOVERY LEARNING

In the following subsections we identify a number of characteristic problems that learners may encounter in discovery learning, and classify them according to the main discovery learning processes; hypothesis generation, design of experiments, interpretation of data, and regulation of learning.

Hypothesis Generation

Coming up with new hypotheses is generally recognized as a difficult process (Chinn & Brewer, 1993) that clearly distinguishes successful and unsuccessful learners (Schauble, Glaser, et al., 1991). An important problem here is that learners (even university students) simply may not know what a hypothesis should look like. Njoo and De Jong (1993a) assessed the "validity" of the learning processes of 91 students of mechanical engineering who worked on a simulation on control theory. They observed the syntactical correctness of the learning processes that students wrote down on "fill-in forms." For example, for the process of generating a hypothesis they examined whether it consisted of variables and a relation between them, not whether the hypothesis was correct in the domain. Njoo and De Jong found an average rate of correctness of 42% for processes generally, and even lower scores for the specific process of generating hypotheses.

A second problem is that learners may not be able to state or adapt hypotheses on the basis of data gathered. Klahr and Dunbar (1988) found that in 56% of observed cases students failed to draw the right conclusions from disconfirming experiments; that is, hypotheses were retained incorrectly on the basis of a negative experimental result. Other studies also emphasize the resistance of learners to theoretical change. Chinn and Brewer (1993) present seven typical learners' reactions to anomalous data, of which only one is the adaptation of the theory on the basis of the data. Chinn and Brewer also cite a large number of studies in which it was found that learners ignore anomalous data (see also Chambers et al., 1994), reject anomalous data, hold anomalous data in abeyance, reinterpret anomalous data and retain an initial theory, or reinterpret anomalous data and make marginal changes to an initial theory (Chinn & Brewer, 1993, p. 4). Also, Dunbar (1993) found evidence in his studies that subjects have an overall difficulty with dropping an original goal, which leads them to persist in holding an initial hypothesis rather than stating a new one. As an explanation, Dunbar mentions what he calls the "unable-to-think-of-an-alternative-hypothesis" phenomenon, meaning that subjects stick to their current hypothesis (despite conflicting evidence) simply because they have no alternative.

These findings may lead to the general assumption that people have a strong tendency to keep their original ideas. However, Klahr and Dunbar (1988) also found a reverse effect: Learners rejected hypotheses in the absence of disconfirming experimental outcomes. This general problem of translating data into theory is illustrated in a study by Kuhn, Schauble, and Garcia-Mila (1992), who found that subjects (10-year-olds) changed their ideas on the causality of a domain variable many times (10 to 11 times) during an experimentation session. The frequent change of ideas can partly be explained by the fact that subjects in this study employed a large repertoire of what Kuhn et al. call "invalid inferences." For example, subjects made inferences about causality on a single instance or made inferences about a variable that had not been changed in two experiments. One aspect that may well influence the ability to adapt hypotheses on the basis of data is the distance between the theoretical variables and the variables that are manipulated in the simulation (Van Joolingen & De Jong, 1997). Glaser et al. (1992) contrasted (a) the environments Voltaville (on

DC circuits) and Refract (on refraction of light), in which a relatively small distance exists between the theoretical variables and the variables that can be manipulated in the simulation, with (b) environments such as Smithtown (on economics), where a larger distance exists between the theoretical variables and the variables that can be manipulated in the simulation. Glaser et al. assert that in the former type of environment it is easier for subjects to see the relation between (a) their manipulations of such variables as lenses, distances, and resistances and (b) the characteristics of the theoretical models.

A third problem in stating hypotheses is that learners can be led by considerations that do not necessarily help them to find the correct (or best) theoretical principles. Van Joolingen & De Jong (1993) describe a phenomenon that they call *fear of rejection*. In an analysis of the use of a so-called hypothesis scratchpad by 31 students, they found that subjects tend to avoid hypotheses that have a high chance of being rejected—for example, a hypothesis in which the relation between variables has a high level of precision. A similar phenomenon was described by Klayman and Ha (1987) and by Klahr, Fay, and Dunbar (1993).

Design of Experiments

A crucial aspect of scientific discovery is the design of experiments that provide information for deciding upon the validity of a hypothesis. Alternatively, if a learner does not yet have a hypothesis, well designed experiments can be used to generate ideas about the model in the simulation. Klahr, Dunbar, and Fay (1991) identified a number of successful heuristics for experimentation in the BigTrak environment, which concerns the operation of a programmable robot. Among their heuristics are the following: Design simple experiments to enable easy monitoring, design experiments that give characteristic results, focus on one dimension of a hypothesis, exploit surprising results, and use the a priori strength of a hypothesis to choose an experimental strategy (Klahr et al., 1991, pp. 388–391). In the literature we find a number of phenomena in which learners use poorly designed experiments.

The first phenomenon, *confirmation bias*, is a learner's tendency to seek information that confirms a hypothesis, instead of trying to disconfirm the hypothesis. In a classic experiment Wason (1960) found confirmation bias for a rule discovery (2-4-6) task in which seeking confirming evidence is not the best strategy to use (Klayman & Ha, 1987). Dunbar (1993) showed, in a simulation environment, that some students have a strong inclination to search for evidence that supports their current hypothesis, and that this inclination may prevent them from stating an alternative hypothesis, even when they are confronted with inconsistent evidence. In an experiment with a simulation of the spread of an influenza epidemic, Quinn, and Alessi (1994) found that only in a small number of cases (one out of six in a sample of 179 subjects) did students conduct experiments with the intention of eliminating hypotheses. In this study students were asked before running an experiment to choose the purpose of the experiment from a series of alternatives presented.

The second phenomenon describes learners who design *inconclusive experiments*. One of the best known examples is described in Wason's (1966) card turning experiment. This phenomenon, which is analogous to the phenomenon of confirmation bias, shows that subjects do not always behave as logical thinkers and do not perform the actions that would be most effective for testing a hypothesis. For instance, in the context of discovery learning with simulations, Glaser et al. (1992) point to a frequently observed phenomenon: Learners tend to vary too many variables in one experiment and, as a result, cannot draw any conclusions from their experiments. Reimann (1991) observed in the domain of optics that subjects perform poorly designed experiments that do not allow them to draw univocal conclusions. In two studies, Van Joolingen and De Jong (1991b, 1993) found that learners often manipulated variables that had nothing to do with the hypothesis they were testing. The percentage of effective experiments could be as low as 22%. Shute and Glaser (1990) and Schauble, Glaser, et al. (1991) report that unsuccessful learners do not gather sufficient data before drawing conclusions.

A third phenomenon is that subjects show *inefficient experimentation behavior*. For example, Kuhn et al. (1992) found that subjects did not use the whole range of potential informative experiments that were available, but only a limited set, and moreover designed the same experiment several times.

A fourth phenomenon describes learners that construct *experiments that are not intended to test a hypothesis*. Schauble, Klopfer, and Raghavan (1991) identified what they have called the engineering approach, in which learners attempt to create some desirable outcome instead of trying to understand the model. An engineering approach, as compared to the scientific approach, leads to a much narrower search and to a concentration on those variables where success is expected. As a consequence, this approach may prevent learners from designing experiments that provide well organized data that are sufficient for discovering all relevant domain relations. This engineering approach was also found by Schauble, Glaser, Duschl, Schulze, and John (1995) and Njoo and De Jong (1993a). A comparable phenomenon was found by White (1993), who reported that students created experiments that were fun (students worked with games in White's simulation environment) instead of experiments that provided insight into the model.

Interpretation of Data

Once the correct experiments have been performed, the data that come from these experiments need to be interpreted before the results of the experiments can be translated into hypotheses in the domain. According to Schauble, Glaser, et al. (1991), successful learners are more proficient in finding regularities in the data than unsuccessful learners. Klahr et al. (1993) found that subjects misencoded experimental data; the rate at which subjects made at least one misencoding ranged from a mean of 35% to a high of 63%, depending on the type of actual rule involved. And indeed, as Klahr et al. state, "compared to the binary feedback provided to subjects in the typical psychology experiment, real-world evidence evaluation is not so straightforward" (p. 114). They reported that the misinterpretation of data most likely resulted in a confirmation of the current hypothesis, thus suggesting that the hypothesis that a subject holds may direct the interpretation of data (see also Chinn & Brewer, 1993; Kuhn et al., 1992).

The interpretation of graphs, a frequently needed skill when interacting with simulations, is also clearly a difficult process. Linn, Layman, and Nachmias (1987) compared a group of students who worked in a "microcomputer-based laboratory" (MBL) with students from traditional classes. In the MBL students carried out experiments in the field of heat and temperature. The output of these experiments was given in the form of dynamically generated graphs. Linn et al. found that students' graphing abilities increased as a result of working with the MBL, but that on the more complicated graphing skills (for example, comparing different graphs) difficulties still existed after the MBL course. Mokros and Tinker (1987) placed students in computer labs where they could generate graphs on the basis of experiments and where they were encouraged to make graphical predictions. Mokros and Tinker found that children's initial problems in interpreting graphs disappeared quickly.

Regulation of Discovery Learning

For regulative processes it is frequently reported that successful learners use systematic planning and monitoring, whereas unsuccessful learners work in an unsystematic way (e.g., Lavoie & Good, 1988; Simmons & Lunetta, 1993). Shute and Glaser (1990) claim that successful learners plan their experiments and manipulations to a greater extent and pay more attention to issues of data management. Glaser et al. (1992) reported that successful discoverers followed a plan over experiments, whereas unsuccessful ones used a more random strategy, concentrating at local decisions, which also gave them the problem of monitoring what they had been doing (see also Schauble, Glaser, et al., 1991). Though Glaser et al. mentioned persistence in following a goal as a characteristic of good learners, these successful subjects were also ready to leave a route when it apparently would not lead to success. Goal setting is also reported as a problem (for subjects with low prior knowledge) by Charney, Reder, and Kusbit (1990). In a more general way Veenman and Elshout (1995) found that, over a number of studies, individuals with a high intellectual ability showed a better working method than individuals with a low intellectual ability, but also that working method made its own contribution to learning outcome on top of intellectual ability. For the process of monitoring, differences between successful and unsuccessful learners are reported by Lavoie and Good, who found that good learners make more notes during learning, and by Schauble, Glaser, et al., who found that successful learners recorded data more systematically.

COMBINING SIMULATIONS AND INSTRUCTIONAL SUPPORT

The previous section presented a number of characteristic problems encountered in scientific discovery learning. A number of researchers and designers have recognized these problems and, in line with the developments in concept discovery learning (see, e.g., Mayer, 1987), have provided learners with support in addition to simulations. In the current section we summarize a number of methods of supporting learners in the discovery process. The first means of support we describe is to provide the learner with direct access to domain information. Subsequently, we present methods that aim to support the learner in specific discovery processes.

Direct Access to Domain Knowledge

A frequently uttered claim about learning with simulations is that learners should know something beforehand if discovery learning is to be fruitful. Insufficient prior knowledge might be the reason that learners do not know which hypothesis to state, cannot make a

good interpretation of data, and engage in unsystematic experimentation (Glaser et al., 1992; Schauble, Glaser, et al., 1991). Several authors have introduced access to extra information as a support measure in a simulation environment, quite often in the form of a (more or less sophisticated) hypertext/hypermedia system (Glaser, Raghavan, & Schauble, 1988; Lajoie, 1993; Shute, 1993; Thomas & Neilson, 1995). Shute (1993) described an intelligent tutoring system (ITS) on basic principles of electricity in which learners could ask for a definition of a concept (e.g., ammeter, ampere, charge, circuit, current) by selecting a term from a menu and follow hypertext links. Shute reported positive effects of the use of this on-line hypertext dictionary on a composite posttest measuring declarative and conceptual knowledge, problem solving, and transfer of knowledge and skills.

A number of authors have pointed to the critical aspect of timing of the availability of information. Berry and Broadbent (1987) found that providing information at exactly the moment it is needed by the learner is much more effective than providing all necessary information before interaction with a simulation begins. Leutner (1993) used a simulation of a fairly complex agricultural system; the students' assignment was to optimize agricultural production. Some students were given information (consisting of domain concepts, facts, rules, and principles) *before* interacting with the simulation, whereas other students were given information (background information on system variables) *while* interacting with the simulation. Leutner found that permanently available information helped learners to acquire domain knowledge but that information provided before the simulation was not effective. For acquiring functional knowledge (the ability to optimize the outcome of the simulation) the same pattern was found, but here the results were less direct, because providing the information before or during the interaction with the simulation was combined with more or less elaborate experimentation advice. Also, Elshout and Veenman (1992) reported that subjects who received domain information before working in a simulation environment (on heat theory) did not profit from this information.

Information must not only be provided by the learning environment but also be invoked from learners' memory. Support measures can stimulate learners to confront their prior knowledge with experimental outcomes. In order to achieve this, Lewis, Stern, and Linn (1993) provided learners with an electronic notation form for noting "everyday life examples" of phenomena they observed in a simulation environment (on thermodynamics).

Support for Hypothesis Generation

Hypothesis generation is a central process in discovery learning. Several studies have created support to overcome the problems that learners have with this process. The Smithtown environment (Shute & Glaser, 1990) offers the learner support for hypothesis generation by means of a hypothesis menu. This menu consists of four windows which present parts of a hypothesis—for example, variables, verbs to indicate change, and connectors. A similar means of support is the hypothesis scratchpad (Van Joolingen & De Jong, 1991b, 1993). Here learners are offered different windows for selecting variables, relations, and conditions. These two approaches offer learners elements of hypotheses that they have to assemble themselves.

A more directive support for creating hypotheses can be found in CIRCSIMTUTOR (Kim, Evens, Michael, & Rovick, 1989), an ITS in the domain of medicine—specifically, on treating problems associated with blood pressure. In this simulation students are asked to state qualitatively what will happen to seven components of the cardiovascular system. As a means of support, they are given a predefined spreadsheet in which to provide their ideas. One step further is to offer learners complete hypotheses. In Pathophysiology Tutor (PPT; Michael, Haque, Rovick, & Evens, 1989) learners can select from lists of predefined hypotheses, arranged in nested menus. Njoo and De Jong (1993a, 1993b) have used similar techniques. They conclude that offering predefined hypothesis to learners positively influences the learning process and the performance of learners. Quinn and Alessi (1994) forced students to write down, before experimenting, a single most plausible hypothesis or a list of multiple plausible hypotheses. The idea is that having more hypotheses available will lead to a strategy of elimination, which could be better than focusing on one hypothesis at a time. Their data showed that the multiple hypotheses strategy did indeed lead to more effective performance (reaching a required state of the simulation), but only if the complexity of the simulation was low. At higher levels of complexity, no advantage of the multiple hypotheses strategy over the single hypothesis strategy could be found. The higher effectiveness of the multiple hypotheses strategy could have been enhanced by the fact that one of the variables included had a counterintuitive result.

Support for the Design of Experiments

To support a learner in designing experiments the learning environment can provide *experimentation hints*. Rivers and Vockell (1987) gave some examples of such hints, like "It is wise to vary only one variable at a time." They provided learners with general experimentation hints of this sort before the learners worked with computer simulations. This did not affect the learning outcome, but it had an effect on the students' experimentation abilities. Hints can also be generated dynamically on the basis of the actual experimentation behavior of learners. Hints are then presented if a learner displays nonoptimal learning behavior. An example of a system containing this type of hint is Smithtown (Shute & Glaser, 1990). Leutner (1993) studied the effect of providing learners with adaptive advice of this kind. He found that if the advice had a limited character, it helped to increase the learner's domain knowledge, but hindered the acquisition of functional knowledge. If the advice contained greater detail, then it also helped to increase the learner's functional knowledge, though the effect was less clear since it was combined with giving extra domain information.

Support for Making Predictions

Whereas a hypothesis is a statement about the relations between variables in a theoretical model, a prediction is a statement about the value(s) of one or more dependent variables under the influence of one or more independent variables, as they can actually be observed in the simulation. One specific way to help learners express predictions is to give them a graphing tool in which they can draw a curve that depicts the prediction. Lewis et al. (1993) provided learners with such a tool. Feedback was given to learners by drawing the correct curve in the same diagram in which the learner's prediction was drawn. Tait (1994) described a similar mechanism, but in his case feedback also included explanations of the differences between the system's curve and the learner's curve. Reimann (1991), in an environment on the refraction of light, provided learners with the opportunity to give predictions at three levels of precision: as numerical data, as a drawn graph, and as an area in which the graph would be located.

Support for Regulative Learning Processes

Regulative processes are the processes that manage the learning process. Regulative aspects such as planfulness and systematicity are regarded as central characteristics of successful discovery learning (Glaser et al., 1992; Schauble et al., 1995). The two most central regulative processes are planning and monitoring (De Jong & Njoo, 1992), both of which can be supported by introducing model progression into the simulation environment. In addition to model progression, we found specific measures for supporting planning or monitoring. Finally, regulative processes can be supported by structuring the discovery process.

Model Progression. The basic idea behind model progression is that presenting the learner with the full complexity of the simulation at once may be too overwhelming. In model progression the model is introduced gradually, step by step. White and Frederiksen's (1989, 1990) work on QUEST is one of the best known applications of *model progression.* In QUEST, electrical systems and models of electrical circuits differ in *order* (qualitative or quantitative models), *degree of elaboration* (number of variables and relations between variables), and *perspective.* While learning with QUEST, learners are confronted with models that advance from a qualitative to a quantitative nature, that are more elaborated, and that transform from a functional to a physical perspective. In this respect the instructional sequence follows the (assumed) transition from a novice knowledge state to an expert one. As far as we know, no controlled evaluation of QUEST has been undertaken. Model progression in which the model increases in complexity for the learner was studied by Swaak, Van Joolingen, and De Jong (1998). SETCOM is a simulation on harmonic oscillation where the model develops from free oscillation, through damped oscillation, to oscillation with an external force. Swaak et al. found that model progression was successful in enlarging the students' intuitive knowledge (but not their definitional knowledge) as compared to an environment without model progression. In a study in a different domain, but with the same type of environment, De Jong et al. (in press) found no effect of providing learners with model progression on top of giving them assignments.

Quinn and Alessi (1994) performed a study in which students had access to a simulation (on the spread of a disease within a population) with four input variables. One group started off with access to all four input variables; one group practiced with three variables before proceeding to the full simulation; and the last group started with access to two variables, proceeded to three, and ended with all four. In all cases students had to minimize the value of one of the output variables. The data revealed that model progression had no overall positive effect on performance. Moreover, model progression proved to be less efficient than providing the students with full complexity at the outset. It should be noted that the domain used by Quinn and Alessi was quite simple; the variables in the model did not interact. In another study on a more complex simulation of a multimeter, Alessi (1995)

found that gradually increasing the level of complexity of the interface was beneficial for initial learning and for transfer. Also, Rieber and Parmley (1995) found, in the area of Newtonian motion, that subjects learning with a simulation that provided increasing control over variables scored significantly higher on a test measuring application of rules than did subjects who could exercise control in its full complexity from the start.

Planning Support. Planning support may, as Charney et al. (1990) have postulated, be especially helpful for subjects who have low prior knowledge. Planning support takes away decisions from learners and in this way helps them in managing the learning process. Support for planning can be given in different ways. Even in the early days of the use of simulations for scientific discovery learning. Showalter (1970) recommended using *questions* as a way to guide the learner through the discovery process. His questions— for example, "Do rats ever reach a point at which they don't learn more?" (p. 49)—focused the learner's attention on specific aspects of the simulation. Zietsman and Hewson (1986) used similar types of questions in conjunction with a simulation on velocity, and Tabak, Smith, Sandoval, and Reiser (1996) used such questions with the aim of setting goals in a biological simulation.

White (1984) helped learners to set goals in a simulation of Newtonian mechanics by introducing *games.* Games, as White uses them, ask learners to reach a specific state in the simulation—for example, to get a spaceship in the simulation around a corner without crashing into any walls (p. 78). White found that learners who learned with a simulation that contained games outperformed learners who worked with the pure simulation on a test of qualitative problems (containing questions of the form "What would happen if . . . ?" or "How could one achieve . . . ?" [p. 81]). The ThinkerTools environment (White, 1993) employs games in a similar way.

De Jong et al. (1994) describe different types of *assignments* that can be used in combination with simulations. Types of assignments include (a) investigation assignments, which prompt students to find the relation between two or more variables, (b) specification assignments, which ask students to predict a value of a certain variable, and (c) "explicitation" assignments, which ask the student to explain a certain phenomenon in the simulation environment. De Jong et al. (in press), using a simulation on collisions, Swaak et al. (1998), using a simulation on harmonic oscillation, and De Jong, Härtel, Swaak, and Van Joolingen (1996), using a simulation on the physics topic of transmission lines, found that students (who were free to choose) used assignments very frequently and that using assignments had a positive effect on learners' gaining what these researchers call intuitive knowledge.

Monitoring Support. Support for monitoring one's own discovery process can be given by overviews of what has been done in the simulation environment. Reimann (1991) provided learners in Refract with a notebook facility for storing numerical and nominal data from experiments. Data in the notebook could be manipulated, so that (a) experiments could be sorted on values for a specific variable, (b) experiments could be selected in which a specific variable had a specified value, and (c) an equation could be calculated over experiments. Also, the student could replay experiments from the notebook. Similar notebook facilities are present in Smithtown (Shute & Glaser, 1990) and Voltaville (Glaser et al., 1988). In SHERLOCK learners can receive upon request an overview of all the actions they have taken so far (Lesgold, Lajoie, Bunzo, & Eggan, 1992). Schauble, Raghavan, and Glaser (1993) presented monitoring support that not only provided an overview of the student's actions, but also offered the opportunity to group actions under goals and to ask for an "expert view" that gave the relevance of the student's actions in the context of a specific goal (e.g., to find the relation between two variables). (These methods in fact supported both monitoring and planning.) In all the examples presented here, learners have to select previous experiments for comparison from the complete set of experiments themselves. Reimann and Beller (1993) propose a system (CABAT) that selects a previous experiment on the basis of similarity and proposes this experiment to the learner for comparison.

Structuring the Discovery Process. Regulative processes can also be supported by leading the learner through different stages of the process. Several studies have compared the effects of structured environments (where structuring is quite often combined with several other measures) with so-called unstructured environments. Linn and Songer (1991) found that providing students with a sequence of experimentation steps ("Before doing the experiment. . .," "Now do the experiment," "After doing the experiment . . .") and with more detailed directions in each of these steps was effective. They report that up to two and four times as many students were able to distinguish between central concepts from the domain (heat and temperature), as compared to students who used an unstructured version of the environment. Njoo and De Jong (1993b) had learners (students of mechanical engineering) work with a

simulation (on control theory) in conjunction with forms that had separate cells for writing down the following: variables and parameters, hypotheses, experiment, prediction, data interpretation, and conclusion. On a test that measured "qualitative insight" the structured group outperformed a group who worked with the simulation environment alone.

Gruber, Graf, Mandl, Renkl, and Stark (1995) gave half of their subjects (60 students of a vocational economics school) instruction in making predictions, comparing predictions to outcomes, and drawing inferences. The other half received no guidance. The simulation used was in the field of economics and involved a jeans factory for which profit should be maximized. On a knowledge test in which students had to make predictions in new situations, the guidance group outperformed the no-guidance group. White (1993), in her ThinkerTools environment, forced subjects to follow a four-phase sequence of activities—"asking questions, doing experiments, formulating laws, and investigating generalizations" (p. 53)—and provided detailed scaffolding in each phase. White found a clear advantage for a simulation-based curriculum compared to a traditional curriculum on a test that measured qualitative predictions in real-world situations. In a number of experiments, Veenman and Elshout compared the learning behavior and learning result of learners working with structured and unstructured simulation environments. In the unstructured simulation subjects did not receive any instructional guidance. In the structured (or "meta-cognitive mediation") condition, subjects received "task assignments" and were prompted to "paraphrase the question, to generate a hypothesis, to think out a detailed action plan, and to make notes of it." Also, after they had performed a series of actions, they were "requested to evaluate their experimental outcomes," to "draw a conclusion elaborating on the subject matter, and to make notes" (e.g., Veenman, Elshout, & Busato, 1994, p. 97). The domains involved were simple electrical circuits, heat theory, and statistics. In an overall analysis of the data of four of their studies, Veenman and Elshout (1995) found no overall effect of structuring the environment. At a more detailed level, they found evidence that low-intelligence subjects with poor working methods profited from structured environments, whereas this was not true for low-intelligence subjects with good working methods or for high-intelligence subjects regardless of their working methods. In this overall analysis, several performance measures (including tests of factual knowledge and problem solving tasks) were combined into a single performance score.

We found two studies in which a comparison was made between a structured simulation environment and traditional, expository instruction. Lewis et al. (1993) required learners using a structured environment to make predictions before doing an experiment and to write down "graph comparisons" and "conclusions" after the experiment. Additionally, these learners were encouraged to write down "everyday examples," "important points," "confusion about" notes, and "example of concept" notes (p. 48). This was done in electronic form using a "Post-it note" metaphor. Lewis et al. found that, in responding to items that required a fundamental understanding of the difference between heat and temperature, students who had used the structured environment outperformed students who had followed the traditional curriculum in the preceding year. In Smithtown (Shute & Glaser, 1990) learners are taken by the hand and led through a fixed sequence of actions that is a little less strict than, for example, the sequence from Lewis et al. (1993). In Smithtown, learners are asked only if they want to make a prediction before experimentation, and they are not forced to do this. Smithtown includes not only structuring, but also a wealth of other supportive measures. An evaluation of Smithtown, using a test that required recall of concepts, failed to show an advantage of Smithtown over a traditional lesson (though learning with Smithtown was far more efficient).

CONCLUSION AND DISCUSSION

In this article we have given an overview of studies in scientific discovery learning with computer simulations of conceptual domains. From studies that empirically examined the discovery learning process we can conclude that a number of specific skills are needed for a successful discovery. Generally, one can say that successful discovery learning is related to reasoning from hypotheses, to applying a systematic and planned discovery process (like systematic variation of variable values), and to the use of high-quality heuristics for experimentation. These skills may have a general character, but can also be more closely related to a given domain (Glaser et al., 1992). Several problems characteristically encountered in the discovery process were identified. For the process of hypothesis generation, a learner's potential weaknesses include choosing hypotheses that seem "safe" and unsuccessfully transforming data into a hypothesis, both when the data are confirming and when they are disconfirming. For designing experiments, we found reports of learners who design inconclusive experiments, who show inefficient experimentation behavior, who follow a confir-

mation bias, and who apply an engineering approach instead of a scientific one. Furthermore, learners quite often have trouble with the interpretation of data as such. A final reported problem is that students are not very capable of regulating the learning process; this is evident in unstructured behavior driven by local decisions rather than an overall plan and in insufficient monitoring of the learning process.

We also examined instructional measures that are used in conjunction with simulations. Quite a few of the studies in which instructional measures were introduced were still in the engineering phase and did not evaluate the effect of the instructional measure in a controlled manner. Other studies in which the effects of adding instructional measures were evaluated used combinations of instructional measures, so that the effect of a specific measure could not be traced. On the basis of the remaining studies, three individual instructional measures can be seen as holding the promise of positively influencing learning outcomes. First, providing direct access to domain information seems effective as long as the information is presented concurrently with the simulation, so that the information is available at the appropriate moment. Secondly, providing learners with assignments (or questions, exercises, or games) seems to have a clear effect on the learning outcome. Thirdly, learners who use an environment that includes model progression perform better than learners who use the same environment without model progression, though it seems that the model needs to be sufficiently complex if this effect is to be evident. For other individual measures (e.g., hypothesis support, experimentation hints, monitoring tools, prediction support) the evidence is not substantial enough to warrant general conclusions. Finally, a number of studies on structuring the environment show that this may lead to more effective learning than using an unstructured environment, though it should be noted that structuring the environment in all these studies not only involved dividing up the learning process into distinct steps, but also included other instructional measures.

A crucial aspect of scientific discovery learning is the instructional goal for which it is used. Following the earliest ideas on discovery learning, it is frequently claimed that scientific discovery learning leads to knowledge that is more intuitive and deeply rooted in a learner's knowledge base (Berry & Broadbent, 1984; Laurillard, 1992; Lindström, Marton, Ottosson, & Laurillard, 1993; Swaak & De Jong, 1996) and that has a more qualitative character (White, 1993). It is also claimed that the results of simulation-based learning are properly measured only by "tests of application and transfer" (Thomas & Hooper, 1991, p. 500). Support for this claim is found in studies by Berry and Broadbent (1984), who showed that while simulations can be effective in teaching the ability to acquire a certain state in the simulation, this does not necessarily mean that the associated conceptual knowledge is learned as well. This lack of a relation between "explicable" knowledge and "functional" knowledge has also been found for simulations on business (Anderson & Lawton, 1992), Newtonian motion (with children; Flick, 1990), kinematics (McDermott, 1990), collisions (De Jong et al., in press; Whitelock et al., 1993), agriculture (Leutner, 1993), a subdomain of economics (Mandl, Gruber, & Renkl, 1994), acceleration and velocity (Rieber, 1996; Rieber et al., 1996), and harmonic oscillations (Swaak et al., 1998).

In the studies that we cited in this overview we find support for the importance of "intuitive" or "deep" knowledge for discovery learning. In studies that compared simulation with expository teaching, Grimes and Willey (1990), for example, used a test containing items that asked for "recognition and understanding," "explicit application," or "implicit application." In this study the simulation group, which showed an overall advantage over the control group, was specifically successful in items measuring implicit application. In Carlsen and Andre (1992), simulation groups performed no better on a posttest than did a no-simulation group; however, when the items were analyzed (by looking at the alternatives chosen) on the mental models that students had acquired, students from the simulation groups showed more advanced models. Rieber et al. (1990) used a test to measure the ability to apply rules from the domain. The simulation group took significantly less time in answering the posttest questions than did a group who had received a tutorial enhanced with questions. According to Rieber et al., this points to more deeply processed knowledge.

In studies where different versions of simulation environments were compared, we again see an effect of the type of knowledge test used. De Jong et al. (in press) and Swaak et al. (1998) used a test of definitional knowledge and also a test measuring "intuitive" knowledge. In the latter test, subjects had to predict what would happen after a change was introduced in a situation, and they had to make this prediction as quickly as possible (see also Swaak & De Jong, 1996). Though learners improved in definitional knowledge when learning with the simulation environments (which also contained expository information), the gain in intuitive knowledge was larger. Also, differential effects of simulation environments came out only on the test of intuitive knowledge.

Finally, the type of knowledge test used also seems to play a role in the studies that compared structured simulation environments with unstructured ones or with the normal curriculum. In Linn and Songer (1991) and Lewis et al. (1993) a test was used that measured qualitative distinctions between central concepts. Njoo and De Jong (1993a, 1993b) used items that measured qualitative insight, and Gruber et al. (1995) and White (1993) used tests in which predictions had to be given (as in De Jong et al., in press, and Swaak et al., 1998). All these studies showed an advantage for the structured simulation environments. In Veenman and Elshout (1995), where learners were tested on a combination of qualitative and definitional knowledge, no overall effect of structuring the environment was found, with an exception for specific group of learners. Finally, in an evaluation of Smithtown (Shute & Glaser, 1990), no difference in effectiveness could be found between a structured simulation environment and a traditional lesson, but here a test measuring recall of concepts was applied. Advantages of simulations seem clear when the instructional goal is the mastery of discovery skills. In Rivers and Vockell (1987), not only was domain knowledge assessed, but also discovery abilities were measured by a number of general tests (e.g., the Watson-Glaser Critical Thinking Appraisal) and by analyzing the trend in scores on a domain pretest. Rivers and Vockell concluded that students from the simulation curricula outperformed the control subjects, especially if the simulations contained guidance in the form of hints that pointed to good discovery behavior (see also Faryniarz & Lockwood, 1992; Woodward, Carnine, & Gersten, 1988).

The development of environments that invite learners to engage in self-directed (discovery) learning and that provide support tools for the learning process continues (see, e.g., Suthers, Weiner, Connelly, & Paolucci, 1995). In our view, therefore, a further and deeper analysis of problems that learners encounter in discovery learning and a further evaluation of specific ways to support learners should be the principal items on the current research agenda in this area. Studies should aim to find out when and how to provide learners with means to overcome their deficiencies in discovery learning—in other words, when and how to provide scaffolding for the discovery learning process.

For these evaluation studies there are three additional points of interest. The first one is that introducing additional support tools is not only meant to enable the learner to perform certain actions, but can also be used to prevent cognitive overload (Glaser et al., 1988, p. 63). However, some instructional measures may also raise cognitive load, by introducing more complexity into the environment. Gruber et al. (1995), for example, suggest that an increase in cognitive load occurs when multiple perspectives are introduced into a simulation environment. Further research on support measures should take into consideration the effects of additional support measures on cognitive load (see, e.g., De Jong et al., in press; Swaak et al., 1998). A second aspect of support tools is that in learning environments these tools can be used as unobtrusive measures, as was recognized by Glaser et al. (1988) in the design of Voltaville. For example, in SHERLOCK (Lesgold et al., 1992) the student goes through the diagnostic problem solving process by choosing from menus of actions. On the one hand, this helps the student in the planning process; on the other hand, this helps the researcher (the system) to assess the student's intentions. In the SHERLOCK environment, information from this measure, which otherwise serves as a planning tool for the learner, is utilized for generating adequate hints. Van Joolingen (1995) describes some principles of how information gathered through a hypothesis scratchpad can be used for assessing the learner's actual state of knowledge. The third point of interest is that the place of simulations in the curriculum should be investigated. Lavoie and Good (1988) suggest that a "Piagetian" approach be used, which implies that simulations are introduced in a first phase of learning, where exploration is allowed, and that concepts are formally introduced later, followed finally by concept application (see also Brant et al., 1991; White, 1993). This suggests a potential use of computer simulation that differs from the classical, hypothesis-driven approach.

Only after sufficient research along the lines sketched in this section has been conducted might an appropriate design theory for instructional simulations arise. Current attempts at such a theory, though interesting, are necessarily fragmentary and incomplete (see, e.g., Thurman, 1993). But when such a theory does indeed arise, discovery learning with simulations can take its place in learning and instruction as a new line of learning environments, based on technology, in which more emphasis is given to the learner's own initiative.

REFERENCES

Alessi, S. M. (1995, April). *Dynamic vs. static fidelity in a procedural simulation.* Paper presented at the Annual Meeting of the American Educational Research Association, San Francisco.

Alessi, S. M., & Trollip, S. R. (1985). *Computer based instruction, methods and development.* Englewood Cliffs, NY: Prentice-Hall.

Anderson, P. H., & Lawton, L. (1992). The relationship between financial performance and other measures of learning on a simulation exercise. *Simulation & Gaming, 23,* 326–340.

Bangert-Drowns, R., Kulik, J., & Kulik, C. (1985). Effectiveness of computer-based education in secondary schools. *Journal of Computer-Based Instruction, 12,* 59–68.

Berry, D. C., & Broadbent, D. E. (1984). On the relationship between task performance and associated verbalizable knowledge. *The Quarterly Journal of Experimental Psychology, 36A,* 209–231.

Berry, D. C., & Broadbent, D. E. (1987). Explanation and verbalization in a computer-assisted search task. *The Quarterly Journal of Experimental Psychology, 39A,* 585–609.

Brant, G., Hooper, E., & Sugrue, B. (1991). Which comes first, the simulation or the lecture? *Journal of Educational Computing Research, 7,* 469–481.

Bruner, J. S. (1961). The act of discovery. *Harvard Educational Review, 31,* 21–32.

Carlsen, D. D., & Andre, T. (1992). Use of a microcomputer simulation and conceptual change text to overcome students' preconceptions about electric circuits. *Journal of Computer-Based Instruction, 19,* 105–109.

Chambers, S. K., Haselhuhn, C., Andre, T., Mayberry, C., Wellington, S., Krafka, A., Volmer, J., & Berger, J. (1994, April). *The acquisition of a scientific understanding of electricity: Hands-on versus computer simulation experience; conceptual change versus didactic text.* Paper presented at the Annual Meeting of the American Educational Research Association, New Orleans, LA.

Charney, D., Reder, L., & Kusbit, G. W. (1990). Goal setting and procedure selection in acquiring computer skills: A comparison of tutorials, problem solving, and learner exploration. *Cognition and Instruction, 7,* 323–342.

Chinn, C. A., & Brewer, W. F. (1993). The role of anomalous data in knowledge acquisition: A theoretical framework and implications for science instruction. *Review of Educational Research, 63,* 1–51.

Coleman, T. G., & Randall, J. E. (1986). *HUMAN-PC: A comprehensive physiological model* [Computer software]. Jackson: University of Mississippi Medical Center.

diSessa, A., & Abelson, H. (1986). Boxer: A reconstructible computational medium. *Communications of the ACM, 29,* 859–868.

Dunbar, K. (1993). Concept discovery in a scientific domain. *Cognitive Science, 17,* 397–434.

Elshout, J. J., & Veenman, M. V. J. (1992). Relation between intellectual ability and working method as predictors of learning. *Journal of Educational Research, 85,* 134–143.

Faryniarz, J. V., & Lockwood, L. G. (1992). Effectiveness of microcomputer simulations in stimulating environmental problem solving by community college students. *Journal of Research in Science Teaching, 29,* 453–470.

Flick, L. B. (1990). Interaction of intuitive physics with computer simulated physics. *Journal of Research in Science Teaching, 27,* 219–231.

Friedler, Y., Nachmias, R., & Linn, M. C. (1990). Learning scientific reasoning skills in microcomputer-based laboratories. *Journal of Research in Science Teaching, 27,* 173–191.

Gall, J. E., & Hannafin, M. J. (1994). A framework for the study of hypertext. *Instructional Science, 22,* 207–232.

Glaser, R., Raghavan, K., & Schauble, L. (1988). Voltaville, a discovery environment to explore the laws of DC circuits. In *ITS-88* [Proceedings of the 1988 conference on intelligent tutoring systems] (pp. 61–66). Montreal, Quebec, Canada: Université de Montréal, Départment d'informatique et de recherche opérationnelle.

Glaser, R., Schauble, L., Raghavan, K., & Zeitz, C. (1992). Scientific reasoning across different domains. In E. de Corte, M. Linn, H. Mandl, & L. Verschaffel (Eds.), *Computer-based learning environments and problem solving* (pp. 345–373). Berlin, Germany: Springer-Verlag.

Grimes, P. W., & Willey, T. E. (1990). The effectiveness of microcomputer simulations in the principles of economics course. *Computers & Education, 14,* 81–86.

Gruber, H., Graf, M., Mandl, H., Renkl, A., & Stark, R. (1995, August). *Fostering applicable knowledge by multiple perspectives and guided problem solving.* Paper presented at the conference of the European Association for Research on Learning and Instruction, Nijmegen, The Netherlands.

Härtel, H. (1994). COLOS: Conceptual learning of science. In T. de Jong & L. Sarti (Eds.), *Design and production of multimedia and simulation based learning material* (pp. 189–219). Dordrecht, The Netherlands: Kluwer Academic Publishers.

de Jong, T. (1991). Learning and instruction with computer simulations. *Education & Computing, 6,* 217–229.

de Jong, T., Härtel, H., Swaak, J., & van Joolingen, W. (1996). Support for simulation-based learning: The effects of assignments in learning about transmission lines. In A. Díaz de Ilarazza Sánchez & I. Fernández de Castro (Eds.), *Computer aided learning and instruction in science and engineering* (pp. 9–27). Berlin, Germany: Springer-Verlag.

de Jong, T., Martin, E., Zamarro, J.-M., Esquembre, F., Swaak, J., & van Joolingen, W. R. (in press). The integration of computer simulation and learning support: An example from the physics domain of collisions. *Journal of Research in Science Teaching.*

de Jong, T., & Njoo, M. (1992). Learning and instruction with computer simulations: Learning processes involved. In E. de Corte, M. Linn, H. Mandl, & L. Verschaffel (Eds.), *Computer-based learning environments and problem solving* (pp. 411–429). Berlin, Germany: Springer-Verlag.

de Jong, T., van Joolingen, W., Scott, D., de Hoog, R., Lapied, L., & Valent, R. (1994). SMISLE: System for Multimedia Integrated Simulation Learning Environments. In T. de Jong & L. Sarti (Eds.), *Design and production of multimedia and simulation based learning material* (pp. 133–167). Dordrecht, The Netherlands: Kluwer Academic Publishers.

van Joolingen, W. R. (1995). QmaPS: Qualitative reasoning for intelligent simulation learning environments. *Journal of Artificial Intelligence in Education, 6,* 67–89.

van Joolingen, W. R., & de Jong, T. (1991a). Characteristics of simulations for instructional settings. *Education & Computing, 6,* 241–262.

van Joolingen, W. R., & de Jong, T. (1991b). Supporting hypothesis generation by learners exploring an interactive computer simulation. *Instructional Science, 20,* 389–404.

van Joolingen, W. R., & de Jong, T. (1993). Exploring a domain through a computer simulation: Traversing variable and relation space with the help of a hypothesis scratchpad. In D. Towne, T. de Jong, & H. Spada (Eds.), *Simulation-based experiential learning* (pp. 191–206). Berlin, Germany: Springer-Verlag.

van Joolingen, W. R., & de Jong, T. (1997). An extended dual search space model of learning with computer simulations. *Instructional Science, 25,* 307–346.

Kim, N., Evens, M., Michael, J. A., & Rovick, A. A. (1989). CIRCSIM-TUTOR: An intelligent tutoring system for circulatory physiology. In H. Maurer (Ed.), *Computer assisted learning: Proceedings of the 2nd International Conference ICCAL* (pp. 254–267). Berlin, Germany: Springer-Verlag.

Klahr, D., & Dunbar, K. (1988). Dual space search during scientific reasoning. *Cognitive Science, 12,* 1–48.

Klahr, D., Dunbar, K., & Fay, A. L. (1991). Designing experiments to test 'bad' hypotheses. In J. Shrager & P. Langley (Eds.), *Computational models of discovery and theory formation* (pp. 355–401). San Mateo, CA: Morgan-Kaufman.

Klahr, D., Fay, A. L., & Dunbar, K. (1993). Heuristics for scientific experimentation: A developmental study. *Cognitive Psychology, 25,* 111–146.

Klayman, J., & Ha, Y.-W. (1987). Confirmation, disconfirmation, and information in hypothesis testing. *Psychological Review, 94,* 211–228.

Kozma, R. B., Russell, J., Jones, T., Marx, N., & Davis, J. (1996). The use of multiple, linked representations to facilitate science understanding. In S. Vosniadou, E. De Corte, R. Glaser, & H. Mandl (Eds.), *International perspectives on the design of technology supported learning environments* (pp. 41–61). Hillsdale, NJ: Erlbaum.

Kuhn, D., Schauble, L., & Garcia-Mila, M. (1992). Cross-domain development of scientific reasoning. *Cognition and Instruction, 9,* 285–327.

Kulkarni, D., & Simon, H. A. (1988). The processes of scientific discovery: The strategy of experimentation. *Cognitive Science, 12,* 139–175.

Lajoie, S. P. (1993). Cognitive tools for enhancing learning. In S. P. Lajoie & S. J. Derry (Eds.), *Computers as cognitive tools* (pp. 261–289). Hillsdale, NJ: Erlbaum.

Laurillard, D. (1992). Learning through collaborative computer simulations. *British Journal of Educational Technology, 23,* 164–171.

Lavoie, D. R., & Good, R. (1988). The nature and use of predictions skills in a biological computer simulation. *Journal of Research in Science Teaching, 25,* 335–360.

Lesgold, A., Lajoie, S., Bunzo, M., & Eggan, G. (1992). SHERLOCK: A coached practice environment for an electronics troubleshooting job. In J. H. Larkin & R. W. Chabay (Eds.), *Computer-assisted instruction and intelligent tutoring systems: Shared goals and complementary approaches* (pp. 201–239). Hillsdale, NJ: Erlbaum.

Leutner, D. (1993). Guided discovery learning with computer-based simulation games: Effects of adaptive and non-adaptive instructional support. *Learning and Instruction, 3,* 113–132.

Lewis, E. L., Stern, J. L., & Linn, M. C. (1993). The effect of computer simulations on introductory thermodynamics understanding. *Educational Technology, 33,* 45–58.

Lindström, B., Marton, F., Ottosson, T., & Laurillard, D. (1993). Computer simulations as a tool for developing intuitive and conceptual understanding in mechanics. *Computers in Human Behavior, 9,* 263–281.

Linn, M. C., Layman, J., & Nachmias, R. (1987). Cognitive consequences of microcomputer-based laboratories: Graphing skills development. *Journal of Contemporary Educational Psychology, 12,* 244–253.

Linn, M. C., & Songer, N. B. (1991). Teaching thermodynamics to middle school students: What are appropriate cognitive demands? *Journal of Research in Science Teaching, 28,* 885–918.

Mandl, H., Gruber, H., & Renkl, A. (1994). Problems of knowledge utilization in the development of expertise. In W. J. Nijhof & J. N. Streumer (Eds.), *Flexibility in training and vocational education* (pp. 291–305). Utrecht, The Netherlands: Lemma BV.

Mayer, R. E. (1987). *Educational psychology: A cognitive approach.* Boston: Little, Brown and Co.

McDermott, L. C. (1990). Research and computer based instruction: Opportunity for interaction. *American Journal of Physics, 58,* 407–415.

Michael, J. A., Haque, M. M., Rovick, A. A., & Evens, M. (1989). The pathophysiology tutor: A first step towards a smart tutor. In H. Maurer (Ed.), *Computer assisted learning. Proceedings of the 2nd International Conference ICCAL* (pp. 390–400). Berlin, Germany: Springer-Verlag.

Mokros, J. R., & Tinker, R. F. (1987). The impact of microcomputer based labs on children's ability to interpret graphs. *Journal of Research in Science Teaching, 24,* 369–383.

Munro, A., Fehling, M. R., & Towne, D. M. (1985). Instruction intrusiveness in dynamic simulation training. *Journal of Computer-Based Instruction, 2,* 50–53.

Njoo, M., & de Jong, T. (1993a). Exploratory learning with a computer simulation for control theory: Learning processes and instructional support. *Journal of Research in Science Teaching, 30,* 821–844.

Njoo, M., & de Jong, T. (1993b). Supporting exploratory learning by offering structured overviews of hypotheses. In D. Towne, T. de Jong, & H. Spada (Eds.), *Simulation-based experiential learning* (pp. 207–225). Berlin, Germany: Springer-Verlag.

Novak, J. D., & Wandersee, J. H. (Eds.). (1990). Perspectives on concept mapping [Special issue]. *Journal of Research in Science Teaching, 27*(10).

Qin, Y., & Simon, H. A. (1990). Laboratory replication of scientific discovery processes. *Cognitive Science, 14,* 281–312.

Quinn, J., & Alessi, S. (1994). The effects of simulation complexity and hypothesis generation strategy on learning. *Journal of Research on Computing in Education, 27,* 75–91.

Reigeluth, C. M., & Schwartz, E. (1989). An instructional theory for the design of computer-based simulations. *Journal of Computer-Based Instruction, 16*, 1–10.

Reimann, P. (1991). Detecting functional relations in a computerized discovery environment. *Learning and Instruction, 1*, 45–65.

Reimann, P., & Beller, S. (1993). Computer-based support for analogical problem solving and learning. In D. M. Towne, T. de Jong, & H. Spada (Eds.), *Simulation-based experiential learning* (pp. 91–105). Berlin, Germany: Springer-Verlag.

Rieber, L. P. (1996). Animation as feedback in a computer-based simulation: Representations matter. *Educational Technology Research & Development, 44*, 5–23.

Rieber, L. P., Boyce, M., & Assad, C. (1990). The effects of computer animation on adult learning and retrieval tasks. *Journal of Computer-Based Instruction, 17*, 46–52.

Rieber, L. P., & Parmley, M. W. (1995). To teach or not to teach? Comparing the use of computer-based simulations in deductive versus inductive approaches to learning with adults in science. *Journal of Educational Computing Research, 14*, 359–374.

Rieber, L. P., Smith, M., Al-Ghafry, S., Strickland, B., Chu, G., & Spahi, F. (1996). The role of meaning in interpreting graphical and textual feedback during a computer-based simulation. *Computers & Education, 27*, 45–58.

Riley, D. (1990). Learning about systems by making models. *Computers & Education, 15*, 255–263.

Rivers, R. H., & Vockell, E. (1987). Computer simulations to stimulate scientific problem solving. *Journal of Research in Science Teaching, 24*, 403–415.

Schauble, L., Glaser, R., Duschl, R. A., Schulze, S., & John, J. (1995). Students' understanding of the objectives and procedures of experimentation in the science classroom. *The Journal of the Learning Sciences, 4*, 131–166.

Schauble, L., Glaser, R., Raghavan, K., & Reiner, M. (1991). Casual models and experimentation strategies in scientific reasoning. *The Journal of the Learning Sciences, 1*, 201–239.

Schauble, L., Klopfer, L., & Raghavan, K. (1991). Students' transitions from an engineering to a science model of experimentation. *Journal of Research in Science Teaching, 28*, 859–882.

Schauble, L., Raghavan, K., & Glaser, R. (1993). The discovery and reflection notation: A graphical trace for supporting self regulation in computer-based laboratories. In S. P. Lajoie & S. J. Derry (Eds.), *Computers as cognitive tools* (pp. 319–341). Hillsdale, NJ: Erlbaum.

Showalter, V. M. (1970). Conducting science investigations using computer simulated experiments. *The Science Teacher, 37*, 46–50.

Shute, V. J. (1993). A comparison of learning environments: All that glitters . . . In S. P. Lajoie & S. J. Derry (Eds.), *Computers as cognitive tools* (pp. 47–75). Hillsdale, NJ: Erlbaum.

Shute, V. J., & Glaser, R. (1990). A large-scale evaluation of an intelligent discovery world: Smithtown. *Interactive Learning Environments, 1*, 51–77.

Simmons, P. E., & Lunetta, V. N. (1993). Problem-solving behaviors during a genetics computer simulation: Beyond the expert/novice dichotomy. *Journal of Research in Science Teaching, 30*, 153–173.

Simon, H. A., & Lea, G. (1974). Problem solving and rule induction: A unified view. In L. W. Gregg (Ed.), *Knowledge and cognition* (pp. 105–128). Hillsdale, NJ: Erlbaum.

Smith, R. B. (1986). The Alternate Reality Kit: An animated environment for creating interactive simulations. In *Proceedings of IEEE Computer Society Workshop on Visual Programming* (pp. 99–106). Silver Spring, MD: IEEE Computer Society Press.

Suthers, D., Weiner, A., Connelly, J., & Paolucci, M. (1995). Belvedere: Engaging students in critical discussion of science and public policy issues. In J. Greer (Ed.), *Proceedings of the AI-Ed 95, the 7th World Conference on Artificial Intelligence in Education* (pp. 266–273). Charlottesville, VA: AACE.

Swaak, J., & de Jong, T. (1996). Measuring intuitive knowledge in science: The what-if test. *Studies in Educational Evaluation, 22*, 341–362.

Swaak, J., van Joolingen, W. R., & de Jong, T. (1998). Supporting simulation-based learning: The effects of model progression and assignments on definitional and intuitive knowledge. *Learning and Instruction, 8*, 235–253.

Tabak, I., Smith, B. K., Sandoval, W. A., & Reiser, B. J. (1996). Combining general and domain-specific strategic support for biological inquiry. In C. Frasson, G. Gauthier, & A. Lesgold (Eds.), *Intelligent tutoring systems* (pp. 288–297). Berlin, Germany: Springer-Verlag.

Tait, K. (1994). DISCOURSE: The design and production of simulation-based learning environments. In T. de Jong & L. Sarti (Eds.), *Design and production of multimedia and simulation-based learning material* (pp. 111–133). Dordrecht, The Netherlands: Kluwer Academic Publishers.

Teodoro, V. D. (1992). Direct manipulation of physical concepts in a computerized exploratory laboratory. In E. de Corte, M. Linn, H. Mandl, & L. Verschaffel (Eds.), *Computer-based learning environments and problem solving* (pp. 445–465). Berlin, Germany: Springer-Verlag.

Thomas, R., & Hooper, E. (1991). Simulations: An opportunity we are missing. *Journal of Research on Computing in Education, 23,* 497–513.

Thomas, R., & Neilson, I. (1995). Harnessing simulations in the service of education: The Interact simulation environment. *Computers & Education, 25,* 21–29.

Thurman, R. A. (1993). Instructional simulation from a cognitive psychology viewpoint. *Educational Technology Research & Development, 41,* 75–89.

Thurman, R. A., & Mattoon, J. S. (1994). Virtual reality: Towards fundamental improvements in simulation-based training. *Educational Technology, 34,* 56–64.

Towne, D. M. (1995). *Learning and instruction in simulation environments.* Englewood Cliffs, NJ: Educational Technology Publications.

Veenman, M. V. J., & Elshout, J. J. (1995). Differential effects of instructional support on learning in simulation environments. *Instructional Science, 22,* 363–383.

Veenman, M. V. J., Elshout, J. J., & Busato, V. V. (1994). Metacognitive mediation in learning with computer-based simulations. *Computers in Human Behavior, 10,* 93–106.

Wason, P. C. (1960). On the failure to eliminate hypotheses in a conceptual task. *Quarterly Journal of Experimental Psychology, 12,* 129–140.

Wason, P. C. (1966). Reasoning. In B. M. Foss (Ed.), *New horizons in psychology* (pp. 135–151). Harmondsworth, UK: Penguin.

White, B. Y. (1984). Designing computer games to help physics students understand Newton's laws of motion. *Cognition and Instruction, 1,* 69–108.

White, B. Y. (1993). ThinkerTools: Causal models, conceptual change, and science education. *Cognition and Instruction, 10,* 1–100.

White, B. Y., & Frederiksen, J. R. (1989). Causal models as intelligent learning environments for science and engineering education. *Applied Artificial Intelligence, 3(2–3),* 83–106.

White, B. Y., & Frederiksen, J. R. (1990). Causal model progressions as a foundation for intelligent learning environments. *Artificial Intelligence, 42,* 99–157.

Whitelock, D., Taylor, J., O'Shea, T., Scanlon, E., Sellman, R., Clark, P., & O'Malley, C. (1993). Challenging models of elastic collisions with a computer simulation. *Computers & Education, 20,* 1–9.

Woodward, J., Carnine, D., & Gersten, R. (1988). Teaching problem solving through computer simulations. *American Educational Research Journal, 25,* 72–86.

Zietsman, A. I., & Hewson, P. W. (1986). Effect of instruction using microcomputers simulations and conceptual change strategies on science learning. *Journal of Research in Science Teaching, 23,* 27–39.

Standards for Research and Program Evaluation

Ethical Standards of the American Educational Research Association

FOREWORD

Educational researchers come from many disciplines, embrace several competing theoretical frameworks, and use a variety of research methodologies. The American Educational Research Association (AERA) recognizes that its members are already guided by codes in the various disciplines and, also, by organizations, such as institutional review boards. AERA's code of ethics incorporates a set of standards designed specifically to guide the work of researchers in education. Education, by its very nature, is aimed at the improvement of individual lives and societies. Further, research in education is often directed at children and other vulnerable populations. A main objective of this code is to remind us, as educational researchers, that we should strive to protect these populations, and to maintain the integrity of our research, of our research community, and of all those with whom we have professional relations. We should pledge ourselves to do this by maintaining our own competence and that of people we induct into the field, by continually evaluating our research for its ethical and scientific adequacy, and by conducting our internal and external relations according to the highest ethical standards.

The standards that follow remind us that we are involved not only in research but in education. It is, therefore, essential that we continually reflect on our research to be sure that it is not only sound scientifically but that it makes a positive contribution to the educational enterprise.

I. GUIDING STANDARDS: RESPONSIBILITIES TO THE FIELD

A. Preamble

To maintain the integrity of research, educational researchers should warrant their research conclusions adequately in a way consistent with the standards of their own

Reprinted from *Educational Researcher,* 10/92, pp. 23–26. Copyright 1992 by the American Educational Research Association.

theoretical and methodological perspectives. They should keep themselves well informed in both their own and competing paradigms where those are relevant to their research, and they should continually evaluate the criteria of adequacy by which research is judged.

B. Standards

1. Educational researchers should conduct their professional lives in such a way that they do not jeopardize future research, the public standing of the field, or the discipline's research results.
2. Educational researchers must not fabricate, falsify, or misrepresent authorship, evidence, data, findings, or conclusions.
3. Educational researchers must not knowingly or negligently use their professional roles for fraudulent purposes.
4. Educational researchers should honestly and fully disclose their qualifications and limitations when providing professional opinions to the public, to government agencies, and others who may avail themselves of the expertise possessed by members of AERA.
5. Educational researchers should attempt to report their findings to all relevant stakeholders, and should refrain from keeping secret or selectively communicating their findings.
6. Educational researchers should report research conceptions, procedures, results, and analyses accurately and sufficiently in detail to allow knowledgeable, trained researchers to understand and interpret them.
7. Educational researchers' reports to the public should be written straightforwardly to communicate the practical significance for policy, including limits in effectiveness and in generalizability to situations, problems, and contexts. In writing for or communicating with nonresearchers, educational researchers must take care not to misrepresent the practical or policy implications of their research or the research of others.
8. When educational researchers participate in actions related to hiring, retention, and advancement, they should not discriminate on the basis of gender, sexual orientation, physical disabilities, marital status, color, social class, religion, ethnic background, national origin, or other attributes not relevant to the evaluation of academic or research competence.
9. Educational researchers have a responsibility to make candid, forthright personnel recommendations and not to recommend those who are manifestly unfit.
10. Educational researchers should decline requests to review the work of others where strong conflicts of interest are involved, or when such requests cannot be conscientiously fulfilled on time. Materials sent for review should be read in their entirety and considered carefully, with evaluative comments justified with explicit reasons.
11. Educational researchers should avoid all forms of harassment, not merely those overt actions or threats that are due cause for legal action. They must not use their professional positions or rank to coerce personal or sexual favors or economic or professional advantages from students, research assistants, clerical staff, colleagues, or any others.
12. Educational researchers should not be penalized for reporting in good faith violations of these or other professional standards.

II. GUIDING STANDARDS: RESEARCH POPULATIONS, EDUCATIONAL INSTITUTIONS, AND THE PUBLIC

A. Preamble

Educational researchers conduct research within a broad array of settings and institutions, including schools, colleges, universities, hospitals, and prisons. It is of paramount importance that educational researchers respect the rights, privacy, dignity, and sensitivities of their research populations and also the integrity of the institutions within which the research occurs. Educational researchers should be especially careful in working with children and other vulnerable populations. These standards are intended to reinforce and strengthen already existing standards enforced by institutional review boards and other professional associations.

B. Standards

1. Participants, or their guardians, in a research study have the right to be informed about the likely risks involved in the research and of potential consequences for participants, and to give their informed consent before participating in research. Educational researchers should communicate the aims of the investigation as well as possible to informants and participants (and their guardians), and appropriate representatives of institutions, and keep them updated about any significant changes in the research program.
2. Honesty should characterize the relationship between researchers and participants and appropriate institutional representatives. Deception is discouraged; it should be used only when clearly necessary for scientific studies and should then be minimized. After the study the researcher should explain to the participants and institutional representatives the reasons for the deception.
3. Educational researcher should be sensitive to any locally established institutional policies or guidelines for conducting research.
4. Participants have the right to withdraw from the study at any time, unless otherwise constrained by their official capacities or roles.
5. Educational researchers should exercise caution to ensure that there is no exploitation for personal gain of research populations or of institutional settings of research. Educational researchers should not use their influence over subordinates, students, or others to compel them to participate in research.
6. Researchers have a responsibility to be mindful of cultural, religious, gender, and other significant differences within the research population in the planning, conduct, and reporting of their research.
7. Researchers should carefully consider and minimize the use of research techniques that might have negative social consequences, for example, negative sociometrics with young children or experimental interventions that might deprive students of important parts of the standard curriculum.

8. Educational researchers should be sensitive to the integrity of ongoing institutional activities and alert appropriate institutional representatives of possible disturbances in such activities which may result from the conduct of the research.

9. Educational researchers should communicate their findings and the practical significance of their research in clear, straightforward, and appropriate language to relevant research populations, institutional representatives, and other stakeholders.

10. Informants and participants have a right to remain anonymous. This right should be respected when no clear understanding to the contrary has been reached. Researchers are responsible for taking appropriate precautions to protect the confidentiality of both participants and data. Those being studied should be made aware of the capacities of the various data-gathering technologies to be used in the investigation so that they can make an informed decision about their participation. It should also be made clear to informants and participants that despite every effort made to preserve it, anonymity may be compromised. Secondary researchers should respect and maintain the anonymity established by primary researchers.

III. GUIDING STANDARDS: INTELLECTUAL OWNERSHIP

A. Preamble

Intellectual ownership is predominantly a function of creative contribution. Intellectual ownership is not predominantly a function of effort expended.

B. Standards

1. Authorship should be determined based on the following guidelines, which are not intended to stifle collaboration, but rather to clarify the credit appropriately due for various contributions to research.

   a) All those, regardless of status, who have made substantive creative contributions to the generation of an intellectual product are entitled to be listed as authors of that product.

   b) First authorship and order of authorship should be the consequence of relative creative leadership and creative contribution. Examples of creative contributions are: writing first drafts or substantial portions; significant rewriting or substantive editing; and contributing generative ideas or basic conceptual schemes or analytic categories, collecting data which requires significant interpretation or judgment, and interpreting data.

   c) Clerical or mechanical contributions to an intellectual product are not grounds for ascribing authorship. Examples of such technical contributions are: typing, routine data collection or analysis, routine editing, and participation in staff meetings.

   d) Authorship and first authorship are not warranted by legal or contractual responsibility for or authority over the project or process that generates an intellectual product. It is improper to enter into contractual arrangements that preclude the proper assignment of authorship.

e) Anyone listed as author must have given his/her consent to be so listed.

f) The work of those who have contributed to the production of an intellectual product in ways short of these requirements for authorship should be appropriately acknowledged within the product.

g) Acknowledgment of other work significantly relied on in the development of an intellectual product is required. However, so long as such work is not plagiarized or otherwise inappropriately used, such reliance is not grounds for authorship or ownership.

h) It is improper to use positions of authority to appropriate the work of others or claim credit for it.

i) Theses and dissertations are special cases in which authorship is not determined strictly by the criteria elaborated in these standards. Students' advisors, who might in other circumstances be deserving of authorship based on their collaborative contribution, should not be considered authors. Their creative contributions should, however, be fully and appropriately acknowledged.

j) Authors should disclose the publication history of articles they submit for publication; that is, if the present article is substantially similar in content and form to one previously published, that fact should be noted and the place of publication cited.

2. While under suitable circumstances, ideas and other intellectual products may be viewed as commodities, arrangements concerning the production or distribution of ideas or other intellectual products must be consistent with academic freedom and the appropriate availability of intellectual products to scholars, students, and the public. Moreover, when a conflict between the academic and scholarly purposes of intellectual production and profit from such production arise, preference should be given to the academic and scholarly purposes.

3. Ownership of intellectual products should be based upon the following guidelines:

a) Individuals are entitled to profit from the sale or disposition of those intellectual products they create. They may therefore enter into contracts or other arrangements for the publication or disposition of intellectual products, and profit financially from these arrangements.

b) Arrangements for the publication or disposition of intellectual products should be consistent with their appropriate public availability and with academic freedom. Such arrangements should emphasize the academic functions of publication over the maximization of profit.

c) Individuals or groups who fund or otherwise provide resources for the development of intellectual products are entitled to assert claims to a fair share of the royalties or other profits from the sale or disposition of those products. As such claims are likely to be contentious, funding institutions and authors should agree on policies for the disposition of profits at the outset of the research or development project.

d) Author should not use positions of authority over other individuals to compel them to purchase an intellectual product from which the authors benefit. This standard is not meant to prohibit use of an author's own textbook in a class, but copies should be made available on library reserve so that students are not forced to purchase it.

IV. GUIDING STANDARDS: EDITING, REVIEWING, AND APPRAISING RESEARCH

A. Preamble

Editors and reviewers have a responsibility to recognize a wide variety of theoretical and methodological perspectives and, at the same time, to ensure that manuscripts meet the highest standards as defined in the various perspectives.

B. Standards

1. AERA journals should handle refereed articles in a manner consistent with the following principles:

    a) Fairness requires a review process that evaluates submitted works solely on the basis of merit. Merit shall be understood to include both the competence with which the argument is conducted and the significance of the results achieved.

    b) Although each AERA journal may concentrate on a particular field or type of research, the set of journals as a whole should be open to all disciplines and perspectives currently represented in the membership and which support a tradition of responsible educational scholarship. This standard is not intended to exclude worthy innovations.

    c) Blind review, with multiple readers, should be used for each submission, except where explicitly waived. (See #3.)

    d) Judgments of the adequacy of an inquiry should be made by reviewers who are competent to read the work submitted to them. Editors should strive to select reviewers who are familiar with the research paradigm and who are not so unsympathetic as to preclude a disinterested judgment of the merit of the inquiry.

    e) Editors should insist that even unfavorable reviews be dispassionate and constructive. Authors have the right to know the grounds for rejection of their work.

2. AERA journals should have written, published policies for refereeing articles.

3. AERA journals should have a written, published policy stating when solicited and nonrefereed publications are permissible.

4. AERA journals should publish statements indicating any special emphases expected to characterize articles submitted for review.

5. In addition to enforcing standing strictures against sexist and racist language, editors should reject articles that contain *ad hominem* attacks on individuals or groups or insist that such language or attacks be removed prior to publication.

6. AERA journals and AERA members who serve as editors of journals should require authors to disclose the full publication history of material substantially similar in content and form to that submitted to their journals.

V. GUIDING STANDARDS: SPONSORS, POLICYMAKERS, AND OTHER USERS OF RESEARCH

A. Preamble

Researchers, research institutions, and sponsors of research jointly share responsibility for the ethical integrity of research, and should ensure that this integrity is not violated. While it is recognized that these parties may sometimes have conflicting legitimate aims, all those with responsibility for research should protect against compromising the standards of research, the community of researchers, the subjects of research, and the users of research. They should support the widest possible dissemination and publication of research results. AERA should promote, as nearly as it can, conditions conducive to the preservation of research integrity.

B. Standards

1. The data and results of a research study belong to the researchers who designed and conducted the study, unless specific contractual arrangements have been made with respect to either or both the data and results, except as noted in II B.4. (participants may withdraw at any stage).
2. Educational researchers are free to interpret and publish their findings without censorship or approval from individuals or organizations, including sponsors, funding agencies, participants, colleagues, supervisors, or administrators. This understanding should be conveyed to participants as part of the responsibility to secure informed consent.
3. Researchers conducting sponsored research retain the right to publish the findings under their own names.
4. Educational researchers should not agree to conduct research that conflicts with academic freedom, nor should they agree to undue or questionable influence by government or other funding agencies. Examples of such improper influence include endeavors to interfere with the conduct of research, the analysis of findings, or the reporting of interpretations. Researchers should report to AERA attempts by sponsors or funding agencies to use any questionable influence.
5. Educational researchers should fully disclose the aims and sponsorship of their research, except where such disclosure would violate the usual tenets of confidentiality and anonymity. Sponsors or funders have the right to have disclaimers included in research reports to differentiate their sponsorship from the conclusions of the research.
6. Educational researchers should not accept funds from sponsoring agencies that request multiple renderings of reports that would distort the results of mislead readers.
7. Educational researchers should fulfill their responsibilities to agencies funding research, which are entitled to an accounting of the use of their funds, and to a report of the procedures, findings, and implications of the funded research.
8. Educational researchers should make clear the bases and rationales, and the limits thereof, of their professionally rendered judgments in consultation with the public, government, or other institutions. When there are contrasting professional opinions to the one being offered, this should be made clear.
9. Educational researchers should disclose to appropriate parties all cases where they would stand to benefit financially from their research or cases where their affiliations might tend to bias their interpretation of their research or their professional judgments.

VI. GUIDING STANDARDS: STUDENTS AND STUDENT RESEARCHERS

A. Preamble

Educational researchers have a responsibility to ensure the competence of those inducted into the field and to provide appropriate help and professional advice to novice researchers.

B. Standards

1. In relations with students and student researchers, educational researchers should be candid, fair, nonexploitative, and committed to their welfare and progress. They should conscientiously supervise, encourage, and support students and student researchers in their academic endeavors, and should appropriately assist them in securing research support or professional employment.
2. Students and student researchers should be selected based upon their competence and potential contributions to the field. Educational researchers should not discriminate among students and student researchers on the basis of gender, sexual orientation, marital status, color, social class, religion, ethnic background, national origin, or other irrelevant factors.
3. Educational researchers should inform students and student researchers concerning the ethical dimensions of research, encourage their practice of research consistent with ethical standards, and support their avoidance of questionable projects.
4. Educational researchers should realistically apprise students and student researchers with regard to career opportunities and implications associated with their participation in particular research projects or degree programs. Educational researchers should ensure that research assistantships be educative.
5. Educational researchers should be fair in the evaluation of research performance, and should communicate that evaluation fully and honestly to the student or student researcher. Researchers have an obligation to report honestly on the competence of assistants to other professionals who require such evaluations.
6. Educational researchers should not permit personal animosities or intellectual differences vis-a-vis colleagues to foreclose student and student researcher access to those colleagues, or to place the student or student researcher in an untenable position with those colleagues.

The Program Evaluation Standards: ERIC/AE Digest*

Sound evaluations of educational programs, projects, and materials in a variety of settings should have four basic attributes:

- Utility
- Propriety
- Feasibility
- Accuracy

"The Program Evaluation Standards," established by 16 professional associations, identify evaluation principles that when addressed should result in improved program evaluations containing the above four attributes. What follows is a summary of the Standards.

Guidelines and illustrative cases to assist evaluation participants in meeting each of these standards are provided in the full report (Joint Committee on Standards for Educational Evaluations, 1994). The illustrative cases are based in a variety of educational settings that include schools, universities, medical and health care fields, the military, business and industry, the government, and law.

UTILITY

The utility standards are intended to ensure that an evaluation will serve the information needs of intended users.

U1 Stakeholder Identification. Persons involved in or affected by the evaluation should be identified so that their needs can be addressed.

U2 Evaluator Credibility. The persons conducting the evaluation should be both trustworthy and competent to perform the evaluation so that the evaluation findings achieve maximum credibility and acceptance.

U3 Information Scope and Selection. Information collected should be broadly selected to address pertinent questions about the program and be responsive to the needs and interests of clients and other specified stakeholders.

U4 Values Identification. The perspectives, procedures, and rationale used to interpret the findings should be carefully described so that the bases for value judgments are clear.

U5 Report Clarity. Evaluation reports should clearly describe the program being evaluated, including its context, and the purposes, procedures, and findings of the evaluation so that essential information is provided and easily understood.

U6 Report Timeliness and Dissemination. Significant interim findings and evaluation reports should be disseminated to intended users so that they can be used in a timely fashion.

*Source: *ERIC Clearinghouse on Assessment and Evaluation.* Washington DC, Eric Document No. ED 385 612; 1995.

U7 Evaluation Impact. Evaluations should be planned, conducted, and reported in ways that encourage follow-through by stakeholders so that the likelihood that the evaluation will be used is increased.

FEASIBILITY

The feasibility standards are intended to ensure that an evaluation will be realistic, prudent, diplomatic, and frugal.

F1 Practical Procedures. The evaluation procedures should be practical to keep disruption to a minimum while needed information is obtained.

F2 Political Viability. The evaluation should be planned and conducted with anticipation of the different positions of various interest groups so that their cooperation may be obtained and so that possible attempts by any of these groups to curtail evaluation operations or to bias or misapply the results can be averted or counteracted.

F3 Cost Effectiveness. The evaluation should be efficient and produce information of sufficient value so that the resources expended can be justified.

PROPRIETY

The propriety standards are intended to ensure that an evaluation will be conducted legally, ethically, and with due regard for the welfare of those involved in the evaluation, as well as those affected by its results.

P1 Service Orientation. Evaluations should be designed to assist organizations to address and effectively serve the needs of the full range of targeted participants.

P2 Formal Agreements. Obligations of the formal parties to an evaluation (what is to be done, how, by whom, and when) should be agreed to in writing, so that these parties are obligated to adhere to all conditions of the agreement or formally to renegotiate it.

P3 Rights of Human Subjects. Evaluations should be designed and conducted to respect and protect the rights and welfare of human subjects.

P4 Human Interactions. Evaluators should respect human dignity and worth in their interactions with other persons associated with an evaluation so that participants are not threatened or harmed.

P5 Complete and Fair Assessment. The evaluation should be complete and fair in its examination and recording of strengths and weaknesses of the program being evaluated so that strengths can be built upon and problem areas addressed.

P6 Disclosure of Findings. The formal parties to an evaluation should ensure that the full set of evaluation findings along with pertinent limitations are made accessible to the persons affected by the evaluation and any others with expressed legal rights to receive the results.

P7 Conflict of Interest. Conflict of interest should be dealt with openly and honestly so that it does not compromise the evaluation processes and results.

P8   Fiscal Responsibility. The evaluator's allocation and expenditure of resources should reflect sound accountability procedures and otherwise be prudent and ethically responsible so that expenditures are accounted for and appropriate.

ACCURACY

The accuracy standards are intended to ensure that an evaluation will reveal and convey technically adequate information about the features that determine worth of merit of the program being evaluated.

A1   Program Documentation. The program being evaluated should be described and documented clearly and accurately so that the program is clearly identified.

A2   Context Analysis. The context in which the program exists should be examined in enough detail so that its likely influences on the program can be identified.

A3   Described Purposes and Procedures. The purposes and procedures of the evaluation should be monitored and described in enough detail so that they can be identified and assessed.

A4   Defensible Information Sources. The sources of information used in a program evaluation should be described in enough detail so that the adequacy of the information can be assessed.

A5   Valid Information. The information gathering procedures should be chosen or developed and then implemented to ensure that the interpretation arrived at is valid for the intended use.

A6   Reliable Information. The information gathering procedures should be chosen or developed and then implemented to ensure that the information obtained is sufficiently reliable for the intended use.

A7   Systematic Information. The information collected, processed, and reported in an evaluation should be systematically reviewed and any errors found should be corrected.

A8   Analysis of Quantitative Information. Quantitative information in an evaluation should be appropriately and systematically analyzed so that evaluation questions are effectively answered.

A9   Analysis of Qualitative Information. Qualitative information in an evaluation should be appropriately and systematically analyzed so that evaluation questions are effectively answered.

A10   Justified Conclusions. The conclusions reached in an evaluation should be explicitly justified so that stakeholders can assess them.

A11   Impartial Reporting. Reporting procedures should guard against distortion caused by personal feelings and biases of any party to the evaluation so that evaluation reports fairly reflect the evaluation findings.

A12   Metaevaluation. The evaluation itself should be formatively and summatively evaluated against these and other pertinent standards so that its conduct is appropriately guided and, on completion, stakeholders can closely examine its strengths and weaknesses.

Approved by the American National Standards Institute as an American National Standard. Approval date: March 15, 1994.

FURTHER READING

Hansen, J. B. & Patton, M. Q.(1994). The Joint Committee on Standards for Educational Evaluation's "The program evaluation standards: How to assess evaluations of educational programs" book review. *Educational and Psychological Measurement, 54*(2), 550–567.

Joint Committee on Standards for Educational Evaluation (1994). *The Program Evaluation Standards: How to Assess Evaluations of Educational Programs.* Thousand Oaks, CA: Sage Publications (available from ERIC/AE).

Stufflebeam, D. L. (1987). Professional standards for assuring the quality of educational program and personnel evaluations. *International Journal of Educational Research, 11*(1), 125–143.

Thompson, B. (1993). *The revised program evaluation standards and their correlation with the evaluation use literature.* Paper presented at the Annual Meeting of the American Educational Research Association, New Orleans, LA, April 4–8, 1993. ERIC Document No. 370 999.

References

Abrami, P. C., Cohen, P. A., & d'Apollonia, S. (1988). Implementation problems in meta-analysis. *Review of Educational Research, 58,* 151–180.

Aksamit, D. L., & Alcorn, D. A. (1988). A preservice mainstream curriculum infusion model: Student teachers' perceptions of program effectiveness. *Teacher Education and Special Education, 11,* 52–58.

Alexander, P. A., Kulikowich, J. M., & Jetton, T. L. (1994). The role of subject-matter knowledge and interest in the processing of linear and nonlinear texts. *Review of Educational Research, 64*(2), 201–252.

Alkin, M. C. (Ed.). (1992). *The encyclopedia of educational research* (6th ed.). Upper Saddle River, NJ: Merrill/Prentice Hall.

Allen, J. D. (1986). Classroom management: Students' perspectives, goals, and strategies. *American Educational Research Journal, 23,* 437–459.

Babad, E., Bernieri, F., & Rosenthal, R. (1987). Nonverbal and verbal behavior of preschool, remedial, and elementary school teachers. *American Educational Research Journal, 24,* 405–415.

Bangert-Drowns, R. L., & Rudner, L. M. (1991, December). *Meta-analysis in educational research: An ERIC digest.* Washington, DC: ERIC Clearinghouse on Tests, Measurements, and Evaluation. (ERIC Document No. ED 339 748)

Barron, A. E., Hogarty, K. Y., Kromrey, J. D., & Lenkway, P. (1999). An examination of the relationships between student conduct and the number of computers per student in Florida schools. *Journal of Research on Computing in Education, 32*(1), 98–107.

Baumann, J. F., Allen, J. B., & Shockley, B. (1994). *Research questions teachers ask: A report from the National Reading Research Center school research consortium* [On-line]. Available: http://curry.edschool.virginia.edu/go/clic/nrrc/ques_r30.html

Beck, I. L., McKeown, M. G., & Worthy, J. (1995). Giving a text voice can improve students' understanding. *Reading Research Quarterly, 30*(2), 220–238.

Benito, Y. M., Foley, C. L., Lewis, C. G., & Prescott, P. (1993). The effect of instruction in question-answer relationships and metacognition on social studies comprehension. *Journal of Research in Reading, 16,* 20–29.

Berliner, D. C. (1987). Knowledge is power: A talk to teachers about a revolution in the teaching profession. In D. C. Berliner & B. V. Rosenshine (Eds.), *Talks to teachers: A festschrift for N. L. Gage* (pp. 3–33). New York: Random House.

Biklen, D. (1993). *Communication unbound: How facilitated communication is challenging traditional views of autism and ability/disability.* New York: Teachers College Press.

Bisesi, T. L., & Raphael, T. E. (1995). Combining single-subject experimental designs with qualitative research. In S. B. Neuman & S. McCormick (Eds.), *Single-subject experimental research: Applications for literacy* (pp. 104–119). Newark, DE: International Reading Association.

Bissex, G. L. (1994). Teacher research: Seeing what we are doing (pp. 88–104). In T. Shannahan (Ed.) *Teachers thinking, teachers knowing: Reflections on literacy and language education.* Urbana IL: National Conference on Research in English and National Council of Teachers of English.

Bogdan, R. C., & Biklen, S. K. (1998). *Qualitative research for education: An introduction to theory and methods* (3rd ed.). Boston: Allyn and Bacon.

Brown, R. B., & Cooper, G. R. (2000, May). School-based management: How effective is it? *NASSP Bulletin, 84*(616), 77–85.

Burns, J. M., & Collins, M. D. (1987). Parents' perceptions of factors affecting the reading development of intellectually superior accelerated readers and intellectually superior nonreaders. *Reading Research and Instruction, 26,* 239–246.

Burns, R. B., & Mason, D. A. (1998). Class formation and composition in elementary schools. *American Educational Research Journal, 35*(4), 739–772.

Bursuck, W. D., & Lesson, E. (1987). A classroom-based model for assessing students with learning disabilities. *Learning Disabilities Focus, 3,* 17–29.

Burton, F. R. (1991). Teacher-researcher projects: An elementary school teacher's perspective. In J. Flood, J. M. Jensen, D. Lapp, & J. R. Squire (Eds.), *Handbook of research on teaching the English language arts* (pp. 226–230). Upper Saddle River, NJ: Merrill/Prentice Hall.

Campbell, D. T., & Stanley, J. C. (1971). *Experimental and quasi-experimental designs for research.* Chicago: Rand McNally.

Carlberg, C. G., Johnson, D. W., Johnson, R., Maruy-ama, G., Kavale, K., Kulik, C., Kulik, J. A., Lysakowski, R. S., Pflaum, S. W., & Walberg, H. J. (1984). Meta-analysis in education: A reply to Slavin. *Educational Researcher, 13*(8), 16–23.

Charles, C. M. (1995). *Introduction to educational research* (2nd ed.). White Plains, NY: Longman.

Clair, N., Adger, C., Short, D., & Millen, E. (1998). *Implementing standards with English language learners: Initial findings from four middle schools.* Providence, RI: Northeast and Islands Regional Educational. Available: http://www.lab.brown.edu/public/pubs/implementing/imp-std.pdf

Clements, D. H., & Nastasi, B. K. (1988). Social and cognitive interactions in educational computer environments. *American Educational Research Journal, 25,* 87–106.

Clery, E. (1998). Homeschooling: The meaning that the homeschooled child assigns to this experience. *Issues in Educational Research, 8*(1), 1–13. Available: http://cleo.murdoch.edu.au/gen/iier/iier8/clery.html

Conoley, J. C., & Impara, J. C. (Eds.). (1994). *Supplement to the eleventh mental measurements yearbook.* Lincoln, NE: The Buros Institute of Mental Measurements/University of Nebraska–Lincoln.

Conoley, J. C., Impara, J. C., & Murphy, L. L. (Eds.). (1996). *Supplement to the twelfth mental measurements yearbook.* Lincoln, NE: The Buros Institute of Mental Measurements/University of Nebraska–Lincoln.

Conoley, J. C., & Kramer, J. J. (Eds.). (1989). *Tenth mental measurements yearbook.* Lincoln, NE: University of Nebraska Press.

Conoley, J. C., & Kramer, J. J. (Eds.). (1995). *Twelfth mental measurements yearbook.* Lincoln, NE: University of Nebraska Press.

Conoley, J. C., Kramer, J. J., & Mitchell, J. V., Jr. (Eds.). (1988). *Supplement to the ninth mental measurements yearbook.* Lincoln, NE: University of Nebraska Press.

Cooper, H. M. (1982). Scientific guidelines for conducting integrative research reviews. *Review of Educational Research, 52,* 291–302.

Cooper, H. M., & Lindsay, J. J. (1998). Research synthesis and meta-analysis. In L. Bickman & D. J. Rog (Eds.). *Handbook of applied social research methods* (pp. 315–341). Thousand Oaks, CA: Sage Publications.

Creswell, J. W. (1998). *Qualitative inquiry and research design: Choosing among five traditions.* Thousand Oaks, CA: Sage Publications.

Darch, C., Kim, S., Johnson, S., & James, H. (2000). The strategic spelling skills of students with learning disabilities: The results of two studies. *Journal of Instructional Psychology, 27*(1), 15–27.

Davis, A., Clarke, M. A., & Rhodes, L. K. (1994). Extended text and the writing proficiency of students in urban elementary schools. *Journal of Educational Research, 86*(4), 556–566.

de Jong, T., & van Joolingen, W. R. (1998). Scientific discovery learning with computer simulations of conceptual domains. *Review of Educational Research, 68*(2), 179–201.

DeLain, M. T., Pearson, P. D., & Anderson, R. C. (1985). Reading comprehension and creativity in black language use: You stand to gain by playing the sounding game! *American Educational Research Journal, 22,* 155–173.

Donoahue, Z., Van Tassell, M. A., & Patterson, L. (Eds.) (1996). *Research in the classroom: Talk, texts, and inquiry.* Newark, DE: International Reading Association.

Duffelmeyer, F. A., & Adamson, S. (1986). Matching students with instructional level materials using the Degrees of Reading Power system. *Reading Research and Instruction, 25,* 192–200.

Eisenhart, M. (1999). On the subject of interpretive reviews. *Review of Educational Research, 68*(4), 391–399.

Eisner, E. W. (1991). *The enlightened eye: Qualitative inquiry and the enhancement of educational practice.* Upper Saddle River, NJ: Merrill/Prentice Hall.

Erickson, F. (1986). Qualitative methods in research on teaching. In M. C. Wittrock (Ed.), *Handbook of research on teaching* (3rd ed.) (pp. 119–161). Upper Saddle River, NJ: Merrill/Prentice Hall.

Fagan, W. T. (1988). Concepts of reading and writing among low literate adults. *Reading Research and Instruction, 27,* 47–60.

Firestone, W. A. (1987). Meaning in method: The rhetoric of quantitative and qualitative research. *Educational Researcher, 17*(7), 16–21.

Firestone, W. A. (1993). Alternative arguments for generalizing from data as applied to qualitative research. *Educational Researcher, 22*(4), 16–23.

Fitzgerald, J. (1995). English-as-a-second-language learners' cognitive reading processes: A review of research in the United States. *Review of Educational Research, 65*(2), 145–190.

Fleisher, B. M. (1988). Oral reading cue strategies of better and poor readers. *Reading Research and Instruction, 27,* 35–60.

Fuchs, D., & Fuchs, L. S. (1986). Test procedure bias: A meta-analysis of examiner familiarity effects. *Review of Educational Research, 56,* 243–262.

Fuchs, D., & Fuchs, L. S. (1989). Effects of examiner familiarity on black, Caucasian, and Hispanic children: A meta-analysis. *Exceptional Children, 55,* 303–308.

Fuchs, D., Fuchs, L. S., & Fernstrom, P. (1993). A conservative approach to special education reform: Mainstreaming through transenvironmental programming and curriculum-based measurement.

American Educational Research Journal, 30(1), 149–177.

Fuson, K. C., Carroll, W. M., & Drueck, J. V. (2000). Achievement results for second and third graders using the standards-based curriculum everyday mathematics. *Journal for Research in Mathematics Education 31*(3), 277–295.

Gall, J. P., Gall, M. D., & Borg, W. R. (1999). *Applying educational research: A practical guide* (4th ed.). New York: Addison Wesley Longman.

Gay, L. R., & Airasian, P. (2000). *Educational research: Competencies for analysis and application* (6th ed.). Upper Saddle River, NJ: Merrill/Prentice Hall.

Geyser, D. J., & Sweetland, R. C. (1991). *Test critiques.* Austin, TX: Pro-Ed.

Gillis, M. K., Olson, M. W., & Logan, J. (1993). Are content area reading practices keeping pace with research? Inquiries in literacy learning and instruction. In T. V. Rasinski & N. D. Padak (Eds.), *Inquiries in literacy learning and instruction. The Fifteenth Yearbook of the College Reading Association.* (pp. 115–123). Pittsburg, KS: College Reading Association.

Glass, G. V. (1976). Primary, secondary, and meta-analysis of research. *Educational Researcher, 5*(10), 3–8.

Goodson, I. F. (1993, March). The devil's bargain: Educational research and the teacher. *Education Policy Analysis Archives,1*(3). Available: http://olam.ed.asu.edu/epaa/v1n3.html

Graue, M. E., & Walsch, D. J. (1995). Children in context: Interpreting the here and now of children's lives. In J. A. Hatch (Ed.), *Qualitative research in early childhood settings.* Westport, CT: Praeger.

Guthrie, L. F., & Hall, W. S. (1984). Ethnographic approaches to reading research. In P. D. Pearson, R. Barr, M. L. Kamil, & P. Mosenthal (Eds.), *Handbook of reading research* (pp. 91–110). New York: Longman.

Guthrie, L. F., Seifert, M., & Kirsch, I. S. (1986). Effects of education, occupation, and setting on reading practices. *American Educational Research Journal, 23,* 151–160.

Gutman, L. M., & Sulzby, E. (2000). The role of autonomy-support versus control in the emergent writing behaviors of African-American kindergarten children. *Reading Research and Instruction, 39*(2), 170–184.

Harris, T. L., & Hodges, R. E. (Eds.). (1995). *The literacy dictionary: The vocabulary of reading and writing.* Newark, DE: International Reading Association.

Hartley, J., & Chesworth, K. (1998). *Qualitative and quantitative methods in research on essay writing: No one way.* Paper presented at "Higher Education Close Up," an international conference from 6–8 July 1998 at the University of Central Lancashire, Preston, United Kingdom. Available: http://www.leeds.ac.uk/educol/documents/000000682.htm

Hatch, J. A. (1995). Studying childhood as a cultural invention: A rationale and framework. In J. A. Hatch (Ed.), *Qualitative research in early childhood settings* (pp. 117–133). Westport, CT: Praeger.

Hiebert, E. H., Colt, J. M., Catto, S. L., & Gury, E. C. (1992). Reading and writing of first-grade students in a restructured Chapter 1 program. *American Educational Research Journal, 29*(3), 545–572.

Hiebert, E. H., Valencia, S. W., & Afflerback, P. P. (1994). Definitions and perspectives. In S. W. Valencia, E. H. Hiebert, & P. P. Afflerback (Eds.), *Authentic reading assessment: Practices and possibilities* (pp. 6–21). Newark, DE: International Reading Association.

Hill, J. W., Seyfarth, J., Banks, P. D., Wehman, P., & Orelove, F. (1987). Parent attitudes about working conditions of their adult mentally retarded sons and daughters. *Exceptional Children, 54,* 9–23.

Hillocks, G., Jr. (1992). Reconciling the qualitative and quantitative. In R. Beach, J. L. Green, M. L. Kamil, & T. Shanahan (Eds.), *Multidisciplinary perspectives on literacy research* (pp. 57–65). Urbana, IL: National Conference on Research in English/National Council of Teachers of English.

Hirtle, J. S. (1993). Connecting to the classics. In L. Patterson, C. M. Santa, K. G. Short, & K. Smith (Eds.), *Teachers are researchers: Reflection and action* (pp. 137–146). Newark, DE: International Reading Association.

Homan, S. P., Hines, C. V., & Kromrey, J. D. (1993). An investigation of varying reading level placement on reading achievement of Chapter 1 students. *Reading Research and Instruction, 33*(1), 29–38.

Hughes, C. A., Ruhl, K. L., & Gorman, J. (1987). Preparation of special educators to work with parents: A survey of teachers and teacher educators. *Teacher Education and Special Education, 10,* 81–87.

Hunsucker, P. F., Nelson, R. O., & Clark, R. P. (1986). Standardization and evaluation of the Classroom Adaptive Behavior Checklist for school use. *Exceptional Children, 53,* 69–71.

Husen, T., & Postlethwaite, T. N. (Eds.). (1994). *The International encyclopedia of education,* 2nd ed. New York: Pergamon/Elsevier Science.

Impara, J. C., & Plake, B. S. (Eds.) (1998). *Thirteenth mental meansurements yearbook.* Lincoln, NE: The Buros Institute of Mental Measurements/University of Nebraska–Lincoln.

Jackson, G. B. (1980). Methods for integrative reviews. *Review of Educational Research, 50,* 438–460.

Jacob, E. (1987). Qualitative research traditions: A review. *Review of Educational Research, 57,* 1–50.

Jacob, E. (1988). Clarifying qualitative research: A focus on traditions. *Educational Researcher, 17*(1), 16–24.

Jacob, E. (1989). Qualitative research: A response to Atkinson, Delamont, and Hammersley. *Review of Educational Research, 59,* 229–235.

Jacobs, J. E., Finken, L. L., Griffin, N. L., & Wright, J. D. (1998). The career plans of science-talented rural adolescent girls. *American Educational Research Journal, 35*(4), 681–704.

Jansen, G., & Peshkin, A. (1992). Subjectivity in qualitative research. In M. D. LeCompte, W. L. Millory, & J. Preissle (Eds.), *The handbook of qualitative research in education* (pp. 681–725). San Diego: Academic Press/Harcourt Brace.

Johnson, R. W. (1993). Where can teacher research lead? One teacher's daydream. *Educational Leadership, 51*(2), 66–68.

Joint Committee on Standards for Educational Evaluation. (1981). *Standards for evaluation of educational programs, projects, and materials.* New York: McGraw-Hill.

Joint Committee on Standards for Educational Evaluations (1994). *The Program Evaluation Standards: How to Assess Evaluations of Educational Programs.* Thousand Oaks, CA: Sage Publications (available from ERIC/AE).

Jones, I. (1997, December). Mixing qualitative and quantitative methods in sports fan research. *The Qualitative Report* [On-line serial], *3*(4). Available: http://www.nova.edu/ssss/QR/QR3-4/jones.html

Jovanovic, J., & King, S. S. (1998). Boys and girls in the performance-based science classroom: Who's doing the performing. *American Educational Research Journal, 35*(3), 477–496.

Joyce, B. (1987). A rigorous yet delicate touch: A response to Slavin's proposal for "best-evidence" reviews. *Educational Researcher, 16*(4), 12–14.

Kamberelis, G., & Bovino, T. D. (1999). Cultural artifacts as scaffolds for genre development. *Reading Research Quarterly, 34*(2), 138–70.

Kamil, M. L., Langer, J. A., & Shanahan, T. (1985). *Understanding research in reading and writing.* Boston: Allyn and Bacon.

Karweit, N. L. (1999). *Grade retention: Prevalence, timing, and effects.* (Report No. 33). Baltimore, MD: Johns Hopkins University & Howard University, Center for Research on the Education of Students Placed at Risk. Available: http://www.csos.jhu.edu/crespar/Reports/report33.pdf

Kerlinger, F. N. (1973). *Foundations of behavioral research: Educational, psychological, and sociological inquiry* (2nd ed.). New York: Holt, Rinehart & Winston.

King, A. (1994). Guiding knowledge construction in the classroom: Effects of teaching children how to question and how to explain. *American Educational Research Journal, 31*(2), 338–368.

Konopak, B. C. (1988). Eighth graders' vocabulary learning from inconsiderate and considerate text. *Reading Research and Instruction, 27,* 1–14.

Kramer, J. J., & Conoley, J. C. (Eds.). (1992). *Eleventh mental measurements yearbook.* Lincoln, NE: The Buros Institute of Mental Measurements/University of Nebraska–Lincoln.

Ladas, H. (1980). Summarizing research: A case study. *Review of Educational Research, 50,* 597–624.

Lancy, D. F. (1993). *Qualitative research in education: An introduction to the major traditions.* New York: Longman.

Langer, J. A. (1984). The effects of available information on responses to school writing. *Research in the Teaching of English, 18,* 27–44.

Langer, J. A., Campbell, J. R., Neuman, S. B., Mullis, I. V. S., Persky, H. R., & Donahue, P. L. (1995). *Reading assessment redesigned: Authentic texts and innovative instruments.* Washington, DC: U.S. Department of Education, Office of Educational Research and Improvement.

Lass, B. (1984). Do teachers individualize their responses to reading miscues? A study of feedback during oral reading. *Reading World, 23,* 242–254.

Lazarowitz, R., Hertz-Lazarowitz, R., & Baird, J. H. (1994). Learning science in a cooperative setting: Academic achievement and affective outcomes. *Journal of Research in Science Teaching, 31,* 1121–1131.

LeCompte, M. D., & Goetz, J. P. (1982). Problems of reliability and validity in ethnographic research. *Review of Educational Research, 52,* 31–60.

LeCompte, M. D., Millory, W. L., & Preissle, J. (Eds.). (1992). *The handbook of qualitative research in education.* San Diego: Academic Press/Harcourt Brace.

Lee, O. (1999). Science knowledge, world views, and information sources in social and cultural contexts: Making sense after a natural disaster. *American Educational Research Journal 36*(2), 187–219.

Leinhardt, G., & Pallay, A. (1982). Restrictive educational settings: Exile or haven? *Review of Educational Research, 52,* 557–578.

Lincoln, Y. S., & Guba, E. G. (1985). *Naturalistic inquiry.* Beverly Hills, CA: Sage.

Linn, R. L. (1994). Performance assessment: Policy promises and technical measurement standards. *Educational Researcher, 23*(9), 4–14.

Lloyd, L. (1999). Multi-age classes and high ability students. *Review of Educational Research, 69*(2), 187–212.

Lyytinen, P., Rasku-Puttonen, H., Poikkeus, A. M., Laakso, A. L., & Ahonen, T. (1994). Mother-child teaching strategies and learning disabilities. *Journal of Learning Disabilities, 27,* 186–192.

MacColl, G. S., & White, K. D. (1998). *Communicating educational research data to general, nonresearcher audiences. ERIC/AE Digest.* Washington, DC: ERIC Clearinghouse on Assessment and Evaluation. ERIC Document No. ED422406.

Madden, N. A., & Slavin, R. E. (1983). Mainstreaming students with mild handicaps: Academic and social outcomes. *Review of Educational Research, 53,* 519–169.

Maeroff, G. I. (1982, March 30). Specific TV shows tied to child's achievement. *The New York Times,* p. C9.

Mandoli, M., Mandoli, P., & McLaughlin, T. F. (1982). Effects of same-age peer tutoring on the spelling performance of a mainstreamed elementary LD student. *Learning Disability Quarterly, 5,* 185–189.

Manning, M., Manning, G., & Cody, C. B. (1988). Reading aloud to young children: Perspectives of parents. *Reading Research and Instruction, 27,* 56–61.

Manzo, A. V., Manzo, U. C., & McKenna, M. C. (1995). *Informal reading-thinking inventory.* Fort Worth: Harcourt Brace College.

Marshall, C., & Rossman, G. B. (1995). *Designing qualitative research* (2nd ed.). Thousand Oaks, CA: Sage Publications.

Martin, L. E., & Reutzel, D. R. (1999). Sharing books: Examining how and why mothers deviate from the print. *Reading Research and Instruction 39*(1), 39–70.

Maxwell, J. A. (1992). Understanding and validity in qualitative research. *Harvard Educational Review, 62*(3), 279–300.

Maxwell, J. A. (1998). Designing a qualitative study. In L. Bickman & D. J. Rog (Eds.), *Handbook of applied social research methods* (pp. 69–100). Thousand Oaks, CA: Sage Publications.

McCarthy, P., Newby, R. F., & Recht, D. R. (1995). Results of an early intervention program for first grade children at risk for reading disability. *Reading Research and Instruction, 34*(4), 273–294.

McCormick, S. (1995). What is single-subject experimental research? In S. B. Neuman & S. McCormick (Eds.), *Single-subject experimental research: Applications for literacy* (pp. 1–31). Newark, DE: International Reading Association.

McFarland, K. P., & Stansell, J. C. (1993). Historical perspectives. In L. Patterson, C. M. Santa, K. G. Short, & K. Smith (Eds.), *Teachers are researchers: Reflection and action* (pp. 12–18). Newark, DE: International Reading Association.

McKeown, M. G., Beck, I. L., Sinatra, G. M., & Loxterman, J. A. (1992). The contribution of prior knowledge and coherent text to comprehension. *Reading Research Quarterly, 27*(1), 78–93.

McNemar, B. S. (1998). The everyday literacy behavior of an adolescent mother for whom English is a second language. In T. Shanahan & F. V. Rodriquez-Brown (Eds.), *47th yearbook of the National Reading Conference* (pp. 274–284). Chicago: National Reading Conference.

Messick, S. (1994). The interplay of evidence and consequences in the validation of performance assessments. *Educational Researcher, 23*(2), 13–23.

Mifflin, L. (1995, May 31). Study finds educational TV lends preschoolers even greater advantages. *The New York Times,* p. B8.

Mills, C. J., Ablard, K. E., & Gustin, W. C. (1994). Academically talented students' achievement in a flexibly paced mathematics program. *Journal for Research in Mathematics Education, 25,* 495–511.

Mitchell, J. V., Jr. (Ed.). (1983). *Tests in print III: An index to tests, test reviews, and the literature on specific tests.* Lincoln, NE: University of Nebraska Press.

Mitchell, J. V., Jr. (Ed.). (1985). *Ninth mental measurements yearbook.* Lincoln, NE: University of Nebraska Press.

Moore, J. (1999). *Some basic concepts in meta-analyses.* Paper presented at the Annual Meeting of the Southwest Educational Research Association, San Antonio, TX, January 21–23, 1999. ERIC Document No. ED426101.

Morrison, T. G., Jacobs, J. S., & Swinyard, W. R. (1999). Do teachers who read personally use recommended literacy practices in their classrooms? *Reading Research and Instruction, 38*(2), 81–100.

Morrow, L. M. (1988). Young children's responses to one-to-one story readings in school settings. *Reading Research Quarterly, 23,* 89–107.

Moustafa, M. (1995). Children's productive phonological recoding. *Reading Research Quarterly, 30*(3), 464–476.

Murphy, L. L., Impara, J. C., & Plake, B. S. (Eds.). (1999). *Tests in print V: An index to tests, test reviews, and the literature on specific tests* (Vol. I and II). Lincoln, NE: The Buros Institute of Mental Measurements/University of Nebraska–Lincoln.

Nattiv, A. (1994). Helping behaviors and math achievement gain of students using cooperative learning. *The Elementary School Journal, 94,* 285–297.

Nelson, J. R., Smith, D. J., & Dodd, J. M. (1994). The effects of learning strategy instruction on the completion of job applications by students with learning disabilities. *Journal of Learning Disabilities, 27,* 104–110.

Neuman, S. B. (1999). Books make a difference: A study of access to literacy. *Reading Research Quarterly 34*(3), 286–311.

Neuman, S. B., & Roskos, K. (1993). Access to print for children of poverty: Differential effects of adult mediation and literacy-enriched play settings on environmental and functional print tasks. *American Educational Research Journal, 30*(1), 95–122.

Newman, R. S., & Schwager, M. T. (1995). Students' help seeking during problem solving: Effects of grade, goal, and prior achievement. *American Educational Research Journal, 32*(2), 352–376.

Nielsen, H. B. (1995). Seductive texts with serious intentions. *Educational Researcher, 24*(1), 4–12.

Nist, S. L., & Olejnik, S. (1995). The role of context and dictionary definitions on varying levels of word knowledge. *Reading Research Quarterly, 30*(2), 172–195.

Okagaki, L., & Frensch, P. A. (1998). Parenting and children's school achievement: A multiethnic perspective. *American Educational Research Journal, 35*(1), 123–144.

Olson, M. W. (1990). The teacher as researcher: A historical perspective. In M. W. Olson (Ed.), *Opening the door to classroom research* (pp. 1–20). Newark, DE: International Reading Association.

Osborne, S. (1985). Effects of teacher experience and selected temperament variables on coping strategies used with distractible children. *American Educational Research Journal, 22,* 79–86.

Pascarella, E. T., Pflaum, S. W., Bryan, T. H., & Pearl, R. A. (1983). Interaction of internal attribution for effort and teacher response mode in reading instruction: A replication note. *American Educational Research Journal, 20,* 269–276.

Patterson, L., & Shannon, P. (1993). Reflection, inquiry, action. In L. Patterson, C. M. Santa, K. G. Short, & K. Smith (Eds.), *Teachers are researchers: Reflection and action* (pp. 7–11). Newark, DE: International Reading Association.

Peshkin, A. (1993). The goodness of qualitative research. *Educational Researcher, 22*(2), 24–30.

Pitman, M. A., & Maxwell, J. A. (1992). Qualitative approaches to evaluation: Models and methods. In M. D. LeCompte, W. L. Millory, & J. Preissle (Eds.), *The handbook of qualitative research in education* (pp. 729–770). San Diego: Academic Press/Harcourt Brace.

Plake, B. S., & Impara, J. C. (Eds.). (1999). *Supplement to the thirteenth mental measurements yearbook.* Lincoln, NE: The Buros Institute of Mental Measurements/University of Nebraska–Lincoln.

Popham, W. J., & Sirotnik, K. A. (1973). *Educational statistics: Use and interpretation* (2nd ed.). New York: Harper & Row.

Putney, L. G., Green J. L., Dixon, C. N., & Kelly, G. J. (1999). Evolution of qualitative research methodology: Looking beyond defense to possibilities. *Reading Research Quarterly, 34*(3), 368–377.

Qin, Z., Johnson, D. W., & Johnson, R. T. (1995). Cooperative versus competitive efforts and problem solving. *Review of Educational Research, 65*(2), 129–143.

Reinking, D., & Schreiner, R. (1985). The effects of computer mediated text on measures of reading comprehension and reading behavior. *Reading Research Quarterly, 20,* 536–552.

Richgels, D. J. (1986). Grade school children's listening and reading comprehension of complex sentences. *Reading Research and Instruction, 25,* 201–219.

Rosenshine, B., & Meister, C. (1994). Reciprocal teaching: A review of the research. *Review of Educational Research, 64*(4), 479–530.

Sanders, J. R., & Joint Committee on Standards for Educational Evaluation. (1994). *The program evaluation standards: How to assess evaluations of educational programs.* Thousand Oaks: CA: Sage Publications.

Santa, C. M. (1988). Changing teacher behavior in content reading through collaborative research. In S. J. Samuels & P. D. Pearson (Eds.), *Changing school reading programs: Principles and case studies* (pp. 185–204). Newark, DE: International Reading Association.

Schneider, W., & Treiber, B. (1984). Classroom differences in the determination of achievement changes. *American Educational Research Journal, 21,* 195–211.

Schwandt, T. A. (1999). The interpretive review of educational matters: Is there any other kind? *Review of Educational Research, 48*(4), 409–412.

Scott, B. N., & Hannafin, R. D. (2000). How teachers and parents view classroom learning environments: An exploratory study. *Journal of Research on Computing in Education, 32*(3), 401–416.

Scruggs, T. E., & Mastropieri, M. A. (1994). Successful mainstreaming in elementary science classes: A qualitative study of three reputational cases. *American Educational Research Journal, 31,* 785–811.

Shanahan, T. (2000). Research synthesis: Making sense of the accumulation of knowledge in reading. In M. L. Kamil, P. B. Mosenthal, P. D. Pearson, & R. Barr, (Eds.), *Handbook of reading research* (Vol. III, pp. 209–226). Mahway, NJ: Lawrence Erlbaum Associates.

Slavin, R. E. (1984a). Meta-analysis in education: How has it been used? *Educational Researcher, 13*(8), 6–15.

Slavin, R. E. (1984b). A rejoinder to Carlberg et al. *Educational Researcher, 13*(8), 24–27.

Slavin, R. E. (1986). Best-evidence synthesis: An alternative to meta-analytic and traditional reviews. *Educational Researcher, 15*(9), 5–11.

Slavin, R. E. (1987a). Best-evidence synthesis: Why less is more. *Educational Researcher, 16*(4), 15–16.

Slavin, R. E. (1987b). Mastery learning reconsidered. *Review of Educational Research, 57,* 175–213.

Slavin, R. E. (1992). *Research methods in education* (2nd ed.). Boston: Allyn and Bacon.

Smith, J. K., & Heshusius, L. (1986). Closing down the conversation: The end of the quantitative-qualitative debate among educational inquiries. *Educational Researcher, 15*(1), 4–12.

Smith, M. L. (1987). Publishing qualitative research. *American Educational Research Journal, 24,* 173–183.

Solomon, D., Watson, M. S., Delucchi, K. L., Schaps, E., & Battistich, V. (1988). Enhancing children's prosocial behavior in the classroom. *American Educational Research Journal, 25,* 527–554.

Sparks, G. M. (1986). The effectiveness of alternative training activities in changing teaching practices. *American Educational Research Journal, 23,* 217–225.

Spindler, G., & Spindler, L. (1992). Cultural process and ethnography: An anthropological perspective. In M. D. LeCompte, W. L. Millory, & J. Preissle (Eds.), *The handbook of qualitative research in education* (pp. 53–92). San Diego: Academic Press/Harcourt Brace.

Stock, W. A., Okun, M. A., Haring, M. J., Miller, W., Kinney, C., & Ceurvost, R. W. (1982). Rigor in data synthesis: A case study of reliability in meta-analysis. *Educational Researcher, 11*(6), 10–14.

Swanson, B. B. (1985). Teacher judgments of first-graders' reading enthusiasm. *Reading Research and Instruction, 25,* 41–36.

Swanson, D. B., Norman, G. R., & Linn, R. L. (1995). Performance-based assessment: Lessons from the health professions. *Educational Researcher, 24*(5), 5–11, 35.

Sweetland, R. C., & Geyser, D. J. (1991). *Tests: A comprehensive reference for assessment in psychology, education, and business* (3rd ed.). Austin, TX: Pro-Ed.

Tallent-Runnels, M. K., Olivarez, A., Jr., Lotven, A. C. C., Walsh, S. K., Gray, A., & Irons, T. R. (1994). A comparison of learning and study strategies of gifted and average-ability junior high students. *Journal for the Education of the Gifted, 17,* 143–160.

Thames, D. G., & Reeves, C. K. (1994). Poor readers' attitudes: Effects of using interests and trade books in an integrated language arts approach. *Reading Research and Instruction, 33*(4), 293–308.

Thompson, M. S., Entwisle, D. R., Alexander, K. L., & Sundius, M. J. (1992). The influence of family composition on children's conformity to the student role. *American Educational Research Journal, 29*(2), 405–424.

Thompson, R. L. (1999). *Reliability generalization: An important meta-analytic method, because it is incorrect to say, "the test is unreliable."* Paper presented at the Annual Meeting of the Southwest Educational Research Association, San Antonio, TX, January 21–23, 1999. ERIC Document No. ED434121.

Valencia, S. W., Hiebert, E. H., & Afflerbach, P. P. (Eds.). (1993). *Authentic reading assessment: Practices and possibilities.* Newark, DE: International Reading Association.

VanDeWeghe, R. (1992). What teachers learn from "kid watching." *Educational Leadership, 49*(7), 49–52.

Van Maanen, J., Dabbs, J. M., Jr., & Faulkner, R. R. (1982). *Varieties of qualitative research.* Beverly Hills, CA: Sage Publications.

Van Scoy, I. J. (1994). Differences in teaching between six primary and five intermediate teachers in one school. *The Elementary School Journal, 94,* 347–356.

Vaughn, S., Schumm, J. S., Klingner, J., & Saumell, L. (1995). Students' views of instructional practices: Implications for inclusion. *Learning Disability Quarterly, 18,* 236–247.

Vukelich, C. (1986). The relationship between peer questions and seven-year-olds' text revisions. In J. A. Niles & R. V. Lalik (Eds.), *Solving problems in literacy: Learners, teachers, and researchers* (pp. 300–305). Thirty-fifth Yearbook of the National Reading Conference. Chicago: National Reading Conference.

Webb, N. M., Ender, P., & Lewis, S. (1986). Problem-solving strategies and group processes in small groups learning computer programming. *American Educational Research Journal, 23,* 243–261.

Wiersma, W. (1995). *Research methods in education: An introduction* (6th ed.). Boston: Allyn and Bacon.

Wilkinson, I., Wardrop, J. L., & Anderson, R. C. (1988). Silent reading reconsidered: Reinterpreting reading instruction and its effects. *American Educational Research Journal, 25,* 127–144.

Wilkinson, L., & APA Task Force on Statistical Inference (2000). Statistical methods in psychology journals: Guidelines and explanations. *American Psychologist* [On-line] *55*(7). Available: http://www.apa.org/journals/amp/amp548594.html

Williams, C. L. (1999). Preschool deaf children's use of signed language during writing events. *Journal of Literacy Research, 31*(2), 183–212.

Wilson, S. (1977). The use of ethnographic techniques in educational research. *Review of Educational Research, 47,* 245–265.

Wolcott, H. F. (1992). Posturing in qualitative inquiry. In M. D. LeCompte, W. L. Millory, & J. Preissle (Eds.), *The handbook of qualitative research in education* (pp. 3–52). San Diego: Academic Press/Harcourt Brace.

Xin, Y. P., & Jitendra, A. K. (1999). The effects of instruction in solving mathematical word problems for students with learning problems: A meta-analysis. *The Journal of Special Education 32*(4), 207–225.

Yochum, N., & Miller, S. D. (1993). Parents', teachers' and children's views of reading problems. *Reading Research and Instruction, 33,* 59–71.

Yopp, H. K. (1988). The validity and reliability of phonemic awareness tests. *Reading Research Quarterly, 23,* 159–177.

Young, S. A., & Romeo, L. (1999). University and urban school district collaboration: Preschoolers and preservice teachers gain literacy skills. *Reading Research and Instruction, 38*(2), 101–114.

Zutell, J., & Rasinski, T. (1986). Spelling ability and reading fluency. In J. A. Niles & R. V. Lalik (Eds.), *Solving problems in literacy: Learners, teachers, and researchers* (pp. 109–112). Yearbook of the National Reading Conference. Chicago: National Reading Conference.

Name Index

Subject Index